THE REIGN OF JAMES I (1603–25) has long been overshado
Elizabeth and the later outbreak of the Civil War. Yet how, v
Jacobean court, are we to understand the world of Jon:
Shakespeare, divine right theory, court scandal and reforn., ₋ᵣᵣ ₋
constitution and reason of state, arguments from necessity and parliamentary
precedent, chivalric nostalgia and classicism, mannerist excess and baroque grandeur?
In this volume an international group of specialists in history, literature and political
theory set about reconstructing the mental world of the Jacobean court and challenging older orthodoxies on Jacobean politics, ideology, religion and culture.

While the volume marks fresh departures in the study of the Jacobean court, it
makes no attempt to offer a comprehensive study of the era. Rather, it presents
chapters of original research, strongly interpretive in character, and sometimes in disagreement. There are three different but highly suggestive interpretations of the role
and writings of the king himself from Jenny Wormald, Johann Sommerville and Paul
Christianson which, taken together, provide the most definitive portrait yet offered of
James as king and theorist. Several essays give important new emphasis to the
neglected early years of James's reign. Other contributions examine the way in which
the court articulated its political ideology, the multiple centres within Jacobean court
culture, and the tensions confronted by its writers and artists. Fresh perspectives on
the origins of and changes in divine right theory are also offered, along with discussions of the court's religious views, the impact of Roman philosophy and common
law on Jacobean court culture, the relationship of court culture to court politics, and
the influence of the court on the literature and art collecting of the period.

Royal court culture in early modern Europe is proving an important and exciting
area of interdisciplinary concern. While revisionism in early seventeenth-century
history has transformed the landscape of early Stuart studies, the new historicism has
also raised major questions for standard interpretations of early Stuart literature. This
volume forms part of the continuing dialogue between historians and literary scholars
and makes an important contribution to the debate among early modern specialists on
the role of the court in determining the pattern of political order and disorder.

THE MENTAL WORLD OF THE JACOBEAN COURT

THE MENTAL WORLD OF THE JACOBEAN COURT

Edited by
LINDA LEVY PECK
Professor of History, Purdue University

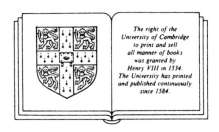

The right of the
University of Cambridge
to print and sell
all manner of books
was granted by
Henry VIII in 1534.
The University has printed
and published continuously
since 1584.

CAMBRIDGE UNIVERSITY PRESS
Cambridge   New York   Port Chester
Melbourne   Sydney

CAMBRIDGE UNIVERSITY PRESS
Cambridge, New York, Melbourne, Madrid, Cape Town, Singapore, São Paulo

Cambridge University Press
The Edinburgh Building, Cambridge CB2 2RU, UK

Published in the United States of America by Cambridge University Press, New York

www.cambridge.org
Information on this title: www.cambridge.org/9780521375672

© Cambridge University Press 1991

First published 1991
This digitally printed first paperback version 2005

A catalogue record for this publication is available from the British Library

Library of Congress Cataloguing in Publication data
The mental world of the Jacobean court / edited by Linda Levy Peck
p.   cm.
ISBN 0-521-37567-3
1. Great Britain – Court and courtiers – History – 17th century.
2. Great Britain – Intellectual life – 17th century. 3. Great
Britain – History – James I, 1603–1625. I. Peck, Linda Levy.
DA391.M37 1992
941.06'1–dc20   90–24160   CIP

ISBN-13 978-0-521-37567-2 hardback
ISBN-10 0-521-37567-3 hardback

ISBN-13 978-0-521-02104-3 paperback
ISBN-10 0-521-02104-9 paperback

CONTENTS

List of illustrations   *page* ix
Preface   xii

1 The mental world of the Jacobean court: an introduction
   LINDA LEVY PECK   1

PART I
RECONSTRUCTING THE JACOBEAN COURT

2 Patronage and politics under the Tudors   21
   WALLACE MACCAFFREY

3 James VI and I, *Basilikon Doron* and *The Trew Law of Free
   Monarchies*: the Scottish context and the English translation   36
   JENNY WORMALD

4 James I and the divine right of kings: English politics and
   continental theory   55
   J. P. SOMMERVILLE

5 Royal and parliamentary voices on the ancient constitution,
   c. 1604–1621   71
   PAUL CHRISTIANSON

PART II
COURT CULTURE AND COURT POLITICS

6 Cultural diversity and cultural change at the court of James I   99
   MALCOLM SMUTS

7 Lancelot Andrewes, John Buckeridge, and avant-garde
   conformity at the court of James I   113
   PETER LAKE

Contents

8 Robert Cecil and the early Jacobean court   134
   PAULINE CROFT

9 The mentality of a Jacobean grandee   148
   LINDA LEVY PECK

10 Seneca and Tacitus in Jacobean England   169
   J. H. M. SALMON

PART III
LITERATURE AND ART

11 The court of the first Stuart queen   191
   LEEDS BARROLL

12 The masque of Stuart culture   209
   JERZY LIMON

13 Robert Carr, Earl of Somerset, as collector and patron   230
   A. R. BRAUNMULLER

14 John Donne, kingsman?   251
   ANNABEL PATTERSON

Notes   273
Index   353

ILLUSTRATIONS

Between pages 178 and 179

1 James I, accession medal, with laurel wreath, describing him as Emperor of the Whole Island of Britain, 1603. Reproduced by permission of the Department of Coins and Medals, British Museum.

2 Bezant: James I in royal robes kneeling with uplifted hands before an altar; before him on the carpet are the four crowns of England, Scotland, France and Ireland, with Latin quotation from Psalm cxvi: 'What shall I render unto the Lord for all the benefits he hath done unto me', 1603. Reproduced by permission of the Department of Coins and Medals, British Museum.

3 James VI, *Basilikon Doron*, autograph page. Royal MS 18 B xv. Reproduced by permission of the British Library.

4 Henry Peacham, *Basilikon Emblemata*. Royal MS 12 A lxvi, f. 38v. Reproduced by permission of the British Library.

5 James I, woodcut. Huntington Library STC 24639 1605.

6 Isaac Oliver, portrait of King James and Prince Henry. Add. MS 36932. Reproduced by permission of the British Library.

7 Reynald Elstrack, engraving of James I in parliament, second state, with shields of English, Scottish and Irish nobility, and portraits of King James, Prince Charles, and English privy councillors. Reproduced by permission of the British Museum, Department of Prints and Drawings.

8 Daniel Mytens, portrait of James I, 1621. Reproduced by permission of the National Portrait Gallery, London.

9 Paul van Somer, portrait of Queen Anne at Oatlands with Inigo Jones gate in background, 1617. Reproduced by permission of Her Majesty The Queen, Royal Collections.

10 Inigo Jones, The Queen's House, Greenwich. Reproduced by permission of the Provost and Fellows of Worcester College, Oxford.

11 Inigo Jones, Penthesileia, masque costume for the Countess of Bedford, Devonshire Collection, Chatsworth. Reproduced by permission of the Trustees of the Chatsworth Settlement.

12 Robert Peake, portrait of Prince Henry with Sir John Harington. Reproduced by permission of the Metropolitan Museum of Art, purchase, Pulitzer Bequest.

13 Somerset House Conference, 1604, group portrait of envoys from England, Spain and the Spanish Netherlands to commemorate peace treaty with Spain. Reproduced by permission of the National Portrait Gallery, London.

14 John de Critz, portrait of Robert Cecil, Earl of Salisbury, in garter robes, Hatfield House. Reproduced by permission of the Marquess of Salisbury.

15 William Larkin, portrait of George Villiers, Duke of Buckingham. Reproduced by permission of the National Portrait Gallery, London.

16 Inigo Jones, New Exchange, drawing of 1618–19, Reproduced by permission of the Provost and Fellows of Worcester College, Oxford.

17 Audley End. Reproduced by permission of the British Architectural Library, RIBA.

18 Inigo Jones, Banqueting House. Reproduced by permission of the Royal Commission on Historical Monuments.

19 Tomb of Henry Howard and Frances de Vere, Earl and Countess of Surrey, 1614. St Michael's, Framlingham. Photo by Adrian Morgan.

20 Daniel Mytens, portrait of Thomas Howard, Earl of Arundel, with sculpture gallery, at Arundel Castle. Reproduced by permission of the National Portrait Gallery, London.

21 Jacopo da Ponte (Bassano Vecchio), 'Beheading of St John', owned by Robert Carr, Earl of Somerset. Reproduced by permission of the Statens Museum for Kunst, Copenhagen.

22 Tintoretto, 'A Maze', owned by Robert Carr, Earl of Somerset. Reproduced by permission of Her Majesty The Queen, Royal Collections.

23 John Speed, Military Map 1603–4, showing locations of battles of the Wars of the Roses with a lengthy genealogical chart displaying James I's descent from William the Conqueror. Reproduced by permission of the Bibliothèque Nationale, Paris.

24 John Speed, *Theatre of the Empire of Great Britaine* (London, 1611), map of England and Scotland with the capital cities of London and Edinburgh. Reproduced by permission of the University of Illinois.

25 John Speed, *Theatre of the Empire of Great Britaine*, map of Ireland. Reproduced by permission of the University of Illinois.

26 and 27 'Watche George', part of insignia of the order of the garter, St

George killing the dragon on one side, watch with one hand on the other. Reproduced by permission of the Department of European Sculpture and Antiquities, Metropolitan Museum of Art.

28 and 29 Mermaid ewer and shell basin, New Year's gift presented by Roger Manners, Earl of Rutland, to Henry Howard, Earl of Northampton. Reproduced by permission of the Victoria and Albert Museum, London.

30 Good Shepherd chalice, owned by Bishop John Buckeridge. Reproduced by kind permission of St John's College, Oxford.

31 Rules for translating the Bible, 1604, issued by King James. Cambridge University Archives. Reproduced by permission of the Syndics of Cambridge University Library.

32 Thomas Lodge, *Workes of Seneca* frontispiece. Reproduced by permission of the Folger Shakespeare Library.

33 Isaac Oliver, miniature of John Donne, 1616. Reproduced by permission of Her Majesty The Queen, Royal Collections.

PREFACE

This volume grows out of a conference on 'The Mental World of the Jacobean Court' held in March 1988 at the Folger Shakespeare Library in Washington, DC and sponsored by the Folger Institute Center for the History of British Political Thought. Several of the essays in this volume began as papers presented at that meeting. It is a rare privilege to be asked to organize a conference at the Folger Shakespeare Library and a great challenge. I want to express my great thanks to Werner Gundersheimer, Director of the Folger Shakespeare Library and Barbara Mowat, Chair of the Folger Institute. The Steering Committee of the Folger Institute Center for the History of British Political Thought invited me to help shape this programme and I am most grateful to J. G. A. Pocock, Lois Schwoerer, Gordon Schochet and Lena Cowen Orlin for this opportunity. To Lena Orlin, Executive Director of the Folger Institute, I owe a special debt of gratitude for her constant help, wise counsel and wit. Carol Brobeck and Gregory Barz of the Folger Institute were of invaluable aid in the preparations for the conference. The meeting was supported by the Research Programs Division of the National Endowment for the Humanities, the John Ben Snow Memorial Trust, the George Washington University and the Exxon Education Foundation.

The conference generated a great deal of excitement and drew a large and distinguished interdisciplinary audience. All of the participants benefited from comments provided by Thomas Cogswell, David Norbrook, David Harris Sacks, Donald Kelley and Gordon Schochet.

I am very grateful to Purdue University, to Vice President Varro T. Tyler, Dean David Caputo and to the history department and its head, John J. Contreni, for allowing me the opportunity to teach a seminar at the Folger and to organize this conference. I wish to thank Joyce R. Good and the history department staff under the direction of Judy McHenry who were, as always, both gracious and efficient in supporting this endeavour.

In editing this volume, I benefited from the very helpful advice of John Guy, John Morrill, Jenny Wormald, David Bevington and John Salmon. To William Davies of Cambridge University Press I am indebted *inter alia* for the suggestion that the book have illustrations, a project that sent me on a voyage of discovery. For permission to reproduce photographs of Jacobean paintings, drawings, metalwork, buildings and tombs, I am most grateful to Her Majesty The Queen, the Marquess of Salisbury, The Trustees of the Chatsworth Trust and the Duke of Devonshire, the Bibliothèque Nationale, Paris, the National Portrait Gallery, the British Museum, the British Library, the Syndics of Cambridge University Library, the Folger Shakespeare Library, the Huntington Library, the Metropolitan Museum of Art, the Royal Institute of British Architects, the Royal Commission on Historical Monuments, St John's College, Oxford, the Statens Museum for Kunst, Copenhagen, the Victoria and Albert Museum and Worcester College, Oxford. I have benefited greatly from the aid of archivists and curators at the British Library, the British Museum, the Huntington Library, the Metropolitan Museum of Art, the Middle Temple and the Newberry Library. I wish particularly to thank Peter Barber and Helen Wallis of the British Library Map Department and Philippa Glanville, Curator of Metalwork at the Victoria and Albert Museum, not only for teaching me about their specialities but also for showing me treasures that made their way into this volume. I wish especially to thank John Millard, Adrian and Tristan Morgan, members of the Church of St Michael's, Framlingham, for their great kindness in photographing the Surrey tomb. I cast my bread upon the waters and was repaid manyfold with great kindness and good will.

This is a fruitful harvest: each of these essays is a new and thought-provoking contribution to the fields of history, literature and political thought. Taken together, *The mental world of the Jacobean court* offers fresh perspectives on early modern politics and culture which it is hoped will stimulate further work on this important period in English and European history.

Linda Levy Peck
West Lafayette, Indiana
September, 1990

1 THE MENTAL WORLD OF THE JACOBEAN COURT: AN INTRODUCTION

Linda Levy Peck

The proclamation of James VI of Scotland as King of England on 25 March 1603 announced the accession of a foreign monarch to the English throne, and brought the creation of a new royal court, the display of new court ritual and culture, new conceptions of kingship and of empire, the imposition of a new elite and a new relationship with the continent of Europe. It constituted a break with the past that the Stuarts sought to smooth over in the interest of political stability and which later historians have been only too willing to accept.[1] But no melding of Scottish thistle with Tudor rose in court iconography could overcome the fact that England had been dramatically transformed when the Virgin Queen breathed her last on 24 March. Improvisation by Robert Cecil in drafting the proclamation of the Scot as 'king of these imperial crowns',[2] lack of other suitable, i.e. powerful and Protestant claimants to the throne, and longstanding concern for a peaceful transition meant that the foreign king was warmly welcomed. But that desire should not keep us from recognizing that something new was created with the beginning of the Stuart dynasty.

Although much attention has been paid to the Elizabethan and Caroline courts, much less has been paid to the Jacobean court, in many ways at once the most problematic and the most fascinating. Its politics and culture have been subsumed by extending the Elizabethan up to 1618, or absorbed by the Caroline, commencing in 1625. A recent work discussing major changes that occurred in the visual arts at the Caroline court began by citing Thomas Howard, Earl of Arundel's trips to Italy in 1609 and 1613.[3] When not absorbed, the Jacobean court has been long derided as drunken and debauched, described most recently as 'one of the least attractive courts in history'.[4] Indeed, the historiography of the Jacobean court was created in the Commonwealth and Protectorate periods to justify the execution of Charles I

1

and the abolition of monarchy. Although attempts began immediately to challenge such interpretations and were later repeated, the revision of the court's reputation began in earnest only recently.[5]

Yet King James made peace with Spain in 1604 after two decades of warfare and reestablished political and cultural contact with the continent; created the plantation of Ulster; incorporated Scots into the English political elite, fought for Union with Scotland and, when that was unsuccessful, ruled Scotland from London and planted viable colonies in the New World;[6] vigorously contested Roman Catholic doctrine and had the Bible translated into English. How, without understanding the Jacobean court, are we to understand the world of the late Shakespeare, Jonson and Webster, divine right theory and pragmatic negotiation between king and political elite, court scandal and court reform, chivalric nostalgia and classicism, mannerist excess and baroque grandeur, appeals to the ancient constitution and reason of state, arguments from necessity and parliamentary precedent? All these, characteristic of the Jacobean court, became decisive elements in the development of seventeenth-century monarchy and court culture. By bringing together specialists in history, literature and political theory, this volume embarks on an attempt to reconstruct the mental world of the Jacobean court.

The royal court and court culture in early modern Europe is currently an important and exciting area of study in history, literature and political theory.[7] Furthermore, in the last decade, revisionist work in early Stuart history by Conrad Russell, Mark Kishlansky, John Morrill and Kevin Sharpe among others has transformed the landscape of early Stuart studies. The new historicism in literature, in works by Martin Butler, Jonathan Goldberg, Jerzy Limon, Annabel Patterson, Stephen Greenblatt and others, has also raised major questions for standard interpretations of early Stuart literature.[8] Other courts have drawn recent attention. David Starkey has recently published a volume of essays, *The English Court*, which focuses especially on the royal Household from the fifteenth to the seventeenth centuries; Malcolm Smuts has addressed the construction of a royalist tradition from Elizabeth to Charles I.[9]

The mental world of the Jacobean court marks fresh departures in the study of the Jacobean court. This volume makes no attempt to 'cover' the era. Rather it presents new research that challenges older orthodoxies on Jacobean politics, ideology, religion and culture. The essays give important new emphasis to the early years of James's reign long neglected by specialists. Strongly interpretive, the articles are, at times, in disagreement. David Harris Sacks has suggested in another context that, 'the practices and values of society . . . are always contested and forever in a dialogue of challenge and reaffirmation'.[10] This volume self-consciously speaks with several voices (much as the Jacobean court itself did). Thus, the volume provides three different but highly suggestive interpretations of the role and writings of the king himself from Jennifer Wormald, Johann Sommerville and Paul Christianson on a canvas that stretches from Scotland to England and the continent.

I

The English court has been defined by historians in strikingly different ways. Perez Zagorin put forward a broad definition in *The Court and the Country* arguing that it included not only all officeholders and courtiers at the centre but all officeholders in the countryside. With such a definition court and political elite became synonymous. Geoffrey Elton focused on the institutional character of the court and the importance of the Privy Council and the Court of Star Chamber at the moment when those institutions of the court began to keep their own records. More recently, in an influential essay, he has stressed that the court was the crucial point of political contact between the monarch and the political elite in sixteenth- and seventeenth-century England.

David Starkey has put forward a new and narrower definition of the court. Drawing on Tudor Household ordinances and the physical layout of Whitehall Palace, he identifies it as only those who were attendant on the king, i.e. his Household and, especially, his Privy Chamber. Within this framework of the politics of access, Neal Cuddy has provided significant new evidence on the political role of the Jacobean Scots who monopolized positions in James's Bedchamber and thereby, he argues, controlled court patronage and, often, court politics.[11] This approach emphasizes the importance of the royal Household to court politics and culture, a point borne out by Roy Strong's important study of the Household, collections and attitudes of Prince Henry. In this volume Leeds Barroll assesses Queen Anne's Household, the major influence in the Crown's cultural patronage. But access to the king's Bedchamber was not the only route to political power.

Here, Wallace MacCaffrey discusses the development of the court as the centre of the state's political patronage. Moreover, Malcolm Smuts, Pauline Croft and I assert that the court was fluid and polycentric: the court was not separate from its context; it flowed back and forth from Whitehall Palace through to the West End of London where the nobility had their city palaces to the Inns of Court that mounted masques to honour the king.

The construction of the court of James I differed in two crucial ways from that of Elizabeth. First it brought a new elite, the Jacobean Scots who did not only serve in the royal Household. In a proclamation at the beginning of the reign the king explicitly noted them as a group that he wished to name to the Privy Council.[12] Secondly, although we will refer for convenience to the court of James I, it was built not around one court but ultimately three: that of the king, the queen and Prince Henry, later replaced by Prince Charles.[13] This multifaceted court spoke with a polyphony of cultural voices. Finally, the court of James I constructed its own myths, its own ceremonies and its own rituals, different from those of the Virgin Queen even if, because of their anti-quarian imagery and Stuart emphasis on legitimacy, they built on Tudor iconography. Jacobean court culture was strongly influenced by the politics and ideology of the 1590s both in England and Scotland, especially increasing concern to combat Catholic and Calvinist theories of resistance to kings and renewed interest in the invocation in political ritual of the symbols of ancient Rome.

In a larger study it would be possible to examine more closely the mentality and informal power structures that animated Jacobean court life, its rites, symbolism, ideology and material culture. Such a study would, among other things, render visible the interaction and the tension between the word and the visual which is present in literature, court ritual and in religious thought. It would demonstrate how the Jacobean court 'translated' classical and conti-nental texts and art, material objects and habits of thought into an English context. In this introduction it is only possible to make some brief comments on its attitude toward the word and the visual, time and space, exteriors and interiors, all-important facets of Jacobean court culture.

II

The written word was supreme at the Jacobean court especially at the beginning of the reign and the king, who had sought to anglicize Scots,[14] had a great hand in trying to control his subjects' language. Within the realm, the accession of James I brought an explosion of print. The new monarch was a new type: the king as *littérateur*. Peter Blayney estimates that thousands of copies of *Basilikon Doron* were printed within the first few weeks of the reign. All the king's writings on monarchy, demonology and religion were reprinted and 'manye books newe wrytten th'admiracion and prayse of him'.[15] In the controversy over the papal interdict of Venice, James and others supported by him wrote on behalf of Venetian sovereignty. The king had works translated and sent to crowned heads all over Europe and brought writers like Marc'Antonio de Dominis and others to England to take part in various battles in this paper war.[16] The king fostered a propaganda campaign as strong as Henry VIII's with Rome. Even if censorship laws were not often enforced, it was always a factor to be reckoned with: James discarded the ecclesiastical canons of 1606 when the clergy were unable to support the Hollanders against Spain without accepting *de facto* monarchy, anathema to the Stuart king.

Word and image were brought together in the medals and coins struck by Renaissance rulers. In 1602 Antoine Rascas de Baggris had stressed to Henry IV the importance of the medal both as royal monument and currency:

It is not wealth, or Power . . . or the extent or length of the Princes' command . . . that give them glory or memory, but only two sorts of things: one being the actions, above all heroic, that produce the subject of glory and memory . . . the other . . . those actions that establish them or give them their perfect last being, by perpetuating them after their century . . . only true and perfect Medals . . . are capable of containing the aforesaid August History and Living Memory of the great Princes . . . as much by portraiture as by writing joined together. And . . . the said Medals alone are again the Monument, the only eternal and the only authentic one and the only one belonging just to the great Princes; and consequently the most perfect for containing, publishing and eternalizing their said glory and memory.[17]

Although both Elizabeth and James I used Roman motifs James I changed English iconography. James I was the first English monarch to portray himself on his coinage as a Roman Emperor (see Plate 1). In his accession medal of 1603 copied perhaps from a miniature by Nicholas Hilliard, he is presented in armour and crowned with a laurel wreath, and lays claim to the title of Emperor in the coin's inscription.[18] Indeed, in the first year of his reign he called himself Emperor of Great Britain which he later dropped as hopes for a 'perfect union' between England and Scotland faded. James imagined that empire as a unitary one. In a church offering called a bezant cast at the beginning of the reign, the king kneels in thanksgiving before an altar with the four crowns of England, Scotland, Ireland and France before him (see Plate 2). The bezant is encircled with a Latin quotation from Psalm 116 which the Geneva and, later, the King James Bible translated 'What shall I render unto the Lord for all his benefits unto me'?[19] God showered favour on the new monarch who similarly was the fountain of favour to his subjects. Word and image were brought together too in graphics such as the woodcut of James early in the reign which carried this benediction: 'Blessed be they that blesse you / And cursed be they that curse you' (see Plate 5).

Not since King Alfred had the king himself played such an important role in translation of sacred writing. As the composers of the 'King James' Bible wrote in their preface, he was the 'principal mover and author' of that work not only because of his support for the enterprise but through his 'religious and learned discourse'. James ordered the translation of the Bible into English shortly after he came to the throne responding to a request made at the Hampton Court conference.

His Majesty wished that some especial pains should be taken in that behalf for one uniform translation (professing that he could never, yet, see a bible well translated in English; but the worst of all, his Majesty thought the Geneva to be) . . . Marry withal he gave this caveat, upon a word cast out by my Lord of London [the Bishop of London], that no marginal notes should be added, having found in them which are annexed to the Geneva translations . . . some notes very partial, untrue, seditious, and savouring too much of slanderous and traitorous conceits.[20]

He had rules drawn up for translators at Oxford, Cambridge and London and promised them ecclesiastical preferment. He insisted that there be no marginalia and 'the old ecclesiastical words [were] to be kept, viz the word church not be translated congregation' (see Plate 31).[21] The King James Bible was designed to speak with authority, to present a single voice without the disputation characteristic of the Geneva Bible. Yet inwardly the Jacobean church was diverse, reflecting, as time went on, a multitude of doctrinal positions from Calvinist to Arminian. Annabel Patterson argues that John Donne was uneasy with the discourse of divine right within which he preached and wrote. And Peter Lake demonstrates that Jacobean bishops like Lancelot Andrewes and John Buckeridge increasingly emphasized the importance of ritual and 'the beauty of holiness'.

The king was highly conscious of the importance of the political language and symbolism of obligation signified by the coronation. He had shaped the coronation of Anne of Denmark as Queen of Scotland including the rite of anointing of which the kirk disapproved. Now for the first time he had the coronation oath translated into English. Although it followed the Latin closely, the English oath made important changes by translating *quas vulgus elegerit* as 'the laws the people have', instead of 'the laws the people shall or have chosen'.[22] The king's promise to uphold the laws was embellished in English to include reference to the royal prerogative.[23] In *The Trew Law of Free Monarchies*, he had written that William the Conqueror 'gave the law and took none, changed the laws, inverted the order of government, set down the strangers his followers in many of the old possessors rooms'. Moreover he had also imposed his language through conquest: 'their old laws, which to this day they are ruled by, are written in his language [William's], and not in theirs. And yet his successors have with great happiness enjoyed the Crown to this day.'[24] James claimed to rule not by conquest but by inheritance. Nevertheless, the decorative emblem of Speed's military map of 1603–4, which takes up almost as much room as the geographic image, showed his descent from William to support his right to rule (see Plate 23).

If the king emphasized the word, other centres within and without the court became more and more interested in a visual culture. Queen Anne, lover of court entertainments, fostered that particularly Jacobean form, the court masque;[25] leaders of the Jacobean church increasingly stressed 'the beauty of holiness'; and Jacobean courtiers collected High Renaissance, mannerist and baroque painting. The religious icon made secular – the portrait miniature – gave way to infinite space and movement as in Rubens's Banqueting House ceiling.

Instead of deifying the Virgin Queen the Jacobean court celebrated family and uxoriousness; even male favourites were brought within an ideology of family as the Duke of Buckingham called James dad and gossip and James I, whose political writings stressed patriarchal authority, signed himself 'dad'. Court weddings among leading noble families arranged by the king were celebrated with court masques and nuptials of members of Queen Anne's Household were consecrated with splendour. At the same time that the king presented his favourite Somerset in marriage to Frances Howard, Queen Anne presented her lady-in-waiting, Jane Drummond, to the Earl of Roxborough in ceremonies costing £30,000. In debate over the union King James told parliament in 1604: 'I am the Husband, and the whole Isle is my lawfull Wife; I am the Head, and it is my body.'[26]

This official view of Stuart kingship was performed in several media. Masques put on before and by the king and the court were central texts of court culture during the reign of James and Charles, and Jerzy Limon provides a reading of their code.[27] Stephen Harrison's *Arches of Triumph* published in 1604 presents the structures that were to greet the king upon his formal entry into London, even though the occasion had to be postponed because of plague. But public entries and progresses which had been so important a part of the public display of the Elizabethan period were gradually cut back under James both because of expense, the king's dislike of public ceremonial and preference for private and informal entertainments such as hunting.[28] If Elizabeth went to dance in the houses of the nobility, James took some of his nobility and favourites to hunt with him. While James encouraged informality at court and personal access, the minister, John Burgess, was imprisoned for saying there were murmurings that the king was not appearing in public. But if James I expended his energies in the written word and in solemnizing himself in written texts, Charles I, like his mother, was more interested in visual culture. This was expressed in his revival of court ceremonial,[29] his patronage of continental artists such as Rubens and Van Dyck, and his collection of Renaissance and baroque paintings which made him the greatest collector amongst English monarchs. In Van Dyck's portraits of King Charles on horseback, his father's taste for hunting was transformed into the mythic image of the ruler subduing nature, the rational overcoming the irrational.[30] Indeed his father's texts were transformed into visual images in the paintings by Rubens for the ceiling of Banqueting House. There James I was apotheosized as Solomon, the symbol of good government, sweeping away the bad, giving judgement and brought to Heaven by God himself. It was the text of *The Trew Law of Free Monarchies* symbolized in baroque imagery.[31]

III

The Jacobean court located itself in time and space in complex fashion. Although it built on the Elizabethan notion that England, and sometimes Britain, was the elect nation, King James identified himself not as Constantine, but as Old Testament exemplars such as David,[32] or as an Old Testament king, Samuel or Solomon. Moreover, his role as the leader of Protestant states developed during the oath of allegiance controversy and the controversy over the Venetian interdict was reflected concretely in time: a clock commissioned to celebrate a diplomatic triumph presents the king, the Prince of Wales and Henry IV holding the Pope's nose to the grindstone.[33] In *The Trew Law* James identified himself with Fergus the Irish chieftain who had subdued Scotland. Moreover, Paul Christianson points out in this volume that the king himself shared the contemporary discourse of the ancient constitution. Nevertheless, as Jonathan Goldberg has demonstrated, the king presented himself most often as a Roman emperor.[34] The king's interest in natural law theory and the Roman law is a constant in his writings. Like continental monarchs who modelled their entries into capitals on major occasions on Roman models (as did Queen Elizabeth at the turn of the century), the king and his court were especially attuned to symbols of the Roman Empire.[35]

At the same time, Roy Strong has emphasized the chivalric revival fostered by Prince Henry.[36] Jacobean courtiers ran at tilts and funeral monuments celebrated the nobility's heraldic and chivalric achievements (see Plate 19). But this revival of the chivalric was complicated by the interest in the Roman and the 'modern': Jacobean members of the Order of the Garter, the highest chivalric order in England, put watch movements in their 'Georges', the image of St George slaying the dragon that symbolized their order (see Plates 26 and 27). They wrapped their walls in tapestries with biblical and classical stories and commemorated themselves after death in Lord Mayor's gowns over knightly armour, in Roman poses, or in French-inspired catafalques by Nicholas Stone with sculpture after the antique holding up the ends.[37] But increasingly as the reign went on, the court became more and more influenced by the Italian Renaissance, mannerism and the baroque. The Earl of Arundel on the Grand Tour in 1612–13 began to collect antique statuary. He adopted a Roman view of his own life when he dedicated his collections to the fame of his family.[38] By the middle of the reign Jacobean courtiers began to patronize the classical Palladian architecture preferred by Inigo Jones.

The study of history had become of increasing interest to the English gentry in the sixteenth century. The educated English, whose libraries were over-whelmingly made up of continental books, collected European histories in the late sixteenth and early seventeenth century. The Elizabethan Society of Antiquaries founded in the wake of the publication of William Camden's *Britannia* in 1586 was made up of officeholders, country gentlemen and heralds led by Camden and Sir Robert Cotton with ties to leading courtiers such as the Earl of Essex and Henry Howard. The Society used original documents and coins to scrutinize the origins of English institutions. Efforts to revive the meetings which had petered out in the first few years of the new reign ended abruptly in 1614 when, as Sir Henry Spelman wrote, 'the king took a mislike' to the Society's meetings not knowing that they did not mean to inquire into *arcana imperii*. The king preferred Edmund Bolton's idea for an 'Academy Roial' under the king's patronage, an historical society with knightly trappings that would not investigate issues such as the origin of parliament (the Antiquaries' topic for 1604).[39] Francis Bacon wrote of history in a manner not unlike contemporary masques, 'For as Statues and Pictures are dumb histories, so histories are speaking Pictures'.[40] Alongside this Neoplatonic statement, however, historians like Camden and Bacon himself became more and more influenced by Machiavelli, Gucciardini and their predecessor in *realpolitik*, Tacitus. Seneca and Tacitus and their description of the Roman Empire's first century was a strong influence in England beginning in the 1590s and continued to inform Jacobean historiography and writing generally as John Salmon demonstrates in his essay. Although Jacobeans drew on medieval legal and political precedent in parliamentary debate, at the same time, they saw themselves as 'modern', as Sir John Holles put it, and living in a time of 'reason of state'.[41]

In the Jacobean era new attitudes toward empire were spelled out which shaped the colonization of Ireland and laid the basis for English expansion across the Atlantic.[42] James's proclamation declaring the union of England and Scotland on 19 May 1603 indicated that he intended to secure it through parliamentary enactment. His plan for the union was, however, made clear: his imperial crown did not mean one king ruling over separate realms. Instead, until the king, with the advice of parliament, could establish the Union, he commanded his subjects to hold 'the two realms as presently united, and as one Realme and Kingdome, and the Subjects of both the Realmes as one people, brethren and members of one body'.[43]

The imperial theme so prevalent in Jacobean ideology and policy was reflected in the way in which James and his court placed themselves in space. The reign's first great map of England and Scotland, decorated with medallions of Britannia and Cunobelinus provided views of the two capitals Edinburgh and London (see Plate 24). John Speed's 'military map' of England and Scotland, 1603–4, simultaneously, depicted the battlefields of the Wars of the Roses and celebrated the legitimacy of the Stuart dynasty.[44] In the upper right-hand sheet, recently discovered at the Bibliothèque Nationale, King James and Queen Anne are presented at the top of a genealogical tree rooted in William the Conqueror (see Plate 23).[45]

The greatest achievement of the reign in map-making was John Speed's *The Theatre of the Empire of Great Britaine* containing maps of England, Scotland and Ireland with individual maps of the counties. Not only did these present all three of James's kingdoms, they also represented the political ideology and social structure of all three.[46] For instance, the map of Ireland shows the Irish gentleman and gentlewoman, the Irish civil man and woman and the 'wild' Irish (see Plate 25). Such emblems reinforced the views expressed when James created the plantation of Ulster in 1611 to root Protestantism in hostile Ireland. The Irish were wild, rather like the painted natives encountered in the New World. As Cicero described life before the beginning of government, they wandered up and down and did not live in settled villages and towns. The plantation would, as natural law theory suggested, draw them down into civil society.

IV

Jacobean architecture is diverse, ranging from the prodigy houses like Audley End to the Queen's House, Greenwich, Inigo Jones's introduction of classical architecture to England, and the Banqueting House, one of the few architectural renovations that remain of the Jacobean building programme for Whitehall Palace (see Plates 17, 10 and 18). Even if form did not always follow function in the seventeenth century (and in a court that accorded decoration religious and theoretical importance, why should it?) Audley End, built by Thomas Howard, Earl of Suffolk, was one of the last of the great country palaces. Its function of entertaining the entire court on progress, was already anachronistic when it was built as James's dislike for public show had been made manifest from the beginning of the reign. If Audley End symbolized one function of the courtier, Arundel House, the home of his nephew projected another. Instead of displaying the might of the Howards in a house that could accommodate the whole court (the stronghold become showplace), the Earl of Arundel made Arundel House the exemplar of Italian and antique culture which he came to love while on the Grand Tour with Inigo Jones. Arundel turned his house into a museum celebrated in Daniel Mytens's twin paintings of the Earl and Countess of Arundel, the Earl pointing to his antique sculpture, the Countess to family portraits displayed in a Jacobean long gallery adorned with Italian chairs called *sgabelli*.[47]

Much attention has been paid to the English country house and Lawrence Stone has distinguished the seventeenth- and eighteenth-century English nobility who preferred the countryside from the French nobility who built city palaces.[48] In fact the Jacobean nobility built city palaces too, among them Northampton House, Buckingham's York House, and Arundel House. Robert Cecil built both Hatfield and the New Exchange as Pauline Croft discusses in her essay: the one, a great prodigy house, the other, part of the development of the Strand and the West End. Commerce and culture combined at its opening with entertainment by Inigo Jones. These houses suggest not only changing tastes but changing conceptions of the role of the nobility, from magnate to courtier and from courtier to virtuoso. In addition they epitomized that focus on House, characteristic of the European aristocracy, which meant, simultaneously, their family and their property, their genealogy and their city palace or country holdings.[49]

Art historians are now approaching interior decoration in ways of interest to all historians. Peter Thornton places furniture and interior decoration within a total environment, discovering how rooms were laid out by contemporaries based on inventories and other records and the relationship of furniture, fabric and objects to the architecture and cultural significance of the buildings in which they were placed. Philippa Glanville provides a social history of the craftsmen who supplied silver metal work to the luxury market and allows us to draw a more complex picture of the life of the Jacobean court and the aristocratic households that formed its polycentre.[50] Art and luxury objects increasingly became the medium of exchange between clients and patrons. This aspect of material culture leads to the question of whether such objects signified only their luxury or whether they simultaneously suggested *vanitas*? In examining *pronkstilleven*, the sumptuous still lifes produced in Holland in the seventeenth century, Sam Segal argues that beneath their extraordinary portrayal of the surface, texture and richness of textile, metal and food there was a moral purpose: to remind their viewers that these works of vanity signified the finiteness of this world.[51] What are we to make of a luxurious mannerist ewer and basin designed to pour rose water through the nipples of the mermaid into a shell basin (see Plates 28 and 29)? Is this only an object of conspicuous consumption, made up by London silversmiths for the Earl of Rutland to present as a New Year's gift to Henry Howard, Earl of Northampton? Or does the subject of the mermaid, a common one in sixteenth- and seventeenth-century imagery suggest as well the wealth, ostentation and siren song sung by the life of the European court?

In 1630 the Dukes of Gonzaga the ruling family of Mantua were down on their luck. Despite failing resources they had continued to decorate the Ducal Palace, already adorned with wonderful frescoes by Andrea Mantegna, with the work of Giulio Romano. They commissioned him to build and to decorate their new summer palace, the Palazzo del Te. When the fortunes of the Gonzaga failed, Charles I, whose wife Henrietta Maria was their relation, bought their art collection confirming a shift in taste that simultaneously created the greatest art collection of any English monarch and made Italy and Italian art the focus of English aspirations. But this taste was not Caroline as often assumed. It was Jacobean.

By making peace with Spain in 1604 James I reestablished ties to Europe and its culture. English ambassadors such as Sir Henry Wotton and Sir Dudley Carleton helped to frame a new taste by using art works as gifts to great courtiers and by putting together collections of painting and sculpture for them to buy.[52] Most earlier analyses have focused on Arundel, Buckingham and Prince Charles as the centre of this new connoisseurship in the late

1610s and 1620s.[53] A. R. Braunmuller demonstrates that Robert Carr, Earl of Somerset, was also an important patron of Italian artists as was Robert Cecil, Earl of Salisbury. Their contribution and that of the Jacobean court generally to this sea-change in English taste should be brought to the foreground.

In 1603 by European standards, English painting was old-fashioned and provincial. Its walls were hung as in the sixteenth century with Low Countries tapestries. By the end of James's reign, in the collections of Cecil, Carr, Arundel, Pembroke and Buckingham, English collectors were competing with continental courts for High Renaissance masterpieces, mannerist and baroque paintings. Much as the Spanish monarch, Philip IV undertook a major building project, the Buen Retiro,[54] so too did James I undertake plans to rebuild Whitehall Palace. Although only the Banqueting House was completed, along with Jones's Queen's House at Greenwich, it signalled the change in Jacobean taste as it became more and more influenced by the Italian. Peter Paul Rubens who had worked at the Mantuan court first came into contact with Jacobean collectors when he painted Alatheia, Countess of Arundel, in 1620. His pupil Van Dyck came to England for the first time in 1620–1. Rubens himself served as a diplomat for the Spanish Netherlands in London in 1620–1 and at that time began discussions with Inigo Jones on a programme that would culminate in his extraordinary paintings for the Banqueting House ceiling. Rubens wrote in 1629, four years after King James's death

This island seems to me to be a spectacle worthy of interest of every gentleman, not only for the beauty of the countryside and the charm of the nation; not only for the splendour of the outward culture, which seems to be extreme, as of a people rich and happy in the lap of peace, but also for the incredible quality of excellent pictures, statues and ancient inscriptions which are to be found in this court . . . Certainly in this island I find none of the crudeness which one might expect from a place so remote from Italian elegance.[55]

V

The essays in Part I examine James I, placing his writings and his performance of kingship in Scottish, English and continental contexts. Wallace MacCaffrey sets the stage for Jacobean politics by suggesting that at their accessions Henry VII and James I faced similar political problems armed with similar political capital: royal patronage. He shows how the structure and dispensation of royal patronage reflected changes in English government under the pressure of warfare and religious upheaval throughout the sixteenth century. Factional struggles resulted from the king's strategy of vesting power in a single minister, whether Wolsey, Cromwell or, during James's reign, the Duke of Buckingham. By the accession of Elizabeth there was 'one universal patron, the king, and one nation-wide pool of suitors'. Clients who sought personal standing in their counties and power at court had to demonstrate their ability to serve the queen. Yet the life and death struggle between Sir Robert Cecil and the Earl of Essex in the 1590s for the present favour of Elizabeth and the future interest of James showed that the political system was still fragile and would be dependent on the personal abilities of the new monarch.

Jenny Wormald analyses James VI and I both as king and theorist, convincingly arguing for the importance of the theoretical writings of James I in *The Trew Law of Free Monarchies* and *Basilikon Doron*. She places them in the context of Scottish political theory, much different from that of England, where they marked a significant departure both from earlier thought and practice. She goes on to suggest, however, that James's writings, which reflected his own experience of rule in Scotland, were written primarily for himself not an English audience. A lover of debate, he did not intend to announce the imposition of absolutism. When *Basilikon Doron* was republished in London in 1603 shortly after the accession of James to the throne, his English subjects snapped up thousands of copies in just a few weeks. Their misreading of the text was the first of a series of misunderstandings between the king and his new subjects.

Changing the focus to King James and continental scholarship, the king's attitude toward the common law and parliament, J. P. Sommerville challenges revisionist views that there were few differences of political principle among Englishmen in the early seventeenth century, rejects the notion that the ancient constitution lay at the centre of English political thinking, and questions the claim that English thought was strikingly insular. Rather he argues that James I's thought must be set firmly against the background of continental controversies and that he was little influenced by English common law. Unlike Jenny Wormald, he claims a continuity in James's theoretical writings both in Scotland and England in all of which he upheld the power of monarchs against theories of deposition. These views were then displayed in James's strong criticism of the House of Commons in 1621. He suggests that James correctly recognized that contract theories of government, which he had long opposed, were held by leading members of the lower House.

Paul Christianson provides a remarkably different picture of James, his court and his parliament from either Wormald or Sommerville. Instead of the playful Scottish monarch writing for himself, or the absolutist theorist of divine right whose views never wavered even after he had achieved the English throne, Christianson argues that James's views underwent a dramatic change. Describing the interplay of the king and the English parliament throughout the reign, Christianson develops at length the view that after his accession to the English throne James became an exponent of a theory of constitutional monarchy made by kings.

Part II takes up the issue of the construction of Jacobean court culture and

13

politics as displayed in the theology of leading bishops, the beliefs and practices of leading courtiers and the importation and interpretation of the Neostoics. Illustrating the complexity of Jacobean court culture, Malcolm Smuts argues that it reflected a much broader range of ideas than previously thought. Rejecting a teleological approach that looks forward to the Caroline period, he criticizes two current models of court culture, one emphasizing a few prominent patrons who imported Renaissance culture from France and Italy, the second isolating the court from the rest of the nation. Rather he argues for a polycentric court culture, setting the court in the context of the London houses of the nobility, the wider world of Westminster, London, and the Inns of Court. Moreover, he points out that cultural influence often flowed from the periphery, whether ambassadors on the continent or the cultural interests of minor courtiers. Indeed, he suggests that innovation originated more on the court's periphery than within the king's Household. He argues that Jacobean court culture included a critique of conventional ideals of courtliness.

Peter Lake offers a sensitive analysis of the works of Lancelot Andrewes, one of the leading Jacobean bishops and perhaps the most prominent court preacher of the reign, and his close associate Bishop John Buckeridge, to demonstrate how they form a crucial link connecting what he calls 'the chain of avant-garde conformist thought' between Hooker and Archbishop Laud. He explores Andrewes's attack on puritan non-conformity and preaching and his focus on the sacrament and prayer, outward demonstrations of the inward search for salvation. He notes the insufficiency of the word in a form of worship that emphasized the visual. Pointing out that all the elements were present in Andrewes's writings that were to be found in the Arminianism of the 1620s and 1630s, he is careful to stress that these were never made a coherent whole in Andrewes's thought nor were puritans persecuted in his dioceses, a significant difference between Jacobean and Caroline ecclesiastical policy.

In her essay on Robert Cecil and the early Jacobean court, Pauline Croft draws on extensive research in newly discovered Cecil manuscripts that she has published for the Camden Society. She challenges the Hurstfield portrait of Cecil as bureaucrat and, at the same time, convincingly rejects the narrow definition of the Jacobean court as Bedchamber. She questions the view put forward recently by Neal Cuddy that Cecil was denied access to King James by his Scottish entourage. Rather, she paints a convincing portrait of Cecil moving easily between Council and court and recognizing the need not only to deal with the king but also with alternative centres of power in the Households of Queen Anne and Prince Henry. She describes Cecil's own rage to build and his understanding of the political use of ritual in the period.

I explore the mentality of the Jacobean grandees, that is the ideas and social attitudes that characterized those noblemen who wielded significant political power at the Jacobean court. Focusing on Henry Howard, Earl of Northampton, I note his close ties with James I whose political outlook he shared. Northampton's education, his writings, his library and his collections demonstrate that his mental world was not primarily English but European. His writings reflected the influence of Aristotle, Cicero and Tacitus, the church fathers, canon law, and Renaissance historiography. He took an active role in the controversialist writings on the Venetian interdict. Moreover, Northampton who placed great stress on his house and the ancient nobility, had an exaggerated sense of rank. For Howard and those like him, the court was the centre of the world and fortune marked the rise and fall of great men. Only fame, reflected in building, collecting and the dominance of house, overcame fortune.

J. H. M. Salmon examines the importance of the work of Seneca and Tacitus in Jacobean England and challenges the applicability of the thesis of Gerhard Oestreich that it became 'the theory behind the powerful military and administrative structure of the centralized state of the seventeenth century'. The influence of Neostoicism through the translations and writings of Justus Lipsius and others who saw important parallels between the Roman context and Europe in the wars of religion, had different consequences in England. After providing a detailed discussion of the increasing number of editions and translations of Seneca, Tacitus, Cicero, Sallust, Plutarch and Neostoic writers in Elizabethan and Jacobean England, Salmon identifies the circles of the Earl of Essex and Prince Henry with the most influential advocates of the Neostoic movement in Jacobean England. He points to the connection of political patronage and the spread of philosophical ideas. He also examines the Neostoic movement in literature, especially the work of Ben Jonson.

Part III turns to important aspects of the patronage and performance of art and literature at the court of James I in the form of the literary patronage of Queen Anne, the artistic collection of the Jacobean favourite, Robert Carr, Earl of Somerset, the court masque and the poetry and prose of John Donne.

Leeds Barroll analyses the cultural patronage of Anne of Denmark and her Household. He argues that her political role and influence on court culture has too often been ignored or dismissed. After examining the Danish and Scottish courts in which Anne grew up, he traces the importance of men and women in the Essex circle in Queen Anne's Household after the succession. He discusses the literary patronage which flowed from the court of Queen Anne especially her most important lady-in-waiting, Lucy, Countess of Bedford. His essay provides important material, too, on the links between the Queen's Household and Robert Cecil, Secretary of State and later Lord Treasurer.

The early Stuart masque-in-performance is the subject of Jerzy Limon's essay. Analysing its spatial construction, he disagrees with previous analysts who have seen the masque as a spectacle staged, as it were, behind a proscenium arch so that the court is the real world, the masque the fictional. He shows why the court too was part of the created model of the universe in the ritual of the masque. Moreover, he goes on to argue in detail that masques were the theatrical transmutation of emblem books suggesting that 'the model of the universe created in the masque is based on the concept of the world as a book, or a text, being a projection of the king's mind'. He notes that Henry Peacham translated James's *Basilikon Doron* into an emblem book in which each picture was based on some part of the king's writings. Not only is the masque staged before the king and to the king, he is part of the masque and its text is the projection of royal wisdom.

A. R. Braunmuller provides an important new view of King James's favourite Robert Carr, Earl of Somerset. Somerset's meteoric rise at court was followed by an even greater fall in 1615. Little or no attention has been paid to the life of a favourite out of favour. Basing his essay on newly discovered inventories, Braunmuller demonstrates that Carr was an important collector of Italian art while in James's graces and, surprisingly, continued to be a literary patron decades after his fall. Carr maintained the loyalty of writers like George Chapman, courtiers like Sir John Holles and the friendship even of George Villiers, Duke of Buckingham. Despite the scandal of the Overbury murder trial, for many Somerset remained the exemplar of 'retir'd virtue'.

Finally, Annabel Patterson brings the volume full circle, as she investigates John Donne's problematic relationship to the discourse of divine right within which he worked. Most of Donne's writing was produced and conditioned by the style of James's court. Patterson insists that Donne the poet cannot be disconnected from Donne the theologian. Challenging newer historical criticism that claims him as an absolutist, she argues that his writings during James's reign were divided between satirical, even subversive, writings and anti-Catholic polemic, despite his own Catholicism, into which James drew him. Patterson places Donne's canon in the context of Jacobean politics and shows that although constrained by censorship, Donne's work yields an ambivalent 'grammar of political consciousness'.

Taken together these essays focus long overdue attention on the Jacobean court. The essays provide the most definitive portrait yet of James VI and I as king and theorist. They give renewed attention to the opening years of his reign in England to suggest how and why a new court culture was constructed and the complex political message it conveyed. Several essays examine the way in which that court articulated its political ideology, the multiple centres within Jacobean court culture and the tensions confronted by its writers and artists. On a larger scale they are part of the emerging scholarship on the relationship of state formation to rituals of power. In reinterpreting the place of the Jacobean court in seventeenth-century British history they also suggest ways in which it is possible to reintegrate political and cultural history.

PART I

RECONSTRUCTING THE JACOBEAN COURT

2 PATRONAGE AND POLITICS UNDER THE TUDORS

Wallace MacCaffrey

When James VI crossed the Tweed to become James I in the spring of 1603 he came, like his ancestor, Henry VII, a stranger to a strange land. Obviously the circumstances of each accession were widely different but many of the problems of kingship that each had to shoulder were, *mutatis mutandis*, of the same genre. Not the least of these problems was the management of royal patronage. Each of these monarchs had to take on the difficult task of mastering an established political elite, of securing their loyalty and cooperation, for it was through these men that he would be able to govern England. The capital which they had to expend in that enterprise was of at least two kinds – the intangible power of personality (with which both Henry VIII and Elizabeth were so richly endowed) and the very tangible material rewards by which the sovereign could hope to give solidity and permanence to that loyalty – the offices, honours, lands and pensions which he had at his disposal. It is this particular kind of patronage with which this chapter is concerned. It seeks to consider the ways in which this enduring element in English political life was reshaped by rulers and events in the generations of James's English predecessors.

Patronage is a large and loose term and the practice of patronage is found in most societies in some form or other. In Tudor society, lacking either extensive market mechanisms or institutional procedures for facilitating personal advancement, the individual had necessarily to seek the personal assistance of some well-placed and well-disposed sponsor. Indeed both supplicant and benefactor had their recognized social roles, governed by accepted conventions of solicitation and acknowledgement. The client's role was defined by his needs; the patron could, of course, accept or reject the individual suitor's request but there was a strong presumption that wealth and influence implied an obligation to exercise beneficence. In other words, the patron–client

21

relationship was not merely a series of random personal contacts but an essential part of the functioning social machinery.

Patronage was both private and official. The nobleman who sponsored a players' company or bestowed a few pounds on a poet was acting out of personal motives, a real interest in the arts or a desire to win applause for a culturally approved role. Political patronage, bestowed by the sovereign or by a minister of state, was unlikely to be disinterested, for the patron had a clear-cut expectation of reciprocal service from his client. Nevertheless, the monarch, like other patrons, was acting out a role which in popular conception presupposed the dispensing of benefits. There was a deep-lying assumption that one of the monarch's essential roles was that of the gift-giver, an echo of the generosity of the war-chieftain, of a Beowulf. In the consciousness of the English political classes the notion of the sovereign as not only the source of power but also as the fountain of grace, which flowed for their benefit, was firmly ingrained.

Political patronage is particularly important in societies where the formal official structure of power is inadequate to ensure full obedience to the ruler's commands. The personal bonds of patronage serve as complements to the official order thus ensuring the ruler's will is carried out. The feudal world of early medieval Europe was such a society.

In England the monarchs had from an early period expanded the authority of their office and proportionately diminished their dependence on the personal loyalty of their nobles. Within the royal entourage they had built a bureaucratic structure in which they were served by officials rather than by clients. But the patron–client relationship with their greater subjects had by no means disappeared. Aristocratic opposition could still thwart royal purposes and noble cooperation was still essential to kings who lacked permanent military and naval establishments. The tensions between the great aristocracy and the monarchs continued and patronage was a valuable emollient in easing them.

The political system of this late medieval age was backward-looking in its assumptions. The magnates, their horizons bounded by the narrow interests of the noble dynasty, viewed the king less as a national leader and more as a great lord to whom they owed personal rather than public obligations. From him flowed the favours which would advance their interests over those of rival families and whose bounty would provide the means to expand their own network of clientage. Equally important, the monarch was the umpire whose powers of mediation were the ultimate guarantor against the naked violence which lurked beneath the surface of this fragile society.

In the century before the advent of the Tudors the system roughly sketched above fell into serious disarray. The fact that four of the seven fifteenth-century kings were usurpers shifted the balance of advantage in favour of the noble client and against the royal patrons and the latter had to woo the loyalty of the aristocracy by using the powers of patronage to shore up their newly occupied thrones. The process can be seen at work in the Yorkist kings, who set out to build a new structure of loyalty on which their dynasty might securely rest. There were two elements in it. In the first full confidence and generous patronage was given to a handful of great regional magnates, such as Hastings, the Howards or the Stanleys. Given the wherewithal in lands and offices, they were expected to build up secondary nuclei of loyalty centred on each of them, thus providing a concentric ring of loyalties, radiating out from the royal centre. The great lords, recipients of royal confidence and royal bounty, in turn guaranteed the obedience of the larger regional communities in which they held sway. At the same time the kings pursued a different tack by building up an inner corps of councillors, household officers and members of the royal family circle. These men, in constant and close contact with the ruler, were more modestly rewarded, often with office rather than land. This second strategy mirrored the view of men like Fortescue who urged the necessity for greater royal independence from the great baronage.

Circumstances had in large part dictated the strategies of the Yorkist kings; the first, usurping, Tudor, faced with similar conditions, reacted in a very different manner. More favoured by the chances of fate and of war he stood upon a national political stage singularly bare of the leading actors. By the 1490s most of the great noble houses which had crowded that stage fifty years earlier had disappeared. Consequently Henry had less need to woo the greater nobles and did not seek, like his predecessors, to build up a new clientele of magnate support. Indeed fear rather than favour was the keynote of his policy and the greater nobility were kept on a tight leash through a form of legal terrorism.

The king was free to pursue more wholeheartedly the strategy essayed by Edward IV, in building up a far more bureaucratic corps of servants over which he presided as chief administrator. With a new freedom of action in the exercise of his patronage, he could now abandon the model of medieval lordship on which Edward IV had still relied and replace it by a new structure, more professional and staffed by men chosen solely for their competence and their usefulness to the king.[1]

With the accession of his son the reins which held the higher aristocracy in control were loosened but the same basic pattern continued. The Crown had broken through the intermediate barriers between the court and the provincial gentry and freed both itself and them from dependence on the great magnates. It could cast its net as widely as it wished in selecting its servants, and aspirants to power or place throughout the country now looked increasingly to the royal court as the sole theatre of their advancement. This required a large-scale reordering of the political stage and of the political drama.[2]

The great figures on the political stage were no longer barons whose aspirations were local and dynastic but ministers of state, court-based, men regularly and closely attendant upon the king, his confidants and the executors of his policy. They were also power-brokers. Their access to the king made them the natural intermediaries to direct the flow of the precious waters of royal grace downwards to the growing multitudes of thirsty suitors. Hence they were not only power-brokers but were themselves also patrons. Aspirants to office or seekers of favour turned to these middlemen as the sponsors who could facilitate their suits by bringing them to the royal attention. For the councillor-patron such a role was at once an outward and visible sign of his own elite status in the political world and an opportunity to build his own network of dependence.

Under Henry VIII centre stage was for thirty years occupied by two successive sole ministers who virtually monopolized the royal confidence. Both of them were men of humble origin. Wolsey as a great ecclesiastic was in a familiar mould but his ambitions and his activities outran those of his clerical predecessors. Cromwell was, of course, a layman and of even humbler background. Under their auspices a new kind of entrant filled the ranks of the royal service. They were, almost to a man, meritocrats who won their honours and advanced their fortunes by their skills as soldiers, administrators, lawyers – all of them men of proven talents, a clientage of service not of favour. Their appearance on the scene mirrors the rapidly changing circumstances of European monarchy in the early sixteenth century.

The needs of vastly expanded warfare imposed radical alterations on state structures. Long years of struggle between the Habsburgs and the kings of France led to a gigantic escalation in the scale of warfare, in the size of armed forces, in new and expensive military technologies, and vastly inflated royal budgets. The necessary consequence was the rise of a professional civil bureaucracy and of professional soldiery. These changes marked a long step away from the dynastic monarchies of the late Middle Ages towards the impersonal bureaucratic states of the seventeenth century.

Although England was only a spasmodic participant in these great wars, they were not without their effect on her affairs. Wolsey's energies were expended in the management of Henry's wars, particularly in the partially successful effort to establish a larger and more flexible income for the king.[3] Cromwell was not called upon to finance or supply armies. The burdens laid on him were even more onerous and much more novel. He was required to break the mould of ancient tradition and bring the church under the sway of the secular power. This meant not only shaping the legal and administrative forms of the new order but manipulating public opinion and private interest in parliament and in the country, revising religious practice, and suppressing all hints of resistance. It was a task of unprecedented complexity and of utter novelty. Moreover, both Cromwell and Wolsey were increasingly aware of the acute problems posed by a rapidly growing population pressing hard on food supplies and flooding the labour market. They initiated the first efforts to use the state's machinery to respond to these pressures, to inaugurate a new era of social engineering.[4]

These developments heralded a long-term change in the very conditions under which government was conducted. The ideological conflicts arising out of the Reformation would alter their shape over time but in one form or another haunt the Crown and its ministers until the end of the dynasty. Regulation of the economic and social order would be an ever-growing preoccupation, as the statute books would bear witness. And after the mid-century the complexities of conducting English foreign relations in the prevailing international anarchy required new skills and a new fund of knowledge. From the 1580s on, war demanded the services of soldiers and sailors. The needs of government were changing rapidly and with them the character of the servants on which it depended. For the English government the stress of these changes was increased by the exclusion of clerics from the civil service, wiping out what for generations had been the largest pool of experienced recruits.

But it was not only the royal patron whose needs had altered. The nature of clients' goals was also shifting. In the past the theatre of those interests had been local. Now their horizons rapidly widened. Although the county remained the arena of gentry life, something like a national political elite began to form around the court and capital, and to a lesser extent parliament, in which local notables from every part of the country met and mingled. Many turned to the Crown's service for a career while those who stayed at home were acutely aware that the realization of family ambitions depended upon a reliable and powerful court connection.

At the highest level of competition, within the Privy Council, the ancient rivalries for land, office and local consequence blended with newer ambitions of a more national character. The fierce rivalries of the 1530s coloured personal competition with the new issues of religion and from that time onwards each clash of faction was at least tinted, often shaped, by differences over the right ordering of the religious polity. What was initially a contest between the old and the new religious faiths became, after 1558, a dispute within the Protestant ranks which in the next decades broadened out into wide differences as to the conduct of English foreign policy.

But to turn from the general to the particular – to the actual course of events in the middle and later decades of the sixteenth century. The pattern of patronage had been shaped from early in Henry VIII's reign by his strategy of vesting a sole minister with his whole confidence, largely to the exclusion of any rival. Such a system, in which one person dammed up the channel through which the royal beneficence flowed, as with George Villiers in the next century, united all other competitors in passionate hostility. From the time when Wolsey's power began to wane down to the end of the reign, politics were dominated by fierce factional competition for royal favour as they would be in the 1620s. But this time the favourite's enemies were twice successful in engineering his fall.[5]

In 1540 as in 1529 the minister's fall did not secure automatic promotion for his enemies nor a new equilibrium in the court. The ensuing royal reluctance to entrust power to any one man ushered in a period of even more intense factional rivalry and nerve-wracking uncertainty and the strife became all the more fierce when it became increasingly unlikely that the king would survive until the prince reached his majority. Henry was able to keep the rivals in play until at the very end of his life he struck down the Howards, and excluded Bishop Gardiner from the executors of his will. But the fragility of a system which depended so completely on the monarch's personal skill in manipulating faction was made all too evident by the events which followed Henry's decease in 1547.

With a boy king on the throne the immense resources of royal patronage, hitherto firmly grasped by the sovereign, became an object of competition among the politicians who jostled for power and position in his Council.[6] The duel between Seymour and Dudley convulsed the political world and, although the latter won, the fragility of his grasp of power was evidenced by the scale of the bribery which he was compelled to use to win support. Titles were dispensed in abundance and much of the royal landed estate dissipated by sale or gift. In 1553 the uneasy instability of these years seemed about to perpetuate itself into the next reign when Northumberland, too dangerously great to yield power, snatched at the throne. His ambitions were checked not only by the firm resistance of Mary but also by the instinctive loyalty of the political elite to the established order. Their rally to Mary, as the embodiment of right order, halted for the moment the drift towards faction-ridden anarchy although her control of an unruly Council was uncertain. The experience of the eleven years between 1547 and 1558 warned all too ominously of the weakness of a monarchy held together by the magnetic powers of a royal personality but it also demonstrated the presence of a new element of stability in the political order which enabled the monarchy to surmount the difficulties of a decade of war, revolt, conspiracy and feeble royal leadership without lapsing into the kind of disorder which wracked the French state for decades to come.

That this did not happen was due in no small part to the advent of a strong-willed ruler who renewed the strength of the monarchy once she ascended the throne. But much was also owed to the nature of the political elite which surrounded the Tudor throne by the 1550s. In the previous twenty or so years there had gradually formed a new community – or perhaps a better way of stating it – a new pool of higher royal servants, a new royal clientage. But it was not tied to the person of one monarch. It had begun to form in the later years of Henry VIII and consolidated itself under his boy successor. Some of its members began their careers in the entourage of Wolsey or the following of Cromwell; all prospered and climbed upwards in the 1540s and 1550s. Among the most successful were Seymour, Dudley, Russell, Paulet, Herbert, Paget, Wriothesley – to name those who made a permanent purchase among the ranks of the peerage for themselves and their posterity. Men of less stature were Sackville, Sadler, Smith, Mason, Sidney and, of course, Cecil. They were all in one sense or other meritocrats, men who had worked their way up the ladder of success by service in one or many capacities to the Crown. For some of them it was the great wars of the 1540s which gave them the chance to prove themselves as soldiers or administrators; others found their careers in the new financial bureaux founded by Cromwell. They were the recipients of royal patronage; a half dozen of them received peerages from the king, but it was a patronage of service rather than of personal favour. They were also, with varying degrees of enthusiasm, adherents or at least *politique* supporters of the new religion. The golden opportunities of King Edward's reign when the urgent needs of the two 'regents', Somerset and Northumberland, threw the balance from patron to client, provided a rich harvest in lands and titles for these men.

The needs of the Tudor government and the expansion of the recruitment pool brought the prospect of a career open to the talents. One at least, Cromwell himself, scrambled up from the lower depths of the social order to the highest level of power. Others came from the middling ranks of the London bourgeoisie or the county gentry. The end of clerical recruitment for royal service widened their opportunities. By the beginning of Elizabeth's reign the very successes of recruitment and service had hardened this corps into something like an establishment, the product of their common experience in the royal service. The weakness of royal leadership in the decade after Henry's death greatly strengthened their position. Wary and tough survivors of dizzying fluctuations in the world of high politics, and possessed of a wealth of administrative and political experience, they had become indispensable. To call them a faction would be a misnomer, for they lacked either leader or coherence of principle. But they were an elite which could not be ignored. Mary, however reluctantly, had to depend upon their service; Elizabeth, almost instinctively, turned to them when she formed a new regime in 1558.

It is worth pausing for a moment to make a contrast with the constellation of French politics at the same moment – the beginning of the 1560s. Across the Channel deep ideological division coincided with a resurgence of magnate strength and feeble royal leadership. In England the new queen faced a political elite of experienced and self-confident politicians on whom she had to rely.

But they were court-based rather than regional or dynastic groupings. Their own personal histories assured a strong tradition of service to the monarchy. Moreover, there was no ideological division among them. The ascendancy of a Protestant polity after 1558 was uncontested (except for the brief flurry of 1569). The Catholics had been unlucky in the death of Cardinal Pole and the absence of a strong secular leader around whom they might have coalesced. Neither the Marian bishops nor such of the lay lords as had lingering loyalties to the old faith were willing to contemplate active disobedience to their sovereign lady although the bishops would have sacrificed their lives for their faith.

The sum of this argument is that the nature of patronage had changed as realm was transmuted to state and kingship to statecraft. There was now one universal patron, the king, and one nationwide pool of suitors. Opportunities were greater but the talents and skills requisite for advancement, more demanding. Access to the king lay through the elite circle of those who, having won the royal confidence, were Janus-like, themselves clients (to their master) and patrons who could open the doors to royal favour. It was, of course, a hierarchic society but talent as much as or more than birth was the key to advancement.

Elizabeth at her coming to power took full account of these changed circumstances. Her Council mingled those whose careers had begun under her father and prospered through both his successors' reigns with those who had emerged under Edward and been forced to withdraw under his sister. She made a bow to the older nobility by including Derby, Shrewsbury and Arundel as councillors although only the last was an active member and an officer of state. The core of the new Council was drawn from the Henrician/Edwardian circle of long-time servants of the Crown, rich in experience, a team of professionals rather than gentlemen amateurs. The sense of continuity was strengthened by generational succession. Dudley, Knollys, Sidney, Cecil, Russell, Howard represented at least the second and in some cases the third generation of courtier families. Many of the men gathered around her council table had served together for twenty years or more and would end their service only with their lives. Many of their successors would come out of the same drawer – Mildmay, Smith, Walsingham, all men with close connections with the Edwardian circle. Bacon and Sackville, the former a connection of Cecil and the latter of the queen, were products of the new bureaucracy created in Henry's reign.[7]

But if the queen displayed a shrewd awareness of political reality in turning to these veterans, she was also to use the freedom of choice her predecessors had won to indulge her own personal preferences. That she could do so was impressive evidence of the monarch's enhanced power. She reordered the political game by altering the pieces on the chessboard. The castles of the old nobility were still in place along with the humble bureaucratic pawns but the bishops were banished and in their places stood one, ultimately two, new pieces, the favourites, Dudley and Hatton.[8] The personal intimate of the sovereign on whom honours and wealth was bestowed was a familiar enough figure. Henry had raised his boon companion (and brother-in-law) Brandon to a dukedom and endowed him with the appropriate means to support it.[9] But Suffolk, although a court figure of note by reason of his title and eminence, was never of central political importance.

What Elizabeth did was to promote Robert Dudley, a man whose only claim to promotion was the delight which the sovereign enjoyed in his presence. Worse still he was a possible royal husband. It was a very risky move, a recipe which might have yielded as indigestible a confection as Mary Stuart's marital adventures a few years later. In Elizabeth's case the ensuing crisis was less catastrophic but nonetheless a dangerous one. Dudley's promotion to the Privy Council opened the way for bitter factional intrigue in the later 1560s. There were now three elements contending for preeminence in the royal circle – the Howard family grouping, the voice of the traditional aristocracy, Cecil and his meritocratic allies, and the *arriviste* Dudley and his dependants. The two former bitterly resented the favourite although for different reasons. However, when the appearance of the heir apparent, Mary Stuart, in England provided the magnet around which faction could crystallize into conspiracy, the result was a reversionary interest based on an alliance between the left and the right, between Leicester and Norfolk, backed offstage by the two Catholicizing northern earls, Northumberland and Westmorland. This ill-conceived patchwork of intrigue came apart quickly when faced by the imperious will of the queen and ended in a farce – a faint echo of the convulsions which were rending the French monarchy. Elizabeth had mastered the factions; more than that she 'legitimated' the favourites by making them work their passage. Both Leicester and Hatton became hard-working and serious servants of the monarchy.

Elizabeth had her cake and ate it; she advanced her favourites to high place in spite of the envious disapproval of their rivals. But she never conceded to them a monopoly of favour or of confidence. They had to share their place in the sun with her more sober servants whose privileged position rested on merit not on personal attraction. It was a hard-earned lesson in royal statesmanship from which her successor might have benefited. The history of Buckingham would be a far different one from Leicester's.

In the wake of these events in the 1570s there emerged a highly idiosyncratic structure of power which blended the queen's personal preferences with the needs of the state in equal proportions. By then Elizabeth had advanced a second personal favourite, Sir Christopher Hatton, to political eminence while Cecil's successor as Secretary of State was another establishment meritocrat,

Sir Francis Walsingham. These two pairs, the professionals, Cecil and Walsingham and the two gentlemen amateurs, Leicester and Hatton, formed a team of royal confidants, an inner cabinet, whose cooperation and sustained energies provided direction and stability both to domestic and to foreign policy for nearly twenty years until the combination was dissolved by death in the early 1590s.

This combination reflected the royal determination to choose her confidants freely; the fact that these four reluctant yoke-fellows worked together in fruitful cooperation for nearly two decades reflects the queen's most important political talent.

Even more than her father she was able to command unfailing obedience to her commands, to exploit her patronage resources in such a way as to provide not only a supportive clientage but also to secure the best possible service for the state. She was able to compel men of unlike background and divergent views to work in harness. Leicester was the queen's intimate; Walsingham, never close to the ruler, was the professional; yet in matters of ideology the two men were close allies. Resolute spokesmen of the evangelical thrust of the reformed faith at home and champion of a Protestant internationale abroad, they stood in direct opposition to the cautious neutrality – one might say isolationism – of Burghley. Neither side had its way; the interventionists lost out in the 1570s; Burghley had to accept war in 1585. What was important was that both points of view had an airing at court; both had access to the royal ear, thus foreclosing the possibility of an aggrieved and excluded faction, such as gave rise to the conspiracies of the Aragonese party in the 1530s.

This harmony at the policy-making level was reflected in the smooth functioning of the patronage system at its lower level. It was an optimal era in which the queen's sturdy loyalty to her servants provided a new stability, in striking contrast to the hag-ridden later years of her father's reign or the confusion of her sister's. Entrants into the political arena knew who the patronage-brokers were. Competition was as fierce as, or fiercer than, ever but the stability of the political climate and the predictability of its weather patterns moderated the conditions of the contest.

The threat inherent in the Leicester–Burghley rivalry was kept in check by the queen; nevertheless both the great rivals remained warily suspicious of each other and each busily pursued the business of building up an extensive clientele. At every vacancy at court competitors for the post looked to the backing of one or another of the great men. In the counties the local officers, JPs or deputy lieutenants, shared the same dependency on the great patronage-brokers. Aspirants to episcopal office or cathedral appointments looked to Burghley or Leicester for their advancement. From the 1560s onwards Ireland became an arena in which the succession of deputies (and the appointments of lesser officers) reflected the varying fortunes of the court factions at home.[10]

As the military establishment grew, from 1585 on, captains in the royal armies made their suit to the same patrons. What was the goal in the creation of these clientages? After the events of 1569–72 it was quite clear that this was not a court where factional combination could manipulate or pressure the queen into a change of direction. English politics would not duplicate the course of events in the Valois court where a dependent clientage could be used as a weapon to break a rival or to bully the royal patron. What then was the object of their strivings? One answer lies in the traditional pursuit of local family eminence. The Cecils expected to dominate the local politics of their home base in Lincolnshire; the Dudleys their bailiwicks of North Wales or Warwickshire. English politicians, however court-oriented, had not lost a strong sense of their local roots and of family ambitions reaching beyond the present generation. The deference of the local gentry and their sense of dependence on a great neighbour was of the very essence of elite status.

Equally important and indeed a part of the same syndrome was the fact that the size of one's clientage was the most obvious affirmation of one's place in the political universe, the visible manifestation of the favour one enjoyed with the queen. In an age of ostentation a great clientage was as necessary a status symbol as the possession of a great house.

Lastly, a less obvious and carefully hidden motive was the lurking nightmare of what might follow the death of the queen. Such fears mounted in intensity in the 1580s amidst the burgeoning plots, real or imagined, which threatened the royal life and led to the Association of 1584, an unofficial response led by the great courtiers and eagerly accepted by the political elite. If the queen were suddenly dead, who would occupy the empty throne? Cecil would have placed the decision in parliament, an arena in which the weight of one's clientage would be an asset of first importance; it would be even more the case if peaceful agreement were not possible and men turned to the arbitrament of arms. In any case there would be a formidable factional struggle and the latent power of a clientage would have to be activated. It was England's good fortune that it never came to that.

The system worked well in taming faction and providing assured guidelines to the thronging suitors for royal bounty. It made for continuity in policy and an atmosphere of stability which was invaluable in these decades of internal stress and external threat. Nevertheless there were signs of strain. The Crown demanded more and more in service from its corps of underpaid (or unpaid) civil servants. The ever-increasing list of statutes which they were expected to enforce, the expanding operation of the poor law, the monitoring of religious conformity, and above all the mounting burdens of war fell very heavily on the shoulders of the county elites and the small corps of central government officials. But the fund of patronage from which they could be rewarded was a fixed one. What was added came from the circumstances of war – captaincies or other posts in the Low Countries or Ireland – but these presumed arduous and expert service and merely temporary reward.

The Crown was well aware of the importance of wholehearted gentry support in peace and in war but also acutely conscious of the meagreness of its patronage assets. Favours were frugally doled out in order to make them go as far as possible while keeping down costs to an overstrained exchequer. The granting of pensions or annuities was kept under close control and they were granted, in very modest sums, largely to old servants, impoverished members of the aristocracy or other deserving cases. Promotions to or within the peerage were very sparingly dealt out; so were knighthoods. Grants of money were virtually non-existent. Aside from local office such as the custody of castles or royal parks, probably the most common form of bounty was a favourable lease of royal lands at a low rent.

The suitors on their side sought traditional goals. Country landowners, secure in their estates, sought enhancement of their local status by the acquisition of a local office, the constableship of a castle or keepership of a park, or the stewardship of a royal manor. They were perhaps easier to deal with than those less fortunate younger sons who hoped for a livelihood at the hands of the Crown. Office under the Crown was uniformly ill-paid, a retainer's fee rather than a salary, and the officeholder necessarily expected to augment his income by informal means, practices which ranged from customary *pourboires* to straightforward extortion which over time gave rise to an accumulation of grievances. In any case the number of offices was finite. Not surprisingly suitors became ingenious in inventing new devices by which their disappointed hope of bounty might be served. They turned to schemes for extracting income by indirect means, not from the Crown itself, but by use of its authority, from the subjects. The most famous (or infamous) of these were the patents of monopoly but there were others, for instance, the much-hated patents for searching out concealed lands. The government's willingness to yield to such persuasions is understandable. Grants of this kind cost the treasury nothing and satisfied the suitor.

Clearly demand was outrunning supply as more and more suitors flooded the court. In 1600 the Privy Council told the Lord Deputy of Ireland 'that in our remembrance the court did never swarm with so many suitors'. It is only one of many indications that the pressure on the Crown for bestowal of its patronage was steadily increasing. With the greedy clamour of courtiers an ever more noisy chorus, the Crown was hard pushed to meet what both the court and country saw as its obligation. As the Privy Council wrote in 1601,[11] 'it standeth not with the reputation of a council of state here at home to forbear to confer some employment upon such as do plead merit to the queen . . . for it is fit that they be so retained in hope as not to abandon their place by despairing of preferment'. They added it was not fit 'that Her Majesty be driven to discontent them'. These quotations reflect the Crown's recognition of the just expectations of the political classes; they also echo its despairing sense of the impossibility of realizing them. The problem, unresolved by the Tudors, was an unwelcome legacy to their Stuart successors.

In the 1590s the relatively stable political universe of the previous two decades was shattered when death claimed three of the four sturdy horses which had drawn the coach of state for two decades past; Leicester in 1588, Walsingham in 1590, and Hatton in 1591. Burghley, the survivor, who might have hoped for a clear stage, bare of all competitors for the royal confidence, on to which he could launch the apple of his eye, the young Robert, found his hopes dashed by the presence of a new favourite. Leicester and Hatton, dead and gone, were now replaced by the youthful Earl of Essex. His fateful appearance on the scene and the fascination which he exercised for the ageing royal spinster led to the revival of faction in the English court, after an interval of two decades, faction of a kind which threatened to destroy the inward harmony of English leadership at a fateful moment of foreign threat and an uncertain succession.

It was not only the tortoise and hare rivalry between the sober young man of business and the wayward, moody and spoiled favourite. There were greater issues at stake. Essex's driving ambition was for martial glory, to be one of the great captains of his age, 'England's glory and the wide world's wonder'. As the spokesman and leader of the party in the Council which constantly urged all-out war with Spain, he urged a struggle not for mere containment but for conquest, in which England would take her place among the great powers of the European world, in the place of a humbled Spain. Over against this party stood the steady conservatism of the Cecils, who sought to limit the struggle to its minimum dimensions, to thrust back the Spanish assault on England but to rely upon the successful efforts of her continental allies, the States and France, to reestablish a counterbalance to Habsburg power in Europe and leave England once again free for a policy of detachment.

There was also a hidden agenda in the rivalry. The queen was now approaching the biblical span and prudent politicians were casting their eyes towards the future. The contest was not only for the favour of the present sovereign but a strategic role at the moment of her death and beyond that assured prominence in the next reign. But who was to be the next ruler of England? James of Scotland was certainly the favoured candidate but nothing was certain. Both sides manoeuvred for positions. Essex boldly wooed the court at Edinburgh. The Cecils, restrained by their official role, were less free to manoeuvre and had to bear the blame for the queen's grudging stinginess towards the Scots king. Had Elizabeth died in the mid-1590s Essex would have had the ear of the new ruler, who at that stage regarded the Cecils very coolly. All they could do was to build up strength at home, by securing support in the Council and in the upper ranks of the civil service, and in the country at large, in the boroughs and the shires. The queen, quite conscious of the rivalry her favour to Essex had excited, was confident she could indulge herself once more, repeating the experience of an earlier generation, playing off the younger Cecil against the reincarnation of Leicester, keeping both on the lead and both under firm control. Essex, like his stepfather, would be tamed to royal service.

It was a tactic which failed. Essex, whose ambitions were very different from those of his stepfather, possessed a temperament ill-adapted to play May to the royal December. The queen wanted to be both mistress and mother; Essex strained at the leash as his hopes for a great martial career soured in the aftermath of Cádiz when England and Spain began slowly to shuffle towards peace. The fatal rupture came in 1598 in the famous scene at the Council table. It did not result in his immediate fall; a reconciliation was patched up. Then, fatefully, his services were urgently required as the Irish rebellion flared up into full-scale civil war, with the expectation of Spanish intervention in the offing. He was at the very height of his popularity and enjoyed a strong clientele among the officers of the army. The risk of entrusting him with the command of the largest army mustered in the queen's reign was obvious but there was no choice. His opponents held their breath as they veered between the hope that Ireland would prove the same burial ground of his reputation as it had already been that of many others and the fear that he would use the weapon in his hand to turn against them. Their fears were not unfounded. He seriously contemplated bringing back a force from Dublin to land in Wales and march on London and he approached James for possible backing, offering in return an assured succession. But Essex was not equal to his opportunities. On his friends' advice he abandoned the thought of a military move and then realized his enemies' dearest hopes by compromising himself with Tyrone. From the moment of his return to England his political career was at an end, thanks to his own shortcomings. Neither the queen nor his enemies ceased to fear him, even in his disgrace. But with the loss of the royal favour, his power to use his clientage as a political weapon was destroyed, however much general sympathy he might still command as the ill-advised farce of February 1601 would show.

The tortoise, slow but purposeful, had beaten the swift but feckless hare. The crisis was resolved from within, so to speak, but it bore witness again to the fragility of a political system so highly personal in character, so dependent on the whims of the royal patron and the behaviour of a small inner elite. The death of Essex and the emergence of Robert Cecil as sole minister to his ageing mistress cleared the way for James's untroubled succession to the English throne and to a political world purged from the ravages of faction.

Henry VII seized the throne by force of arms; James enjoyed a peaceful accession amidst universal acclamation. No less important was the changed nature of the political order over which the Scottish king was now to preside. The preeminence of the Crown over its greater subjects was beyond question and the freedom of the sovereign to choose his servants untrammelled. The gates of the court stood freely open to all aspirants for royal favour and as a consequence the Crown could command the services of a talented and experienced corps of administrators. The tensions of faction, inherent in the system, were contained within the Privy Council under the firm hand of the queen. It was a system which had worked well under the strains of religious division and foreign war. Yet it depended ultimately on the performance of the prince. Elizabeth, for all her talents, had blundered in her assessment of the Earl of Essex and good luck more than royal skill had saved the monarchy from the threat of open violence. She bequeathed to James a fair political inheritance but one which would require the most delicate fine-tuning if it were to function harmoniously.

3 JAMES VI AND I, *BASILIKON DORON* AND *THE TREW LAW OF FREE MONARCHIES*: THE SCOTTISH CONTEXT AND THE ENGLISH TRANSLATION

Jenny Wormald

The Trew Law of Free Monarchies was published in 1598. It is significant that the only writings in English of the period of the reign of Elizabeth that definitely formulate a doctrine of absolute monarchy were written by a Scot in Scotland, and by a man who suffered from the drawback of being himself a King.[1]

Thus in 1928 did J. W. Allen debar James VI from serious consideration, because of the twin disabilities of Scottishness and royalty. Much more recently, and much more surprisingly, this political theorist received even more dismissive treatment from Quentin Skinner, whose *Foundations of Modern Political Thought*, published in 1978, omitted the king's works entirely from his list of primary sources, mentioned him only four times in the course of the book, and coped with the 'Scottish problem' in the index by referring to him simply as 'James I, King of England'. Yet, even if we were not now far removed from the perception of James VI and I as the pedantic buffoon, beloved of Sir Anthony Weldon and Sir Walter Scott,[2] it would still remain true that the writings of a king have a peculiar, indeed a unique importance. Not since Alfred had a ruler combined the practice and the theory of kingship in his own person; and if all political theory, to a greater or lesser degree, is a response to immediate political reality, the view from the throne has its own peculiar fascination and relevance to the debate about that fundamental question which underlies all theory, the nature and source of power. It would be an unwise historian, in this age of revisionism, who attempted to resurrect 1603 as a crucial milestone on the road to civil war. Yet it was the date chosen by Dr Sommerville as the starting-point for his compelling analysis of *Politics and Ideology in England, 1603–1640*, that thought-provoking work which, as Dr Christianson has pointed out in his recent review, offers both 'a perspective not entirely dissimilar to the old whig interpretation' and 'the best formal analysis of English political theory in early

Stuart England that has ever appeared in print'.[3] So if 1603 is not the essential prelude to the battlefield, it still has its place in the history of ideological conflict.

This is surely because the mental world of the English court – and the world beyond the court – were jolted on to a new level of theoretic debate simply because of a foreign king whose leisure pursuits included not only the normal royal enthusiasm for hunting (if, as they saw it, to an obsessional degree) but the very abnormal one of writing books. It was an aberration made all the worse because, as Nicholas Fuller said in the parliament of 1610, he was 'in truth very wise yet is he a straunger to this government', so that the Commons had to take to themselves the awesome responsibility to be 'true to the King and true to ourselves, and let him know what by the laws of England he may do'. This was not, of course, just an 'ideological' comment. It related to that potential flashpoint, impositions; and it was made on 22 May, in response to the deeply worrying speech by the king on 21 May. The crunch comes in Fuller's insistence that the reason why the Commons had to remind the King of England about the laws of England was that 'the king speaks of France and Spain what they may do'; and the same point was made by Thomas Wentworth, citing Fortescue on the difference between France and England, 'in that . . . by the law of England no imposition can be made without assent of parliament as in France etc. etc'.[4]

It was of course quite clever of Fuller and Wentworth to single out these frightening creatures, the Catholic and arbitrary kings of France and Spain. But they were only partially quoting. For what James had said the previous day was that 'all kings Christian as well elective as successive have power to lay impositions, I myself in Scotland before I came hither, Denmark, Sweden that is but newly successive, France, Spain, all have this power. And as Bellarmine abuses me in another sense *solus rex Angliae timet*, so shall *solus rex Angliae* be confined? Besides to call in question that power which all your kings have ever had, which two women have had and exercised, I leave it to yourselves to think what dutiful subjects ought to do in it'.[5] And there is the huge distinction between king and English MPs. The MPs argued their case on the basis of Fortescue and English law. The king, in asserting his, moved in a huge sweep from Scotland round the other major continental monarchies, Catholic and Protestant, and even threw in a reference to Bellarmine before arriving at English government – and petticoat government at that.

What could better illustrate the problem: the deep, and probably unbridgeable ideological gulf between a traditional attitude memorably satyrized in Flanders and Swann's song, 'The English are best' and the approach now translated into the English political world, which was grounded in continental, and Scottish, theories of kingship, as well as Scottish practice. Because of that approach, of course, tactlessness was writ large virtually every time James opened his mouth in England; and tactlessness hardly made for mutual trust. This was sad, because at the political level, there was actually much less to frighten the English in their king's understanding of his role than his language suggested. It was indeed unfortunate that James picked up English constitutional rhetoric with such enthusiasm and then turned it into a constant reminder of his passionate interest in an ideological debate which was very definitely not English. It masked all too effectively the king's ability to separate when necessary his love of theorizing from his firm grasp of the real world of politics. The Commons leapt like hungry trouts at the gaudy fly of continental theory. They paid no attention to the much less colourful little fly also cast by the king in his speech: his unwelcome complaint that 'fourteen weeks have now been spent in the parliament, yet you cannot allege nor say that for the principal errand you have bestowed so many days, nay scarce half so many days as weeks have been spent in the parliament'.[6] The theorist had a very practical point to make to the castigators of his theory.

Therein surely lies the supreme irony. For not only was James naturally unaware that his unusual leisure pursuit would provide wonderful evidence for the whig historians of later centuries. He was also unaware that it would deeply disturb his English subjects, for two reasons. First, it is highly doubtful if the two great works on kingship written in Scotland were primarily designed to inform his future English subjects of their king's extreme views of his kingship. Second, it is arguable that his major misreading of his kingdom of England lay not so much in his assumption that it was the land flowing with milk and honey, as in his expectation that there he could indulge the pleasure of talking political 'shop' as well as the theological 'shop' which he had enjoyed in Scotland. For the English took themselves all too seriously. They made the mistake of taking their new king too seriously also.

To illustrate this, let me begin with the mental world of Scotland. For what has never been given sufficient emphasis is that not only was it highly unusual for a king to write books. It was remarkable in the extreme for a Scottish king to do so, not because of a lack of an intensive and up-to-date education – James was, after all, taught by one of Europe's leading scholars, George Buchanan – but because before the sixteenth century there had been, in sharp distinction to England, virtually no tradition of political theorizing: no Magna Carta, no Provisions of Oxford, no theoretic justification such as accompanied the depositions of Edward II and Richard II, no Fortescue or Thomas Smith, and certainly no history of demands by those Scottish lairds, whose English equivalents sat in the lower house of parliament, for rights and privileges. And whereas only Richard III and Henry VII are missing from the line of seven English kings from Edward III to Henry VIII (and to the list can be added Henry VI's son Edward Prince of Wales) who were the recipients of at least one letter of advice to princes,[7] Scottish kings were not. There were, in the fifteenth century, Scottish contributions to the *speculum principis* genre, such as the anonymous poem known as *The Harp* which contained the singular advice that the king should choose his councillors because of ability rather than birth; Gilbert Hay translated the pseudo-Aristotelian *Secreta Secretorum*, but this was a work commissioned not for a king but by the Earl of Orkney; and only John Ireland's *Merroure of Wisdome*, which drew heavily on five sermons preached by Gerson to Charles VI, was actually intended for a king, James IV.[8] But for the clearest example of a specific connection we have to wait until a king himself turned writer, when James VI produced his manual of Scottish kingship for his son Henry.

This does not mean that Scotland was wholly without political theory. A country which produced a document as moving and dramatic as the Declaration of Arbroath of 1320 can hardly be dismissed as lacking ideological awareness. But the Declaration is itself an excellent guide to the nature of Scottish political theory. It was an appeal to the pope, John XXII, by the barons of Scotland that the ban of excommunication on their king, Robert Bruce, should be lifted, and Robert recognized as ruler of an independent kingdom, in no way subservient to England. To illustrate their utter resistance to English claims of overlordship, they asserted that if Robert – the king who had led them to freedom – were to depart from this cause, they would depose him and choose another in his place.[9] This was indeed resistance theory. But it was hypothetical resistance not to a tyrant but to a deserter, in one particular circumstance. Even more important, it was a theory drawn up in order to persuade a foreign power. It admirably demonstrates how different was the Scottish approach from the much more internalized attitude of the English; for the English explained things to themselves. And the Scottish approach had not substantially changed when the next great burst of theorizing took place in the 1560s, provoked by the crisis created by Mary Queen of Scots. Once again, the Scots were explaining themselves to a foreign power, this time Elizabeth.

By then, however, there were two new elements. First, the theorizing of King James was not Scotland's earliest experience of continental ideas being brought to bear on Scottish kingship. For sound political reasons – the fright the Scots had had when the succession to the Crown collapsed in 1290, and the sustained and aggressive English attempts at colonialism which followed – succession by primogeniture had been emphatically established. The Crown was entailed twice in the fourteenth century, in 1318 and 1371, according to rules of primogeniture, and never again was there a dynastic threat to the Scottish royal house. One might, indeed, ruminate in passing on the curious fact that the much more sophisticated kingdom of England so signally failed to sort out that most fundamental issue of how men became kings that it plunged itself into political mayhem in the fifteenth century. Meanwhile, and more to my purpose, there was another kind of crisis going on in Europe: papal mayhem, and the Conciliar Movement. And it was conciliarist theory which belatedly threw its shadow across accepted norms of Scottish kingship in the early sixteenth century. For one of the great latter-day conciliarists was the Scot John Mair, theologian and historian, teacher at Paris and subsequently principal of the universities of Glasgow and then St Andrews.

Mair wrestled with the problem of the source and nature of authority, not always consistently, but in the end clearly enough assigning to the ruler – ecclesiastical or secular – a role subordinate to and contained by the state. He recognized the need for, or at least advantages of, a prince of sorts; for, as he said, republics tended to be short-lived. And on occasion he did seem to veer towards assigning very considerable power to the ruler; as J. H. Burns has pointed out, his argument that it was best to have a monarch who would not only guide but, having taken counsel of wise men, decide, whether they agreed or not, might have been stated by Bossuet. But when he faced the question of whether the supreme power which is absolute and belongs only to Christ could ever be brought down to earth, his answer was that there was indeed a power which was not just superior but supreme – *potestas fontalis* – and that power was vested in the community. And the state, and the monarchy, which he used to illustrate this most fully was Scotland; in his *History of Greater Britain*, this concept was applied with ruthless logic to argue for the power of the state over the king, the right of deposition, and the elective nature of kingship.[10] As a political theorist Mair was more influential in the academic circles of Europe than in his native country. But if his impact was relatively limited, there was another's which was not. Mair's greatest European pupil was John Calvin. His greatest Scottish one was George Buchanan, future tutor of James VI. Both turned against the teachings of their master. Yet by a different route, Buchanan did arrive at conclusions about power in the state very similar to Mair's.

Buchanan's theory, particularly as applied to Scotland, derived more directly from a contemporary of Mair, Hector Boece, another luminary of Paris, principal of the new university of Aberdeen, and friend of Erasmus. Boece produced the same answer, by way not of logic but of an invented source, Veremundus, and an equally invented line of forty kings, each deposed because of their vicious lives, by the people of Scotland. And while the cool and logical Mair had little influence, the much more riotous Boece – far more popular in his own day, when he was given the royal patronage denied to Mair – was a wonderful source. None of it particularly mattered in the first half of the sixteenth century. But Boece's writings came to matter very much indeed in the late sixteenth century. He provided the witches for *Macbeth*; and he provided, for Buchanan, the necessary basis for the 'Ancient Constitution' of Scotland, by which 'the people' elected and deposed kings. The fact that the ancient Scots apparently got the choice wrong forty times over seems to have worried no one. Much more to the point, Buchanan could use ideas of Mair (without, as it were, adequate footnotes), and reinforce them with the supposed facts of Boece, to demonstrate to Elizabeth that the people of Scotland were justified in deposing Mary in 1567; and he could then go on to add his weight to the contractual theories advanced by the Huguenot writers of the 1570s.[11] He could also, of course, teach – indeed, hammer – such theories into his own great pupil, King James.

The second, and, for the Scots, crucial new element was religion. For Mary's unique – and uniquely irresponsible – stance as a ruler who insisted on one religion for herself while allowing, and even paying for, another for her subjects, created a uniquely radical strand in Scottish reforming thought from the beginning, in the assertion of the superiority of the spiritual over the temporal power, and the extension beyond the natural leaders of secular society of the right and duty of resistance. The leading figure here was, of course, John Knox, with his appeal in 1558 to the nobility to 'hear the voice of the Eternal your God' and fulfil their divinely ordained role to act against an ungodly magistracy; and if they failed, Knox appealed beyond them to the commons, so that 'vox populi', invoked in England in 1327 to justify the deposition of Edward II, was now introduced to Scotland as the defender of the true religion against idolatry – except that when that defence turned into iconoclasm in Perth in May 1559, Knox's commons promptly became 'the rascal multitude'.[12] Yet despite the fright which the reforming leaders had when seeing 'vox populi' in action, they, like Buchanan, continued to appeal in the most general terms to the people; in practice, both were looking to the nobility, but they never limited the responsibility for action against ungodly rule to the lesser magistracy, as continental theorists like Beza and Philippe Du Plessis-Mornay did. Thus Knox could reduce Mary to stunned silence by insisting on his right to dictate her choice of husband as a subject born within the realm. And in the General Assembly of 1564, the former Dominican and minister of Edinburgh, John Craig, followed up a lengthy debate between Knox and Mary's secretary Maitland of Lethington about the right of the ministers to remove Mary, by citing the debate he had been present at in the university of Bologna in 1553, when it had been successfully held that all rulers could be deposed by their subjects if they broke their oaths to them; in answer to a 'claw-backe of the corrupt court' who objected that Bologna, being a commonwealth, was irrelevant to the kingdom of Scotland, he argued that 'everie kingdome is a commoun wealth . . . albeit everie commoun wealth is not a kingdome', and came close to Ponet by asserting that in each, the negligence of the people as well as the tyranny of princes might mean that laws contrary to God could be made, and yet that people or their posterity 'could justlie crave all things to be reformed, according to the originall institutioun of kingdoms and commoun wealths; and suche as will not doe so deserve to eate the fruict of their owne foolishnesse'.[13]

The Scottish context of *Basilikon Doron* and the *Trew Law* was therefore, from the point of view of their author, confusing and potentially very dangerous. In the long term, he inherited a kingdom in which, in theory and in practice, politics had been very low-key. Mainly because of their personal strength and ruthlessness, his Stewart predecessors between 1424 and 1542 had ruled with great authority, but the repeated minorities which beset the Stewart dynasty had militated against the move towards absolutist rule, with its ideological underpinning, already detectable in the French and Spanish kingdoms by the fifteenth century. This did not mean that the other end of the ideological spectrum, the elective and contractual theories of Mair and Buchanan, in any way disturbed the theoretic basis of a monarchy so firmly grounded, since the early fourteenth century, in the principle of primogeniture. But there was another aspect of Scottish political life which did more closely correspond with their ideas. One important consequence of the intermittent exercise of royal rule was that the localities remained unusually autonomous, by the standards of the major kingdoms of the sixteenth century; and they were presided over by men whose local power and influence were, from the mid-fifteenth to the early seventeenth century, given formal written recognition in the numerous bonds and contracts made between lords and their followers.[14] Mair and Buchanan did not significantly change, let alone dictate, the realities of Scottish politics (even in the sensational events of January 1649, it was the English, not the Scots, who were to agree with Buchanan that a people could bring a tyrannous king before the courts, try him, condemn him and kill him). Rather, they were subsuming the Scottish contract, as it had existed in practice at least since the fifteenth century, into their political theory. But the very existence of these contracts, as the fundamental means of social control, created a context in which contractual theories of kingship, when pushed hard for immediate political motives, could evoke vibrant echoes. More than that, they enabled the Scots of the late sixteenth century to move naturally towards a covenanting theology. It was the heirs of both theorists and politicians of the sixteenth century who were to draw up that supreme example of the Scottish bond, the National Covenant of 1638. More immediately, however, James also suffered from his short-term inheritance.

He can hardly be said to have been fortunate. He succeeded a ruler who was politically discredited and personally scandalous, but who was still alive, and wanted her throne back. In particular, he was vulnerable to aspersions on his legitimacy because of Mary's supposed affair with David Riccio. Hence Henry IV's famous sneer at the Scottish Solomon, son of David, and the insults hurled at him in Perth on 5 August 1600, the day of the Gowrie conspiracy, as the 'son of seigneur Davie'; these things may give us a clue to his curious choice of phrase in the *Trew Law*, when describing the effect on the law of the conquest of England by the 'bastarde of Normandie'.[15] He was educated – savagely – by the man who was Mary's most outspoken and vicious critic, and whose personal attack on her had been subsumed into a political theory which made James's power ultimately dependent on the will of the community; as the first coinage of his reign succinctly put it, 'pro me si mereor in me' (for me; against me if I deserve it), the phrase referring to the sword on the coins. At his coronation, when he was aged thirteen months, it was promised on his behalf that he would uphold the Protestant faith, and this, to the Protestant reformers, undoubtedly meant acting as the godly magistrate under their direction. Between them, his mother, his tutor, and the leading Protestants had reduced his position, at least in theory, to one of a subservience which would have been unacceptable to any of his predecessors, and was certainly unacceptable to him.

Basilikon Doron and the *Trew Law* have been castigated as unoriginal, even dismissed as stating no meaningful theory.[16] In one sense, they were unoriginal, as they were bound to be. For there was nothing new about the question whether power could be absolute and, if so, whether it was vested in the monarch or the community, even if in the late sixteenth century the focusing of the ruler's sacerdotal power as something precise and potentially immense had brought a new intensity to the debate. James had learned the contractual theory from Buchanan. But he was also aware of something very different; for by 1577 the royal library contained a copy of Guillaume Budé's *Institut du Prince*, and it also contained Bodin's *République*, and both offered him an answer utterly opposed to Buchanan's. How soothing it must have been to turn from the thunderings of Buchanan, with his terrifying stories of what had happened to wicked kings – which gave James nightmares years later – to assertions such as 'Maiestie or Soveraigntie is the most high, absolute, and perpetuall power over the citizens and subiects in a Commonweale . . .'.[17] But when, twenty years later, James adopted in his own writings the theories of the 'absolutists' rather than the 'contractualists', he was, in the Scottish context, doing something very original indeed. For he gave to Scottish monarchy an ideological base wholly different from anything in the past; and he gave it not just as a theorist, but as the man who had to translate theory into practice. And it is this which explains the difference between *Basilikon Doron* and the *Trew Law*.

Space does not allow discussion of the practice, the subtlety and skill with which James restored royal authority in the state, and gained ascendancy over the extremists in the church, the hard-line group of Presbyterians known, from their leader Andrew Melville, as the Melvillians.[18] But the chronology of the gradual imposition of the new ideological base can be briefly sketched in. As Ian Stewart has shown, the 'Buchanan' propaganda of the first coinage gave way to royal propaganda, and the dates are instructive. In 1578, the year when the last of James's regents, the harsh and Anglophile Earl of Morton, fell from power, with the eleven-year-old king cheerfully asserting his ability to rule, and showing the first signs of saying no to Elizabeth, the coins for the first time used the famous Scottish motto 'Nemo me impune lacessit' (no one may meddle with me with impunity); ten years later, his coins announced 'florent sceptra piis regna his Iova dat numeratque' (sceptres flourish with the pious; God gives them kingdoms and numbers them); and in 1591, the new gold piece gave the name of Jehovah in Hebrew, with the inscription 'te solum vereor' (Thee alone do I fear), while the silver had a pair of scales over a sword, declaring 'his differt rege tyrannus' (in these a tyrant differs from a king).[19] Meanwhile, other propaganda methods had been brought into use. In 1583, when James, unlike in 1578, was genuinely emerging from his minority, he asserted his intention to be a 'universal king', above faction.[20] It was an intention which was to be fulfilled – to the fury, *inter alia*, of Cecil in the first decade of his English rule. In 1610, he burst out furiously to Sir Henry Yelverton that 'it fareth not with me now as it did in the Queen's time . . . for then . . . she heard but few, and of them I may say myself the chief, the king heareth many, yea of all kinds. Now as in hearing too few, there may be danger, so in hearing so many cannot be but confusion';[21] but confusion to Cecil was, and had long been, for James, the intelligent assertion of the over-riding authority of the king.

Moreover, the ruler who was to upset his English Commons by high-handed statements about his power, deliberately invoked the authority of his Scottish parliament in order to establish the authority of the king as he understood it. In 1584, parliament gave its support to enhancing royal prestige, when it passed two acts dealing with the king's estate. The first 'perpetuallie confirmis the royall power and auctoritie over all statis alsweill spirituall as temporall within this realme in the persoun of the kingis maiestie our soverane lord his airis and successouris', who will be 'Juges competent to all persounis . . . of quhatsumevir estate degrie functioun or conditioun . . . spirituall or temporall'. The second promised the full rigour of the law against any who uttered calumnies 'to the dishonour hurt or preiudice of his hienes his parentis and progenitouris', and specifically called in for suppression Buchanan's *De Iure Regno apud Scotos* and his *History of Scotland*; it was James's view of kingship, not Buchanan's, to which his subjects must now subscribe. But along with this went an attempt to repair the damage done by Mary not just to the prestige of monarchy but to Scottish government as a whole; her misuse of parliament was now to be rectified by the king's assertion of the 'honour and the auctoritie of his supreme court of parliament continewit past all memorie of man unto thir dayis as constitute upoun the frie votis of the thrie estatis of this ancient kingdome'.[22]

In practice, the authority of the supreme court of parliament was both built up and contained with immense skill. In the great parliament of 1587 the dignity of parliament was given considerable emphasis; this included its visual dignity, for James, following a precedent set by James II, took it upon himself to design clothes fitting for MPs, and the opening and closing public ceremony of the Riding of Parliament through Edinburgh undoubtedly became in his reign a splendid affair. At last an effective system of shire elections was introduced, which both met the rising aspirations of the lairds to turn up and give their voices, and at the same time imposed limits on the numbers who could actually do so.[23] And meanwhile in a series of acts in 1587 and the parliaments of the early 1590s, control of composition, notably of that crucial committee the Lords of the Articles, and control of business were relentlessly extended. It was effective; and yet it did not produce the kind of tension which marked James's dealings with his English parliaments. Perhaps there was a considerable safety-valve in the fact that James had not yet adopted English rhetoric; only after 1603 did his Scottish parliaments discover that their 'soverane lord' had greatly elevated his style, and now expected them to regard him as 'his sacred majestie'; more generally, only after 1603 were there signs of unease about what his sacred majesty, remote in England and raising the level of the actions of royalty as well as its language, was up to.[24]

Before 1603, his achievements did not of course solve all problems. But they marked a significant move towards the creation of a new Scottish context, after the troubles and confusions of the previous two decades. During the twelve years after the 1584 parliament, the king gradually translated the claims made there into practice. After 1596, apart from the extraordinary and quixotic Gowrie affair, his control of church and state was becoming irresistible. And after 1596, he settled down to write about it.

The texts of both his political tracts are well known. Neither is a long work; the *Trew Law* in particular is very short, so much so that it has recently been reprinted under the surprising title of *The Minor Prose Works of James VI and I*. Both are highly readable. And both are firmly set within the context of Scottish kingship. There the similarities end. The *Trew Law* deliberately – perhaps even defiantly – takes up the familiar Scottish theme of contract, and gives it a twist; the subtitle *The Reciprock and Mutuall Dutie betwixt a free King and his naturall Subiectes* has nothing whatsoever to do with a contract which may be broken by the inferior party if the superior does not fulfil his part. It was a new interpretation of 'reciprock'. It also rewrites Scottish history. Boece's forty kings, so crucial to Buchanan's theory, no longer exist. But the arguably historical figure of Fergus, fifth-century King of the Scots of Dalriada, is invoked to prove that 'as our Chronicles beare witnesse', this king from Ireland and his successors settled in a country 'skantly inhabited' and 'skant of civilitie', and therefore kings in Scotland 'were before any estates or rankes of men within the same, before any Parliaments were holden or lawes made; and by them was the land distributed (which at the first was whole theirs) states erected and decerned & formes of government devised & established. And so it follows of necessitie, that the Kinges were the authors & makers of the lawes, and not the lawes of the Kings'. It was an appeal to history and logic of which Mair would surely have approved, even if his own logical approach – that despite rules of primogeniture, the first king must have been elected – resulted in a very different conclusion. Indeed, James himself allowed for Mair's idea, when he insisted that his Scottish 'model' was not universal. In other societies 'in the time of the first age', men were chosen to rule and protect their fellows. But not in Scotland, which stands somewhere between such societies and others, which were 'reft by conquest from one to another, as in our neighbour countrie in England, (which was never in ours)'. The parenthetical clause looks somewhat specious, for James had already acknowledged that Fergus arrived with his followers from Ireland and 'maid himself maister'. But the inconsistency could be resolved by the fact that he clearly saw Fergus and his followers, unlike the Saxons or the Normans, as coming in peaceably, to be welcomed by the few existing barbarous inhabitants; it was a particular and very muted kind of 'conquest', in which Fergus introduced law and government where previously there had been none, whereas the Conqueror 'changed the lawes (and) inverted the order of governement'.[25] His argument against Buchanan's theory therefore remained valid. But if this theory was to be answered on historical and logical grounds, that of Knox and Melville meant scripture; and Samuel's terrible warning to the Israelites about what their insistence on having a king would bring down on them was duly rehearsed.

This may appear a less than happy method of asserting divine right – as unhappy, indeed, as the forty mythical kings as props for the authority of the people – but it certainly established the case that what the Lord gave, the people must accept. There is no doubt whatsoever that the *Trew Law of Free Monarchies* was an unequivocal defence of the theory of the divine right of kings. And inasmuch as it was written by a king, it raised the possibility, and indeed, especially among his English subjects, the spectre, that this was the thinking of a man who was in a position such as Mair and Buchanan could never be, of translating theory into practice. But one does not need to turn only to James's political actions to find that fears about his understanding of his office were often exaggerated. We only have to read the end of his book. His most terrible warning was not to subjects who must accept the will of God. It was to the monarch. The tyrant would not escape punishment:

but by the contrary, by remitting them to God (who is their only ordinary judge) I remit them to the sorest and sharpest Schoolemaister that can be devised for them. For the further a king is preferred by God above all other ranks and degrees of men, and the higher that his seate is above theirs: the greater is his obligation to his maker . . . The highest benche is sliddriest to sit upon.

Indeed, the absolute insistence on the providence of God led him to acknowledge the loophole in his own theory. The evocative homeliness of the 'sliddriest benche', so typical of much of James's writing, gave way to the compelling need, equally typical, to explore the full implications of his argument; and in one of the most deliberately powerful passages in the book, he went on:

neither thinke I by the force & argument of this my discourse so to perswade the people, that none wil herafter be raised up, and rebel against wicked Princes. But remitting to the justice and providence of God to stirre up such scourges as pleaseth him, for punishment of wicked kings (who made the verie vermine & filthy dust of the earth to bridle the insolency of proud Pharaoh).

It may then 'please God to cast such scourges of princes and Instruments of his furie in the fire'. But the hand of God could reach out to punish the tyrant even in this life, and would surely punish him in the next. There were to be men in England who felt that this king was slipping out of human control. The *Trew Law* tells us about the awesome control imposed on the king who was controlled only by God.[26]

Basilikon Doron is very different. It is a manual of kingship, firmly set in the *speculum principis* genre. Indeed, the immediate model may have been the work believed to be Charles V's *Political Testament* to his son Philip; certainly an Italian version of it was sent to James in 1592 by an Italian scholar and fugitive from the Inquisition, Giacomo Castelvetro, who had turned up in Scotland in 1591, hoping for the job of the king's Italian teacher.[27] In any event, it is a practical handbook and emphatically not a statement of highly developed political theory. Only in the first section, called 'A Kings Christian Duetie towards God', is there an overt nod towards divine right: 'for that he made you a little God to sitte on his throne, and rule over other men'.[28] But it is a very little nod; most of the section is about the king and his God. In the second part, 'A Kings Duetie in his Office', it becomes very clear that James's major concern, in developing the theory of the *Trew Law* and in setting out his advice here, was the Melvillians, those 'vaine Pharasaicall puritanes', who will cry 'Wee are all but vile worms, & yet wil judge and give law to their king, but will be judged nor controlled by none: Surely there is more pride under such a ones black-bonnet nor under great Alexander's Diademe.' He had reason to know. He also had reason to know of both the dangers and the advantages of aristocratic power, and advised his son to harness the one and use the other, as indeed he had done with considerable success. His lack of understanding of economic matters comes out in his moan – the eternal moan of the 'layman' – about high prices and poor quality as the fundamental problem. His passionate desire for peace is equally apparent, although he admits and advises on unavoidable war. His discussion of marriage would of course send any modern self-respecting feminist into paroxysmic fury, but is in fact, by contemporary standards, a moderate and reasonable account, leavened with humour and a certain affection.[29] And the third part, on 'Indifferent Things', deals with the ideal lifestyle of a king: moderation – the same keynote – in all things, in food, language, recreation, even armour which provokes the unashamedly unheroic, if eminently practical comment that it should be light for easier 'away-running'. Hunting is highly praised; silly pedantry condemned.[30] What above all informs this remarkable book is not its theory of kingship. It is its low-key and admirable commonsense and wit.

Both works, however, posed considerable problems. Naturally James while King of Scotland was of considerable interest to the English; and the accounts of English diplomats give us a clear picture of a very effective ruler, controlling factions, controlling parliaments, asserting his will. So far, so good. But he was also the author of books which laid down a view of kingship, from the controlling of property to the making of law; and that was anything but good. Elizabeth believed, as much as James did, in kingship by divine right, and had no hesitation in warning her subjects off areas which were reserved to the monarch; but she was 'mere English', and she never offended English susceptibilities by making the claims, and showing an indifference to the rules, which the king from Scotland was to do.[31] It is inconceivable that she would ever have insisted, as James did in his famous exchange with Sir Edward Coke, that in effect he could be 'judge competent', as the 1584 act had said, because 'the law was founded on reason, and that he and the others had reason as well as the (English) judges'; and he then went on to make matters worse by retorting, when Coke pointed out that for all his great endowments, English law demanded long study and experience, that this put him under the law 'which is treason to affirm'.[32] It did not help very much that *Basilikon Doron* could on occasion be pressed into service by those whom James made profoundly uneasy; in 1610 Nicholas Fuller cited its advice to Prince Henry to be careful not to impoverish his subjects – something which in practice James appeared all too guilty of doing. It is a nice illustration of Maurice Lee's reminder that '*Basilikon Doron*, like scripture, can be used for many purposes'.[33] But on the whole, the translation of James's Scottish writings into the English context, reinforced by some of James's own assertions after 1603, contributed to, if they did not wholly create, an atmosphere of unease. Yet it can be argued that this was not so much, as the English thought, because the king did not understand them. It was because they did not understand the king.

Few authors write only for themselves; and it may appear inconceivable that James, who was not a modest man, could have done so. Yet, as I shall suggest, it does appear that, at least at the time of their conception, neither of James's tracts was designed for an open readership, and neither was written with an English readership particularly in mind. In later years, James did write for his public; the *Apologie for the Oath of Allegiance* and the *Premonition to all Christian Monarchies* are obvious cases in point. But these were very different works, deliberately designed to refute papal claims and therefore naturally composed for a European market. This was not the case with the Scottish writings. Indeed, there are various clues about James's approach to writing – and to controversy – which suggest that the political tracts of 1598–9 should be viewed, initially at least, as the product of a mind at work rather than a closed and fixed one having already determined on the theme he had decided to lay before the world. Not the least of these clues is the manuscript of *Basilikon Doron* itself, a delightful piece of evidence of an author searching for words and ideal expression of arguments, scribbling, scoring out, scribbling again – and the whole lovely mess, which would call down the wrath of any tutor were a student to present it as an essay, bound up in purple velvet, and stamped in gold leaf with thistles, the Scottish emblem, and the royal initials, as befitted a king. There is also James's justification for a piece of early writing, his *Paraphrase on Revelations* (1588), which is 'asvell to teach my self as others'.[34] And it is arguable that the *Reulis and Cautellis of Poesie* (1585) and the *Daemonologie* (1597) were written in a state of anything but certainty, the first because of the dawning awareness that he could not match the great circle of poets in the Scottish court, the second because of the dawning fear that even if witchcraft existed, many of those who had died for it in Scotland had not been witches.

We have, then, a picture of a man who turned to writing to clarify his thought, who found writing a release; as Bishop Goodman later said of him, 'he did love solitariness, and was given to his study'.[35] *Basilikon Doron* and the *Trew Law* do not absolutely parallel the *Reulis* and the *Daemonologie*, but they should surely be seen in similar terms: that is, they were written for refreshment and for pleasure, for the sheer delight in temporarily shutting the door on a world which, in his early years, had posed so many problems, but which were now being overcome, and could now be analysed by the pen. *Basilikon Doron* was certainly written for Prince Henry. But both were surely written primarily for King James. It may even be that he was following in the footsteps of two great rulers of the past who had turned to writing; for the *Meditations* of Marcus Aurelius, and Alfred's *Boethius* and *Augustine* were composed because of the awareness of these men that the vanity and pride that might too easily accompany great power must be controlled by internal contemplation. Much more prosaically, there was also the consideration that *Basilikon Doron* would greatly upset the Melvillians; as indeed, when they became aware of it, it did.[36]

It is not only the appearance of the manuscript of *Basilikon Doron* which is suggestive of an author not principally motivated by the desire to rush into publication. The *Trew Law* was anonymous when first published in 1598; the author called himself 'C. Philopatris' (a hybrid which is, incidentally, hardly a tribute to Buchanan's teaching of the classics!). Moreover, the passage describing the effect of the Norman Conquest on English law and government was, as James can hardly have failed to be aware, one which touched on a somewhat raw English nerve. James was not averse to the occasional assumption of Scottish superiority, such as his change of New Year's Day to 1 January in 1600, to bring Scotland into line with 'all utheris weill governit commoun welthis and cuntreyis', though he must have realized when he said this that his hoped for succession to the country which, unlike well-governed ones, retained 25 March, could not be much longer delayed.[37] But that was very different from the pointed contrast between Scotland and the conquered, subservient England; and this surely indicates that this book was not intended as a means of trumpeting to his future subjects his political theory of divine right. The fact is that we make too much of the *Trew Law* because it sounds very familiar. But it was not the final and comprehensive statement of the deeply convinced and unshakeable divine right theorist, bound by the confines of his own theory. We only think that because after 1603, James expressed his ideas, and refined them, a great deal more than he had done in Scotland, in response to the English common lawyers. Before 1603, it was not even typical of his utterances. It was brought into being as a direct reaction to the secular theory of Buchanan and the much more dangerous religious theories and claims of the Melvillians.

Basilikon Doron was written in thorough-going Middle Scots, a fact which, as the editor of the Scottish Text Society edition, Dr James Craigie, rightly points out, is itself worthy of note; for already some thirty years earlier John Knox's *History of the Reformation* had been written in a version of Scots which showed distinctly anglicizing tendencies, the late sixteenth century witnessed a continuation of the process in both literary and non-literary writings, and James himself in his great plea for Union in 1607 used linguistic similarity as one of his arguments for the common ground between his kingdoms of England and Scotland. All this does suggest a very private approach when James wrote *Basilikon Doron* in 1598; indeed, the immense secrecy which surrounded it and the fact that James wrote what he called his 'testament & latter will' because he was in fear of death – as Charles V had been when he wrote his testament – were described to Cecil by his agent George Nicolson, who begged him to keep quiet about it.[38] When the ideas began to emerge from the study for the first printing in 1599, the text was indeed anglicized; even so, James himself swore the printer, Robert Waldegrave, to secrecy, and only seven copies were produced, for designated people: his wife, his son, his son's tutor, the reasonably reliable Marquis of Hamilton, and the three northern Catholic earls who had caused him such trouble in the early 1590s but who were now cooperative subjects, Huntly, Erroll and Angus.[39] And then in March 1603 the situation changed entirely. The book appeared on the London market.

I have previously described this – impressionistically – as 'becoming a best-seller'; his new subjects wanted a sight of 'the king's book'. But I had no idea of the scale of it until Peter W. M. Blayney, who has made a very detailed study of the printing of *Basilikon Doron*, told me of his findings and very kindly allowed me to make use of them. They are dramatic in the extreme. The *Trew Law* was also published in that year, after *Basilikon Doron*, and in two of the three printings the king's name did appear. But it was very small-scale compared to the huge success of *Basilikon Doron*. One copy of Waldegrave's Edinburgh edition was sent to London before Elizabeth's death on 24 March. Only four days later, on 28 March, the publisher John Norton and five partners 'entered' the work in the Stationers' Hall, thus registering their claim to copyright. By 13 April, eight 1603 editions were almost certainly out; at that point plague hit London – and the booktrade – and very little was produced from then until 30 May. Dr Blayney estimates that there were between 13,000 and 16,000 copies printed: up to 10,500 of the Norton editions, two pirate editions by one Edward Allde, who printed 3,000 and was fined on 13 April for doing so and for undercutting the price of the official editions, and in addition copies of the Waldegrave edition made available on the London market. The printer of all the official editions was Felix Kingston, who began by roping in other printers in order to get the sheets ready but then took over the enterprise almost exclusively. Norton himself, publisher of all eight editions, was a friend of Cecil; and, as Dr Blayney suggests, Cecil – no doubt anxious to please his new master – may have been involved in bringing the initial Waldegrave copy to London before Elizabeth's death and its registration with the Stationers' Company immediately afterwards. This friend in high places, however, did not save Norton from being up before the court of the Stationers' Company on the same day as Allde, 13 April, not for under-cutting, but for overcharging. The king's book was undoubtedly a best-seller.

Whether it was a popular read is a quite different matter. Normally very few copies survive from the editions of books which capture the market: one or two from the first edition, a few more from the second, and so on. In the case of *Basilikon Doron*, a lot survives from each edition, and this suggests that it was bought, perhaps read once, and put on the bookshelf.[40] This seems to me to raise a very interesting possibility. By March 1603, James does seem to have decided that his book should be made generally available to his future subjects; in the 1603 Edinburgh edition he referred to Elizabeth as being still alive, and apologised to his English readers for anything which might offend them in a text written originally for private purposes, commenting on Scottish affairs, and not intended for general publication.[41] The highly significant fact is that the work he chose to make available was not the theoretic and potentially controversial *Trew Law*; that simply trailed in behind *Basilikon Doron* later in 1603. Although like the *Trew Law, Basilikon Doron*, as he now acknowledged, did contain things which might appear critical of the English, it was nevertheless the book brought into circulation because it was his account of the practical exercise of royal authority, realistic, moderate rather than arbitrary, compromising. That was the style of kingship which he wanted to demonstrate to his new subjects. If they did not read it, then it explains an error which has been remarkably persistent: the belief that an English king called James I wrote a book about absolute kingship called *Basilikon Doron*. The idea gains support from the fact that after the frenzied printings of the first two and a half weeks of the reign, there was virtually no interest in England for further editions. It was taken up on the Continent; some thirty translations into Latin, French, Italian, Spanish, Dutch, German and Swedish – as well as one in Welsh – were produced in James's lifetime. But it did not appear in England again until the publication of the *Workes* in 1616. So the English seem, on the whole, to have treated it as the equivalent of a coronation mug.[42] But it was not a coronation mug. It was a guide to their new king. It was, in other words, not just a missed opportunity. It was an opportunity which James, the stranger, the incoming foreign king was keen to offer, as reassurance; and it went very badly awry.

The sad thing was that once this had happened, the problem could only be compounded. For James was certainly more than a solitary author. He was a delighter in controversy. In Scotland, it had been theological controversy – sometimes impassioned, even bad-tempered controversy, but always with the spice of enjoyment. There is a revealing little thumbnail sketch of a row between the king and one of the Melvillian ministers, John Davidson, in 1598 – a row in which, incidentally, Davidson, like Andrew Melville himself on a much more famous occasion, clutched at the king's sleeve. It could hardly be said that they parted in agreement. But as they parted, 'the king turned backe, and taking him by the shoulder, said, "Mr Johne, yee sall be welcomer with me becaus yee are plaine." '[43] Not the least of James's difficulties in the new world of England was that the English were not so plain.

Moreover, they took him too literally, at every turn. They failed to make allowance for bursts of irritation and visible exaggeration in the heat of argument, of which the exchange with Coke, and the famous outburst at Hampton Court are obvious examples. And, perhaps precisely because he was a notable political theorist as well as a leading political figure, they failed to make sufficient allowance for flexibility of mind – that flexibility which produced works as different in character as *Basilikon Doron* and the *Trew Law* within a year, and twelve years later, in the parliament of 1610, the very well-received speech of 21 March on the nature of monarchy which was far more acceptable than either, commanding 'the great Contentment of all Parties'. This reaction, among MPs all too ready to show their touchiness, and the text of the speech itself, suggest that Dr Sommerville's view of it as 'little more than pleasantries' may be an understatement.[44] It was surely more than that, a genuine assertion of James's belief that kingship did indeed involve vast powers, but that wise kings did not invoke them without concern for the law and for the bond between monarch and subjects. But I have already referred to a speech of 1610, made exactly two months later, which did not create contentment; flexibility included irritability and, with it, the tendency to emphasize theory when practice caused frustration. Inevitably that made it difficult for his English subjects – especially the English common lawyers – to distinguish between theory and practice.

There were even occasions when it was hard for them to see the theory for what it was. In the genial and hopeful atmosphere surrounding the opening of parliament in 1621, James took up the delicate question of the nature of monarchy and parliament. He told his parliament that 'Things proper to your-selves are the making of laws in that nature as he [the king] shall call for them. The king, he is the maker of them and ye are the advisers, councillors, and confirmers of them . . . '. The very idea of the king as the maker of laws no doubt struck horror into his listeners. One wonders whether they had listened attentively to an earlier passage: 'for kings and kingdoms were before parlia-ments . . . but when people began to be willing to be guided by laws, then came the first institutions of parliaments'.[45] It was the appeal to logic expressed in very similar terms two decades earlier in the *Trew Law*. Indeed, if anything, it was a modified version of that earlier claim. But the modification was not enough. James was not claiming that he alone could 'make' law. But it was possible to interpret him as believing that he could; and that, to his English subjects, was profoundly disturbing.

Yet in reacting as they did, they missed not one but two crucial points about King James. It was not only that he never translated his most extreme theoretic claims into practice. It was also the fact that the political issue which con-cerned him most when he succeeded to the English throne was not divine right monarchy at all, but union. And this brings me finally to a much neglected figure, James's major ally in the union project, the great Scottish lawyer Sir Thomas Craig of Riccarton. Craig was an enthusiastic unionist, influenced not only by the king, but by the vision of union expressed by Protector Somerset in his influential *Epistle* of 1547.[46] It was to be a union of equal partners. That meant asserting Scotland's antiquity and independence as a kingdom, as against the dismissive views of the vassal status of the Scottish kingdom most recently expressed by Holinshed. Craig gives us a wonderful little description of the eternal reaction of the Scot when faced with assertions of English superiority: having read Holinshed, 'I found my Choler begin to rise, and that it happened to me exactly as Holinshed had foretold; for there is nothing, says he, which will vex a Scotsman more, or that he takes worse, than to tell him, that Scotland is a Fee-Liege of England.' But he was concerned with far more than the defence of Scottish independence. This friend and legal adviser of the king was the one notable exception to the general rule that debate in Scotland was religious debate. His political theory was very moderate. An admirer of Bodin, he nevertheless stopped far short of Bodin's view of kingship; indeed, he managed to maintain good relations with James despite the fact that he could describe George Buchanan as 'my very intimate friend'. For Craig, the law was of two kinds, mutable and immutable. The Prince could alter the first, for the good of the state; for it related to particular times and circumstances, and must change as they changed. But the immutable law is that which always binds the Prince, because he has sworn to observe it, by sacred oath; and 'as God himself is invoked witness of the Oath given, so he will avenge the violation of it. The Prince has not made his promise to men, but to the Omnipotent God, who can and uses to require a strict account of it.' And what did Craig mean by the Prince? 'When I speak of a Prince, I mean a Prince in the Parliament or Great Court of the kingdom. For then he has the Rights of Majesty more eminently, because otherwise he cannot make a law, that obliges the subjects, nor impose Taxes upon them.'[47] Despite the very different emphasis of the *Trew Law* and, indeed, many of the assertions James made to his English subjects after 1603, this view, advanced by a man close to the king, trusted and respected by him, was not one from which the king would have dissented. But neither was it a view which made its mark on his English subjects. The English translation of James's Scottish views was not a happy one. But that was not simply because the Scottish views were unacceptably extreme.

King James adored theological debate. In Scotland and England he got plenty of it. In Scotland, when he turned to political theory, he was, apart from Craig, a more isolated figure. When he entered the English world, he found a preoccupation with political issues which to him was both stimulating and entertaining. James's Scottish subjects were well aware that their king was a man of wit and humour. Even the hostile Anthony Weldon paid grudging tribute to that. But it is not something which James's English subjects – or later historians of King James I – have particularly appreciated. The difficulty was that royal enjoyment, even occasional tail-twisting, could only add to English worry.

4 JAMES I AND THE DIVINE RIGHT OF KINGS: ENGLISH POLITICS AND CONTINENTAL THEORY

J. P. Sommerville

After the Civil War, the historian Sir Roger Twysden looked back on the parliamentary history of England. He gave particular emphasis to the reign of James I, arguing that the king was the first monarch in over 200 years to dissolve parliaments abruptly and while their business was still incomplete. Twysden also argued that James was the first king in almost a century to leave any substantial gap between meetings of parliament. He was largely correct. The sudden dissolutions of the meetings of 1614 and 1621 meant that those assemblies were virtually abortive, and the hard work which had gone into preparing legislation was wasted. The seven-year gap between those two parliaments was also unusually long – easily the longest in living memory. Indeed, in strict legal theory it was arguable that neither of those two meetings counted as a parliament, and so that there was no *legal* parliament between 1611 and 1624 – a period of thirteen years, and easily the longest gap in parliament's entire history. By law, parliament ought to have been summoned annually, a fact which many Englishmen were soon to recall – if, indeed, they had ever forgotten it. The rapid dissolutions of parliament by James's son in the 1620s, and his refusal to call a parliament in the eleven years before 1640, were amongst the major grievances levelled against his regime on the eve of the Civil War.[1]

To understand why James failed to call more parliaments it is necessary to investigate his political ideas. Recent methodological studies on the history of ideas have emphasized that the great texts of theory cannot fully be understood unless we set them in the context of the political and social history of the times in which their authors lived. Ideas, in short, have to be understood against the backcloth of political events. The converse is also true. In other words, to grasp what a political event meant for those who participated in it, it is necessary to know something about their ideas. This is not to suggest that profound philosophies explain political actions. They rarely do. But it is to suggest that if we want to know why somebody acted in a certain way, we must find out enough about their general mental outlook to discover what counted as their reason for action.[2]

The purpose of this chapter is to examine the political ideas of one man – King James I – in the hope of shedding light on some of his political actions, such as his conduct towards parliament. Another reason for surveying James's ideology is that little attempt has been made to do this for a very long time. Indeed, McIlwain's account, published in 1918, is still probably the fullest and best.[3] Analysing the king's political thoughts is no mere antiquarian enterprise. Recent debate on the history of England in the early modern period has concentrated on the work of so-called revisionists. Though they disagree on many points of detail, the general revisionist argument is that English history had little to do with any high conflicts of principle, and much with personal animosities, factional struggles at the royal court, and the pressures of war on an antiquated and ramshackle administrative system.

Revisionists rebut the notion that the seventeenth century in England witnessed the defeat of the Crown's attempts to establish an absolutist form of government, or the victory of a system which centred on the rule of law, the accountability of the executive to a representative parliament, and the protection of individual liberties from encroachment by the central administration. In rebutting this interpretation, revisionists have in effect cut off the modern world from its moorings in the seventeenth-century past, and by implication challenged some of the most cherished self-images of our age. If the story of the last four centuries or so is nothing more than a tale of back-door intrigues and petty personal vendettas, then many widely held views on the origins and meaning of modern western civilization must be abandoned – though this, of course, does nothing to show that revisionism is false.[4]

Now, revisionist arguments rest upon one basic contention – that there were very few differences of political principle amongst Englishmen in the early seventeenth century. According to the revisionist account, which owes a great deal to the work of J. G. A. Pocock, a single political ideology prevailed in England. The leading representatives of this ideology were Sir John Fortescue in the mid-fifteenth century, and Sir Edward Coke in the early seventeenth. Its main features were, firstly, insularity. Continental modes of thought were rejected, and the English common law reigned supreme over men's minds. This law consisted of ancient custom. The second feature of the ideology was a great reverence for the past. By investigating the past, revisionists maintain, Englishmen believed that they could discover the ancient constitution which alone defined the rights of the king and the liberties of subjects. Belief in a balanced constitution, revisionists argue, lay at the very centre of English political thinking. Of course, there were a few disputes over the exact point of balance. But the ideal itself commanded almost universal adherence. Consequently, major clashes of political principle were impossible.

It might be helpful to illustrate the revisionist outlook with just a few quotations, though these could easily be multiplied. Professor Pocock tells us that '[t]hose who supported what the Stuart kings were doing did not normally regard their ruler as a sovereign maker of law . . . and consequently did not argue that the laws flowed from his will'. Rather, they rested their case on an immemorial law – and belief in this law was (so Pocock informs us) 'not a party argument' but 'the nearly universal belief of Englishmen'. He also lays great stress on the insularity of English thinking. According to J. P. Kenyon, 'with remarkable unanimity early seventeenth-century Englishmen believed that they were bound to abide by the ancient constitution, which had existed without change time out of mind. By that constitution the monarch had certain prerogatives, the subjects certain rights – particularly rights of property – and neither could be infringed without a dangerous imbalance resulting'. Kenyon acknowledges that James I made some notorious statements which sound absolutist. But he insists that the king's absolutism was 'confined to the realm of theory', and argues that in practice 'he was always careful to operate within the framework of the Common Law'. Moreover, in his later years, says Kenyon, he abandoned even the theory of absolutism.[5]

Austin Woolrych takes a line very similar to that of the revisionists, claiming that even in his earlier years James accepted that his power was not absolute, though he occasionally adopted the rhetoric of absolutism. Finally, Conrad Russell emphasizes the remarkable extent to which ideological unity prevailed even at the end of the turbulent 1620s. Though parliaments diminished in usefulness to the Crown in the early seventeenth century, the king did still call them. Professor Russell seeks the reason in ideology. It was, he argues, the influence of Sir John Fortescue which secured parliament's survival.[6]

The central problem with these arguments is that there were, in fact, *several* ideologies (and not just one) current in early Stuart England. Some people did indeed claim that ancient custom guaranteed irrefragable rights to both ruler and ruled. Others, however, believed that kings derive their powers not from old laws but directly from God, and that the monarch could infringe any purely human law if he judged this necessary. Others, again, claimed that the king drew his authority from a grant by the people, and held that the monarch was subject to contractual obligations. These points deserve to be stressed. It makes sense to study individual thinkers against the background of the ideological climate of their times. This climate, in the case of early Stuart England, was *not* one of unity and harmony.[7]

Let us turn now to the political ideas of James I. Whatever the truth of the revisionists' views on English political thought in general – and these views are open to many objections – they do not apply to the king. James's ideas were far from insular. The king's political outlook must be set firmly against the background of continental controversies, and was scarcely, if at all, influenced by the common law. His outlook explains much about his actions. James was not a split personality, and his practice was not sealed from his thoughts. The king's early thinking was shaped in large part by Scottish Presbyterianism. In theory, the Scottish church claimed only spiritual power over kings. In practice, it used its power to depose James's mother from the throne, and to place stringent limitations upon his own authority. James resented this, and reacted vigorously against Presbyterian ideas. During the king's formative years, France was torn apart by civil wars in which the king's close relatives, the Guise family, played a major part. In the course of those wars both the Huguenots and the zealous Catholics of the League argued that it was legitimate for subjects to take up arms against a tyrannical or heretical ruler. Both claimed that kings derived power from the people, and that the people could resume power if their monarchs infringed the conditions on which it had first been granted to them. Catholics also argued that the pope could use his spiritual authority to intervene in temporal affairs by deposing Protestant rulers. One pope excommunicated Elizabeth of England, and another deprived Henry of Navarre of the right to succeed to the throne of France. In the thinking of some Catholics, a deposed king was no better than a usurper, and could be killed by anyone. Both Henry III and Henry IV of France were assassinated by Catholic fanatics. James's own fears of assassination are well known, and in view of the Gunpowder Plot and the writings of Catholics they were not unrealistic.[8]

James was Britain's most scholarly king, and wrote five main works of political theory – two in Scotland, and three more after his accession to the Crown of England.[9] In all these books he argued against theories of legitimate resistance which circulated in Scotland and on the Continent. Advising his son and heir in 1598, James warned him against the writings of the Scottish resistance theorists Knox and Buchanan. Seventeen years later, in the longest and last of his political works, James focused on the ideas of the Catholic Cardinal Du Perron. The cardinal had delivered a speech in the French Estates General at the beginning of 1615, in which he attacked a proposal of the Third Estate to have it set down as a fundamental law of France that the king could never in any circumstances be resisted or deposed. Du Perron regarded this proposal as an unwarranted infringement of papal claims to be able to depose heretical rulers. He did not want to argue that the pope held direct temporal power over kings. But he did claim that popes possessed spiritual jurisdiction over monarchs, and that if need arose they could use their spiritual authority to intervene in temporal matters, say by deposing kings. This theory of the 'indirect' power of the pope in temporal affairs was defended by many

Catholics, including Suarez and Bellarmine, but it did not convince the king. According to James, the distinction between a direct temporal power over kings, and a spiritual power which could extend into the temporal realm was mere nonsense. If the pope had authority over kings in certain circumstances, and if he could decide just what those circumstances were, then it really did not matter whether you called his authority spiritual or temporal. Either way, the king would end up deposed, and quite possibly dead.[10]

In taking up his pen against Du Perron, James intended to vindicate the rights of all Christian rulers against papal pretensions. That was also the aim of the two books which he wrote in defence of the oath of allegiance of 1606, and which were largely directed against another cardinal, Bellarmine. In the king's opinion, Bellarmine's political ideas were false not merely because he subjected kings to the pope, but also because he subjected them to the people. In 'setting up the people above their natural king', he said, Bellarmine laid 'an excellent ground in divinity for all rebels and rebellious people'. Kings, James argued, derived their powers immediately from God, and not from the people. His central intellectual concern throughout his career was to protect the rights of kings everywhere against the assaults of Jesuits and puritans.[11]

The books against Du Perron and Bellarmine were intended to contribute to a European-wide controversy over the powers of monarchs. Like most of James's writings they were translated into Latin, the international language of learning. The second reply to Bellarmine was addressed to all the princes and states of the Christian world. The king attempted to have sumptuously bound copies of it presented to all the sovereigns of Europe – sometimes with embarrassing results, since many Catholic rulers felt reluctant to accept a work which the pope had rapidly placed on the Index.[12]

James was extremely sensitive about his continental reputation, both as an author and as a truly orthodox monarch. This led him to intervene in European affairs on a number of occasions, sometimes causing difficulties for his ambassadors. He meddled in the internal affairs of France in the case of the article of the Third Estate of 1614–15 – the article against which Du Perron spoke. He intervened in Dutch affairs in the famous case of Vorstius, a Professor at Leiden whom James considered a heretic, and whose dismissal he secured in 1612. In the same year he acted as arbitrator in a dispute about the theological doctrine of justification between the French Protestants Du Moulin and Tilenus. A few years later he interfered in the affairs of the Spanish Netherlands in connection with a book entitled *Corona regia* – a Catholic mock-panegyric on the king which scoffed at his bandy legs, and which explicitly accused him of indulging in homosexual practices. James sent a special envoy to Brussels to demand the punishment of the author. The envoy was unsuccessful, since it was difficult to establish who the author was, though the diplomat Sir Henry Wotton tried to ascertain his identity over a period of eight years and even suggested kidnapping the printer and bringing him to England, where it would be easier to make him talk.[13]

The English diplomatic service did use strong-arm tactics on foreign soil in the case of the German, Kaspar Schoppe, in 1616. Schoppe had written a particularly offensive attack on one of James's books. When the ambassador to Spain found that Schoppe was in Madrid, he arranged for him to be beaten up. The idea was to cut off his nose and ears, but he managed to escape with a cut on the face and some bruises.[14]

The king's desire for fame abroad led him to take part in continental scholarly debate, and later to read large quantities of European books – in part with the idea of seeing how the reputation of his own works was progressing. He also offered patronage to continental intellectuals, and a number of authors dedicated works to him in the hope of rewards. In 1615, for example, an Italian Franciscan sent a messenger to James with a book advocating a union of Christian princes against the Turks. Since James was much in favour of schemes for union he was very pleased with the book – until he was shown a passage in it alleging that he was a secret Catholic. At that point the messenger prudently fled. More successful was the Dutch scientist, Cornelis Drebbel, who dedicated a perpetual motion machine to the king. Drebbel was given a pension and James put his scientific skills to practical use by placing him in charge of the special effects at court masques. A more famous scientist, Joannes Kepler, sent and dedicated work to the king, and in return was invited to the royal court.[15]

But James's interests lay far less in science than in political and theological debate. He employed foreign research assistants, and invited some leading European scholars to come to England. The views of the people he invited make clear the king's own intellectual preferences. James advised his son that if he did write books he should have them revised by skilled men. The king took his own advice on this. His assistants were often foreigners (or else such Englishmen as Lancelot Andrewes, who were steeped in continental learning). When James composed his second reply to Bellarmine he received help from John Barclay, whose antecedents were Scottish but who had himself been brought up in Lorraine, where his father William was a professor of law. William Barclay was author of *De regno* – one of the most famous of early modern defences of monarchical authority against ideas of legitimate resistance, and the work which coined the term 'monarchomach'. William himself came to England briefly after James's accession, but it was John who profited most from royal favour, receiving a pension and other gifts from the king and the Earl of Salisbury. James's reply to Du Perron was originally published in French, and the man responsible for polishing its style – and also perhaps for much of the writing – was the Huguenot, Pierre Du Moulin. Some years before this, Du Moulin had already written two works in defence of James's ideas.

James gave him money and also a Welsh living, a prebend at Canterbury, and a doctorate at Cambridge University. His influence over the king was lamented from different perspectives both by Lancelot Andrewes – one of the king's favourite bishops – and by the Spanish ambassador Sarmiento.[16]

Another Frenchman to gain the king's favour was Isaac Casaubon, one of the greatest of early modern classical scholars. When Venice was put under Interdict by the pope in 1606, the authorities there invited Casaubon to write a book in their defence. This was published in 1607 and Richard Bancroft, Archbishop of Canterbury, gave the king a copy of the book, which not only asserted the independence of secular rulers from ecclesiastical interference, but also laid down as an unquestionable principle the Bodinian doctrine that in every state there must be an absolute and indivisible sovereign. Casaubon opposed papal claims by arguing that in all states the governing authority derived its powers solely from God and not from the people. James was so taken with Casaubon's ideas that he invited the Frenchman to England in 1610, and Casaubon spent the rest of his life there. James gave him the task of reading all new continental publications on church–state relations and similar questions, and of reporting on them to the king. Casaubon also produced controversial works supporting the king's attitudes, and collaborated closely with James in drawing up a defence of the king's religious views.[17]

James took a great interest in the controversy over the Venetian Interdict, since it raised issues which were close to his heart. One of these issues was the relationship between secular rulers and the church. The scholars who defended Venice argued that the church had no right to interfere in the temporal concerns of states. They also claimed that secular rulers drew their power from God alone, that they could not be actively resisted by their subjects, and that they were supreme lawmakers in their states. The idea that the legislative power of sovereigns is limited, whether by contract or by ancient custom, was absent from their thought. James liked their theories, and in 1612 he invited the most famous defender of Venice, Paolo Sarpi, to come to England. Sarpi declined, but a few years later his friend Marc'Antonio De Dominis accepted a similar invitation, and he stayed in England from 1616 to 1622. While in England he published two massive volumes on church–state relations in which he took an uncompromisingly absolutist line. The books were dedicated to the king and published by the royal printer. James was also very impressed by Joannes Marsilius, whose writings he read, and whose ill-health he lamented in 1612. Though Sarpi refused to emigrate, he was keenly interested in the controversy which resulted from James's writings, obtaining newly published copies of many of the books, and corresponding with Casaubon, whom he encouraged in his controversial efforts.[18]

Another of Casaubon's correspondents was Hadrian Saravia, who was of Flemish extraction, but who had already long been naturalized as an

Englishman by the beginning of James's reign. Like Du Moulin, Saravia was a canon of Canterbury. He was one of the translators of the Authorized Version of the Bible. In a book first published in 1593 and reprinted in 1611 Saravia trenchantly asserted the sovereign power of the kings of England, attacking the idea that the English form of government was mixed or limited. William the Conqueror, he said, had ruled as an absolute conqueror, and later monarchs had held the same powers. Indeed, he argued that an absolute sovereign was a necessary feature of every state, and his reasoning on this point was close to Bodin's. The ideas of Bodin were also highly influential on the thinking of another foreigner in England – Alberico Gentili, the Regius Professor of Civil Law at Oxford. In 1605 Gentili published a treatise *De potestate regis absoluta* – 'on the absolute power of the king'.[19]

James involved himself in continental intellectual debate, read the works of European scholars, and invited a number of leading figures to England. He was especially closely associated with a group of thinkers who emphasized that rulers were not accountable to the church or the people, and who claimed that in every state the sovereign alone made law. By contrast, there is little evidence that the king owed any great intellectual debt to English scholars, and, in particular, to common law thinkers. The most reliable guides to the influences on the king's mind are undoubtedly the king's own writings. James was happy to parade his learning by citing authors to confirm his ideas, and in his printed *Workes* he refers to some 200 writers. Of these, scarcely any were recent English scholars – the main exception being the king himself, since he referred to his own books several times. He also cited a few medieval English chroniclers, and some of the authors who had taken Henry VIII's side on the question of the Royal Supremacy. Of more recent writers, he referred to Reginald Scot, whose sceptical views on witchcraft he rejected, and to several English Catholics whom he similarly cited only to criticize. James referred with approval to only three recent British authors apart from himself. These were the Earl of Northampton, whose printed speech after the Gunpowder Plot put forward ideas similar to the king's own; Lancelot Andrewes, whose controversial works were written under the king's close supervision; and John Gordon, Dean of Salisbury, a kinsman and flatterer of the king.[20]

There is virtually no mention in James's writings of the thought of common lawyers – though conventional wisdom tells us that common law attitudes dominated the political outlook of most English thinkers. Of course, James knew of the work of Coke, and his quarrels with the judge over the nature of royal power are famous, as is the fact that James wanted Coke's law reports to be purged of passages which undervalued the royal prerogative. Less well-known, but equally striking, is the king's relationship with John Selden – perhaps the most eminent of common law scholars, and along with Coke one of the leaders of the House of Commons in the debates which led up to the

Petition of Right in 1628. Early in James's reign Selden wrote a number of works on legal and scholarly matters. These included an edition of Sir John Fortescue's *De laudibus legum Angliae*, perhaps the single most important book in shaping the constitutional views of lawyers. Then in 1618 Selden published a *Historie of Tithes* which offended many of the clergy. As a result he was summoned before the king. According to Selden's own later account, James had not only never met him before, but never so much as heard his name. Nor does there seem to be any evidence that he had heard of Fortescue either. Manifestly, the king was seriously out of touch with common law scholarship.[21]

If the keynote of the common lawyers' approach to English politics lay in the belief that both monarch and subject draw their power from an ancient constitution, discoverable by historical investigation, then James did not share that approach. The king used history selectively, and to support conclusions which he had reached by other means. In arguing against the pope's alleged right to depose sovereigns, James did indeed cite many examples taken from medieval history. But his point in doing so was simply to substantiate the subordinate argument that papal claims had been widely rejected in the past. The king's main argument was that the pope's powers had no foundation in Scripture or reason. We are often told that in the years before the Civil War Englishmen looked to history as the golden repository of political truths, and that it was only the war itself which gave rise to talk in terms of the natural rights of all men rather than the legal rights of Englishmen. That claim will bear reexamination, for many pre-Civil War authors observed that questions of right and wrong simply cannot be answered by reference to past facts alone. James certainly believed that precedents had to be interpreted carefully, especially if they tended to diminish royal rights. He cited the civil law to show that no contrary customs, of however long duration, could deprive kings of their powers. James warned Sir Edward Coke against arguing on the basis of what happened in the times of weak kings such as Richard II and Henry VI when 'the crown tossed up and down like a tennis ball'. As often, the king was virtually quoting himself here. Earlier, he had cautioned the French against accepting Du Perron's arguments, which implied that 'Popes may toss the French King his throne like a tennis ball'. James himself had no intention of becoming a tennis ball, whether it was popes or common lawyers who wielded the racket.[22]

Historically, said James, kings had come to power by a variety of means, including election and conquest. But he thought that however monarchs had at first acquired their crowns, their authority was derived from God alone. God gave kings a monopoly of political power within their realms. This meant that the political privileges of subjects were necessarily derived from the king. The exemption of the clergy from civil jurisdiction in certain cases, for example, existed because the king had willed it, and not in virtue of any law independent of the monarch. The same applied to the privileges of other groups within the realm, including parliament itself.[23]

When members of parliament attacked royal policies, James was quick to see resemblances between their arguments and those of the Catholic theorists against whom he had written. In 1610, for example, the Commons attacked the king's right to collect impositions, which were extra-parliamentary levies on exports and imports. He claimed that in questioning this right they were unwarrantedly distinguishing between the King of England and foreign sovereigns – for foreign monarchs did collect impositions. The same unwarranted distinction, he told parliament, featured in the writings of Bellarmine, since the Cardinal had denied James's claim that there was a community of interest between all European monarchs in opposing papal pretensions. It was only the King of England, Bellarmine had sneeringly said, who feared the pope's powers. In similar fashion, thought James, the Commons were now telling him that it was only the King of England who could not collect impositions. Against both, he affirmed that his own powers were identical with those of other sovereigns. His right to levy impositions, he declared, was 'one of the points of regality', which he could not give up even if he wanted to. All kings, he believed, were empowered by God to govern their realms for the public good and to raise revenues when they found this necessary. Manifestly, this argument had little to do with any supposedly ancient constitution. Equally manifestly, it was the very reverse of insular – and it was an argument expressed not just by James but also by a good many others, especially churchmen.[24]

It is sometimes said, indeed, that James 'was careful always to operate within the framework of the Common Law'.[25] It has even been suggested that in 1610 he became a convert to constitutional thinking. Certainly, in a famous speech to parliament the king distinguished between the earliest times before laws had been set up – when monarchs could rule as they pleased – and later periods after settled legal arrangements had been introduced, and when kings would sin if they wantonly broke the law. James did not, however, derive this position from common law principles. In his *The Trew Law of Free Monarchies* of 1598 he had already argued that although 'the King is above the law, as both the author and giver of strength thereto; yet a good king will not only delight to rule his subjects by the law, but even will conform himself in his own actions thereunto'. There is no reason to suppose that James changed his mind on any fundamental question of political theory after his accession to the throne of England.[26]

Some of the king's ministers found it useful to try to establish legal precedents for royal actions whose legality was doubtful. In Bate's case, the legality of an imposition on currants imported by the merchant Bate was upheld in the Exchequer. It might be thought that this indicates that James was always assiduous in submitting his claims to legal arbitration. This is doubtful. For one thing, Bate's case was no satisfactory legal basis for the great expansion in impositions which took place in 1608, as Pauline Croft has ably demonstrated. Again, the king himself based his main argument for impositions not upon the common law, nor upon Bate's case, but, as we have seen, upon the rights of all monarchs – rights derived from the law of nations. He observed that his two predecessors – Mary and Elizabeth – had collected impositions, and in his view they had every right to do so – though they had of course reigned long before the trial of Bate. The great lawyer Sir John Davies likewise grounded the royal right to levy impositions in the law of nations, and not in the common law.[27]

At times, the king did speak very highly of the common law. Far more than his son Charles, James was capable of compromise, and of giving voice to polite if imprecise formulae in the hope of encouraging his subjects to make him generous grants of cash. That the king was sometimes willing to compromise should cause us little surprise. He had no desire to rule as a despot, nor to win the detestation of his subjects. James resented attempts to limit his prerogative, but he had no wish to exercise that prerogative in an arbitrary or capricious fashion. Moreover, he believed that the common law did not in fact restrict royal rights. 'No law,' he said, 'can be more favourable and advantageous for a king, and extendeth further his prerogative, then it doeth.' So when James acknowledged the virtues of the common law he was not in any way admitting that royal power is limited. As Jenny Wormald has rightly observed, the king's use of words or phrases reminiscent of common lawyers should not be seen as evidence that he had adopted the *substance* of Coke's thinking: 'it was a veneer, overlaying his very different approach'.[28]

There was, in fact, no place in James's political outlook for the idea of an ancient constitution underlying the rights of both sovereign and subject. It is doubtful that he even understood the doctrine of the ancient constitution. James's political universe was one in which good Christians united against anti-monarchical Presbyterians and Jesuits. He regarded people who questioned royal power not as well-intentioned citizens who wanted to revise or restore small points of detail in an otherwise agreed constitution, but as potential rebels and traitors who were little better than Jesuits. To question royal power, he thought, was implicitly to claim jurisdiction over kings, and ultimately to assert the right to depose and kill them. When the Commons questioned impositions, James called to mind Bellarmine and the papal deposing power. For in his opinion any attack on royal authority implied that the attacker – whether pope, or Presbyterians, or parliament – was assuming the right to sit in judgement on the king. To question the king's power in one area – say, over impositions, or over ecclesiastical policy – was potentially to usurp jurisdiction over him in all areas. That idea underlay the king's repeated warning to his subjects that though they might point out to him cases in which the exercise of his powers was proving onerous, they should not call in question the powers themselves.

When the Commons did question impositions in 1610, James told them that by doing so they made him a mere shadow of a king, with no more power than the Doge of Venice. 'No Christians,' he said, 'but papists and puritans were ever of that opinion', and using an image that had earlier been employed by Saravia (and was later borrowed from him by the notorious Roger Maynwaring), James informed them that 'you cannot so clip the wing of greatness', since 'if a king be resolute to be a tyrant, all you can do will not hinder him'. As 'it is atheism and blasphemy to dispute what God can do', he declared in 1616, 'so it is presumption and high contempt in a subject to dispute what a king can do or to say that a king cannot do this or that'.[29]

Such sentiments – and, of course, the king's actions – convinced people that he was bent upon a policy of changing the form of government in England in the direction of absolute monarchy. In 1604 members of the Commons observed the increase of royal power with alarm in their Apology, and a Catholic document of about the same period referred to James's bad treatment not only of the papists but also 'of the whole commons in general', adding that 'nothing is more miserable than to see the faces of all sorts of men grinded with the former oppressions, and distracted with the fear of new mischiefs to ensue'. In 1609 the Spanish ambassador reported that the king had determined to make his will absolute and was therefore breaking all the venerable laws of England and oppressing his people with high taxation. The following year the House of Commons argued that impositions did indeed threaten the established constitution.[30]

But there is little reason to think that James himself believed that he was changing the English constitution. He thought that monarchs had always held sovereign power, in England as elsewhere, though some of his predecessors had not exercised it as effectively as they might have done. In the king's opinion it was ideas of limited monarchy and legitimate resistance which were novel. He thought he detected such ideas not only in Jesuits and puritans abroad, but also in the English parliament. It would have come as news to James that he was living in an age of ideological harmony and consensus.

In two ways, though, he did mis-read the ideological climate. For though he recognized that there were people who disagreed with his own political views, he grossly underestimated their number and importance. Like his son Charles, he thought that the Commons acted unpleasantly towards him because they had been led astray by a small number of seditious men. If the truth were explained to his subjects, he felt, they would loyally obey him. Arguably, this was a major reason for the failure of absolutism in England. James and

Charles were so convinced of the truth of their political views that they thought other people would be too, and could not seriously believe that disobedience on a wide scale was possible. Richelieu, by contrast, realized that many people would need to be persuaded of the truth of absolutist ideas, and that they might find a standing army a particularly convincing argument. Secondly, James's belief that there was no logical stopping-point between attempting to limit royal power in a specific small area, and resisting or deposing the king, sometimes led him to react far more violently than was sensible.

The king's language illustrates the depth of his resentment at attacks on his powers by members of the House of Commons. Commenting on his first parliament, he said that he had suffered 'more disgraces, censures and ignominies' from it 'than ever Prince did endure'. 'No house save the house of Hell' could have treated him as the Commons had done, he declared in 1610. It was only with difficulty that his councillors persuaded him to call parliament again in 1614, and when members of the Commons renewed the attack on impositions, as well as on the Scots, James dissolved the meeting before it had accomplished anything. In 1621 he likewise broke with parliament before it had been able to do much. That dissolution is worth examining in a little more detail – and such an examination will serve to draw together the main themes of this chapter, and to illustrate some of the weaknesses of revisionist re-assessment.[31]

In 1621 the House of Commons debated foreign policy, and in particular the projected marriage between the Prince of Wales and a Spanish princess. The king told them to drop the topic, since foreign policy and royal marriages were under his exclusive control. The Commons replied that by ancient law they had the right to discuss any matter which concerned the public good. James responded that free speech, like the other privileges of parliament, was derived from the grace of the monarch, was limited, and could be revoked if it was abused. When the Commons passed a Protestation declaring that the privilege of free speech and other parliamentary privileges existed as matters of right – and not grace – James dissolved the parliament and tore the Protestation from the Commons' Journal with his own hand. It has been suggested, by Conrad Russell, that the dissolution of the 1621 parliament had much to do with the machinations of the Marquis of Buckingham. Buckingham had profited greatly from monopolies. The 1621 parliament investigated the activities of monopolists, and Buckingham feared that they would bring charges against him. So he arranged for his client Sir George Goring to initiate discussion of foreign policy in the House of Commons. The Commons knew that Goring was Buckingham's servant, and so assumed that Buckingham and the king himself were inviting them to discuss the question. In fact, the king had nothing to do with Goring's motion, and was outraged by the Commons' action. This analysis may be correct. Certainly Buckingham was quite capable of wrecking a parliament to save his own skin. But even if the dissolution of the 1621 parliament was the consequence of a plot by Buckingham, the scheme would plainly not have worked unless a radical divergence of opinion on the nature and origins of parliamentary privilege had already separated the king from many in the House of Commons.[32]

So what were the principles which led James to dissolve the session of 1621? The king later spelled them out in a proclamation and a declaration on the dissolution. He argued that it was just a few members who had engineered the actions of the Commons as a whole, and talked about the 'captious and curious heads', the 'mutinous and discontented spirits', the 'Tribunitial Orators' who had caused all the trouble in the House. As usual, thought James, these seditious men had used the pretext of religion (which was raised in connection with the prince's projected match) to attack royal powers. In 1616 he had warned Star Chamber against Justices of the Peace who 'in every cause that concerns prerogative give a snatch against a monarchy, through their puritanical itching after popularity'. In his mind, there was little difference between the political ideas of puritans and Jesuits – and he famously declared that 'Jesuits are nothing but Puritan-papists'. The king detected puritanical and Jesuitical attitudes in the stance which the House of Commons took up on the question of its own privileges in 1621.[33]

The Commons asserted that their privileges were not derived from the monarch. They claimed that it was each house of parliament alone – and not the king – which had jurisdiction over its privileges. James believed that what underlay these claims was an outlook indistinguishable from that of Scottish Presbyterians or Cardinal Bellarmine – a point which he made forcefully in his declaration on the dissolution. Of course, the Commons claimed sovereign power only in the area of their own privileges, and at first glance this might not seem very threatening to the king. But James felt that their claims could be dangerously extended to cover virtually any aspect of government. In effect, he said caustically, the Commons were usurping 'all power upon earth', and their case was distinguishable from the pope's only in that they stopped short of asserting possession of the keys of heaven and Purgatory as well.[34]

People who claimed power independently of the king in one area had a habit of allowing that area to expand alarmingly. James gave two examples. 'For so', he said, 'did the Puritan ministers in Scotland bring all kind of causes within the compass of their jurisdiction, saying, That it was the Church's office to judge of slander, and there could no crime or fault be committed but there was a slander in it, either against God, the king, or their neighbour. And by this means they hooked in to themselves the cognisance of all causes.' In just the same way, he continued, Bellarmine's notion that the pope had no direct temporal power over kings, but that his spiritual sovereignty allowed him to use temporal means to help save souls, in effect gave the pope 'all temporal jurisdiction' over monarchs. And, again in just the same way, the arguments of the House of Commons would make them omnipotent in England. They had, he said, left nothing 'unattempted in the highest points of sovereignty . . . except the striking of coin'. Their disloyal speeches also threatened to bring the Protestant religion into disrepute in Catholic countries. For James, one of the most attractive features of the religion established in England was the great emphasis it placed upon the God-given duty of submission to monarchs. The actions of the Commons would give papists grounds for associating Protestantism with rebellion. 'And we would be sorry', said James, 'that that aspersion should come upon our religion, as to make it a good pretext for dethroning of kings, and usurping their crowns.'[35]

The strong language which the king used in criticizing the Commons of 1621 makes clear the anger that he felt at their conduct. What they had done, he declared, constituted 'an usurpation that the majesty of a king can by no means endure', and he said that 'we cannot with patience endure our subjects to use such anti-monarchical words to us'. James was certainly angry, and it is sometimes suggested by revisionists that emotional outbursts explain many of the cases of friction between king and Commons in the years before the Civil War. But James's reaction to what the Commons did in 1621 was no mere irrational tantrum. He was angry because he believed that he knew precisely where the Commons was being pushed by its seditious manipulators. It was being pushed towards republicanism. The important point, which deserves to be underlined, is not that James was angry but that he treated the opinions of the Commons as though they were indistinguishable from those of Jesuits. The fact that he published his views, and that he did not mince words, indicates that he expected people to agree with him. But of course many did not. As Sir Roger Twysden later commented, it was unwise for James 'on those terms to show a discontent with the representative body of this whole kingdom'. People who believed that the English form of government was mixed or limited monarchy were understandably aggrieved at James's statements. They resented being accused of holding anti-monarchical opinions, for they regarded themselves as loyal supporters of the monarch. They also disliked the king's opinions, which many saw as a threat to the established constitution. James tore the Protestation from the Commons' Journal, but he could not tear the ideas which it codified from the minds of members of the House. There were moves to revive the central points of the Protestation in every parliament of the 1620s.[36]

For James, the ideas which underlay the Protestation were alarmingly similar to the seditious theories of papists and Presbyterians. It is easy to assume that he was wholly mistaken, and that the bulk of Englishmen shared the outlook of Sir Edward Coke, who believed that ancient custom defined the rights and obligations of both king and subjects but gave the latter no power to resist their ruler. Why, if Englishmen were in fact hostile to ideas of contractual monarchy and licit resistance, did James fail to appreciate this? Was he a victim of his own ideology, trapped behind spectacles whose distorting lenses made even Coke resemble a Jesuit?

Certainly, James's own views did lead him to misconstrue the attitude of some of those who opposed his policies. But he construed the ideology of others correctly. That is to say, a number of the king's subjects did in fact believe that royal power had been granted not by God alone, but by the people through an original contract. Such men include Sir Robert Phelips, John Pym and Sir Edwin Sandys. In this chapter, we have seen that the king's political ideas differed drastically from those of Sir Edward Coke. So too did the ideas of a great many other Englishmen, and even amongst common lawyers Coke's views held no monopoly.[37] There was a variety of political viewpoints in early Stuart England, and James knew this. But he tended to identify opinions which differed from his own with the theories of the Jesuits.

The case of James I provides a cogent counterexample to the revisionist thesis that harmony reigned in early modern England, and that all believed in the doctrine of the ancient constitution. There are a good many other counterexamples – so many, in fact, that it is plain that the revisionist approach itself requires urgent modification. Several ideologies competed for the minds of Englishmen in the early seventeenth century. Any account of the mental world of the Jacobean court which ignores this truth is certain to be fatally flawed.

5 ROYAL AND PARLIAMENTARY VOICES ON THE ANCIENT CONSTITUTION C. 1604–1621

Paul Christianson

Among the representations of monarchy, the panels painted by Peter Paul Rubens for the ceiling of the Banqueting House at Whitehall provide, in intricate baroque visual discourse, a rich portrayal of majesty which, in vigour of execution, grandeur of scale, and complexity of symbolism rivalled any other contemporary European production.[1] From the vantage point of the 1630s, Rubens fashioned a rosy, retrospective view of the powers and accomplishments of his patron's father. The three central panels deal directly with James VI and I, the central rondel portraying a vision of his ascent into heaven and the flanking rectangular canvases representing him as uniting all of Britain under a single monarch and bestowing peace and plenty upon his realms.

Perception of these posthumous images of James has always depended strongly upon the theoretical conceptions brought to the text by the observer; no uninterpreted literary or visual text has ever existed. Most interpreters have seen these paintings as reflecting the absolutist divine right monarchy espoused by the early Stuart kings of England. The early writings of James VI, especially *The Trew Law of Free Monarchies* (Edinburgh, 1598) and the *Basilikon Doron* (Edinburgh, 1599), have become the key texts not only for unlocking the mysteries of the Whitehall ceiling, but also for establishing his own and his son's views on monarchy. For example, Roy Strong has argued that a number of these panels refer:

to what is without doubt the key source-book for the iconography of the ceiling, James I's own exposition of monarchy by Divine Right, the *Basilikon Doron*, written for the edification of his son, Henry, Prince of Wales. The central theme of this can, for our purposes, be summed up by the opening couplet of the sonnet placed at the very beginning:

> God gives not kings the style of Gods in vain,
> For on his throne his scepter do they sway . . .[2]

71

Stressing the 'absolute', divine right monarchy of the early Stuarts, literary and art historians alike have laboured together to buttress this variation on the old Whig interpretation of early Stuart England.[3] Recently they have received the able assistance of Johann Sommerville, an accomplished historian of political thought.[4] The line from the *Basilikon Doron* to the masques and paintings of the reign of Charles I has appeared undeviating.[5] What James wrote in the 1590s governed royal political thought during the first four decades of the seventeenth century.

This chapter challenges the assumption that, for the early Stuarts, divine right meant absolutism, which in turn meant arbitrary rule by the Crown. It will argue that by focusing upon the products of the 1590s and 1630s, historians appear to have brought a distorted perspective to a series of texts from the first three decades of the seventeenth century and have seriously misread the constitutional discourse of James I and his new subjects. The world of James I in England did not replicate that of Charles I, or even that of James VI in Scotland. While the British monarch continued to employ absolutist discourse in his disputes with Catholics, to defend the 'theology' of absolute monarchy against external powers, he needed and employed a different discourse when dealing with the governance of England.[6] In a speech to both Houses in 1610, James drew upon the language of the common law to fashion a model of 'constitutional monarchy created by kings' in which monarchs limited their own powers by creating laws and the institutions of governance. Although this interpretation proved helpful in defending royal prerogatives and initiatives, it also engendered, in reaction, conflicting interpretations of English governance as a 'constitutional monarchy governed by the common law', in which the common law stood above kings and parliaments and distributed both royal prerogatives and the liberties of the subjects, and 'mixed monarchy', in which sovereignty was shared from the very beginning by kings, nobles, and freemen. The first of these received systematic expression in a speech against impositions made by Thomas Hedley in the session of 1610, the second in John Selden, *Jani Anglorum Facies Altera* (London, 1610).[7] This chapter charts the articulation and competition amongst these three interpretations in various treatises and in speeches made in the parliaments of 1604–10, 1614, and 1621, to argue that constitutional debates which took place in England from 1610 through 1621 more often pitted rival versions of the ancient constitution against each other than theories of absolutism versus constitutionalism.

Before examining the speeches of James I and the replies of his English subjects, however, a glance at the absolutist ideas of James VI is necessary. 'Absolute monarchy' had a number of meanings in early seventeenth-century Europe and England.[8] First, as James Daly demonstrated over a decade ago, it indicated that the English monarch derived his or her power from God and held the highest position of power in the land independent of any foreign ruler. In this sense, an 'absolute monarchy' meant an independent realm with a king; it did not rule out a mixed monarchy in which the 'one' shared sovereignty with the 'few' and the 'many', to use the categories of Aristotle so popular in the Renaissance. Within the English context, only a few Catholic writers, such as Robert Parsons, disputed this view. 'Absolute monarchy' meant something else, however, in theories that derived the power of kings from God, placed all sovereignty in the hands of one ruler, forbad any attempt to resist the actions of the monarch as rebellion, and placed the prince, if not above the laws of God and nature, certainly above the law of the land. One of the most important defenders of this sort of 'absolute monarchy' was James VI of Scotland.

For the present purpose, *The Trew Law of Free Monarchies* provides the best insights into the political theory of James VI. In this treatise, James briefly set down 'the trew grounds, whereupon I am to build, out of the Scriptures, since *Monarchie* is the trew paterne of Divinitie . . . next from the fundamental Lawes of our owne Kingdome . . . thirdly, from the law of Nature, by divers similitudes drawn out of the same'.[9] The scriptures showed that: 'Kings are called Gods by the propheticall King *David*, because they sit upon GOD his Throne in the earth, and have the count of their administration to give unto him.'[10] Kings hold their power from God and account to him alone. Nature reinforces the rule of one through patriarchy: 'By the Law of Nature the King becomes a naturall Father to all his Lieges at his Coronation: And as the Father of his fatherly duty is bound to care for the nourishing, education, and vertuous government of his children; even so is the king bound to care for all his subjects.'[11] As well as fitting into the assumptions of a patriarchal society, the image of father and children resonated with language commonly used to describe the relationship of God with his people. History provided many illustrations of such theory (or 'theology', as James called it) in action.[12]

In the 'fundamental laws' of Scotland, kings held both a logical and historical priority of place. Recounting the establishment of a kingdom in Scotland by Fergus and his followers, James combined a negative blast against the writings of George Buchanan, his tutor, with a positive vision of the Kings of Scotland as lawmakers:

So the trewth is directly contrarie in our state to the false affirmation of such seditious writers, as would perswade us, that the Lawes and state of our countrey were established before the admitting of a king: where by the countrarie ye see it plainely prooved, that a wise king comming in among barbares, first established the estate and forme of governement, and thereafter made lawes by himselfe, and his successors according thereto.

The kings therefore in *Scotland* were before any estates or rankes of men within the same, before any Parliaments were holden, or lawes made: and by them was the land distributed (which at the first was whole theirs) states erected and decerned, and formes of governement devised and established: And so it followes of necessitie, that the kings were the authors and makers of the Lawes, and not the Lawes of the King.[13]

A wise king accepted by barbarians created the kingdom of the Scots; his successors distributed the land, made the laws, and established the institutions of government. The laws of God, nature and Scotland therefore combined to place sovereignty in the hands of the king. In return, subjects had the duty to obey. Although a similar theory of absolute monarchy continued to resonate through the arguments used by James I against the claims of Catholic divines, it found little or no articulation in his public speeches.

After coming to England, James accommodated his image of monarchy to fit the laws and history of his new kingdom. In the earliest of his widely available public speeches, that he delivered in the House of Lords at the opening of his first parliament on 19 March 1604, James displayed caution. Twelve years later, he would claim that: 'When I came into *England* . . . I resolved therefore with *Pythagoras* to keepe silence seven yeeres, and learne my selfe the Lawes of this Kingdome, before I would take upon mee to teach them unto others . . . '[14] True to this retrospective interpretation, in his earliest public address James thanked the assembled Lords and Commons for 'your so joyfull and generall applause to the declaring and receiving of me in this Seate (which GOD by my Birthright and lineall descent had in the fulnesse of time provided for me)' and called for a better union between England and Scotland: 'I am the Husband, and all the whole Isle is my lawfull Wife; I am the Head, and it is my Body; I am the Shepherd, and it is my flocke . . . '[15] Although the language picked up on imagery used in the king's earlier treatises, it avoided extending the principle of legitimate descent into a claim of royal sovereignty above the law. Still a new king in England, James I hesitated to pronounce on the English constitution at this date.

In a speech to parliament delivered in 1605, however, some of the king's earlier diffidence had dissipated. Indeed, he displayed at length his recently gained knowledge of English parliaments:

And as to the nature of this high Court of Parliament, It is nothing else but the Kings great Councell, which the King doeth assemble either upon occasion of interpreting, or abrogating old Lawes, or making of new, according as ill maners shall deserve, or for the publike punishment of notorious evill doers, or the praise or reward of the vertuous and well deservers . . . [16]

The king clearly displayed the supreme role of parliaments in the 'abrogating of old' and 'making of new' laws and other public matters of great consequence and provided a foretaste of the feast to come in 1610. By assuring the assembled members that 'you are heere assembled by your lawfull King to give him your best advises, in the matters proposed by him unto you', James depicted a legislative process in which the Crown held the initiative; however, he also recognized the right of members to 'propone any thing that you can after mature deliberation judge to be needefull, either for these ends already spoken of, or otherwise for the discovery of any latent evill in the Kingdome, which peradventure may not have commen to the Kings eare', that is, to declare grievances and 'propone' or put forward remedies which could take the shape of laws.[17] The performance and content represented another gracious attempt at accommodation to English custom.

In some of the early programmes of his reign, such as the union, the call for a codification and reform of the common law, and the increase of impositions, some of the king's new subjects perceived a threat to the common law of England.[18] James addressed the first of these concerns in a major speech delivered in 'Great Chamber at White-Hall' on 31 March 1607, where he clearly made England the senior partner in this enterprise: 'for Scotland I avow such an Union, as if you had got it by Conquest, but such a Conquest as may be cemented by love'; in other words, England should treat Scotland as a conquered realm; according to the most common application of the 'law of nations' to Christian realms, this meant that Scotland would keep its own particular customs.[19]

James spoke of the union of laws largely from a universalist perspective and viewed the common law as a 'municipal law', just one local variation on the universal principles best expressed in the law of nature and capable of improvement if codified, extended, and interpreted according to civil law principles.[20] Although aiming at reconciliation and praising the common law, James clearly did not have a sympathetic understanding of the unwritten nature and case law principles of English custom:

I must needs confesse by that little experience I have had since my comming hither, and I thinke I am able to proove it, that the grounds of the Common Law of England, are the best of any Law in the world, either Civil or Municipall, and the fittest for this people. But as every Law would be cleare and full, so the obscuritie in some points of this our written Law, and want of fulnesse in others, the variation of Cases and mens curiositie, breeding every day new questions, hath enforced the Judges to judge in many cases here, by Cases and presidents, wherein I hope Lawyers themselves will not denie but that there must be a great uncertaintie, and I am sure all the rest of you that are Gentlemen of other professions were long agoe wearie of it, if you could have had it amended . . .[21]

Within a decade, a host of common lawyers would come to the defence of the certainty of English judgements.[22] However, the call for a codification of the common law by parliament did have the support of such luminaries as Sir Edward Coke and need not have seemed a threat.[23] Nevertheless, confirming some of the fears of common lawyers, James spoke positively of the civil law prerogative of sovereigns to grant citizenship, for 'in such a question wherein no positive Law is resolute, *Rex est Judex* for he is *Lex loquens*, and is to supply the Law', but then hastened to decline to put this privilege into action.[24] In 1607, James had not yet learned to speak in common law discourse.

This changed dramatically, however, in a creative speech delivered to both houses on 21 March 1610. Clearly echoing one side of the medieval common law legacy, the branch that stressed the creative initiatives of kings, James fashioned a case for 'constitutional monarchy created by kings'. This speech arose within the context of attacks made in the Commons against arguments presented in *The Interpreter*, a book recently published by John Cowell, the professor of civil law at Cambridge. In one passage, Cowell had argued that the King of England was 'Above the Law by his absolute power' and in another that: 'simply to binde the prince to or by these laws [the laws of England], were repugnant to the nature and constitution of an absolute monarchy'.[25] These pushed to an extreme the not entirely dissimilar ideas expressed in the *Trew Law*. Attempting to maintain some continuity with his published writings and yet to adapt his theory to the English situation, King James opened by comparing the powers of kings with that of God:

The State of MONARCHIE is the supremest thing upon earth: for Kings are not onely GODS Lieutenants upon earth and sit upon GODS throne, but even by GOD himselfe they are called Gods.[26]

Kings derive their authority from God. This metaphor remained a powerful part of the argument throughout the speech, but now took a new twist.

A transitional sentence in which the British monarch distinguished between the unlimited powers of 'Kings in their first originall' and the limited powers of 'setled Kings and Monarches, that doe at this time governe in civill King-domes' marked the shift. Just as God had come to govern 'his people and Church within the bounds of his reveiled will':

So in the first originall of Kings, whereof some had their beginning by Conquest, and some by election of the people, their wills at that time served for Law; Yet how soone Kingdomes began to be setled in civilitie and policie, then did Kings set downe their minds by Lawes, which are properly made by the King onely; but at the rogation of the people, the Kings grant being obteined thereunto. And so the King became to be *Lex loquens*, ['a speaking law'], after a sort, binding himselfe by a double oath to the observation of the fundamentall Lawes of his kingdom: *Tacitly*, as by being a King, and so bound to protect aswell the people, as the Lawes of his Kingdome; And *Expresely*, by his oath at his Coronation: So as every just King in a setled Kingdome is bound to observe that paction made to his people by his Lawes, in framing his government agreeable thereunto, according to that paction which God made with *Noe* after the deluge, *Here after Seed-time, and Harvest, Cold and Heate, Summer and Winter, and Day and Night shall not cease, so long as the earth remaines.* And there-fore a King governing in a setled Kingdome leaves to be a King, and degenerates into a Tyrant, assone as he leaves off to rule according to his Lawes.[27]

This passage worked the themes and imagery of earlier speeches and writings into a new interpretation in which 'kings set down their minds by laws', binding upon themselves and their successors.[28] The coronation oath was a formal 'covenant' by the king to observe 'the fundamental laws of the kingdom' and held just as strongly as 'that paction which God made with *Noe* after the deluge', which would last until the end of the earth. This looks like a direct contradiction of Cowell's contentions.

The stress placed upon the covenants of God and kings, a covenant made by the ruler of the universe to restrict the exercise of his powers within the laws of grace and nature and the corresponding covenant made by kings with themselves and their successors to exercise their powers within the laws and institutions of the realm, changed the relationship of an individual king to the law in a 'civil kingdom'. Kings ruled by arbitrary will only at the start of societies; in making law and creating civil polities, they restricted their own freedom of action and that of their successors.[29] Just as God chose to channel his grace through the church, so kings chose to exercise their power through courts of law and parliaments; like God, they could not go back on their word. In one imaginative leap, James had subverted the derivation of political power from the people argued in the standard constitutionalist position, appropriated the strengths of constitutional government (stability and the consent of the community of the realm), and maintained a creative initiative for monarchs.

Although pointedly declaring his faith in the common law, the king also expressed a desire to preserve the study of the civil law at English universities, both as a civilizing influence and as a means of discourse with foreign nations.[30] Here he mirrored the receptionist view of the common lawyers: the common law had 'received' useful portions of the civil or canon laws and allowed these to operate within the limits established by custom or statute. To distance himself from Cowell and assuage any fears that he meant to favour the civil law, James stressed:

My meaning therefore is not to preferre the Civill Law before the Common Law; but onely that it should not be extinguished, and yet so bounded, (I meane to such Courts and Causes) as have beene in ancient use; As the Ecclesiasticall Courts, Court of Admiraltie, Court of Requests, and such like, reserving ever to the Common Law to meddle with the fundamentall Lawes of this Kingdome, either concerning the Kings Prerogative, or the possessions of Subjects, in any questions, either betweene the King, and any of them, or amongst themselves, in the points of *Meum & tuum*.[31]

This passage, with its emphasis upon the firm support for monarchy provided by the common law, proclaimed that James had abandoned both the natural law absolutism and much of the universalist mentality displayed in his earlier works, a point also stressed in his recognition that: 'the King with his Parliament here [that is, in England] are absolute, (as I understand) in making or forming any sort of Lawes.'[32] However, sensitive common lawyers may have perceived a threat in the king's reiterated plea that aspects of the common law 'be purged & cleared' by 'the advise of Parliament'.[33] James asked for three major reforms: first, the writing of the law in English, second, the production of 'a setled Text in all Cases', and third, the review and reconciliation of statutes, reports, and precedents.[34] Although such a codification would have diminished the powers of judges and juries to create customs, it also would have enhanced the recognition that the monarch, peers and representatives of the commons made law. Although James voiced a constitutional position, his stress upon the royal creation of and initiative in parliaments left plenty of room for debate over the nature of the ancient constitution of England.

In addition, more than hints of civil law discourse continued to trouble relations between King James and members of his first parliament. Despite royal warnings, members of the House of Commons continued to attack the judgement of the Exchequer in Bate's case upholding the legality of impositions. Informed of this, the king returned from Thetford and on 21 May lectured members of the lower House that he had not meant 'to forbid you to complain if there were inconvenience or heaviness, inequality, disproportion or disorder in matter of trade', but 'you should not go to the root and dispute my prerogative and call in question that power which I have in possession, confirmed by law, derived from my progenitors and which my judges have denounced [i.e. pronounced] . . .'[35] Although defending his right to impositions from English precedents, James could not resist a comparative perspective and asserted that 'all kings Christian as well elective as successive have power to lay impositions.'[36] In addition, he warned against the dangers of limiting the discretionary powers of the Crown: 'You must not set such laws as make the shadows of kings and dukes of Venice; no Christians but papists and puritans were ever of that opinion.'[37] Having defended royal rights against attacks made in the Commons, James ended this portion of the speech by offering a token of peace, the promise that he would not increase impositions during his lifetime without first consulting parliament.[38] However, this pledge came too late to dampen the fears of members of the lower House.

The interpretations voiced by King James soon engendered replies from those learned in the common laws of England. On 22 May several members of the House of Commons, including Nicholas Fuller, Sir Edwin Sandys, Thomas Wentworth and James Whitelocke, raised the spectre of the ancient constitution in danger; in the insular voice of his colleagues, Fuller noted that although 'the King were in truth very wise yet is he a stranger to this government' and offered to remedy this situation: 'The King speaks of France and Spain what they may do, I pray let us be true to the King and true to ourselves and let him know what by the laws of England he may do.'[39] The dispute over the right of the Commons to debate the legitimacy of impositions ended with a tactical withdrawal by the king in a conference with members of the House held on 24 May.[40] Concerns over the constitution reached a climax in the powerful debate over impositions held in committees of the whole House which lasted from 23 June to 2 July and featured long, learned speeches by such worthies as Sir Francis Bacon, Sir John Doderidge, Heneage Finch, Nicholas Fuller, William Hakewill, Sir Henry Hobart, Thomas Hedley, Sir Roger Owen and James Whitelocke.[41] Supporting their cases with full lists of precedents, most of these speakers attacked the prerogative right to levy impositions, but Attorney General Hobart, Solicitor General Bacon, and Sergeant Doderidge skilfully attacked the precedents cited by the opponents of imposing and defended the prerogative of the Crown as upheld in Bate's case.[42] Moving out from specifics to the crux of the matter, Hedley fashioned a compelling interpretation of the common law and its relation to the royal prerogative, the powers of parliament, and the liberties of English subjects.[43]

Drawing its wisdom 'strength, honor, and estimation' from the test of time, according to Hedley, the common law embraced both reason and immemorial custom: 'the common law is a reasonable usage, throughout the whole realm, approved time out of mind in the king's courts of record which have jurisdiction over the whole kingdom, to be good and profitable for the commonwealth'.[44] A subtle interplay of maxims and immemorial custom built continuity and flexibility into the laws. The rationality of maxims assured that 'no unreasonable usage will ever make a custom (pleadable in law)', while the ability to overrule judgements assured that the mere 'reason or opinion of 3 or 4 judges' could not make law.[45] The continual questioning of judgements did not mean, as King James had claimed, that case law lacked certainty; an examination of 'all the suits in law' would reveal that for every case 'delayed for doubtfulness of the law, there have been 1000, nay 10,000, proceeded and ended without any question or doubt at all in law'.[46]

Instead, Hedley argued, the unwritten nature of the common law produced greater certainty than either statutes or civil law which needed continual interpretation.[47] 'Confirmed by time', immemorial custom far better upheld the liberties of freemen and 'establisheth kings and their regal power' than could any law created by 'the wisest lawgivers or parliament or council', for such law was not 'reversible by that power that made it'.[48] The common law stood above and distributed power to both kings and parliaments. This meant that any attempt to replace the refined wisdom of generations with the fallible judgements of one parliament, as in the 'reforms' advocated by King James, threatened the very nature of the common law.

While bolstering specific arguments against impositions, Hedley fashioned a subtle, complex interpretation of 'constitutional monarchy governed by common law'. Although Hedley did not directly attack, he certainly subverted the interpretation of 'constitutional monarchy created by kings' advocated by

King James some two months earlier. By removing the sole capacity to make law from the hands of a single or collective sovereign, his stress upon the superior wisdom of time also subverted the arguments of natural law absolutists and mixed monarchists, who argued respectively that kings and kings in parliaments created laws. This coherent speech provided one of the earliest and most complete articulations of what J. G. A. Pocock identified as the 'ancient constitution' of the 'common law mind'.[49] Recently, Christopher Brooks has argued that this mentality did not exist in the sixteenth century and 'was not the product of a deep rooted mentality', but 'a response to a particular set of political, religious, and legal conditions', including the arguments on monarchy presented by James VI and I.[50] My own analysis of the prefaces of the *Reports* of Sir Edward Coke and Sir John Davies would suggest that neither provided as early, complete or sophisticated a version of Pocock's 'ancient constitution'.[51] This would suggest a major role for Thomas Hedley in creating what became the defence of the liberties and privileges of free Englishmen as part of an immemorial 'constitutional monarchy governed by common law'.

The scope and clarity of Hedley's representation of the English constitution contrasted with the much more episodic and concrete general sections of the speeches against impositions made by other prominent common lawyers. For example, in a lengthy, powerful speech, William Hakewill addressed the problem of the origins of custom duties, arguing that just because scholars 'cannot tell how or when they began', one could not justly 'conclude that they began by the kings absolute power', as had James and some of the spokesmen in the Commons for the royal prerogative of imposing.[52] Instead, Hakewill argued, such common law practices as trial by jury, twenty-one as the age of majority for males, and 'a yeere and a day given to sue an appeale' began either 'by a tacit consent of the king and people, and the long approbation of time beyond the memory of man' or 'that most of them might begin by act of parliament'.[53] This attempt to occupy the territory between the positions of original contract, immemorial custom and mixed monarchy hedged a good number of theoretical and historical bets. Frankly admitting that any attempt to chart such customs back to acts of parliament ran into the problem of a lack of archival evidence (at least before the first parliament 'in our bookes', that of 9 Henry III, held in 1225), Hakewill bravely noted that chroniclers wrote about parliaments in the reigns of John, Richard I, Henry II and Henry I, and that evidence for parliaments existed in the laws of William the Conqueror and of King Ine.[54] Although not entirely consistent, Hakewill's argument creatively attempted to bind together the powers of parliament with the immemorial laws of the land.

In another lengthy speech against impositions, James Whitelocke also combined the ancient customs of the common law with the various powers of parliament. Noting that the 'king out of parliament' exercised many prerogatives, Whitelocke argued that even greater powers accrued to the 'king in parliament', including the 'power to make laws', the 'power to judge without appeal', and 'this right of imposing'.[55] This cleverly turned a fairly standard distinction between the prerogative powers of the Crown and those powers exercised in parliaments against the legitimacy of imposing. By tracing the powers of the king in parliament back to the beginnings of civil government in England, however, Whitelocke extended putative customary usage into an ancient constitutional distribution of powers and privileges which originated with the establishing of the kingdom of England:

Can any man give me a reason, why the king can only in parliament make lawes? No man ever read any law whereby it was so ordained; and no man ever read that any king practised the contrary. Therefore it is the originall right of the kingdome, and the very natural constitution of our state and policy, being one of the highest rights of soveraigne power.[56]

A similar ancient right applied to the liberties of the people, including their consent to all taxation:

That the king of England cannot take his subjects goods without their consent, it need not be proved more than a principle. It is *jus indigenae*, an old homebred right, declared to be law by divers statutes of the realm.[57]

Here, old native law, declared but not created by statutes, upheld the rights of English subjects. Taken as a whole, Whitelocke's arguments seemed to avoid an immemorial common law and stressed instead a 'natural' constitution which established a mixed polity at the origin of the kingdom; although this polity used the common law to uphold the prerogatives of the Crown and the rights of subjects, it placed the sovereign law making power in the hands of the king-in-parliament. Combining brief, striking, references to mixed monarchy and an original constitution with concrete English evidence, Whitelocke provided a fascinating glimpse (less complete and coherent than Hedley's more lengthy argument) of an interpretation of England as a mixed monarchy.

Echoes of Hedley's interpretation and Whitelocke's imagery soon resounded in two general sections of the petition on temporal grievances presented to King James at an audience in Whitehall by the House of Commons on 7 July 1610. In voicing principles which would delegitimize what they saw as a recent overextension of proclamations, the Commons noted that English subjects accounted it 'dear and precious' to be 'guided and governed by the certain rule of law, which giveth both to the head [the king] and members [subjects] that which of right belongeth to them'.[58] This interpretation of the 'certain rule of law' praised the ancient governance of England by the common law:

Which, as it hath proceeded from the original good constitution and temperature of this estate, so hath it been the principal means of upholding the same in such sort, as that their kings have been just, beloved, happy, and glorious, and the kingdom itself peaceable, flourishing, and durable so many ages.[59]

Here 'estate' meant state or polity; 'original good constitution and temperature' a well-balanced sharing of powers and responsibilities worked out at the origin of civil rule in England. The 'original good constitution' of the state helped to create good kings and a stable, prosperous realm. It also provided the people with the privilege of assessing those taxes collected by their monarchs and 'that indubitable right of the people of this kingdom not to be made subject to any punishments that shall be extended to their lives, lands, bodies or goods, other than such as are ordained by the common laws of this land, or statutes made by their common consent in parliament'.[60] This significant section of the petition drew upon a mixture of ideas from Hedley and Whitelocke to argue a strong case for a rule of the common law in which particular liberties of subjects stood established from the very beginning.

Another general paragraph divulged the sources of this coherent interpretation of the 'rule of law' by openly merging Whitelocke's 'very natural constitution of our state and policy' into Hedley's interpretation of 'constitutional monarchy governed by the common law':

The policy [i.e. polity] and constitution of this your Majesty's kingdom appropriates unto the kings of this realm, with the assent of the parliament, as well the sovereign power of making laws, as that of taxing or imposing upon the subjects' goods or merchandises, wherein they justly have such a propriety, as may not without their consent be altered or charged. This is the cause that the people of this kingdom, as they ever shewed themselves faithful and loving to their kings, and ready to aid them in all their just occasions with voluntary contributions, so have they been ever careful to preserve their own liberties and rights when anything hath been done to prejudice or impeach the same . . . And though the law of propriety be original and carefully preserved by the common laws of this realm, which are as ancient as the kingdom itself, yet those famous kings, for the better contentment and assurance of their loving subjects, agreed that this old fundamental right should be further declared and established by act of parliament, wherein it is provided that no such charges should ever be laid upon the people, without their common consent, as may appear by sundry records of former times.[61]

Of course, the attempt to conflate 'taxing' and 'imposing' clearly begged the question under dispute. More important, however, this passage argued that the 'constitution' of England distributed particular powers to kings and subjects through the 'common laws of this realm' which were 'as ancient as the kingdom itself'.[62] The general sections of the petition of 7 July 1610 not only worked numerous specific grievances gathered by members of the House of Commons into a powerful, compact vision of the ancient constitution, they demonstrated that Hedley's interpretation could create harmony out of a variety of constitutional voices.

Within a few months, another major interpretation of the ancient constitution appeared in the *Jani Anglorum Facies Altera* of John Selden.[63] Drawing upon themes found in the speeches of Hakewill and Whitelocke, Selden fashioned a more systematic, better documented interpretation of the ancient constitution as a mixed monarchy in which kings, clergy, nobles and freemen had shared sovereignty from the very beginning.[64] Monarchy and Germanic customs arrived in England with the Saxon invasion and provided a lasting framework for the ancient constitution. Saxon kings proclaimed law with the advice of the leading men of the realm.[65] Consultation took place within an institutional system which derived from the Germanic *wapentakes* described by Tacitus; these became 'the Wiðδena gemoðes, *i.e.* Meetings of the Wise Men, and Micil sinoðes, *i.e.* the Great Assemblies' of the Anglo-Saxons and, in turn, were called parliaments under the Normans.[66]

During the centuries following the Norman Conquest, feudal laws blended with Saxon customs to produce a potent, vital constitution presided over by the three estates of king, magnates and representatives of the commons, all gathered together in parliaments, the symbol and reality of England's mixed monarchy. With appropriate glances both backward and forward at significant spots along the way, Selden detailed the development of this pattern up to the death of Henry II, always preserving a place for parliaments as the place where new laws were made and old laws changed or repealed.[67] The publication of Selden's Latin treatise added a third major interpretation of the ancient constitution, that of mixed monarchy centred on both common law and the shared sovereignty exercised in parliaments. 'Mixed monarchy', 'constitutional monarchy governed by the common law', and 'constitutional monarchy created by kings' appear to represent the most important voices which vied for supremacy in the constitutional debates of early seventeenth-century England.

Although the parliament of 1614 discussed many of the same issues as the session of 1610, it did not produce any significant, new constitutional discourse. Stressing his desire to make this a 'parliament of love', offering to hear grievances, presenting eleven bills of grace, and repeatedly asking for supplies, James made a number of speeches to members of the Lords and Commons.[68] Despite the king's conciliatory gestures, members of the lower House reopened the question of impositions.[69] The refusal of the Lords to hear the arguments of the Commons, however, stopped any further proceedings on this matter.[70] A number of additional disputes took place in this parliament, such as the attacks in the Commons against the new order of baronets (including an incredible claim that the Crown could not erect new titles of honour), attempts by the Commons to punish Richard Neile, Bishop of Lincoln, for two speeches made in the Lords, and a threat by the Commons to work on no other business until Neile was punished.[71] James patiently bore the attacks upon the baronetcy without dispute. Advised by Lord Chancellor Ellesmere to defend their privileges, the Lords stoutly refused to countenance complaints against Bishop Neile.[72] The threat to desist from all other business, however, goaded the king into action. Informed by the speaker, James warned the Commons against encroaching upon the royal prerogative of calling, dissolving, proroguing and adjourning parliament and suggested to the 'good antiquaries' and 'nimble lawyers' engaged in 'searching out precedents' to strengthen the privileges of the lower House that 'if he would hunt what other kings have done, he might find some-what for himself'.[73] Clearly, the king felt much more at home in discussing the antiquities of England now than he had earlier in his reign. Ironically, this speech seemed to anticipate some of the issues which would arise in the parliament of 1621.

During the years immediately preceding and succeeding the parliament of 1614, all three of the major interpretations of the ancient constitution received firm support. In the prefaces to the eighth, ninth and tenth *Reports* of 1611, 1613, and 1614, Sir Edward Coke developed portions of Hedley's 'constitutional monarchy governed by the common law', especially by linking the laws of the Saxons through the confirmations of William I, Henry I, Stephen, and Henry II, the Great Charters of John and Henry III, and through the treatises of such great common lawyers as Glanville, Bracton, Fleta and Fortescue, to his own day. In his *Primer Report* of 1615, Davies developed other aspects of Hedley's interpretation, especially the importance of time as a test of law and the superiority of the immemorial, unwritten custom over all institutions of government.[74] Together these treatises by Coke and Davies provided most of the evidence for that classic interpretation of the ancient constitution created by Pocock.[75]

Within this decade, Selden's interpretation of mixed monarchy also received further development and support, in three major works. *Titles of Honor* (London, 1614) integrated the insights and method of humanist legal history of the Continent into the discussion of the English constitution. The notes to Selden's critical edition of Sir John Fortescue, *De Laudibus Legum Angliae* (London, 1616) reduced all western European law to an original 'state' (or constitution) and custom. His image of the English 'state' as a 'ship, that by often mending had no piece of the first materialls' and yet still remains 'the same' and his demonstration that the common law itself was a mixture of such customs as the laws of Wessex, Mercia and the Danelaw, exemplified this new position. *The Historie of Tithes* (London, 1618) provided considerable historical evidence that, when it came to real and personal property, the customary and statutory laws of western Europe had always stood supreme over the canon and Roman laws.[76] By employing the historical methods of continental legal humanists to interpret the law and constitution of England as one variation on a wider European pattern, Selden used the most up-to-date scholarly tools to defend an ancient constitution in which the king, nobles and freemen had shared sovereignty from the origins of civil government.

The interpretations supported by Coke, Davies and Selden would not stand uncontested, however. On 20 June 1616, in a speech delivered to the assembled justices of the central common law courts in the Star Chamber, King James extended the theory of 'constitutional monarchy created by kings' to cover all English magistrates. Deriving the powers of kings from God, of all judges from the king, James I echoed some of the discourse of James VI:

From this imitation of GOD and CHRIST, in whose Throne wee sit, the government of all Common-wealths, and especially Monarchies, hath bene from the beginning setled and established. Kings are properly Judges, and Judgement properly belongs to them from GOD: for Kings sit in the Throne of GOD, and thence all Judgement is derived.[77]

However, this derivation of the logical and chronological priority of kings from the authority of God served to support an argument for 'constitutional monarchy created by kings', not absolute monarchy. James used it primarily to provide a foundation for the exercise of justice in 'all well setled Monarchies, where Law is established'; in such jurisdictions, 'Judgement is deferred from the King to his subordinate Magistrates'.[78] Delegating some of their authority, European monarchs appointed judges to interpret the law and administer justice.

This Deputation is after one manner in *France*, after another here, and even my owne Kingdomes differ in this point of government: for *Scotland* differs both from *France* and *England* herein; but all agree in this, (I speake of such Kingdomes or States where the formalitie of Law hath place) that the King that sits in Gods Throne, onely deputes subalterne Judges, and he deputes not one but a number (for no one subalterne Judges mouth makes Law) and their office is to interprete Law, and administer Justice. But as to the number of them, the forme of governement, the maner of interpretation, the distinction of Benches, the diversitie of Courts; these varie according to the varietie of government, and institution of divers Kings . . .[79]

Both institutions and constitutions varied from one European monarchy to another, but all judges derived their authority from and spoke with the tongue of the king. The kings of England had erected all manner of central and local courts and continued to appoint the justices who enforced the common law in common law courts, the canon law in church courts, and the civil law in such courts as the Admiralty.

Clearly aware of concerns over his universalist mentality, James 'resolved, as Confirmation in Majoritie followeth Baptisme in minoritie; so now after many yeeres, to renew my promise and Oath made at my Coronation concerning Justice', to uphold 'the Common Law of the Land, according to the which the King governes, and by which the people are governed'.[80] The justices received an admonition to administer justice boldly, uprightly and indifferently. This meant incroaching 'not upon the Prerogative of the Crowne', but upholding 'the Common Law kept within her owne limits, and not derogating from these other Lawes, which by longer custome have beene rooted here; first, the Law of GOD and his Church; and next, the Law Civill and Canon, which in many cases cannot be wanting'.[81] Here, James indirectly criticized some of the recent actions of Sir Edward Coke, Chief Justice of the King's Bench.[82] Reminding the judges that they were 'no makers of Law, but Interpretours of Law, according to the true sense thereof', James chided Coke and his colleagues to:

observe the ancient Lawes and customes of *England* . . . within the bound of direct Law, or Presidents; and of those, not every snached President, carped now here, now there, as it were running by the way; but such as have never beene controverted, but by the contrary, approved by common usage, in times of best Kings, and by most learned Judges.[83]

While his audience might disagree over who were the 'best Kings' and the 'most learned Judges', James appealed to English legal historical experience, not to an abstract theory of divine right. On the basis of 'ancient custome', the itinerant justices were admonished to act as 'the Kings eyes and eares in the countrey' by reporting to the Chancellor on the justices of the peace when they came back from circuit.[84] In return for this supervision of magistrates and strict enforcement of the law, the king demanded that all subjects 'give due reverence to the Law'.[85] Throughout this speech, James continued to develop and apply his interpretation of the English constitution with appeals to historical precedent.

Although King James and a number of common lawyers had voiced at least three discrete interpretations of the ancient constitution during the second decade of the seventeenth century, neither confrontation nor closure had yet arrived. In practice, Selden's interpretations of 'mixed monarchy' continued to interact and overlap in rather untidy ways with Hedley's 'constitutional monarchy governed by the common law'. Neither directly confronted the royal interpretation of 'constitutional monarchy created by kings'. Since Coke and Davies were leading legal servants of the Crown at the time that they published their treatises and since prudent people with political ambitions of any sort could not directly challenge the known ideas of the monarch, such reticence hardly seemed surprising. Although Lords Chancellor Ellesmere and Bacon had worked out interpretations very similar to that of the king, neither they nor James had openly or directly challenged the interpretations voiced by Hedley, Davies, Coke, and Selden.[86] By the end of the decade, however, such spokesmen as James, Coke, and Selden had gained considerable experience in drawing upon evidence from the history of England to define and refine their positions. This, along with more immediate concerns, may have helped to account for the alacrity of constitutional debate in the next parliament.

On 30 January, James opened the first session of the parliament with a brief lesson on the nature and origins of parliaments in Europe:

A parliament in general is a thing compounded of a head and a body; the head is the monarch that calleth it, the body is the three [e]states called together by that head. Now in all monarchies, parliaments have been used and were not instituted before them (as many foolishly have imagined) but long after that monarchies were established, were they created. For kings and kingdoms were before parliaments, and are relatives; but when people began to be willing to be guided by laws, then came the first institution of parliaments.[87]

This passage directly confronted interpretations which placed the law or parliaments above or even coterminal with the rule of monarchs; as James had stated in 1610, kings preceded and created both laws and parliaments. By characterizing the interpretations so recently defended by Coke, Davies and Selden as foolish imaginations, the king issued a challenge to the common lawyers.[88] Arguing that 'none but monarchies have parliaments', James also claimed that such republics as 'the Switzers and the Low Countries and Venice are aristocratical governments' and 'have no parliaments', a technically correct point which created a somewhat misleading impression by refusing to equate provincial and municipal with national assemblies.[89]

Moving from the wider to the English context, the king spoke to his 'three estates' in turn, addressing the peers to whom 'it belongs to acquaint, advise, and counsel the king in weighty affairs of the kingdom', the bishops 'because they have the charge perpetual and cure of the church, and are lords, barons of lands and inheritances', and members of the 'House of Commons, consisting of knights of the shires and burgesses'.[90] Stressing that the writ summoned members 'to advise and deliberate with the king upon high and urgent affairs of the kingdom', he noted that 'the king is ever representatively sitting in the Higher House of parliament'.[91] The Commons had the special responsibilities of petitioning the king for the redress of grievances and affording 'supply and sustenance to his necessities, what they think the country may afford and think fit'.[92] No longer shy in talking about the English constitution, James spent the largest portion of his speech on the normal business of parliaments, the need for good laws, the strengthening of religion, and provision of supply. Near the end, he specifically warned the members of 'the Lower House, I would not have you meddle with complaints against the King, the church or state matters, nor with prince's prerogatives. The parliament was never called for that purpose.'[93] Emphasizing a cooperative spirit, James ended with a plea for harmony between the head and body: 'That the world may see how happy a sympathy there is between the king and his subjects, to his own felicity within, his fame abroad, the reverence among his people, and honor from his subjects.'[94] Clearly, however, this concord would have to proceed on the king's terms.

Early in the session, the House of Commons started to work on both the supply of the king and the presentation of grievances, which led to the passage of an early double subsidy and to attacks upon the abuses of royal patent holders. After moves in several directions, the Commons turned to investigation of the activities of Sir Giles Mompesson who held patents on the licensing of inns, gold and silver thread, and concealed Crown lands. Not yet aware of an acceptable way to bring charges against such an official, members of the House also began to investigate precedents on the judicature of parliaments, with William Noy and William Hakewill carrying out the research and Sir Edward Coke moving from the committee that 'we are resolved according to former precedents to address ourselves to the Lords, for so it was in Henry the Sixth's time'.[95] The House arranged to present its evidence of wrongdoing and its suggestions for action to the Lords at a joint conference held on the afternoon of 8 March.

Before his report on 27 February, Coke had argued in the committee that parliament was a 'Court of Counsell and a Court of Pleas', that is, a place for advice and for deciding cases; accepting historical accounts that parliaments had first consisted of one house, he noted that when 'the Howses were divided, the indevisible things remayned with the Lords.' This meant that 'Pleas continued in the Upper-Howse long after the Stattute' which Coke presumed had created the separate Houses. Although the Commons had from 'ancient' times examined 'greevances' and tried 'the matter of fact' in such matters, 'they have often resorted to the Lords for Judicature', following a variety of proceedings. He ended by noting that: 'There hath beene noe judgement in this kind since 2 Henry 6.'[96]

In his speech to the Lords on 8 March, Coke pushed for punishment of offending officials and argued that 'there is a power of judicature or judicial proceedings' in parliament of four sorts, before: (1) the king and Lords, (2) the Lords alone, (3) the Lords and Commons and (4) the Commons alone. For the first, he cited precedents from the reigns of Edward I, Richard II and Henry VI; for the second, precedents from the reigns of Edward III and Richard II; for the third an example from the reign of Richard II; and for the fourth Arthur Hall's case from the reign of Elizabeth and a case of a fine from the reign of Henry VIII. Then, drawing upon the *Mirror of Justices* to show that King 'Alfred, *anno* 873, made an act to have 2 parliaments in one year', an ordinance from the reign of Edward I 'to have one parliament in two years' and an act from the reign of Edward III for annual parliaments, Coke advocated frequent parliaments for removing 'abuses and corruptions' in the 'commonwealth'.[97] Both of these speeches displayed the power of antiquarian research in early seventeenth-century political discourse; the second, especially in the reference to Alfred, displayed that mentality of the ancient constitution seen in the prefaces of some of the *Reports*. By stretching his earlier argument in his speech to the Lords, however, the great justice probably overplayed the hand of the Commons.

Two days later, King James appeared in the House of Lords with the excuse that since Sir Edward Coke had said 'that I alwayes sitt in this place amongst you by representacion, and theirfore I conceive I may much more come personally when I will', and asked Lord Chancellor Bacon 'make report unto me what passed at the conference'.[98] After listening to Bacon's account, the king explained his own distaste with 'projects and projectors', his desire to have 'a lawe made against theis thinges', his own warnings to Mompesson, and his willingness to allow the Chancellor and Treasurer 'to answere for themselves'.[99] Congratulating the Commons on their discretion, he gave the Lords his permission to proceed to investigation and judgement against his servants:

Now my Lords, I have somewhat to say to you: you neede not search presidents whether you may deale in this business without the lower howse for there is no question yours is a house and a court of Record. You neede not stick uppon it, for the lower house, they are but a howse of customes and orders and their house hath come from yours, for though heretofore a long tyme since you were but all one house, yett uppon the division all the power of judicature went with your howse.[100]

James defended the difference between the Lords and Commons in judicature on the same historical grounds used by Coke in a committee of the Commons a fortnight earlier.[101]

Oblique references to the arguments of Coke, however, did not mean that the king accepted all of the assertions made by the common lawyers in the Commons. Warning that 'though Sir Edward Coke be very busie and be called the father of the Law and the Commons' howse have divers yonge lawyers in it, yet all is not law that they say', James admonished the Lords to follow the advice of the judges on points of law, to accept only 'presidents of good kings' tymes such as my Grandfather King Henry the 7th, or King Henry the 8th . . . [or] the late Queene Elizabeth . . . and not ether of Henry the 6th, a poore weake Prince governed by his counsell or of Richard the 2, who was murthered'.[102] The last point received a careful repetition at several points, once with the additional caution that: 'I thinke him an enemie to monarchy and a trayter to me that menciones my actions with such kings as I have tould you.'[103] Throughout the speech, James sought to subvert the 'false' and uphold the 'true' interpretations presented by the former chief justice. This distanced Coke from his position as a privy councillor and subordinated Coke's view of the law to the interpretation of the king, judges and peers. With its challenging discourse on the ancient constitution carefully tempered by its zeal for reform, the king's speech exuded a judiciously confident air of conciliation.

The presumption that King James or Sir Edward Coke had to convince the peers of 1621 to take up and defend the privileges which they could claim by historical precedents does scant justice to the evidence. Even before the question of judicature had arisen, the Lords had appointed a committee, then a subcommittee, and then hired a number of expert antiquaries, including John Selden, to produce a formal statement of its procedures and privileges.[104] The first concrete result of this new association appeared in the draft roll of standing orders for the House reported in March 1621 by Sir Henry Elsyng and Selden. These orders described the sitting, procedure, committees and other customs of the House.[105] They allowed Archbishop of Canterbury George Abbot to defend the jurisdiction of the Lords to punish Sir Henry Yelverton, the former Attorney General, for a speech he made in the Lords which James had argued touched the honour of the king, on the grounds that to remove him would break 'the liberty and priviledges of their house' and 'make them imagine your Majestie mistrusteth them to doe you justice', something which brought forth the reply from James that: 'My Lords, I like not as the Lower House you to stand upon reason and precedents.'[106] Before the end of this parliament, the upper House would stand well above the lower in both the clarity of its procedures and the defence of its privileges.

The second product of the antiquaries hired by the Lords, a report on privileges which included a long section on parliamentary judicature, bore the marks of Selden's learning. Probably finished in early June and among those papers seized at the time of Selden's arrest during the recess, it resided in the hands of the Lord Keeper until released after considerable prodding by the Lords after the second session opened on 20 November 1621; on 30 November, Selden officially presented this report in the form of a book written in a fair hand.[107] The privileges mentioned included both 'those speciall rights which concern them as they are one estate in the upper house of Parliament' and those 'special rights that concerne the Barons' individually.[108] The first embraced such perquisites as proxies, freedom from law suits during the sitting of parliament and the power of judicature, while the second extended to trial by peers, keeping a set number of chaplains, freedom from such civil actions as imprisonment for debt, account, or trespass and giving evidence by a protestation upon honour instead of upon oath. For each privilege, Selden furnished some, often ample, documentation from appropriate primary sources.

The most sweeping and well-covered privilege was the revival of original and appellate judicature by the Lords. This long section consisted almost wholly of long quotations of relevant precedents from the Rolls of Parliament. The only commentary came in two introductory paragraphs which stood at the opening of the chapter and proclaimed its purpose:

The power of the Judicature belonging to the Lords of Parliament is chiefly seene in their Jurisdiction uppon Writts of Error and their Judgements of offences as well Capitall as not Capitall which tend to any publique mischiefe in the State.

Of their Judgements of such offences manie examples are of former tymes in the Records of Parliament and out of them are here selected some such as most of all conduce to the opening of the course of accusation, the forme of the Defendants answering, the usuall wayes of triall and other incidents in their various kinds of Judgements which are to be found arbitrarie in cases not capitall soe that they extend not to the life or Inheritance, and in capitall offences soe arbitrary that the forme of the death inflicted sometimes varyes from the ordinary course used in the common Law for suche offences.[109]

From such an understated argument sprang the most significant increase in power gained by one of the constituent parts of parliament in the period before 1640, the revival of the judicature of the Lords. This included three main areas: the reversal of cases from the King's Bench on a writ of error, original civil justice upon petition, and, of course, impeachment.[110] Although faced by competing claims during the early stages of this struggle, the upper House rested its privileges firmly upon the unchallenged scholarly research of Selden and Elsyng.

In comparison, the attempts made by the Commons to uphold the privileges of their House looked reactive and less than systematic. Although some frictions had arisen during the first session, a serious dispute over this issue arose on 3 December, with the preparation of a petition in the Commons on religion, foreign affairs and the marriage of Prince Charles. Warned by Sir Edward Sackville and Sir Richard Weston, Chancellor of the Exchequer, not to include the prince's marriage and the declaration of war against Spain in the petition, the majority of the House persisted.[111] Enraged at 'some fiery and popular spirits of some of the House of Commons' for presuming 'to argue and debate publicly of the matters far above their reach and capacity, tending to our high dishonour and breach of prerogative royal', James sent a pre-emptive reply which forbad members from meddling 'with anything concerning our government or deep matters of State', specifically mentioning that they were not to deal with the marriage of the prince to the 'daughter of Spain', 'the honour of that King or any other our friends and confederates', and any particular matter pending before 'our ordinary courts of justice'.[112] Not much conciliation here.

The letter caused enough shock to merit three readings and a decision to postpone work on all other business while preparing an answer.[113] The petition and a declaration explaining the actions of the Commons passed on 7 December and was presented to the king at Newmarket on 11 December; conciliatory in tone, the declaration explained that the Commons 'did not assume to ourselves any power to determine any part thereof, nor intend to encroach or intrude upon the sacred bounds of your royal authority, to whom and to whom only we acknowledge it doth belong to resolve of peace and war and of the marriage of the most noble Prince your son', but only to express their cares and concerns.[114] When it came to their liberties, the Commons took a stand which both sounded firm and invited compromise from the king:

And whereas your Majesty doth seem to abridge us of the ancient liberty of Parliament for freedom of speech, jurisdiction, and just centure of the House, and other proceedings there (wherein we trust in God we shall never transgress the bounds of loyal and dutiful subjects), a liberty which we assure ourselves so wise and so just a king will not infringe, the same being our ancient and undoubted right, and an inheritance received from our ancestors; without which we cannot freely debate nor clearly discern of things in question before us, nor truly inform your Majesty; in which we have been confirmed by your Majesty's most gracious former speeches and messages.[115]

The language was carefully chosen; the 'liberty of Parliament' was an 'ancient and undoubted right, and an inheritance from our ancestors'. This resembled such earlier declarations made by the Commons as the draft 'Apology' of 1604 and the petition of temporal grievances of 1610.

Having taken a strong stand on several occasions in this parliament, James VI and I displayed no willingness to back down. He sent back a lengthy, direct reply which claimed that: 'In the body of your petition you usurp upon our prerogative royal, and meddle with things far above your reach, and then in the conclusion you protest the contrary; as if a robber would take a man's purse and then protest he meant not to rob him.'[116] Unconciliatory from the start, James voiced strong displeasure with the discourse used by the Commons to defend their liberties:

And although we cannot allow of the style, calling it 'your ancient and undoubted right and inheritance', but could rather have wished that ye had said that your privileges were derived from the grace and permission of our ancestors and us (for most of them grow from precedents, which shews rather a toleration than inheritance), yet we are pleased to give you our royal assurance that as long as you continue yourselves within the limits of your duty, we will be as careful to maintain and preserve your lawful liberties and privileges as ever any of our predecessors were, nay, as to preserve our own royal prerogative.[117]

Although purporting to assure the Commons that the king would maintain their 'lawful liberties and privileges', this passage reiterated the interpretation that the laws, institutions of government, and privileges of parliament derived from the 'grace and permission' of monarchs, not from immemorial custom nor an original 'state' or constitution of the realm. In a letter delivered to the Commons, James repeated much of the passage quoted above and added that:

whatsoever liberties or privileges they enjoy by any law or statute shall be ever inviolably preserved by us, and we hope our posterity will imitate our foosteps therein.

And whatsoever privileges they enjoy by long custom and uncontrolled and lawful precedents we will likewise be as careful to preserve them and transmit the care thereof to our posterity.[118]

The 'grace and permission of our ancestors' fit into 'constitutional monarchy created by kings', but the expression of a 'hope' that his successors would preserve the liberties of the Commons hedged upon the binding power of the covenant announced by James in his speech of 21 March 1610. This more than implied that such royal grace could be continued or withdrawn at the will of the monarch. Without much difficulty, a seventeenth-century observer could have interpreted this as an absolutist argument. Perhaps it provides a key to the discourse which developed in the reign of Charles I.

Reactions to this royal missile took place immediately, with Coke attempting to prove from a case dating to the reign of Henry VI that the Commons held their privileges 'by law, by Act of Parliament'.[119] Sir Randolph Crew drew an analogy from the common law to argue that: 'We have our privileges of right not of grace. This were to make us from freeholders of inheritance to make us Coppiholders *ad placitum*, or rather, tenants att will.'[120] The scholarly lawyer, William Hakewill, adding that the request by the Speaker's petition for the privileges of the House at the beginning of the session was an innovation of 'Queen Elizabeth's time', further developed the link with the common law: 'Priviledges of this house are part, nay a principall part, of the lawe of the kingdome. The freedome of our persons in lawe is called the Custome of England. This is a lawe of lawes; and these that wee insist upon are inseparable incidents of a Parliament.'[121] Numerous members called for the formation of a committee to draft a defence of these privileges as a matter of right, not grace. During a debate in a committee of the whole House on 18 December, Sir Robert Phelips made reference to the 'protestacion *1ᵐᵒ Jacobi*', that is, the draft 'Apology' of 1604, as a pattern; William Noy supported the idea that they should 'looke what was done in *1ᵐᵒ*, if there bee any defect wee may goe farther'; others made additional suggestions, and the protestation was assembled, 'put to the question and passed the committee'.[122] In the afternoon, reassembling as the House, the Commons passed the protestation and entered it into the Journal.[123]

Despite the citations of numerous precedents, only a brief, unsupported assertion of the 'liberties, franchises, privileges, and jurisdictions of Parliament' as the 'ancient and undoubted birthright and inheritance of the subjects of England' appeared. Without consulting the peers, the Commons claimed the right to treat of 'affairs concerning the King, State, and defence of the realm and of the Church of England, and the maintenance and making of laws, and redress of mischiefs and grievances' as 'proper subjects and matter of counsel and debate in Parliament' and the 'freedom of speech to propound, treat, reason, and bring to conclusion the same' on behalf of 'every member of the House of Parliament'. Then, they asserted this broadly defined freedom of speech, including a 'freedom from all impeachment, imprisonment, and molestation (other than by censure of the House itself) for or concerning any speaking, reasoning, or declaring of any matter or matters touching Parliament or Parliament-business', for the 'Commons in Parliament'.[124] Like the 'Apology' of 1604 from which it drew, the 'Protestation' of 1621 represented a hurried assertion of purported liberties which lacked both the clear interpretation of the ancient constitution voiced by Thomas Hedley in 1610 and the support of the weighty quotation of evidence assembled by John Selden in 'The Priviledges of the Baronage in England' of 1621. Too hurried to make a careful statement of their liberties, the Commons resorted to the lawyer's common rhetoric of hyperbole.

Clearly, by 1621 no single representation of the ancient constitution had obtained a position of hegemony; instead, debates over the liberties of the House of Lords and the House of Commons had transformed the tentative, implicit contrasts among the constitutional interpretations articulated in 1610 into an open, explicit debate which would reach one peak in the parliament of 1628–9.[125] Through a thick description and analysis of public speeches and letters by King James VI and I, treatises by common lawyers, and speeches, petitions and resolutions in the House of Commons in the parliaments of 1604–10, 1614 and 1621, this chapter has attempted to provide a brief representation of these patterns of discourse on governance voiced by significant spokesmen in early seventeenth-century England. It has argued that James VI and I, Thomas Hedley, and John Selden fashioned the three major interpretations of the English constitution, 'constitutional monarchy created by kings', 'constitutional monarchy governed by the common law', and 'mixed monarchy', in 1610 and that these continued to shape English constitutional discourse for more than a decade.

Although somewhat diffident about commenting on the English constitution early in his reign, James had become aggressive in defending his interpretation by 1621. His speeches and letters outlined a theoretical and historical account in which kings derived their authority from God, held absolute power at the beginnings of civil rule, and created law, property and the institutions of government. Along with the people in general, English parliaments, which first included lords, clergy and freemen in one great council, obtained their liberties and privileges as a matter of grace from monarchs. This reading of the texts would suggest that a continuous tradition of absolutist theory did not link *The Trew Law of Free Monarchies* to the representations of power painted by Rubens for the Whitehall ceiling because James VI had modified his voice on governance in order to incorporate the discourse of the common law of England after becoming James I. Although some suggestions of absolutist theory entered King James's discourse on governance in 1621, a fuller application of this position to aspects of English governance would await the guiding hand of Charles I in the 1630s.

Responding to the theoretical voices of the king, common lawyers fashioned two interpretations of the English constitution which deliberately avoided the derivation of authority from monarchs alone. In a speech in the House of Commons, Thomas Hedley advocated an interpretation of 'constitutional monarchy governed by the common law' in which an immemorial common law, confirmed by continued usage over time, distributed prerogatives to the king and liberties to the people. Hedley's interpretation elevated the common law above both kings and parliaments. In a series of treatises, John Selden rejected immemoriality and fashioned the most detailed historical account of England's laws and constitution published in the early seventeenth century around the theme of a 'mixed monarchy' in which the monarch, lords, clergy and freemen had shared power from the very beginning and made law through custom in the courts and statute in the high court of parliament. In treatises and speeches in parliaments, other common lawyers (including James White-locke and Sir Edward Coke) mixed these interpretations together or voiced less coherent interpretations, so that many contemporaries would have perceived 'mixed monarchy' and 'constitutional monarchy governed by the common law' as variations on a single theme. The analysis and evidence presented in this essay suggests that the constitutional debates which took place in England between 1610 and 1621 more often pitted rival interpretations of the ancient constitution against each other than theories of absolutism versus constitutionalism.

PART II
COURT CULTURE AND COURT POLITICS

6 CULTURAL DIVERSITY AND CULTURAL CHANGE AT THE COURT OF JAMES I

Malcolm Smuts

The cultural history of the court of James I can hardly be regarded anymore as a neglected topic, after the appearance in the past two decades of several important articles and monographs on court masques, paintings, poetry and architecture.[1] Our understanding of that history has been coloured, however, by a preoccupation with two major figures – Ben Jonson and Inigo Jones – and by a tendency to interpret developments in James's reign as a prelude to the 'artistic renaissance' that occurred under Charles I. We associate Jacobean court culture with Jonsonian masques, Jonesian architecture and the burgeoning interest in European art that foreshadowed Charles's great collection and the English career of Van Dyck. Approaching the subject in this way inevitably distorts it somewhat, by giving undue prominence to forms that were not entirely representative of the period. In scholarship focused on the Caroline period or on the careers of Jones and Jonson the distortions may not matter very much, but to understand the culture of James's court as a subject in its own right one needs to be especially careful about reading history backwards, or judging it by the work of a few great artists.

The problem is particularly acute because Jacobean court culture was far less cohesive than that of either Elizabeth's or Charles's reign. It is not easy to characterize a court that produced both Audley End and the Banqueting House, for example, since they reflect entirely different approaches to architecture (Plates 17 and 18). Audley End is a late example of the sort of courtyard house favoured by English lords since the fifteenth century.[2] Its turrets and outer gate are still faintly reminiscent of a medieval castle, while other features, like the great windows and the ornamental strapwork along the roofline, derive from more recent fashions in prodigy house architecture. In every important respect, however, it derives from indigenous traditions which can be traced back, through the country houses of other Jacobean and Tudor peers and courtiers, to the late Middle Ages. The Banqueting House, by contrast, is a compact and meticulously classical building that owes everything to Italian models and to Jones's reading of Vitruvius, and nothing to native architecture. The two buildings look as if they came from different worlds, although they were in fact constructed within five years of each other, the one by James's Lord Treasurer and the other by James himself.

Equally dramatic contrasts exist between the classicist poetry of Jonson and the neo-chivalric poetry of Drayton, or the portraiture of Larkin and Peake and that of Mytens and van Somer. Within the Jacobean court neo-classicism and neo-medievalism, provincialism and cosmopolitanism, existed side by side, sometimes in the work of the same artist. The simplest way of sorting out the bewildering variety is by distinguishing the new from the old, the Tudor survivals and revivals from baroque and classicizing trends that seem to point to later developments. Doing so, however, can beg any number of questions.

Despite an accumulation of detailed knowledge, our overall picture of culture at James I's court therefore remains somewhat out of focus. This essay represents an attempt to clear away some of the preconceptions that, I will argue, have obscured understanding of the subject and to suggest lines along which a more fruitful approach might proceed.

I

What exactly do we mean, in the context of James I's reign, by the term 'court culture'? Most previous scholarship has adopted one of two models, neither entirely adequate. One, epitomized by the work of Frances Yates and Roy Strong, stresses the roots of English court culture in an international tradition deriving ultimately from the court academies of late Renaissance France and Italy. That tradition spread throughout Europe in the course of the sixteenth century, reaching England belatedly through the efforts of a few prominent royal and aristocratic patrons and the artists they supported.[3] These patrons were motivated not only by the aesthetic appeal of European Renaissance culture but by the conviction, which they absorbed from the Neoplatonic philosophy prevalent within French and Italian courts, that cultural works possess mysterious powers to transform society and politics. To a Neoplatonist all political order ultimately derives from divine Ideas which the human mind can only grasp indirectly, through images. The right kind of art, literature and music will harness the force and beauty of those Ideas, thereby promoting justice, harmony and civic virtue. Thus by refashioning the arts a ruler may also refashion the minds of his subjects and control their behaviour. This attitude reached its fullest development in what Yates has termed 'the Hermetic tradition', with its roots in ancient concepts of the occult and its nebulous visions of a future golden age of peace and progress, based upon human control over the spiritual powers that govern the universe. Hermetic ideas

100

were deeply influential within the academies of Medicean Florence and Valois France, and shaped dynastic imagery all over Europe, including Elizabethan and Jacobean England. They helped foster a view of the arts as tools of state-craft, whose reform would bring about a great age of national glory.[4] Court festivals, paintings, buildings and even landscape gardens all expressed this lofty vision, which ultimately lay behind the cultural innovations of the Stuart court.

This interpretation undoubtedly contains elements of truth: specialized studies have repeatedly documented the presence of Hermetic and Neo-platonic strains in Jacobean court art and literature.[5] It is misleading, however, to overemphasize the degree to which Jacobean court culture was indebted to any single Renaissance tradition. Even the most cosmopolitan and Italianate Jacobean artists were shaped by a wider and more eclectic background than some scholars have recognized. Among the forty-six books once owned by Inigo Jones and now preserved at Worcester College, Oxford, there are no titles by Pico or Ficino. The only works deeply influenced by Renaissance Neoplatonism in Jones's library are treatises on art and architecture. But Jones did own Italian or French translations of Plato's *Republic*, Aristotle's *Ethics*, and works on moral philosophy by Plutarch and Xenophon. He also owned a number of histories, including volumes by Herodotus, Polybius and Guicciardini.[6] His library suggests that courtly Neoplatonism may have meant less to him than other classical and Renaissance traditions whose influence upon Stuart court culture has never received systematic treatment.

It is, in any case, a mistake to identify court culture entirely with the out-look of a few advanced patrons and cosmopolitan artists. James's court never produced an academy responsible for developing and promulgating an official cultural philosophy and approved canons of taste. In fact it never developed any effective system for supervising cultural patronage.[7] It lacked the basic tools needed to pursue a cohesive cultural policy and implement program-matic reforms, such as the Medici and the Bourbons promoted on the Conti-nent. It is therefore very misleading to draw close parallels between court culture in England and in places like Tuscany and France, where patronage was much more centralized. In England each major court patron freely pursued his or her own interests without direction or control, a fact which helps explain the remarkable heterogeneity that resulted.

There is also room for more scepticism about the ambitious claims a few seventeenth-century theorists and several modern scholars have advanced on behalf of the political significance of masque texts and images.[8] Few courtiers seem to have taken masques very seriously as tools of statecraft. The views of Bacon, who dismissed them as toys, and the rather earthy comments of newsletter writers like Chamberlain and Carleton, undoubtedly convey dominant English court attitudes better than the claims of Ben Jonson and various Italian writers.[9] Nor can we assume that the presence of Hermetic and Platonic symbolism in court culture *necessarily* implied a commitment to deeper philosophical attitudes. By the seventeenth century such symbolism was a conventional feature of court entertainments throughout Europe which, like any artistic convention, might be used with varying degrees of seriousness and conviction.[10] Masques certainly expressed political ideas, but this does not mean that their metaphoric language straightforwardly expressed the ways in which kings and courtiers normally thought about politics.

None of this should suggest that masques and other cultural forms had no political significance, only that uncovering their significance requires a more extensive investigation than many scholars have supposed. Masques were not only symbolic spectacles but important rituals, entertainments and social events in which leading courtiers participated. Consequently even seemingly trivial details in a performance might take on political meaning, by conveying something about the configuration of power and influence at Whitehall. Indeed masques could sometimes help to sustain or alter that configuration. The difficulty confronting the historian lies in the difficulty of knowing which aspects of a performance struck contemporaries as revealing or important, rather than merely conventional and decorative or boring and irrelevant. It is a problem that can never be overcome so long as masques are treated as isolated texts whose importance as vehicles for court attitudes is taken for granted. Only by refusing to take masques at face value and investigating them in terms of evidence gathered from other sources illustrating the court's ambience and mentality can we begin to appreciate their true place in Jacobean political culture.[11]

II

A second model of court culture is found in the work of P. W. Thomas, Perez Zagorin and Lawrence Stone. These scholars do attempt to portray culture as an outgrowth of larger social and political conditions. Yet they have little sympathy for the court, which they invariably treat as an isolated hothouse environment, harbouring a society that was frivolous, corrupt, fond of novelty and luxury, sexually permissive and imbued with a cosmopolitan sympathy for popery and absolutism.[12] Despite its occasional surface brilliance, they argue, court culture remained essentially shallow, brittle and out-of-touch with the nation's real aspirations.[13] Although the examples taken to support this characterization normally come mainly from Charles's reign, the Jacobean and Caroline periods are rarely sharply differentiated.

Anyone really familiar with the early Stuart court must, I think, realize that this portrayal oversimplifies. It characterizes the entire court through a few selective quotations and anecdotes, glossing over the diversity of political, cultural, religious and moral outlooks that any close study will uncover.

Equally important, it greatly exaggerates the gulf separating the court from other social, political and cultural milieux, especially in the London area. No effective barriers separated courtiers from other peers and gentlemen in the metropolis: royal servants and country squires up for the Season lived in the same neighbourhoods, rubbed elbows in the city's theatres and other gathering spots, and sometimes formed close bonds. Poets and artists retained by the Crown almost always lived in their own houses in the capital, and often worked for patrons who were not courtiers. Any attempt to distinguish sharply between the court's culture and that of fashionable London will therefore run into difficulties. To give a few examples, where does one place Jonson, who wrote court masques but also plays for London's theatres and poems for country peers and gentry, or Donne, who never really belonged to the court after his dismissal from Egerton's household, but who certainly influenced court literature? How does one classify antiquarians like Camden and Sir Robert Cotton, who accepted court patronage and lived closer to the court than many privy councillors, but who also had close bonds with scholars and gentlemen who were in no sense courtiers?[14] The only solution, it seems to me, is to admit that Whitehall was one among several centres of a larger social and cultural environment, that engulfed the court without ever becoming totally dependent upon it.[15]

To understand Jacobean court culture properly we must, therefore, abandon the notion that it developed within an exclusive, self-contained setting, somehow cut off from the nation at large. Instead of concentrating on assumed differences between the court and the rest of England, we need to look much more carefully at the court's internal structure and dynamics, and at the ways in which its members could have absorbed ideas and tastes from other milieux. In making this argument I am adopting an approach in some ways similar to and in other ways very different from that of an important recent study edited by David Starkey.[16] Unlike most previous studies, Starkey attempts to reconstruct the court systematically and sympathetically. Yet Starkey defines the court so narrowly that his book ends up revealing relatively little about how it interacted with other environments. The court's geography, Starkey argues, consisted of a few rooms within Whitehall Palace: the royal Bedchamber and Privy Chamber, the Council Chamber, and the privy gallery that ran between them. Its personnel comprised a very select group of less than fifty individuals – the privy councillors and Privy and Bedchamber servants – who had access to these rooms.

Reducing the court to this restricted sphere will raise numerous problems for the cultural historian. The most obvious is that relatively little cultural activity took place within the Bedchamber and the Privy Chamber. Even court masques were normally performed in the Banqueting House, a public room of the royal palace; and much of what we customarily think of as court culture usually took shape outside Whitehall altogether. Any cultural geography of the court must surely include the studios of court artists, the study in which Ben Jonson wrote his masques, and the galleries of people like the Duke of Buckingham and the Earl of Arundel. Yet by Starkey's definition none of these places belonged to the court.

The problems posed by Starkey's approach lie deeper than this, however. As their name implies, the privy apartments were a place where the monarch might retreat from public life, among a select group of companions and advisors. But a royal court was not only a king's refuge; it also existed to surround him with pomp and ceremony, a fact Starkey recognizes but does not explore in his recent volume.[17] Many forms of court culture were bound up with the public and ceremonial aspects of royal life. Equally important, the court was a national centre of politics and high society, which attracted prominent visitors from all over England. It was a 'point of contact' between the royal entourage and the political nation at large, as G. R. Elton has shown.[18] In the seventeenth century the phrase 'going to court' did not always mean entering the Privy Chamber: it could also mean travelling to Westminster and seeking access, not only to the king but to others who might influence him. To understand the court's dynamics we need to pay attention not just to activities in the privy apartments, but to the constant round of entertaining, intrigue and patronage-hunting that extended well beyond Whitehall's gates.

It is, in fact, crucial to recognize that English court life in this broader sense was never confined within any particular locale or rigorously controlled by a small inner circle. In this respect Whitehall was very different from Louis XIV's Versailles. Even James's most intimate companions did not live permanently in his palace: Bedchamber servants normally kept their own London houses, while privy councillors always built up their own clienteles and maintained very large households in or near the capital. Important social and cultural events sometimes took place in courtiers' residences, rather than at the king's. Thus in January of 1617 James's first English Bedchamber servant, the Earl of Montgomery, produced a masque at his residence in Enfield, with a number of important courtiers in the cast.[19] James did *not* attend, but he soon heard of the performance and summoned Montgomery's masquers to repeat it at the royal palace of Theobolds. In ways like this, court life ebbed and flowed between the king's palaces and the many other locations where courtiers gathered.

The Jacobean courtier inhabited a polycentric world, revolving not only around the privy apartments but a number of other institutions, prominent among them the households of court peers. A few aristocratic palaces, like Salisbury House until 1610 and York House during Buckingham's ascendancy, were almost as central to the court as Whitehall itself. Others, like Prince Henry's St James or Arundel House in the 1620s, became focal points of opposition to royal favourites and policies.[20] But such opposition did not entail rejecting the court as an institution: far from it. The Strand palace of a discontented prince or nobleman often represented an alternative model of the court, both in political terms and with respect to matters of taste, style and ambience. Prince Henry and the Earl of Arundel pointedly enforced much stricter rules of decorum within their households than James did in his, while also patronizing Italian cultural fashions in which the king showed less interest. Arundel House and St James became paradigms of a courtly ideal of cosmopolitanism, moral order and formality, which James had failed to implement.

Each major household also dispensed its own patronage, sometimes with significant results. Arundel's role as an art patron is justly famous; but the Earls of Salisbury and Pembroke, the Duke of Buckingham and other peers were also active patrons, about whom much less is known. The court's great aristocratic households influenced each other and undoubtedly shaped the king's patronage, though in ways that remain somewhat obscure. In some cases the taste of major court patrons was also shaped by provincial noblemen with ties to court patrons: we cannot assume that cultural fashions that took root at court always began there. The whole subject of how such fashions developed and travelled from one household to another deserves much closer scrutiny.[21]

Further out toward the court's periphery lay the Inns of Court, from which many young courtiers tried to launch their careers, and Paul's Walk, where courtiers and others gathered to exchange news and gossip. English embassies abroad also had cultural links to the court, not only because ambassadors sometimes helped procure paintings and foreign books, but because diplomatic service was often a stepping stone in a courtier's career.[22] More than one important figure at the late Jacobean court had spent years overseas in British embassies. Cultural institutions, like the more fashionable London theatres and the Society of Antiquaries, were also to some extent pulled within the court's orbit, despite James's justified suspicions of both. Of course many of these institutions did not technically belong to the court at all and, except for the embassies, none were subservient to it. But they all contributed to the complex milieu that had grown up around Whitehall. The gossip of Paul's Walk and the cultural amenities of London were as much a part of the Jacobean courtier's world as the privy gallery itself.

The court's culture was also immeasurably enriched by the cultural and intellectual interests of many lesser courtiers and place-seekers. In any strictly political history of James's court people like John Donne, Sir Dudley Carleton or the king's physician, Sir Theodore Mayerne, would play secondary roles at best. But Donne's poetry, Carleton's art-collecting and Mayerne's extensive scientific and artistic pursuits and connections illustrate the varied interests and attainments of minor Jacobean courtiers, who sometimes had more impact on cultural life than much more prominent figures.[23]

Throughout James's reign, important innovations in court culture tended to originate toward the court's periphery or within its secondary centres, much more often than in the king's Household. London's theatres, the literary and intellectual coteries of the Inns of Court, the antiquarian movement, English ambassadors abroad and the patronage of a few noblemen all influenced the evolution of cultural trends more decisively than royal preferences and initiatives. Many of the individuals who most affected court taste did *not* come from courtly backgrounds, and had great difficulty finding a court niche for themselves. Thus Donne, Jonson and Inigo Jones all emerged from plebeian or minor gentry origins and spent years trying to win court patronage, with mixed results.[24] Even the Earl of Arundel was usually a more peripheral figure at court than most accounts have assumed, and his precocious interest in European art was shared by others, like his father-in-law, the Earl of Shrewsbury, who were scarcely courtiers at all.[25]

Of course, courts always recruited talent from beyond their own ranks, but more than recruitment was involved in this case. In most cultural fields James provided minimal leadership.[26] Nevertheless the Crown remained the kingdom's most lavish and prestigious cultural patron. In the absence of strong direction from the monarch the court's culture inevitably responded to forces impinging on Whitehall from outside, including the preferences of secondary court patrons, cultural fashions developing at the Inns of Court and elsewhere in London, and foreign models of aristocratic culture encountered by Englishmen on the Grand Tour. Also important were the ambitions of poets and artists who sought court patronage not only for obvious financial reasons, but because the court's approval would automatically lift them above their rivals. Ben Jonson and Inigo Jones set out quite deliberately to refashion English poetry and architecture by conquering the court and using it to enhance the prestige of their own work. In the end they succeeded well enough to help reorient English upper class taste in both court and country, well beyond the reign of James I. The court was not the source of Jonesian and Jonsonian classicism so much as the vehicle through which these styles established their commanding place in English high culture.

III

Even if this picture is somewhat overdrawn, there can be no doubt that the Crown and the court's other great patrons often followed cultural trends rather than initiating them. This means that we need to reexamine some widely held attitudes concerning the social and political dimensions of court culture. It is often assumed that court culture must have reflected the viewpoint of the king and a few others closely associated with him. At worst it was

106

the elegant propaganda of an absolutist dynasty. But even when not overtly propagandistic it embodied the outlook of a small parasitic coterie whose wealth and power derived from James's bounty.

This view depends on the erroneous assumption that at court cultural influences, like power and patronage, travelled in only one direction: from the top down and the centre outward. It may have some validity with respect to works like the masques, which were essentially creations of royal households.[27] The larger evolution of tastes and mentalities in and around the court was never effectively controlled, however, by the Crown or the royal entourage. Far from reflecting a single cohesive outlook, cultural trends and attitudes often provide valuable evidence of tension and conflict *within* court society. I will conclude with three rather different illustrations to support and amplify this claim.

The first concerns cultural images of court society and politics.[28] One might logically expect a court culture to project a flattering vision of court life, but this was often far from the case in Jacobean England. Anyone who seriously reads Jonson's court poetry, or Bacon's essays and histories, or even the letters of a great minister like the Earl of Salisbury, will repeatedly encounter jaundiced views of how courts operate.[29] Indeed much of the bad press the Jacobean court has always received derives from writings by courtiers, or people trying to become courtiers, complaining about the extravagance, duplicity and venality of their own milieu.

At least part of the reason for this fact must be sought in the highly ambiguous nature of the relationship between the court's leaders and its rank and file. Lesser courtiers looked to the king and his favourites as potential patrons, but also resented them for not bestowing favour more quickly and profusely. Even those who achieved high office often felt insecure about their position. Anxiety, jealousy and frustrated ambition were proverbially common at court, and often led to real bitterness.

Another common feature of court life was a passion for news and gossip about the king and those around him, stemming not only from natural curiosity but from the need to keep abreast of developments that might affect careers.[30] The newsletter is one of the most typical products of early Stuart court society, even if it quickly became popular among rural landowners.[31] Written news, however, represents only a small portion of what circulated by word of mouth. Often the news was harmless enough, but when a court scandal (like the Overbury affair) broke, or when the man reporting it had an axe to grind, it could become salacious.

This tense concern with the affairs of the court's elite demonstrably affected literary trends. Jacobean plays often depicted fictional court intrigues which audiences readily interpreted as veiled allusions to contemporary events. The Scots around James I were particular favourites with dramatic satirists, much to the king's fury. Jonson complained, in the prologue to *Volpone*, that he could not write a play without having members of his audience read libellous meanings into it.[32] The important thing is not so much whether the playwrights intended to make such allusions, but the fact that the play-going public – which included many courtiers – enjoyed finding them. The spice of scandal, the thrill of seeing libels enacted on the stage, drew fashionable people to the theatre.

The influence in late Elizabethan and Jacobean England of Roman satirists and satiric historians – notably Tacitus – stemmed from the same preoccupations. These authors became fashionable because the political and social vices they described seemed highly reminiscent of contemporary court life. Once established, in turn, the fashion for Tacitus guaranteed that courtiers would examine their surroundings through cynical eyes, forever ready to detect sordid intrigues and signs of spreading corruption. Much of the literature written at court is a product of this mentality. Even in the Tudor period court poets and intellectuals had attacked court vices. Under James classical influences reinforced and deepened this tradition of moral criticism, while fostering the development of more direct and naturalistic styles in both poetry and prose. The Elizabethan taste for Petrarchanism, allegory and rhetorical artifice gave way before an emphasis on plain speech, psychological insight and vividly immediate portraits of corruption.[33] Donne's satires, Jonson's court poems and Roman tragedies and the essays and historiographical works of Bacon – to take but three examples – incisively dissect the corrosive effects of luxury, ambition and power upon a ruling elite.

This point needs emphasis because many scholars still tend to associate classical influence with incipient republicanism, and to assume that neo-classical political languages reached England primarily through the ideas of radical parliamentarians.[34] Such a view obscures some of the most important channels through which Roman thought shaped English culture and political discourse, long before the Civil War appeared on the horizon. It also drastically oversimplifies the political discourse of the early seventeenth century. Until after the conclusion of the Civil War Englishmen habitually thought in terms of a court-centred polity. Pointing out the pitfalls of that polity was not a call to revolution so much as a prudent recognition of the facts of political life. Jacobean intellectuals were obsessed with corruption at court for the same reason that Hanoverian intellectuals were obsessed with corruption in parliament: because it seemed an ineradicable and potentially fatal weakness at the heart of the constitution. Anyone involved in early Stuart politics therefore needed to learn how courts fostered corruption and how the corruption they fostered might be combated. And the king needed to learn most of all. From this point of view the writing of anti-court satires might appear a prime duty of a court author, as it undoubtedly did to Ben Jonson.

My second illustration concerns patterns of conspicuous consumption. It was axiomatic in Renaissance and baroque Europe that kings and their courtiers must display magnificence, in entertainment, festivities, clothing and countless other ways. The forms courtly magnificence took varied widely, however. Some shifts in cultural taste involved changing attitudes toward the types of display appropriate to kings and courtiers. Indoor masques, for example, represented a very different sort of magnificence from outdoor pageants, such as those associated with royal entries and public tournaments. In general James's reign witnessed a gradual movement away from traditional public varieties of magnificence in favour of private forms, like masques and art collections, accessible only to those who gained admission to the king's palaces. There were enough exceptions, however, to show that the court had not entirely made up its mind. Henry was much fonder of outdoor pageantry than his father, a reflection, no doubt, of his desire for popularity. His investiture as Prince of Wales was an exceptionally lavish public ceremony. But so was James's coronation entry in 1604 and Princess Elizabeth's wedding in 1613: James did not always avoid great public ceremonies.

The ambivalence of Jacobean court attitudes is also evident in the ways court literature sometimes attacked forms of public display intrinsic to court life. One example is the polemics which Jonson, Bacon and others directed against ostentatious dress. Expensive and elaborate costume had always been a form of competitive self-assertion in which the monarch's servants had to engage. The more important the occasion the more elaborate clothing became, and the more attention observers paid to it. The gold and silver lace on Princess Elizabeth's wedding dress cost £1760.[35] Writers associated with the court nonetheless frequently criticized expensive clothing. In part that criticism reflected disdain for imported luxuries and foreign fashions. Frequently it also involved a moralistic distrust of luxury and extravagance, reinforced by humanist convictions that one ought to judge people by their ideas and actions rather than by outward appearances. 'It is not powdering and perfuming and every day smelling of the tailor that coverteth to a beautiful object', as Jonson put it, 'but a mind, shining through any suit, which needs no false light either of riches or honors to help it'.[36]

This was a very old theme, but it seems to have taken on new life at the Jacobean court. Why? Part of the explanation may be that fashions in dress became even more elaborate in James's reign than they were during most of the Tudor period, thereby giving rise to a backlash.[37] But at least in one important case there also appear to have been more personal motives. In the late 1610s the Earl of Arundel deliberately adopted a simpler style of clothing, which became something of a trademark.[38] He associated this style with the 'old nobility' and this gives a clue to his motives. He wished to distinguish himself from the court's newly minted noblemen, especially the Duke of Buckingham, whose sartorial magnificence was excessive even by Jacobean standards.

109

What one finds, in short, is not a culture characterized simply by extravagant ostentation, as the old stereotype would have it. It is instead a culture in which the scale and the type of display appropriate to the great has become an issue. Clothing is simply one example: the cost of banquets, masques, public pageants and building all excited negative comment within the court itself. I have argued elsewhere that the work of Jones, Jonson and others in fact reflects a shift toward a more austere concept of the sort of display in which royalty and noblemen should engage: an attitude broadly congruent with Arundel's disdain for ostentatious dress.[39] The style of the Banqueting House is markedly less flamboyant than that of Hatfield and Audley End, just as the court paintings of Mytens and van Somer tend to place less emphasis on magnificent accoutrements of rank than most court portraits of the early and mid-1610s.

My final illustration concerns the cultural ramifications of debates over foreign policy. It is of crucial importance that James's reign was an era of peace that followed nearly twenty years of war. For the question of how long Britain should remain at peace shaped any number of other areas of court life. Not only was the Jacobean peace a major theme of masques and panegyrics: it also affected the ways ordinary courtiers defined their conduct and their relationship to the king. The careers of Sir Walter Raleigh and Lord Herbert of Cherbury vividly display the dangers and frustrations faced by men trying to fulfill in James's reign the neo-chivalric courtly ideals personified by Elizabethans like Sir Philip Sidney and the second Earl of Essex.[40] But the change in tone at court was in fact more equivocal than these examples might suggest, since important leaders, including Prince Henry, favoured a more warlike orientation than the king.

This policy disagreement had extensive cultural ramifications. It is no coincidence that Henry enjoyed jousting much more than his father, or that he patronized Drayton's epic on the reign of Henry V, whereas James rarely patronized epic poetry of any sort.[41] Even after Henry's death one finds courtiers advocating war, not only from concern for religion or the military balance of power in Europe, but because they believed that war would improve English culture and morals. Bacon argued on more than one occasion that a prolonged peace will breed effeminacy and corruption. Ben Jonson's 'Epistle to a Friend to Invite him to the Wars' expresses much the same view, castigating the venality and sexual debauchery of the age, which Jonson implicitly associates with peace. Sir Robert Cotton, on the other hand, regarded military men as dangerously prone to faction, and militaristic culture as a threat to political stability.

Thus Jacobean courtiers realized full well that culture and politics were ultimately interdependent. But the whole court never committed itself either to one policy or to a single, corresponding cultural style. Even the work of individuals like Ben Jonson and Inigo Jones displays ambiguities. Through the king's masques they developed a classicist celebration of the Jacobean peace; yet in *Prince Henry's Barriers* they also managed to fuse classical and chivalric themes in a celebration of military heroism. If James, rather than Henry, had died in 1612 the work of both might have developed in very different directions, and the overall style and tone of the court's culture would certainly have altered. It may not be coincidental that Jonson never finished the epic poem about the heroes of England's past that was destroyed when a fire consumed his manuscripts in 1623. He may have felt that conditions under James I were simply unpropitious for the heroic verse he wanted to write. Understanding the relationship of culture and politics at court requires an awareness of the internal disputes, over policy issues and larger philosophical convictions, that always divided James's servants from each other. Art, literature and theatrical entertainments often participated in an ongoing political contest. They were used not only to defend and glorify royal actions but implicitly to criticize them and suggest alternatives. At a deeper level culture participated in the process through which some courtiers adjusted their behaviour and aspirations to prevailing political conditions, while others defiantly resisted such adaptation. Poetic rhetoric, differences in taste and contrasting lifestyles all helped to define competing ideals of nobility that were related to political disputes but also transcended them.

IV

Jacobean court culture will always be misunderstood so long as scholars portray the court as a homogeneous body dominated by a single outlook. For Stuart court society was remarkably complex and heterogeneous. It always included men and women from varied social backgrounds, who disagreed with each other about politics, religion, culture and everything else of importance. Far from being an isolated hothouse environment, it was a magnet for ambition and talent, the central arena where people struggled for power and prestige. Along with neighbouring London, it was also the only true national centre of upper-class society. This meant that novel ideas and cultural fashions among the kingdom's landed elite inevitably found their way to court, wherever they might originate. In a period like the early seventeenth century, when aristocratic lifestyles were undergoing deep change, the court inevitably reflected a diversity of tastes and values. Young innovators like Prince Henry and Arundel, older and more traditional English noblemen and Scots like James himself and virtually all of the Bedchamber servants, each brought their own cultural preferences to court and became models of different patterns of courtliness. Poets and artists competed for court favour, offering a variety of styles and orientations from which to choose.

The resultant cultural diversity is even more apparent in James I's reign than in other periods. Cultural developments in London and contact with Mediterranean Europe had much less impact upon the Elizabethan court than upon James's. Elizabethan court culture was therefore more insular and more uniformly aristocratic in both its tone and its origins than that of the early seventeenth century. Under Charles the pronounced and relatively uniform tastes of the king and a few other patrons close to him acted as a kind of filter, admitting some influences while screening out others. In Jacobean England one finds a remarkable assortment of urban and aristocratic, native and foreign influences converging on a court that had not yet established a dominant cultural attitude. The result was an extraordinarily rich and varied landscape, that we can begin to understand only by relinquishing the myth that a uniform Jacobean court culture ever existed.

7 LANCELOT ANDREWES, JOHN BUCKERIDGE, AND AVANT-GARDE CONFORMITY AT THE COURT OF JAMES I

Peter Lake

The conventional defence of the Elizabethan church from its puritan critics was formulated within certain conceptual limits, limits set by what might best be termed the English reformed tradition. For our present purposes the central features of that tradition were a doctrine of double predestination, a vision of the church and its evangelical mission centred on preaching and a view of the world stretched tight between the true church of Christ and the false church of Antichrist. The leading conformist apologists – John Whitgift, John Bridges, Thomas Cooper, Matthew Sutcliffe amongst them – were as committed to that reformed tradition as their puritan opponents. On the basis of this common reformed heritage Elizabethan conformists erected a defence of the status quo founded on the idea of things indifferent and on the need, in such matters, to obey the commands of the Christian prince. They defined puritans almost exclusively in terms of their attitude to the power of the prince and to the government and ceremonies of the church, and not in terms of their doctrinal beliefs or style of piety. Thus, the polemical image of puritanism current in the 1590s concentrated on disobedience to the prince in matters of ceremony and on the allegedly subversive implications of Presbyterian populism and clericalism.

However, while this remained the dominant mode of conformist argument, thanks to Richard Hooker, there was another more emotionally compelling and comprehensively religious style of conformity available, in the public domain, by the middle of the 1590s. Whatever Hooker's own position on the issue of predestination (and this clearly shifted over time and arguably never achieved stable coherence) he can be seen almost to have invented the style of piety associated with the rise of English Arminianism and the ecclesiastical policies pursued by Charles I, Laud and their supporters during the personal rule. A broadly based vision of the Christian community, propounded in

113

conscious contrast to the division between the godly and the profane which was taken to be central to puritan piety and Presbyterian ecclesiology; a view of the visible church centred far more on the sacrament and on public worship than on preaching; a justification of the ceremonial arrangements of the English church that transcended the realm of *adiaphora* and instead attributed a positively religious role and significance to the rituals and observances of the church – all these can be found fully developed in Hooker's thought. Moreover, they were developed in deliberate and overt opposition to an image of puritanism that was not limited to the realms of ceremony and external government but included a whole style of piety – word-centred, predestinarian, concerned with separating the godly off from the ungodly rather than celebrating the mystical union which bound all baptized members of the national church together as members of Christ's body.

In *Anglicans and Puritans?* I argued that Hooker's position was new, at least in the context of Elizabethan conformist thought, if not in that of English protestantism *tout court*, and that consequently Hooker occupied a somewhat exposed and lonely position during the 1590s.[1] If that is right then two questions emerge; what links can be discerned between Hooker and later English Arminianism and in particular what happened to this Hookerian style of piety during the reign of James I? There is a long and a short answer to those questions. The short answer is Lancelot Andrewes and it is with his court sermons and those of his friend, eulogist and literary executor John Buckeridge that I shall concern myself here.

There are two reasons, then, for talking about Lancelot Andrewes. The first is that he does provide a personal as well as an ideological link between the world of Hooker and the world of Laud. A personal friend of Hooker, he almost certainly had manuscript copies of the unpublished parts of the *Polity* in his possession after Hooker's death. He was also regarded as 'our Gamaliel' (the phrase is Richard Montague's) by the Durham House group, that faction of Arminian or anti-Calvinist divines centred on the household of Richard Neile, Bishop of Durham. The second is that he was a very prominent court preacher of James's reign; he preached at nearly all the great feast days – Christmas, Ash Wednesday, Good Friday, Easter Sunday and Whitsun – from around 1605 until his death and, probably even more importantly at the Jacobean court, on the anniversaries of the Gowrie conspiracy and the powder plot.[2] Here, then, is a very central strand in the religious ideology of the court.

Central it may have been, but it would be absurd to suggest that it was the predominant strand. The Jacobean church scarcely possessed a unitary official religious ideology. James himself saw to that; as Ken Fincham and I have argued James set out, by balancing ecclesiastical factions, to establish his regime on as broad a basis of support as possible. The church was to be united around the assertion and defence of James's God-given powers as a Christian king against the threats posed to them by the Presbyterians on the one hand and the papists on the other. However, within the ideological limits thus set by the king a considerable latitude remained for the expression of different and indeed mutually exclusive styles of divinity. As the reign went on different groups and factions sought to exploit one aspect or other of the king's religious and political susceptibilities in order to push royal policy in what they took to be the right direction. Ken Fincham and I have sketched elsewhere the outline of those factional and ideological manoeuvres.³ Here I want to concentrate on just one of the contending ideologies of the Jacobean court – that contained within the court sermons of Lancelot Andrewes.

Let us start, perhaps perversely, with what Andrewes hated, with the trends in contemporary religious thought and practice he most disliked and feared. Let us start, in short, with Andrewes's image of puritanism. This was composed of various strands which need to be teased out and related to one another very carefully if Andrewes's position is to be understood. Andrewes loathed puritanism which he conventionally saw as organised around a Presbyterian threat to order and hierarchy in the church and to the power of the prince in church and state.⁴ He similarly loathed puritan non-conformity, seeing it, with earlier conformists, as part of the devil's plot to undermine the church, as the first step on a slippery slope that led from seemingly trivial ceremonies to schism and even heresy.⁵

So far so bad, but Andrewes hated other things as well. Throughout his sermons he denounced those who reduced religion to the transfer and assimilation of information. People now behaved 'as though Christian religion had no law-points in it, consisted only of pure narratives – believe them and all is well'. Here were only certain 'dogmatical points, matters of opinion'. For such people divinity had become mere 'sophism and school points and at the best a kind of ecstasy about God'. Piety was the repetition of 'curious and quaint terms and set phrases wherein a great part of many men's religion do now-a-days consist'. Faith was the virtue most in demand and faith was now defined in largely intellectual terms. People who embraced such opinions 'entitled themselves gnostics, that is men of knowledge' and despised all those who could not talk like them as 'simplices, good, simple souls'. Buckeridge noted the same trend, warning that 'true religion is no way a gargleism only, to wash the tongue and mouth, to speak words; it must root in the heart and then fructify in the hand, else it will not cleanse the whole man'.⁶

For Andrewes such opinions could have only one result – hypocrisy – the sin of the pharisees, whose knowledge had been great but had yielded almost no practical fruits. They had attempted to conceal that by making a great outward show of formal piety. But that piety had consisted only of a series of outward works and observances of their own making rather than any duties required of them by God. Andrewes was not repudiating the role of works in true piety, far from it. Rather he was making an implicit distinction between the works of charity, piety and worship enjoined by God and those merely formal marks of apparent zeal, devised by hypocrites like pharisees and the puritans, in order to mark themselves off from their contemporaries. The resulting confusion between their own will and works and those of God Andrewes described as a form of spiritual idolatry; a worship not of images but of their own imaginations. Since the reformation Andrewes claimed that this tendency has been 'the disease of our age . . . There hath been good riddance made of images; but for imaginations, they be daily stamped in great number, and instead of the old images set up, deified and worshipped carrying the names and credit of the "apostles doctrine", government etc.'[7]

That last remark led straight back to Presbyterianism and the multifarious forms of worship produced by puritan non-conformity. But it led elsewhere too. Andrewes saw the cult of the sermon as the classic contemporary example of a pharisaical outward godliness. For at present, according to Andrewes, the church was full of 'sermon hypocrites'. The result was what Andrewes called a 'scenical, theatrical, histrionical godliness'. Amongst the preachers this involved 'volubility of utterance, earnestness of action, straining the voice in a passionate delivery, phrases and figures'. Amongst the laity it produced a similarly extrovert emotionalism. 'With some spring within, their eyes are made to roll, and their lips to wag, and their breath to give a sob; all is but Hero's pneumatica, a visar, not a very face; "an outward show of godliness, but no inward power of it at all".' So bad had things become that 'the corps, the whole body of some men's profession, all godliness with some, what is it but hearing a sermon? The ear is all, the ear is all that is done, and but by our ear-mark no man should know us to be Christians.' According to Buckeridge 'oratories' were turned 'into auditories, and temples into schools, and all adoration and worship into hearing of a sermon; as if all, soul and body, were turned into an ear, or as if all religion and sacrifice that must be sent up to God, were only this, to know the message that God sends down by his servants'. The age was obsessed with taking in knowledge by the ear. 'In at our ears there goes I know not how many sermons, and every day more and more if we might have our wills.' But nothing in the way of good works came out of us. 'All in hearing in a manner, none in doing what we hear.' Men pray to know God's will not to know how to do God's will. The result was not merely a lack of good works, too often seemingly godly persons used their incessant hearing of the word as a cover for sin. 'So they serve God, and hear lectures, as the term is, they take themselves liberty to pay no debts, to put their money out to usury, to grind their tenants; yea, and so they miss not such a lecture in such a place, they may do anything then.'[8]

It is possible to give a slightly greater theological precision to Andrewes's critique of this style of divinity. For Andrewes predestination was the crucial example of a doctrine about which abstract speculation was inappropriate. In a number of crucial asides Andrewes denounced the presumptuous certitude of those who 'with their new perspective . . . think they perceive all God's secret decrees, the number and order of them clearly'. 'Are there in the world that make but a shallow of this great deep, they have sounded it to the bottom. God's secret decrees they have them at their fingers ends, and can tell you the number and the order of them just, with 1, 2, 3, 4, 5.' 'Therefore', Andrewes concluded, 'we are not curiously to enquire and search out of God's secret touching reprobation or election, but to adore it.'[9]

Not only did such speculative flights of fancy represent a clear infringement on the majesty of God, they could also have dangerous practical consequences. Buckeridge claimed that a divinity filled with 'curious, idle and philosophical questions' could only end in disaster; although he chose as his example of this outcome the popish doctrine of transubstantiation. Applied to predestination such methods could produce the notion that God was the author of sin, or that he was like a tyrant 'sentencing men to death only for his pleasure, before they have offended him at all'. Such views could lead only to despair or to presumption. Amongst Andrewes's contemporaries the latter was distinctly the more likely outcome. 'A great many', he wrote, 'think that presumption in being secure of their salvation is good divinity.' This led to a fatal security or presumption grounded on the assumption, held by many, that they were 'God's darlings, and God doth so dote on them that he will not suffer them in any case to receive the least hurt that may be'. The result was that such men left out crucial stages in the progress of the Christian to salvation. They argued that 'there is but one degree or step in all Christianity, it is no more but out of the font to leap straight into heaven; from predestination we leap straight to glorification, it is no matter for mortification, there be no such mean degrees'. Such people made 'a short cut and step to Christ straight, and lay hold on him by faith without any more ado' and thus 'vainly imagine to come to remission of sins, per saltum, over repentance's head'.[10]

Preachers of this school fatally unbalanced the message of Christianity, playing up the gospel at the expense of the law and God's mercy at the expense of his justice. They made a similar mistake on the subject of Christian liberty. Fear of superstition and hypocrisy had now driven people to a licentious liberty. Fasting was now equated with superstition and outward observance with hypocrisy. Having, in the name of Christian liberty and the mercy of God, turned their backs on repentance and the works of repentance (like fasting) such professors, when they wished to find evidence of their own assurance of salvation, turned inward. Instead of inspecting what they had done, the state of their works (and here it seems likely, that Andrewes was referring to the works of charity, mortification and worship enjoined by God and not the puritans' own pharisaical obsession with hearing sermons), they inspected the state of their minds and souls. In this way they entered a labyrinth of subjectivism that led almost inevitably to hypocrisy and presumption. 'It is not good trying conclusions about our souls', claimed Andrewes. 'As for what is in the heart . . . "who knows it?" Not we ourselves; our own hearts oft deceive us.'[11]

For John Buckeridge such presumption could not but have an effect on people's public demeanour in church. Buckeridge identified pride as 'the commonplace of all sects' and located in 'pride and an assurance without ground' the cause of that irreverence which led the godly to refuse to kneel at communion, receiving instead 'pompously and gloriously . . . as co-heirs and fellows, as if they were Christ's equals'. The contemporary obsession with the inward at the expense of the outward, with faith and not with works, with the gospel not the law caused many Christians to behave as though God had made only their souls and not their bodies and offer him only spiritual and not physical or outward reverence. Andrewes bewailed contemporary ecclesiastical mores; 'covered we sit, sitting we pray; standing, or walking, or as it takes us in the head, we receive; as if Christ were so gentle a person, we might touch him, do to him what we list, he would take all well, he hath not the power to say noli to anything' and had rather to suffer 'the hand of presumption', 'the scornful eye', 'the stiff knee' without redress. Buckeridge claimed to 'fear those . . . elephants that have no joints in their knees, have sworn and vowed that they will not kneel to God, and his Christ, that they may make it known that they esteem their own fantasy more than they do the oath of God, who cannot repent'. Such irreverence, he warned, 'trenches deep, almost to Arianism, to deny all worship to Christ'.[12]

Similarly, the obsession with Christian liberty had led to the abandonment or neglect of outward ceremonies in the worship of God. It was a 'plausible theme not to burden the church with ceremonies; the church to be free, which hath almost freed the church of all decency'. The refusal to kneel either to pray or to receive the sacrament was justified all too often in terms of the casting out of 'the spirit of bondage'. This process of emancipation from the bondage of superstition could be and was being taken too far, so far that it was producing (the opposite extreme from superstition) an irreligious profaneness, which, in fact, was even more inimical to true religion than superstition itself. Buckeridge took up the point, praising the Elizabethan reformers for not founding a new church but merely restoring the old 'to her ancient purity'; rather than flying from 'one extreme to another', 'from superstition to profaneness' they had preserved a 'golden mean', neither retaining 'all ceremonies, lest religion might seem to be nothing else but external pomp and gesticulation' nor 'rejecting all, lest religion, having lost all external majesty, might appear naked and soon decay at the heart'.[13]

Andrewes's indictment of his contemporaries did not end with the delineation of a certain style of piety or pattern of religious irreverence; it expanded to take in the political sphere as well since the religious attitudes outlined above had, for Andrewes, directly secular effects. For Andrewes the concepts of popularity, hypocrisy and presumption provided the connection between these two spheres. Thus puritan hypocrisy was linked directly to popularity. 'There is no animal so ambitious, no chameleon so pants after air, as doth the hypocrite after popular praise; for it he fasts, and so hungry and thirsty he is after it as you shall hear him even beg for it . . . hypocrisy is ever popular . . . to be magnified up and down the peoples' mouth, that is even the consummatum est of all this stage devotion.' Yet this same drive for popular praise and support was at the bottom of puritan non-conformity and for Andrewes it led straight to popular sedition and rebellion. 'Why should any love to be "contentious"?' asked Andrewes, 'Why? It is the way to be somebody. In time of peace, what reckoning is there of Wat Tyler, or Jack Straw? Make a sedition, and they will bear a brain with the best . . . This makes we shall never want contentious persons, and they will take order we shall never want contentions.' For Andrewes, of course, popularity was also a central feature of Presbyterianism.[14]

Not only hypocrisy and popularity, but also presumption and irreverence were at the heart of the political threat presented by puritanism. Andrewes identified presumption as a crucial feature of his opponents' attitude to predestination and assurance. He now extended this diagnosis to include the tendency to encroach on the prerogatives and private affairs of kings. Buckeridge and Andrewes both compared reverence in the presence of God in church to reverence to the person of the prince, implying irreverence in one sphere would inevitably lead to irreverence in the other.[15] Thus in one passage Andrewes extended the injunction *noli me tangere* not only to include God and the things that were God's but also kings and their 'affairs and secrets of state' 'points too high, too wonderful for us to deal with'. In the paragraph immediately following that passage Andrewes proceeded to associate this sort of presumption against kings with the presumption that led to rationalist speculation about the divine decree. The need for reverence transcended the first of the 'king's two bodies' and encompassed the king's state, family and affairs. After all, Andrewes asked, 'is there no touch but that of the violent hand? The virulent tongue, doth not that touch too? And the pestilent pen, as ill as both . . . Yes, they be Satan's weapons, both tongues and pens have their points and their edges and . . . cut like a razor'. For Andrewes the barking of such detractors was tantamount to sedition. 'For they that in the end prove to be seditious, mark them well, they be first detractors . . . "Meddle not" with these detractors.' Meddling like sedition was, for Andrewes, 'a sin of presumption' and as such 'destructory, a destroying sin' for those guilty of it. Nor was there any doubt in Andrewes's mind who were the arch meddlers and detractors of the day – they were the puritans. It was they who, mistaking the promptings of their own spirit for those of the Holy Ghost, were 'ever mending churches, states, superiors – mending all, save themselves.' So bad had things become, Andrewes lamented in 1610, that every 'tongue is walking and every pen busy, to touch them and their rights which they are to have, and their duties they are to do'. In front of the jabbering multitude the puritan preachers preened themselves, 'men indeed of tumultuous spirits, but in show zealous preservers of the peoples' liberties', taking every opportunity to attack and insult over the rights of princes.[16]

On this subject Andrewes allowed himself one of his few directly topical references, remarking in 1616 that 'marriage matters' particularly those involving 'a queen of a contrary religion' were often the occasion for men to 'grow godly on a sudden and wax very zealous as the fashion is' all the while using the issue as an occasion 'to serve many purposes'. The allusion here to the fuss over the Spanish match was clear; and in that convulsion of popular religious prejudice orchestrated by puritan ministers through the pulpit and press Andrewes had the perfect example of puritan populist presumption. Moreover the height of the agitation over the match coincided with the English reverberations of the synod of Dort. Andrewes's most explicit denunciations of predestinarian presumption date from 1619 and 1621 respectively. They help to show us how, for Andrewes, the presumption and irreverence in predestinarian speculation were linked to puritan populist sedition. Indeed, in one typical aside Andrewes made the association between predestinarian theology and subversion even more explicit, denouncing in 1616 those who held that 'one that is not in state of grace can have no right to any possession or place. For they of right belong to none, but to the true children of God; that is, to none but themselves.'[17]

It is time now to turn away from what Andrewes hated and to look at what he liked. Against the drily intellectual definition of faith as knowledge allegedly canvassed by his contemporaries Andrewes juxtaposed a practical knowledge of Christ. According to Andrewes 'the perfection of our knowledge is Christ'. 'For as from the brazen serpent no virtue issued to heal but unto them that steadily beheld it, so neither doth there from Christ but upon those that with the eye of faith have their contemplation on this object; who thereby draw life from him, and without it may and do perish for all Christ and his passion.' Here Andrewes placed especial stress on Christ crucified, for if the perfection of our knowledge was Christ then the 'perfection of our knowledge in touching Christ is the knowledge of his cross and passion'. It was important that we should look at Christ on the cross because we would see there first a picture of our own sins, for it was our sins which were directly responsible for his death. Secondly, we would see painted in equally vivid colours, indeed carved in the wounds of his side and hands, Christ's love for us. The effects of this sight in us should be repentance and sorrow for sin, a desire for amendment of life and a love for Christ who had suffered so on our entirely undeserving behalf.[18] From Christ on the cross Andrewes then turned to Christ rising from the tomb, harrowing hell, and triumphing there over death. Just as Christ rose from the tomb so should we rise from the grave of sin and produce good works. Lastly Andrewes presented to his audience Christ endowing the apostles with the gifts of the spirit at Whitsun. This referred us to the gifts of the spirit available to us in and through the visible church. Whitsun, as the baptismal day of the church, reminded us that we must account on the last day for the spiritual gifts wrought in us by Christ through the Holy Ghost.[19]

This heavily Christocentric approach to the problem of Christian knowledge was clearly intended by Andrewes as a stark contrast to what he saw as the empty predestinarian theorizing, the formal theological speculation which passed amongst too many of his contemporaries for faith. Direct apprehension of the physicality of Christ's sufferings and of the awesome power of his rising should have directly practical effects in the believer. It should induce not merely right opinion, but also a structured progression of feelings, leading the individual toward repentance, amendment of life and the consequent production of good works. Andrewes was insistent on this point; it was a huge mistake to maintain, as some did, that 'our conversion' should be 'conceived as a turning of the brain only'. 'Take heed of this error, as if repentance were a matter merely mental or intentional. It is not good notions in the brain, nor good motions in the mind will serve, these are but the sap within; look to the branches, what see you there? Look to *proferte*, what is brought forth.' Buckeridge agreed; 'faith comes by hearing, but faith, hope and charity, justice and religion, are not hearing, but the fruits of hearing'. Andrewes compared repentance to a tree; just 'as the fruit of the forbidden tree had envenomed our nature, the fruit of this tree to expell it, to recover and cure us of it'. Thus it was the fruits of repentance that mattered, it was they which were 'medicinable, of the nature of counter poison', and, of course, the fruits of repentance were good works; works which Andrewes listed as '1. the works of devotion, as prayer; 2. works of chastisement of the body, as fasting; 3. works of mercy as alms.' Buckeridge, too, held that we should offer ourselves to God as sacrifices of 'humility of soul', 'humiliation of body' and alms for the poor. 'There by these fruits here, and by these fruits only, all shall go, for none is in heaven but by it. Sinners both they in heaven and they in hell; only this difference, they in heaven had these fruits, they in hell had them not. And then seeing they will be then all in all, *proferte fructus igitur.*'[20]

But if his insistence on the need for a practical knowledge of Christ crucified, rather than a merely theoretical knowledge of a corpus of right doctrine enabled Andrewes to emphasize the need for repentance and good works, it was also through this Christocentric approach that he was able to distance himself from the doctrines of merit and free will. For however essential for salvation good works might be Andrewes went out of his way to emphasize that, as he put it, our best righteousness was the moral equivalent of a menstruous cloth. It was only in and through Christ that our works were able 'to please God'. This was true in two senses. To begin with whatever virtues we might be able to claim were not moral habits rooted in our own nature, but spiritual gifts infused into us from outside; gifts which took their value from their source, the Holy Ghost and not from us. Moreover, even having received the gifts of the spirit we were still unable to obey the law sufficiently to win salvation by our own merits. It was only the law mitigated 'in the hands of the mediator' (Christ) that even men regenerated by the spirit could hope to keep. Andrewes here distinguished between inherent and imputed righteousness to explain his position. To be saved all had to be able to lay claim to inherent righteousness, which Andrewes defined as 'righteousness done', in other words righteous acts actually performed by the individual believer. Yet before the judgement seat of God 'righteousness in that sense will not abide the trial'. There we needed the perfect righteousness of Christ to be imputed to us if the scales of divine justice were to be tipped in our favour.[21]

Such statements left no room for any hint of merit or desert in our dealings with God. For while God would accept our works in Christ there was no sense in which he was bound to do so. 'If he would, he might refuse; and that he doth not, it is but of his mere goodness; all are but accepted.' 'God counts them worthy and his so counting them makes them worthy; makes them so, for so they are not of themselves, or without it, but by it so they are. His taking our works of righteousness well in worth, is their worth.' Buckeridge agreed; our sacrifices of praise, fasting and alms were acceptable to God only in and through Christ, and as far as Buckeridge was concerned that undercut all popish notions of merit. The resulting position allowed both men to strike what they took to be a balance between the two extremes of presumption and desperation. To avoid presumption Andrewes administered a healthy dose of the law, as an antidote to the excessive servings of the gospel dished out by his contemporaries. For 'gospel it how we will, if the gospel hath not the legalia of it acknowledged, allowed and preserved to it; if once it loose the force and vigour of a law, it is a sign it declines, it grows weak and unprofitable, and that is a sign it will not long last'. The law thus preached by the clergy was internalized by the laity as 'fear'. Since faith had a natural tendency 'of itself to take an unkind heat' (that is to engender too blithe or enthusiastic an assurance of salvation) such fear, far from being a bad thing, had been 'by God ordained' to 'cool' faith 'and keep it in temper, to awake our care still and see it sleep not in security'.[22]

However, since even the regenerate could not hope fully to keep the law, too much law in the pulpit produced desperation, or, in Andrewes's phrase, 'too much terror'. Conversely, its opposite, a diet composed entirely of the gospel led to 'too much security'. We should, therefore, not 'only love him [God] as a father but fear him as our lord and king. And this mixture shall keep us in the way of salvation, we shall neither too much despair, nor presume of his goodness.' True faith was thus to be found mid-way between distrust and presumption. For Buckeridge, too, true faith was a mean between overweening, pharisaical, assurance, on the one hand, and desperation, on the other. Only by maintaining a balance between a joyful praise of God's mercy and goodness and a tearful apprehension of our own sinful inadequacies could we be driven up 'the ladder of practise' which alone led from baptism to salvation. This was the 'ordinary means' to salvation and paradoxically it was only by espousing it that one could gain a genuine sense of assurance.[23]

Now it could reasonably be observed here that having made such a fuss about the puritans' presumptuous obsession with assurance and security Andrewes had in fact ended up precisely where Dr Kendall's experimental predestinarians ended up – with a secure sense of assurance based on the godliness of their own conversation.[24] But the crucial point for any proper understanding of Andrewes's thought is that he worked out his position in conscious contradistinction to what he took to be the coldly intellectualist view of faith, the aridly predestinarian style of divinity, the presumptuous security and hypocritical subjectivity of many of his contemporaries. Now the resulting image of Calvinist piety can hardly be accepted as an objective description of contemporary evangelical Calvinist or moderate puritan belief and practice. It was a caricature cobbled together for polemical purposes. Like all caricatures it only worked because it resembled reality. However, the question of just how good or bad the likeness was is neither here nor there for my present purpose. What does seem certain is that Andrewes's loathing of the trends and tendencies thus caricatured was a major determinant in the construction of his own position. Thus even here where he seemed at his closest to the Calvinists his dislike of their hypocritical subjectivism led him to conclusions very different from theirs about the path to true assurance. Arguing that repentance could only be known from its fruits Andrewes denied that individual Christians should be left alone to determine which penitential acts best suited their particular sins. That was a task best left to the clergy. Elsewhere he went on to develop this notion into a full-blown doctrine of priestly absolution.[25]

We can best see how far Andrewes's practical, Christocentric approach drove him from conventional Jacobean Protestantism in his view of the interrelationship between the word, prayer and the sacrament in the public worship of God. To start with Andrewes's attitude to the word, he could, when it suited him, talk of preaching in the most exalted language. As Andrewes remarked since God 'saves not any but those he teaches' and preaching was the means by which he taught us, preaching was essential to salvation. 'There is a door shut, this is the key; no opening, no entrance without it, none at all. For . . . how can they possibly be saved, except they call upon God; or call upon him except they hear.' 'Twenty times in the gospel is the preaching of the word called the kingdom of heaven, as a special means to bring us thither.' Andrewes was able to combine this very exalted vision of the role of the word preached with his earlier denunciations of the sermon-centred piety of his contemporaries because while he held knowledge to be essential for salvation, the things it was necessary to know were neither very numerous nor difficult to grasp. The current obsession with points of doubt and difficulty was therefore completely misguided. It led, Andrewes claimed, to the notion that 'the points of religion that be manifest' were 'certain petty points, scarce worth the hearing. Those – yea those be great, and none but those, that have great disputes about them.' That was completely wrong. 'Those [points] that are necessary he [God] hath made plain; those that are not plain, not necessary.' Preachers ought therefore not to concentrate on increasing the knowledge of their flocks, continually introducing them to new and more complex doctrinal cruxes, they should rather act as 'the Lord's remembrancers', occupied as much in 'calling to their minds the things they know and have forgot, as in teaching them the things they know not, or never learnt'. They should, in short, spend their time, as Andrewes did in many of his court sermons, in presenting the figure of Christ as an object of faith, adoration and emulation.[26]

Preaching then might provide us with the key of knowledge, with Christ as an object of faith and emulation, without which no one could be saved but that was scarcely the end of the matter. In fact, it was only the beginning of a true profession of Christianity. After all, the whole point of hearing the word was to purge us of sin and enable us to lead a godly life and the word alone could perform neither of those tasks. As Andrewes observed, 'prophets spake but purged not. Purging was ever the priests office.' It was true that the word did have a 'mundifying virtue . . . but, not that only, or principally. For medicine which purgeth ex proprietate, his flesh and blood go to it.' Buckeridge, too, stressed that present in the sacrament was not 'somewhat of God, but God himself, to whom it is proper to be the physician and the physic, the food and the feeder of our souls'. 'By the force and effect of this sacrament we receive power against sin and Satan and ability to serve God, in holiness and righteousness, and the neglect thereof giveth advantage to our spiritual enemies, whereby we are entangled in many temptations and fall into many sins.' Thus, while the word might convince us of the need to believe in Christ, to repent and lead a good life, it was only through the medicine of the sacrament that we could be purged of sin and receive the enabling grace essential if we were indeed to live the life of a Christian.[27]

124

Preaching appealed through the sense of hearing to the mind. It was, therefore, entirely dependent for its efficacy on the attention of the hearers. Andrewes saw the hand of Satan in the contemporary tendency to put all the service of God onto preaching since this was the one ordinance in divine worship which reduced all the participants, save the preacher, to passivity and depended entirely on the attention and mental acuity of its recipients. Even when a sermon was listened to its effects, while they might be intense, were also likely to be short-lived. The effects of the sacrament, Andrewes observed, 'are permanent, and stick by us'. They did so because they appealed to senses rather more basic and less cerebral than the sermon. In the sacrament, wrote Andrewes,

there we taste, and there we see; 'taste and see how gracious the lord is.' There we are made to 'drink of the spirit', there our 'hearts are strengthened and stablished with grace.' There is the blood which shall 'purge our consciences from dead works', whereby we may die to sin. There the bread of God, which shall endue our souls with much strength; yea, multiply strength in them, to live unto God; yea, to live to him continually; for he that 'eateth his flesh and drinketh his blood, dwelleth in Christ and Christ in him'; not inneth, or sojourneth for a time, but dwelleth continually. And, never can we more truly, or properly say, in Christo Jesu domino nostro, as when we come new from that holy action, for then he is in us and we in him, indeed.

Buckeridge, too, saw the sacraments as 'the channels and conduits wherein God's mercies and graces do run and are conveyed to us'. At communion we were 'more nearly conjoined to God, and participate most of his graces' more intensely than at any other time in our lives. For Andrewes while preaching, in appealing to the ear and the mind, could be called the 'outward means' to bring us to God, the sacrament, because of its ability to penetrate directly within us, could be called the 'inward means', able directly to affect and operate on both 'the understanding part' and 'the seat of the affections'.[28]

Preaching, while thus complemented and completed by the sacrament, was also similarly aided by prayer. Prayer along with the word and sacraments was, according to Andrewes, a divinely ordained 'artery to convey the spirit unto us' it was 'the conduit or bucket of grace'. It was the means by which we expressed our desire to draw Christ in 'which very attraction or desire hath a promise by the mouth of our saviour Christ himself, that his heavenly father will give the Holy Ghost . . . "to them that will make petition, seek and sue, open their mouth and pray for it".' Thus like the sacrament prayer was a source of enabling grace.[29]

Prayer was, therefore, the natural accomplice of preaching. Together they formed a two-way street linking God to man and man to God, 'the one prophecy, being God's tongue to us, the other, invocation, being our tongue to God . . . prophecy breaths it [the spirit] unto us, prayer breaths it out again . . . prophecy doth infuse, pour in at the ear, invocation doth refundere, or "pour back again" in prayer, out of the heart.' Ministers should therefore discharge the duty of angels, not only descending to earth from heaven to teach the people the will of God but also ascending from earth to heaven 'to make intercession for the people' via prayer.[30] While the prayers of the priest had a peculiar efficacy due to his divinely ordained role as intercessor or mediator for his flock,[31] the laity also had to pray and thus public prayer gave them an active role, one unavailable to them in preaching. 'It is the oratory of prayer poured out of our hearts shall save us, no less than the oratory of preaching poured in at our ears', concluded Andrewes. This being so Andrewes then advanced the argument that far from being merely equal to preaching public prayer was the end for which preaching was but the means. Certainly a sterile cycle of preaching pursued for its own sake led nowhere; prayer was 'the higher end; the calling on us by prophesy is but that we should call on the name of the lord. All prophesying, all preaching is but to this end.' John Buckeridge made the same point when he observed that 'reading and preaching are *doctrinam cultus*, not *cultus ipse*, the doctrine that teacheth and the way that leadeth to God's worship but not properly the worship itself. For worship offereth and sendeth somewhat upward to God and these do only bring somewhat downward from God to us and serve to feed the understanding and stirr up the affection.'[32]

This 'sacrificial' aspect of worship united both prayer and the sacrament and set them apart from and indeed above preaching in the public worship of God. At a sermon 'God rather serveth us and attends us and entreats us by his ministers' but at prayer we served God. For Andrewes prayer represented our 'reasonable service of God, because we do therein acknowledge not only our own wants and unworthiness, but also that as God hath in his hands all manner of blessings to bestow upon us, if we sue to him for them "he will withold no good thing" from us'. Prayer was, therefore the ultimate acknowledgement of human unworthiness and impotence and of divine power and beneficence. As such it could not but stand at the centre of divine worship. For Buckeridge, 'there can be no act of divine worship and religion without prayer'; since 'prayer offereth up and tendereth the worship itself unto God'. The set 'liturgies and forms of divine worship' of the primitive church bore 'the names some of the apostles, others of the ancient fathers' and were by all men's confession 'very ancient'. It was, therefore, as Andrewes observed, no accident that in the church of England, as well as amongst the Greeks and Hebrews, the term prayer had come to stand for the whole of divine service and no accident that God himself called his church 'a house of prayer'.[33]

Both Andrewes and Buckeridge extended this argument about prayer's superiority over the sermon as a form of worship to the sacrament. Buckeridge developed the point to its fullest extent in a full-blown doctrine of eucharistic sacrifice. For Buckeridge 'the sacrament is a part of God's worship not as

126

reading or meditation is but as prayer, and the like, which properly offer divine adoration unto God. For why? The sacrament is a visible sign of an invisible grace; in which, as God offereth to us his son in his death and passion, and the graces of the Holy Spirit, so we offer to him ourselves.' As baptism 'doth regenerate and consecrate us to God' so

the eucharist doth offer us up in sacrifice to him. And this sacrament may better be called an act of religion or piety than the sacrifice of the Lord's passover, since that was typus agni paschalis, a type of the paschal lamb, and here are offered . . . the members of the paschal lamb. And this offering up of ourselves to him is indeed the true and daily sacrifice of the Christian church, which, being the mystical body of Christ, cannot offer Christ's natural body, which Christ offered once for all upon the cross, but offereth his mystical body, that is herself, by Christ her high priest and head, unto God.

Prayer too offered up a sacrifice to God of 'praise and thanks' but the greatest such sacrifice was, for Buckeridge, 'the eucharist in which we chiefly praise and thank God for this his chief and great blessing of redemption'.[34]

Such a vision picked up and developed Andrewes's insistence on the works of repentance as sacrifices offered to God for our sins – our bodies offered through acts of amendment and self punishment like fasting, our substance offered through the giving of alms to the church and to the poor and our souls offered through the works of religion like prayer. All these now came together in the sacrifice of the eucharist, a sacrifice which, Buckeridge emphasized, must take place not on a table but on an altar.[35]

For both Andrewes and Buckeridge the upward traffic of praise and thanksgiving contained in prayer and the downward traffic of instruction and exhortation contained in preaching came together in the sacrament. Here the downward trickle of divine grace, whereby we were gradually incorporated into Christ – as wax was melted into a candle[36] – and into one another, was answered by the daily sacrifice of ourselves in praise and thanksgiving for the benefits thus conferred. It was this vision of the mystical body of Christ gradually growing in both size and purity through the process of self-consumption in the sacrament that stood at the very heart of Andrewes's and Buckeridge's vision of true religion. According to Andrewes and Buckeridge the sacrament was the 'food of angels'. Since it was a preparative for our final union with God in Christ, the moment when we received the sacrament represented the closest that we could approach to that union in this life. Buckeridge quoted Chrysostom in the same vein.

At that time (the time of the consecration of the sacrament) the angels stand by the priest and the universal order of the heavenly powers do raise up cries and the place near the altar is filled with the choirs of angels in the honour of him that is immolated . . . While thou beholdest the lord offered up and the priest sacrificing and the present multitude to be dipped and made red with that precious blood dost thou think that thou dost converse among mortal men on earth? Or rather that thou art suddenly translated into heaven.

Some of the passages quoted above concerning the sacrament might be taken to be congruent with the Prayer Book, which saw the sacrament as a sacrifice, albeit only as one of praise. Indeed, Buckeridge sometimes went out of his way to stress that the sacrament was a sacrifice only of prayer, praise and contrition, a sacrifice undertaken by Christ's mystical body, the church, of itself to God, not a repetition of the unique sacrifice of Christ's natural body on the cross.[37] However, it is not at all clear that the same could realistically be claimed for passages like this one from Chrysostom. Of course, Buckeridge was 'only quoting' Chrysostom, just as he similarly quoted other fathers in the same vein, on the same subject. If challenged, he could always use his own more moderate formulations to undercut the thrust of the somewhat literal and bloody patristic outpourings about the sacrifice of Christ in the eucharist, with which he had studded his text. Of course, the very ambiguity (and defensibility) of the resulting position was the whole point. We are, perhaps, dealing here with a divinity of plausible deniability.

In any event there can be no doubt that the sacrament stood at the very centre of Andrewes's and Buckeridge's piety. Here was the place where Christ as the head of his mystical body, the church, was most immediately and efficaciously present to the members of that church. As such it represents the acme of Andrewes's and Buckeridge's general view of the visible church as a holy or sacred institution both containing and showing forth the saving presence of God to a sinful humanity. Here the church militant and the church triumphant met in the real presence of Christ, their common head, in the sacrament. It was this vision of the presence of God in his church that under-lay the last crucial feature of their style of divinity which I want to discuss – their insistence on what might be called the beauty of holiness, a reverent, ceremonious and uniform public worship of God.

Here again we return to Andrewes's and Buckeridge's insistence that religion was not a thing of the mind or spirit alone. Buckeridge claimed that outward bodily reverence both expressed and helped to form or create internal spiritual reverence. Soul and body were joined in 'mutual excitation; for the soul doth always excite the body as the musician strikes the instrument and the body doth sometimes call home and awaken the soul that wandereth and is heavy in the service of God . . . ' Just as bodily creatures needed out-ward means and symbols (like the sacrament) through which God's grace could be imparted to us, so we had to give immediate physical expression to our reverence toward God.

He will not have the inward parts only, and it skills not for the outward members, though we favour our knees and lock up our lips. No, mental devotion will not serve,

128

he will have both corporal and vocal to express it by. Our body is to afford her part, to his glory; and the parts of our body, and namely, these two, the knee and the tongue. Not only the upper parts, the tongue in our head, but even the nether also, the knee in our leg.

Thus prayer should be merely mental or silent; 'as we ourselves have not only a soul but a body also, so our prayer must have a body; "our tongue must be the pen of a ready writer". We must at the time of prayer bow our knees, as our saviour Christ did. We must "lift up our hearts with our hands". Our eyes must be lifted up to God "that dwelleth in the heaven". And as David says all our "bones" must be exercised in prayer.' Buckeridge agreed that kneeling was the appropriate gesture for prayer since it was 'the gesture of suitors and petitioners that desire to receive, and of those that offer and desire to be received and accepted at God's hand'.[38]

The same arguments made kneeling the proper gesture with which to receive the sacrament. Kneeling was also necessary in order to give outward expression to our fear and reverence in the presence of God, which presence, although it was suffused throughout the world, was of course most obvious and intense in the church. 'His presence is his tabernacle, or his temple, the place which he hath chosen to dwell in.' But if God was present in his church he was most present in the sacrament. Buckeridge observed,

When God appeared to Jacob at Bethel, Jacob said, surely God is in this place and I knew it not . . . This is none other but domus dei and porta coeli, the house of God and the gate of heaven, and God calleth himself the God of Bethel. But this mystery goes further; it is not domus, but mensa dei, not the house only, but the table of God, not porta, but cibus coeli, not the gate only, but the food of heaven; yea, Christ that is God and man, is here offered and received, and therefore as that was a locus terribilis, a dreadful place, so this is actio terribilis, an action, not of familiarity, which breeds presumption and presumption begets contempt, but of dread and reverence and therefore to be undertaken with all devotion of soul and humiliation and kneeling of body.[39]

Outward ceremony was not only a means to express reverence before the presence of God in his church, it was also a means to ensure the continuation of that presence through the outward demonstration of the church's unity. It was, Andrewes observed, only natural that the Holy Spirit – the very element of unity and love both between the persons of the Trinity and between God and man – should be attracted by unity and repelled by its absence. And for Andrewes it was, of course, axiomatic that such unity should take an outward physical as well as an inward spiritual form. We should be

not only 'of one mind', that is, unanimity but also 'in one place' too, that is, uniformity. Both in 'the unity of the spirit', that is, inward and 'in the bond of peace', that is, outward . . . God's will is, we should be, as upon one foundation, so under one roof; that is his doing . . . For say what you will, division of places will not long be without division of minds. This must be our ground. The same spirit, that loveth unanimity, loveth uniformity; unity even in matter of circumstance, in matter of place. Thus the church was begun, thus it must be continued.[40]

So great an emphasis did Buckeridge place on outward ceremony and reverence that he denied that the ceremony of kneeling was in itself a matter of indifference, rendered necessary by the authority of the church. For him it was 'a duty or part of God's worship, not to be omitted in solemn and public adoration but in case of evident necessity'. Andrewes did not go quite that far but it is clear from what has been said already that his defence of outward reverence and uniformity in general and of ceremonies such as kneeling in particular transcended the claim that they represented a legitimate use of a lawful authority over things in themselves indifferent. He tried to ground the practice of bowing at the name of Jesus directly on the authority of scripture and supported the practice of kneeling by citing the psalms as well as the prayer book and the perpetual practice of the church. Moreover, Buckeridge used a doctrine of immemorial custom to collapse the traditions of the church on kneeling into the practice of the apostles, arguing that since the earliest patristic references to kneeling called it a custom its origins must needs stretch beyond the fathers 'and take beginning from the apostles or succeeding apostolical men'.[41] Here the tendency to claim the aura of scriptural or apostolic authority for central features of the ecclesiastical status quo which, on the issues of episcopacy and tithes, conformists had already taken over from the Presbyterians, was being applied to the ceremonies of the church as well. In the process the area of genuine *adiaphora* was being greatly reduced and the room for compromise or cordial disagreement between moderate puritans and conformists of the sort which typified the Jacobean church in the localities was shrinking away almost to nothing.[42]

More generally the Christocentric orientation of both men's divinity served to confer renewed meaning and significance on the great feasts of the church; for Andrewes, the progress of Christ from 'the cratch to the cross' and of the liturgical year from Christmas to Whitsun mirrored the spiritual progress of the individual to a true profession of Christianity. Each feast thus became an occasion for meditation on the figure of Christ at a distinct stage of his spiritual journey and an example of Christ's immanent presence within his mystical body the church, a presence both enhanced and shown forth by the reception of the sacrament with which, Andrewes insisted, each of the great Christian festivals should be celebrated. Finally, the whole thrust of his style of piety, toward the sacraments and public prayer and away from an obsession with sermons, served to confer an enhanced value on the ordinary observances of the English church and in turn to cast an even deeper shadow of opprobrium on those who neglected, omitted or still worse criticized or denounced those rites and observances.

We have, therefore, in the piety of Andrewes and Buckeridge the necessary link in the chain of avant-garde conformist thought which runs between Hooker and Laud. In Andrewes's view of the undesirable, divisive and subversive elements and tendencies within English Protestantism we have an almost perfect replication of that identification of Calvinism with puritanism and of puritanism with Presbyterianism, popularity and subversion which figured so prominently in the works of Richard Montague. In Andrewes's and Buckeridge's insistence that Christ died for everyone, that in the sacraments all were offered potentially saving grace, in their emphasis on the need for repentance and the works of amendment, their rejection of what they took to be the carnal security and presumption inherent in Calvinist notions of assurance nearly all the necessary elements were assembled for a full-scale Arminian critique of Calvinist doctrine on the issue of predestination. Finally, in their insistence on the central role of the sacrament and public prayer in the worship of God, their intense concern with external uniformity and the beauty of holiness and their revaluation of the value and significance of the traditional feasts of the church they prefigured many of the central policies of the Caroline church.

However, it is important at this point not to get too carried away. Lancelot Andrewes was not Richard Montague or William Laud. While his court sermons can indeed be cited to demonstrate a continuous avant-garde conformist tradition linking Hooker with Laud, they do not demonstrate that the policies of the 1630s were not novel or that the Arminian takeover of the church in the 1620s was an optical illusion or a puritan invention. In Andrewes's sermons all the major ingredients of the puritan plot against all order and authority described by Richard Montague and any number of pamphleteers during the 1630s may have been present but Andrewes himself did not assemble them into such an image. He scarcely used the term puritan and many of the passages cited in the first part of this essay occurred not in concentrated bursts of anti-puritan rant but were scattered widely throughout the corpus of his writings. Similarly, while all the necessary elements for an Arminian assault on Calvinist predestinarianism were present in Andrewes's sermons, once again they are scattered here and there. Andrewes himself never produced such a concentrated critique. Such a critique can be drawn, by implication, out of many of his statements, just as the conceptual linkages between his different religious dislikes can be analysed to reveal not merely a shopping list of isolated hatreds and aversions but a unitary vision of religious deviance best labelled puritan. The fact still remains that, however great the conceptual, linguistic and logical connections between these disparate passages of doctrinal and political criticism, Andrewes himself never drew them together. Indeed, when he indulged in public, indeed in royally sponsored, works of

131

polemic against the papists he denied that puritans, whom he identified with Presbyterians, were of a different religious or doctrinal persuasion from mainstream Protestants or that they refused to acknowledge the royal supremacy – someone defending the head of the English and Scottish churches could hardly do less.[43] When performing virtually in the royal name and certainly under the royal nose Andrewes did not fluff his lines. Nor were the vast majority of his sermons even published in his lifetime. It is similarly true that, as Ken Fincham has shown, however close Andrewes's opinions were to the informing principles behind the policies of the personal rule, in none of the dioceses where he was bishop did he pursue either a draconian campaign against puritan nonconformity or seek to enforce anything resembling the altar policy of the 1630s.[44]

Why not? It might be argued that the answer should be sought in Andrewes's character. Andrewes, it might be said, was a man chronically devoid both of political sense and gumption, unwilling to take the necessary risks to fight for what he believed in. It is certainly true that Andrewes had precisely such a reputation amongst his contemporaries.[45] However, there was surely more to it than that. Men like Andrewes and Buckeridge certainly gained access to the very heart of the ecclesiastical and secular establishments under James I. Moreover, as this chapter has shown, once established at court, they felt able to give expression to their singular religious opinions and preferences. But they could only do so within certain political and ideological limits laid down by the king.[46] Of these the most obvious was the tacit, and at times explicit, injunction not openly to attack the substance of Calvinist doctrine on predestination nor to spread overtly Arminian opinions on that subject. Since, as we have seen, the rationalist analysis of controversial or controverted doctrines, particularly predestination, was not high on Andrewes's list of religious priorities, that limitation may have meant more to his Calvinist contemporaries than it did to him. More seriously, the balance of forces within the Jacobean church meant that men like Andrewes and Buckeridge could not turn their theoretical opinions and preferences into practical policy without stirring up a storm of protest and, in order to face down that protest, they needed the personal backing and authority of the king, which was something upon which they could not rely. Buckeridge almost admitted as much in print when, having threatened the 'sectaries, separatists and refractories' who refused to observe the ceremonies of the church with the 'severity of laws', he had to concede somewhat wistfully that James was 'another Moses, meek and mild above all the men that are upon the face of the earth'. Given what Buckeridge almost certainly wanted to do to the puritans that was probably not the egregiously flattering remark it might at first appear to have been. Likewise, Andrewes's last sermon before the king, preached at Christmas 1624, can be construed as simply another attack on the lax, gospel-based style of piety that Andrewes lambasted so often in his sermons. But it can also be read as a sidelong critique of the lack of discipline and decent uniformity in the Jacobean church; 'the reverend regard, the legal rigour and power, the penalties of it are not set by. The rules – no reckoning made of them as of law writs, none, but only as of physic bills; if you like them you may use them, if not lay them by. And this comes of drowning the term "law". And all for lack of praedicabo legem.'[47] It is, perhaps, not too hard to see in this the outlines of the Jacobean church as Dr Fincham and Professor Collinson have described it, only viewed here from a rather more astringently conformist perspective than that adopted in their work.[48]

However, in the absence of a royal green light, Andrewes and Buckeridge were left to snipe at their adversaries, if not from the side lines, then at least not quite from the centre of power. Andrewes's sermons show conclusively that throughout his reign James had available to him a vision of the church, very different from that proffered by the likes of George Abbot and James Montague. Andrewes's vision amounted to a rather pointed critique of the sort of church which the king had allowed the balance of forces at court and in the country to produce. James might like listening to Andrewes and allow him his shafts of sarcasm and polemical, anti-puritan and anti-Calvinist aggression, but until the 1622 instructions to preachers Andrewes had precious little in the way of practical achievements to show for all his eminence as a court preacher. James clearly knew what sort of church Andrewes and Buckeridge wanted and was prepared to listen to them talk about it for hours on end, but he was not prepared to act on their advice.

In consequence, they had to wait on events to push royal policy in directions more congenial to them than to their enemies at court. In part, at least, that was what the sermons discussed here were trying to do. Buckeridge's sermon and treatise on kneeling were preached and printed in 1617 in an attempt to take advantage of the articles of Perth and the king's forthcoming showdown with Scots Presbyterianism. The sermon even contained a hint on the advantages of religious uniformity between the two kingdoms which looks forward to the disastrous policy pursued by Charles and Laud in the 1630s.[49] Similarly, as we have seen, Andrewes responded when and as he could both to the threat posed by Dort to the balance of religious forces in England and to the furore over the Spanish match. Both men did what they could, within the limits placed upon them by James and the influence of their enemies at court. As Ken Fincham and I have argued,[50] it was a strategy that ultimately paid off handsomely during the 1620s. It would, however, take a combination of the crisis over the match, the bravery or ambition of Richard Montague and the genuine religious convictions of Charles I to do the job properly. In the meantime, it is reasonable to conclude that Andrewes and Buckeridge had done the best they could to keep the avant-garde conformist cause alive at the court of James I.

ROBERT CECIL AND THE
EARLY JACOBEAN COURT

Pauline Croft

In April 1601 King James VI of Scotland faced a major crisis in his carefully planned strategy to ensure his succession to the English throne. He had placed his hopes of English support in his chief contact and informant, the Earl of Essex, but in February 1601 Essex staged a crazily incoherent rising in London which collapsed within twenty-four hours. On 8 April, James briefed his envoys now that matters had changed so much for the worse. Not only had he lost his ally Essex, he had begun to fear that other worrying developments south of the border could complicate matters even further. Although the run of appalling harvests that had plagued the 1590s had ended, England was still suffering from all the pressures of war, high food prices and population growth. James was concerned by what he saw as a growing disaffection between 'the Queen and the people', a rising popular distaste for 'the present rulers in the Court'. Although the king was by far her most likely heir, Elizabeth had never confirmed the Stuart succession and any discussion of it was banned as treason. In the new situation it was imperative that he should increase support for his claim among the Privy Council. Of these 'her principal guiders', there was one above all whose attitude concerned James. This was Robert Cecil, Secretary of State and Master of the Wards, whom James described as 'king there in effect', particularly now that Essex, his only possible rival, faced the block.[1] If the King of Scots wished to succeed Elizabeth he somehow had to come to terms with the man who effectively ruled England. James's trump card was his blood right as the only remaining male heir of Henry VII; Cecil's was the power to bring about the transition smoothly, to the great benefit of both kingdoms. Each man needed the other, and in May 1601, Robert Cecil took his career, perhaps even his life, in his hands and joined in the secret correspondence with James which had already been initiated by Lord Henry Howard and others. Rapidly the king's earlier

134

hostile tone moderated and he was soon describing Cecil as 'so worthy, so wise and so provident a friend', assuring him moreover that such praise was not merely 'Italian complementoes'. On 24 March 1603, it was Cecil who read out the proclamation both at Whitehall and in the city of London announcing the king's accession. From Edinburgh, on learning of the queen's death, James at once sent Cecil an informal interim ratification of the position of all Elizabeth's Council, adding in his own hand 'How happy I think myself by the conquest of so wise a counsellor I reserve it to be expressed out of my own mouth unto you.'[2]

The king's gratitude was genuine, and on Cecil's side the relief at James's trouble-free arrival in England was immense. Years later, without the slightest sense of incongruity, he could refer to it as comparable to the nativity of Christ. The engineering of a peaceful succession, after all the fears and uncertainties of the 1590s, was to remain a strong personal bond between them, and it must count as their greatest joint achievement. But the relationship between the king and the secretary, who finally met face to face at York in April 1603 on James's journey south, would inevitably generate problems. In the later years of Elizabeth's reign, Cecil had been by far the most influential member of the Privy Council and the key figure in the administration of the realm. Though he thought of himself as surrounded by 'vipers' at court, his predominance was apparent to all. He worried constantly about the precarious financial situation of the Crown, complained that he lived in purgatory 'oppressed by a world of business', but he enjoyed the queen's total confidence. Although at times he privately deplored her unwillingness to act decisively, he was mostly able to control both domestic and foreign policy.[3] With the arrival of James, this unique position was undermined. Instead of an ageing, vacillating woman who for years had felt a genuine affection for him, not least as Burghley's son, Cecil now faced a man in the prime of life, whom he knew only by correspondence. James had strong opinions of his own, and a very high estimate of his kingly abilities, as well as a circle of close friends and longstanding advisors. It was obvious that he would listen to many voices, not just to that of the secretary.

As the weeks of the new reign wore on, James made further changes. He placed five Scots on the English Privy Council, and deliberately widened the circle of Englishmen with access to power. Lord Henry Howard, soon to be Earl of Northampton, was pointedly made a privy councillor in the hall of Cecil's own great house at Theobalds. One of James's very first actions, while still in Scotland, had been to order the release from the Tower of the Earl of Southampton, leader of the remnants of Essex's faction. The Earl of Northumberland, generally acknowledged as the spokesman for moderate Catholics was promoted to the Privy Council.[4] Cecil retained both the Wards and the secretaryship of state, but he seemed likely in future to be only one of half a dozen senior advisors. Another aspect of the Stuart regime, a striking novelty which complicated the situation yet further, was the revival of the Bedchamber as a focus of influence and patronage. Under both Mary and Elizabeth, power had been concentrated in the hands of the Privy Council. The queen's ladies rarely meddled in politics, even if occasionally they attempted to advance the careers of relatives and friends. James by contrast was surrounded by the gentlemen of his Bedchamber, brought with him from Edinburgh, whose services he insisted on retaining and whose Scottishness he refused to dilute by adding new English appointees. The Bedchamber, powerful under both Henry VIII and Edward VI, now returned as a focus of faction and intrigue in political life, further undercutting Cecil's previous near-monopoly of influence.[5] All this was dangerous enough but the worst possibility, which could not be ruled out, was that within a few months of being securely established on the English throne, James's gratitude might wane and Cecil find himself not merely demoted but dismissed. Even though he had survived the immediate transition into the new reign virtually unscathed, he could not rely on the automatic continuance of his position. Cecil would have to prove his worth afresh, adapting to the king's wishes and his ways of doing business if he was to remain in power.

The changes brought about by James's accession included not merely an expanded Privy Council and the intrusion into court life of a group of Scots, but also a complete change in court routine. Although famed in her earlier years for her progresses amidst her people, in her old age Elizabeth rarely moved much beyond the palaces within easy reach of London. No longer able to ride easily, she spent most of her time at Greenwich in the summer and Whitehall in the winter, with short, sedate removes to Richmond or Oatlands and visits to dine with old friends such as Dr Julius Caesar at Mitcham or Lord Admiral Nottingham in Chelsea. The furthest she ventured in 1601 was to the Paulets at Basing House in Hampshire before returning the thirty miles back to Windsor.[6] James was far more adventurous, and also more anxious to avoid his plague-ridden capital. In the summer of 1603, just after the long journey down from Scotland, he embarked on what the Household official responsible for his transport wearily described as 'that labyrinthical progress'. The king and his entourage visited Richmond, Nonsuch, Woodstock, Farnham, Basing, Wilton and Winchester before arriving back at Hampton Court a week before Christmas. Picking up his pen at midnight on 17 September Cecil described to his old friend the Earl of Shrewsbury 'our camp volant, which every week dislodgeth, [and] makes me often neglect writing'. A few days later he lamented that they were driven 'up and down so round as I think we shall come to York'. At the ancient palace of Woodstock, unused for many years, only the king and queen, the privy chamber ladies, and some three or four Scottish counsellors could be accommodated. All the English privy councillors were forced to stay eight miles away in Oxford.[7] The peripatetic pattern of the first year of the reign was continued as James spent more and more of his time away from London, moving from one hunting lodge to another. In 1605 Levinus Munck, Cecil's chief secretary, bitterly complained of the extreme inconvenience of 'these arrant removes', while other members of the Privy Council bemoaned their exhaustion from late nights and of having to answer their official letters without secretarial help. James's lifestyle not only wore out his companions but also caused considerable friction in the localities, for the demand for purveyance to support the king and his retinue drained whole areas dry. Local protests included the tying of a letter of complaint onto Joler, one of James's favourite greyhounds, briefly kidnapped for the purpose. In private, Cecil admitted that rural anger at the presence of the court, whose rapacious and wasteful officials exhausted regional supplies, was all too justified.[8]

By 1605 the king had established a routine whereby he spent about half the year away from his capital, mostly on hunting trips to his favourite lodges at Royston and Newmarket. He maintained that his health necessitated constant outdoor exercise, while at the same time assuring the Privy Council that he would return promptly to London if events required it. Although initially both the court and the council accompanied the king, the council later stayed behind, sometimes joining James on summer progresses but rarely attending him for any length of time while he was hunting. Even on progresses the chase dominated the daily routine, to the dismay of those who found it hard to share the king's enthusiasm. 'I have no news to send you but that we are all become wild men wandering in a forest from the morning till the evening', wrote the Earl of Dunbar resignedly to Cecil in August 1607 from Beaulieu in Hampshire.[9] At Royston and Newmarket it was virtually the sole activity, and the king would move from one lodge to another if the supply of game failed or the weather made the ground too hard. As a result the small entourage who shared James's rural pursuits was almost entirely made up of fellow huntsmen. Although technically described as 'the court', it can scarcely be regarded as such in the usual sense. One result was that 'court culture' in these years was as much the creation of the great aristocratic households of London as of the monarchy itself, and thus subtly different in many of its emphases. Recent discussions of English court culture which have failed to appreciate the distinction are seriously flawed as a result. Contemporaries were aware of the difference. Dudley Carleton noted in September 1604 that the king was going down to Royston 'and with him only his hunting crew', while in contrast when the king, the queen, the Bedchamber and the Household were all together at Greenwich in spring 1605 it was remarked on as a 'complete court'.[10] Moreover the king's extended absences necessitated a radically new pattern of business. Under Henry VIII and Elizabeth, court, council and power had been virtually one entity in one place. The Jacobean Privy Council continued to meet at Whitehall but for substantial parts of the year the privy lodgings were empty. Tacitly acknowledging the need for a royal presence, James instructed his councillors to meet at his wife's court once a week. But only when he was on one of his brief visits back to London was there the old pattern of access, with the king and his leading advisors to be found informally discussing foreign policy late at night after a visit by the Venetian ambassador.[11] Such an intermittent style of court life had not been seen for generations and its consequences were disturbing. Contact with relatively isolated places like Royston and Newmarket was not easy. The posts were overstretched and important papers were on occasion lost in transit or left behind when the king moved on. On some matters James's second thoughts would arrive days later, after documents had already been drafted or decisions implemented. There were frequent fears for his safety, both from hunting accidents and even from assassination. Perhaps most worrying of all, matters that previously could be discussed tactfully and tentatively, sounding out the monarch's reactions before proceeding further, now all too often had to be formalized from the outset in writing. The anxious tone to which this gave rise can be seen in the surviving correspondence between James and his Privy Council, especially in the letters begging him to limit his expenditure.[12]

However uncongenial the novel pattern established by James, the secretary of state had no choice but to adapt to it. In many ways he was ill-equipped to do so. Cecil was small in stature with a humped shoulder and a far from robust constitution. Although he enjoyed hawking he had no taste for hunting, and in any case found little time for outdoor recreation, despite the advice of his old friend Shrewsbury that it would do his eyesight good. He was a workaholic and a worrier, admitting that he was always inclined to do too much rather than too little. Groomed by his father to succeed to the management of state affairs, he was both profoundly deferential towards the English monarchy and deeply protective of what he saw as the best interests of the English commonwealth. He was prone to pangs of self-pity, comparing himself to the biblical Martha toiling in the kitchen at Bethany while Mary abandoned housework to listen to Jesus.[13] All this contrasted sharply with the canny, physically energetic and hugely self-confident James who openly rejoiced that his accession had admitted him to 'a paradise of pleasure'. However, the king's absences in the country and Cecil's diligence in Whitehall should not mislead us into describing their relationship in terms of a figurehead monarch with a modern British prime minister. It is true that James was intermittently idle, giving orders that his hunting was not to be interrupted and teasing Cecil for his supposed omnicompetence. Yet at the same time the king required daily packets of letters, often awaiting the post-horn with avidity and sending back brisk demands for further detail on topics that attracted his attention.[14] Although distant from Whitehall he maintained a shrewd if occasionally erratic oversight of government business, particularly on ecclesiastical and foreign policy. The resulting correspondence between Cecil and the king, in many ways a continuation of that earlier secret relationship begun before 1603, reveals both James's usual goodwill towards his chief minister and his heavy sense of humour, very unlike Cecil's own taste for irony. Although unperturbed by the appellation of 'little beagle', the secretary showed flashes of resentment at others such as 'fool', 'mouse', 'parrot-monger' and 'monkey-monger' which the king favoured. Cecil was not alone in being the object of such boisterously derogatory epithets, but the contrast between James's extravagant vocatives – 'my littil wiffe waffe', 'my little beagle . . . that lyes at hoame by the fyre quhen all the goode houndis are daylie runnung on the feildis' – and Cecil's cool endorsement, 'His Majesty to me', sums up much of the difference in their personalities.[15]

If James was not a figurehead monarch, Cecil should not be viewed simply as a bureaucrat. Sir Robert Naunton perceptively described him as 'a courtier from his cradle' and he expertly played his part, sending the king gifts of fine grapes, peaches and melons grown in his own gardens, presenting curiosities such as monkeys and marmosets to the royal family, giving court suppers, masques and entertainments, and enjoying expensive gambling sessions. When he wrote to James he took care to make his business letters as amusing as possible. The king regarded him as good company after dinner and wished he would come to Royston more often. Cecil also dealt with innumerable minor chores, such as keeping an eye on the young lion whelp in the Tower which James wished to have trained as a pet. From the beginning of the reign, he prepared his mansion at Theobalds as a hunting lodge for the king, eventually handing it over when James suggested an exchange of property. Cecil knew that the skills of the courtier were vital for political advancement and when his son, the young Viscount Cranborne, spent too much of his grand tour in Paris rather than in attendance on Henri IV, he was chastised. To Cecil the French court was an essential part of Cranborne's education; the capital city was merely tourism.[16]

The years after 1603 saw a great increase in court display, the costs of which fell not only on the royal finances but also on those who had to keep up with the rise in conspicuous consumption. Pressure to do so played a significant part in that notable greed which has been seen as a hallmark of the entire Jacobean political establishment. Already by December 1604 the Privy Council was warning the king that after the expenses of riding out to greet him on his journey south, the ceremonial entry into London, the coronation, and for members, the two successive Garter ceremonies on St George's day, there were not many at court who were willing or able to undergo further heavy charges. But Cecil could scarcely allow himself to fall behind. In particular

James's marked predilection for ancient nobility, a group which did not include the *arriviste* Cecils, necessitated by way of compensation a strong presence on his part at great ceremonial occasions. Although he was dealing with correspondence from Knights of the Garter from at least 1603 onward, Cecil was not made a member of the order until 1606, significantly behind such other leading courtiers and council members as Lennox, Southampton, Pembroke, Northampton and Mar, and even then with rumours of protests from the kings of France and Denmark that the honour should be confined to those of preeminent nobility of rank and blood. It can scarcely be coincidental that when Cecil was at last given his Garter, he devoted the previous weeks almost entirely to ensuring that his elevation at Windsor should stun spectators and participants alike with its magnificence, so much so that it was reported as surpassing the coronation itself. Thereafter he used the Garter motto 'Honi soit qui mal y pense' on his personal seal, and he is depicted in the lavish robes of the order in the striking formal portraits by John de Critz and Marcus Gheeraerts, much admired by his friends, that still hang at Hatfield.[17]

The Garter was not the only aspect of court life to be appropriated as a visual demonstration of status. Cecil was fully aware of the importance of ceremonial display and its intimate relationship to political power. His immense building programme, by far the greatest of its age, began with Salisbury House in the Strand, continued with Cranborne House in Dorset and the New Exchange (Britain's Bourse) in the rapidly expanding west end of London, and culminated in Hatfield House in Hertfordshire. In five years the earl spent about £60,000, a gigantic sum which came near to exhausting even his vast resources. These great new edifices served to reaffirm his position, not least by underscoring his links with the royal family. In April 1609 the king, the queen, Prince Henry, Princess Elizabeth and the Duke of York all came to the extravagant and fantastical opening ceremony for Britain's Bourse, a name devised by James himself. James visited both Hatfield and Cranborne in 1611, and at Hatfield apartments were constructed to enable both the king and the queen to stay there at the same time.[18] However the most notable example of the use of spectacle and ceremony for specific political ends was to come with the installation of Henry as Prince of Wales in 1610. The reversionary interest represented by the first young male heir to the throne for over fifty years was always a matter of deep concern to Cecil, although he never failed to express his joy at 'that blessing of a lasting succession' which the king had brought with him from Scotland. In May 1603, James had publicly received the young son of the late Earl of Essex, greeting him most warmly and proclaiming him 'to be the eternal companion of his eldest son the Prince of Wales'. To Cecil, intent on ensuring the status of his own son William, a revival of the Essex interest under Henry's aegis could pose a significant long-term threat. It was essential for both his own and William's future that he cultivate the prince, and by the expenditure of much effort he succeeded in building up a relationship in which there was real personal warmth. Henry felt able to appeal to Cecil and Lord Chamberlain Suffolk against his parents when he was forbidden swimming lessons. Cecil proffered carefully chosen presents, particularly horses, and was punctilious in waiting on the prince. He took the trouble to brief Henry on foreign affairs and provided his teenage friends with introductions when they travelled abroad. Henry's growing interest in paintings gave Cecil a genuine bond in common with the prince. He was happy to facilitate the cultivation of Henry's taste, showing him items from the Cecil collection, while English ambassadors abroad were instructed to keep an eye open for old masters at reasonable prices, for purchase by either the prince or the secretary of state. Cecil was also endeavouring to ensure that younger members of his family should be members of the prince's circle, repeatedly protesting the devotion of his son Cranborne to Henry's service, whilst his favourite nephew Sir Edward Cecil corresponded with the prince on military matters, another of Henry's enthusiasms.[19] However, as Henry grew older, and especially after Cecil became Lord Treasurer in 1608, the relationship underwent increasing strain. Cecil found himself walking a tightrope, for at the same time as he was assuring Henry of his loyalty he was attempting to exercise some control over the rising costs and chaotic organization of the prince's household. In 1610, as the heir's majority drew near, Cecil expressed major unease at the extra charges inevitable in the setting up of a separate court for Henry, especially as he acknowledged that only James himself could dictate the size of the prince's future income, 'that being only proper for . . . no subject to perform towards him'. The two threads of the political use of ceremony on the one hand and the significance of the reversionary interest on the other came together in the midst of the 1610 session of parliament. As Cecil propounded his scheme for a Great Contract to rescue the royal finances, all business was halted for a week whilst Henry was created Prince of Wales. No such ceremony had taken place for over a hundred years so despite the air of antiquity many of the details must have been largely invented for the occasion. Cecil stood on the king's left hand and read out 'distinctly and audibly' the patent of creation, while James placed a gold circlet on Henry's head, gave him a gold ring for his finger and bestowed on him a rod of gold. The Lords were a sea of formal scarlet robes while most of the Commons showed their enthusiasm with a more varied but equally notable sartorial display of their own, to the extent that country members who had not made a sufficient effort with their appearance felt uncomfortable. As early as October 1609 the prince was declaring his willingness to trust Cecil 'with the care of his creation', while in his speech at the opening of the session in February 1610, rebutting those who had queried the point of holding the ceremony within the context of a parliament, Cecil revealed the extent of his own researches into the history of the creations of successive English Princes of Wales. All the signs point to Cecil as the inspirer and organizer of the official installation ceremonies of June 1610, probably aided by his two close friends Suffolk and Worcester who as Lord Chamberlain and Earl Marshal respectively took leading roles.[20] The parliamentary pageantry at Westminster, which was followed at court by days of fireworks, masques and tilting, was deliberately designed to produce a surge of loyal affection towards the already popular young prince. Underlying the splendour of the occasion was the hope that it would induce a greater willingness to vote supply towards rising royal expenditure. In this way Cecil deployed public spectacle to lubricate the parliamentary process, just as he had used the Garter ceremonies of 1606 to underline his own political power. Yet such were the Lord Treasurer's financial worries that at the same time as he was stage-managing Henry's elevation to the princedom of Wales, he was privately delaying the grant of livery of lands to the prince. In the event despite all its magnificence the carefully devised ritual failed in its purpose for the session of 1610 proved fruitless. Even worse, over the next two years all Cecil's fears were to be justified, for between 1610 and 1612 Henry rapidly outstripped his allowance. In money matters if in nothing else the prince resembled his father, and on his death he was heavily in debt.[21]

Cecil also needed to pay attention to Queen Anne, not least because she remained in favour with her eldest son even after her relationship with James himself had cooled. Although it has been alleged that Anne for years bore Cecil a secret resentment, the evidence instead suggests a mostly amicable relationship. Cecil had immediately written to proffer her his devotion on James's accession and throughout the rest of his life was an active high steward of her estates. She consulted him on suits submitted to her and, conversely, others sought the queen's intercession for Cecil's favour. Lady Walsingham, one of his closest women friends, was the Keeper of the Queen's Robes and a lady of her Privy Chamber. Cecil presented Anne with splendid gifts and received presents in return. He attended her at social occasions such as the baptisms of her friends' children, and rushed to condole with her on the deaths of her two small daughters. To him was entrusted the commissioning of Princess Sophia's touching cradle tomb in Westminster Abbey. Towards the surviving elder daughter, Princess Elizabeth, he behaved with courteous attention, ensuring that as she grew older she received the jewellery appropriate to her station. In return she wrote him careful thank-you letters in French. The king used Cecil to pass on numerous personal messages to Anne, and in the extremely delicate episode of which only the barest outlines can be discerned, when rumours circulated of the queen's infidelity, it was Cecil and Dunbar (whom she had known for years in Scotland) who were sent by James to speak in confidence to her. Sir Walter Cope, probably the closest of all Cecil's associates, spent a fruitless morning in 1604 hunting for players and jugglers to amuse the queen. He finally summoned expert help only to be told by Richard Burbage that there was no new play that Anne had not seen. Fortunately, Cope wrote in a quick note to Cecil, 'they have revived an old one called "Love's Labour Lost" which for wit and mirth he says will please her exceedingly'. If on occasion Anne and Cecil disagreed, her animosity seems to have been brief for she was a diligent visitor during his final illness.[22] Once again in his dealings with Anne of Denmark we are reminded that Cecil was just as much leading courtier as supreme man of business. His connection with the king, the queen, the prince and the princess was that of attendant, servant and confidant.

The royal family were the heart and the *raison d'être* of the court, but around them was the ramshackle, corrupt department of the Household. Here Cecil faced a major difficulty. Burghley had controlled the Household by occasional purges but Cecil never achieved the dominance over it that his father had wielded. After Burghley's death in 1598 the situation deteriorated, and it worsened still further after 1603 with the great expansion of court personnel. Repeated complaints both in parliament and in the localities over purveyance and the dishonest practices of Household officers led to the promulgation of numerous but ultimately ineffective reforming ordinances. The principal officers of the Household were Cecil's fellow privy councillors Knollys and Wotton, but although they signed the council's letter of 1606 to the king, urging Household retrenchment alongside other economies, their own slackness was a leading cause of the escalation of costs. Expenses rose horrendously, to become what Cecil despairingly described as '*Ignis Edax*, a devouring fire', while the number of servitors increased to become 'a little army compared to former times'. In January 1611 he made a last attempt to urge James to restrain the Household officers, in whose hands lay 'the power of prevention', in contrast to himself and the officers of the Exchequer who were 'only able to demonstrate at the year's end, the characters which do decipher that there was spent too much'.[23] The plea was largely ignored, and when Cranfield later attempted to curb Household expenditure he too came up against deeply entrenched interests. In effect no one controlled the Household; it had become a sprawling organic entity with its own momentum of growth.

The problems of the Household were worsened by James's accession but they were not of his making, for he had inherited a corrupt system from Elizabeth. The novelty of James's court, as already indicated, was the presence of a male Bedchamber staffed with the king's Scots intimates who had opportunities for the exercise of considerable patronage and influence. Faced with the Scottish presence after 1603, Cecil showed extreme discretion. He worked diligently for the Union, although he knew that the English nobility was reluctant to support it, and the tenor of his private views may perhaps be gleaned from his dry comment to his old friend Shrewsbury, whose chief seats were in Yorkshire and Derbyshire. 'Now my lord, for a parting blow, know this . . . that you are now a northern subject to the king of Great Britain, and that I am a true South Briton'. At court, where Cecil often mediated in aristocratic quarrels, he was particularly quick to intervene when friction arose between the two nations. 'My lord Cecil was umpire between us', commented Sir Robert Carey of the incident when Dunbar forced him to cede the captaincy of Norham Castle. Cecil ensured that Dunbar paid a price acceptable to the reluctant Carey but lower than the latter's first demand.[24] Unfortunately, Cecil's tact was not matched by the House of Commons, and in pressing the unwilling James to summon another session of parliament to tackle the financial crisis in 1610, the Lord Treasurer was well aware that one key obstacle was the king's distaste for any criticism of his Bedchamber. As part of his efforts to bring the king to consent to a parliament, Cecil wrote for him a set of confidential treatises, 'such things as the time and that occasion doth require', with information and arguments designed 'against the time when these things come in question'. The treatises as a whole are remarkable for their frankness, but one of the most daring and also most carefully phrased passages occurs in the sixth treatise, written sometime between 12 January and 9 February 1610. In it Cecil grasped the nettle of English hostility to the Scots, that ancient animosity already sharply articulated by Sir Christopher Pigott in the Commons in 1607. He outlined for James's scrutiny his prepared answers to 'any frivolous objection' that might be made against the king's fellow-countrymen. If it was said that they should live at home, 'what can be a more just reply to such a one, than to ask him whether he would be glad that he that was their king, and now is ours also, should live there too?' The appalling thought of London as a distant dependency of a court permanently resident in Edinburgh should be enough to silence any such comment. However, instead of the almost wholly Scottish entourage which James had so far maintained, Cecil suggested 'a selected number of choice servants of both kingdoms . . . able to serve your Majesty in a noble and generous fashion'. In return for ceding their monopoly of Bedchamber influence the Scots would be given capital to pay off their debts, and also annual pensions a third higher than those of their English equivalents, ostensibly 'both because they are further separated from their own private estate and revenues than the other, as also in respect of difference (possibly) in their means and abilities'. After all, no king 'could so far degenerate from all true generosity' as to neglect his first friends; and it was a matter not 'of private but of public consequence to maintain such particular men as are necessary for the service of princes'. To Cecil, from whose thoughts the old fear of an uncertain succession was never far distant, no such burden of maintenance could be 'compared to the innumerable felicities derived from the safety and peace in our fortunes and consciences, so long thirsted after and now enjoyed'. If the problem of the Scots could be settled, 'then is that object of distaste taken away, and on the contrary one step to the Union gained by the Union of hearts'. Cecil took a considerable risk in pointing out that it had been 'the harsh effects and ill order of your Majesty's gifts' which had earlier 'troubled the passage of this desired Union' but went on to soften the impact of his criticism by hinting that James's dearest project might still be a political possibility, despite the comprehensive failure of 1604–7. He flatteringly described the Union as in the long term inevitable, since 'law and nature fully resolved to bring forth and nourish that beloved child, which must be the life and strength of this island'.[25]

It is abundantly clear from this evidence that Cecil was alert to the major political liability represented by the Scottish entourage and had given much thought to solving the problem. It is noteworthy, however, that his striking bluntness elsewhere in the treatises on the king's excessive bounty is matched by the caution of his discussion of the Scots and the generous financial package of debt-relief and pensions which he felt compelled to offer. Cecil was under no illusion about Scottish influence at court. In a recent valuable study of the entourage, it has even been suggested that the power of the Scots was in fact so great that by 1608, Cecil had not only largely been deprived of informal access to the king, but that 'the Bedchamber eventually broke Salisbury as it was to break other great officers who tried to use it or work through it'.[26] This is surely a serious exaggeration. Personal access to the king was limited by James's absence on hunting expeditions, not by Bedchamber power. Far from finding himself excluded from the royal presence, Cecil was pressed by the king to leave London and visit him more often at Royston. There is no evidence that when James and Cecil were in the same place at the same time, the latter was ever denied full access with all the old familiarity. Moreover, the theory of Bedchamber influence relies very heavily on the model of Henry VIII's reign, when the royal signature was very much under Privy Chamber control. Despite his absence from the king's side Cecil experienced no difficulty whatsoever in procuring James's signature. The letters from Sir Thomas Lake and other members of the entourage at Royston or Newmarket refer constantly to the return of documents signed by the king which had been sent out in the previous packet by Cecil. Perhaps most significant of all, in 1608 at a time when it is alleged that Cecil was being reduced to merely formal contact with the king, he completed his unparalleled monopoly of office by adding the lord treasurership, vacant after Dorset's death at the council table. Since this was most crucial position in the financial administration of the country, and James himself had repeatedly stressed his acute awareness of the problems of his revenues, the appointment hardly fits any theory of diminishing influence. On the contrary the original uncertainties of Cecil's situation in

1603 had been dispelled by 1608, as can be seen in the excellent working relationship which he had built up with both the king and new councillors such as Northampton and Dunbar.[27]

It must also be pointed out that the claim that 'the Bedchamber broke Cecil' is based on a flawed reading of the evidence for the collapse of the great contract, which focuses almost exclusively on the very scantily documented opposition to it at court while ignoring the massive criticism which the project encountered in parliament. Whatever the attitude of the Bedchamber, the great contract would have run into severe difficulties in the Commons, above all because of the interwoven problem of impositions. The argument also ignores the extent to which Cecil retained control after the collapse of the Contract. The failure of his plan for a parliamentary solution to the financial crisis was of course a major blow, and it led to a series of bitter tongue-lashings from the king. However, James was not a vindictive man and after his initial outbursts of anger he made no further moves to humiliate his Lord Treasurer. In particular the notion that by the end of 1610 Cecil's position had become purely formal, the shadow of power rather than the substance, fails to consider foreign policy, always of paramount concern to the king personally. The years from 1610 to 1612 were dominated by the question of suitable marriage alliances for Prince Henry and Princess Elizabeth. Cecil was in charge of the complex negotiations over these, and there is much evidence to suggest that as a result, his intimacy with the king and the royal family was strengthened rather than weakened. Furthermore, suitors continued to flock to him, always a sure sign of continued influence.[28] However, if Cecil largely retained political power, it cannot be doubted that the Bedchamber did thwart most of his repeated attempts to curb its profligacy, with the attendant inroads into crown reserves. But if patronage and financial gain are to be the sole criteria of Jacobean power then Cecil himself was still far ahead. He retained the mastership of the Court of Wards, which even after his own reform of its practice in January 1611 remained the most lucrative and influential single office, while as Lord Treasurer he was uniquely placed to tap large private loans and kickbacks from the farmers of the customs. Significantly, it was at the end of 1610, after the débâcle of the great contract, that he received from James the grant of the silk farm for nineteen years, which gained him an extra £7,000 per year without any effort. In the last two years of his life his annual income was at least £25,000, and the landed estate he left to his son more than compensated for the fact that most of Burghley's lands had been left to the Earl of Exeter, Cecil's elder half-brother. By his own efforts he had placed his descendants, the younger branch of the Cecil family, in the highest ranks of the English aristocracy. His building programme, as outlined earlier, was the most grandiose of the early seventeenth century.[29] Members of the Bedchamber did well for themselves, but not as well as Cecil.

What brought the years of power to an end was neither the Bedchamber nor the Great Contract, but the stomach cancer from which the lord treasurer was already visibly suffering by the summer of 1611, when he consulted the king's doctor Sir Theodore Mayerne. But even in the last year of his life, whenever his health allowed him he still dominated the machinery of state as the unchallenged chief minister of the king. In March 1612 Chamberlain reported that Cecil was convalescing in Kensington; 'he forsook the court to be more private at home, but he cannot avoyde the perpetuall visits that still follow him', including those of the king, the queen and the prince. Shortly afterwards he returned for a few days 'to embrace business again, which found a great want of him', and just before his last journey to Bath, besides addressing the Tuesday and the Saturday council meetings, 'he had longe speach with the King once or twise before his going'. This does not seem the picture of a broken and disgraced man who had forfeited his sovereign's confidence. Rather as his memorialist Tourneur put it, 'He had a full mind in an imperfect body . . . he depended on maiesty, without the Mediacone of any second greatnes; which is an honour, the moste noble to a mans self and the sureste to his Kinge.'[30]

9 THE MENTALITY OF
A JACOBEAN GRANDEE

Linda Levy Peck

A few days before his death in 1614, Henry Howard, Earl of Northampton, Lord Privy Seal and Lord Warden of the Cinque Ports, travelled by coach from Greenwich to London accompanied by dozens of retainers. Describing this procession and his elaborate last rites, Chamberlain commented sourly *sic transit gloria mundi*.[1] The Spanish Ambassador was more fulsome: to the King of Spain, Phillip III, Gondomar extolled Northampton as a connoisseur whose London mansion was one of the finest in Europe. 'In consideration of the Earl's courage, virtue, prudence and refinement he was for all this accounted the first gentleman of the kingdom and with reason.'[2] Allusions to the power of great men are frequent throughout the sixteenth and early seventeenth centuries and there are significant similarities amongst the leading noblemen and favourites at the Jacobean court. Almost all built prodigy houses, Salisbury at Hatfield, Northampton at Northampton House in the Strand, Suffolk at Audley End, Pembroke at Wilton. Almost all spent enormous amounts on display which included royal entertainments, clothing and art. Almost all were patrons of writers, divines, historians, poets. Several began important collections of European paintings and sculpture culminating in the great collections of Thomas Howard, Earl of Arundel, Robert Carr, Earl of Somerset, George Villiers, Duke of Buckingham and King Charles himself. However much they might differ on religion and foreign policy, they created for the English nobleman a new persona, the grandee.

Grandes, the leading nobility of Castile, called 'cousin' by the King of Spain, usually had very large estates over which they exercised virtual seigneurial authority. Their higher status amongst the nobility was recognized in law.[3] The English word 'grandee', applied to Spanish and Portuguese noblemen, appears to have come into English usage in 1598 in the writings of the English Catholic controversialist Father Parsons. Sir Francis Bacon wrote

148

more generally of 'grandees and noblemen' in his *Advancement of Learning* (1605).[4] Although grandee lacked the legal distinctions of Spanish usage and the requirement of large land holdings, it nevertheless conveyed in some cases the aura of Spain and Catholicism. The Earl of Pembroke, himself one of the greatest peers in England, called Buckingham a grandee. Distinct from magnate and oligarch, grandee continued to be used in England into the Restoration and the eighteenth century.

To plot the mental world, the complex of ideas and the web of political and social attitudes of one Jacobean grandee, this essay explores the Earl of Northampton's attitudes toward authority, nobility, family and self.[5] As an intellectual, Northampton was in a class by himself among the Jacobean nobility. But in his attitudes toward family, display and the practice of court politics he shared the unstated assumptions of the group. Scion of the Dukes of Norfolk and Cambridge don, Northampton was a product both of late Renaissance learning and aristocratic culture. In the 1590s he formed an alliance with James VI of Scotland founded upon James's hopes for the English throne and Northampton's for political power. The ties between the ageing aristocrat and the king were historical: he and his brother had suffered for the cause of Mary, Queen of Scots; scholarly: Northampton attacked George Buchanan as vigorously as James; and pragmatic: Northampton situated himself first in the network of Essex and then of Cecil to lay the basis for the political structures of the new reign.[6] Extravagant of language, extremely susceptible to slight, and fearful of ridicule, Northampton had a tender concern for the prerogatives of the nobility. Yet the role he created differed significantly from that his grandfather, Thomas Howard, third Duke of Norfolk, played at the court of Henry VIII. Although Northampton's library has been broken up, his palace torn down, his Greenwich house burned and his paintings and tapestries dispersed, fragments of evidence allow us to reconstruct the symbolic and material culture within which he dwelt.

I *Readings and writings*

The wheel of fortune which brought the Howards to dizzying heights under Henry VIII dashed them to the ground with the execution of Northampton's father, the poet, Henry Howard, Earl of Surrey, and the imprisonment of his grandfather, the third Duke of Norfolk in 1546. The year before Norfolk had Stephen Gardiner ask Roger Ascham to secure a tutor for his grandchildren.[7] During Edward's reign, Henry Howard studied with John Foxe and the humanist Hadrian Junius who published extensively on historical topics. On the death of Edward VI, and the release of his grandfather Norfolk from the Tower, Howard was sent to live with the Marian Bishop John White. Bishop White was himself a protégé of Bishop Stephen Gardiner, serving as the executor of his will and preaching his funeral oration. Within that episcopal household Howard spent his impressionable teenage years. At Mary's death and Elizabeth's accession, Howard was removed from the Catholic White's household and sent to Cambridge. He studied at King's and ultimately became Reader in Rhetoric and Civil Law at Trinity Hall where be lectured in Latin and worried that 'the clock is even uppon the pointe to strike 1 and I altogether unphounded [*sic*] for my lectore'.[8] He was the only nobleman to teach at either university in the Tudor or early Stuart period.

In his earliest surviving work, a treatise on natural philosophy written from Trinity Hall in 1569, Northampton commended 'that most excellent work of the Count of Castiglione called the Courtier'.[9] Castiglione prescribed an education that would make the courtier not only an ornament of the court but also the king's political advisor. Furthermore the humanist ideal of the orator, skilled in the rhetoric and values of the ancients who could provide counsel to the king found a natural home in Renaissance states that conducted their politics and diplomacy through formal speeches and debates.[10] Northampton achieved what many other humanists sought, political power as 'the perfect orator'.[11] In 1605 Sir Francis Bacon asked the Earl of Northampton to present the *Advancement of Learning* to King James to whom he had dedicated the work because James 'I dare avouch . . . to be the *Learnedst King* that hath Reigned; I was desirous, in a kind of Congruity, to present it by the Learnedst Counsellor in this kingdom.'[12] By the end of the sixteenth century, however, the humanist had escaped his moorings as exemplar of virtue and been transformed into the scholar willing to support any side with his learning.[13] This was the task Northampton assigned to the scholars, such as Sir Robert Cotton, who were his advisors, and the one that he adopted himself. As Cotton wrote to him in 1602, 'thus much I have hastily gathered, not knowing by your paper which way you labour to fortify'.[14]

The widely held view that in early Stuart England politics were couched in the language of the ancient constitution has been challenged recently by the argument that there were three distinct and competing political discourses: royal absolutism, social contract theory and immemorial custom.[15] Northampton demonstrates a more complex position which proved contradictory only under the pressure of later political conflict. At the centre of his politics was a discourse of absolutism based on natural law theory that drew explicitly on the writings of Jean Bodin. How he understood that discourse is of intense interest. It nestled, if uneasily, next to the assumptions that the nobility ought to serve as the king's natural counsellors and that the bishops had a broad secular jurisdiction. Finally, he argued that, in relation to parliament, the king chose to retain only 'a negative voice'.[16] Northampton believed that the king was above the positive law. At the same time in a distinction not unlike the one that James I drew between the origins of monarchy and kings in settled kingdoms, Northampton suggested that the king would want to act

150

as a royal monarch not as a tyrant. Citing Bodin, Northampton argued that the royal monarch would obey the laws of nature and of God and secure the persons and 'propriety' of his subjects.[17]

Northampton was impressed with Bodin whom he called 'greatly read and deepeley learned'.[18] Like Sir Robert Filmer he worked on a tract on monarchy that drew on and debated Bodin. Northampton did not privilege Roman history but culled historical examples from different societies from the ancient to the contemporary to construct his politics in much the same way as Bodin did. Indeed, he often used Bodin's examples without acknowledgement. Gabriel Harvey had commented in or about 1579 that one could not enter a study in Cambridge without finding a scholar reading Bodin or Louis Le Roy. He might easily have been talking about Northampton who had been his university examiner.[19]

Northampton participated in every major political and religious debate of his time: supporting the legitimacy of women rulers, justifying the authority of the bishops against the Presbyterians, arguing the power of the king against the temporal power of the pope, challenging astrology and contributing to the education of princes literature. He recorded the progress of his thinking in formal tracts, collections of *sententiae*, writings on political theory and letters.[20]

Alongside a humanist agenda shaped by his reading and his education, Northampton had a heightened view of nobility and a Tacitean, perhaps even Machiavellian, view of politics joined to the English historical drama of the rise and fall of great families as exemplified in *The Mirror for Magistrates*. Thus he marshalled arguments from Aristotle to Machiavelli allowing for princely dishonesty: 'Machiavell supposeth that it is enough for Princes to putt on an outward Maske of conscience and religion however they bee otherwise affectedly Inwardly.'[21] Although he condemned such practices, it was a mask he himself sometimes wore. In the midst of an age of religious and political upheaval, he conceived his world as dangerous and in flux.[22] In response to travail he drew on the Stoics.

Fluent in Greek and Latin, French, Italian and Spanish, Northampton read widely in the classics, the Church fathers, canon law, Renaissance historiography, heraldry, natural law theory and Catholic and Protestant controversialist literature.[23] Amongst his favourite writers in works he wrote in the 1580s and 1590s were Plato and Aristotle, Cicero and Plutarch, Seneca and Tacitus. Despite his admiration for Bodin he sometimes disagreed with him and he attacked George Buchanan and Justus Lipsius.

Northampton's library, about which we have only scraps of information, reflected the classics and works of the late Renaissance and the Counter-Reformation. In 1615, his nephew, the Earl of Arundel, bought Northampton's library and other household-stuff for £529.[24] Because lists of Arundel's holdings include purchases from several sources, they offer insight if only opaquely into Northampton's library. Nevertheless, some can be identified. Three were New Year's gifts. Sir Robert Cotton, his most important advisor and one of the leading English antiquaries of the period, presented a copy of Agostino Tornielli's *Annales Sacri et Profani*. In this oversize, lavishly illustrated work, Tornielli, an Italian bishop, told the history of the world from its origins. This was a work after Northampton's heart, learned and encyclopaedic. Another year, Cotton gave the Earl several volumes of *La Corónica General de España* by the Spanish historian, Ambrosio de Morales. Percival Harte, a Kentish gentleman and patentee for Venetian glass, presented him with a history of Cremona by Antonio Campi, the Italian painter and architect, addressing Northampton as the most illustrious among the learned.[25] Other works that can be identified certainly as Northampton's were a Paris edition of Arnobius, the fourth-century Church father who wrote against non-believers, Philippe Moreau's work on French heraldry, of interest to Northampton because of his own work on the office of Earl Marshal and his writings on heraldry, and a Jesuit drama of 1605, 'Bavius et Maevius, ille ut delirus Alcymista', by the well-known German Jesuit professor Jacob Gretser. Gretser was a strong supporter of Cardinal Bellarmine in the propaganda war with James I over the new English oath of allegiance.

In addition, there are a cluster of works in Arundel's collections that concern royal authority in church and state written between 1605 and 1610 which are most likely to have been Northampton's, such as a sermon by William Wilkes, a royal chaplain, entitled *Obedience or Ecclesiastical Union* and James I's *Apologie for the Oath of Allegiance of 1607* which refers to the Gunpowder Plot. An early manuscript catalogue of Arundel's library includes the 1608 Paris edition of Cardinal Bellarmine's works in four volumes and Jacob Gretser's Latin defence of Cardinal Bellarmine published at Ingolstadt in 1607.[26] Moreover, Arundel's library included multiple copies of books which cannot be identified directly with Northampton, but which he cited in his writings. Thus Arundel had six editions of Livy's *Historia*, four of Machiavelli's *Historia Fiorentina* and two of his *Discorsi*, and several works by Bodin including *Methodus ad facilem historiarum cognitionem* and *Six Livres de la République* in French and Italian.[27] A book of psalms dated 1614 with the binding of Pope Pius V may have marked Northampton's return a few months before his death to Roman Catholicism.[28]

When his older brother, Thomas Howard, fourth Duke of Norfolk, was attainted for intriguing with Mary, Queen of Scots, and executed in 1572, Henry was removed from Cambridge and brought to court. While Queen Elizabeth apparently showed him some favour, he was soon suspected himself of communicating with Mary, Queen of Scots and the Spanish ambassador, and he was arrested and his papers repeatedly searched.

Although in his first treatise of 1569 he had claimed to write for a learned and private audience, from the 1570s to the 1590s he sought to regain access to royal favour by producing works designed to appeal to the queen and the court. In 1574 he attacked Thomas Cartwright and, in the process, argued for the secular jurisdiction of the English bishops.[29] He celebrated the queen in a Latin work, 'Regina Fortunata' in 1576. While his friend Charles Arundel was explicitly attacking the Earl of Leicester in the notorious *Leicester's Commonwealth*, Howard implicitly did so in his answer to John Stubbs's *Gaping Gulf* (1580) and *A Defensative against the Poyson of Supposed Prophesies* (1583).[30] Howard argued that the intent of those who opposed the queen's proposed marriage to the duc d'Anjou was to force the queen to marry at home, specifically to marry Leicester. Referring to the 'tyrannies' of some who enjoyed the queen's favour, he wrote 'were [there] not the reverent regard and fear of offending Her Majesty, they should find themselves abandoned by all honest and virtuous men . . . which for fear of intolerable injuries are now constrained to yield plausible speeches out of a cankered mind'.[31] No doubt such expressions explained why these works won not reward but rebuke.

Between 1577 and 1590 Howard wrote the most extensive work in the sixteenth-century debate on female monarchs. Yet the Council, probably Walsingham, questioned his loyalty, wondering whether he meant to uphold the right of Queen Elizabeth or Mary, Queen of Scots, for whom he also wrote.[32] Like many of his contemporaries, Northampton thought the court the centre of the world. Even after decades of effort, he was out of favour, as far away from Elizabeth, he told her, as America.

Northampton found a more favourable audience in James VI of Scotland. The two wrote on the same issues in the 1590s. Before the king composed *The Trew Law of Free Monarchies* and *Basilikon Doron*, Northampton prepared a work on monarchy that drew heavily on Bodin's *Six Livres de la République* and translated Charles V's advice to Philip II. The latter manuscript (possibly supposititious) circulated in late sixteenth-century Europe. Howard dedicated the work to Queen Elizabeth and it is possible that he shared it with King James. James received an Italian copy of the manuscript in the early 1590s, and it has been suggested that it had some influence on *Basilikon Doron*.[33] That the king read Northampton's work on monarchy at this time has not yet been established; that their political and intellectual interests coincided cannot be doubted.

II *Authority: church and state*

For Northampton upholding authority in church and state was fundamental and public utility the end of government policy.[34] The civil law informed his writings but like the French jurists of the late sixteenth century, he sought to place both Roman law and the customs of different nations in their historical context.[35] He addressed issues of contemporary political concern in Europe, the origin of political power, the relationship of the king to the law, the role of the king in parliament, the power of the bishops and the rights of female rulers.

Northampton always supported the ecclesiastical hierarchy with which he identified. He had close ties to Catholics at court under Elizabeth and connections to the Spanish for many decades, but no evidence yet links him with with the Catholic offensive of William Allen and Robert Parsons in the late sixteenth century.[36] In the Admonition controversy of the 1570s Thomas Cartwright published a strong attack on episcopacy to which John Whitgift, later Archbishop of Canterbury, replied. So did Northampton who portrayed himself in *Defense of the Ecclesiasticall Regiment in England* (1574) as Cicero in his invectives against Catiline and Verres. He attacked Cartwright for depriving the queen 'of her just supremacy' and questioning the bishops's titles, jurisdiction and livings. St Paul was not as precise as Cartwright and neither were the Protestant martyrs Archbishop Thomas Cranmer and Bishop Ridley. Arguing that ritual was as important as preaching, Northampton justified episcopal vestments, kneeling at communion, the celebration of holy days, signing the cross and fasting in celebration of Christ's majesty. Unity of mind and opinion should be kept even with 'due severity'.[37] He attacked Cartwright for claiming 'nothing . . . but liberty . . . where every man will . . . level his doings buy [*sic*] the president of no superior'. Howard made his views clear: no bishops, no peers. Cartwright's demands for purification were at odds with the history of the English church such as Pope Gregory's instructions to Augustine on his mission to convert England that he throw down idols but not destroy churches.[38] Moreover, historical change justified innovation in matters indifferent to doctrine.

Northampton supported the bishops' right not only to serve as counsellors to the monarch but to exercise a broad secular jurisdiction that went beyond Elizabethan doctrine:

Bishops may intermeddle in civil causes . . . nothing may be done without the warrant of God's sacred word, and the interpretation of the law must be required of the priest . . . For subjects are not bound whatsoever Princes charge them but . . . that which they teach according to the law of God.[39]

This rationale for resistance to the monarch remained undeveloped in Howard's writings.[40] Thirty years later in a speech to parliament in 1604 Northampton applauded James's religious policies in Scotland, 'restoring the state of the bishops in his own dominions and . . . [reducing] the Scottish elderships to Episcopal uniformity'. Northampton always supported the position of the bishops on bills presented in parliament.[41]

Howard laid out his views on kingship in two manuscripts, the 'Dutiful

Defense of the Lawful Regiment of Women', begun in the late 1570s and presented to the queen in 1590 and an unfinished manuscript on monarchy written during Elizabeth's reign. Constance Jordan has argued that those opposed to female rule relied on arguments from natural law.[42] Northampton used natural law theory, along with historical example, scripture and writers from Plato and Aristotle, Livy, Xenophon and Tacitus to Machiavelli, to support women monarchs. This extensive tract, which has never been published, responded not only to John Knox's *First Blast of the Trumpet against the Monstrous Regiment of Women* but also to George Buchanan, Justus Lipsius and Jean Bodin whose *Six Livres de la République* came out the year before Northampton was asked to write his treatise by an unnamed Elizabethan privy councillor, probably Burghley. Howard claimed to have

proved by the lawe of nature that excellency in guifts is not impropriate to Males, That the difference which is betweene the guifts of men and weomen consisting onely in proportion of more or less ought not in any sort to weaken their tytles to imperiall Authority by the right of inheritance, that . . . all countreyes under heaven have generally admitted female heires.

Howard attacked Knox's claim from Genesis that women were not created 'capable of regiment'. He argued that 'before the fall of Eve there was noe purpose of subjection in any kynd . . . women weare endowed with reason which is the rule of government as well as men, that they had equall dominion over creatures, that possession was given to both'. Even after the fall, the curse of 'bringing forth with payne and yielding duety and obedience to men concerneth none but wyves'. Women could command in one respect though they were subject in another.[43]

It was primarily on inheritance and succession that Northampton rested his case for women rulers. Howard claimed that Plato and Aristotle had been misused by such opponents of female rule as Justus Lipsius.[44] Aristotle provided examples of inheritances by women in Greece and elsewhere and did not distinguish between the inheritance of goods and offices. 'Nations not effeminate but martiall . . . gave like allowance of prerogative and honnor to the sexe of women.'[45] Howard admitted that were succession by election it might be possible that a man might be more fit. But 'a right invested by succession of blood dependeth not upon comparison of qualities . . . When private men of wealth and quallitie decease, wee seeke not for the wisest Senators, or the strongest wrastler to bee heire, but for the next of blood. The like course we must hold in disposing state inheritable by discent' (f. 35ff). While praising Bodin, 'I reverence the knowledge of the man, I admire his reading. I commend his diligence', he questioned Bodin's assertions about recent English politics. Howard argued that Bodin was at pains to find some other country besides France that prevented female succession to the Crown' (f. 83). He concluded because monarchs received their authority from God to whom they were responsible, 'wee are bound to reverence the sacred Image of divine authoritie in mortall Princes whether they bee men of judgement, women of experience, children of great hope or opposite in all these guifts and to acknowledge ordinary power by ordinary obedience' (f. 126).

Howard insisted that the king was not subject to the law. Nevertheless, he acknowledged limitations on the monarch based on practice, custom and policy.

[K]ings are in truth exempted by prerogative of their imperial estate from the censure of laws positive, yet by the grounds of nature, the precedents of lawful monarchies, the people's expectations and their own inward conscience they stand no less bound in the sight of God than the meanest subject in the Realm to respect and keep those rules which concern their policy.[46]

In the late sixteenth century as Northampton took up these themes, he put forward a position akin to James VI's on monarchy and advice to princes. He treated the coronation oath in much the same way that James did: 'the prince sweareth not to his subjects though he swear before them'.[47] Howard located political power in the king not in the people as argued by Catholic and Protestant resistance theorists. Originally kings' powers were unlimited. The first monarch was established in Assyria under Nimrod.[48] Arraban, captain of the King of Persia's guard, had declared to Themistocles, that the king was 'the image of the living God' and Plutarch said that the first princes had no other point of honour 'but to force men against their wills and to hold them lyke slaves in subjection . . . It appeareth plainly both by Bodin lib 3 cap 3 and by the texte of the lawe . . . that the princes made lawes and repealed them, put in officers and removed them at their pleasure.'[49]

Northampton attacked George Buchanan's arguments circumscribing the power of the king because political power was located in the people under Roman law: 'with better right ore coulor might the people of Rome resume the poweres which theie gave to Cesar then our people challenge a prerogative above princes which in truth they never had for of God alone they hold their crownes and to him only are theie accountable'. For Scotland, Northampton drew on a favourite example of James VI, that of Fergus, to whom the Scots made a solemn vow 'forever to be trew which was so religiously observed afterward as till this present from 333 years before Christ excepting . . . certain bastardes none but the right offspring of King Fergus hath governed'.[50]

Despite his debt to Bodin, Northampton's formulation of the king's role in parliament sounded surprisingly like Richard Hooker's in the unpublished Book 8 of his *Of the Laws of Ecclesiastical Polity*.

Whereas Bodine reasoneth that wheare it is not in the power of one to make Lawe the state must needs be populare, I denie the argument because it is required by the civile law that Quod omnes tangit ab omnibus debet approbari and therefore in our state of Englande our princes have dulie reserved to themselves a negative voice and thought it reason that the people should be made acquainted with the causes of the lawe and yeld their assent that afterwards theie might be the more obedient and overruled by the measure of their own approbation.[51]

The history of baronial revolt and the tradition of political thought had produced a language of liberties in England that Northampton tried to assimilate to Bodin's political theory. He did not articulate the implications of Bodin's notion of undivided legislative sovereignty; instead, he took over Bodin's assertion of limitations on the monarch based on natural law.

Thus, in his manuscript treatise on monarchy Northampton adopted Bodin's distinctions between tyrannical, lordly and royal monarchy.

The difference of one state of king from another ought not to be taken as Aristotle doth fondlie by the meanes wherbie thei come to raigne whether it be succession, force, lette, corruption or anie such but by their manner of government whether it be lordlie ore tyrannicall . . . The definition which is sette downe of a kinge by Aristotle is to vanne and ridicoulouse that he is a king which ruleth according to the liking of his subjects and againe that when a king beginneth to rule otherwise he becomes a tyrante. I call him a right king whiche is readie to employ his goods his bloud and lyfe for his people . . . Plinie reported that the gods themselves take example by the Life of Traiane . . . who doth not more value the title of Aristides called the juste than of William the Conqueror.[52]

A tyrant 'treading underfoote the lawes of nature abuseth the libertie of subjects that are free borne as if they were slaves and the goods of other men as if they weare his owne'. A lordly monarch controlled both his subjects' persons and goods. The only examples of lordly monarchy still in existence were in Ethiopia and Asia and the Moscovite kingdom. But a royal monarch, while not subject to his people, recognized the property rights of the free-born 'leaving to them all liberties both of their person and goodes'. But in a royal monarchy the king should deal as a father with his children.[53]

The issues of sovereignty and reason of state as presented in the works of Machiavelli and Bodin were central to political thought in sixteenth- and seventeenth-century Europe. Northampton was an early supporter of the absolutist theories which came into vogue in England from the 1580s on. He always supported the idea of unity, authority and obedience in church and state, 'one fold, and one shepherd, in perfect unity for ever and ever Amen'.[54] The world of the mind in which Northampton lived was thus not primarily English. It stretched back to Babylonia, to Berosus whom he called 'the most ancient historian we have',[55] ancient Greece and Rome, and encompassed the history and the learned world of contemporary Europe. It was based primarily on natural law theory and civil law texts. English history was frequently invoked in his writings and he relied on Sir Robert Cotton for advice and for historical precedents to use in his official writings.[56] But Northampton's was primarily a continental culture.[57]

We have then the sketch of the mental world of an unusually learned nobleman who had, with the accession of James I, finally achieved the goal of the Renaissance courtier as advisor to the prince at the age of sixty-three. Castiglione said of old courtiers that although it might not become them to dance, feast and sport, yet they could instruct the prince and indeed take for their models Plato and Aristotle, the latter the instructor of Alexander the Great.[58] Northampton played the role of 'The Perfect Orator' at the Jacobean court on several occasions where he used his learning to support James's views on kingship.

III   *'The perfect orator'*

Two of Northampton's Jacobean controversialist writings, the first on the Spanish peace treaty, the second on the Gunpowder Plot and the trial of Father Garnet help us to understand his public role. Northampton was well known to his contemporaries as leaning toward Catholicism.[59] Not only would Northampton encourage other Catholics to support the Stuart monarchy but he would use his 'learned pen', as King James and his bishops had, against the papacy and against resistance theory.[60]

The Earl was one of the five English treaty commissioners who met six Spanish and Spanish Netherlands representatives at Somerset House in 1604 to negotiate peace. In the group portrait celebrating the peace, he holds a folded paper symbolizing his role as orator. At the first meeting, the

Earl of Northampton, in a speech in the Latin tongue, fraught according to the manner of the times, with many quotations and allusions to the sacred scriptures and the Grecian and Roman literature . . . congratulated his audience on the prospect of peace; set forth the pacific dispositions as well as prosperous fortune of his Brittanic majesty, expatiated on the duty of sacrificing all passions whether of individuals or the times, to the general good of mankind.[61]

In the Spanish Peace Treaty Negotiations, as in advice on financial and naval policy and the Court of Earl Marshal, Northampton relied on Sir Robert Cotton for historical briefs and precedents. At least as important to Northampton's argument as English historical precedent, however, was natural law theory.[62]

One of the central issues was the English right to trade to the East and West Indies. The Spanish refused on the grounds that the pope had shared out the new world between Portugal and Spain. Northampton went beyond Cotton's brief to question the pope's right to deal with secular matters. He claimed he could avow 'the greatest doctors both of the civil and canon law' to uphold freedom of the seas, but focused on the work of Fernando Vazquez, an important sixteenth-century natural law theorist, professor at the Catholic university at Louvain and a servant to the Spanish king. Countering claims of the Venetians and Genoese to the seas off their coasts, Vazquez argued that originally all property had been held in common. While land had undergone division, the sea remained in common possession, an argument used in 1605 by Northampton at the negotiations and developed by Hugo Grotius in 1609.[63] Northampton contended 'that it did not rest in the liberty of any prince or potentate under heaven to limit or stint the scope of traffic or intercourse which nature had left at liberty.' The pope, of all potentates, was least fit and worst qualified to decide the debates because he drew the warrant of his preeminency from Christ whose kingdom was not of this world and therefore could not be maintained by the sword.[64]

In 1606 Northampton published an extensive treatise on the relationship of the papacy and secular powers as part of the Crown's justification of its trial of the Gunpowder Plotters and Henry Garnet, the Jesuit who had heard the confession of one of the plotters. Northampton upheld the freedom and authority of the sovereign prince and attacked Catholic resistance theory.[65] King James was so pleased with the argument of what he called 'The Earl of Northampton's Book'[66] that he had it translated into French, Latin and Italian and sent to other crowned heads of Europe. James himself continued this argument in a series of works which justified the new oath of allegiance crafted after the Gunpowder Plot. Repeatedly referring to the proceedings against the Gunpowder Plotters and 'The Earl of Northampton's Book', he claimed that Northampton had refuted the defence of Father Garnet mounted by Cardinal Bellarmine, the leading Catholic controversialist.[67]

If, as John Pocock has argued, texts are events, the contexts in which they exist change the meaning of their language. 'The Earl of Northampton's Book' not only justified Garnet's trial and execution but also responded to the controversy over the papal interdict of Venice. According to the Venetian ambassador, Northampton told him that any merit in his treatise on Garnet was due to reading the work of Antonio Querini. Querini, a Venetian aristocrat and member of the government, was the most important layman among the Venetians to take part in the immense controversialist literature the Interdict produced beginning in 1606.[68] The Querini tract was distributed by the Venetian government late in that year, the same year that 'The Earl of Northampton's Book' appeared. While Paolo Sarpi was later seen as the force behind Venetian resistance, in the early days of the resistance Querini was one of those singled out for primary blame by Rome.[69] The Querini influence is probably overstated by either the ambassador or the Earl. Yet Northampton did criticize 'the great artillery of your sentences and decrees against the States and Persons of all Princes', which may have referred to the papal interdict imposed in May 1606.

William Bouwsma has argued that Venice represented 'the central political values of Renaissance republicanism, which she made available to the rest of Europe in a singularly attractive and provocative form'.[70] But Northampton was not a republican and he did not adopt the language of republicanism. Rather, he approved Querini's argument for Venetian liberty in the language of the sovereignty of the prince.[71] The power of the Venetian republic as prince resembled that put forward by absolutist theorists and included the prince's dominion over the property of his subjects.[72] In these sorts of terms, Venetian republicanism was attractive to James and Northampton.[73]

With James's accession Northampton put forward a view of monarchical authority similar to the king's in which there was no room for limits or power-sharing with the church. For papal claims to 'deprivation of right, suspension from rule, or sequestration from royalty . . . I take to be that ball of wildfire, which hath caused so great loss of lives and states by combustion in monarchies'.[74] He argued elsewhere that the monarch could not be questioned or resisted. Furthermore, the monarch's actions could not be challenged by his subjects. In his last work, a tract in the king's name against duelling, Northampton relied on designation theory, one of the mainstays of the Jacobean theory of the divine right of kings. 'Subjects are presumed to have put the sovereigns in trust at their first election.' Northampton wrote that 'princes may be truly said to hold rather a shadow than a strength of power, that leave it in the subjects' liberty either to scan their directions or to scan their authority . . . the majesty and prerogative of kings . . . acknowledge no superior but God only'.[75] While Northampton's speeches in parliament recognized the importance of the role of members of the House of Commons, his earlier language of the monarch's 'negative voice' and the liberties of the subjects' persons and goods no longer found utterance.[76]

IV   *Public utility*

Northampton's work as a privy councillor, especially his approach to administrative reform, was pragmatic, based on public utility and the politically possible. Northampton spent a year attacking venality in the navy, questioning witnesses and annotating confessions himself. He recruited a circle of advisors made up of antiquaries, especially Sir Robert Cotton, and merchants, most notably Lionel Cranfield, to advise on the making of policy. While his commonplace book may be filled with treatises on kingship, his other writings were concerned with parliamentary bills, Household reform and, between 1612 and 1614, when the Treasury was put into commission, with finding means to finance the monarch in the absence of parliamentary subsidies. In 1605 Matthew Hutton, Archbishop of York, wrote to Northampton worried about royal finances. Because of the wasting of treasure he argued that England would become 'the poorest kingdom in Europe and the chief blame will be laid upon you great councillors . . . now it hath pleased God to make you a great councillor of state and the best learned of any especially'.[77]

Northampton brought together his political theory and administrative experience during the debate over the Great Contract in 1610:

Proportion should rather be the rule of our imitation than precedent . . . for so long as empire and subjection are relatives, supplies and satisfactions must be concomitant according to . . . necessity. Wherefore whether we leave precedents or follow precedents, whether princes . . . hand[s] be open or close, yet this rule must ever hold, that so long as subjects live under monarchy they are bound to maintain the monarch.[78]

Even as Northampton denied parliament's right to withhold supply, he counselled the king to limit expenditures. As the leading commissioner of the Treasury between 1612 and 1614, Northampton provided detailed suggestions for increasing revenues. His reports, politically informed, discarded sale of office for the Crown's profit as 'doubtful and dangerous'. So sensitive to rank himself, Northampton helped develop and sell the new title of baronet after the failure of the Great Contract in 1611. He urged James to 'abstain from granting reversions . . . and from giving any new, till the gross which is now too heavy for the state, be drawn down'. He and his fellows requested that royal grants be 'reviewed by his Majesty's learned counsel who out of their judgement will observe what may be spared for the king's benefit'. Northampton ordered surveys of expenditures and requested a quarterly review of pensions: 'that the list be reviewed every quarter to see how many die and what is spared'.[79]

Northampton was attuned to political considerations in the exercise of royal authority. He urged that enclosure come only by consent and increases in revenue from wardship should not total more than £50,000 'a higher strain will cause great clamour'. He urged royal officials 'to feel the pulse of the subject'.[80] Nevertheless, in the end, as he put it in debate over the Great Contract: 'shall the kingdom be able to maintain war under Elizabeth and not maintain the ordinary charge under James. Shall his Majestyes bounty not be regarded but condemned, which in former times we would have thought the greatest virtue? As long as there is a Monarchy it must maintain the Monarch.'[81]

V *Interiors: house and nobility*

Norbert Elias has suggested that the French nobility thought not in terms of family but of their 'house',[82] meaning both their family and their property, their genealogy and their city palace or country holdings.

The Howard faction is something of a fiction. Northampton challenged the Lord Admiral, Charles Howard, Earl of Nottingham, for control of the Jacobean navy, was contemptuous of Nottingham's son[83] and distant from the

Howard de Bindon branch. His older brother, Thomas Howard, fourth Duke of Norfolk, left him nothing, not surprising since Northampton was his younger brother but he had had some expectations. Norfolk did not even mention him in the touching letter he wrote to his sons shortly before his execution. During the Elizabethan period Howard was both fond of and dependent on his sister Katherine and became close to his nephews, the sons of Thomas Howard, fourth Duke of Norfolk, especially Thomas, later Earl of Suffolk. He fostered the relationship of Suffolk's daughter Frances with Robert Carr, Earl of Somerset. While Northampton expressed affection to his close friends, amongst his many letters there are few that show family affection.

Loyalty to his house, or family considered in time, was another matter. He arranged for the reburial of his mother and father, saying that the latter coffin need not be large (Surrey's head had been struck off for treason). He erected imposing tombs for them in Framlingham, Suffolk, site of other sixteenth-century Howard monuments. The tomb of plaster and gilt shows Surrey and Frances de Vere, daughter of the Earl of Oxford, surrounded by their five kneeling children adorned with heraldic shields but without religious iconography. Northampton wrote the inscription which puts into words this visual portrayal of filial piety.[84] It permeated many of his writings both under Elizabeth and under James in which he referred to his house as having fallen to 'the meanest in Manassas'. His speeches to parliament and his encomia to the king repeatedly linked the restoration of his house to King James.[85]

As Northampton adapted humanist learning to contemporary issues of diplomacy and politics, he also drew on Tacitus and Machiavelli to understand political manoeuvring at court. Northampton had been caught up in the factional politics of the late Elizabethan court. In 1569 and 1570 Leicester had urged Thomas Howard, Duke of Norfolk, to persevere in his suit for marriage to Mary, Queen of Scots and then was complicit in his fall resulting in his execution.[86] Northampton urged Cecil to undermine Sir Walter Raleigh and Cecil's brother-in-law William, Lord Cobham, in the same way

as my Lord of Leicester dealt with my brother – finding his humour apt to deal with Scotland, when he thrust him into treaty about those affairs, assuring himself that either he should lose the queen for the present, or the other queen for the future – so must you embark this gallant Cobham by your wit and interest, in some course the Spanish way, as either may reveal his weakness or snare his ambition . . . For my own part I account it impossible for him to escape the snares which wit may set, and weakness is apt to fall into.[87]

Cobham and Raleigh did indeed fall victim either to ambition or to Cecil and Northampton's wit. When Lady Raleigh reminded him of his own family's woes he replied with cruel satisfaction:

I could thank your Ladyship for putting me in mind of the griefs and sores of my own honourable family (because nothing more contenteth and pleaseth the dispositions of men than to look back to the rocks and billows of the sea after they are arrived in safe harbour) . . . none of those was either committed thither nor convicted after they came thither upon so just grounds as we committed Sir Walter.[88]

Northampton's view of nobility was heightened, combining both a traditional belief in nobility by birth and the humanist notion that nobility was to be identified with merit and virtue.[89] He had a tender concern for the prerogatives of the peerage reflected in his work on the Earl Marshal's court from the 1590s on.[90] Although he was later to depend on Lionel Cranfield and other merchants for advice, Howard harshly attacked the increasing numbers of those granted arms in the 1590s by describing commerce as an infection:

If Mary the sister of Moses were excluded seven days out of society for feare of infection, how many days or years should we demand our probationers that are derived and drawne out of shopps and warehouses . . . If none but the high priest might decide the differences intere lepram et lepram how dare our heralds in the clearing of base blood which is a kind of leprosie forestall the sentence of their superior.[91]

The nobility were the king's natural counsellors. In May 1603, James I issued an order under the signet explaining that he had increased the size of the Privy Council, to acknowledge the position of the nobility and the Scots. The king's language about the 'ancient nobility whose birth and merit makes them more capable than others' is similar to that adopted by Northampton in his maiden speech in the House of Lords where he lauded James by noting 'the many scions of true noble houses planted at the council board, upon our saviors own presumption that thistles cannot bring forth figs'. Significantly the order was made at Howard House, the home at that time of Suffolk and Northampton.[92]

Northampton's exaggerated sense of rank made him especially sensitive to signs of deference. The Constable of Castile came to sign the treaty of peace with England in 1604. Northampton, long a Spanish supporter, was sent by the king to greet him. He wrote ecstatically that the Constable 'did not only meet me at the stairhead in his Inn at Gravesend three rooms from his own but that very first night at the taking of my leave after some half hours visitation . . . in despite of all my resistance, he brought me back not only those three rooms but down the stairs and to the very door of the street'.[93] The Constable also took note of Northampton's personal sufferings and referred to Mary, Queen of Scots, as the Queen Martyr.

In contrast, Northampton himself paid deference only when necessary. As a young man he insisted that he preferred to write privately for one than publish for many and later, in a line that would not have sounded strange coming from Coriolanus, he wrote 'I was never apt by nature, to crave acquaintance with a private person without urgent cause, much less at random a multitude.'[94] He insisted that a government official and gentleman dismantle part of his house in order for Northampton to enhance the views at his Greenwich house. He used the power of the Privy Council and Star Chamber to the consternation of contemporaries, to challenge Ben Jonson for *Sejanus*, James Whitelocke, the lawyer, for questioning the competence of the court of Earl Marshal, and a group of gossiping gentlemen who claimed that he had been insincere in his challenge to Cardinal Bellarmine.[95]

At the same time, Northampton used the rhetoric of flattery insistently to monarch and favourite and others of influence. Contemporaries criticized the Earl as a flatterer; Edmund Bolton, a sometime client of the Earl's, when recommending models of English from Sir Thomas More, Surrey and Wyatt to Shakespeare, Samuel Daniel and Drayton and Beaumont, suggested 'Henry, Earl of Northampton, son of that Surrey, for some few things, a man otherwise too exuberant and wordfull.'[96] Northampton's flattery was not, however, unique. Salisbury used similar language in writing to Prince Henry and John Marston's *The Fawn* suggests that this is a traditional vice which had peculiar relevance to the Jacobean court.[97]

Unlike his grandfather the third Duke of Norfolk, Northampton's power was not at all military, but political, obtained solely through the king's favour and political patronage. Those dozens of servants and retainers who escorted him at the end of his life reinforced his status not his military power. He kept in close touch with East Anglia and the Cinq Ports, but his residences were near the court, in the Strand and in Greenwich, not in Norfolk and Suffolk. Unlike his father, attainted for quartering the royal arms but, along with Norfolk, guilty rather of contending with the Seymours for control of Henry VIII's heir, he claimed no power independent of the monarch.

Nevertheless, at the end of his life Northampton had, he thought, so thoroughly cemented prince and house that he was able to write 'the last clause in my testament shall be to bind my executors to engrave upon my monument for a lasting memorium when I am dead that the wisest and best king that ever England had was pleased to divide between the uncle and the nephew the two golden keys of great treasure, to one of his kingdom and of his chamber to the other, both his person and his state, resting by this obligation of indissoluble trust . . . in the faith of one family'.[98] Northampton, who had taken the ideal of *The Courtier* for his own and mused that any means to achieve it were legitimate, at once personifies a member of the service nobility and suggests the grandees at the court of Spain whose hold Count Olivares sought to break in the 1620s. After Northampton's death his nephew Suffolk dominated court politics along with the favourite Somerset. It was Buckingham who most effectively moulded the roles of courtier, counsellor and favourite into one.

164

VI *House and collections*

Fame overcame fortune. The Earl built Northampton House just two years after James's accession and furnished it lavishly with contemporary European and Asian luxuries, Turkish carpets and wares from China, Brussels tapestries, some especially grand given him by the Archduke, others, even richer, originally given by the Archduke to the Earl of Dorset. The king granted him the keepership of Greenwich Park and on the foundations of an ancient tower Northampton built a very beautiful house.[99] While Northampton dressed austerely in black, he slept grandly in purple. In London his bedstead

of *China* worke blacke and silver branched with silver with the Armes of the Earle of Northampton upon the head peece, the toppe and valance of purple velvett striped downe with silver laces and knottes of silver, the frindge blewe silke and silver with 8 cuppes and plumes spangled suteable, the 5 curtanes of purple taffeta with buttones and lace of silver, the counterpoint of purple damaske suteable laced, with two featherbeds and one fustian downe bed, a woolbed, a French quilte, one fustian blanckett, and another blanckett, one bowlster, and two pillowes.

It was the bed he died in.[100] In Greenwich, his 'blacke field bedstead painted with flowers and powdred with golde, with the Armes of my Lord of Northampton upon the head' had a 'valence powdered with blewe starres and spangles' and was covered with 'a quilte of poppingey greene sarcenett lined with blewe calicoe stitched with blacke silke'. It was sold after his death to the Earl of Somerset.

Northampton surrounded himself with ornament. He had a 'china guilt cabinet upon a frame' apparently of black lacquer with gilt decoration, one of the earliest ornamental cabinets which was used to display virtù. His extensive collection of jewels included the ruby James sent him from Scotland as a token at his accession and a diamond presented by the Elector Palatine. He owned miniatures in richly jewelled frames, one of Queen Elizabeth set in agate, diamonds and rubies and another of the Earl of Essex set in a tablet of gold. He bought andirons of Nuremberg work and had a couch bound with leather like a rich book binding.

He also collected the most up-to-date information on space and time: he owned maps of Rome, Amsterdam and Antwerp as well as Speed's large map of England, Scotland and Ireland. His Molineux globes of the world, one terrestrial, one celestial, were covered with green taffeta curtains. Amongst his clocks and watches was an unusual 'watche George', in which he combined the timepiece with the representation of St George and the dragon, symbol of the order of the garter to which he was admitted early in James's reign. Northampton's inventory of plate lists great show pieces given by courtiers and ambassadors as New Year's gifts but relatively few dishes, suggesting that most of the former were received late in life when he became a privy councillor. He owned the 'Howard grace cup', a medieval jewelled relic connected to Sir Thomas à Becket. Amongst his silver was a large basin and ewer in the form of a shell and mermaid. The mermaid was designed so that rose water flowed through her nipples.[101]

The power of monarchy and house are reflected in Northampton's collection of paintings.[102] Unfortunately it is not possible to identify the many religious paintings that he had or the fourteen 'Venetian pictures of one bigness' that were listed in his inventory. But of the more than 100 at Northampton House, his palace in the Strand, and at Greenwich, fifty were portraits, many of his family, including eight pictures of the house of Norfolk from John, first Duke of Norfolk to Lord Maltravers (Henry Frederick, eldest son of Thomas, Earl of Arundel). Many of the portraits were of women in the Howard family.

In addition, there were paintings of Queen Elizabeth, the Earl of Essex, and of Essex's children, Louis XIII, Prince Maurice and 'the French Queen', Prince Henry on horseback,[103] King James and Mary, Queen of Scots. In fact the Earl had *five* portraits of Mary, Queen of Scots, as many, if not more, than her grandson Charles I accumulated.[104]

Throughout Northampton House there were religious paintings, several of the Three Kings paying homage to the baby Jesus, of St Francis flanked by the Virgin and Christ with the Cross, folding triptychs of the Pietà and of Christ spilling his blood into a golden fountain. The Earl's portrait collection included Bishop Stephen Gardiner, Bishop Wareham and St Anselm. In his bedroom, hung with Cardinal Wolsey's Brussels work tapestries, there were just three paintings, of the passion of Christ, of Mary – Queen of Scots – and of King James, the earthly equivalent for Northampton of the holy family.

VIII *Decoding the self*

Who did Northampton think he was? Or to put it another way, how did he invent himself? In writings to Elizabeth and to James he invoked the image of the old hermit.[105] It betokened an image both of removal from the queen's presence but also, in the figure of St Jerome, of study, contemplation and wisdom. St Jerome was also a scourge of heretics and, in the Renaissance, identified with the cult of the Virgin.[106] As he composed his will on his deathbed, Northampton recalled both St Jerome and Alexander the Great. In *Basilikon Doron*, James had urged Prince Henry to keep the book next to him as Alexander had kept the *Iliad*. According to Justin, Alexander was asked as he was dying who should succeed him, and replied 'the worthiest'. To King James, Northampton left a silver cup engraved with the words 'detur dignissimo', i.e. 'let it be given to the worthiest'.[107]

His devotional works, his role as religious controversialist, his charitable foundations established along monastic lines, suggest a religious vocation and

166

perhaps, had England remained Catholic, Howard would have played a role similar to that of Bishop Stephen Gardiner. In secret correspondence between Somerset and Overbury he was referred to as the Dominican.[108] Alongside the bishops, he became the English equivalent of Cardinal Bellarmine.

Yet there were many layers to this complex and contradictory man. As matchmaker between his niece, Frances Howard and the favourite, Somerset, Northampton resembled Pandarus in *Troilus and Cressida*, a role not unlike his grandfather Norfolk's who presented two of his nieces to Henry VIII. Self-consciously, the man who wrote a book *Against the Poyson of Supposed Prophesies* presented himself in an entertainment for Queen Elizabeth not only as the old hermit but as Merlin, wiseman and magician.[109] Amongst his tapestries were a series of the sibyls representing wisdom and secret knowledge. Secret knowledge was important to Northampton, whether in the form of astrology, or Jesuitical doctrines of equivocation for which Father Garnet was attacked but which Northampton practised himself or of the Jacobean monarchy with its emphasis on *arcana imperii*. While Northampton's mental world shared a focus on authority, family and history with English gentlemen generally, his was a discourse significantly different from that of many of his contemporaries even as it mirrored his monarch's.

Grandees such as Salisbury, Suffolk, Arundel, Pembroke, Lennox, Carlisle, Somerset, Buckingham served as patrons to antiquaries, poets, dramatists and artists. Those who were favourites of James I, such as Lennox, Hay, Somerset and Buckingham, were ornaments of the court and presented themselves at court very differently from Northampton, Salisbury and, later, Arundel. To Northampton and Salisbury's sober black cloaks, they contrasted brilliantly coloured outfits to catch the eye of the king: Carr had over fifty.[110] Arundel received not only Northampton's library but his example as connoisseur and his circle of scholars.[111] There was a significant change in emphasis however. Northampton's interest was caught more by the word; Arundel's, like Carr and Buckingham, by the visual. For all grandees, however, fame, expressed in deeds, in writing, in bricks and mortar, in stone, in marble, in painting, overcame death.

The Earl of Arundel dedicated his collections to the continuation of the fame of his family.[112] Arundel commissioned the sculptor Nicholas Stone to create Northampton's elaborate tomb. Stone erected a monumental work of black marble with the four Cardinal Virtues in white stone surrounding the structure with the effigy of Northampton kneeling in prayer on the top. For the life-size statues of the four Cardinal Virtues which surrounded it, Stone drew inspiration from the Arundel Marbles, which the Earl had just brought back from Italy.[113] Northampton's tomb proclaimed him *inter nobilitas literissimo* and the Latin inscription on the tomb, composed by William Camden, focused on his lineage, office and religion.[114] Sir Robert Sidney thought him more mourned in Europe than in England.[115] There were even rumours that he had not died but that he had been smuggled out of the country and lived beyond the sea. Such a feat would be worthy of Merlin. Yet such rumours were not idle gossip. A year after Northampton's death, Secretary of State Winwood ordered William Trumbull to investigate whether the Earl's estate was supporting Catholic charities in the Low Countries.[116] Such an end suggests how suspicious many of his contemporaries were of a nobleman and a culture so thoroughly rooted in the Europe of the Counter-Reformation.

10 SENECA AND TACITUS IN JACOBEAN ENGLAND

J. H. M. Salmon

During the wars in France and the Netherlands in the late sixteenth century the Neostoic movement cut across confessional boundaries to provide a practical system of ethics to fortify the individual against the misfortunes of the time. The movement spread across Europe, deriving its inspiration less from the original founders of the Stoa, Zeno, Cleanthes and Chrysippus in the third century BC, than from Seneca and Epictetus in the age of Tacitus. Indeed, Tacitus's own relentless exposure of human motives in his history of the principate, including the relationship between Seneca and his pupil, Nero, was annexed to the corpus of Stoic writings, and added political bite to Neostoic morality.[1] The foremost exponent of late sixteenth-century Neostoicism, Justus Lipsius, was also the greatest Tacitean and Senecan scholar of his time. Through his pen the surviving parts of both the *Annals* and the *Histories* of Tacitus became a kind of analogue for the travails of late sixteenth-century Europe. When classical antiquity was employed as a screen to view the problems of the late Renaissance, Seneca and Tacitus came to be preferred to Cicero and Livy, and the shift in moral and political thought brought with it a change in literary taste. This has been abundantly demonstrated for France, Germany, Italy, the Netherlands and Spain.[2] The same cannot be said of modern discussion of the vogue for Seneca and Tacitus in late Elizabethan and Jacobean England. Seneca has been treated in terms of literary allusions; Tacitus in terms of historiography and, to less extent, of political ideas.[3] A new dimension of Jacobean mentality becomes visible when English interpretations of Seneca and Tacitus are placed in the context of Neostoicism in general and court faction in particular.

Gerhard Oestreich has described the European Neostoic movement as an ideology of statesmen, soldiers and scholars, providing 'the theory behind the powerful military and administrative structure of the centralised state of the seventeenth century'.[4] This is not a judgement that can readily be applied to Stuart England, where Neostoicism had a far less positive role to play. The reason for this is partly that the English disciples of Seneca and Tacitus were usually members of circles soured by suspicion and defeat, and partly that the Senecan and Tacitean ideas they took from Lipsius and his continental disciples contained ambiguities that allowed a more negative application to English politics.

The relationship between pagan Stoicism and Christianity embodied several of these ambiguities. However loyal to Stoic precepts, Lipsius himself was singularly inconstant in his confessional allegiances. His 1574 edition of the historical works of Tacitus was the fruit both of his Catholic studies in Rome and his Lutheran sojourn in Jena. His original Neostoic compositions, *Constancy* and *Six Books of Politics*, appeared in 1584 and 1589 during his Calvinist phase at Leiden. His Senecan commentaries and his edition of the essays and letters of Seneca were published in the last fifteen years of his life, when he resided as a Catholic in Louvain. *Constancy* was essentially a system of practical ethics that adapted Stoic assumptions to an undogmatic Christianity. The old legend that Seneca had corresponded with St Paul died hard, and even Lipsius, with all his critical acumen, refused to deny it categorically. In common with other Neostoics, he was aware of the difficulties in any attempt at reconciliation. He discussed the way in which the ancient Stoics had defined fate, and tried to show that Panaetius and Seneca had used the term as if it were divine providence.[5] Lipsius had to acknowledge that the Stoic doctrine declaring all faults to be equal was inconsistent with the Christian distinction between venial and mortal sins, and he also condemned Stoic approval of suicide as unChristian.[6] He did not, however, discuss the most important anomaly of all: the conflict between a Christian's dependence upon divine charity and the Stoics' use of reason and will to subdue the passions and shield the self from the external world.

Constancy was a tract for the times which invoked Tacitus to show that the Rome of the *Annals* and the *Histories* had endured comparable, if not worse, persecutions, atrocities and civil wars.[7] Lipsius explained in the preface that the work was based upon Seneca and Epictetus, and intended to provide solace and to teach survival amid contemporary suffering and chaos.[8] This negative aspect involved another ambiguity, transmitted from Stoic antiquity, between participation in public affairs and withdrawal in pursuit of personal tranquillity. Some of the Stoics, Seneca included, had served the state, and it was their opponents, the Epicureans, who had advocated cultivating one's own garden. Yet the advice of Epictetus, ἀνέχου καὶ ἀπέχου ('endure and abstain') was also a part of the Stoic legacy, and the burden of Seneca's message was the self-sufficiency of the individual. If *Constancy* counselled the individual to endure the hardships of tyranny and civil war through fortitude and private prudence, Lipsius's *Politics* offered a pragmatic guide to statecraft through public prudence. Seneca and Tacitus were again invoked in tandem, but in *Politics* the priorities were reversed and Tacitus took the leading role. In the fourth book Lipsius developed his theory of *prudentia mixta*, which held that a moderate amount of deceit and subterfuge was a necessary ingredient in any government. Tacitus supplied an inexhaustible fund of Roman examples of prudence applied and misapplied, and Lipsius constantly interwove his observations on statecraft with Seneca's reflections upon morality in every kind of political circumstance. This parallelism culminated in Lipsius's *Manuductio ad Stoicam Philosophiam* of 1604, and the following year Lipsius reduced his political and moral philosophy to a series of adages and examples in *Monita et Exempla*, the most widely read and frequently plagiarized of all his publications.[9]

Thus Lipsius incorporated Tacitus into the Neostoic movement, and in his frequent parallels between the darkest moments of first-century Rome and the Europe of his own day endowed Stoic sentiment with certain negative aspects for those pessimistic enough to apply it to their own society. Montaigne, Guillaume du Vair, and Pierre Charron also contributed to Neostoicism and cited Seneca and Tacitus in the spirit of *similitudo temporum*. Their works were also well known in England,[10] but it was Lipsius who pointed the way to its particular impact there. His confessional uncertainty enabled English Catholics as well as Protestants to enlist him in their causes, and his ambiguity between private and public prudence allowed those who failed to achieve their ambitions to bend Neostoicism into less constructive channels than those apparent on the Continent. This outcome can be traced through the networks of court patronage and faction, and initially its association with the Sidney circle seemed to promise a very different result.

Sir Philip Sidney met and corresponded with Lipsius, who dedicated to him a work on Latin pronunciation.[11] An earlier and much closer friend was Philippe Du Plessis-Mornay, counsellor of Henri de Navarre and director of Huguenot propaganda. Mornay anticipated Lipsius in the attempt to blend Stoicism and Christianity. Sidney himself began a translation of Mornay's *De la vérité de la religion Chrétienne* (1581), which was completed by Arthur Golding and published soon after Sidney's heroic death in the Netherlands in 1586. Mornay sought to establish a widespread pagan consciousness of the existence of a beneficent creator, and asserted that Zeno, Seneca and Epictetus had believed in the 'unity and infiniteness of God'.[12] In 1576 Mornay's Stoic-inspired *Excellent discours de la vie et de la mort*, which included a version of Seneca's *De Providentia*, was put into English by Edward Aggas as *The Defence of Death*. Sixteen years later Sidney's sister, Mary Herbert, Countess of Pembroke, retranslated it and had her client, Samuel Daniel, prepare a new English version of *De Providentia* known as *A Letter to a Countess*.[13] Another translator of Mornay was Samson Lennard, who had been beside Sidney on the fatal field of Zutphen. Lennard also translated Pierre Charron's *De la sagesse* (1600), and dedicated it to Prince Henry in 1606.[14] The translator of the most influential of all the Neostoic works, Lipsius's *Constancy*, was also linked with the Sidneys. Sir John Stradling dedicated his English version of 1594 to his uncle, and the latter's ward married Sir Philip Sidney's younger brother, Robert. Lipsius's *Politics* also appeared in English in 1594 in a version prepared by William Jones.

Sidney's connections with Queen Elizabeth's most trusted ministers, his role as a leader of the European Protestant movement against Counter-Reformation catholicism, and his influence upon the literary fashions of his day ensured that Neostoicism entered English intellectual life without the darker shades it subsequently acquired. This may have been partly due to the fact that Lipsius's assimilation of Tacitus into the movement took some time to enter English consciousness. Tacitus did attain an early vogue in Oxford, but Sidney treated the moral implications of his history with suspicion. When Robert Sidney followed in his brother's footsteps at Christ Church in the late 1570s, Sir Philip urged him to seek out Henry Savile as his mentor, and to broaden his political understanding by reading Bodin, Dio Cassius and Tacitus, paying heed to 'the venom of wickedness' he would encounter in the latter.[15] As it turned out Tacitus became at least as well known as Seneca within the Sidney circle after Sir Philip's death, especially when the leadership of the group was assumed by Elizabeth's new favourite, Robert Devereux, Earl of Essex. Sidney left not only his sword and his widow to Essex, but also his friends and clients. These included Fulke Greville and Charles Blount, Baron Mountjoy, who pursued an interest in Senecan tragedy with the Countess of Pembroke.[16] Mountjoy had fought beside Sidney in the Netherlands, and became the lover of Essex's sister, Penelope Rich, once the object of Sidney's poetic admiration. Roger Manners, Earl of Rutland, who had married Sidney's daughter, was also a member of Essex's retinue and a patron of Neostoic writers. Francis Bacon, Henry Cuffe, John Hayward, Richard Greneway, Henry Savile, and Henry Wotton were all followers of Essex who tended to stress Tacitus rather than Seneca.

Savile and Greneway were the two English translators of Tacitus, Savile of the *Histories* and the *Agricola* in 1591, and Greneway of the *Annals* and the *Germania* in 1598. Savile's text was combined with Greneway's in the 1598 and subsequent editions.[17] At Oxford Savile took an interest in Henry Cuffe, and when the rebellious Cuffe had been expelled from Trinity for defying the master, arranged for him to become a fellow of Merton, where Savile had been appointed warden in 1586. Cuffe was briefly professor of Greek, and then left the university to act as Essex's secretary, attending him at Cádiz and in Ireland. Meanwhile Savile became provost of Eton through the favourite's influence. Essex's loss of the queen's favour, and then his disgrace after his premature return from Ireland, led to his revolt and execution in 1601. This catastrophe proved to be a turning point in the development of the Neostoic movement in England, and in large measure the Tacitean strand had prepared the way for it. Cuffe seems to have encouraged the spirit of faction and discontent in the earl's entourage and it may not be fanciful to see him as the centre of the group who politicized the cult of Tacitus and gave it the bitter edge it preserved in subsequent decades. Francis Bacon, while paying tribute to Cuffe's scholarship, mentioned his 'turbulent and mutinous spirit against all superiors', and recorded how Essex, after his own condemnation, confronted Cuffe in the Tower and called him 'one of the chiefest instigators of me to all these my disloyal courses into which I have fallen'.[18]

There was not, of course, the slightest hint in the prefatory matter to Savile's text that Tacitus in English garb might encourage sedition. Montaigne had called Tacitus 'a seminary of moral, and a magazine of politique discourses for the provision and ornament of those that possess some place in the managing of the world'.[19] It was in this spirit that Savile had dedicated it to the queen, knowing 'the great account your Highness most worthily holdeth this history in'. In his address to the reader Savile made the lesson rather more explicit. He rehearsed the lessons that could be drawn from each of the three emperors who contended for power after the death of Nero. 'In them all', he concluded, 'and in the state of Rome under them, thou mayest see the calamities that follow civil wars, where laws lie asleep and all things judged by the sword.'[20] Before the beginning of the surviving fragments of the *Histories* Savile inserted twelve pages of his own composition on the fall of Nero, covering the lost concluding section of the *Annals*. Disputed succession and the associated possibility of civil war were a source of considerable anxiety in Elizabeth's last years. A number of English works appeared at this time concerned with the wars between Marius and Sulla, Caesar and Pompey, and Antony and Octavian. The same motif inspired contemporary works on English history.[21] Greneway's Tacitus was less concerned with succession problems, and more with the techniques of tyranny, conspiracy and survival in a world where virtue was at a discount. With no sense of foreboding, he dedicated his translation of the *Annals* to Essex, and struck an even more ingenuous note than Savile when he stressed the utility of Tacitus, making a dutiful nod to Cicero's praise of history in the process:

For if history be the treasure of times past, and as well a guide as image of man's present estate, a true and lively pattern of things to come, and as some term it, the work-mistress of experience, which is the mother of prudence, Tacitus may by good right challenge the first place among the best. In judgment there is none sounder for instruction of life for all times to those which oft read him judiciously, nothing yielding to the best philosophers.[22]

If Savile was correct in his assumption that the queen esteemed Tacitus at the time she accepted the dedication of the *Histories*, she found reason to change her opinion when Tacitean 'politic history' became associated with the Essex faction. Within Essex's retinue Sir John Hayward became one of the more notorious practitioners of the genre. His *First Part of the Life and Reign of King Henry IV* (1599) roused Elizabeth's ire when she read his account of the deposition of Richard II and his critical remarks about that ruler's poor judgement. According to the well-known story in Bacon's *Apophthegms*, she asked whether Hayward could be charged with treason:

Mr Bacon, intending to do him a pleasure, and to take off the Queen's bitterness with a jest, answered: 'No, Madam, for treason I cannot deliver opinion that there is any, but very much felony.' The Queen, apprehending it gladly, asked: 'How, and wherein?' Mr Bacon answered: 'Because he hath stolen many of his sentences out of Cornelius Tacitus.'[23]

A new edition of the work was banned, and after the failed coup Hayward found his history being used by Sir Robert Cecil and Sir Edward Coke as proof that the plot had been long premeditated. The speeches invented by Hayward were taken as evidence of the intentions of the conspirators. Bacon himself contributed to this impression by suggesting that the work had had Essex's prior approval.[24]

Those at Essex House who had stood aloof from Cuffe's extremism, such as Francis Bacon, Fulke Greville and Henry Wotton, retained their interest in Seneca and Tacitus after the disaster. Nor was the darker aspect of the cult so evident in their writings. Wotton had shown off his knowledge of Seneca in his correspondence during his first visit to the Continent.[25] When he subsequently entered Essex's service in 1594, he was sent to France by the earl on a delicate mission to conceal compromising material entrusted to Antonio Perez, Philip II's former minister, who earned a reputation as a fervent Tacitean.[26] After attending Essex on the Cádiz expedition and in Ireland, Wotton returned to Italy, where, soon after his patron's treason, he expressed his despair at the tragedy in an eloquent Latin letter to his friend, the scholar Isaac Casaubon. Later, as James I's ambassador to Venice, he cited Tacitus at times in his despatches.[27] Seneca and Tacitus doubtless continued to be read at Eton, where Wotton became provost two years after Savile's death in 1622.

Bacon likewise remained a Tacitean, but he was no blind admirer of ancient Stoicism. In a letter composed for Essex's signature in 1595 he offered advice to the young Earl of Rutland, who was embarking on his first grand tour of Europe. In it he commended Stoic control of the passions, but added: 'The Stoics were of opinion that there was no way to attain this even temper of the mind but to be senseless, and so they sold their goods to ransom themselves from their evils.'[28] On the other hand, Bacon entirely approved of Lipsius's approach to politics, for he wrote another letter of advice on Essex's behalf at this time suggesting a reading list for a young client going to Cambridge in which he endorsed the *Politics* of Lipsius as the best epitome of the subject.[29] Bacon often cited Tacitus in his *Essays*, especially in those entitled 'Of Simulation and Dissimulation' and 'Of Seditions and Troubles'. Seneca was also frequently invoked, but Bacon criticized the emphasis he and other Stoics placed upon preparing for death.[30] Tacitus was also to feature in Bacon's *Advancement of Learning*, in his speeches in James I's initial parliament, and in his begging letters to the king in 1612 and 1616.[31] Bacon's respect for Tacitus blended with his admiration for Guicciardini, who shared the Roman historian's disenchanted view of human nature and had modelled his own historical writing on Tacitus when the latter's works were becoming widely known in Italy in the first half of the sixteenth century. Their joint influence was apparent in Bacon's *History of the Reign of King Henry the Seventh*, written after his impeachment.[32]

In the immediate aftermath of Essex's revolt Senecan fortitude and the dark side of Tacitean politics seemed to complement each other. Bacon, Greville and Robert Sidney cooperated with the Privy Council. Cuffe suffered the same fate as his master. As Essex's clients, Hayward and Savile were briefly imprisoned. Roger Manners, Earl of Rutland, and his brothers were fined. Mountjoy, Essex's lieutenant and successor in Ireland, was pardoned. The confluence of Neostoicism and the Tacitean current at this time is well illustrated by the essayists Robert Johnson and Sir William Cornwallis. Little is known of the former, but his 1601 essay, 'Of Histories', seems to have represented the attitudes of the survivors. Johnson saw the lessons of the past as a means of reinforcing Stoic principles. He cited the positive virtue represented by Cleanthes, Zeno's successor at the Stoa, as something that delighted the mind, strengthened resolution, and encouraged the kind of martial ardour evident in ancient Athens and Sparta. There was a reverse side to the coin, and though less attractive it was equally necessary:

Another kind there is like labyrinths, relating cunning and deceitful friendships, how rage is suppressed with silence, treason disguised with innocence . . . and although they may be distasted by those who measure history by delight, yet they are of the most use in instructing the mind to like accidents . . . In this rank I prefer Tacitus as the best that any man can dwell upon.[33]

William Cornwallis issued his first group of essays in 1600, and a second collection, together with *Discourses upon Seneca the Tragedian* in the following year. Despite their rebarbative style, the *Essays* reappeared with additions in later years. Although he served Essex in Ireland, he was not involved in the earl's treason, and received a knighthood in 1602. On the one hand he had connections with the Sidney tradition through the Harington family, to whose ladies he dedicated some of his essays; on the other with the Catholic Henry Howard, of whom his father, Charles Cornwallis, was a client. Howard, who, surprisingly, had ties with Essex, had been readmitted to the royal court in 1600 after a period when he was suspected of favouring Spanish interests, but he had nothing whatever to do with the plot in the following year.[34] In their search for patrons the Cornwallises illustrate the way in which the Neostoic and Tacitean cult found Catholic as well as Protestant followers. No one typified its attitudes better than William Cornwallis, and the more his expectations as a courtier were disappointed, the more strongly his Stoicism was reaffirmed. In his younger days he had been attracted to the chivalric romances that were popular in the Sidney circle. His tastes changed, as he confessed in the essay 'Of the Observation of Things': 'If in Arthur of Britain, Huon of Bordeaux, and such supposed chivalry, a man may better himself, shall he not become excellent with conversing with Tacitus, Plutarch, Sallust, and fellows of that rank?'[35]

To judge from the number of citations in the *Essays*, Seneca and Tacitus were Cornwallis's favourite authorities. Although he seldom mentioned modern writers, political pragmatists such as Lipsius, Guicciardini and Commines received his approbation. Many essays on themes such as resolution, patience, fortitude and temperance were thinly disguised adaptations from Seneca. In 'Of Essays and Books' Cornwallis ranked Seneca as the supreme moralist, and went on to praise Tacitus as a historian who could look unblinking at the vices of Seneca's age. In one of his later essays, 'Of Fortune and her Children', Cornwallis quoted Seneca's *De Tranquillitate Animi* to reproduce the old Stoic tension between pursuing worldly ends and insulating the self by withdrawal: 'There is liberty in a solitary obscure life more precious than any commodity that rests in the hands of those strivers for the world, and that is mine.'[36] This was no academic resumption of the eternal debate between the merits of the *vita activa* and the *vita contemplativa*, but rather a reflection of the conflicts and disappointments that carried over from the Elizabethan to the Jacobean age. Cornwallis's Neostoicism was essentially negative, and the consolation he offered his readers involved contempt for those who trod the path of ambition. In 'Of Imitation' he wrote: 'The age after us that shall see both fashions to please the senses and to get riches, and must be our judges, I am afraid will determine the times of old, times begetting philosophers and wise men, and ours an age of cooks and tailors.'[37] In the same spirit Cornwallis's *Discourses* extracted maxims from Seneca's tragedies, and gave them a cynical slant. 'Among poets', he wrote, 'Seneca's tragedies fit well in the hands of a statesman, for upon that supposed stage are brought many actions fitting the stage of life, as when he saith *Ars prima regni est posse te invidiam pati*'.[38] For Cornwallis fear was the world's governing principle. Princes ruled by it, and without it the bestial proclivities of humankind would cause universal anarchy. Hence the first discourse developed Seneca's line *Odia qui nimium timet regnare nescit; regna custodit metus.* As for virtue, Cornwallis, like Tacitus, thought it could only be found in the past:

It seems virtue once had the empire of the world, for antiquity shows many coins of [such] stamp, but even this age so fears her power, as everyone will wear her livery, though few do her service. The worst, though they love vice, yet adorn their ill will with the counterfeit colour of virtue.

With a political cynicism matching his moral pessimism, Cornwallis integrated his two prime authorities, blending the egoistic fortitude of Seneca with Tacitus's acceptance of the corrupting influence of power.

At his advent James I not only forgave the partisans of Essex but showered honours upon them. Bacon, Greville, Savile and Wotton were knighted. Robert Sidney became a baron and Mountjoy Earl of Devonshire. At the same time the king showed favour to the Howard family. Henry Howard became Earl of Northampton and played a major role in the Privy Council, particularly in bringing Raleigh to trial for treason and in prosecuting the conspirators of the Gunpowder Plot. Charles Cornwallis received a knighthood and pursued the new policy of peace with Spain as ambassador to Madrid. After his return in 1609 he entered Prince Henry's household as treasurer. However, most of those who gravitated to the court of King James's elder son had been associated with Essex. Before his premature death in 1612 Prince Henry seemed to have inherited from Sidney and Essex the mantle of the Protestant cause in Europe.[39] The pacific policies of the king, combined with the advancement of his Scottish favourites and of the Howard faction stimulated tensions comparable with the bitter last years of Elizabeth. The Main and Bye Plots of 1603, followed two years later by the conspiracy of Catesby, an active participant in Essex's rising, created an atmosphere of uncertainty, while the scramble for place and pension intensified rivalries and conflicts. Such was the setting in which the negative aspect of the Neostoic movement evident at the end of Elizabeth's reign continued to manifest itself. A memoir on Prince Henry by Sir Charles Cornwallis conveys the climate of contention, suspicion and deceit. He describes the courtiers and place-seekers as 'the moths and mice of court at that time . . . maligners of true virtue and only friends to their own ambitions and desires'.[40] When Prince Henry died, Sir Simonds d'Ewes heard many compare his demise with the poisoning of Germanicus.[41] The growth of Tacitean influence in preceding years explains the popularity of the image.

Among those in the prince's household who continued the Sidney–Essex tradition were Sir Thomas Chaloner, his governor and chamberlain, who had once been Essex's agent in France and Florence, and Lionel Sharpe, Essex's former chaplain. John Hayward became the prince's historiographer. A constant attendant was the Earl of Rutland, husband of Sidney's daughter, who secured a place for his client, Sir Robert Dallington. One of the prince's companions was Essex's young son, who had previously been entrusted to the care of Sir Henry Savile at Eton. Another was John Harington, son of Baron Harington of Exton, the governor of Prince Henry's sister, Elizabeth. The Haringtons were related to the Sidneys through young John Harington's grandmother, Lucy Sidney. Sir John Harington of Kelston, a cousin who was once an intimate of Essex the traitor, had been in trouble with the old queen for his satires. He played some part in the prince's education. Lucy Harington was perhaps the most famous of them all as Countess of Bedford, one of the great ladies and literary patrons of the court. Ben Jonson, Samuel Daniel and George Chapman received her support.[42] John Florio, another client of the Haringtons, obtained a place at court and dedicated his translation of Montaigne's *Essays* to Lucy Harington. Sir William Cornwallis, whose own essays have already been examined, was associated with the group not only through his father's position as treasurer of the prince's household but also through his marriage to Jane Meutys, the Countess of Bedford's companion. Finally, Joseph Hall, the so-called 'English Seneca', was one of the prince's chaplains.

This network, loosely bound by patronage and family, had a common interest in the lessons provided by Seneca and Tacitus. There were, of course, many beyond the circle who were attracted by Neostoicism, and many others at the court of Prince Henry who gave no sign of seeing their own age as the analogue of first-century Rome. Literary critics have written much on the manner in which Jacobean letters, and particularly drama, reflected the reality of the royal court and its offshoots. Historians, in reaction, have sometimes scorned the idea that the palace, like the stage, was 'sinister, bloody, cynical and corrupt'.[43] Certainly, it seems extreme to assert that Whitehall under James I was actually like Rome under Tiberius, but it is understandable, given the vogue of the Lipsian parallel and the plots and conflicts already mentioned, that some at the time came to believe it to be so. What began as a literary convention took on the specious guise of moral truth. Ben Jonson's play *Sejanus* is a case in point.

Jonson had his patrons in the Sidney–Essex circle, and developed a particular obsession with Roman history. His *Poetaster* of 1601 set the scene in the last years of Augustus. This play was not simply the dramatist's way of settling old scores with rival poets: it was also a rather sour commentary on the queen's last years, and Jonson, like his friend William Cornwallis, himself assumed Stoic attitudes.[44] After the first performance of *Sejanus* by Shakespeare's company in 1603 Jonson was called before the Privy Council and interrogated by Henry Howard. Although he vigorously denied any reference to English affairs, the suspicion remained that Essex had been the model for the stage version of Tiberius's ambitious and unprincipled favourite.

PLATE 1 *James's Accession Medal, with laurel wreath, describing him as Emperor of the Whole Island of Britain, 1603.*

PLATE 2 *Bezant, 1603. James I in royal robes kneeling with uplifted hands before an altar; before him on the carpet are the four crowns of England, Scotland, France and Ireland, with a Latin quotation from Psalm cxvi: 'What shall I render unto the Lord for all his benefits unto me', Geneva Bible.*

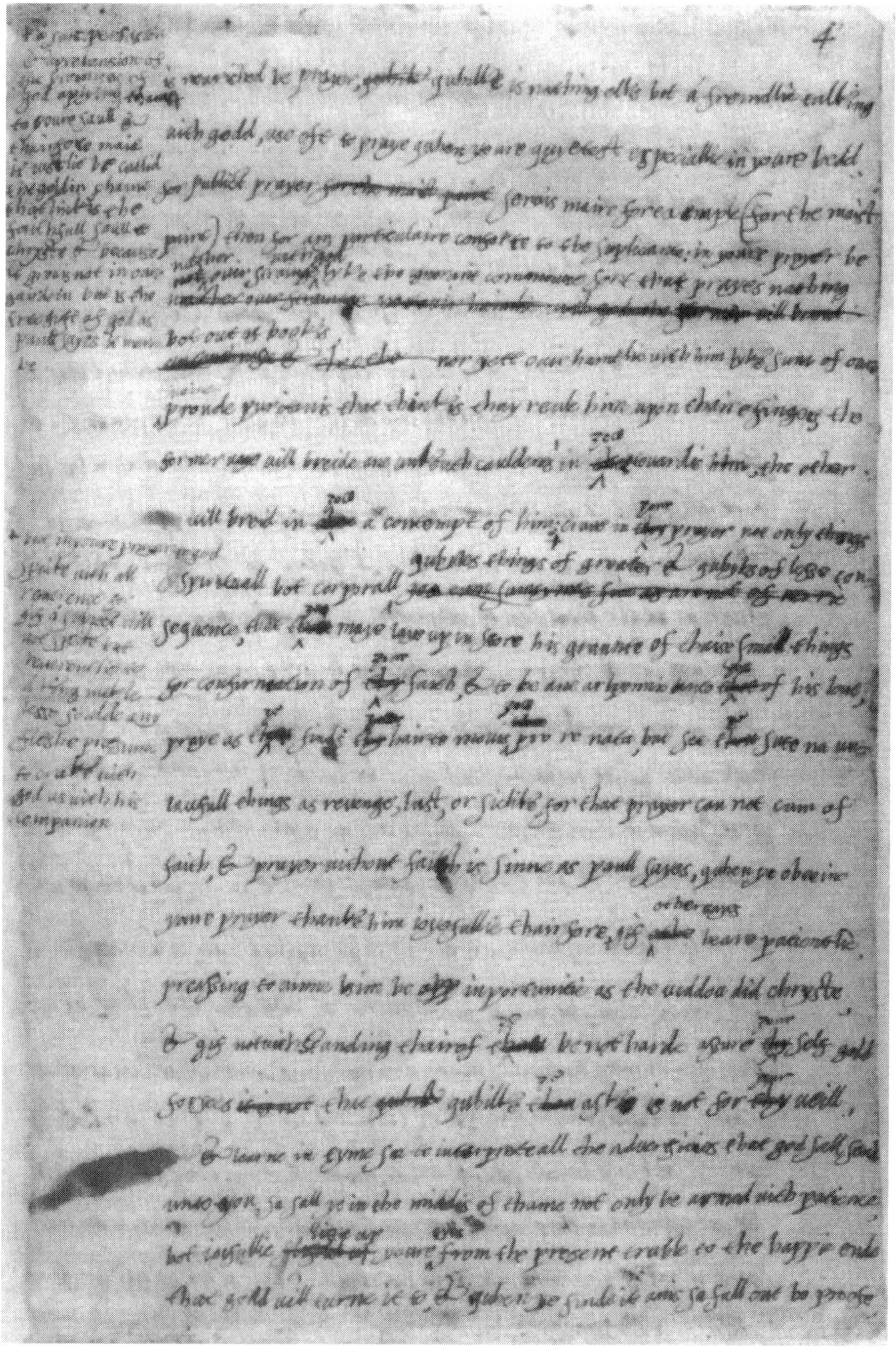

PLATE 3 *James VI, 'Basilikon Doron', autograph page.*
British Library, Royal MS 18 B xv.

PLATE 4 *Henry Peacham, 'Basilikon Emblemata'. British Library, Royal MS 12 A lxvi, f. 38v.*

ATE 5 *Woodcut of James I.*
ntington Library STC 24639
05).

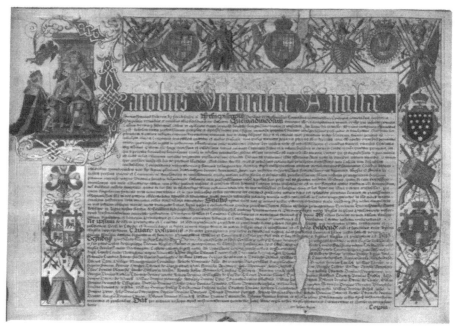

PLATE 6 *Portrait of King James and Prince Henry by Isaac Oliver. B.L. Add. Mss. 36932.*

PLATE 7 *Engraving of James I in Parliament, Reynald Elstrack, second state, with shields of English, Scottish and Irish nobility, and portraits of King James, Prince Charles, and English privy councillors.*

PLATE 8 *Portrait of James I by Daniel Mytens, 1621.*

PLATE 9 *Portrait of Queen Anne at Oatlands with Inigo Jones gate in background, 1617, by Paul van Somer.*

PLATE 10 *Inigo Jones, The Queen's House, Greenwich.*

PLATE 11 *Inigo Jones, 'Penthesileia', masque costume worn by Countess Bedford. Devonshire Collection, Chatsworth.*

PLATE 12 *Robert Peake, Portrait of Prince Henry with Sir John Harington.*

PLATE 13 *Somerset House Conference, 1604, group portrait of English, Spanish and Spanish Netherlands envoys to celebrate peace treaty with Spain.*

PLATE 14 *John de Critz, Robert Cecil, Earl of Salisbury, in Garter Robes, Hatfield House.*

PLATE 15 *Portrait of George Villiers, Duke of Buckingham, by William Larkin.*

PLATE 16 *Inigo Jones, New Exchange, drawing of 1618–19.*

PLATE 17 *Audley End.*

PLATE 18 *Inigo Jones, Banqueting House. Royal Commission on Historical Monuments.*

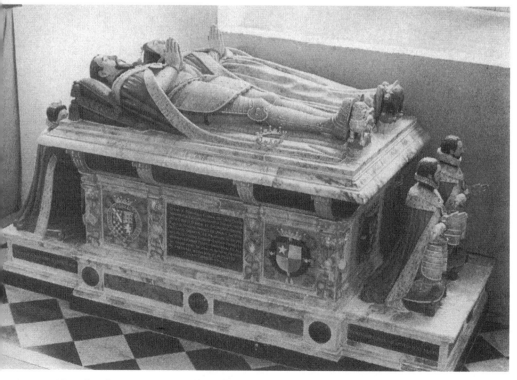

PLATE 19 *Tomb of Henry Howard and Frances de Vere, Earl and Countess of Surrey, 1614. St Michael's, Framlingham.*

PLATE 20 *Daniel Mytens, Portrait of Thomas Howard, Earl of Arundel, with sculpture gallery, at Arundel Castle.*

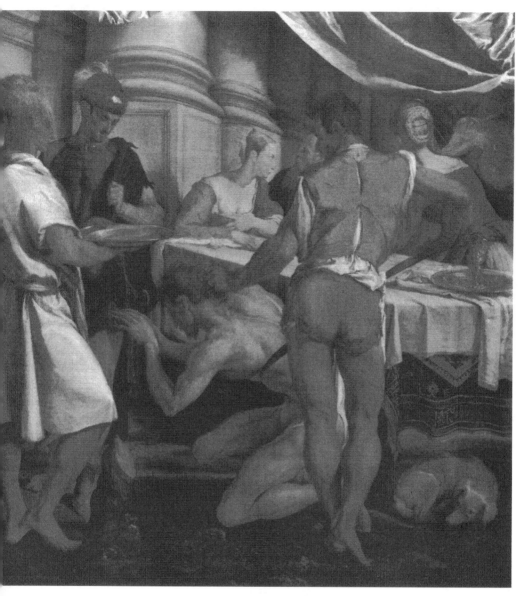

TE 21 *Jacopo da Ponte (Bassano Vecchio), 'Beheading of*
ohn' (Copenhagen), owned by Robert Carr, Earl of Somerset.

PLATE 22 *Tintoretto, 'A Maze', owned by Somerset.*

PLATE 23 *John Speed, Military Map 1603–4, showing locations of battles of the Wars of the Roses with a lengthy genealogical chart displaying James VI and I's descent from William the Conqueror.*

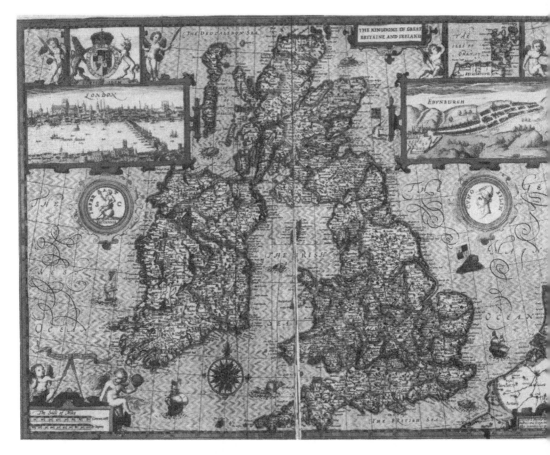

PLATE 24 *John Speed, 'Theatre of the Empire of Great Britaine, 1611', map of England and Scotland and the capital cities of London and Edinburgh.*

PLATE 25 *Irish social groups, John Speed,
Map of Ireland, 'Theatre of the Empire of
Great Britaine, 1611'.*

PLATES 26 and 27 'Watche George', part of
insignia of the Order of the Garter, St George
killing the dragon on one side; watch with one
hand on the other.

PLATES 28 and 29 (right) Mermaid ewer and
shell basin, New Year's gift presented by Roger
Manners, Earl of Rutland, to Henry Howard,
Earl of Northampton.

PLATE 30 *Good Shepherd chalice, owned by Bishop John Buckeridge.*

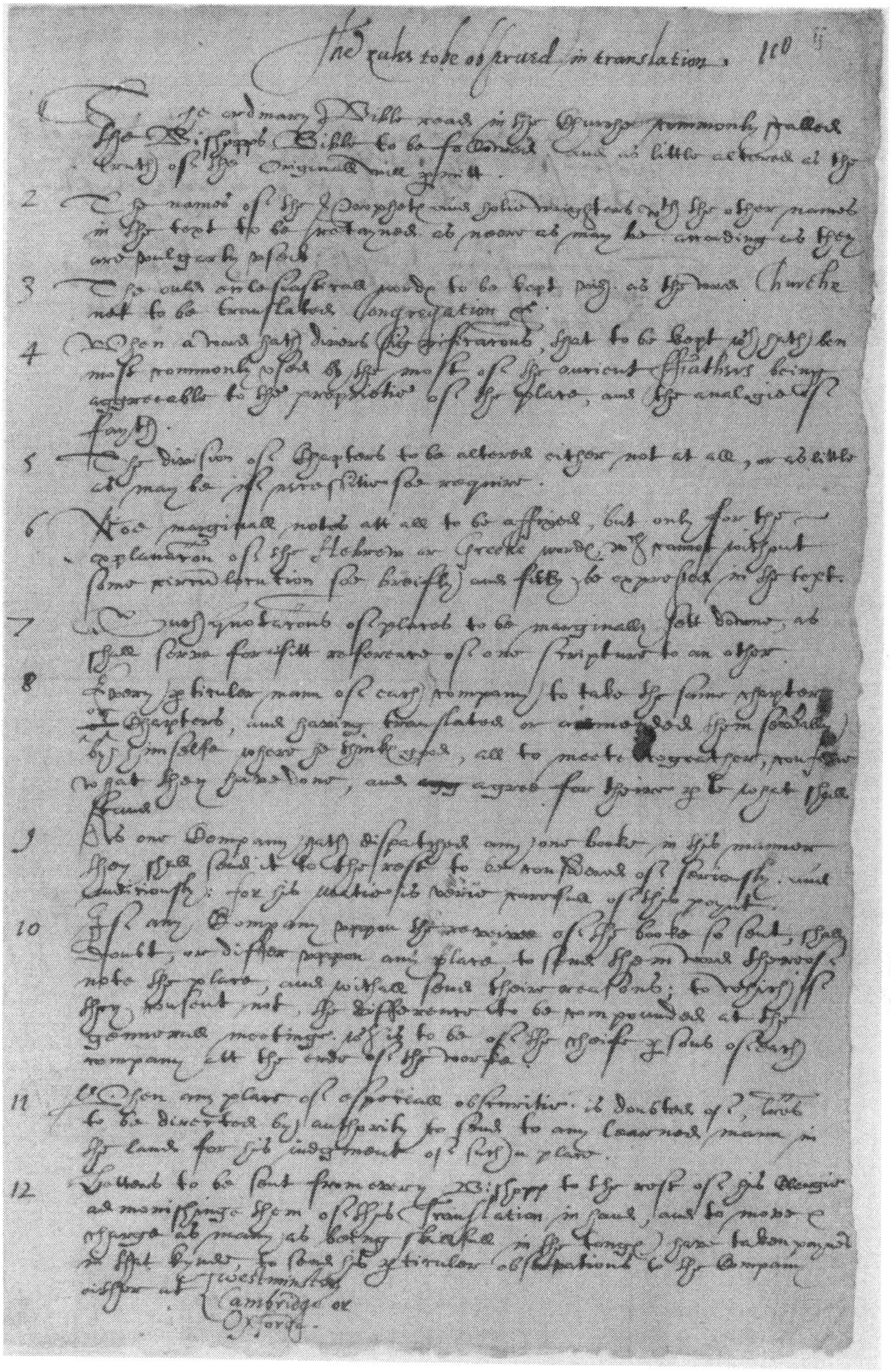

PLATE 31 *Rules for translating the Bible, 1604, issued by King James.*

PLATE 32 *Frontispiece Thomas Lodge's 'Workes Seneca'.*

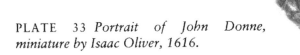

PLATE 33 *Portrait of John Donne, miniature by Isaac Oliver, 1616.*

When Jonson revised and published the play in the immediate aftermath of the Gunpowder Plot, he took the precaution of adding a postscript calling the piece 'a mark of terror to all traitors and treasons'.[45] In his note to the reader he stressed the historicity of the play, and in the margins of the text inserted references to Tacitus, Suetonius, Dio Cassius, Seneca and Juvenal taken from the best Latin editions. There were, indeed, only trivial departures from the historical record, and there were some speeches lifted wholesale out of Tacitus, which caused Jack Marston to scoff at pedant playwrights who 'transcribe authors, quote authorities, and translate Latin prose orations into English blank verse'.[46]

Sejanus has been aptly described as 'a play of whispers, of informers, toadies, flatterers and spies, who congregate in small impenetrable groups'.[47] Compared with an anonymous play published in 1607, *The Stately Tragedy of Claudius Tiberius Nero*, which provided the audience with vivid horrors and perversions,[48] *Sejanus* was a discreet affair, leaving violence and libidinous excess offstage, to be conveyed by conversation and innuendo. What matters here is not correspondence with real events and personalities in contemporary England, but atmosphere and the correspondence of roles. Reminiscent of the function of the group of Tacitean 'politic historians' is the role of Cremutius Cordus. Thus Sejanus to Tiberius in the second act:

> . . . Then there is one Cremutius
> Cordus, a writing fellow they have got
> To gather notes of the praecedent times
> And make them into Annals; a most tart
> And bitter spirit (I heare) who under coulor
> Of praysing those, doth tax the present state,
> Censures the men, the actions, leaves no trick,
> No practice unexamind, paralells
> The times, the governments; a profest champion
> For the old liberty. (Tiberius) A perishing wretch.[49]

It is in *Sejanus* that so many of the English devotees of Seneca and Tacitus seem to find an echo. Ben Jonson's other Roman tragedy, *Catiline* (1611), follows on the heels of Thomas Heywood's translation of Sallust, and begins in the style of Senecan tragedy with the ghost of Sulla delivering a warning against the perils of faction and civil war. It has been convincingly linked to the conspiracies in the decade before its composition.[50] Jonson's image of Rome in the last century of the republic and the first of the empire connects at every point with the parallels drawn to their own times by the English Neostoics. The opening lines of *Sejanus*, where the two outmoded and virtuous senators, Silius and Sabinus, discuss the ethics of the court of Tiberius, closely resemble the negative account of the late Elizabethan and the Jacobean courts in the writings of Cornwallis and others yet to be examined:

Silius. 'Tis true: indeed this place is not our sphaere.
Sabinus.   No, Silius, we are no good inginers;
We want the fine artes, and their thriving use
Should make us grac'd or favor'd of the times:
We have no shift of faces, no cleft tongues,
No soft and glutinous bodies that can stick
Like snailes on painted walls; or on our brests
Creepe up, to fall from that proud height, to which
We did by slaverie, not by service, clime.
We are no guilty men, and then no great;
We have nor place in court, office in state,
That we can say we owe unto our crimes;
We burne with no black secrets, which can make
Us dear to the pale authors; or live fear'd
Of their still waking jealousies, to raise
Ourselves a fortune, by subverting theirs.[51]

Jonson's play made much of the contrast between the virtuous courtier of bygone times and the unscrupulous seeker of fame and fortune. Having failed to obtain the latter, Sir William Cornwallis used Tacitus to recognize the necessity of conflict and deceit, and Seneca to confirm his own renunciation of the path to power. Another associate of Prince Henry's court, Sir Robert Dallington, employed Neostoicism to justify the way of the world and to signify his own contentment with it. His skill in finding patrons, and his facility with his pen, enabled him to escape from the status of an obscure Norfolk schoolmaster to become the cicerone first of the Earl of Rutland and then of his brother, Lord Roos. The byproducts of his European travels with the Manners family were his published guides to France and Tuscany – guides remarkable for their shrewd observation of political and social mores.[52] So skilful was Dallington in those arts of the courtier which Cornwallis affected to despise that, on the death of Prince Henry, he successfully transferred to the household of Prince Charles. Having presented the manuscript of his *Aphorisms Civil and Military* to the former in 1609, he dedicated the published version to the latter in 1613.

Dallington was clearly a survivor, and his *Aphorisms* put more stress upon prudential politics and the formulae for success than the sour grapes expressed in Cornwallis's *Essays*. Yet the difference between them was one of attitude rather than sources and format. Their common technique was to begin with an epigram, and to build upon it reflections in which citations from the ancients expanded the topic in ever-increasing circles. The method arose from the taste for maxims or *sententiae* extracted from moralists and historians, and Seneca and Tacitus afforded a mine of such material. Montaigne declared Tacitus so useful because his history was 'fraught with sentences',[53] and

Lipsius had turned the genre into an art with his *Monita et Exempla*. There were many books of epigrams and aphorisms, some of them, such as the collections of Francesco Sansovino and Remigio Nannini, available in English.[54] Dallington's aphorisms were similar to Nannini's, for they followed up observations on particular maxims with examples from Guicciardini's *History*. Many of Dallington's adages were derived from Tacitus, Seneca, Plutarch and Sallust, sometimes by way of Lipsius. Indeed, he claimed in his address to the reader that the aphorisms were cemented together by 'Lipsius solder'.

Dallington steered a careful course between cynicism and moral principle in accordance with Lipsius's definition of *prudential mixta*:

All moralists hold nothing profitable that is not honest. Some politic[ian]s have inverted this order and perverted the sense by transposing the terms of the proposition, holding nothing honest that is not profitable. Howsoever those former may seem too straight laced, these [latter] surely are too loose. For there is middle way between both which a right statesman must take.[55]

The tag for this was the theme from the second book of Cicero's *De Officiis*: *Nullum utile est quod non sit honestum*. It was supplemented by related quotations from Seneca, Tacitus, Sallust, Juvenal and others, and exemplified from Guicciardini with an episode involving Cesare Borgia. In another passage, taken direct from Lipsius's *Politics*, Dallington justified dissimulation in statecraft:

Upon the theatre of public employment either in peace or war, the actors must of necessity wear vizards, and change them in every scene, because the general good and safety of a state is the centre in which all their actions and counsels must meet: to which men cannot always arrive by plain paths and beaten ways.[56]

Dallington provided here another supporting reference to Lipsius on prudence, and then cited a passage in *Annals* XIV:44, where Tacitus argued that injustice must necessarily be done to an individual when the common good was at stake. This paragraph was a notorious point of reference for those who saw Tacitus as an apostle of reason of state.

While Cornwallis pessimistically accepted the decay of virtue, and Dallington justified moderate deceit, another Neostoic swung to an extreme of misanthropy. He was Thomas Gainsford, the author of an unpublished manuscript entitled *Observations of State and Military Affairs for the most part collected out of Cornelius Tacitus*.[57] Its title page is dated 1612, but the fact that it is addressed to 'Sir Thomas Egerton, Knight' suggests that it was begun earlier, since the Lord Keeper became Chancellor and Baron Ellesmere in 1604. Apart from his service in Ireland and later publication of miscellaneous histories and romances, little is known about Gainsford. The opening remarks in *Observations* suggest that he was a bitter and disappointed man.

181

He had evidently offended Ellesmere's mother-in-law, the Countess of Derby, and he had scandals attached to his name, for he referred darkly to 'faults sequestered under colour of state', and to 'detractions' that made him 'resemble an adder in a path, wherein the encounter occasioneth a sudden fear'.

Gainsford does allude to Tacitus from time to time, and he makes several references to Roman history, but he is clearly writing about his own times under cover of a commentary upon antiquity. Many seeming abstractions apply to contemporary English issues, such as mentions of monopolies and trading in offices, and a remark about conflicting loyalties on the eve of a rebellion that suggests the split in Essex's entourage at the time of the abortive coup.[58] Some of Gainsford's maxims are common Senecan coin, such as 'a good prince governed by evil ministers is as dangerous as if he were evil himself'.[59] Others display conventional Stoic sentiment, such as 'miseries are tempered with patience; felicity corrupteth'.[60] Gainsford makes the standard denials that his Stoicism preempted Christian belief, but holds that history shows little difference between pagan and Christian rulers. In all times and in all places self-interest prevails and power corrupts, 'as though princes were contented to be admitted scholars in God's academy, but will take no more lessons than will serve their own turns'. It is not surprising that, for Gainsford, 'positions of state break through the wall of our consciences'. He expects nothing virtuous in human nature: 'It is the property of man's nature to hate those they have hurt.'[61]

As the manuscript moves through such topics as 'policies of state', 'secrets of court', 'tyrants', 'evil councillors', 'innovation', 'ambition', 'revolts', and 'reformation of a commonwealth', Gainsford's focus wanders between prince, courtier and subject. He even defends ordinary folk against the oppressive laws of the time. 'What are these', he asks, 'but contradictions of the truth, which yet the politics of state would fain colour over with adulterate excuses of custom, establishment of peace, prevention of innovation, contempt of regal authority, dispersion of good order, neglect of superiors, and discovery of turbulent spirits?'[62] Sometimes he advises the tyrant how to deceive and punish; sometimes he coaches the dissident in the art of rebellion by feigning defence of liberty and the common people; and sometimes he tells the courtier how to rid himself of rivals. What Gainsford provided was a textbook for survival in a predatory world:

The safest way to live under tyrants is to do nothing, because of nothing no man is to yield an account. Otherwise, to do evil is dangerous, to do ill is not always secure, and to be changeable the next step to deformation.[63]

It was possible, of course, to pay tribute to Tacitus without any close connection with the Essex inheritance and without any particular avocation for

Stoicism. Such was the case with the two founding members of the Society of Antiquaries, William Camden and Sir Robert Cotton. Camden declared in the preface to his *Annals of Queen Elizabeth* that he had learnt his methods from Tacitus,[64] but as he was writing contemporary history, and had trouble enough with his account of the deposition of the king's mother, Mary Queen of Scots, he avoided cynical maxims and Roman parallels. In any case, he had received his mission from Burghley to celebrate the reign of a greater queen, and he had no intention of allowing the troubles of Elizabeth's last years to colour his narrative. Cotton's situation was rather different. He became far more involved in politics than Camden, and he managed to shift from one great patron to another, serving Northampton, Somerset and Arundel, with all the skill of a Roman courtier. His admiration for Tacitus was a part of his obsession with all things Roman. He even catalogued the manuscripts in his celebrated library under the names of the early emperors.[65] When it came to writing history, rather than collecting antiquities, his method was the reverse of Camden's. His *Short View of the Long Life and Reign of Henry III* (1627) was more a list of maxims than a narrative of events.

Just as there were some who respected Tacitus without Seneca, there were others who admired the philosopher but not the historian. Joseph Hall was a most unusual member of Prince Henry's household, and represents as much sweetness and light as English Neostoicism could muster. Hall was named 'our spiritual Seneca' by Sir Henry Wotton, and the term 'the English Seneca' was often applied to him. One of his early works was even translated into French as *Le Sénèque Chrétien*.[66] He began as a satirical poet in the style of Juvenal during Elizabeth's last years, and published the three works that earned him his reputation as a Christian Stoic early in the reign of James I: *Meditations and Vows Divine and Moral* (1605), *Heaven upon Earth or True Peace and Tranquillity of Mind* (1606), and *Characters of Virtues and Vices* (1608). His mission was declared in the dedication of *Heaven upon Earth*: 'I have undertaken a great task, to teach men how to be happy in this life. I have undertaken and performed it, wherein I have followed Seneca and gone beyond him: followed him as a philosopher, gone beyond him as a Christian, as a divine.'[67] He realized, as perhaps Lipsius did not, that Stoic self-reliance was incompatible with the need for divine grace, and rejected Seneca's teaching on tranquillity, finding inward peace impossible in face of consciousness of sin and fear of evil. Only reconciliation with God could comfort the sinner.[68] Hall's *Characters* was adapted from the ancient genre invented by Theophrastus, whose text by the same title had been edited by Isaac Casaubon, and who was mistakenly assumed to have belonged to the Stoa.[69] Others had tried their hand at the personification of virtues and vices, but none were as successful as Hall. His work was directly in contrast with the cynical tone noted at Prince Henry's court. He began his 'Description of a Good and Faithful Courtier' with the words: 'Our courtier is no other than virtuous and serves the God of Heaven as his first Maker, and from Him derives his duty to these earthen gods.'[70] In similar tone he described flattery, the stock-in-trade of those around him at the court, as 'nothing but false friendship, fawning hypocrisy, dishonest civility, base merchandise of words, a plausible discourse of the heart and lips'.[71]

Hall became a considerable anti-Catholic polemicist, and was nominated by James I to attend the Dutch Calvinist Synod of Dort in 1618. In later life he defended episcopacy, and as Bishop of Norwich was persecuted by the Long Parliament in the civil war. His career was very different from that of the leading English Catholic interpreter of Seneca, Thomas Lodge, although there were some odd similarities in their early literary development. There was also a curious chance encounter between them. In 1605 Hall had gone to the Spanish Netherlands with Sir Edmund Bacon, and there, as he recalled in his memoirs, he 'met an English gentleman, who, having run himself out of breath in the Inns of Court, had forsaken his country, and therewith his religion, and was turned both bigot and physician'.[72] Lodge was indeed in exile in Brussels at this time, and Hall's derogatory description fits his varied career. Hall went on to report the altercation that ensued when Lodge engaged in 'hyperbolical predication' about miracle cures he alleged had occurred at a shrine of the Virgin at Sichem nearby. It so happened that at this very time Lipsius was publishing his own testimony in support of these miracles – an action that earned him the scorn of many of his colleagues.[73] As earlier noted, Lipsius's own religious shifts help to explain the appeal of Neostoicism to both Catholics and Protestants.

Lodge voyaged to North America in 1585 and 1591. In subsequent years, while registered at Lincoln's Inn, he acquired some reputation as a satirist and dramatist. His play about Marius and Sulla, *The Wounds of Civil War* (1594), contributed to the taste for using Roman history to offer English political lessons. In *Wit's Misery and the World's Madness* (1596) Lodge anticipated Hall by using the genre of Theophrastus to personify the seven deadly sins. He then turned to medicine, and at the same time began his career as a translator. His translation of the works of Josephus was dedicated in 1602 to Lord Howard of Effingham, and contained an address to the reader on 'the use and abuse of history' which stressed the Stoic virtues and called upon the historian to teach morality to his readers.[74] Lodge's 1614 version of Seneca's prose works is in many ways a monument to the Jacobean Neostoic cult. He had returned to England, and as a Catholic had taken the oath of allegiance to James I. Evidently he continued to rely upon the patronage of the Howards, for the 1620 edition of his Seneca was dedicated to the recently disgraced treasurer, Thomas Howard, Earl of Suffolk, to whose family's service, Lodge declared, 'I have inseparably consecrated my best labors.'[75]

The frontispiece to Lodge's rendering of Seneca (Plate 32) represents pictorially the various aspects of English Neostoicism. It depicts the philosopher's death, combining in a single scene the gruesome phases described by Tacitus. The details were familiar to English readers from Montaigne's account of the passage, or from Greneway's translation of the *Annals*,[76] but the frontispiece provides something more, a miniature pantheon of Stoic worthies. Below the balcony containing the death scene are the shades of Zeno and Chrysippus, the founders of Stoicism. Beneath them is a panel showing a philosopher turning his back on worldly affairs and labelled *Honores exilium*, an apt comment for Lodge as well as Seneca. On either side of this are effigies of Socrates and Cato Uticensis, who, if not Stoics themselves, had died the Stoic deaths related by Diogenes Laertes and Plutarch. Among the Senecan essays that follow in the text are the celebrated pieces on providence, constancy, tranquillity, clemency, life's brevity, consolation and the twenty-fourth epistle preparing the mind for death. This translation is based upon Lipsius's 1605 Latin edition. Indeed, the spirit of Lipsius pervades the whole book. Lodge includes Lipsius's life of Seneca, derives his commentaries from those of Lipsius, and even adds a tail-piece of Stoic errors that is an adaptation of Lipsius's discussion of the difficulties in reconciling pagan Stoicism with Christianity.[77]

Another English Catholic who made a notable contribution to Neostoicism was John Healey. In 1610 he published both his version of St Augustine's *City of God* (which, of course, had no connection with Stoicism) and a new translation of Epictetus's *Manual*.[78] A second edition of the *Manual* in 1616 was accompanied by Healey's English version of the *Characters* of Theophrastus, based on Casaubon's Latin text. Anglicans tended to decry the Catholic Neostoics. For instance, the high churchman, Anthony Stafford, who was well read in the works of Lipsius, especially his *Manuductio*, and who endorsed Stoic attitudes in general, accused the Catholic heirs of Lipsius of going too far and forgetting their Christianity.[79] Both Lodge and Healey were more charitable than this towards Protestant Neostoics. Lodge translated a commentary upon *Divine Weeks and Works*, the popular epic poem by the Huguenot Salluste du Bartas. Healey admired Du Plessis-Mornay and translated his lament for his dead son. He also prepared an English version of Hall's utopian work *Mundus alter et idem* (1605).[80] There was a more optimistic note in Lodge and Healey, as there was also in the work of Hall. All three taught virtue, not dissembling. Yet the more significant element in English Neostoicism was the darker side of Stoicism that accompanied the infusion of Tacitean thought and its application to court politics. It was the more negative practitioners of the cult who deserved the critics' reproach of neglecting Christian obligations.

The spread of Neostoicism did not go unchallenged. Hostility to Seneca drew upon the critical view presented by Dio Cassius, against which

Montaigne composed his defence of the philosopher, denying that he had been, as Dio Cassius and his modern adapters had claimed, 'covetous, given to usury, ambitious, base-minded, voluptuous, and under false pretences and feigned shows, a counterfeit philosopher'.[81] While denigrating the character of Seneca was one form of criticism, the Neostoics were also attacked for their lack of Christian humility, their asceticism and their insensitivity. Bacon's comments to this effect have already been mentioned. Weightier criticism came from James I himself, who in *Basilikon Doron* wrote of 'that Stoic insensible stupidity that proud inconstant Lipsius persuadeth in his *Constantia*'. The 1603 edition dropped the personal mention of Lipsius, and substituted 'wherewith many in our days, pressing to win honor in imitating that ancient sect, by their inconstant behaviour in their own lives belie their profession'.[82] The Puritan Gabriel Powel wrote of 'that blockish conceit that would have men to be without affection, howbeit of late it hath been newly furbished by certain upstart Stoics',[83] and George Thomson, perhaps exploiting the royal disapproval, assailed Lipsius directly with *Vindex Veritatis adversus Justum Lipsium* (1606).

James I's opinion of Tacitus was indicated in a conversation he had with Casaubon in 1610. The king doubted that Tacitus deserved his reputation for political wisdom, and Casaubon repeated the criticism he had advanced in his edition of Polybius that Tacitus merely provided a breviary of evil actions.[84] If it had survived, the king's response to a letter sent to him in 1612 by Traiano Boccalini might provide further evidence of the king's distaste for the Taciteans. Boccalini enclosed the first volume of his *Ragguagli di Parnasso*, where he satirized the controversy over Tacitus. He differed from the Counter-Reformation practice then current in Italy of linking Tacitus with Machiavelli in the service of godless immorality, and his *Osservazioni sopra Cornelio Tacito* made this clear. However, his 'News from Parnassus', while placing an eloquent defence in the mouth of Lipsius, also expressed the case for the prosecution. It condemned reason of state, and blamed Tacitus for teaching princes how to be tyrants and subjects how to dissemble their disloyalty.[85]

James clearly had some antipathy to the Taciteans despite the favours he bestowed on them at his accession. This was apparent in his endorsement of the views of Edmund Bolton, a Catholic who had had links with Northampton. Bolton knew the *Ragguagli*, and took up in earnest the ironic case constructed against Tacitus by Boccalini. In 1624 Bolton published *Nero Caesar or Monarchy Depraved*, in which he praised the administration of the empire in the early part of Nero's reign and, while not denying Nero's bloody excesses, characterized the plots against him as contrary to divine injunctions against rebellion. His object was to illustrate James's belief in the divine right of kings, and to demonstrate that the worst ruler was better than the anarchy of revolt. *Nero Caesar* was an answer to earlier plays, derived from the history of Tacitus, that stressed the duplicity of rulers and their favourites, or idealized resistance in the name of republican virtue. It was dedicated to the Duke of Buckingham with the words: 'Royal approbation of the thing (with the greatest improbation of Nero) hath made it so honorably capable of best acceptance, as it may well be called his Majesty's.' In fact the manuscript had been sent to the king two years before publication, and it has been maintained that it was not only approved but touched up by James himself.[86]

Near the end of the reign Degory Wheare published in Latin the lectures he had recently given at Oxford as the first incumbent of the professorship established by William Camden. His subject was the art of history. When he came to Tacitus, the equivocal reputation that Tacitus's English disciples had acquired decided him not to venture his own judgement but to cite testimony for and against the historian of Roman tyranny. To defend the usefulness of Tacitus, Wheare quoted the dedication to the German emperor, Maximilian II, with which Lipsius had prefaced his edition of Tacitus's *Opera Omnia*:

Let everyone in him [Tacitus] consider the courts of princes, their private lives, counsels, commands, actions, and from the apparent similitude that is betwixt those times and ours let them expect the like events. You shall find under tyranny flatterers and informers, evils too well known in our times, nothing simple and sincere, and no true fidelity even amongst friends; frequent accusations of treason, the only fault of those who had no fault; the destruction of great men in heaps, and a peace more cruel than any war.[87]

Against Lipsius Wheare set the equally prestigious opinion of Casaubon, citing from the preface to his edition of Polybius the comments on Tacitus that Casaubon had repeated to James I. To advocate reading the *Annals* as a lesson in Stoic fortitude and the technique of survival under tyrants was ill-advised, for modern rulers were not like Tiberius and Nero, and such Roman examples induced not prudence and constancy but a creeping corruption, as 'little by little they sink into our minds'.[88] A few years after Wheare's lecture, Isaac Dorislaus chose Tacitus as the subject of a similar series at Cambridge endowed by Fulke Greville. The authorities considered the topic so subversive that the lectures were suspended.[89]

Wheare's caution is understandable, given the reputation of many of the English Taciteans and the king's distaste for the cult to which they belonged. The attitude of James I ensured that in England those positive aspects of the Lipsian movement, which on the Continent contributed in some measure to the ideology of state building, were ultimately without influence. Instead, Tacitean Neostoicism became a vehicle for discontent in Jacobean court circles. The particularly English confluence of the streams of Senecan and Tacitean ideas, which occurred at about the time of the Essex coup, differed somewhat from Lipsius's intermixing of the two. With Lipsius the way lay open for rational statecraft and the prudential participation of the subject as the servant of the absolutist state. It was not so with those English malcontents who devised their own blend of Senecan and Tacitean influence under the pressure of plots, rivalries and disappointments in late Elizabethan and early Jacobean times. For them Tacitus politicized Senecan philosophy and gave it a cynical bent, while Seneca strengthened the lessons, already suggested in Tacitus's history of Roman tyranny and civil war, that private prudence and withdrawal were the best policies.

Some of the conflicts within the Jacobean court spilled out on a wider stage, and the Tacitean aspect of the Neostoic movement contributed to the bitterness with which they were expressed. Under Charles I Sejanus became a popular name of opprobrium for the Duke of Buckingham. Sir John Eliot applied the label to the duke in parliament in 1626, and the king, who was as quick as his father to resent the implication that he resembled Tiberius, sent Eliot to the Tower.[90] In 1628 Pierre Matthieu's biography of Sejanus, whose duplicitous and bloody ways had been surpassed only by those of his master, appeared in two separate English versions to satirize Buckingham, both of them entitled *The Powerful Favourite or the Life of Aelius Sejanus*. When the duke was assassinated in that same year, there were many who hoped for a solution to the constitutional impasse. It was not to be, and when Eliot went back to the Tower for his final act of defiance, it was appropriate that Sir Robert Cotton thought to send him a copy of Lipsius's *Constancy*.[91]

PART III
LITERATURE AND ART

11 THE COURT OF THE FIRST STUART QUEEN

Leeds Barroll

Queen Elizabeth's death brought important alterations in the status of noble women to the royal court of England. Though female, she had operated as a monarch, a role essentially patriarchal, and thus she played the part of the symbolic head of the male aristocracy. And while surrounding herself with a Privy Chamber that at the end of her reign had come to be a *familia* largely composed of women, Elizabeth was strict in drawing a line beyond which her women could not pass in trying informally to affect policy. At the same time her Privy Chamber was virtually a 'closed shop' with women of the Howard, Carey, Radcliffe, Stafford, Brooke and Knollys families being omnipresent.[1] Ladies outside of this circle had small chance for advancement; women within the circle had limited opportunity to exert influence.

When King James came to the throne, however, a male replaced a female as the symbolic leader of the male aristocracy. Further, he brought with him a royal woman who was not, as in the last four decades, the monarch, but the royal female person whose role merely established her as the principal member of the female gender in England. Nevertheless this position held some significance for ambitious noble women, for Anne of Denmark, as royal consort, required the formation of a new and second court, the court of the queen.

Paradoxically, then, the accession of James in 1603 could activate, for the first time in decades, the political aspirations not only of some male courtiers, but, more importantly, of a number of ambitious and talented women. True, some, such as Lady Cobham and the recently deceased Countess of Nottingham, had attained positions of unofficial influence around Queen Elizabeth, but her court had been remarkably stable, not a place for temporary ascendancies. When Queen Anna (she never called herself 'Anne') arrived, however, the situation for noble women now altered. No matter how many males might serve such a queen as gentleman ushers, stewards, or in Crown positions such

191

as Lord Chamberlain or Treasurer, a Queen Consort was not otherwise required to give official recognition to men: her role seemed, rather, to require a formal circle of women whose existence could resemble the presence of the male officials who served the monarch. For ambitious and highly-placed women, then, the arrival of a Queen Consort who, furthermore, had no history of local attachments, created a situation in which a number of new positions were now open.

I propose here a preliminary examination of this situation, the formation of this vastly underestimated new court of the Queen Consort in the initial years of King James's reign, first sketching Anna's background and some of her activity in Scotland, then tracing the identity of some of the noble women and men who made up the queen's English circle early in James's new reign, and finally suggesting the potential influence of her court upon English culture. Most pronounced with respect to the drama and literature of the period, this influence nevertheless extended to Crown affairs since it included Henry Prince of Wales during his own short lifetime. Thus, although Queen Anna's circle has greatest significance for students of literature and the arts, the political activity of this interesting woman invites as much scrutiny as her cultural patronage.

Literary historians have hitherto agreed in ascribing to Queen Anna a curious personality. Roy Strong, writing as recently as 1986, observed that 'on the whole, Anne lived for pleasure, passing her time moving from one of the palaces assigned to her to the next . . . She deliberately avoided politics, devoting herself instead to dancing, court entertainments, and the design and decoration of her houses and gardens.' Prince Henry, heir apparent, was, we gather, familiar with her character, for 'even at sixteen he was keenly aware of his mother's pettiness'.[2] Thus students of the English Renaissance are not accustomed to viewing Queen Anna's domain as an important part of the artistic scene, even though the translator John Florio and the poet Samuel Daniel are both long known to have been Grooms of her Privy Chamber,[3] nor have scholars seemed to realize the collective power of patronage represented among the queen's courtiers and their own circles. Yet as Queen Anna was organizing her court, she was, intentionally or not, establishing the formal structure for a concentrated network of patronage in the arts. In view of this, an overemphasis upon James's own literary influence presumably motivated by his scholarly interests may seriously misrepresent the actual situation at the Stuart court and greatly underestimate the role of his queen.

Anna's activities prior to her coming to England, for example, do not bear out traditional characterizations. Certainly the environment in which she spent her youth would not forecast an adulthood oriented to trivialities. Anna's father was Frederick II, King of Denmark and Norway, whose support of learning is well known to Danish historians. Frederick's most important benevolence in this respect was his patronage of Tycho Brahe. Frederick funded Tycho's famous castle-laboratory, Uraniborg, on the island of Hveen. Designed with the help of a number of scholars, this observatory was regarded as one of the most advanced buildings in Europe.[4]

Anna's mother was a highly gifted woman, Sophia, daughter of Ulric III, Duke of Mecklenberg. Interested in the arts and the sciences, she too, for example, had supported Tycho (he was, in fact, the son of Queen Sophia's Mistress of the Wardrobe). Sophia visited Hveen several times, and on one of these visits took up a suggestion made to her by Tycho about his friend the historian Anders Sorensen Vedel (Velleius). At Tycho's urging, the queen encouraged Vedel to gather together his collection of old Danish ballads and have them published: they still remain an important source of early Danish folk-literature.[5]

Anna, born 12 December 1574, was one of seven children. The organization of her family, especially the role of Sophia, is suggested in a letter to Lord Burghley describing the queen as 'a right virtuous and godly princess which with a motherly care and great wisdome ruleth the children'.[6] But King Frederick died in 1588 and Sophia claimed the right of governing Denmark and Norway as Dowager Queen through the minority of Christian IV, the oldest of Anna's younger brothers – now eleven. The Danish Privy Council refused Sophia this power and appointed four guardians to rule the country until Christian would come of age, although, interestingly, they did allow her to receive ambassadors. Otherwise, Sophia held her own court at Nykjobing where she devoted part of her time to the study of astronomy, chemistry and other sciences. Anna thus had in her parents, especially in her mother, available role-models of some intellectual and political weight.

Less than a year after her father's death Anna, now fifteen, was married by proxy to James VI of Scotland. After some delays caused by the weather, James sailed to the Continent to claim her and Queen Sophia invited the couple to Copenhagen.[7] James visited Hveen to meet Tycho Brahe and was impressed enough by his visit to Uraniborg to write three poems about the great astronomer.[8]

Anna was crowned in Scotland on 17 May 1590. Then began a period in her life in which, with her mother Sophia as her only prior model, she would attempt to define a position as Queen Consort in the sixteenth-century Scottish court. The sixteen-year-old queen would not bear a child for four years,[9] and seems to have moved vigorously into court politics, although her few biographers and other historians of the period have failed to focus on this important aspect of her life. The queen had her own lands and strongholds in marriage-settlement (Dunfermline, Leith and Falkland), but her valence in the Scottish court is best assessed in terms of the general political background of the last decade of James's Scottish reign.

In his efforts to return the Scottish crown to the status it had enjoyed during the time before the troublesome period extending from the end of the reign of James V, the new James had to contend with three general problems. These were (1) the political challenges of those earls resisting the broad entente generally prevailing between the Crown and the Scottish magnates who were indispensable to it; (2) the efforts by the kirk to gain autonomy and then political power in Scotland through an elected internal hierarchy responsible in theory only to God; and (3) the destabilization continually threatened by blood-feuds among the nobility, revenge-patterns often innocent of any broad political goals.[10] James met (1), the political challenges from individual nobles, either by eventually destroying or neutralizing the more threatening earls such as Bothwell, or the Gowries. Meanwhile he continued to stabilize Crown authority by creating or maintaining offices that functioned as lightning-rods to absorb attack: Maitland's chancellorship, for example, and, after his death, the 'Octavians' onto whom James displaced anti-monarchist sentiments. (2) The kirk James engaged and eventually pushed from the political arena through counter-polemic or by carefully chosen confrontations effected when the kirk was careless in selecting the circumstances of their own resistance-displays. (3) Blood-feuds James controlled through the interplay of central power with the localities in which feuding was chronic.

Queen Anna, coming upon this general scene in 1590, seems to have manipulated weight in several of these precarious balances. In December 1590, for instance, she developed what seems to have become a lasting friendship with the Countess of Huntley, a woman close to her in age, but also the wife of one of James's childhood friends and most important earls, albeit Catholic.[11] The countess herself was, as were, importantly, most of Anna's friends, a person of almost impeccable credentials from James's viewpoint: Henrietta *née* Stuart, the daughter of James's second cousin and great favourite Esmé Stuart who, arriving from France in 1579, had become an important influence upon the thirteen-year-old James. Before the Earl of Gowrie (the father of those James would later have to deal with) effected his famous ten-month kidnapping of James in 1582, the young king had created Esmé Stuart Duke of Lennox. But during the kidnapping, Lennox was forced to leave Scotland, dying shortly thereafter in Paris in 1583. Yet he left four children whom James was most careful to protect or advance for the rest of his life.[12] The two daughters he married to members of the small group of his former childhood friends: the Earls of Mar and Huntley. The latter, George Gordon, 6th Earl of Huntley, became the husband of Henrietta Stuart who, although formally a Protestant owing to her father's careful recantation, was thus married to the most powerful among the Catholic earls of Scotland, a group that included the Earls of Erroll, Crawford, Maxwell and Claude.[13]

194

Huntley had received his education at the Valois court and his wife, Henrietta, had also been raised in France to which she would return in her widowhood and where she would die. Raised in her father's sophisticated and intellectual milieu, the Countess of Huntley herself was noted in Presbyterian Scotland for the receptions she gave and must in those early years have been an important companion to Anna who herself spoke French perhaps better than English and was used to continental surroundings.[14] Because Henrietta was seen by Scots as a Catholic, Anna's friendship with her was frequently criticized. But although the countess from time to time would be denied the court when her husband was in conflict with James, Anna stayed loyal to her.[15] Indeed, as late as 1599 the Countess of Huntley would still be described as close to Anna who by then, of course, had widened her social influence.[16]

It was this intimacy with the Countess that may have initiated the young queen into her first political activity. A year after her coronation, in 1591, we find Anna joining a group of nobles at the Scottish court to petition the recall of Henrietta's brother, Lodovick Stuart, 2nd Duke of Lennox, who had struck the Laird of Logie with his sword in the king's presence and been forbidden the court. The result was that 'the Queen shall write to him [Lennox] to come to her'.[17] Anna also intervened in blood-feuds to the extent of urging Huntley's punishment for slaying the Earl of Moray. But Anna's political activity in Scotland was shaped, in the long run, by enmities with two personages: first, Chancellor Maitland, and then, one of the nobles who was the king's closest supporter, the Earl of Mar.

In the first instance, at some point in 1592, Maitland seriously offended Anna. As she later indicated, the cause of her anger was his 'rash words to the King of Scots . . . narrowly touching her'. In this situation Anna had, by August 1593, at age nineteen, aligned with her against Maitland (for their own reasons) such disparate figures as the Duke of Lennox, the Earl of Mar, the Earl of Bothwell (James's almost murderous anti-monarchist enemy) and Lord Home. Independent assessments confirm the seriousness of the situation: it had been reported to Burghley as early as January 1592 that Scotland 'so now stands as there is but the King and Queen and the Chancellor, that the King must forsake and leave the Chancellor, or leave the Queen, for the Queen blames wholly the Chancellor'. Indeed, Anna's pressure on the man regarded by historians as one of Scotland's great chancellors continued so heavy that Maitland in November 1592, wanted to go to England and live privately. Even then, reports went, 'the Queen of Scots has required the Queen of England to show the Chancellor no favour or reception in England'.[18] Anna was still working against Maitland in April 1593. 'Sundry ministers have travailed lately and divers times with the Queen to pacify her wrath against the Chancellor that he might be restored to her good countenance and return to the Court to serve the King who greatly desires his service.' But apparently, Maitland 'does not like and does not find any safety to come to court before he shall recover the Queen's favour, and thereon be reconciled with the Duke and the Master of Glamis'.

Finally, King James concluded that 'only the Queen of England's letter to the Queen of Scots shall work the Chancellor's peace' and directed a letter to Queen Elizabeth to this effect. Maitland pressed the English agent, Robert Bowes, to do the same thing, and Bowes communicated with Burghley seeking advice. Meanwhile, Maitland himself wrote to Queen Anna, 'in very humble sort'. It did no good. So Queen Elizabeth communicated with Anna, by 20 May 1593, but Anna yielded only as far as to begin negotiating with Maitland. Even so, it was not until 30 November 1593, that Maitland was formally reconciled with the queen. A week later, Bowes, the British agent, wrote to Burghley that 'the Chancellor directs his course to please the Queen, and that by the means of the Queen and the Chancellor the court shall be reformed [reorganized]'.

I have detailed this two-year situation to suggest Queen Anna's political adroitness: regardless of the rights or wrongs involved, it is clear she had succeeded in making herself a force that required attention. And even when the direction of her political activity changed, her persistence did not. Two months after the end of her conflict with Maitland, on 19 February 1594, Anna gave birth to Prince Henry, an event that was to precipitate the queen into serious differences with King James and with the Earl of Mar. For the Scottish Privy Council, two days after the birth, nominated the Earl of Mar to assume the same office his father and grandfather had held before him: the formal guardianship of the heir apparent who would thereafter be kept at the Castle of Stirling.

Anna's reaction to this decision, given her own background, is not surprising. Her family, we recall, had remained a unit until the King of Denmark's death when Anna's younger brother, the heir apparent, was removed to different custody. Whether or not these memories affected Anna, the fact remains that a little over a year after Henry was born, the twenty-one-year-old queen attempted to break Mar's guardianship. In March 1595 she requested the king to assign her the keeping both of the prince and of Mar's castle of Stirling. Two weeks later she abandoned her request because of James's adamancy (Bothwell, for example, had not yet left England) and because Chancellor Maitland, who, significantly, had himself been supporting her, withdrew from the situation.

But even though she desisted at this time, and despite her understanding of the fact that James's life may have depended upon keeping the child Henry out of the hands of Bothwells or of Gowries, Anna never ceased in her efforts to regain Henry. Indeed she revealed a politically relentless streak that was to be noted again much later by the Venetian ambassador to England. Thus, in May 1595, Roger Aston, an English correspondent of Cecil but also a close hunting companion to James in Scotland and a member of James's court, reported to the English agent that 'the Queen speaks more plainly than before and will not cease till she has her son'.[19] We have 'two mighty factions', he continued. 'What will be the end God knows'. In July the sides had defined themselves: Chancellor Maitland and seven nobles with the queen, all opposed to the king, the Earl of Mar, his cousin, Thomas Erskine, and Sir James Elphinstone, the possession of the prince being the ostensible issue.[20]

The tension continued for several more weeks.[21] Robert Cecil received a report in August that 'the country is now constantly divided into two factions, one for the King and another for the Queen'. All the parishes of Scotland were observing a fast 'for the amendment of the present danger'. But then one of Anna's Danish ladies returned from Denmark with a communication from Queen Sophia commanding Anna 'to obey the King's will in all things, as she would have her blessing'. Whether this or Anna's own intention carried the day is not clear. But in the middle of August 1595, Anna superficially reconciled herself with the Earl of Mar.[22] She was 'something hard' with him at the beginning, for, as she told the king, 'the cause of her earnest suit was that she thought she could not be crossed by any subject, but that she had as much credit as might countervail any'.

In 1596, after bearing her second child, Anna resumed political activity, joining the court consensus in persuading King James to allow the Earl of Huntley to return from Europe where he had gone in March 1595 after King James had been forced to move on him and Bothwell at the instigation of the anti-Catholic kirk after Huntly's murder of the Earl of Moray. And little more than a year later, in December 1597, Robert Cecil heard Anna 'is presently and will be still [dealing], in matters of importance to the greatest causes'. Again, in 1598: 'Always the Queen knows all.'[23]

The Gowrie Plot of 4 August 1600 again polarized James and Anna because the Earl of Gowrie's two sisters, Barbara and Beatrix Ruthven, were ladies 'in chieftest credit' with the queen. When James returned from that famous episode in which he was almost assassinated, he immediately caused the Ruthven sisters to be 'thrust out of the house'. Several weeks later, Princess Margaret died at the age of two years and eight months. In these fragile times important officials suggested to the king that Anna herself had been connected with the Gowrie plot.[24] The Master of Grey wrote to Robert Cecil on the subject.

The King and the Queen are in very evil menage and now she makes to take upon her more dealing than hitherto she has done. At public table she said to him that he was advised to imprison her, but willed him to beware what he 'mintit' at for she was not the Earl of Gowry. He said he believed she was mad. She answered that he should find she was neither mad nor beside herself if he 'mintit' at that he intended.

(*SPS*, XIII, p. 721)

Despite the serious quarrel between them, Anna reportedly became very loving with James as her latest pregnancy came to term – so reconciled were they, in fact, 'that no man dare deal in that matter farther'. Prince Charles was born 19 November 1600, on the evening of the day when the condemned corpses of the two brothers of Anna's former ladies-in-waiting were hanged, drawn and quartered in retroactive punishment for the Gowrie Plot.[25] Even so, for the remaining time prior to James's accession to the throne of England the royal domestic situation seems to have stabilized, 'the Queen constant in her dislike of her conceived enemies, yet not able to hurt them. For now they rule more absolutely than ever'.[26]

Two remarkable final episodes in Scotland emphasize the traits in Queen Anna that underlay her political behaviour in Scotland and would shape her courtly activity in England: persistence and personal loyalties. The first episode manifests her continued fidelity to Beatrix and Barbara Ruthven, Gowrie's sisters. Two months before Queen Elizabeth's death, on an evening in January 1603, Beatrix was smuggled into the palace as part of a group coming to visit the queen. Stowed 'in a chamber prepared for her by the Queen's direction', Beatrix had 'much time and conference' with Anna. When King James discovered this, he seems to have been badly unsettled by the security implications, for he ordered workmen to seal up 'all dangerous passages for coming near the King's chamber'. All the queen's servants were then called into the chapel and enjoined 'on pain of death' and made to swear to have no dealings with the Ruthvens 'without the King's and Queen's [*sic*] direction and privity'.[27] Nevertheless, Anna seems to have made a point.

The second episode occurred just after James became King of England, taking with him to London the nobles who had, in Scotland, been of his own 'faction'. True, the Duke of Lennox was an old ally of Anna, but the other Scottish advisors of the new English king were without exception her old enemies, including the Earl of Mar, Sir George Home, Sir James Elphinstone of Barnton (the future Lord Balmerino) and Edward Bruce, Lord of Kinloss.[28] In May 1603, Anna, still in Scotland, four months pregnant, and on the eve of her progress into England, made a journey to the Castle of Stirling in her most direct and final attempt to gain custody of Prince Henry. Joined at Stirling by a party that included John Hamilton, James Cunningham, 7th Earl of Glencairne, John Master of Orkney, Alexander Livingstone, Earl of Linlithgow and Alexander, 4th Lord Elphinstone, the queen demanded access to the castle.[29] But Mar's mother, the Dowager Countess of Mar, now guarding the castle, 'gave a flat denial' to the queen's demand for Prince Henry. At this refusal, as the Venetian Secretary in England heard it,

The Queen flew into a violent fury, and four months gone with child as she was, she beat her own belly, so that they say she is in manifest danger of miscarriage and death.[30]

She did indeed miscarry. When James received news of this in England where the queen was awaited, he dispatched the Earl of Mar to Scotland with a commission for the queen to travel under Mar's escort to England. Anna, however, would not receive him, requiring that he convey to her through a second party the letters he was carrying from the king. Mar insisted on discharging his secret commission personally, yet the queen still refused him and wrote to James. In response, James sent, on 14 May, letters both to the Earl of Mar and Anna that were carried north by the Duke of Lennox himself, James for the moment having stripped himself of his two closest advisors in this emergency.

Mar was informed in these letters that he was needed in England and Lennox, whom the queen evidently trusted, was commissioned to escort Anna together with Prince Henry on the progress south into England. Thus, had it not been for Anna's actions, Henry might well have remained in Scotland at the Castle of Stirling, at least until his accession as Prince of Wales in 1610. Indeed, when Henry arrived in England, Mar's demand implied this: he insisted that he and all his descendants be permanently and formally discharged of any future responsibility for Scottish heirs apparent. He received this discharge from the Scottish Privy Council and, in the end, Anna's relentlessness had again made itself manifest.[31]

But this was the only political gain she secured from the accession; she lost the nobles – and the situations – that had made her a force to be reckoned with at the Scottish court. James only brought with him those lords who were in his close circle, those who had generally sided with Anna not being included in the Scottish nucleus that went to England. At the same time, the vastly different English political situation hardly lent itself to the manipulation of factions to the extent possible in Scotland. Anna's activities were thus confined to ceremony. And even though her political bent would occasionally exercise itself in these greatly altered circumstances,[32] her associations were to be primarily with English noble women and their own contacts among the male peerage, for she brought none of her noble Scottish women with her.

In the end, however, Anna may have handled her political sterilization with some acumen. For her choice of ladies, while of great significance for the art and literature of the period, as I shall argue here, would also prove instrumental in effecting a close association with the maturing Prince Henry, an association that would have been of considerable importance had Prince

Henry lived to become king, for Anna was never wholly inactive politically, even given the nature of the new English court.

James had ordered the English Privy Council to select a few ladies to ride north to escort the new queen into England, and those chosen reflect the power-structure in England at the accession: the Countesses of Worcester and Kildare, Lady Scrope and Lady (Anne) Herbert, among others. The Earl of Worcester, Queen Elizabeth's Master of the Horse, had carried her marriage-congratulations to James in 1590, and the countess had probably attended Queen Elizabeth. Lady Anne Herbert was the Countess of Worcester's daughter-in-law; Lady Anne's mother was also Robert Cecil's aunt, Lady Russell.[33] Kildare, widow of an Irish earl, was Nottingham's daughter and now married to Lord Cobham, Warden of the Cinque Ports. Lady Scrope was Philadelphia Carey, sister of Nottingham's late wife and of the 2nd Lord Hunsdon. Married to Thomas, 10th Baron Scrope, Keeper of Carlisle, who waited on King James in Northumberland during his progress south, she had been a close attendant of Queen Elizabeth from 1588 until her death.[34]

The Privy Council plan for Anna's ladies was deconstructed by a party of women who had not been selected but who had already travelled north in a significantly preemptive action.[35] This second group included Lucy Russell, Countess of Bedford and her mother, Anne Kelway Harington. And because the Countess of Bedford was destined, in a lightning strike, to 'capture' the new queen, it is important to recall Lady Bedford's own far-reaching connections with a group of nobles who, though out of political power, were among the most significant patrons of literature and drama in England.

Lady Bedford was a member of what might be termed the 'Essex group', that circle of nobles united around the figure of the late earl, for Lucy Russell was married to one of the three earls who rode with Essex in his rebellion (the other two being Southampton and Rutland). Other members of the 'Essex group' included Sir Robert Sidney, brother of the dead and idealized Sir Philip Sidney whose widow Essex had married, and brother of the literary Countess of Pembroke who edited Sidney's *Arcadia*. The young Earl of Pembroke, son of the Countess and nephew of Robert Sidney, socialized with this Essex group after the earl's death. The Sidneys, in turn, were first cousins of the Countess of Bedford's father, Sir John Harington of Exton, and the Countess of Bedford was herself friendly with Barbara Sidney, Sir Robert Sidney's wife, and was godmother to one of their children. Lady Bedford was also close to Essex's sisters, Penelope Rich (whose lover was Charles Blount, Lord Mountjoy, future Earl of Devonshire) and Dorothy, Countess of Northumberland who indeed had named one of her daughters Lucy.[36]

Many in this group supported intellectual activity. Sir Robert Sidney's great house, Penshurst, was celebrated in a poem by Ben Jonson for its hospitality to the arts and its practitioners. The young Earl of Pembroke helped Inigo Jones travel and study in Italy, sent £20 a year to Ben Jonson for books, knew the great actor Richard Burbage, one of Shakespeare's fellows, and would be a dedicatee of the Shakespeare First Folio of 1623.[37] Burbage and Shakespeare would also execute an Accession Day Tilt *impresa* for the son of the Earl of Rutland, another member of the group, while the Earl of Southampton is, of course, well known as dedicatee of Shakespeare's two early poems. He and the Earl of Rutland, seem also to have supported the translator John Florio. Another member of the group, Mountjoy, Penelope Rich's lover and the future Earl of Devonshire, is well known as a patron of Samuel Daniel and, according to Sir Robert Naunton was 'much addicted' to reading and 'a good piece of a scholler'.[38]

Of the women in the group, Penelope Rich, Essex's sister, had a number of works dedicated to her, including those of the composers John Dowland and William Byrd, while the painter Nicholas Hilliard named his daughter after her. Another woman, the Countess of Rutland, Sir Philip Sidney's daughter, is described by Ben Jonson as 'nothing inferior to her father in poetry', while his *Forest* 12, an 100-line Epistle to her, observes that 'with you, I know, my offering will find grace'.[39] It was a third woman, the Countess of Bedford, however, who seems to have been most involved in patronizing the arts and letters of the period. The poet Michael Drayton, tutor in the house of her parents, the Haringtons, had begun dedicating work to Lucy when she was thirteen.[40] John Florio not only dedicated his first publication, an Italian dictionary, to the Countess (as well as to the Earls of Rutland and Southampton), but also finished his famous translation of Montaigne as a resident in the Countess of Bedford's house, observing that the Countess had introduced him to the scholarly Theodore Diodati and Matthew Gwynne, his collaborators in the project.[41]

The social cohesion of the Essex group is manifest in several instances before the accession of Queen Anna. A letter conveying news to Sir Robert Sidney when he was on duty in the Low Countries describes, for example, a supper at Essex House, 14 February 1598, where the company included 'my Ladies Leicester, Northumberland, Bedford, Essex, Rich: and my Lords of Essex, Rutland, Mountjoy, and others. They had two plays which kept them up till 1 o'clock after midnight.' Four years later, 1602–3, just prior to the accession of James, the Countess of Bedford's father, Sir John Harington, had guests for the holidays:

Sir John Harington means to keep a royal Christmas in Rutlandshire having the Earls of Rutland and Bedford, Sir John Gray and Sir Henry Carey with their ladies, the Earl of Pembroke, Sir Robert Sidney and many more gallants.[42]

With Southampton in the Tower and Essex dead, much of the group was still together including Sir Robert Sidney with his niece (the Countess of Rutland) and his nephew (the young Earl of Pembroke) at Burleigh-on-the-Hill enjoying the hospitality of the father of the Countess who would become Queen Anna's most influential lady.

As early as 15 June 1603 it was clear how Queen Anna had chosen among the two groups of ladies who had ridden north to meet her. Thomas Edmondes observed that the new queen 'hath hitherto refused to admit my Lady of Kildare, and the Lady Walsingham, to be of her Privy Chamber, and hath only as yet sworn my Lady of Bedford to that place'. Later in the same month Lady Anne Clifford observed that the queen 'showed no favor to the elderly ladies, but to lady Rich and such like company', while, in July, Dudley Carleton noted that 'the ladies Bedford, Rich, and Essex' were especially in favour.[43]

Other remarks confirm this developing relationship between Queen Anna and the Countess of Bedford. Lady Anne Clifford, who was fourteen at the time, noted in this June of 1603 that 'my Lady of Bedford' was then 'so grand a woman with the Queen as everybody much respected her, she having attended the Queen from out of Scotland'. And later in the month, on 28 June, Dudley Carleton wrote to Sir Thomas Percy that the queen's court was 'very great of ladies and gentlewomen, but I hear of none she hath admitted to her Privy Chamber or in place near about her, save the Lady Bedford, who was sworn of the Privy Chamber in Scotland, and Lady Kildare, to whom she hath given the government of the Princess'.[44]

The case of the Countess of Kildare, who, we recall, was one of the ladies sent by the Privy Council to escort Queen Anna south, would only reinforce indications of Bedford's growing influence. Daughter of Nottingham, the most influential earl in England at the death of Queen Elizabeth, Lady Kildare had been an appropriate choice for guardian of the future Elizabeth of Bohemia. But in July 1603 the Bye and Main Plots deeply implicated Kildare's husband, Lord Cobham, and thus necessitated the removal of his wife from the person of the seven-year-old Princess Elizabeth. It is significant that at that point the young Princess was now trusted to Lord and Lady Harington, the parents of the Countess of Bedford, and indeed it was under their tutelage that the future Elizabeth of Bohemia grew up.[45]

The queen's evident trust in the Countess of Bedford's circle seems also to have effected an appointment important for arts patronage at Anna's new court. Separate from the king's, this court had its own subsidy and officials who, in many respects, were the counterparts of officials in the court of the monarch.[46] One such was a Lord Chamberlain. At the court of the king, one of the Lord Chamberlain's minor officers was the Master of the Revels who controlled and dealt with the London actors, also summoning them for performances at court every year. That the *queen's* Lord Chamberlain may have had similar responsibilities (if no 'Master of the Revels') now seems also clear from fragmentary documents that show him signing warrants of payment to professional acting companies in 1615.[47] Hence, for students of literature as well as for those concerned with the parameters of literary patronage, the process of appointing Anna's Lord Chamberlain in the summer of 1603 is of some cultural significance.

The chamberlainship, in fact, became an issue in the middle of Anna's progress south, for Sir Thomas Edmondes wrote to the Earl of Shrewsbury on 15 June that James was extremely irritated at the queen 'for conferring the place of her Chamberlain (to the which Sir George Carew was recommended) on one Mr. Kennedy, a Scottish gentleman, of whom the King hath very ill conceit'.[48] Carew's own candidacy is easily understandable, considering the influence of Robert Cecil early in the reign. Mountjoy's second-in-command in the final suppression of Tyrone in Ireland, Sir George Carew had ties to Cecil, his career prospering until Carew was eventually created Earl of Totnes.[49] But although Anna did replace Kennedy, she did not favour Carew for the position. On 14 August Sir Robert Sidney was rumoured, and in October 1603 indeed confirmed as the queen's Lord High Chamberlain and Surveyor General. And at that time, Sir George Carew became the queen's Vice Chamberlain and Receiver.[50]

Sidney himself was close enough to the Essex group for Southampton to be the godfather of his daughter and Penelope Rich to be the godmother of his son. But he must have gained his entrée to Queen Anna via the Countess of Bedford at whose father's house he had, we have seen, spent the previous Christmas. And since Sidney and Bedford were two of the most active and influential supporters of artists and writers in this period, the cultural significance of Queen Anna's court immediately becomes apparent.

The group of ladies finally gathered around the queen by the middle of summer 1603, furthermore, suggests a wide range of contacts extending beyond the Countess of Bedford and Robert Sidney. For Anna may not have wished to or been able to draw her ladies from only one particular well. King James had interests in her court if only because his powerful early supporters in England such as Cecil and the Howards, Nottingham, Suffolk and Northampton, had to be honoured by compliments to their wives, children or relatives. Thus, the composition of the queen's court also inevitably included those persons whom the king wished to place there (Cecil was her Lord High Steward). And many of these other women, as we shall see, also had significant cultural connections.

The queen had moved well along towards organizing her court by 4 July 1603, but specific names beyond those of the Countess of Bedford and Penelope Rich do not surface until the following winter when the Earl of

Worcester, Master of the Horse, would refer to three of the queen's court circles. These he described as the 'Bed Chamber', the 'Drawing Chamber', and the 'Private Chamber' as if in descending order of importance.[51]

'Bed-Chamber':	The Countess of Bedford
	The Countess of Hertford[52]
'Drawing-Chamber':	The Countess of Derby
	The Countess of Suffolk
	Penelope Lady Rich
	The Countess of Nottingham
	Susan de Vere
	[Audrey] Lady Walsingham
	[Elizabeth] Lady Southwell
'Private Chamber':	'All the rest.'
'Maids of honour':	Cary
	Middlemore
	Woodhouse
	Gargrave
	Roper

(Lodge, III, pp. 188–9)

One notes from this list that the ladies of the 'drawing-chamber', although subsidiary to Bedford and Hertford, obviously comprised an inner circle despite the fact that several seemed to be appointments from the king's side. For example, the Countess of Suffolk was wife of James's new Lord Chamberlain. And although Penelope Rich was already congenial to Anna herself, she was germane to King James's general lionization of the Earl of Essex's family. (Indeed, James had issued a proclamation that Lady Rich's precedence would be that of the oldest Earls of Essex, i.e. over all daughters of all earls except those of the Earls of Arundel, Northumberland, Shrewsbury, and Oxford.)[53]

Elsewhere in the above list, the Countess of Nottingham was now Margaret Stuart, one of the two children of the murdered 2nd Earl of Moray whom James and Anna had taken under their protection. Margaret had recently married the newly-widowed Earl of Nottingham at whose house James was proclaimed Queen Elizabeth's successor. Lady Southwell was Elizabeth *née* Howard, daughter of the same Earl of Nottingham and widow of Sir Robert Southwell, Vice-Admiral for Norfolk and Suffolk under his father-in-law, Nottingham. Lady Southwell would soon remarry, but for now, her wealth and her father's name defined her status.[54]

In this same inner circle, Elizabeth Countess of Derby, twenty-eight, had for the last nine years, been married to the 6th Earl of Derby, who had inherited the title when his brother, the former Lord Strange and then 5th Earl, had died without a male heir.[55] Elizabeth and Susan de Vere were sisters, nieces of Sir

Robert Cecil through their mother, and daughters of Edward de Vere, 17th Earl of Oxford, so their inclusion among the queen's ladies may have been through Cecil's influence. But Susan, turned sixteen in May 1603, became a great favourite of Queen Anna. In a year and a half she would marry the Earl of Pembroke's younger brother, Philip (soon to become Earl of Montgomery and, with his brother, a favourite of King James), in a wedding of two favourites that would be the court event of Christmas 1604.[56]

These new women were also patrons of the arts, or allied to patrons. Elizabeth Countess of Derby's husband penned 'comedies for the common players', and she wrote to Cecil in 1599 to help protect Derby's acting company. It was for her wedding in 1595, some scholars have suggested, that Shakespeare wrote *A Midsummer Night's Dream*.[57] Her mother-in-law was the famous Dowager Countess of Derby, a cousin of Edmund Spenser and a person interested in dramatic activities: Marston and Milton wrote masques for her. Elizabeth's father, the 17th Earl of Oxford, had kept a dramatic company for which John Lyly had written his comedies and, of course, he was mentioned by Francis Meres as one of the best writers of tragedy. Oxford's other daughter, Susan de Vere, also one of Anna's ladies, the future Countess of Montgomery, seems also to have been active as a patron. Ben Jonson wrote Epigram 104 about her, while George Chapman inserted a dedicatory leaf to her in the 1609 edition of his translation of the *Iliad*. She was also dedicatee of Lady Mary Wroth's *Urania*, written by the daughter of Anna's Lord Chamberlain, Robert Sidney.[58] Penelope Rich, another of Anna's ladies before she was forbidden the court had, as we have seen, long been a patron. Among other works, the English translation of Montemayor's *Diana* bore her name.

In these early Stuart years that define the limits of this essay, the queen and her court not only came to constitute a centre of patronage, but they also established an important connection with the heir apparent, Prince Henry. The relationship in fact invalidates Roy Strong's thesis in his recent book on Prince Henry that the prince was alienated from his two parents – as if he almost autonomously created himself an influence upon the arts in England before his premature death in 1612. For the story Strong tells is organized so as to dismiss the queen and her court from any significant consideration at all in the history of the Prince of Wales. Such a narrative is, I argue, a misreading of available documents.

One such document is a portrait. At his accession King James, making his public gestures of favour and goodwill towards the Essex family, as with Penelope Rich, also favoured Essex's son. He appointed the twelve-year-old boy life-time Companion to Prince Henry.[59] This relationship is expressed in a painting at Hampton Court palace by Robert Peake the Elder. This depicts Prince Henry in hunting costume standing over a slain deer. Assisting him is a youth, the young son of the deceased earl. Because the prince wears the George rosette, having been inducted as a Knight of the Garter on 2 July 1603, the painting was probably executed that first summer of the reign, the background suggesting Oatlands, site of the prince's first household. But this painting is apparently a copy by Peake himself of an original that now hangs in the Metropolitan Museum of Art in New York. In this original the youth with Prince Henry is not the young Essex but the younger brother of the Countess of Bedford.[60] That is to say, the prince is depicted with John Harington, a twelve-year-old boy not necessarily chosen by King James but most probably allowed access by the queen whose ranking lady was the boy's older sister.

This portrait is but one instance of the queen's continuing interest in Henry who moved into his own household during the early months of the reign.[61] Because of the outbreak of plague in the area of Oatlands in September, Prince Henry, presumably with his governor, Sir Thomas Chaloner, travelled with Queen Anna when the royal family withdrew to the west of England.[62] But the setting for the prince changed a year later: Lady Lumley (Elizabeth Darcy) wrote to the Countess of Shrewsbury:

The Prince's house is dissolved, and I perceive there will be great industry used to get Mr. Murray of his place: Sir Thomas Chaloner's board is quite taken away, and the young youths about the Prince go most of them to the university except the two earls, and Mr. Harrington . . . There was speech that the Prince should have an able man to look to him in Court, whereto my Lord of Shrewsbury was named; but now I hear the Queen will look to him herself.[63]

'Mr. Harrington' was, of course, the young John Harington, the Countess of Bedford's brother and the figure in the original Peake painting, one of the several youths permitted to remain with Henry under the supervision of the queen.

Thus at this time – in the first several years of the reign – the queen had some degree of control over both Prince Henry and Princess Elizabeth, and used the agency of the Haringtons, parents of her chief lady. Not only were the Haringtons bringing up the Princess Elizabeth, but Bedford's younger brother gradually forged a highly significant tie with the future king. In 1609 the ambassador from England to Venice would pay a formal call upon the Doge, conveying a message that emphasized young John Harington's standing not only with the prince, but also with Sir Robert Cecil, now the Earl of Salisbury. Harington, he wrote

is a youth but little over sixteen [*sic*], son of Lord Harington . . . The sister of this young gentleman, the Countess of Bedford is the Queen's favourite maid-of-honour [*sic*]; and the Princess, Her Majesty's only daughter, is brought up at the house of Lord Harrington, father of the youth, whose mother is governess to the Princess. Add to this that it is thought certain that the young man will marry Lord Salisbury's only daughter, and being the right eye of the Prince of Wales, the world holds that he will one day govern the Kingdom . . . When the Prince with tears in his eyes, took him to the King to ask leave of absence, his Majesty said to him 'What hast thou done John' – that is his name – 'that thou art so master of the Prince's favour – tell me what art thou hast used.'[64]

Thus throughout Anna's early reign in England, up to the time she lost two children in 1612 – Prince Henry dying and Princess Elizabeth leaving the country with her new husband the Elector Palatine – the relationship of the prince and princess to the court of the queen through the Countess of Bedford's family was quite close. Had not Prince Henry died so early, in fact, John Harington, his older sister the Countess of Bedford, and even Queen Anna herself might have exerted considerable influence over the evolving court of the next King of England.[65] Instead, the queen, one presumes, had to remain content with such influence as she could eke out through her relationship with James and through the contacts of her women.

In the end, however, Anna's significance to the early Stuart court was not negligible. On the one hand, while the new English situation had stripped her of her power to use factionalism as a tool, she may have achieved a state where such a tool was unnecessary to her relative freedom of action. Even so, she never wholly refrained from political behaviour. Her intercession, for example, placed James Hay (the future Earl of Carlisle) as a Gentleman of the King's Bedchamber early in the reign (August 1603).[66] She was also a loyal friend of Sir Edward Coke even in his difficulties. She joined Prince Henry in support of Sir Henry Wotton for Secretary of State and Somerset was afraid to oppose them. She supported the Earl of Pembroke for the Lord Chamberlainship against Somerset's candidacy and later dissuaded James from pardoning Somerset after his fall, supporting Buckingham. 'Since the fall of her enemy, the Earl of Somerset', Contarini would point out in a confidential report of 1618, 'Mr. Villiers has risen, supported by her and dependent upon her', and in her later years Anna was even capable of frightening Northampton.[67] Indeed, in 1607, Nicolo Molino, the Venetian ambassador, had already observed an English Anna who was, then, not very different from the Scottish queen: 'full of kindness for those who support her, but on the other hand she is terrible, proud, unendurable to those she dislikes'.[68]

But, in the end, it is the queen's cultural activity that is most significant. Too complicated wholly to assess at this stage in the present writer's review of the subject, Anna's situation suggests a number of lines of influence and literary patronage orbiting and intersecting her sphere. The Earl of Pembroke, who became James's Lord Chamberlain, a well-known patron, was, for example, closely involved with her court.[69] Robert Sidney, Earl of Leicester, was his uncle. The same Pembroke was a friend too of the Countess of Bedford,

Anna's chief lady, while, of course, Pembroke's younger brother was married to Susan de Vere. Further, the queen's own interests encouraged an atmosphere of culture. She encouraged John Florio from whom she learned to speak Italian with great fluency.[70] And, as Parry has noted, she not only provided Inigo Jones with his first full-scale monumental commission, but she patronized Isaac Oliver and in 1617 drew into her service Paul van Somer, the most advanced painter in England before the coming of Mytens and Van Dyck. She had a taste for music (apparently shared by her son Henry) and kept a number of the best French musicians. The masques that so occupied Ben Jonson and Inigo Jones professionally seem, thus, almost the least of Queen Anna's cultural activity. They lasted for only the space of one night a year, but certainly not even in every year of Anna's reign, and though the queen, in surveys of the period, is almost always defined by them, these shows seem only the proverbial tip of the iceberg. For Anna's many artistic associations were complex and significant: indeed, one can even detect a common thread of influence and interests that connects her with Prince Henry, the Earl of Arundel, Buckingham and Charles I, a topic in itself warranting further study.[71]

12 THE MASQUE OF
STUART CULTURE

Jerzy Limon

In a recent definition of the masque, David Lindley stated that at its heart 'is the appearance of a group of noble personages dressed in elaborate disguise to celebrate a particular occasion and to honour their monarch. They perform some specially designed . . . masque dances, and then take out the members of the court audience in the communal dance of the revels. The fundamental job of the masque writer is to provide a fiction to explain the disguised arrival'.[1] Because this fiction, surviving in several pages of printed texts, is based on long-forgotten Renaissance codes of meaning, one fundamental task of a critic is to elucidate its 'hidden meanings'.

Practically all the printed texts of masques, their topicality notwithstanding, direct the implied reader to other systems, without which the masque text cannot be decoded. These systems include ancient Greek and Roman mythology (and Renaissance mythographies); contemporary emblem books such as Ripa's *Iconologia*; scripture; Hermetic philosophy; Stuart ideology, as expressed, for instance, in King James's own writings; ritualistic courtly behaviour, another signifying system of signs always manifested during the masque spectacle; and last but not least the conventions of court theatre and its mechanistic and illusionistic stage.

Without the knowledge of the latter, a reader will be baffled – to say the least – by the extraordinary events that occur within the created worlds of the masque. Moreover, without the knowledge of rules by which the masque world was originally created in actual performances, a reader may well miss the nature of this peculiar model of the universe that the masque-in-performance reveals. For the masque-in-performance is a *different* text – in the semiotic sense of the word – from the surviving printed texts which may be called the literary masque; they belong to two different systems, theatre and literature, and employ different modes of expression.

This essay concentrates on the masque-in-performance and singles out common features of all masques staged at the Stuart court. Focusing on the theoretical meaning and theatrical use of space in the masque, it discusses the several spheres into which the masque divided the created world and their different functions. Furthermore, it develops the argument that masques were the theatrical equivalent of an emblem book. Understanding these features is also essential to our understanding of the literary masque and to any discussion of Stuart culture in general.

Theatre historians emphasize that the importance of masque lies in the fact that in their productions illusionistic scenery was first introduced in England. In an enclosed space, specifically in a cube open on one side towards the non-stage world, objects are displayed according to geometric and mathematical rules, creating an illusion of depth greater than that of the actual cube, and – strictly speaking – of an infinite space. This perspective stage appeared after Renaissance discoveries in optics and astronomy. Erwin Panofsky strongly insists in a controversial essay that only after space was conceived of as continuous, endless and geometric was it possible for the artist to draw his space as entirely projecting into the depth of the picture.[2] Cusanus's revolutionary idea that *any* point could be treated as a central point from which the space might be considered marks an important shift. Turning away from earlier philosophical concepts, Cusanus claimed that both God and the world are infinite spheres. To present an infinite human world on canvas or on stage was congruent with this new philosophical concept and linear perspective with its vanishing point would serve as the most appropriate convention for the pictorial representation of 'truth'. To understand the mathematics and geometry of space and the physical laws of optics meant that one might gain insight into the very nature of the universe and of God.[3]

Alongside such views the Renaissance habit of thinking in terms of universal analogy must be taken into account when discussing the nature of the masque-in-performance. A basic correspondence was asserted between the microcosm of man and the macrocosm of the universe and this pattern was present everywhere. Thus, the laws that govern the universe could be discovered in plants, in animals, or in man and all could serve as a model of the world. Works of art could visually present a model of that kind. 'I am a little world made cunningly of elements' wrote John Donne in his *Holy Sonnets* (V); 'thou seemst a world in thyself, containing heaven, stars, earth, floods, mountains, forests and all that lives' states Drummond of Hawthornden in *A Cypress Grove*;[4] and Thomas Nabbes wrote *Microcosm. A Moral Maske* (1637), which – as the title suggests – combines morality and masque traditions, and where the dramatic conflict is caused by misbehaving Elements, who refuse to succumb to the rules of the 'harmony of parts'.

Ernst Cassirer noted that Renaissance philosophers frequently employed

210

analogy and expressed themselves largely in linguistic terms stylized with 'poetic' diction, mythological parallels and symbols rich in imaginative element. Indeed, their idea of the truth or falsity of a statement seems to have been linked to the degree of richness in 'poetic' elements. Significantly, it was not only the philosopher and scientist studying the nature of the universe but the poet as well who, by universal analogy, was able to discover and express the common pattern in the world created by God.[5]

The court masque then may be treated as a model of this universe, created by the educated poet, the artist who designed scenery, the composer and choreographer. Neoplatonists believed that divine reality, of which our world is merely a poor imitation, its perfect harmony, proportion, goodness and virtue, could be envisioned by the artist through his imagination and communicated to the recipients of his art.[6] The most important part of the process of artistic creation was the *invention*, or discovery of a main idea and its attendant images. Invention could draw from other works (as masques often did), but it could also be *imagination* in its highest form (as masques often were), when the artist or the poet (or both) conceives of a vision identical with, or close to, a Platonic absolute: the imaginative vision is supposed to be a glimpse of an absolute reality.[7] This explains why the printed texts always stress who is responsible for a masque's 'invention', and the person involved is not necessarily the one that actually writes the text to be printed.[8] For instance *Tempe Restord* (1631) ends with the following comment: 'All the verses were written by Mr. *Aurelian Townesend*. The subject and Allegory of the Masque, with the descriptions, and Apparatus of the Sceanes were invented by *Inigo Jones*, Surveyor of his Maiesties worke.' The poet provided the verses only, and the masque was 'invented' by the artist who should therefore be treated as the main author.

Thus there were sundry reasons why court masques, being highly imaginative 'inventions', could be treated as unique insights into not only courtly matters ('the present occasion'), but also into the nature of the universe, revealing the laws that govern it. As Roy Strong stresses in his excellent book on Renaissance festivals, court spectacles generally presented an ideal world

in which nature, ordered and controlled, has all dangerous potentialities removed. In the court festival, the Renaissance belief in man's ability to control his own destiny and harness the natural resources of the universe find their most extreme assertion. In their astounding transformations, which defeat magic, defy time and gravity, evoke and dispel the seasons, banish darkness and summon light, . . . they celebrate man's total comprehension of the laws of nature . . . in its fullness of artistic creation [this] was a ritual in which society affirmed its wisdom and asserted its control over the world and its destiny.[9]

With minor reservations these words could apply to the Stuart masques: in the latter case, however, it was not the society's wisdom, but the king's that – with the support of his superhuman powers – controlled the harmony and order of the world and its destiny.

Let us then take a closer look at the bizarre world of the masque, where, quite contrary to the laws of empirical reality, stars can dance and sing, islands can float like sailboats, rocks can open and close, revealing beautiful palaces; the bottom of the ocean will uncover mysterious worlds and people will undergo miraculous metamorphoses as in Ovid or in Kafka, turning into animals, plants, beasts and, when need be, into bottles; the stage-set can transform itself, and instantly change from a castle to a landscape, or a seascape, or a moonscape, or to an allegorical or emblematic composition. The laws that govern this highly imaginative world are not accidental, or merely aimed to evoke wonder: they are a part of the created model of the universe, which ought to reveal its true nature during the actual performance of a masque.

Even a brief glance at the surviving texts of the masques will show that the created or artistic world is basically divided into three spheres: the divine or metaphysical, the sphere of the court, and the non-court world. The metaphysical sphere is inhabited by mythological gods who rule over the whole universe, and also by a number of allegorical characters that usually stand for the virtues that mortals should follow; the court sphere is inhabited by select human and superhuman beings ruled by a monarch whose power and authority comes from the first sphere; and the outer sphere is inhabited by ordinary humans, and all sorts of vices, who occasionally enter the sphere of the court, but take part only in the so-called 'antimasques'. This tripartite structure of the created universe is vertical, of course: the gods and allegories always *descend* from the divine sphere to the world of the court (and never to the 'lower' court), and the existence of heavens is additionally confirmed in dialogue, songs and speeches and is visually presented on stage. The illusionistic stage functions here as a sort of magical box, or, perhaps, as a new scientific instrument, that enables encounters of the divine beings with the court. The latter is naturally located in the middle, between the metaphysical sphere and the mundane, non-court world. The very structure of this universe is significant: communication between the ordinary, human world and the representatives of the divine sphere is possible *only through* the mediation of the court; a direct link of the commons with divinity is not foreseen in this model of the universe. And this rudimentary law operates in other ways too: divine messages of various kinds are conveyed only to the court, and only through this medium can these be transmitted further down.

The boundaries between the three spheres are clearly marked by the organization of space in the masque-in-performance. It is possible to distinguish two basic types of organization of space in theatres. One, composed of two 'open' spaces (forming one space of the theatre), the other – of two 'enclosed' spaces. The first type is familiar to all students of ancient Greek or of Elizabethan theatres, and is characterized by an open stage surrounded – at least on three sides – by an amphitheatrical auditorium. In a theatre of this type there is a multitude of equal viewpoints and 'perspectives'; furthermore, this stage does not 'hide' anything from the spectators, does not create any physical or optical illusion as far as its dimensions and shape are concerned. It does not 'pretend' to be anything else, and a convention has to be employed to transform this stage space into, say, a hall or a street (this phenomenon is sometimes referred to as 'verbal scenography'). The two spaces are divided only by the difference in their ontological status: one is the created, artistic reality, the other is the empirical reality of the spectators. However, the openness of space in that kind of theatre is in fact of double nature: that of the stage towards auditorium and the auditorium towards the stage.[10] This leads to an illusionary reduction of the boundary and distance between these two spaces and two groups of people: the actors and the spectators. The latter phenomenon, in turn, leads to the well-known illusion of communal participation in the performance. Thus, the theatre world is created by two open spaces, and it is distinct from anything outside this world, from the non-theatre.

The second type of space organization in theatre is based on a different concept: we are presented with a closed stage, which hides a number of its features, and is rigidly separated from the auditorium. The latter forms the second closed space in this theatre. The stage is a cube open on one side only to the auditorium, and – with the help of stage-design – it presents an illusionistic space, which seems infinite when viewed from the right station point, as it is called in descriptive geometry, and is also reminiscent of a painting framed in a proscenium arch. This type of space and its inner organization by the rules of linear perspective determines a single 'best' location for the spectator. The stage of this sort is always equipped with a large area invisible to spectators, where – among other things – all stage machinery is concealed, a factor which additionally stresses the isolation of the stage world from the auditorium. In other words, the stage tells the spectator where he or she is allowed to sit, or stand, and what he or she is allowed to see. Court theatre created for the staging of masques is basically a transitional fusion of the two types of space organization, described above.

Critics used to treat the masque-in-performance as a spectacle staged, as it were, in a nineteenth-century theatre, where the boundary between the fictitious and empirical realities were clearly marked by a raised stage, by proscenium and proscenium arch. Because illusionistic scenery was used in masques it had been assumed that the action of these spectacles, including what was said or sung, took place within the stage set and on the proscenium. However, more recent work by Stephen Orgel, Roy Strong and others takes note of the fact that the most important acting area was not what we would normally call the stage, but the so-called 'dancing place'. This is true not only because dances occupied in fact most of the time of the masque-in-performance, but also because many important speeches and songs were actually presented in the area below the perspective stage and close to the king, who was seated in a throne on a raised platform, directly opposite the centre of the stage, often referred to as the 'state'. The surviving text of *The Masque of Twelve Months* (1612) tells us, for instance, that in the opening scene 'the heart opens, and Bewty issues . . . the two Pulses beating before them towards ye King. Beinge neare, Beauty speaks . . . '[11] Similarly, in practically all other masques there are characters descending from above, or entering from the sides, or from below, and taking steps down to the dancing floor in order to address the king, or to present songs and dialogues immediately in front of him.[12]

Much of what happened in the masque-in-performance took place, therefore, not within the illusionistic stage, but in front of it, i.e. on the narrow proscenium,[13] and on the dancing floor: a large rectangular area in the middle of the hall, surrounded on three sides by spectators and backed with the stage picture. Allardyce Nicoll in his influential *Stuart Masque and the Renaissance Stage* observed long ago that the masquers habitually descended upon the 'dancing place', 'while frequently, in the very course of the masque action, characters were made to move downward and approach the royal throne'. Nicoll further noted that occasionally 'dispersed scenery' was employed on the dancing place, as in *Tethys' Festival* which had a 'tree of victory' represented by a 'bay at the right side of the state, upon a little mound there raised'.[14] We should therefore treat the dancing floor as an important acting area in the productions of masques. Since the perspective stage was raised (and we have now reasons to treat this as one of the two stages used in actual productions), most of the action, and all of the dances, took place on a level below the stage, i.e. below the stage picture. With few exceptions all the speaking parts were played by professional actors, and songs were sung by musicians; the most important roles in these spectacles, the roles of the masquers, were always mute. Moreover, most of the dialogues belong to antimasques which were usually presented in other acting areas than the stage proper. To a certain extent the perspective stage was predominantly 'mute' and it was basically pictorial in character, providing illusionistic space from which mythological and allegorical characters descend upon 'earth'.

This organization of the acting space is similar to the typographical layout of printed emblems, where the poetic or narrative part, is always set below the engraving to illustrate a given emblem. Furthermore, the perspective of the illusionistic stage picture could not possibly include the characters, or stage properties, on the dancing floor. If we were to treat both acting areas as one, the discrepancy between the natural and distorted optic laws would become apparent. Whatever or whoever appears on the dancing floor is not deformed

214

by the stage-designer in order to create an illusion of depth. Since the spectators are seated on three sides of this acting area, there is a multitude of possible 'perspectives', and no single one is privileged.

In this sense, the hall floor, between the 'state' and the raised stage picture, forms an open stage, familiar to all frequenters of the public theatres. Thus the stage picture and frame do not mark the boundary between the fictitious, or artistic, and 'real' worlds: all they mark is the inner division of the created world which is composed of two visible spheres linked physically by the magical powers of the stage box. The heavenly sphere is brought closer to the world of the court, and it is presented basically as a three-dimensional picture, governed by the rules of linear theatre perspective. These rules stress the Platonic ideal revealed in this geometric, perfectly proportioned world, the harmony of which is additionally corroborated by the 'divine' music. Opposed to this 'artificial' (in the seventeenth-century meaning of the word) sphere is the court, which is 'real' only in the sense that the laws that govern this world are reminiscent of empirical reality. There is also a third sphere – the implied earthly non-court world, from which either antimasque or ordinary human characters enter into the court world; they enter either from the sides, which mark the physical boundaries of the court world, or from below the stage, which stresses the vertical hierarchy of the created universe even more strongly.

The masque-in-performance is not autonomous after the fashion of a self-contained fiction performed before spectators who belong – as it were – to a different reality, but is rather an institutionally autonomous performance of a ritual,[15] in which all present take part. As David Woodman observed, 'the ceremony that drew the audience into the revels resembled a magical ritual, both audience and masquers entering into a celebration through which nature was controlled, and villainous enchanters subdued'.[16] While the masque may be seen as a peculiar manifestation of courtly behaviour, it is also, to use Roy Strong's phrase, 'liturgy of state', which becomes of particular importance in Protestant countries where the Reformed church did not make extensive use of elaborate ceremonial, involving images, paintings and sculpture. In this sense the masque-in-performance filled an obvious gap in Stuart iconography and propaganda. As David Norbrook rightly observed, 'the increasingly elaborate concluding scenes of Jacobean and Caroline masques, in which Jones's scenery transformed courtiers into images of transcendent truths, formed a secular counterpart to the cult of religious images'.[17] In this way the masque becomes a useful medium for Stuart ideology in general, and it comments at times on current political issues in particular. It is not surprising that the most important guests in these spectacles were foreign ambassadors. From the point of view of Stuart interests, the perspective setting adds not only the third but also a divine dimension to their ideology.

215

Keir Elam has noted that dramatic worlds are immediately recognized by the audience as counterfactual, but embodied as if in progress in the actual here and now. Any other approach, or misunderstanding of this convention, will result in one's mistaking the stage for actuality. The separation of the two worlds is stressed additionally by their *asymmetrical* character, which means that their relationship of accessibility is one-way: it is the spectators who can see into the created world on stage, overhear even the most personal confessions and witness embarrassing scenes, but the spectators' world is not seen into – or even noticed – by the characters on the stage.[18] This convention makes the two realities conspicuously distinct. However, in modern theatre practice we often witness attempts to nullify the asymmetry rule, by which actors interact directly with spectators. But this is, in fact, yet another convention, creating another illusion: the auditorium is simply incorporated into the artistic reality of the performance and thus 'tricks' the audience into believing that it is really his own world.[19] In the masque this convention, or trick, is used constantly: the spectators are led to believe that their world is the 'real' world and appears in opposition to the superfluous world of the stage. But in fact they are incorporated into this fictitious reality, as is always the case in a ritual. In this way the masque audience is transformed into a stage character, who 'impersonates', for instance, the court hierarchy (the closer one sits to the king, the higher one's court position is), or represents the earthly instrument of the king's power. The king, of course, is also a stage character who plays the triple role of spectator, the implied author of the 'magic' at court, and 'a little god' equipped with super-human wisdom and power.

Stephen Orgel notes that it is only 'the characters in Jonsonian antimasques, played by professional actors [who] are nearly always unaware that there are spectators' (the only exception to be found in *Love Restored*).[20] In the antimasque the asymmetry rule is fully applied: the two worlds of the stage and the auditorium are clearly distinct.[21] However, the antimasque is a topsy-turvy world and the antimasque characters cannot really communicate with characters from the masque proper: they are usually scared or chased away by the appearance of the latter, and consequently the chaos or the evil of the antimasque is brought to order or otherwise neutralized. The only communication possible in this tripartite world is between the court sphere and the metaphysical sphere, and between the court and the non-court. Thus, for instance, when Iris appears 'above' in the *Masque* staged at Coleoverton in 1618 (?), all the antimasque characters 'run out distractlie'.[22] In the earlier *Masque of Queenes* (1609), during a wild dance of the Witches, 'on the sodayne, was heard a sound of loud music, as if many Instruments had given one blast. With which, not only the *Hagges* themselves, but their Hell, into which they ranne, quite vanished; and the whole face of the *Scene* alterd', by which twelve masquers were discovered in the House of Fame.[23] In *Pleasure Reconciled to*

Virtue the Pigmees of the second antimasque dance around a sleeping Hercules 'at ye end whereof they think to surprize him: when sodainly being wak'd by the *Musique*, and rowsinge himself, they all run into holes'.[24]

Only one sphere and only one acting area of the created world of the masque is organized according to the rules of linear perspective – this is the three-dimensional stage box. In early masques, this is exclusively a divine sphere, presented as harmonious, proportional, geometric and infinite space. As opposed to this, the world of the court is finite, enclosed by the walls of the hall, by the floor and the ceiling; it is equipped, however, with one open wall, through which, as if through a window, it is possible to see the metaphysical order of this universe. This presents the court as the seer of truth. As an acting area, the 'divine' sphere (which in later masques will alternate with human worlds presented within the illusionistic stage) is used primarily for discoveries (of gods and masquers) and for descents from the 'heavens' or from any other allegorical location (in the *Masque of Beauty*, Reason descends from the top of the 'microcosm'). With hardly any exceptions, the movement of the characters in this highly structured (hence signifying) space is two-dimensional: up and down to the sides, as if on a flat surface of a painting on canvas. Except for one possible instance[25] not a single character enters or exits through the back of the perspective stage. This would ruin the whole artistic concept of the organization of the stage space. Since the latter was relatively shallow, the actors could not act anywhere near the back of the stage, because by doing so they would expose the optical illusion and reveal the distorted pro- portion of 'diminishing' set elements. Only the very front of the stage design, i.e. the vertical plane framed by the proscenium arch, could be proportioned in accordance with the natural dimensions of the non-stage world.

If no action, then, took place towards the back of the perspective stage, the proscenium, in turn, was too narrow – as we know from surviving designs – to accommodate any major stage action.[26] This leaves the so-called 'dancing place' as the main acting area, and – characteristically – the second general movement in the masque-in-performance is outward from the stage picture towards the court's centre – the king. The central position of the monarch is additionally marked by the laws of perspective. As Stephen Orgel has pointed out, the king's eye is directly opposite the vanishing point and on the height of the illusionary horizon. Thus, the whole space between the king and the stage picture is the main acting area, surrounded on three sides by spectators. It should also be noted that it is only the king and those select few surrounding the monarch who actually face the stage picture; the vast majority of spec- tators are seated with their sides to the stage picture and are in fact facing the dancing floor.

However, as indicated above, the boundary between this stage and the audi- torium is an illusionistic artistic device, a trick, because in fact the entire hall is incorporated into the created world, along with the spectators. This hall always appears as 'here' in masques, as opposed to the implied 'there' of the stage picture or of the non-court. The court as a whole may, in addition, be given explicit allegorical meaning, as in *Love's Triumph Through Callipolis* (1631) where it stands for the city that is in fact the only invariable element of the overall stage-design; it cannot 'disappear', because it is the here and now of the court, and all other elements of the setting in the stage picture are always presented *in relation* to Callipolis, i.e. the court. Fame in *Time Vindicated* (1623) praises the king directly for restoring the divine age on earth and promises to 'fill this world of beautie here, your Court',[27] similarly, Cupid addresses the king:

> You, Sir, that are the Lord of Time,
> Receive not as any crime
> 'Gainst Majesty, that Love and Sport
> Tonight have entred in your Court.[28]

And in *The Masque of Augurs*, Apollo calls the king with the familiar

> Prince of thy Peace, see what it is to love
> The powers above
> Jove hath commanded me
> To visit thee.[29]

In all the masques the court seems to be nothing but the court, and the king and his courtiers seem to be nothing but themselves. This creates the illusion of a 'real' world. However, the laws that govern this sphere of the created world are substantially different from the physical laws that govern empirical reality. To begin with, all the people of the court world have a miraculous insight into the metaphysical sphere, by which they can see mythological heavens inhabited by gods, they can see floating islands approaching English shores, they can see the underwater kingdoms of Neptune and Oceanos. The entire celestial world, which is said to govern the universe, is brought – as through a magical and powerful telescope – close to them, enabling them to see with their own eyes what is happening on the Moon. All of the above could also occur in a public theatre, but there these insights would not be distinctive for any particular group of people; anyone can come and watch the spectacle. The case is totally different in masques-in-performance: these were staged by the court for the court, and no one else, with the exception of honoured guests, was admitted. The masque could be 'experienced' only by those closest to the monarch; and one could not simply 'buy a ticket' and enter, one had to be invited.

What distinguishes the masque-in-performance from other types of theatre is that the masque never reenacts a historical moment: it is happening here and now, a fact that is stressed by the temporal and spatial unity of the entire hall space. In drama time is always compressed (even if the classical unities are observed), or stretched, or cut and on those occasions when it seems to be congruous with the empirical time of the spectators, it is in fact a reconstruction of a different time (past or future). In the masque-in-performance as in a ritual there is only one temporal dimension which joins all the spheres of the created world. Sometimes, however, and especially in antimasques, there appear 'scenes' that take place somewhere else, i.e. outside the court hall, and at a different time: in all these cases (few as they are) we may talk of elements of *drama* added to what is basically a ritualistic courtly event.

Secondly, allegorical and mythological characters (and sometimes even the souls of the blessed) may enter into the court world with ease, by simply descending from their heavens. This feature is asymmetrical: none of the mortals, not even the king, has the ability to enter the divine sphere. This can happen only after one's death. Thirdly, the metaphysical characters communicate various messages to the king and to the other courtiers present. This again, does not work the other way round: neither the king nor any of his courtiers ever say anything to their visitors from outer space. The fourth difference between the 'real' court and the masque court is that the masque king is equipped with super-human qualities and powers, and one can see them in operation in the created world (and only during the actual performance). For example, in many masques, the king is said to be the source of light and harmony, and this should not be taken as a metaphor, because many of the newcomers to the court are literally 'blinded' or 'stunned' by this light.[30] Even if the individual and sceptical courtiers did not actually see the fluorescent monarch, they are – after all – only mortals and it is only the divine beings that can fully see into his true nature. Furthermore, it is the king's mere presence (who by laws of divine geometry is placed in the centre of the court world) that brings order and (literally and physically) governs this world. It is the king's very presence that enables flowers to be transformed into human beings, or brings spring in winter. Many masques stress that the source of the king's super-human powers lies in the divine sphere; this is corroborated by the laws of perspective that link the monarch, and only him, with divinity.

Critics have often observed that the discovery and descent of the masquers was the most important moment in the whole spectacle; in point of fact, the whole masque may be said to have been written to provide an explanation for the appearance of the masked nobles. Yet not enough attention has been paid to the function of the masquers within the created world. Who are they, anyway? Obviously they are a part of the metaphysical sphere, and by entering the court with hidden identities, they cannot be treated as individuals (the prince, the queen, or Lord so-and-so), but rather as paragons representing the courtly virtues. To follow these virtues means to secure one's way into the divine sphere. In Thomas Middleton's *The Masque of Heroes* we are explicitly told that the masquers are, in fact, 'Heroes deified for their virtues'. They descend in order to show others an example to follow: 'They all descend to have their worth/Shine in imitation forth'. In James Shirley's *The Triumph of Peace*, the masquers are called 'the sons of Peace, Law and Justice', and the 'children' of the king's 'reign'. In this sense the masquers function as mirror reflections of the king's virtues. They are said to be offsprings of the king's wisdom, and this quality enables them to perform an important function within the created world. It is through them that the king's super-human powers can be seen in operation. Their appearance literally brings harmony and order and objectively reveals the divine origin of royalty. After their dances with the ladies of the court, the masquers usually return to where they came from and disappear with the closing of the scene. Whenever the masquers do not return to the metaphysical world, they take off their masks, marking the end of the spectacle and their becoming mortals again, identifiable individuals, who simply join the others at a subsequent banquet. Thus, through the king's wisdom and virtue a place among gods is secured for the most notable courtiers. At the very end of the Middleton masque, quoted above, TIME – who is one of the characters – 'makes his honour to the Ladies':

> Live long the Miracles of Times and yeeres,
> Till with those Heroes, You sit fixt in Spheres.[31]

In spite of all its seemingly mimetic qualities, then, the court of the masque cannot be treated as an empirical reality opposed to the fictional world on stage. Both are parts of the created model of the universe. Ben Jonson considered these highly illusionistic, and certainly non-mimetic spectacles as 'mirrors of man's life'.[32] What he actually meant was that the laws that govern this artistic reality are – by analogy – the same as those governing the microcosm of man (who governs his body in the same way as the king his nation), the geocosm of earth, and the macrocosm of the universe. With the closing of the scene, after the final dance and final speeches, with the disappearance of the stage picture, the court goes through the final transformation: it instantaneously returns to its 'real' ontological status, i.e. to the empirical reality. The ritual is over.

The function of the stage picture created by the masque, however, requires further analysis because it sheds important light on Stuart culture. When discussing the similarity of early nineteenth-century Russian theatre to painting, Yuri Lotman noted that: 'The analogy between painting and theatre was manifested above all in the organization of the spectacle through conspicuously pictorial means of artistic modelling, in that the stage text tended to unfold not as a continuous flux . . . imitating the passage of time in the extra-artistic world, but as a whole clearly broken up into single "stills" organized synchronically, each of which is set within the decor like a picture in a frame.'[33] This description may just as well be applied to the masque-in-performance. What we have there is a series of scenes, in which each stage picture is not only similar to painting in general, but reminiscent of the graphic arts and emblem books in particular. It is not surprising that the masque has been labelled a 'speaking picture'. There is more to this simile than one may suppose. Indeed, the masque-in-performance may be seen in fact as a theatrical 'equivalent' of an emblem book. Semioticians like Keir Elam use the concept of *ostension* to mean an action in which 'in order to refer to, indicate or define a given object, [instead of describing it] one simply picks it up and shows it to the receiver of the message in question . . . This ostensive aspect of the stage "show" distinguishes it, for example, from narrative, where persons, objects and events are necessarily described and recounted.'[34] The masque-in-performance, however, besides being a courtly theatrical spectacle, lies also in the tradition of a courtly ritual, in which the basic formula remains the same and is repeated in every masque, but details of the 'invention' are variable and often have to be 'supported' by the word, which describes and explains its 'hidden meanings'; this explains the double nature of the masque: dramatic and narrative.

The latter feature is fully revealed in most of the masques: in their performance we find both elements – the theatrical ostension, by which 'living emblems' and the 'mechanics of the world' are presented to spectators by predominantly pictorial means, and which may be decoded without a description[35] and the verbal element, which in numerous speeches, dialogues and songs is in fact narrative in character, describing the events, people, allegories and the visual images that they accompany. This double nature of the masque has intrigued scholars or, rather, irritated them, and we often encounter comment about the 'non-dramatic' quality of these texts such as 'the theatrical machine has a life of its own, and one that is . . . quite *separate* [italics are mine] from the life of Jonson's text' and that 'the scene, whether symbolic or realistic, was related to the text but not integrated with it'.[36] Such a view might be appropriate if the masque is treated as a minor form of drama. But drama it is not; it is a courtly ritual, constantly rewritten, but invariably dealing with the infinite depth of the king's divine wisdom.

In speaking about the similarity between the masque-in-performance and pictorial arts, we must not forget basic differences. To begin with, following the rules of perspective and optics in general, a stage picture creates an illusion by which a three-dimensional setting 'pretends' to be a two-dimensional painting, or engraving, disguised as a three-dimensional space.[37] In other words, the stage picture wants to be seen as a two-dimensional painting constructed in accordance with the rules of linear perspective. In contrast to this, a perspective painting not only creates the illusion of three dimensions, but also *re-creates* a perspective view 'seen' or imagined by the painter sometime in the historical past; the painter, who is usually not seen within the frame, but who is implied by the painting itself, functions as a 'witness' to the historically true or fictitious scene he represented. The ideal viewpoint for an onlooker is in fact the very point from which the painter viewed (or imagined) his scene. Yet it is quite obvious that the viewer and the painting (or, rather, the scene it represents) belong to different temporal realities. In the masque-in-performance, however, the perspective scenes are located *hic et nunc* and are not re-creations of anyone's view or vision that occurred in the historical past. The king is not seated in the place from which somebody earlier saw the unfolding stage pictures. The magical box generates pictures that do not 'bring to life' past events, but constitute entirely new events in the 'now' of the temporal dimension of the court.

Roman Jakobson's category of *transmutation*, or intersemiotic translation is relevant to this analysis of the masque-in-performance; when a text created within one system (say an emblem book, which in fact would be a fusion of two systems: graphic arts and literature) is reconstructed with materials of another system (in our case theatre art) it loses its specific literary qualities and gains specific theatrical ones. In the case of masque-in-performance, the perspective three-dimensional stage is in most cases an example of trans-mutation of an emblem book picture (either actual or invented *ad hoc*) into the 'language', or system of theatre.[38] The illusionistic stage picture may therefore be treated as a scenographic transmutation of a two-dimensional emblem icon, and the dialogues, speeches and songs may, consequently, be treated as theatrical transmutations of the emblem mottos. The basically literary origin of this transmutation explains why both pictorial and verbal components of the masque may with ease be analysed philologically. From this point of view, the masque-in-performance is to a great extent a text about another text (being 'the book of the king's wisdom').

In Ben Jonson's *Hymenai* (1607), a new emblematic scene is discovered with Juno sitting on her throne with Jupiter above, the Rainbow or Iris below, and eight 'ladies' on the sides; we are told in the printed text that 'All which, upon discovery, REASON made *narration of* [italics are mine]'.[39] And in what follows, REASON in a lengthy speech in verse actually describes what is seen in the 'picture' and elucidates the significance of its particular elements. Thus, a theatrical equivalent of an emblem from a book is created. In this respect one may agree with Roy Strong's comment that 'Jones's scenery was essentially the action of the masque which its dialogue, songs and dances elucidated and moralised . . . Every stage picture he presented was a symbol composed of a composite series of hieroglyphs'.[40] And long ago Allardyce Nicoll observed that 'the audience gathered at Whitehall, trained in the study of emblems and *impresa* . . . can have looked upon the masques as nothing but a series of living emblems or have listened to their verses as aught else than a string of mottoes'.[41]

Even the dances were often 'emblematic' in character, as when the dancers formed certain geometric figures, a circle, a 'chain' or an initial or somebody's name. Their painting-like quality is sometimes stressed in descriptions in the printed texts. In Jonson's *Pleasure Reconciled to Virtue*, for instance, the dancers are asked to 'put all the aptness on/Of figure, that proportion/or colour can disclose'; and we are told that even if the rules of painting were lost, they could be reconstructed on the basis of the dance (which implies that that particular dance was an ideal transmutation of a painting):

> That if those silent Arts were lost,
> Designe, and picture, they might boast,
> > from you a newer ground,
> Instructed by the heightning sence
> Of dignitie and reverence,
> > in their true motions found.

The picture-like character of the stage and its 'bookish' origins are additionally stressed by its frame – what later became known as the proscenium-arch. As Richard Southern described it: 'for the first time in history a *frontispiece* was made to frame-in the stage picture. One saw the show *through* it. This frontispiece was, in Jones's hands, an emblematic decoration at the front of the stage, designed separately for each show [which makes it a part of the stage text – J.L.], and consisting of two side pieces adjoining the walls of the hall and flanking the scene, with a cross-piece connecting their tops and reaching up to the ceiling.'[42] What is striking in this description, and in the surviving designs, is the close similarity of this concept of framing the stage picture to the contemporary framing borders or architectural designs of graphic (and often emblematic) frontispieces in printed books.

Rosemary Freeman in her *English Emblem Books* noted in passing that 'emblems entered the masques in ways other than through personifications.' The scene was often painted with small emblematic designs arranged in much the same fashion as they were in the engraved frontispieces of books.'[43] Margery Corbett and Ronald Lightbown point out that in the Renaissance the most popular frame for title-pages was the classical recess flanked by architectural wings, set on a base and topped with a pediment. The title was often enclosed in a cartouche which hung from the architectural frame or was attached to the top.[44] Similarly, in a number of masques the title appears within the architectural frame. The underlying principle for this on title-pages was to create a front or façade to the book. In the later sixteenth and seventeenth centuries these were often enriched with allegorical figures, emblematical attributes and symbols. Similarly, in the masque-in-performance allegorical and mythological figures appear in the designs for the proscenium arch as do other basically graphic elements.

The two-dimensional graphic character of the 'frontispiece' in the masque is additionally stressed by the introduction of a flat curtain, which was separately designed for each spectacle. The painted curtain, framed by an architectural 'arch' has to be treated as part of the design. Even the meagre evidence we have for the use of curtains in masques proves that at least sometimes they were pictures in themselves. In the *Masque of Flowers*, for instance, we are told that there 'appeared a *Travers* painted in *Perspective*, like a wall of a Cittie with battlements, over which were seene the Tops of houses. In the middle whereof was a great gate and on either side a Temple . . . in either of which opened a little gate.'[45] If the architectural inventions of title-pages use fantastic and highly ornamented forms, so too do the designs for the frontispieces in masques as the surviving designs, published by Orgel and Strong illustrate.[46] Placed on the title page, these portals and triumphal arches 'symbolise the formal entrance to the work within'.[47] In the case of the masque-in-performance the proscenium arch and the curtain would create a theatrical equivalent, or transmutation of a title-page, being a formal entry to the worlds within. It is, perhaps, not without significance that the stage frame in printed masques is usually called 'Arch Triumphal', as in *Somerset's Masque* or in *Lovers Made Men*.

However, that was not the only possible meaning of a title-page. When emblematic title-pages began to appear in England in the late sixteenth century, they were closely connected with the contents of the book for which they were made. As authorities on the subject have observed: 'Generally the design was not confined to the expression of one idea or one theme. It was the vehicle for the thoughts of the author on his work, but might also seek to give an indication of its scope, and include pictorial representations which could be understood only by perceiving the book, thus stimulating the reader's curiosity. All the themes were carefully interwoven into the set patterns for the design of title-pages, according to an inner logic, to make up the meaning of the whole.'[48] The same description could in fact be applied to the frontispieces in masques, for they were meaningful introductions to the worlds within. Even the scarce evidence we have for the actual stage frontispiece designs tells us that at least sometimes these designs repeated certain motifs from the rich interior decorations of the Banqueting House, thus identifying particular stage texts with the iconographical and ideological programme of the entire space of the hall.[49] Ben Jonson considered the frontispiece design for his *Lovers Made Men* – to give just one example – important enough to have its description included in the printed text:

The Front before the Scene, was an Arch-Triumphall. On the top of which, Humanitie placed in figure, sate with her lap full of flowers . . . holding a golden chaine in her left hand: to shew both the freedome, and the bond of Courtesie, with this inscription.

SVPER OMNIA VULTUS.

On the two sides of the Arch ⎫
Cheerefulnes, ⎬ her servants
and Readines, ⎭

Cheerefulnes, in a loose flowing garment, filling out wine from an antique piece of plate; with this word	Readines, a winged Mayd, with two flaming bright lights in her hands and her word,
Adsit laetitia dator	Amor addidit alas
[Let the giver of joy be present – J.L.][50]	[Love gave wings – J.L.]

The emblematic character of title-pages led to the appearance of explanatory verses, which first occurred in England during the reign of James.[51] Similarly in those printed masques in which the frontispiece is described, the description usually includes explanatory comments, as the example given above illustrates.[52]

Thus, to sum up, the emblematic frontispiece in the masque-in-performance is reminiscent of emblematic title-pages in printed books. In this particular case the theatrical 'title-page' is iconographically (and through inscriptions) closely linked with the contents of the 'theatrical book of emblems'. As the curtain is dropped, or drawn to the sides, we pass over the title-page, and are presented with several three-dimensional pages of this 'book', a sequence of living emblems accompanied by living mottos. The book, owing to the miraculous power of the magical box of the stage, reveals itself to the spectators, and allegorical and mythological characters step down from its pages on to the court floor and interact with the courtiers. Naturally, the book needs the author (as the magic needs its source), and he is here implied by the rules of perspective: it is the king's eye, or his mind that is equipped with supernatural power that enables the contents of his 'book' to appear in the magical box. Thus the model of the universe created in the masque is based on the concept of the world as a book, or a text: a projection of the king's mind or a mystery that the king's mind is uniquely able to penetrate. Because the masque is a theatrical transmutation of a book, it may therefore be treated as a text about a text. We know of another attempt of this kind: Henry Peacham 'translated' James's *Basilikon Doron* into an emblem book, three manuscripts of which have survived to our times. These were originally presented to the king and Prince Henry. The emblems are in Latin, and each accompanying picture is based upon some part of the king's instructions and supported by quotations from the classics.[53] In this sense all the masques presented at the Stuart court may, and perhaps should, be treated as one text. Their emblematic interrelationship has not been sufficiently studied and is certainly worth a closer scrutiny. For instance, in Jonson's *Hymenai* Atlas and Hercules appear supporting the heavens; the extant text of this particular masque does not really explain why Atlas and Hercules have been brought together and one needs to read the later *Pleasure Reconciled to Virtue* to discover that Atlas is associated with wisdom and Hercules, traditionally with virtue. Thus the firmament of the masque world in *Hymenai* is supported by Wisdom and Virtue, the union of which is a recurrent motif in other masques as well and epitomized in King James himself.[54]

Since the masque is based on the concept of the world as a book, it may be analysed as a book, that is philologically. This is, in fact, proven by numerous printed texts of masques, where we have a whole *apparatus criticus* added, with elaborate marginal notes, footnotes, lengthy quotations and with references to dozens of ancient and contemporary sources. The latter occasionally include direct references to King James's works. For instance, an obvious allusion to the instructions for the prince as they are laid out in *Basilikon Doron* may be found in Ben Jonson's *Haddington Masque*:

> A Prince, that draws
> By 'example more, than others do by laws:
> That is so just to his great act, and thought,
> To do, not what Kings may, but what Kings ought.
> Who, out of piety, unto peace, is vow'd;
> To *spare his subjects*, yet to quell the proud,
> And dares esteem it the first fortitude,
> To have his passions, foes at home, subdued. [italics mine]

As D. J. Gordon first noticed, the Virgilian 'Parcere subiectis' is the last line in *Basilikon Doron*.[55] The concept of seeing the world as a book was in fact quite common in Renaissance literature and thought. Man himself was a book, the Book of Nature, or the Book of God.[56] John Donne wrote in one of his sermons that 'The World is a great Volume, and man an Index to, that Book; Even in the Body of Man, you may turne to the whole world.'[57] The king's wisdom found an appropriate reflection as a living emblem book, for emblem books were considered by contemporaries as epitomes of wisdom of almost divine dimension. As Francis Quarles wrote in the Introduction to his book of emblems: 'An Emblem is but a silent Parable . . . Before the Knowledge of Letters, God was known by *Hieroglyphics*. And, indeed, what are the Heavens, the Earth, nay every Creature, but *Hieroglyphics* and *Emblems* of his Glory?'[58]

Samuel Daniel explained in his *Vision of the Twelve Goddesses* that the goddesses of his invention will appear in human shapes, so that it would be easier to 'read' their 'mysticall *Ideas*, dispersed in that wide, and incomprehensible *volume of Nature*' [italics are mine]. And Ben Jonson in *Newes From the New World Discover'd in the Moone* draws the readers' attention to the king, whose greatness can be 'read' (and this word is used) 'as you would doe the booke/Of all perfection . . . ' In Jonson's *Pleasure Reconciled to Virtue*, the first living emblem opening the masque is 'the mountain Atlas, who had his top ending in the figure of an old Man, his head and beard all hoary and frost . . . ' Now, this mountain, as we learn from the text is the 'hill of knowledge', an epitome of wisdom, where twelve princes 'have been bred' ('near Atlas' head' – we are informed). One of the princes is an offspring of Hesperus, by which name King James appears in the text. In this way a significant equivalence is created between the mountain of wisdom (and its ancient head), where the fictitious prince has been educated, and the royal court of Britain and its head, i.e. King James, where the real prince has been brought up, nourished with the fruits of his father's wisdom.[59] In the same masque, the masquers are discovered on the 'lap of the mountain', and a choir asks them to descend to earth, pointing to the allegorical significance of Atlas:

Ope, aged Atlas, open then thy lap,
And from thy beamy bosom strike a light,
That men may *read* in thy mysterious map
   All lines
   And signes
Of royal education, and the right . . . [my italics]

Thus we are asked to *read* from the 'mysterious map' of royal wisdom. Everything that the masquers do is meaningful, as opposed to the 'actions of mankind' that are 'but a labyrinth or maze'; even their dance is full of wisdom:

[Dedalus:] So let your dances be entwin'd,
Yet not perplex men unto gaze;
But measur'd, and so numerous too
As men may *read* each act you do;
And when they see the graces meet,
Admire the wisdom of your feet:
For dancing is an exercise
   Not only shows the mover's wit,
But maketh the beholder wise,
   As he hath power to rise to it. [italics mine]

Similarly, the reader of emblem books was expected not merely to look at the pictures and learn; he was also asked to imitate what he saw when the emblem represented an exemplar.[60] Thus, when a courtier was invited to dance with the masquers, he imitated the divine perfection of the latter's movements.[61]

While 'reading' the book of royal wisdom during the masque performance, spectators became in fact incorporated into it, for they constituted a significant part of the projected model of the world. As Orgel and Strong put it, the perspective scenery (and as we know more than perspective scenery) transformed '*audiences* into *spectators*, fixing the viewer, and directing the theatrical experience toward the single point in the hall from which the perspective achieved its fullest effect, the royal throne . . . Jones's theatre transformed its audience into a living and visible emblem of the aristocratic hierarchy: the closer one sat to the King, the "better" one's place was, and only the King's seat was perfect. It is no accident that perspective stages flourished at court and only at court, and that their appearance there coincided with the reappearance in England of the Divine Right of Kings as a serious political philosophy'.[62] The masque, it may be added, proves the validity of this philosophy, reveals its 'objective' power, and stamps it with a divine seal of *nihil obstat*.

But there is even deeper significance in the concept of the world as a book, for this concept is in fact congruous with one of the distinctive features of the type of culture developed in Renaissance England. The importance attached in the masque to minute and seemingly trifling details, their enormously rich and elaborate iconography is a good starting point for a larger work on the subject, or for the conclusion of this one. From the semiotic point of view, the masque-in-performance may be treated as a peculiar form of courtly behaviour or as a ritualistic spectacle, capable of generating content, and not as a symbolic one, for a symbol usually presupposed an external, relatively arbitrary expression of some content.[63] Yuri Lotman and Boris Uspensky observed: 'To a culture directed towards expression that is founded on the notion of *correct* designation and, in particular, correct naming, the entire world can appear as a sort of text consisting of various kinds of signs, where content is predetermined and it is only necessary to know the language; that is to know the relation between the elements of expression and content. In other words, cognition of the world is equivalent to philological analysis.'[64]

The masques hardly say anything 'new': their content is predetermined by the existing Stuart ideology, and what counts is the level of expression: how the book of royal wisdom is translated into the system of signs of theatre. What counts is the 'invention', because the content is known and readily available in other texts. Even the 'present occasion' (one of the favourite topics in masque criticism) is only a pretext to present the recurrent motif of the king's wisdom which, in turn, generates peace, divine harmony, and announces the beginning of the millennium. And the printed texts of masques provide a great deal of evidence that the cognition of the created world is, indeed, equivalent to philological analysis. For this model of the universe is a theatrical transmutation of emblem books that 'come to life' during the performance. They are self-explanatory to all those who know the language of the emblems; they may with ease be decoded by the learned. For those who do not fit into the latter category, the printed texts, in most cases provide full explanation of the difficult passages.[65]

Moreover, cultures directed primarily towards expression have this concept of themselves as a correct text, and not as a system of rules that generates texts; and each type of culture generates its own particular ideal of Book and

Manual, including the organization of those texts. Consequently, 'with orientation towards rules, a manual has the appearance of a generative mechanism, while with orientation towards text, one gets the characteristic (question–answer) format of a catechism, and the anthology (a book of quotations or selected texts) comes into being'.[66] A good example of this would be the book King James ordered to be written in which the basic doctrine of the divine right of kings is explained in the form of questions asked by a school-boy, and answers given by his teacher.[67] In this context, the Renaissance emblem books may be treated as an anthology or (predominantly Neoplatonic) catechism. In this sense the masque-in-performance presents the Book of the culture that made its appearance possible. We already know the author of this book. Since in this culture the world appears as a text, immaculate precision in naming things becomes of vital importance. Hence, we see such concern with attributes, colours and forms in the masques-in-performance (and this does not apply to the printed texts, which often neglect such details). Similarly, there is no place for arbitrariness in the emblem book. An incorrect designation can be identified with a different context, which creates the basic opposition within this culture between 'correct' and 'incorrect'. Thus, for example, the world of antimasque has its own system of signs, but an 'incorrect' one. This is the only source of evil and chaos in the masque world. Anything that is 'incorrect' stands in opposition to the 'correct' and consequently has to be treated as anticulture and should be either destroyed or eliminated from the court world. And so it happens that the antimasquers are always scared or chased away before the masque proper begins.

The laws that govern the created world in masque are presented as eternal. The created model of the universe does not foresee any possibility of, or even need for, any kind of change. The recurrent motif of disorder, or chaos, troubling the court world, and stemming from the antimasque or anticulture, is only of a temporal nature. The laws that govern this universe, in fact the king's presence itself, bring back order and harmony. This model is not geared to knowledge about the future, the future being presented as a stretched out 'now'. It is metaphorically referred to as 'perpetual spring'. And all this is confirmed and given greater authority by infallible gods.

13 ROBERT CARR, EARL OF SOMERSET, AS COLLECTOR AND PATRON

A. R. Braunmuller

Robert Carr's career as royal favourite to James I is most often remembered for his leaving of it. Within the space of two and one-half years, Carr achieved an earldom, married the recently divorced Frances Howard, was convicted with her for the murder of his friend Sir Thomas Overbury and sentenced to the Tower, disgraced and stripped of all public influence. As Jacobean observers enviously remarked, Carr's rise from minor gentry status to high place was sudden and entirely due to his being 'the King's minion'. Modern historians have been content to accept this view, with the further criticisms that 'his intelligence was shallow', he had 'no ability', and his single most significant political activity (in the Parliament of 1614) was a role for which he was 'totally unfitted', largely obstructionist, and subservient to the aims of his powerful Howard in-laws.[1] Vulgarly, for contemporary and modern writers, Carr was just another pretty face.

Robert Carr's gaudy passage through the Jacobean political firmament has distracted attention from other aspects of his career, in particular his place in Jacobean aesthetic culture and, after his fall, on the margins of politics. Yet, Carr's art-collecting and, more surprisingly, his literary patronage continued for three decades after his conviction in 1616. Conventional in some ways as they are, these activities require that we reevaluate both the man and his place in the Jacobean world. As a collector of art works – jewels, tapestries, pictures, statues, metalwork – Carr responded to the dictates of both fashion and the artistic agents who more and more intensively competed in European art markets on behalf of James's courtiers.[2] With help from those agents and others, Carr displayed an avant-garde taste, accumulating, for example, an impressively large collection of sixteenth-century Italian and northern paintings. Styles of collecting among the English and Anglicized Scottish elite changed in the first fifteen years of James's English reign: the Tudor taste for

230

portraits and religious allegories gave way to collections of secular and classical subjects, landscapes and narrative histories.[3] Here the obvious comparisons with Carr are Prince Henry, Thomas Howard, Earl of Arundel, and (later) Prince Charles; the contrasts such collectors as John, Lord Lumley and his Tudor coeval Henry Howard, Earl of Northampton.[4] For some years before Carr began buying European pictures and perhaps during the period of his earliest purchases, Robert Cecil, Earl of Salisbury, gathered an eclectic collection that included several Italian paintings on allegorical and mythological subjects.[5]

In 1609, William Cecil, later second Earl of Exeter, advised the Earl of Shrewsbury to buy certain Roman and Venetian paintings 'If your Lordship desire to increase your magnificence', and Carr's collecting, too, was partly motivated by Jacobean mania for display.[6] Indeed, it has been claimed that 'ostentatious Venetian collecting had come [*c.* 1635–9] to be expected of the courtier closest to the Stuart throne'; yet Carr's collecting also had a private aspect: the works were destined for domestic chambers, be they public or private.[7] By contrast, Carr's literary patronage was inevitably public and therefore more decisively affected by his fall. Jacobean authors very rarely dedicated works to prisoners in the Tower, perhaps because they feared charges of *lèse majesté*.[8] Conforming to this pattern, dedications to Carr divide into two unequal parts: before his imprisonment in late 1615 and after his release in January 1622. The special circumstances of the literary patron, the patron's participation in a quasi-dialogue with the authors who sought and found his support, make it possible to infer an active and continuing public role for Robert Carr, or at least to infer that other people attributed such a role to him.

I

Carr began to purchase works of art a few years after his contemporaries first recognized him as more important than, or different from, the men who preceded him as King James's favourites. Unlike such earlier favourites as Sir James Hay (who sponsored Carr at the Coronation Day celebration in 1607 when the traditional story holds James first noticed him), Carr seemed to want, or James appeared to want to grant him, a central role in both political decisions and the distribution of royal bounty.[9] As early as 15 September 1612, Sir Thomas Overbury suggested to William Trumbull, the English agent at Brussels, that Carr would find it 'acceptable service' if 'upon the death of any great men in that country', Trumbull could help Carr 'to any good bargain of excellent hangings at the second hand, or pictures or any household stuff which they have there better than ours'. In reply, Trumbull assured Overbury he would try to purchase some paintings from the Duke of Arschot's estate for Carr, but mentioned high prices and stiff local competition. The next year, Trumbull wrote Carr directly about some tapestries Carr wanted woven in the Low Countries, giving incidental insight into the availability of custom-made and off-the-peg tapestry subjects and asking for Carr's own choice in the matter:

it is requisite that you send me word whether you will have bespoke, or great imagery or any such other work as you shall fancy most . . . It may please you to remember where you have seen any fair modern hangings in England; and to inquire where they were made; I will get you the like . . . so that you will vouchsafe to send me the name of the history by which they are called.[10]

In mid-1615, also from the Low Countries, Sir Henry Wotton sought to improve his prospects by sending Carr a Netherlandish painting. Wotton expects Carr to understand the difference between northern and Italian styles:

I am bold by this gentleman to entertain your Lordship with a piece of perspective [landscape? architectural interior?] which is a very busy kind of work and therefore think patient and phlegmatic hands do commonly more excel therein than Italians who rather affect draughts of spirit and action. But this piece which I now send hath a little life more than ordinary by addition of the personages which made me make choice of it for your better delectation.[11]

Another ambassador, Sir Thomas Roe, was not so immediately fortunate in his hopes to win Carr's patronage through art:

I offered . . . to provide you with rarities, for I thought all the East Indies had been a shop, but I was deceived . . . here is nothing but very mean, the stuff of gold like players' clothes, and extreme dear . . . the carpets of Persia . . . are so rare that they are taken up for the king: But I hope to obtain some whereof your lordship shall command all, or what you please.[12]

Carr's best-known activity as a collector is his intended purchase of numerous paintings and statues gathered by the artistic entrepreneur Daniel Nys in Venice.[13] By the early months of 1615, working on behalf of Carr's secretary John Packer and under the supervision of Ambassador Dudley Carleton, Nys had collected an extraordinary group of Italian pictures and two thousand ducats' worth of statuary that eventually required twenty-nine cases for shipment to London.[14] Combining Nys's list with Carleton's summary invoice, we find that the paintings included: *Susanna* [*and the Elders*, presumably], *The Benediction of Jacob*, *Bethseba*, *The Samaritan Woman*, *Ceres*, *Bacchus*, *and Venus*, and *Labyrinth*, all ascribed to Tintoretto; Veronese's three paintings of the *Life of Hercules* and two 'poetical histories'; Bassano Vecchio's (i.e. Jacopo da Ponte's) *Beheading of St John* and *Creation* [*of the Animals*]; Titian's 'molto raro' *Venus*; Schiavone's *Shepherds*. The shipments of paintings and statuary apparently left Venice for London around the date of Carleton's invoice, 25 April 1615; precisely when they arrived is unclear, but the paintings and statues evidently followed separate paths once in England, although all had originally been meant for Carr.[15]

About the time these art works were *en route* for London, Carr's position as favourite and his importance as a source of political patronage had begun to look uncertain: 'never', wrote Sir Ralph Winwood, 'was the court fuller of faction'.[16] Two or three weeks after Carleton's Venetian invoice, Carr's loyal but resolutely pragmatic client Sir John Holles admitted, 'there is a new favourite [George Villiers] springing, who makes much noise and great expectation, [so] that all the fortune followers in that place seem to be distracted, and surely the new man exceeds in number; the other [Carr] fills less room, but weighs more', and ten days later John Chamberlain wrote Carleton, 'he makes more show now the world thinks him in the wane than ever heretofore'.[17] Carr's status waned and flowed through the spring and summer of 1615, but innuendo and accusation about Sir Thomas Overbury's death leaked slowly into public knowledge.[18] After Robert Carr's benightedly futile attempt to discover (and presumably to destroy) evidence of his wife's complicity in the murder, both Carr and Frances Howard Carr were committed first to a mild form of arrest (18 October) and then to the Tower.[19]

As the legal consequence of Carr's arrest, Lord Treasurer Howard ordered Sir Henry Fanshawe and John Osborne to inventory the earl's possessions.[20] Carr occupied the Whitehall Palace apartments that had been the Princess Elizabeth's before her marriage and departure for the Continent in 1613.[21] The inventory identifies at least forty-one rooms (including service quarters, but excluding 'the Cockpitt' and 'the Bowling ally'); although it itemizes the contents of 'my Ladies bedd Chamber', the inventory does not mention a bedroom for Carr, who had been a Gentleman of James's Bedchamber since 1607 and therefore lodged, presumably, with the king when he resided in Whitehall.[22]

Amidst the revealing impedimenta of a lavish household, the flock and livery beds, the close stools, andirons and kitchen spits, the long cushions, the high chairs, the stools, the almost endless lists of doublets and hose and hangers, the Persian, Turkey and Egyptian carpets, there appear numerous undifferentiated books (with parchment covers, or paper), tapestries, and pictures, framed and unframed. The inventory mentions, for example:

Of pictures of yard boorde [broad], or thereabouts
Of dozen pictures of lesser size 99[23]
Five pictures of the whole length [i.e. life-size or full figure]
Four pieces of tapestry hanging of the story of the wars of Troy
Six pieces of hangings of new tapestry 13 foot deep with a border of beasts, birds, and fishes
Eight pieces of hangings of new tapestry nine foot deep with a border of beasts, birds, and fishes

A. R. Braunmuller

Two pieces of hangings of a Roman story 13 foot deep of tapestry
Six pieces of shallow hanging of the new work
Six pictures[24]

A later folio adds tapestries that 'came from the Blackfriars [either the earl's town house or the house where his countess was in the custody of Sir William Smith] since the first inventory was taken':

Six pieces of hangings of *Moses* & *Aaron* of Tapestry
Four pieces of hangings Bull bear & horse. Tapestry
One old piece of hangings tapestry[25]

Some, at least, of the art works were impressive enough, or acquired recently and therefore sufficiently well documented, to receive detailed treatment. Sir Henry Fanshawe and John Osborne specified what they found 'In the Bowling ally':

X A little long piece of the story of the Sheaperds
  A greate table of the 3 wise men
  A greate table of Sampson & Delila
  An other great table of the woman taken in adultery
  Another great table of the story of Lazarus
X A great table of the Creation
X A large table of Venus & Cupid
X A great table of Susanna & the Elders
X A great table of Isaack blessing Jacob
X A great table of the Queene of Sheba coming to Salomon
X A table of Bacchus Ceres & Venus
  A great table of Venus & Adonis
X A great piece of Christ & the woman of Samaria
X A great Labyrinth
  A peice of St Lawrence of the gridiron
[in margin: These peices that are crossed were deliv'ed back to Sr Dudley Carlton the 18th of January 1615 {i.e. 1616} by warrant from my Ld Trer date the 17th of January 1615 {1616}].[26]

Carr's taste, or the taste his agents assumed appropriate for him, evidently favoured biblical and classical subjects; given his subsequent difficulties, the 'modern' sexual and transgressive motifs are ironically appropriate.

Assuming Carleton dispatched all the pictures he listed in April 1615 and assuming they arrived in Whitehall, the marked pictures represent nine of the fifteen he had assembled. It is not too difficult to explain their return: although Carr had possession, these pictures had apparently not been paid for, and Carr's father-in-law, Lord Treasurer Thomas Howard, Earl of Suffolk, ordered that they should be 'delivered back' to their rightful owner. That redelivery was not so easy as the note implies, nor did Carleton's ownership go unchallenged. An undated note from Edward Sherburn, who helped

234

Carleton with the recovery and resale of the pictures, describes Suffolk's refusal to release some 'parcels' (a word commonly used to describe the pictures) of Somerset's without the express order of the commissioners investigating the Overbury murder.[27] In 1616, spreading news by word of mouth as well as by letter, John Chamberlain told Edward Sherburn of a rumour that letters had surfaced testifying Carleton had *given* the pictures to Carr; in the event, the rumour was moot, since Sherburn reports, 1 November 1616, 'his Majesty hath also bestowed upon his Lordship [Arundel] all my Lord of Somerset's pictures, which are valued at the least worth £1000'.[28] Negotiations over the pictures returned to Carleton were lengthy and required the lubrication of at least one rather expensive gift, but Sherburn finally helped Carleton sell twelve pictures for £200 to Arundel, who had Inigo Jones's assistance in evaluating the purchase. Henry, Lord Danvers, had earlier paid £32 for several paintings from the same group, including, apparently, the da Ponte *Creation* which Danvers later decided was 'too grave' and hoped to exchange for 'some toys fit to furnish a lodge'.[29]

Even with Nys's and Carleton's unusually detailed descriptions, tracing the subsequent history of these pictures is difficult and mostly hypothetical, given changing attributions and the popularity of most of the subjects (hence the likelihood of multiple copies). It seems probable, however, that *A Maze* [or *Labyrinth and Pleasure Garden*], a picture now at Hampton Court (see Plate 22), ascribed to Tintoretto and in one of Charles II's frames, is the 'Labirinto del Tintoretto' of Nys's list of 25 April 1615.[30] Bassano Vecchio's 'Decolatione di S. Giovane' on the same list apparently entered Arundel's collection, was sold in Amsterdam (1684), and eventually became the Jacopo da Ponte *Beheading of St John* now in Copenhagen (see Plate 21).[31] Thereafter the trail becomes exiguous. Arundel's inventory of 1655 contains a Tintoretto *Benediction of Jacob*, two scenes from the life of Hercules by Veronese, a Titian 'Sleeping Venus, Life Size', *St Lawrence*, and an anonymous 'Chiaroscuro' painting of the Samaritan woman.[32] Just as the Tintoretto *Labyrinth* remained in, or returned to, the royal collection, it is possible that some of Carr's paintings were retained by James, or more likely, were given to Prince Charles.[33]

The luxury and liberty of Robert Carr and his countess's imprisonment were maliciously noted, but beyond some hangings, silver plate and a few books, they seem to have taken little that might be called works of art to the Tower, perhaps because they feared that, if they were convicted, their possessions would become the property of Sir George More, the Lieutenant of the Tower, as legal custom dictated.[34] To the Tower, however, Carr did take one precious possession, a 'George' (the jewelled emblem worn on a ribbon or chain about the neck) and the garter representing his knighthood in the Order of the Garter.[35]

Collecting jewels, medals, and other classical and modern rarities became *de rigueur* for the stylish Jacobean aristocrat. The 1615 inventory evidently became a kind of running list of Carr's valuables, and his collection of jewels contained many Georges and garters, including 'A large Agot [agate] George compased round with diamants' and 'A George with an Agot having a Roman head compased on the one side with diamants the other with Rubies'.[36] The George did not have a fixed form; other jewels or medals could be combined with a representation of St George. Thus, a George 'having a Roman head' is not quite the oddity it might seem, if it were an ancient cameo made over into a pendant of the Order of the Garter. This elaborate jewel may be the one 'belonging to the crown' that Secretary Windebank peremptorily demanded from Carr on 15 May 1631. Windebank rebuked Carr for his treatment of an earlier request: 'His Majesty . . . is very ill satisfied with the answer you returned . . . this your Lordship's carriage his Majesty much resents', and Windebank's draft includes a blunt reminder of Carr's dependence upon James and Charles: 'your having been many years in some nearness to his Majesty's father to whom you owe your fortune [you] should better understand how to treat with your sovereign'.[37]

Carr finally returned the jewel, 'not without great reluctation', and it was dispatched at once to the king.[38] Abraham Van der Doort's inventory of 'all your Majesty's Agate stones . . . being 4 in all' includes:

A large, oval, cracked and mended agate stone of 4 colors, one on the top of another, first brown and then white, and brown again and then white, wherein is cut an emperor's head in a laurel side faced, kept in a leathern case, which agates your Majesty had when you were Prince.

Van der Doort adds a note: 'This was cracked and broken in former time by the Lady Somerset when her husband was Lord Chamberlain [i.e. 10 July 1614–2 November 1615] <before it came to the King's hands. Delivered [to Van der Doort] by the King himself.>'[39] This stone remains in the royal collections and is regarded as a precious gem of about the first century AD; it is tempting to suppose that it might be identical with the 'George with an agate, having a Roman head compassed on the one side with diamonds, the other with rubies' in the list of Carr's jewels.[40] (It is even more tempting to imagine the circumstances under which Frances Carr might have broken the gem.)

The inventory of Carr's possessions begun in December 1615 allows one further glimpse of his taste. On 19 September 1615, the earl sent plate weighing 755 ounces to Mr Williams, goldsmith, to be pawned in order 'to make plate for the christening' (of the child who proved to be Anne Carr); two basins and ewers 'Norembeck' (i.e. Nuremberg) were also sent as 'patterns for those he was to make'.[41] Nuremberg was the stylistic leader in baroque metalwork, and the last two items of another list in the same inventory appear to be the objects Mr Williams copied for Anne Carr's christening: 'A Bason and Ewer Nurrombrig worke gilt the ewer like an Olophant in black leather Cases'; 'Another Bason and Ewer Norrombrig work with a great rugged pearle in the Middest of the bason, the Ewer round with a sprigg like a branch on the Topp in black leather Cases'.[42] Whatever Carr's failings, and they seem to have been many, he loved display and his daughter, for whose marriage to William Russell, later fifth Earl and first Duke of Bedford, he agreed an astonishingly large dowry (£12,000).[43]

I have found two later descriptions of Carr's collection: a note of hangings and named but unattributed pictures 'lent' to Carr's old friend Mr (later Sir) Henry Gibb, 25 July 1619, and an elaborate, vellum inventory of items sold to Philip Herbert, Earl of Pembroke, 24 March 1637, when Carr was trying to raise his daughter's dowry.[44] These lists substantially improve and complicate our knowledge of Carr's collecting. 'The Prison of St Peter done by the Spanyerd' in the 1637 inventory, for instance, may record a very early English interest in Spanish painting.[45] Both lists contain numerous portraits (30 out of 35 titles in the 1619 list, approximately 78 out of 136 in the later one), and the portrait subjects testify to a wide interest. As in Northampton's collection, there are some Howard family members: 'The Earle of Surrey' (1637) and '4 of the howardes of the house of northfolk' (1619), for example. The 1637 inventory cites portraits of three naval heroes – Drake, Hawkins, and Thomas Cavendish 'wch sayled aboute the worlde' – displayed 'In the wayting Roome', while elsewhere a visitor might have seen Ferdinand Cortes, 'Amerigo Vespucci', Columbus, and 'John Doria a Genowaise'; the lists include British figures celebrated for accomplishments on land as well as at sea: Philip Sidney, Edward Dyer, Edward Kelley (the alchemist, presumably), 'Buchananus' (King James's turbulent tutor), Jane Shore. If portraits of Suarez and Ignatius Loyola and Pope Julius II seem slightly odd possessions for an Anglo-Scottish Protestant, they shared the walls with Bishops Gardiner and Fisher, 'Oxensterne' (i.e. Axel Oxenstierna, Swedish statesman), Castruccio Castracani, Machiavelli, 'Virgilius the poet', Aristotle, and Du Bartas.[46] There are, in addition, more common subjects – 'The Twelve Emperors', kings of France, of Spain, and of Poland, 'The picture of the Prince of Orange in a round frame by Mr Johnson' and (in an adjacent room) 'The picture of him that killed the Prince of Orange', a duke of Burgundy, a duke and duchess of Savoy, royal mistresses and the like – though only three portraits of English royalty are identified, and all are women: 'Catherina Reg matter maria Reg' (Catherine of Aragon); 'Henry the Seavenths Mother' and 'Wife to Kinge Edward the second, and Mother to Edward the third'.[47] By 1637, Carr had accepted the continental interest in famous buildings and cities alongside the older British interest in famous people; 'the greate Chamber' of Carr's

Chiswick mansion was furnished entirely in paintings of places: Pontefract Castle and 'The Castell of St Angell', London, Westminster, Greenwich, and Lambeth, for example, along with a souvenir of home, 'The Cittie of Edenburgh'.

Sir Henry Wotton's expectation in 1615 that Carr might like paintings from the Low Countries may now be thoroughly substantiated. The 1637 inventory contains portraits and genre paintings by Netherlandish artists: alongside the usual sprinkling of attributions to Tintoretto and Titian, Veronese and Bassano Vecchio, five paintings are attributed to Antonis Mor, court painter to Philip II, another five to Willem Key, and there are four classical subjects attributed to one or the other of the Valkenborch brothers. Here at last is evidence of a taste for sea and landscape and genre painting: 'A little ship piece', 'Sixe little landskipes', 'A little piece with wine bread and cheese', 'A man stealing fowls done by Paul Flemminge', 'A kitchen piece done by Blomen' (i.e. Abraham Bloemaert?), 'A piece of fowls and fruit done by Schneiders' (i.e. Franz Snijders, who specialized in both). By its nature, the 1637 inventory advertises, perhaps overvalues, Carr's collection, but it is still remarkable that so many paintings have attributions, often quite careful ones – 'done by Conyet [Gilles Coignet, 1540–99?] a disciple of Titian', or a ' . . . picture supposed to be done by More', for example. Granted that the most prestigious possible pedigrees would increase the pictures' value, 'a schedule to an indenture by which the property comprised therein is passed is of the highest authority', and these attributions seem to testify to a knowledgeable owner, or a careful curator, or at the least, good records.[48] Further, the inventory suggests an interest in the artists as well as their cultural products: 'Michael Angelo the famous painter', 'A picture of a painter . . . half length', 'The picture of the famous painter Paulus Brill' and self-portraits by Mor and 'George Pembi'.

More remarkable still, the 1637 inventory testifies to the durability of Carr's collection, or to put it another way, shows how little his political and economic difficulties affected his artistic property. At least ten of the paintings in the 1619 list reappear in the 1637 inventory, and Edward Sherburn was clearly wrong to claim that King James had given 'all' of Carr's pictures to Arundel in 1616: the six titled pictures in the 1615 Whitehall inventory that were not 'delivered back' to Dudley Carleton appear in the last inventory, four ascribed to Tintoretto, two to Titian. The 1615 and 1637 lists mention two sets of hangings identically described, and the latest inventory contains what seems to be a basin and ewer used as a model for Anne Carr's christening plate: 'one great Bason hamered out variously which is the Historie of Hannibal and Scipio with an Ewer wch represents an Elephant wth a Castell vpon his back, wrought by the famous John Metzer of Norinberg'.

While Carr's collection was smaller than the more famous ones gathered by Arundel, Buckingham and Charles Stuart, it was nonetheless fashionable and extensive, begun when there were few other collectors to guide his taste and evidently growing until its dispersal as part of Carr's self-impoverishment for his daughter's sake.[49] Carr's collection reflects a rather different figure from the bumptious, arrogant, infatuated, reckless playboy of contemporary and modern accounts even as it illuminates an important and still poorly understood moment in the history of English collecting.

II

Earlier, I described the relation between author and patron as sometimes constituting a quasi-dialogue conducted through the dedications of literary works, a dialogue of which we have only one side, the author's. While author and patron are economically and, often, socially unequal and the author a petitioner for bounty, the very one-sidedness of the dialogue, the patron's temporary status as a captive audience, allows an author to create the patron, to present a view of how the patron is or ought to be understood.[50]

From a few dedications to Robert Carr, it is possible to infer contemporary estimates of him and his career, estimates sometimes no less blunt than those in Secretary Windebank's letter demanding the return of the king's gem, but at the same time rather different from the typical modern view of Carr or the view of Jacobean satirists and Commonwealth antagonists. Almost a decade after Carr's imprisonment, Abraham Darcie, a Geneva-born hack and rogue, sought the patronage of seven important individuals for his translation of Pierre Du Moulin's moralistic and consolatory text, *The Teares of Heraclitus: or, The Misery of Mankinde: the vanitie of his life, and the inconstancie of worldlings* (1624).[51] One issue, probably the first, is jointly dedicated to the Earls of Oxford, Northumberland, Suffolk, Somerset, Southampton and Hertford and to Sir Edward Coke. Darcie chose these patrons, he writes, because

I know your Honors to have more, then any Lord of this Age, acknowledged the inconstancy of this world, made tryall of it's [*sic*] vanity and misery, opposed and resisted the dangerous assaults thereof, tasted the bitternesse of his gall, more then the sweetnesse of his pleasures: and (as I may say) followed Fortune through the impetuous stormes of her most furious tempests.

(A8r–v)

Darcie may have been, as he writes, 'a poore Stranger', but he shows himself knowledgeable enough about the dedicatees, some of whom had suffered politically motivated imprisonment (Oxford, Northumberland, Southampton, Hertford), some disgrace and loss of office (Suffolk, Somerset, Coke).[52]

Thomas Heywood was in most respects Darcie's opposite, but he repeats and elaborates the argument for dedicating a work to a patron whose own public experience might make that work appropriate reading. In 1631,

239

Heywood enlarged and republished a book long out of print, Sir Richard Barckley's *Discourse of Felicitie*. He dedicated it to Robert Carr, who was now living an uncomfortable and severely restricted life in Chiswick; Heywood forthrightly declares the dedication's appositeness:

Most requisite it is, that all *bookes* should be protected by such noble *Patrones*, whose Dispositions and Indowments have a sympathy & correspondence with the Arguments on which they intreate. The Title of this, is *summum bonum*: to the attaining of which, those which best know you, can give assured testimony, that your *Matutini*, and *Lucubrationes* . . . are devoutly intended . . . I have added . . . such needefull ornaments . . . as best suit with the humour and fashion of the time; selecting you the sole *Mecaenas* of so weighty and worthy a worke, whose serious contemplations are aymed at Reality, not Forme, as studying to be actually that, which others strive to seeme in appearance.

(2A2r–v)[53]

Whatever Carr may have been – glamorous favourite, arrogant courtier, convicted murderer – Heywood presents him now as the courtier's antithesis.

Incomparably more talented than Heywood, George Chapman develops the claim Heywood makes: there exists some special link between the subject-matter of the book and the patron's own circumstances or personality. What distinguishes the Darcie and Heywood dedications – and as we will see Chapman's – from run-of-the-mill petitions for money or favour is the emphasis on the *nature* of this link; it is not a mere ceremonial or complimentary association, but an ethical, even admonitory, one. The patron cannot escape the identity the suppliant author thrusts upon him. In the case of Robert Carr, the 'compliment' of Darcie's and Heywood's dedications turns precisely upon the patron's failure, his fall from power and great place into a life that offers only the rewards of humble submission and 'retired virtue'.

To explore Chapman's frank subversion of the inequalities in the patron–poet relation, we should remember that he had extensive experience of aristocratic and royal patronage. In the late 1590s, Chapman dedicated two partial Homeric translations to the second Earl of Essex; after Essex's execution in 1601 and probably after mid-decade, Chapman successfully enlisted Prince Henry as principal patron for the Homer.[54] The public careers and promise of both dedicatees influenced the translations; according to Chapman's dedication of *Seaven Bookes of the Iliades* (1598), for example, Essex was a

Most true *Achilles* (whom by sacred prophecie *Homere* did but prefigure in his admirable object) and in whose unmatched vertues shyne the dignities of the soule, and the whole excellence of royall humanitie . . . [55]

Alongside these great patrons, there were many subsidiary ones, and in 1611, about a year before Prince Henry's death in November 1612, Chapman made his first approach to Robert Carr. During the print run of his translation of Homer's *Iliad*, Chapman added a sonnet 'To the Most Honord, and Judiciall honorer of retired vertue, Vicount Rochester, &c.'

> You that in so great eminence, live retir'd
> (Rare Lord) approve your greatnesse cannot call
> Your judgement from the inward state requir'd
> To blaze the outward; which doth never fall
> In men by chance raisd, but by merit still.
> He seekes not state, that curbs it being found:
> Who seekes it not, never comes by it ill;
> Nor ill can use it. Spring then from this ground,
> And let thy fruits be favours done to Good,
> As thy Good is adorn'd with royall favours;
> So shall pale Envie famish with her food;
> And thou spread further by thy vaine depravours.
> True greatnesse cares not to be seene but thus;
> And thus, above our selves, you honour us.

Chapman strikes a note that will continue for the remainder of his dedications: Carr honours 'retired virtue' and lacks the blaze of outward state one might expect from a meritless man raised by chance or by external forces only. He has an 'inward state' superior to the court-honour and respect customarily given to any one in high place. Instead, Carr is a worthy man raised by merit, a man who 'curbs' the pomp and display many might suppose appropriate to his status. Chapman does not forget the purpose of his sonnet – reward ('thy fruits be favours done to Good') – but urges it as a natural consequence of the royal favour dispensed to Carr's own goodness. By redistributing the royal favour, Carr starves Envy: the more he is falsely depraved, the more his true merit will be manifested. This second subject, the envy necessarily but vilely attendant upon greatness, will join retired virtue as the main themes of Chapman's dedications from this point through Carr's imprisonment. Upon the patron's release, the dedications will generally promote both subjects: withdrawn virtue as the best response to, and envy as the universal explanation for, political failure.

The poet's views reflect contemporary comment on Carr's modesty, his reticence, at least at this stage in his career. About the time of Chapman's sonnet, Marc Antonio Correr, the Venetian ambassador, described Carr as 'a youth of a most modest nature', and four years later (October 1615), Gondomar, the Spanish ambassador and too astute a diplomat to have friends or to take sides, commented, 'although the Earl has been solitary (*retirado*), and a man with few friends, yet he has been moderate, without offending or injuring anyone'.[56] Carr's behaviour, or the public perception of his behaviour, changed in the four or five years of his greatest prominence. He was originally seen as retired, as bearing his influence quietly and modestly;

later, complaints of arrogance and self-display become common.[57] One possible inference, then, is that Chapman's 1611 sonnet is not misguided or ill-informed compliment, but a feasible, even a convincing, interpretation of the favourite's public self. To anticipate my argument about Carr after the fall, we might extrapolate a complementary withdrawal *from* arrogance and courtiership *back* to a style of life similar to that during the 'early' period of Carr's career.

Chapman's most controversial address celebrates the marriage (26 December 1613) of Carr, now Earl of Somerset, to Frances Howard, whose first marriage had been nullified on the grounds of the Earl of Essex's impotence. King James had arranged that first marriage and had then, five years later, laboured hard to dissolve it, offending the consciences of the Archbishop of Canterbury and several other members of an investigative commission the king eventually had to pack in order to gain the result he desired. Most observers were incredulous that Frances Howard could be declared – even by a vote of 7-to-5 – *virgo intacta*, and most regarded the episode as an offensive display of the favourite's domination over James.

The marriage proved a difficult rhetorical and tactical problem for several prominent poets. Ben Jonson, who had written a fine masque for the first marriage, wrote another for this one, but he deleted direct references to the wedding from the folio text published (1616) immediately after the couple's imprisonment. Jonson never printed his ambivalent poem congratulating Carr; only an autograph copy survives, pasted inside a Jonson second folio that may have belonged to Carr himself.[58] John Donne, soon to abandon his hopes for a grand secular post and to accept his great career as a churchman, had assiduously sought Carr's favour for the past two years, but his poem acknowledging the marriage was so tardy he had to write another explaining why.[59] Like Donne, Samuel Daniel was simultaneously receiving the patronage of Carr and his enemy, Lucy, Countess of Bedford. Carr had stepped in as patron of Daniel's *First Part of the Historie of England* after Salisbury's death, and Daniel was to remain, privately rather than publicly, a loyal supporter of Carr after his fall.[60]

Chapman's epithalamion, *Andromeda Liberata, or The Nuptials of Perseus and Andromeda* (1614), and its dedication display none of the doubts that afflicted his fellow poets. The entry for his poem in the Stationers' Register demonstrates, however, that others were less certain of the public reaction to marriage and poem. Uniquely among all the works entered in that register up to 1640, Chapman's poem was licensed for printing by no fewer than four members of the Privy Council – 'the Duke of Lennox, the earle of Suffolke, the earle of Marr, Sir Julius Caesar'. Licensing was ordinarily the prerogative of various clerics, and of the four councillors who licensed Chapman's poem, only one, Lennox, licensed even a single other work. That these four men should favour a poem supporting the marriage is understandable: Suffolk was the bride's father, Mar an old friend and confidant of James, Julius Caesar one of the most enthusiastic members of the commission that nullified her first marriage and Sir John Holles testified that Lennox had privately urged the marriage 'in [Frances's] behalf'.[61] So many authoritative names in the Register may be an aggressive act, a move in the propaganda war to vindicate the favourite's position, his marriage and, by extension, the power and sway of his allies – these very four men, for instance. Alternatively, some party to the transaction, perhaps Lawrence Lisle, the publisher, might have wanted reassurance that the poem represented the ruling party line.[62] Chapman's pugnacious dedication and the poem's inflammatory adulation do not bear out Walter Greg's claim that 'Chapman evidently sought to put it under the protection of powerful members of the Privy Council'.[63]

Worries about offence, if there were such worries, came from the Privy Council or the publisher, not the poet. Chapman at once addresses his patrons' unpopularity. His dedication begins with a majority-of-one argument, a conventional claim that the more popular an idea the less likely it is to be true:

> As nothing under heaven is more remov'd
> From Truth & virtue, then Opinions prov'd
> By vulgar Voices: So is nought more true
> Nor soundly virtuous then things held by few . . .
>
> (ll. 1–4; *Poems*, p. 305)

This *in medias res* opening assumes the reader ('The Right Worthily Honored Robert', 'the Ladie Frances', or anyone else) already knows what the 'vulgar Voices' are saying, knows, that is, how thoroughly unpopular the marriage and its antecedents are.[64] Chapman concludes the dedication with the same advice he gave in the *Iliads* sonnet: Carr is to 'thirst' for 'inward *Goodnesse*' 'Till *Scandall* pine', and '*Bane-fed* envie burst' (ll. 154, 158–9); his wife is to

> make our factious brood
> Whose forked tongs, wold fain your honor sting
> Convert their venomd points into their spring:
> Whose owne harts guilty, of faults faind in yours
> Wold fain be posting off: but arme your powers
> With such a siege of vertues, that no vice
> Of all your Foes, *Advantage* may entice
> To sally forth, and charge you with offence,
> But sterve within, for very conscience
> Of that Integritie, they see exprest
> In your cleere life . . .
>
> (ll. 161–71; *Poems*, p. 308)

243

The poem retells the myth of Perseus and Andromeda, with Andromeda's 'barren rock' allegorized as the very same vulgar opinion castigated in the dedication. Given the official claim that Essex's impotence justified the divorce, readers quickly supposed that rather than rescuing Frances from the slings and arrows of public obloquy, making (or re-making) an 'honest woman' of her, Carr had in fact rescued his wife from a loveless, sexless marriage. The interpretation may be vulgar, but it is also obvious and congenial to popular distaste for recent events. Chapman was forced into an unpersuasive, but dogmatically defensive, *Free and Offenceless Justification of . . . Andromeda Liberata* (also 1614) in which he claimed that the obvious interpretation of his poem could not be right because it made no sense to describe a man, the Earl of Essex, as a 'barren rock'!

Little more than a year after the poem, Edward Coke's zealous investigation of Overbury's murder, and the trials and convictions that followed it, destroyed Carr's influence. Despite the catastrophe that had befallen him (still less than thirty years old in 1615), his calm manner in prison before his trial and his patient bearing during a very long day in Westminster Hall earned some rather grudging respect. John Castle wrote James Miller that awaiting trial Carr 'still seems not to be shaken with these storms . . . If this constancy and carelessness be of innocency, I should admire him as a man that hath his mind of an admirable building. But if it proceed from insensibleness, I will pity him as more wretched than those that have been found nocent.' At the trial itself, Carr remained dignified and resolute in his own defence: 'The only thing of note in him was his constancy and undaunted carriage in all the time of his arraignment; which as it began, so did it continue to the end, without change or alteration'.[65]

'Constancy and undaunted carriage', fortitude and courage in adversity, well describe the way Chapman's dedications represent Carr after his release from the Tower in January 1622. Chapman's loyalty continued in the dedications to *Pro Vere, Autumni Lacrymae* (1622) and *The Crowne of all Homers Workes* (1624–5?) and, if Solve's speculations are correct, in the *Tragedy of Chabot*'s political propagandizing.[66] Carr's political circumstances and Chapman's poetical ones invite a new rhetorical strategy: patron and poet are one, equal in suffering, equal in fortitude. Patron and poet suffer detraction, barbarism, misunderstanding – all of Chapman's lifelong complaints, now for the first time publicly shared by his patron, though for different reasons.

Chapman's dedication to *Pro Vere* asserts his loyalty: in disgrace, Carr's 'acceptive and still-bettering *Spirit*' remains

> My *Wane* view, as at *Full* still; and sustaine
> A *Life*, that other subtler *Lords* disdaine:

Bring *Suttlers* more, to *Braggart-written* Men,
(Though still deceiv'd) then any truest *Pen*.

(ll. 18–22; *Poems*, p. 339)

Though Carr may remain a full moon for Chapman, both men have waned in their respective spheres of poetry and politics. 'Subtler lords', who are also court '*Suttlers*', supplying metaphoric provisions of praise and sycophancy, have abandoned both fallen favourite and needy poet, although Chapman's '*Wane* view' (punning on 'one', that is, unitary, constant) has not been affected by Carr's fall:

Pro Vere was written and printed in the summer of 1622 (*Poems*, p. 465) and concerns the English strategic position *vis-à-vis* the European forces arrayed against James's son-in-law, the Elector Palatine; it concentrates on Horace Vere's entrapment in Mannheim, from which he eventually retreated with honour in September 1622.[67] The desperate military situation is not so very different from Carr's, first imprisoned, then released but forbidden to attend court, and now rattling from one Howard country house to another:

All lest *Good*, That but onely aymes at *Great*,
I know (best *Earle*) may boldly make retreat
To your *Retreat*, from this Worlds open *Ill*.

(ll. 1–3; *Poems*, p. 339)

Nor, of course, is it so different from Chapman's own situation, both figuratively as the embattled poet and, it seems, quite practically, as a poverty-stricken man himself exiled from London during the period 1614–19.[68]

When others' scorn or indifference harrowed him, Chapman sought refuge in poetry and hermetic consolation. Dedicating *The Crowne of all Homers Workes* (1624–5?), he now offers Carr that consolation, or a chastened version of it:

Since then your Lordship settles in your shade
A life retir'd, and no Retreate is made
But to some strength (for else tis no Retreate,
But rudely running from your Battaile's heate),
I give this [the translation] as your strength:
    your strength, my Lord,
In Counsailes and Examples, that afford
More Guard than whole Hosts of corporeal power,
And more deliverance teach the fatall Howre.
    Turne not your medcine then to your disease,
By your too set and sleight repulse of these,
The Adjuncts of your matchlesse Odysses . . .

(ll. 42–52; *Homer*, II, 508, font reversed)

The martial metaphor vividly exaggerates both the patron's situation and the poet's, but Chapman leaves no doubt that he sees Carr's situation in military terms when he devotes over thirty lines (84–116) to an extended simile comparing Carr's retreat-to-strength to Sir John Norris's exploits on the continent. In fact, court-war is worse than open-war:

> So fight out, sweet Earle, your Retreate in Peace;
> No ope-warr equalls that where private Prease
> Of never-numberd odds of Enimie,
> Arm'd all by Envie, in blinde Ambush lie
> To rush out like an open threatning skie,
> Broke al in Meteors round about your eares.

(ll. 105–10)

Contemplative withdrawal – political exile or poetic meditation – offers no easy answers and demands fierce energies, as Chapman had always claimed. Envy will always ambush goodness. Yet in Homer (and by extension, perhaps in Chapman), Carr has a source of moral assurance and strength:

> Retire to him [Homer, the *Hymns*] then for advice, and skill
> To know things call'd worst Best; and Best most ill;
> Which knowne; truths best chuse; and retire to still.

(ll. 81–3)[69]

Failed politician and waning poet now retreat, or Chapman would have it so, to the same source of strength.

The unhappy see-saw of Chapman's attempts to secure patronage amply justifies his sense that he has been banished from the 'fields of life': a series of disasters quite divorced from his poetry and from his own abrasive personality recurrently denied him sponsorship when public, merited success appeared certain.[70] Just as Essex's seemingly bright prospects influenced the way Chapman approached him and the way he translated Homer, so Carr and his special circumstances gave Chapman the opportunity to unite poetry's subject and political life – this time to link the genuine poet's isolation with an equivalent political exile. While Chapman did seek other aristocratic patrons, he remained loyal to Carr throughout his rise, his fall, and his ambiguous restoration to a half-liberty. Part of the motive lies, simply, in identification of poet with patron; Chapman believed, or wanted to believe, that they shared equal if different disappointments and similar compensations.

The last literary work dedicated to Robert Carr is William Davenant's first published play, *The Tragedy of Albovine, King of the Lombards* (1629), a derivative and apparently unacted drama. Davenant's dedication claims Carr

read this Tragedie, and smil'd upon't, that it might live . . . My Numbers I not [*sic*] shew unto the public Eye, with an ambition to be quickly known . . . but that the world may learn, with what an early haste, I strive to manifest my service to your Lordship.

He signs himself 'Your humblest Creature'.[71] Among the quarto's commendatory poems are one by 'Ed. Hyde', the future Earl of Clarendon and Davenant's room-mate at the Middle Temple, and another by 'H. Howard', presumably one of Carr's in-laws. Hyde specifically compliments the choice of patron: 'Thy Wit hath purchas'd such a Patron's name / To deck thy front, as must derive to Fame / These Tragic raptures . . . '[72]

Davenant's critics have puzzled over the dedication to what one calls 'the somewhat faded Earl of Somerset', but there is nothing especially remarkable about either dedication or commentary poem until we read the play itself.[73] It revolves around the sexual competition and political imbroglios of King Albovine and the character he repeatedly calls 'my boy', his favourite, Paradine.[74] Grimold, Gondibert, and Volterri, all old soldiers, form a carping chorus:

GONDIBERT: He [Paradine] is our king's minion, sleeps in his bosom.
GRIMOLD: True, and the royal fool greets him with such
    Ravenous kisses, that you would think he meant
    To eat his lips.
GONDIBERT: The captive captivates the conqueror.

(Act 1, p. 21)

Paradine himself says Albovine 'bruis'd me in his arms' (Act 3, p. 49), and Hermegild describes how Albovine

    hath of late hung thus –
Upon my neck; until his amorous weight
Became my burden: and then lay slabbering o'er
My lips, like some rheumatic babe.

(Act 5, p. 90)[75]

Even more than a decade after Carr's fall, it is hard to imagine that he, and others (like Edward Hyde and his fellow puffers of the play), could fail to recall what so many contemporaries had seen in Carr's relation with King James: 'The Prince leaneth on his arm, pinches his cheek, smoothes his ruffled garment, and, when he looketh at Carr, directeth discourse to divers others . . . '[76] Later and more prejudiced writers elaborate, probably with some factual basis:

I have seen *Somerset* and *Buckingham* labour to resemble [women] in the effeminacy of their dressings. Though in w– [whorish?] lookes and wanton gestures they exceeded any part of woman kind my Conversation did ever cope withall . . . the Kings kissing them after so lascivious a mode in publick [led some to speculate about royal behaviour in private] . . . I have heard that Sr *Henry Rich*, since *Earle of Holland*, and some others refused his Majesties favour . . . *Rich* loosing that opportunity . . . by turning aside and spitting after the King had slaber'd his Mouth . . . [77]

In *Albovine*, 'the arts of court' (Act 3, p. 49) and especially the favourite's relation with the king are recurrent issues. Hermegild, a melodramatically evil counsellor, advises Paradine:

> they that aim
> At victory in Court must practise smooth
> And subtle arts. Wise favourites do walk
> I'th'dark, and use false lights.
>
> (Act, 2, p. 45)

Paradine never completely abandons his martial honesty, or his loyalty to Albovine; throughout, Paradine's actions and speeches combine the naiveté and idealism, the easy credulity and adolescent egotism of the typical Fletcherian hero. He also, it seems hard to deny, exhibits qualities of the 'good' favourite (loyal, honourable, unsuspecting) and the 'bad' favourite, who practises smooth and subtle arts, who walks in the dark and uses false lights. Paradine thus combines qualities Carr and his friends might wish to attribute to himself and qualities they might wish to attribute to the man who supplanted him, George Villiers, Duke of Buckingham, the favourite of James and Charles I assassinated the year before (1628) the play's printing.

For Davenant to dedicate his play to Carr and (we may assume) to hope for reward requires that Carr and his supporters parse Paradine's actions and speeches, dividing them between the long-discarded favourite and the recently dead one. At first glance, the enterprise seems unlikely, even self-defeating.[78] *Albovine*, despite its crude sensationalism, apparently indicts weak kings and servile courtiers.[79] Yet Chapman, a much greater if less socially adept artist, likewise bluntly exploited Carr's outcast status and turned his patron's fall into an allegory of both poetry and politics. The dedication of *Albovine* to Robert Carr may be explained in several ways. Perhaps Carr did not read the play and Davenant's dedication lies, but this explanation seems unlikely if 'H. Howard' really is a member of Carr's extended family. Alternatively, we may infer that Carr enjoyed, or at least approved, plays representing his relation with James (and again this reaction was presumably not Carr's alone, given the Howard and Hyde prefatory poems); that inference in turn suggests the favourite–monarch relation was not so demeaning as later writers imagine, and contemporaries were capable of dissecting a dramatic 'favourite' into various component allusions.[80] Representing James's relation with Carr and Buckingham, it seems, was an acceptable form of nostalgia for the past, or, more interestingly, criticism of the present; published in the aftermath of Buckingham's sensational murder, the play may covertly if implausibly urge Charles to reinstate Carr as favourite.[81]

Historical as well as literary evidence suggests we should see more nuance in Carr's later career than modern writers suppose, particularly when we consider how he viewed his relation with his successor. More than a decade after his fall, Carr sought Buckingham's help in gaining the lands and income James had promised in 1616:

I conceyve that you will have sum sense of my oversights and fynd out rather reasons of excuse for me such as may cover my errors then to lay them open by giving me cause to plead for myself, for you know who must be a party therto and that it concerns him unto whom wee were both of us all Men most bounde, and who is bounde herein by no ordinary Ingagments, nor shall I need hereunto to adde what I understand myself to be in reference to you, and how much the bonds betwixt thos that ar of one profession or Society hold more firmely then thos do that ar held the neerest, nor will I pretend any [expectations] I have had of a better usage and confidence in the King, his sonne the King present [Charles I] and in yourself to whom I confesse I could not conceyve that I should ever need to mak other suit, then only to mak knowen what I had to desyre . . . [82]

Strikingly, Carr describes the relation of former to current favourite as one exceeding even kinship: 'the bonds betwixt thos that ar of one profession or Society hold more firmely then thos do that ar held the neerest'. As Secretary Windebank's letter demanding that Carr return the royal jewel shows, the favourite's 'nearness' to the monarch could also be invoked to coerce obedience, but James himself partly confirms Carr's claim: 'ye have deserved more trust and confidence of me than ever man did: in secrecy above all flesh, in feeling and unpartial respect, as well to my honour in every degree as to my profit. And all this without respect either to kin or ally or your nearest or dearest friend whatsomever, nay immovable in one hair that might concern me against the whole world'.[83] One episode, almost certainly the last, in Carr's postlapsarian dealings with Buckingham encapsulates their paradoxical relation. Despite the world's opinion that Buckingham had been 'much crost' by Carr more than a decade before, and despite Carr's later, largely unanswered, pleas for Buckingham's help, the former and the present favourite were friendly enough to make Buckingham visit Chiswick to take his leave of Carr about a week before journeying to Portsmouth and assassination.[84]

III

Robert Carr's art-collecting and his literary patronage force us to reevaluate his activity in those spheres; further, Carr's career after his fall requires us to reassess the favourite's role as it was perceived in early Stuart society. While English advisors and diplomats and their European agents doubtless helped form his artistic taste, he also ordered purchases independently, and he understood conspicuous display well enough to amass the costly clothing, tapestries, rugs, jewels, metalwork and furniture we know he possessed. Moreover, in the period of Carr's ascendancy, the period of his earliest documented purchases of art works, there were few British collectors of recent European art on whom he might have modelled his activities.[85]

In the most revealing literary dedications to Carr, we see the perception of his public behaviour as it changes through the period of his rise, fall and the long twilight of his career. More striking still are what the dedications and the works they preface imply about Jacobean ambivalence toward the king and his favourites. Chapman and Heywood understood courtiers as "*Suttlers* . . . to *Braggart-written* men' and the favourite's role as 'Forme . . . appearance'; the fallen favourite's task was 'contemplations . . . aymed at Reality'. The contrasts between Carr then and Carr now and the language his client authors use – 'retired virtue' (Chapman), or the religious overtones of 'retreat' (Chapman), 'the inconstancy of this world' (Darcie), '*summum bonum*', '*Matutini*', '*Lucubrationes*' (Heywood) – reveal their uneasiness before Carr's ambiguous status as once and perhaps future royal favourite. He remained rich enough and potentially influential enough to be a desirable patron, but at the same time his value as ethical exemplum came from his having lost the favourite's power, a power his writer-clients at once anathematize and court. *Albovine* manifests this ambivalence in its schizoid portrayal of 'the favourite' – good and bad, dangerous and beneficial to the commonweal, sycophantic and honest. Davenant seems to solve the double-bind by dividing the imaginary favourite into a representation of Buckingham, a 'bad' favourite, and of Carr, the 'good'. Carr's activities as collector and patron, then, reveal a more individual and more politically volatile figure than traditional accounts present. Throughout his life, Carr remained a semi-public figure, an individual whose patronage was worth seeking, an individual whose career commanded attention long after his political eclipse and exile to Chiswick 'with promise not to looke toward the Court'.[86]

14 JOHN DONNE, KINGSMAN?

Annabel Patterson

THE MUCH OF PRIVILEG'D KINGSMEN, AND THE STORE

OF FRESH PROTECTIONS MAKE THE REST ALL POORE.

Elegy 14

As perhaps *the* author in whom literary criticism was once most deeply invested, John Donne has been curiously out of fashion since that discipline rediscovered the explanatory value of 'history'. Because Donne entered the canon as a lyric poet (since lyric has been the least inviting of the genres to the New Historicism) the social and political dimensions of his writings were longer neglected than was the case for Jonson, once thought of as his less successful rival in the mysterious business of 'schooling', setting the style of Jacobean poetry. Built into the very editions on which our scholarship and pedagogy relies has been the decree that Donne was 'essentially' a poet,[1] which has not only severed Donne's most famous poetry from his sermons, in a myth of maturation and renunciation to which Donne himself contributed, but has also inhibited the project of resituating him in the cultural environment that made him, with his own collaboration, what he was. In 1986 it was still possible for Thomas Docherty to produce a book that, while chastising others for ignoring 'the historical culture which informed [Donne's] writings, and the ideology which conditioned the act of writing or "authority" itself',[2] contained one sentence on *Biathanatos*, and remained entirely silent on the works, from *Pseudo-Martyr* and *Ignatius his Conclave* to the more political sermons, in which Donne engaged directly with contemporary problems of authority in both church and state.

Yet more than any other Renaissance poet, Donne challenges us to conceive of subjectivity in environmental terms, to see how socioeconomic and political circumstances interact with a particular temperament to produce the historical person, who is both partly conscious of the rules by which he must play and partly the director of all his roles.[3] And if any single writer might be said to exemplify 'the mental world of the Jacobean court' as well or better than James himself, Donne is he. Donne was, like his sovereign, a learned controversialist, whose intelligence was bent to the most contentious and hence most historically specific issues of his day; but what makes Donne paradigmatic in a way that James himself, at the centre, could never be is his deep ambivalence about the world in which he both desperately wanted and deeply disdained to participate.

This raises the question of how much of Donne's career as a writer was coterminous with James's reign. The problem of dating posthumously published poems has been bedevilled by Ben Jonson's statement that Donne had written 'all his best pieces ere he was twenty-five years old',[4] an unreliable generalization that was, however, reinforced by later critics in the sentimental hope that all Donne's satirical forays into both politics and erotics could safely be stowed away in the category of student high jinks, in the Lincoln's Inn period. But *The Canonization* distinguishes between the 'Kings reall, or his stamped face',[5] that is to say, his image on coinage, as *Elegy 10* speaks of love impressing his heart 'As Kings do coynes, to which their stamps impart/The value.'[6] More significantly, *The Sunne Rising* and the lesser known *Loves Exchange* refer to the king's hunting, an unmistakable code (shared with *King Lear*) that specifies James as the royal referent.[7] Likewise the speaker in *Elegy 15* includes in his maledictions against the man who betrayed the lovers into quarrelling the hope that 'his carrion coarse be a longer feast/To the Kings dogges, then any other beast'.[8] *Pseudo-Martyr* (1610) refers to 'any such hunting as [the Jesuits] will call intemperate'.[9] Likewise *The Courtier's Library*, a parodic bibliography based on Rabelais, written in Latin, and never published in Donne's lifetime, contains in its preface the following address to the courtly aspirant:

The engagements natural to your life at court leave you no leisure for literature . . . [sleep, dress, meals and amusements]. But still you condescend to keep up an appearance of learning, to enable you occasionally to praise with grace and point your fellow-menials, the royal hounds.[10]

In this context the specifically Jacobean clue, 'the royal hounds', is unmistakably presented in a contemptuous light, implying the conventional relationship between fawning dogs and flatterers.

I shall return at the end of this essay to the cultural messages found in the *Songs and Sonets* and the *Elegies*, poems whose assumed 'early' composition has affected all sorts of critical and editorial decisions. But the inquiry must begin with those writings, both poems and prose, which we know to have belonged to James's reign. This category includes the two ambitious *Anniversaries* (1611 and 1612), poems on the death of a patron's child that Donne expanded into vast statements on his world, religious, scientific, political; his epithalamia, both in 1613, for Princess Elizabeth and the Elector Palatine, and for Robert Carr, Earl of Somerset and Lady Frances Howard; 'Good Friday,

Riding Westward', self-dated 1613; almost half of his verse letters; and the *Essays in Divinity*, which show Donne in transition between what his son called 'Civill business' and his later career in the church, sometime between 1611 and 1615.[11]

One of the earliest of Donne's verse letters was sent to Sir Henry Wotton as he left for his embassy to Venice on 13 July 1604, and its language reflects, as well as the complimentary function of the poem, the optimism that generally accompanied the opening of the new reign, the political honeymoon. Donne referred there to 'those reverend papers' that gave Wotton his commission, 'whose soule is/Our good and great Kings lov'd hand and fear'd name,'[12] the symbolic combination of text, person and office in the royal signature. But by no means all of the Jacobean writings retain this idealistic stance. The posthumously published *Paradoxes and Problems* probably divide themselves between the two reigns, with several of the *Problems* apparently written in 1607. Closely connected to these was *Biathanatos*, an extraordinarily extended 'Paradox' on the legitimacy of suicide, which was written about 1608 and never published during his lifetime. *The Courtier's Library*, mentioned above, certainly followed the trial and execution of Essex in 1601, and may have been revised in 1610 or 1611.[13] In 1614 Donne's sardonic 'Newes from the Very Countrey' was included in the first of the editions of Sir Thomas Overbury's *Characters*. And even the *Essays in Divinity*, as we shall see, contain (like the fourth satire) gibes at royal favourites and financial mismanagement, which helps to explain why Donne's son dedicated them to Sir Henry Vane in 1651, suggesting that 'the manner of their birth may seem to have some analogie with the course you now seem to steer . . . being so highly interested in the publick Affairs of the State'.[14]

Donne's middle age, then, was marked by contradiction: on the one hand a continuation into the new reign of satirical, even subversive and unpublishable writings that he himself later designated the products of Jack Donne; on the other the anti-Catholic polemic into which he was drawn, despite his Catholic upbringing, apparently by James himself, and that earned him the Deanship of St Paul's. While Walton's story of how Donne was persuaded to write *Pseudo-Martyr* may contain elements of fiction, one of his own personal letters records how, in January 1610, he hurried down to Royston where the king was hunting to offer him a presentation copy of the just published work.[15] As the eventual result of having demonstrated his command of ecclesiastical polity, and of the church appointments that followed, there are of course the Jacobean sermons. Although Donne himself did not publish any large collection of his sermons, between 1623 and 1626 there appeared first *Three Sermons upon Speciall Occasions*, then *Foure* and then *Five*, their publication and republication indicating the importance Donne took them to have in public affairs, and the title of the volumes indicating the extent to which he had accepted the role of an 'occasional' preacher, the high priest of public events, if not of public policy. In its largest form the volume marked the transition between James I and Charles I (by including Donne's first sermon before Charles after his accession). It was a transition keenly felt by Donne, who learned how difficult it was to adjust his style of preaching to a new and in some ways more hypersensitive royal patron.[16] But even in his 1622 sermon to the Virginia Company Donne recorded the ethical dangers of tying the pulpit to secular purpose:

Birds that are kept in cages may learne some Notes, which they should never have sung in the Woods or Fields; but yet they may forget their Naturall Notes too. Preachers that bind themselves alwaies to Cities and Courts, and great Auditories, may learne new Notes, they may become occasionall Preachers, and make the emergent affaires of the time, their Text, and the humours of the hearers their Bible.[17]

The vast majority of Donne's work was, then, produced 'under' and in some sense directly because of James I, and was conditioned by the style of James's court, character, politics, publications, and James's dealings with parliament. And while Donne's 'literary' reputation in this century was originally constructed on the basis of poems, known, guessed or stated to have been written in Elizabeth's reign, a different, Jacobean Donne has gradually emerged, based on the modern biography of R. C. Bald, which revealed all too clearly, by Bald's own moral standards, the unedifying spectacle of Donne's absorption by ambition and the Jacobean patronage system.[18]

But while at the level of documentary probity this new story of Donne's career was infinitely more reliable than Isaac Walton's earlier hagiography, at the interpretative and evaluative level it has left us with problems equally severe. In the aftermath of John Carey's iconoclastic *John Donne: Life, Mind and Art*[19] and Jonathan Goldberg's *James I and the Politics of Literature*[20] we now face, as hagiography's converse, the spectacle of John Donne the careerist, marked by a devouring ego, acting always from expediency, and obsessed with a desire to replicate his sovereign's status and style in his own life and writings. We have been told of the 'thwarted, grasping parasitic life that Donne was forced to lead'; that after Donne's ecclesiastical promotion 'he grew repressive, as people generally do with age and success' (p. 11); and that 'the egotism manifest throughout his career is what impels the poetry'.[21] This form of psychobiography seeks to account for everything Donne wrote as the fallout of two fatal decisions, which in Carey's chronology are melded into one: the decision to abandon his family religion, probably, it is suggested, shortly after the death of his brother Henry while in prison for consorting with a Jesuit priest in 1593; and the decision to seek advancement at all costs. And the bad conscience he suffered while practising the arts of apostasy and ambition produces its symptoms in the imagistic texture of his poems. Carey noted (correctly) that James's presence and doings are insinuated into private poems that appear to deny their importance; but he also believed that this denial was always effected, as it is in 'The Sunne Rising', or 'The Anniversarie', in terms of the speaker's claim himself to royal status, to monarchical absolutism: 'What the real court and the real king may be doing stays at the back of his mind, and as if to counteract this the poem evolves its announcement of personal kingship . . . Royalty glowed in the depth of his consciousness . . . In giving his unqualified allegiance to James, Donne answered the need of his imagination';[22] and Goldberg repeated this observation with the statement that 'Donne's self constitution is absolutist.'[23]

I do not wish to deny the psychological force of this proposition. Carey's approach has considerable explanatory force with respect to Donne's playing with the terms (martyrdom, recusancy, idolatry, canonization) by which his abandoned and outlawed religion had now to be understood; and Carey was particularly acute on the way intelligence is shaped by early repression, on the 'sense of perilous trespass' that made Donne an outsider who both despised those whose rules rejected him and longed for incorporation.[24] But on the question of Donne's politics the story has now to be retold once more with a different emphasis. For from the records that Donne left us to consider (and from some that he never intended for the scrutiny of anyone except his closest friends), it is impossible to produce a single-minded person, let alone a coherent pattern of behaviours. The story of Donne in the reign of James is a story of self-division and self-contradiction; and we will learn more about Jacobean intellection and introspection by noticing the contradictions than by trying to smooth them away. This essay, therefore, has a double objective; to do better justice to Donne by demonstrating that he was never so simply the king's man as the newer historical criticism has asserted; and to suggest that some of the current paradigms in history proper could be profitably modified by looking at 'literary' evidence. In particular, when among the historians of this period the major competing models for a theory of motivation are principle versus self-interest,[25] it may be useful to show how difficult it is, in certain complex political careers (and even for the protagonist), to adjudicate between them.

In 1619, putting his life in order before departing for Germany as a member of the embassy James was sending to Bohemia, Donne wrote to the other Sir Robert Carr, the cousin of the king's favourite and one of Donne's closest friends, and sent him the manuscript of this unpublishable work, along with a letter that, perhaps better than any poem, tells the story of Donne's ambivalences:

It was written by me many years since; and because it is upon a misinterpretable subject, I have always gone so near suppressing it, as that it is onely not burnt: no hand hath passed upon it to copy it, nor many eyes to read it: onely to some particular

255

friends in both Universities, then when I writ it, I did communicate it: . . . Keep it, I pray, with the same jealousie; let any that your discretion admits to the sight of it, know the date of it; and that it is a Book written by *Jack Donne*, and not by *Dr. Donne*: Reserve it for me, if I live, and if I die, I only forbid it the Presse, and the Fire: publish it not, but yet burn it not: and between those, do what you will with it.[26]

This letter attempts the impossible: to delineate a space 'between' the only known alternatives for self-expression, between 'the Presse' and 'the Fire', open publication and absolute self-censorship. By the same token, we can imagine a self-characterization somewhere between Jack and the Doctor, in the sense that neither of the two can exist without drawing on the other's resources; as Jack's book has been kept by the Doctor in a marginal category strangely described as 'onely not burnt', so Donne himself exists in an auto-biographical limbo between past and present.

And in that 'onely not burnt' text, *Biathanatos*, Donne's thoughts are recorded in a way that is both supremely his own and supremely Jacobean. A religious case of conscience is settled by way of a political analogy, but one, it appears, of the same paradoxical structure as the treatise it supports. The personal liberty of conscience that permits a rational man to take his own life in defiance of the natural law of self-preservation is equated, not, as one might more easily imagine, to the liberty of the subject – that great and contentious topic of Jacobean parliamentary discourse – but to its equally contentious opposite, royal prerogative. The text insists perversely that 'mans liberty' can be understood in terms of an illimitable sovereign power:

. . . as neither the watchfulnesse of Parliaments, nor the descents and indulgences of Princes, which have consented to lawes derogatory to themselves, have beene able to prejudice the Princes *non obstantes*, because prerogative is incomprehensible, and over-flowes and transcends all law . . . so, what law soever is cast upon the conscience or liberty of man, of which the reason is mutable, is naturally condition'd with this, that it binds so long as the reason [for the law's introduction] lives.[27]

Now it might be possible to argue that Donne was here constituting himself in monarchist, absolutist terms in order to deflect his sense of powerlessness within the system; and/or that the statement that royal prerogative is unbounded is to be taken at face value, as proof of Donne's literal acceptance of the Stuart doctrine of the divine right of kingship. But neither of these meanings seems compatible with the genre of the paradox, whose substance is a profound alienation from commonly accepted belief, and which in Donne's practice elsewhere requires the reader at least to experience the temptation to read every statement in reverse, as a mirror image of itself. Nor, if we suppose that in this major paradox Donne was expressing a real, though controversial and indeed unpublishable conviction of his own, is it likely that he would so toy with the concept of personal liberty as to *equate* it with precisely that power that was most inimical to freedom of religious practice in his own state? And indeed the language here, both in the main text and the marginal gloss, is slippery. To call the prerogative 'incomprehensible' is potentially a subversive pun, combining what cannot be understood with what cannot be contained.[28] This implication is corroborated by the following statement that the prerogative 'over-flowes and transcends all law'. And in the marginal gloss, the effect of condensation is of a certain syntactic, and perhaps semantic *balance* between the powers of the sovereign and the liberties of the subject: 'As nothing can annull the prerogative of Princes', wrote Donne, 'so no law doth so destroy mans liberty, but that he returnes to it, when the reason of [for] the law ceases.'

This was a structure of political thought and discourse that was increasingly common from 1604 through 1610, especially among Donne's friends and associates. His reference to the 'watchfulnesse of Parliaments' might appear to be evaluatively neutral, but outside knowledge tells us that Donne, who himself would soon be returned as a member for Taunton in the truncated session of 1614, belonged at roughly the time of writing *Biathanatos* to a group that included, though by no means exclusively, several members of the House of Commons. More significantly, several of *those* were already well known, and some would later become notorious, as parliamentarians who consistently opposed what they saw as unwarranted extension of the royal prerogative.[29] On 15 May 1610, for instance, James had sent a message to the Commons to prevent them from debating any further his prerogative in the matter of impositions, or additional taxes levied on imports. John Hoskyns, one of Donne's companions at the Mitre Tavern, challenged the newly mystified doctrine of the prerogative which Northampton and some of the higher clergy, in their separate ways, were attempting to place in the category of *arcana imperii*. 'Methinks', said Hoskyns on 18 May, 'our answer should be that we may dispute [the prerogative] . . . And as to the phrases of infinite and inscrutable, they be things that belong to heaven and are not upon earth and he that looks for them here upon earth, may miss them in heaven.' And Christopher Brooke, who had given away the bride at Donne's secret marriage, and himself been thrown into prison in consequence, added (with the same careful balance as Donne's marginal comment): 'As I am always unwilling to argue the prerogative of my sovereign; so am I not willing to lose the liberty of a subject. The prerogative is great yet is it not endless nor boundless, but justice and equity are the bounds and limits of it.'[30]

In his letter entrusting *Biathanatos* to his friend, Donne defined suicide as the 'misinterpretable subject'. The same could be said both of the royal prerogative, and of Donne's statements about it, which were both like those of his friends, and yet not so easy to place in the ideological spectrum.[31] The fear of misinterpretation was one of Donne's most frequently expressed anxieties; and while it undoubtedly spoke to an age of official censorship, it also authorizes us to read his writings as *problems* in interpretation. This is no less true of *Pseudo-Martyr*, for all its status as an official text published with the king's encouragement, and dedicated to him. We know that Donne had entered the controversy over the Oath of Allegiance at the urging of Thomas Morton, which may have been seconded by James himself. Apparently it was not without internal resistance. His dedication of *Pseudo-Martyr* to James begins, 'As Temporall armies consist of Press'd men, and voluntaries, so doe they also in this warfare',[32] leaving it open to inference which category he himself belonged to. There is certainly evidence here of sycophancy: Donne describes himself as turned into an exhalation drawn upwards by the solar influence of the king's 'Bookes', a metaphor for his 'ambition, of ascending' to the king's presence in some permanent capacity.[33] Yet prior to the dedication, Donne addressed the ordinary reader in a way that suggests the pressures upon him; for to prove his sincerity he inserted an admission of his Catholic upbringing, transforming a conventional rhetorical gambit into a gamble. 'I have beene ever kept awake', he wrote, 'in a meditation of Martyrdome, by being derived from such a stocke and race, as, I beleeve, no family, (which is not of farre larger extent, and greater branches,) hath endured and suffered more in their persons and fortunes, for obeying the Teachers of Romane Doctrine, than it hath done.' Although the context is rejection, the language is that of family pride and solidarity; an inference confirmed in the 'Preface to the Priestes, and Jesuits', where he asserted that his conversion to the 'locall Religion' had only recently occurred, because he had had to 'wrastle both against the examples and the reasons' of those who had brought him up. And he distinguishes between those who by 'nature' had authority over him, and others 'who by their learning and good life, seem'd to me justly to claime an interest for the guiding, and rectifying of mine understanding in these matters'.[34] The open project was to show his readers how deeply meditated was the Protestant stance from which he now spoke; the silent one was to remind all of his three audiences, king, Jesuits and general readers, that 'learning and good life' are non-denominational.

That Donne refused to include his family in the massive attack he would mount against the Jesuit mission is confirmed by his treatment of Sir Thomas More, a model and inspiration for later members of this deeply Catholic family.[35] It was one of James's own concerns to shatter the More legend and disperse the aura of sanctity it emitted. In his *Triplici Nodo*, the royal reply to the pope's breves and to Cardinal Bellarmine, James quoted More's defence before the House of Lords, and concluded that by 'his owne confession it is plaine, that this great martyr himselfe took the cause of his owne death, to be onely for his being refractary to the King in this said matter of Marriage and Succession; which is but a very fleshly cause of Martyrdome, as I conceive'.[36]

To which Donne replied in *Pseudo-Martyr* as follows: 'Sir Thomas Moore, of whose firmeness to the integrity of the Romane faith, that Church neede not be ashamed' (p. 108). The comment is inserted parenthetically in an attack on the doctrine of Purgatory; yet what Donne destroys with one hand he restores with the other – integrity – as a property of both the Roman faith and the martyr who chose to die for it.

But *Pseudo-Martyr* contains a larger statement than this of Donne's resistance to his self-assumed role as the king's polemicist. In his 'Preface to the ... Jesuits', Donne insisted that he was not venturing into theological disputes, but narrowing his concerns to the single issue of whether Roman Catholic subjects were required to obey the secular authority, or whether the pope could release them from that obedience. But precisely on this central issue – the theory of political obedience – Donne seems remarkably independent. His strategy throughout was to compare the claims made by James and Pope Paul V respectively, and to assert that those of the pope were more excessive than those of the king; yet the inference remains that those of the king may be *somewhat* excessive. For instance, having stated that when princes assume 'high stiles' they 'do but draw men to a just reverence, and estimation of that power, which subjects naturally know to be in them', whereas popes 'by these Titles seeke to build up, and establish a power, which was ever litigious and controverted', Donne continued:

And the farthest mischiefe, which by this excesse Princes could stray into, or subjects suffer, is a deviation into Tyranny, and an ordinary use of an extraordinary power and prerogative, of so making subjects slaves, and (as the Lawyers say) *Personas Res*.

(p. 43)

It is hard to believe that he intended this to be reassuring!

It was, in fact, the ordinary use (to raise revenue) of an extraordinary power that the opposition group in the Commons perceived as particularly dangerous. For however careful James had been in his early statements in England to present himself as a constitutional monarch, by early 1610 he had managed to give a contrary impression. On 21 March James addressed the new session of parliament with a speech that referred to 'doubts, which hath bene in the heads of some ... whether I was resolved in the generall, to continue still my government according to the ancient forme of this State, and the Lawes of this Kingdome: Or if I had an intention not to limit my selfe within those bounds, but to alter the same when I thought convenient, by the absolute power of a King.'[37] Those doubts had been raised, in part, by an excessive reliance on proclamations during a long prorogation, and their publication in a single volume on 3 February 1610,[38] which gave the impression of *codification* just prior to parliament's opening. At that opening, on 15 February, Salisbury referred to those ill-affected persons who, 'hearing of a course taken to bind up all the printed proclamations into a book to the intent there may be the better notice taken of those things which they command, have been content to raise a bruit that it was intended at this parliament to make the power of proclamations equal to the laws'.[39] During the session there were frequent references to 'the four grievances, prohibitions, proclamations, Wales four shires, impositions'.[40]

And especially in his speech of 21 May James exacerbated those doubts and bruits (and revealed the connection between three of those grievances, impositions, proclamations and prohibitions) by his sharp and coercive tone. 'You must not set such laws as make [kings] the shadows of kings and dukes of Venice', he said; and again, 'You cannot so clip the wing of greatness. If a king be resolute to be a tyrant, all you can do will not hinder him.'[41] Although some modern historians have seen this speech as conciliatory (and Paul Christianson makes that argument elsewhere in this volume), James himself said at the outset that his tone was negative: 'I must complain of you to your-selves and begin with a grievance instead of a gratulation.'[42] And its effect, John Chamberlain reported to Dudley Carleton, was 'so litle to theyr satisfaction, that I heare yt bred generally much discomfort; to see our monarchical powre and regall prerogative strained so high and made so transcendent every way, that yf the practise shold follow the positions, we are not like to leave to our successors the freedome we received from our forefathers.'[43] 'Transcendent', we remember, was the term that Donne used of the 'incomprehensible' concept of prerogative in *Biathanatos*, entrusted to Carr as unpublishable nine years *after* his own defence of obedience.[44]

But even in that defence, which appeared just a few months before James so slapped the wrists of the Commons, Donne was apparently insinuating 'doubts' of his own. For *Pseudo-Martyr* delivered a just perceptible challenge to James on the question of monarchy's origins, from which, of course, depended the different theories of limited or unlimited sovereignty. In *The Trew Law of Free Monarchies*, certainly one of those royal 'Bookes' that Donne cited as his inspiration, James had set himself to dispose of the 'seditious' arguments based on Samuel's warnings to the Israelites against their desire for a king, by interpreting this scriptural episode as the origin of monarchy, 'a paterne to all Christian and well founded Monarchies, as beeing founded by God himselfe', and by reading Saul's warnings not as the basis for a theory of a two-way contractual monarchy, with the people's right to remove a tyrant, but conversely as the founding text of obedience no matter what. Monarchy once chosen, and its potential dangers forewarned against, is chosen for ever.

Donne's response was cautiously contradictory; for he constructed his own account of the origins of monarchy in a way that James, if he read it carefully, could have scarcely approved, and might even have seen as a warning. In the crucial chapter VI, on obedience itself, he advised against the claim that either the papacy or the monarchy draws its authority 'Immediately from God'.[45] The only direct transfer from God is the inclination 'imprinted in mans Nature and Reason' to obey, as 'immediately infus'd' from God, any power that preserves peace and religion. And although, Donne adds, God has 'testified abundantly that Regall Authoritie . . . is that best and fittest way to those ends', it is by no means the only way:

For those diffrences which appeare to us in the divers formes, *are not in the essence of Soveraignty*, which hath no degrees, nor additions, nor diminutions, but they are onely in those instruments, by which this Sovereignty is exercised . . . And therefore the governement amongst the Jewes *before* Saule, was fully a Kingdome in this acceptation: nor did they attend any new addition to this power, in their solicitation for a King. (italics added)

Donne, therefore, claimed divine sanction for *all* forms of government that conduce to peace and the Christian religion, deriving that sanction from human reason; and although he asserted that monarchy was the most perfect form of sovereignty that human reason had thought up, its superiority was only relative. And, he added, although 'some States in our time seeme, to have Conditionall and Provisionall Princes, betweene whom and subjects, there are mutuall and reciprocall obligations; which if one side breake, they fall on the other, yet that soveraignty, which is a power to doe all things available to the maine ends, resides somewhere'. That 'somewhere', and the reminder of precisely those 'Conditionall and Provisionall Princes' to whom James refused comparison, has the effect of keeping alive in the pamphlet the conceptual possibility of alternative models of government; alternatives scarcely rendered unthinkable by Donne's concluding qualification, that sovereignty '*if* it be in the hands of one man, erects and perfects that Pambasilia of which we speake'.[46]

J. P. Sommerville, in providing us with what is probably to date the clearest account of the competing theories of government and sovereignty in the earlier seventeenth century, several times cites Donne, apparently in the belief that he belonged on the side of the theorists of absolutism:

Many writers – including Donne, Maynwaring, Willan, Rawlinson and Field – endorsed the view that Adam's power had been kingly . . . If the power of the first fathers had been kingly, it followed that the doctrines of original democracy and of the contractual origins of regal authority were false.[47]

But in fact the statement in *Pseudo-Martyr* to which he alludes *combines* a theory of original democracy ('if a companie of Savages, should consent and concurre to a civill maner of living, Magistracie, & Superioritie, would necessarily, and naturally, and Divinely grow out of this consent') with the statement that 'Adam was created a Magistrate.'[48] And his rejection of the transference theory ('Regall authority is not therefore derived from men, so, as at that certaine men have lighted a King at their Candle')[49] is part of a rejection, as 'a cloudie and muddie search', of all arguments as to the human origins of sovereignty, 'since it growes not in man'. Certainly John Donne, Jr, did not believe that the belief in Adam's magistracy was automatically a belief in kingship by divine and unlimited right; for when he dedicated the *Essays in Divinity* to Vane, he remarked (as one addressing a revolutionary general):

And although it bee objected, that the Sword be no good Key to open the Gates of Heaven, yet it was thought fit to protect and defend Paradise, and keep out even ADAM himself, who was the first and lawfull Heir, and who had for ever enjoyed his Prerogative, if he had not exceeded his Commission, in devouring that which he was forbidden to taste.[50]

He evidently intended Donne's readers to apply this reproach to Charles I.

Despite these irruptions into the text of *Pseudo-Martyr* of what look like arguments *with* James I rather than for him, the treatise as a whole was obviously intended to be taken as a loyal exercise in Protestant nationalist propaganda. As such, it conflicts with *The Courtier's Library*, where Donne's butts include Protestant spokesmen Martin Luther and John Foxe, anti-Catholic polemicists Matthew Sutcliffe and Edward Hoby, and Richard Topcliffe, one of the vilest agents of anti-Catholic persecution, whose name appears also in some of the manuscripts of Donne's fourth satire. But *The Courtier's Library* also includes a strange item whose contents connect both to the fourth satire, to the troubled speaker 'who dreamt he saw hell' at the Elizabethan court,[51] and, more intensely, to the work that immediately followed *Pseudo-Martyr*, the *Ignatius his Conclave*, entered in the Stationers' Register in January 1611. For the *Conclave* is described by an anonymous speaker who fell into an 'Extasie' and 'saw all the roomes in Hell open to [his] sight', with Ignatius Loyola as *diabolus in cathedra*. And in the sardonic *Library* (like the *Conclave* written in Latin) the courtier is encouraged to read a book entitled *The Quintessence of Hell; or, The private apartment in Hell, in which is a discussion of the fifth region passed over by Homer, Virgil, Dante and the rest of the papists, where, over and above the penalties and sensations of the damned, Kings are tortured by a recollection of the past.*[52] It looks, then, as if Donne continued to imagine the court in infernal terms, as much under James as Elizabeth, a fact that destabilizes the contrast drawn in the *Conclave* between a demonic Loyola down below, and the European monarchs, specifically James and Elizabeth, against whom (so the *Conclave* claims) the primary malice of the Jesuits is directed.

But the *Conclave* is in almost every way a radically unstable text. Published anonymously, first in Latin and then in a still anonymous translation by Donne himself, it was in both versions a tiny octavo, self-declared a satire, and mockingly dedicated, not to James, but to 'the two Adversary Angels, which are Protectors of the Papall Consistory, and of the Colledge of Sorbon'. Yet the book insists on establishing a mirror relationship with *Pseudo-Martyr*. Continuing the strategy Donne had developed for the fourth satire, where the authorial voice divides itself between the poem's 'I' and the seditious courtier who corners him, the *Conclave* pretends in its address 'To the Reader' to distinguish author from editor, while insisting that the author's identity is unknowable.

'Dost thou seeke after the Author?' asks the preface, 'It is in vaine.'[53] For the only thing known of him was conveyed to the fictional editor by a friend of the author's, in a letter, as follows:

The Author was unwilling to have this book published, thinking it unfit both for the matter, which in it selfe is weighty and serious, and for that gravity which himselfe had proposed and observed in an *other* booke formerly published, to descend to this kind of writing . . . At the last he yeelded, and made mee owner of his booke, which I send to you to be delivered over to forraine nations, (a) *farre from the father*: and (as his desire is) (b) his last in this kinde. Hee chooses and desires, that his *other* booke should testifie his ingenuity, and candor, and his disposition to labour for the reconciling of all parts. This Booke must teach what humane infirmity is.[54]

This extraordinary passage tells us more about the motives for returning to the Jesuits than Bald's hypothesis that the later work was a spillover, that Donne 'had been unable to use a whole sheaf of the more extreme and ridiculous utterances of his opponents' which are here displayed to best advantage.[55] For the father from whose jurisdiction this squib escapes may be either its author or the patriarchal figure who commanded Donne's *other* book and dictated the gravity of its utterance. That second meaning admits the pressures on the self of the domains of law and authority, those territories entry into which Lacanian theory has identified with social and linguistic maturity, and subsumed under the Name-of-the-Father. But if Donne intuits the point at which psychoanalysis will merge with sociology, he offers himself and his readers a strategy for self-management that Lacanian theory, with its stress on irreparable bondage, overlooks. Dividing himself between author and editor, reluctant utterer and eager promoter, dividing his utterance between *this* book, written in the alienated voice of satire, and the *other*, written from the 'reconciling' perspective of the official propagandist, Donne found a way to speak ambivalence. And though by this strategy Donne may not have been able to reconcile all parts of himself, his appeal to 'humane infirmity' is both disingenuous and ingenuous at the same time, demanding for himself the toleration that his project denied to others.

The text of the *Conclave* is no less peculiar than its preface. As the preface reminds us of Donne's origins ('how hard a matter is it for a man . . . so thoroughly to cast off the Jesuits, as that he contract nothing of their naturall drosses, which are Petulancy, and Lightnesse')[56] the ironies of the text are so rebarbative that it looks suspiciously as if the author had reserved to himself the Jesuit strategy of 'Mentall Reservation, and Mixt propositions', otherwise known, since the trial of Father Garnett, as the 'art of equivocation'.[57] The *Conclave* consists in a demonic competition, presided over by Lucifer, between all the greatest innovators in contemporary thought, in theology, science, or the 'Arts', 'or in any thing which . . . may so provoke to quarrelsome and brawling controversies: For so the truth be lost, it is no matter how.'[58] Among the contestants, then, are Copernicus, Paracelsus, Machiavelli, Aretino, Columbus, and Ignatius Loyola, who will win; and in the course of putting his own case forward Machiavelli complains that the followers of Ignatius 'have brought into the world a new art of Equivocation . . . have raised to life againe the language of the Tower of Babel, so long concealed, and brought us againe from understanding one an other'.[59] Conversely, Ignatius, who has argued against Copernicus's claims as insufficiently perverse ('those opinions of yours may very well be true'[60]) attacks Machiavelli (his most formidable rival) on the grounds that his teachings have worked against the kingdom of Rome:

. . . for what else doth hee endeavour or go about, but to change the forme of common-wealth, and so to deprive the people (who are a soft, a liquid and ductile mettall, and apter for our impressions) of all their liberty: & having so destroyed all civility and republique, to reduce all states to Monarchies; a name which in secular states, wee doe so much abhor.[61]

This astonishingly backhanded compliment to monarchies implies that they come into existence by depriving the people 'of all their liberty' and 'having . . . destroyed all civility'. Yet the irony cannot be intended to function by a simple discrediting or inversion of all that Loyola says, for that would nullify his malice and deprive the pamphlet of its point. If other texts of Donne's are slippery, this one is positively glacial; with the author absent and anonymous, there is no place for the reader to set her feet securely.

But equivocation is not restricted to Donne's Jacobean prose, and appears even in poems that would seem to have completely abandoned that territory of personal freedom to which Donne keeps alluding, in however peculiar a tone. We know, for instance, that Donne profited from the greatest scandal of James's reign, in which Frances Howard's divorce from the third Earl of Essex and remarriage to Somerset, was made still more disreputable by the murder of someone who had resolutely opposed it. On 14 September 1613, Sir Thomas Overbury died in the Tower, poisoned, it was later charged, by the countess through her accomplices. Donne, in the meantime, had not only sought out Somerset as a new patron, but had accepted the position as his secretary that Overbury's imprisonment had vacated. By mid-December rumours were circulating that there had been foul play; so that Donne already knew how he had fulfilled one of the most horrible of the charges laid by the seditious speaker in his own fourth satire, where the first-person persona learns unwillingly 'who by poyson/Hasts to an Offices reversion'.[62] Yet early in 1614 Donne contributed semi-anonymously to the second edition of Overbury's *Characters*, a collaborative volume that became *the* best-seller of 1614, capitalizing on what was known and what was suspected of his all-too-convenient death in the Tower. We also know that Donne was late in contributing his own verse tribute to the Somerset–Howard marriage. He may have been very late indeed. Although the 'Ecclogue' that prefaces the epithalamium is dated 26 December 1613, the date of the marriage, we know from his private correspondence that Donne did not begin it until several weeks later. The function of the 'Ecclogue' is, in fact, to explain the delay in the poem's completion and delivery; and it provides the most sharply delineated version in Donne's work of that formally divided self to which he apparently had recourse when attempting to deal with ambivalence, here personified as Idios ('one's own', 'pertaining to one's self') and Allophanes ('appearing otherwise', or, perhaps, 'the face of the Other'). In their dialogue, Allophanes reproaches Idios for his absence from court on this great occasion of the marriage, only to be told that even in the country Idios so reveres the king and his style of government that he is not, in spirit, 'from Court'.[63] Yet the language in which Allophanes records the virtues of James and Somerset treads that slippery line whereby the claim for good is rendered as a denial of the converse imputation. It is a court 'where it is no levity to trust, [?] /Where there is no ambition, but to'obey, /Where men need whisper nothing, and yet may'; and the question of Somerset's own role in that structure is addressed in the most oblique manner possible:

> . . . the King's favours are so plac'd, that all
> Finde that the King therein is liberall
> To them, *in him*, because his favours bend
> To vertue, to *the which they all pretend.* [?]
>
> (ll. 81–4)

These lines 'pretend' to unsay those lines in Donne's second satire which speak of lying 'Like a Kings favourite, yea like a King' and which the editor of the 1633 volume of Donne's *Poems* thought too dangerous to print.[64] While the discreetly unnamed recipient of the king's favours supposedly is merely the conduit of those favours to 'all' who desire them, and the king's liberality supposedly proven by the favourite's selfless virtue, the mobility of 'all' as a qualifier may expand to include suitors, Somerset, king, all. All are then governed by the disabling and concluding verb 'pretend', which obviously claimed its innocent meaning of 'profess' while admitting the suspicious one, the one that, as the language evolved, drove out the neutral connotation. It is then not entirely surprising that the language Idios himself uses to explain his delayed eulogy is more elegiac than celebratory:

> . . . I knew
> All this, and onely therefore I withdrew.
> To know and feele all this, and not to have
> Words to expresse it, makes a man a grave
> Of his owne thoughts; I would not therefore stay
> At a great feast, having no grace to say.

> (ll. 91–6)

If one reads these lines *without* a prior assumption that Donne when he wrote them was utterly cynical, they express rather clearly and painfully the particular version of the inexpressibility *topos* that actual and self-inflicted censorships had arranged. The crucial 'whisper', in Donne a sign of political opposition or 'sedition',[65] is here introduced (through denial) in order to explain the mortal gap between knowing all, and telling only part of it; while the powerful and indecorous image of the marriage celebrant becoming a 'grave of his own thoughts' reintroduces the necrophilic imagination ('in this standing wooden chest . . . let me lye in prison, and here be coffin'd')[66] of Donne's first satire, and reveals, after all, what generic affiliates this pretended pastoral confesses to.

This brings us to the meaning of Donne's participation in the ill-fated parliament of 1614. To apply for a seat would probably have been seen as independence from Somerset, who in new alliance with the Howards was against calling a parliament at all. That *parlamentum inchoatum* (as John Chamberlain called it)[67] was undermined by suspicion that the proceedings had been rigged.[68] Some modern historians have discounted the invidiousness of 'undertaking', and defended the motives of Sir Henry Neville, who attempted to persuade James to call another parliament on the grounds that the dissolution of the previous one was causing dissent and harming England's reputation abroad.[69] Neville had committed himself to negotiate with the 'patriots' in the House of Commons on the basis of his friendship with them, and, in exchange for certain 'graces', such as forgiven loans, 'protections' against bankruptcy, and a commitment that no impositions should subsequently be levied except through parliament, to neutralize their opposition. He claimed to speak 'as one that lived and conversed inwardly with the chief of them that were noted to be the most backward and know their inwardest thoughts in that business'; and, in a phrase that subsequently entered the language as a new concept in political thought, he added: 'So I dare undertake for most of them, that . . . [the king] shall find those gentlemen willing to do him service.' But while it was probably true, as Roberts and Duncan argued, that the Commons was capable of distinguishing between such an undertaking, and any attempt actually to pack the House by manipulating the election, and while Neville himself, whose 'Advice' to the king[70] was subsequently circulated in the House, was cleared of any wrongdoing, there were certainly some who believed that undertaking, as the institutionalization of the deal, was inimicable to genuine parliamentary process. As Sir John Holles complained to Lord Norris on 28 April:

a schism is cast into the House by reason of some interlopers between the K. and the Parliament, whom they term undertakers, so named, because they have promised that the Parliament shall supply the King's want to his contentment . . . nor for that they envy these undertakers' reward but that they foresee a perilous consequence by this precedent to the State, when kings heartened by this success shall hereafter practise the like; and sprinkling some hires upon a few shall . . . so by little and little steal away the liberty and at the next opportunity overthrow Parliament itself.[71]

Even before the Privy Council had advised James to issue the writs for the election, Donne himself had written to a friend that 'It is taken ill, though it be but mistaken that certain men (whom they call undertakers) should presume either to understand the house before it sit, or to incline it then, and this rumour beforehand . . . must impeach, if it do not defeat their purposes at last.'[72] Despite the cautious neutrality of this statement, its very occurrence shows that Donne was concerned on behalf of the parliament's success. While we cannot tell from this letter *whose* purposes he supported, Donne, who received his seat through Sir Edward Phelips (no doubt through the request of his son, Sir Robert, who was one of Donne's personal friends), could well have shared the dilemma of Sir Robert and other opposition leaders,[73] that if they pursued the charge of undertaking too zealously, too many of their own group would in fact be revealed to have benefited in some way from the court patronage system, and so be forced, defensively, into political defection. Sir John Holles himself, who had no patron since the death of Prince Henry, and who despised the Scottish favourites at court, had sometime in 1614 applied for assistance to Somerset.

There is no record of Donne's having spoken in the Commons, though he was named to important committees. One, in May, was to prepare a conference with the Lords so that both Houses could present a joint petition to the king against monopolies. The others were a series of select committees appointed to cope with a constitutional crisis, in which Richard Neile, Bishop of Lincoln, declared that the Commons had no business meddling with impositions, that they were a *noli me tangere*. 'Proud Prelate', said Sir William Strode in the Commons; and Sir Edward Hoby, 'Woe to that Time, where an humble Petition of the grieved Gentry of England shall be called an entering upon the King's Prerogative.'[74] But both Ellesmere, Donne's former employer, and Sir George More, his father-in-law, defended Neile. The pressures on everyone were evident, and Donne more than others must have experienced those pressures as the pull of divided allegiances.

For Bald, the absence of evidence that Donne participated in the debates meant that he did not, although the official records are, to say the least, elliptical. '*No doubt*,' wrote Bald, arguing from silence, 'he judged it the part of discretion not to run the risk of expressing himself too openly or of giving offence. He seems to have been a good committee-man [and what a derogatory phrase that is] but he *probably* kept out of the debates *quite deliberately*, lest he should spoil his chances with the King or the leading members of the Government.'[75] By the time Carey retold the story, that 'no doubt' and 'probably' have hardened into statement: 'Christopher Brooke and other *former* friends of Donne vehemently opposed these abuses of royal power. Donne discreetly held his tongue.'[76] But silence is notoriously hard to argue from. Is it merely by coincidence that one of Donne's love poems goes under the title of 'The Undertaking' and begins (and ends) as follows?

> I have done one braver thing
> Then all the Worthies did,
> And yet a braver thence doth spring,
> Which is, to keepe that hid.

(pp. 9–10)

This brings us, as promised, back to the supposedly 'early' *Songs and Sonets* and the *Elegies*. When Carey (who also realized that many of the lyrics were probably Jacobean) performed his powerful analysis of the image patterns in Donne's love poetry, and noticed how frequently love relations are conducted from a position of monarchical power, he overlooked the fact that these poems are actually riddled with political terminology, by no means all of which situates the speaker on the side of royal absolutism.

It is when one collects these terms into relation with each other, into what one might call a grammar of political consciousness, that the unstable tone of the canon as a whole becomes noticeable. To begin with the question of favourites, between the evidently hostile reference in *Satire 2* and the ambiguous epithalamium for Somerset, there are a series of references to this problem, more topical for a Jacobean audience than an Elizabethan one. When we remember that Donne was, like several of his friends, a follower of Essex, we might see an Elizabethan reference in *Elegy 12*, which compares an enforced separation of lovers to the workings of 'blinded Justice', which 'when Favorites fall,/Strike them, their house, their friends, their followers all'. But *The Anniversarie* opens with the statement that 'All Kings, and all their favorites . . . [are] elder by a yeare', and that opening relationship, so evidently *not* between royal spouses, continues its implied analogy to that of the lovers in the poem, who count themselves 'safe' because 'none can doe/Treason to us, except one of us two'. *Elegie 6* opens by reversing the relationship:

> Oh, let mee not serve so, as those men serve
> . . .
> As those Idolatrous flatterers, which still
> Their Princes stiles, with many Realmes fulfill
> Whence they no tribute have, and where no sway.
> . . . Oh then let mee
> Favorite in Ordinary, or no favorite bee.[77]

And the *Essays in Divinity*, certainly a Jacobean text, contain the following remarkable analogy for the doctrine of election:

To enquire further the way and manner by which God makes a few do acceptable works; or, how out of a corrupt lumpe he selects and purifies a few, is but a stumbling block and a tentation . . . will any favorite, whom his Prince only for his appliableness to him, or some half-vertue, or his own glory, burdens with Honours and Fortunes every day, and destines to future Offices and Dignities, dispute or expostulate with his Prince, why he rather chose not another, how he will restore his Coffers; how he will quench his peoples murmurings, by whom this liberality is fed; or his Nobility, with whom he equalls new men . . . ?[78]

This passage, with its clear reference to the problems in dispute between James and his parliaments from 1604 through 1614, is the *other* side of the untrue compliments in Donne's 1614 *Ecclogue*, 'Where the Kings favours are so plac'd, that all/ Finde that the King therein is liberall/To them', in Somerset, and 'Kings (as their patterne, God) are liberall . . . /Enlarging narrrow men.'[79]

More significantly still, the term *prerogative* recurs, virtually as a theme word, in ways that would have had less meaning in Elizabeth's reign, but are fully resonant with the special circumstances of Jacobean culture and politics. And it recurs in contexts which show that Donne had taxation, as a disputed aspect of prerogative, on his mind. In the fourth satire he had punned on 'the prerogative of my Crowne', the coin he paid to get rid of a dangerous and seditious companion, who 'like a priviledg'd spie' he imagined to be drawing him into equally treasonous thoughts.[80] But in *A Valediction: of the booke*, using the metaphor of scholarship as a basis for writing the definitive history of his love-affair, Donne gives it institutional or constitutional force:

> Here more then in their bookes may Lawyers finde,
> Both by what titles Mistresses are ours,
> And how prerogative these states devours,
> Transferr'd from Love himselfe, to womankinde,
> Who though from heart, and eyes,
> They exact great subsidies,[81]
> Forsake him who on them relies,

> And for the cause, honour, or conscience give,
> Chimeraes, vaine as they, or their prerogative.[82]

It scarcely needs pointing out that to speak of the prerogative as devouring the state, or as a vain chimaera, was not to align oneself with monarchical absolutism. In *Loves Deitie*, the poet complains that 'every moderne god will now extend/His vast prerogative, as far as Jove', and calls it a 'Tyrannie' against which his own posture is that of 'Rebell and Atheist too'.[83] And in *Loves Exchange*, already mentioned as a poem of Jacobean reference, he agrees not to 'sue from thee to draw,/A *non obstante* on natures law,/ These are prerogatives, they inhere/In thee and thine.'[84] The *non obstante*, or 'notwithstanding [any statute to the contrary]' was a term brought into prominence in the debates of 1610, when Heneage Finch, insisting that 'the prerogative of the king is not infinite', and that because it had been augmented in the past through parliament it could also be diminished, used the phrase *non obstante* nine times. He concluded, focusing on the issue of protections, that 'though a protection were granted in such a case with a *non obstante*, the judges will not allow such protection, for the king cannot protect him contrary to the law'.[85] This casts a rather different light on the statement in *Essays in Divinity*, that 'Nature is the Common law by which God governs us, and Miracle is his Prerogative. For Miracles are but so many Non-obstantes upon Nature. And Miracle is not like prerogative in any thing more then in this, that no body can tell what it is.'[86] If one suspects a certain irony here (remembering the 'Chimeraes' of the *Valediction*), one's suspicion is confirmed by the later statement that 'multiplicity of laws . . . is not so burdenous as is thought, except it be in a captious, and entangling, and needy State; or under a Prince too indulgent to his own Prerogative';[87] a statement that John Donne, Jr clearly remembered when he dedicated the book to Vane.

But perhaps the most complex example of how contemporary politics infiltrated the mental world of Donne (as a Jacobean poet) is the *Second Anniversarie*, a poem we know, along with its partner, *An Anatomy of the World*, to have been published in 1612 in honour of Elizabeth Drury, dead in her teens and not known personally to Donne; an *occasion*, therefore, for a meditation on what was wrong with the world that he knew, which was virtually everything. And in accordance with Donne's plan in these poems to balance his universal critique with extreme idealism, to make Elizabeth Drury, however inappropriately, the epitome 'the best that [he] could conceive', the *Second Anniversarie* presents her as a perfect form of government:

> Shee, who being to her selfe a State, injoy'd
> All royalties which any State employ'd;
> For shee made warres, and triumph'd; reason still
> Did not o'rthrow, but rectifie her will:

270

> And she made peace, for no peace is like this,
> That beauty, and chastity together kisse:
> She did high justice, for she crucified
> Every first motion of rebellious pride:
> And she gave pardons, and was liberall,
> For, onely her selfe except, she pardon'd all:
> She coy'nd in this, that her impressions gave
> To all our actions all the worth they have:
> She gave protections; the thoughts of her brest
> Satans rude Officers could ne'r arrest.
> As these *prerogatives* being met in one,
> Made her a soveraigne State; religion
> Made her a Church; and these two made her all.[88]

It would have been impossible for Donne's readers in 1612 not to notice, in this analysis, one by one, of the categories of the royal prerogative, what is missing: making war and peace, giving pardons, even protections; but not, significantly, impositions. Given this omission, one must also question Donne's *avoidance* of the easier metaphorical alignment between ideal woman and ideal monarch, and its replacement by the concept of a 'soveraigne State'.

Finally, then, we should consider a love poem in which Donne himself was not sovereign but very much subject to Eros, and in which that relationship was expressed in terms not of prerogative but its counter-principle in English constitutional theory – personal liberty. In *Elegy 17* the speaker complains that while in the good old days of erotic conquest men were essentially polygamous, now, in an honour culture:

> The golden laws of nature are repeald,
> Which our first Fathers in such reverence held;
> Our liberty's revers'd, our Charter's gone.
>
> (p. 102)

Nevertheless, in this newly restrictive context, 'Onely some few strong in themselves and free/Retain the seeds of antient liberty' and continue the old tradition of libertinage. Donne's language here echoes that of the opposition in the 1610 parliament, which frequently cited Magna Carta as the source of those ancient liberties which the new stress on prerogative looked in danger of abrogating. On 23 June 1610, Nicholas Fuller stated that impositions 'appear to be contrary to the laws of the realm and directly contrary to the great Charter, which laws having once a settled allowance cannot be altered, changed, or made void by act of prince or people, but by mutual consent in parliament of prince and people'; on 28 June Thomas Hedley drew his last argument 'from the ancient freedom and liberty of the subjects of England, which appeareth and is confirmed by the great Charter of the liberties of England'.[89] Yet the poem, as it speaks of 'resisting hearts', itself resists

271

solution. From a statement that such a return to the ancient liberty is only a different form of 'subjection' to his 'Soveraigne' Eros, Donne imagines a time when that liberty/subjection will be discarded also:

> For our allegiance temporary is,
> When firmer age returns our liberties.[90]

And in the last redefinition liberty becomes a patient and contented monogamy. If the poem was a ruse by which to express a residual political independence, its behaviour is as inchoate as the public forum in which such principles were debated; more likely it functioned in Donne's own mind as a therapeutic displacement into wit of contradictions that, in their real location, he was quite unable to resolve.

If then, as I have implied, Donne's membership in the 1614 parliament might have been construed as a last bid for personal freedom, events conspired against him. The Addled Parliament expired, and the following year Donne finally bowed to the king's pressure and agreed to take orders, so that a clerical appointment might follow. It was not, evidently, a happy decision. The first sermon that he preached, at Greenwich, on 30 April 1615, was upon the text of Isaiah 52.3 'Ye have sold your selves for nought, and ye shall be redeemed without money.' And, talking to himself, Donne pointedly addressed the Jacobean appointee:

Let no man present his Dotals, his Court-rolls, his Baculs, his good Debts, his titles of honur, his Maces, or his Staves, or his Ensignes of power and Office, and say, call you all this nothing? Compare all these with thy soul, and they are nothing . . . Thou that thoughtest thy self strong enough in purse, in power, in favour, to compass any thing, and to embrace many things, shalt not finde thy self able to attain to a door-keepers place in the kingdome of heaven.[91]

NOTES

1 The mental world of the Jacobean court: an introduction

1 This is a longstanding view. See for instance Conrad Russell, *The Crisis of Parliaments* (Oxford, 1971) in which the Elizabethan age stretches to 1618.

2 STC 8297; J. F. Larkin and Paul Hughes (eds.), *Stuart Royal Proclamations* (2 vols.; Oxford, 1973), I, pp. 1–4. For the combination in 1603 of thistle and rose see Philippa Glanville, *Silver in England* (London, 1987), p. 212.

3 Boris Ford (ed.), *The Cambridge Guide to the Arts in Britain* (Cambridge, 1989), IV, p. 27. Evidence for Arundel's 1609 trip remains elusive. Mary Hervey, *The Life, Correspondence and Collections of Thomas Howard, Earl of Arundel* (Cambridge, 1921).

4 David Starkey (ed.), *The English Court* (London, 1987), p. 2. This negative view of the court began even during its existence. See 'Truth Brought to Light', *Somers Tracts* (2nd edn, London, 1809), II, pp. 262–400; Anthony Weldon, *The Court and Character of King James* (London, 1650); Arthur Wilson, *The History of Great Britain Being the Life and Reign of King James I* (London, 1653); Francis Osborne, *Traditional Memoirs of the Reign of King James I* (London, 1658). For the royalist counter-attack see [William Sanderson], *Aulicus Coquinariae* (London, 1650). In reply to Weldon, Goodman composed *The Court of King James I*, first published by J. S. Brewer (2 vols., London, 1839).

5 See A. G. R. Smith (ed.), *The Reign of James I* (London, 1973); Joel Hurstfield, 'The Morality of Early Stuart Statesmen' in *Freedom, Corruption and Government in Elizabethan England* (Cambridge, Mass., 1973). Roger Lockyer, *Buckingham* (London, 1981); Linda Levy Peck, *Northampton: Patronage and Policy at the Court of James I* (London, 1982); Jenny Wormald, 'James VI and I: Two Kings or One?', *History*, 68 (1983), 187–209.

6 For relations with the continent see Simon Adams, 'Spain or the Netherlands? The Dilemmas of Early Stuart Foreign Policy' in *Before the Civil War*, ed. Howard Tomlinson (London, 1983), pp. 79–101 and Thomas Cogswell, *The Blessed Revolution, English Politics and the Coming of War, 1621–1624*

(Cambridge, 1989); on Scotland see Maurice P. Lee, *Government by Pen: Scotland under James VI and I* (Illinois, 1980); on the union between England and Scotland see Bruce Galloway, *The Union of England and Scotland, 1603–1608* (Edinburgh, 1986); on the plantation of Ireland see T. W. Moody, F. X. Martin and F. J. Byrne (eds.), *A New History of Ireland* (Cambridge, 1976); Michael Perceval-Maxwell, *Scottish Migration to Ulster in the Reign of James I* (1973); and Nicholas Canny, *Kingdom and Colony in the Atlantic World, 1560–1800* (Baltimore, 1988).

7 Norbert Elias, *The Court Society*, trans. Edmund Jephcott (Oxford, 1983). Although first published in 1939 this is the first publication of this work by the influential sociologist in English; A. G. Dickens (ed.), *The Courts of Europe, Politics, Patronage and Literature, 1400–1800* (London, 1977); Stephen Orgel and Roy Strong, *Inigo Jones, The Theatre of the Stuart Court* (2 vols.; London, 1973); Roy Strong, *Art and Power: Renaissance Festivals, 1450–1650* (Berkeley, 1984); Guy Fitch Lytle and Stephen Orgel (eds.), *Patronage in the Renaissance* (Princeton, 1981); Sean Wilentz (ed.), *Rites of Power* (Princeton, 1985); Kevin Sharpe and Stephen Zwicker (eds.), *Politics of Discourse* (Berkeley, 1987).

8 On revisionism see Conrad Russell, *Politics and Parliaments* (Oxford, 1979); Mark Kishlansky, 'The Emergence of Adversary Politics in the Long Parliament', *Journal of Modern History*, 49 (1977), 617–40; John Morrill, *The Revolt of the Provinces* (London, 1976); Kevin Sharpe (ed.), *Faction and Parliament* (Oxford, 1978). Among recent works in literature see Martin Butler, *Theatre and Crisis 1632–1642* (Cambridge, 1984); Jerzy Limon, *Dangerous Matter* (Cambridge, 1986); David Norbrook, *Poetry and Politics in the English Renaissance* (London, 1984); Jonathan Goldberg, *James I and the Politics of Literature* (Baltimore, 1983); Stephen Greenblatt, *Renaissance Self-Fashioning* (Chicago, 1980); Annabel Patterson, *Censorship and Interpretation* (Madison, 1984).

9 Jonathan Brown and J. H. Elliott, *A Palace for a King: The Buen Retiro and the Court of Philip IV* (New Haven, 1980); Malcolm Smuts, *Court Culture and the Origins of a Royalist Tradition in Early Stuart England* (Philadelphia, 1987); David Starkey (ed.), *The English Court* (London, 1987); see also V. Scattergood and J. W. Sherborne, *English Court Culture in the Later Middle Ages* (New York, 1983).

10 'Searching for "Culture" in the English Renaissance', *Shakespeare Quarterly*, 39 (1988), 488.

11 See Neal Cuddy, 'The Revival of the Entourage', in *The English Court*, ed. D. Starkey (London, 1987), pp. 173–225.

12 The king desired to prefer members of the ancient nobility and 'not to forbear to prefer such of our subjects of Scotland at this time as we shall have occasion to use, and desire to grace about us', P.R.O. S.O.3/2, 10 May 1603.

13 See Linda Levy Peck, *Court Patronage and Corruption in Early Stuart England* (London, 1990), pp. 68–74.

14 See chapter 3, Jenny Wormald, 'James VI and I, *Basilikon Doron* and *The Trew Law of Free Monarchies*: The Scottish Context and the English Translation'.

15 *Les Reports del Cases in Camera Stellata, 1593 to 1609* (London, 1894), pp. 179–82.

16 See Johann Sommerville, *Politics and Ideology in Early Stuart England* (London, 1986), pp. 19, 24–5.

17 Quoted in Louis Marin, *Portrait of the King*, trans. Martha M. Houle (Minneapolis, Minn., 1988), pp. 123–8.

18 See Peck, *Court Patronage and Corruption in Early Stuart England*, introduction and chapter one. Erna Auerbach, *Nicholas Hilliard* (London, 1961), pp. 149–50, 193. Jonathan Goldberg points out that James had used this Roman motif in his 1590 wedding medal in Scotland and quotes Arthur Wilson who likened James to Augustus and attributed the troubles of the reign to peace and plenty which led to dissoluteness, *James I and the Politics of Literature*, pp. 46, 50.

19 Both medals are from the British Museum, Department of Coins and Medals. James made bezants, church offerings named after Byzantine coins, both for himself and Queen Anne. Only this impression still exists.

20 Quoted in Ward Allen (ed.), *Translating for King James* (Kingsport, 1969), p. 4 and B. F. Westcott, *A General View of the History of the English Bible*, 3rd edn, rev. by W. A. Wright (London, 1905), pp. 108–9.

21 See CUL, University Archives 11A (C.4, III.a,b): the letter from the Bishop of London, Richard Bancroft, to the Vice Chancellor of Cambridge University, John Cowell, reiterated the king's insistence that rules 3 and 4 be followed (see Plate 31). Alfred W. Pollard, *Records of the English Bible* (Oxford, 1911), LXII–LXIII and pp. 37–64.

22 Robert S. Hoyt, 'The Coronation Oath of 1308', *English Historical Review*, 71 (1956), 353–83.

23 Percy E. Schramm, *A History of the English Coronation* (Oxford, 1937), pp. 99–100; J. Wickham Legge, *English Coronation Records* (London, 1901), pp. 240–1; *The Coronation Order of King James I* (London, 1902), pp. 35, 40, 41.

24 C. H. McIlwain (ed.), *The Political Works of James I* (Cambridge, Mass., 1918), p. 63.

25 See, for example, Barbara J. Lewalski, 'Lucy, Countess of Bedford: Images of a Jacobean Courtier and Patroness' in Kevin Sharpe and Stephen Zwicker (eds.), *Politics of Discourse*, pp. 52–77.

26 Quoted in McIlwain, *The Political Works of James I*, p. xxxv.

27 On court masques there is a vast literature; see, for example, Roy Strong and Stephen Orgel, *Inigo Jones, The Theatre of the Stuart Court* and the bibliography in David Lindley (ed.), *The Court Masque* (Manchester, 1984).

28 Stephen Harrison, *Arches of Triumph* (London, 1604); see Malcolm Smuts, *Court Culture and the Origins of a Royalist Tradition in Early Stuart England* (Philadelphia, 1987), p. 53.

29 For the revival of court ceremonial see Father A. J. Loomie, *The Notebooks of Sir John Finet* (New York, 1987).

30 See Smuts, *Court Culture and the Origins of a Royalist Tradition in Early Stuart*

England, p. 176; for a discussion of the portraits of Charles I on horseback see Roy Strong, *Van Dyck: Charles I on Horseback* (London, 1972); Oliver Millar, *Van Dyck in England* (London, 1982). This image had been presented in the work of Sydney and Chapman but had not previously been exploited by the monarchy. I am grateful to A. R. Braunmuller for discussion of this point.

31 See Roy Strong, *Britannia Triumphans* (London, 1980); Per Palme, *Triumph of Peace* (London, 1957). Strong argues that the ceiling is based on *Basilikon Doron*.

32 See Arthur H. Williamson, *Scottish National Consciousness in the Age of James VI* (Edinburgh, 1979).

33 I am grateful to Philippa Glanville, Curator of Metalwork at the Victoria and Albert Museum for this information.

34 Jonathan Goldberg, *James I and the Politics of Literature* (Baltimore, 1983), pp. 33–50 and *passim*.

35 See Roy Strong, *Spectacle of Power* (London, 1973).

36 Roy Strong, *Henry, Prince of Wales and England's Lost Renaissance* (New York, 1986).

37 See Adam White, 'Nicholas Stone and Early Stuart Sculpture' in *The Cambridge Guide to the Arts in Britain*, ed. by Boris Ford, IV, p. 269 on the Roman effigies of Sir George and Francis Holles in Westminster Abbey and the monument to Henry Howard, Earl of Northampton; Linda Levy Peck, 'Court Patronage and Government Policy: The Jacobean Dilemma', *Patronage in the Renaissance*, eds. Guy Fitch Lytle and Stephen Orgel (Princeton, 1981), p. 43, on Sir Edward Barkham whose funeral monument shows him wearing his Lord Mayor's gown over knightly armour.

38 See David Howarth, *The Earl of Arundel and his Circle* (New Haven, 1985); Mary Hervey, *The Life, Correspondence and Collections of Thomas Howard, Earl of Arundel* (Cambridge, 1921).

39 Linda Van Nordern, 'The Elizabethan College of Antiquaries' (PhD. thesis, UCLA, 1946); Kevin Sharpe, *Sir Robert Cotton* (Oxford, 1979); Linda Levy Peck, *Northampton*, pp. 119–21 and 'The Mentality of a Jacobean Grandee', below.

40 Quoted in F. J. Levy (ed.), Francis Bacon, *The History of the Reign of King Henry the Seventh* (Indianapolis, 1972), p. 254, Bacon to Lord Ellesmere, April 1605.

41 P. R. Seddon (ed.), *The Letters of Sir John Holles*, Thoroton Society (3 vols.; Nottingham, 1975–83). Visiting the fallen favourite Somerset in the Tower Holles wrote

seeing in others miseries, as in a glass, we may behould the misfortune, to which all men that live under the will of another be subject . . . this . . . which modernly is termed reason of state is an arrow, which flyeth over every mans head, and no man can escape it without miraculous fortune, if he stand in the way; for sum mens ruins ar as necessarie for Princes dessignes, as other mens services.

Seddon, *Letters of Sir John Holles*, II, pp. 171–2, Holles to Lord Norris, 1 July

1617. Holles suggested that this rule is 'all the religion, and state discipline in this age'. See also III, pp. 525–9.

42 See, for example, Nicholas Canny, *Kingdom and Colony in the Atlantic World, 1560–1800* (Baltimore, 1988).

43 J. F. Larkin and P. Hughes (eds.), *Stuart Royal Proclamations* (2 vols., Oxford, 1973) I, pp. 18–19, 19 May 1603.

44 See Helen Wallis and Gunter Schilder, 'Speed Military Maps Discovered' in *The Map Collector*, issue no. 48 (Autumn, 1989), pp. 22–6.

45 In discarding the canons of 1606, however, because they recognized the legitimacy of *de facto* monarchy, King James insisted that he ruled strictly by lawful inheritance and not by conquest.

46 See J. B. Hartley, 'Meaning and Ambiguity in Tudor Cartography' in *English Map-Making, 1500–1650*, ed. Sarah Tyacke (London, 1983), pp. 35–8.

47 See G. Jackson-Stops, *The Treasure Houses of Britain* (New Haven, 1985), pp. 134–5; Peter Thornton, *Seventeenth-century Interior Decoration in England, France and Holland* (New Haven, 1978), p. 185.

48 See Lawrence Stone, 'Residential Development of the West End of London' in *After the Reformation*, ed. Barbara Malament (Philadelphia, 1980), p. 174.

49 Norbert Elias, *The Court Society*, p. 50.

50 Thornton, *Seventeenth-century Interior Decoration* (New Haven, 1978); Philippa Glanville, *Silver in Tudor and Early Stuart England*, Victoria and Albert Museum (London, 1990).

51 See Sam Segal, *A Prosperous Past* (The Hague, 1988). See, for example, the silver candlestick in the form of a cornucopia; in the candlestick there is, however, only a candle stump, no. 62 and 62n. I am grateful to Simon Schama for this reference.

52 See, for example, Oliver Millar, *Van Dyck in England*.

53 See, for example, David Howarth, *The Earl of Arundel and his Circle*; Oliver Millar, *Van Dyck in England*.

54 Jonathan Brown and J. H. Elliott, *A Palace for a King* (New Haven, 1986).

55 Quoted in Christopher White, *Peter Paul Rubens, Man and Artist* (New Haven, 1987), p. 225.

2 Patronage and politics under the Tudors

1 For the late fifteenth century and early sixteenth see R. L. Storey, *The End of the House of Lancaster* (London, 1966); J. R. Lander, *Crown and Nobility, 1450–1509* (London, 1976); Charles Ross, *Edward IV* (Berkeley and Los Angeles, 1974), and *Richard III* (Berkeley and Los Angeles, 1981); S. B. Chrimes, *Henry IV* (London, 1972). See also the initial chapter of John Guy, *Tudor England* (Oxford, 1988).

2 On the Tudor royal Household and its political role see David Starkey *et al.*, *The English Court* (London, 1987) and David Loades, *The Tudor Court* (London, 1986).

3 Roger Schofield, 'Taxation and the limits of the Tudor state' in *Law and*

Government under the Tudors, ed. Claire Cross, David Loades, and J. J. Scarisbrick (Cambridge, 1988).

4 For the policy of Thomas Cromwell see the work of G. R. Elton; in particular *Reform and Renewal* (Cambridge, 1973) and *Reform and Reformation: England 1509–58* (Cambridge, Mass., 1977).

5 G. R. Elton, *Studies in Tudor and Stuart Politics and Government* (Cambridge, 1974), I, 189–230.

6 Dale Hoak, *The King's Council in the Reign of Edward IV* (Cambridge, 1976).

7 For general detail of individual councillors see the *DNB* and *Complete Peerage*. For particular biographies: Samuel R. Gammon, *Statesman and Schemer: William, First Lord Paget, Tudor Minister* (Newton Abbot, 1973); F. G. Emmison, *Sir William Petre, Tudor Secretary* (London, 1961); A. J. Slavin, *Politics and Profit: A Study of Sir Ralph Sadler* (Cambridge, 1966); Stanford E. Lehmberg, *Sir Walter Mildmay and Tudor Government* (Austin, Texas, 1964); Amos C. Miller, *Sir Henry Killigrew: Elizabethan Soldier and Diplomat* (Leicester, 1963); Mary Dewar, *Sir Thomas Smith: A Tudor Intellectual in Office* (London, 1964).

8 For early Elizabethan politics see W. T. MacCaffrey, *The Making of the Elizabethan Regime* (Princeton, 1968); 'England: The Crown and the New Aristocracy 1540–1600', *Past and Present*, no. 30 (1965), pp. 52–64.

9 S. J. Gunn, *Charles Brandon, Duke of Suffolk, 1484–1545* (Oxford, 1988).

10 For Ireland see Nicholas Canny, *The Elizabethan Conquest of Ireland, 1565–76* (Hassocks, 1976).

11 *Acts of the Privy Council of England*, ed. John R. Dasent (London, 1890–1970), XXXII, 188; XXX, 455.

3 James VI and I, *Basilikon Doron* and *The Trew Law of Free Monarchies*: the Scottish context and the English translation

I would like to thank Professor J. H. Hexter, Dr Pauline Croft, Professor Conrad Russell and Mr Patrick Wormald for all their help in the preparation of this paper. I also owe much to the comments on it made at the conference on 'The Mental World of the Jacobean Court' in the Folger Shakespeare Library – in which it was such a pleasure to take part – and on the version subsequently given to the Tudor and Stuart Seminar in the Institute of Historical Research, London. Above all, my warm thanks to Professor Linda Levy Peck, exemplary critic and editor.

1 J. W. Allen, *Political Thought in the Sixteenth Century* (London, 1928), p. 252. For the writings discussed here: *Basilikon Doron of King James VI*, ed. J. Craigie (Scottish Text Society, Edinburgh, 1944–50), 2 vols.; *The Trew Law of Free Monarchies* is in *Minor Prose Works of King James VI and I*, ed. J. Craigie and A. Law (Scottish Text Society, Edinburgh, 1982), pp. 57–82. Both are also printed, in English, in *The Political Works of James I*, ed. C. H. McIlwain (Cambridge, Mass., 1918; reprint, 1965), pp. 3–70; the introduction, pp. xv–cxi, is a masterly analysis of James's thought.

2 Sir Anthony Weldon, *The Court and Character of King James*, in *The Secret History of the Court of James I*, ed. Sir Walter Scott (Edinburgh, 1811), II, pp. 1–20. Scott's own views are made all too clear in his novel *The Fortunes of Nigel* (Edinburgh, 1822).

3 J. P. Sommerville, *Politics and Ideology in England, 1603–1640* (London, 1986). P. Christianson, 'Political Thought in Early Stuart England', *Historical Journal*, 30 (1987), 960.

4 *Proceedings in Parliament, 1610*, ed. Elizabeth Read Foster (New Haven, 1966), II, pp. 109, 108.

5 *Ibid.*, II, p. 102.

6 *Ibid.*, II, p. 101.

7 Jean-Philippe Genet, 'Ecclesiastics and Political Theory in Late Medieval England: The End of a Monopoly', in *The Church, Politics and Patronage in the Fifteenth Century*, ed. R. B. Dobson (Gloucester, 1984), pp. 31–2.

8 'The Harp' is printed in *Liber Pluscardensis*, ed. F. J. H. Skene (Edinburgh, 1877–80), I, pp. 392–400. *Gilbert of the Haye's Prose MS* (1456), II, *The Buke of the Ordre of Knychthede and The Buke of the Governance of Princis* (Scottish Text Society, Edinburgh, 1909). J. H. Burns, 'John Ireland and *The Merroure of Wyssdome*', *Innes Review*, 6 (1955), 77–98. R. J. Lyall, 'Politics and Poetry in Fifteenth and Sixteenth Century Scotland', *Scottish Literary Journal*, 3 (1976), 5–29. R. A. Mason, 'Kingship, Tyranny and the Right to Resist in Fifteenth Century Scotland', *Scottish Historical Review*, 66 (1987), pp. 125–51. Sally L. Mapstone, 'The Advice to Princes Tradition in Scottish Literature, 1450–1500' (DPhil., Oxford, 1986); I have much benefited from reading this thesis, and from discussions with Dr Mapstone.

9 Sir James Fergusson, *The Declaration of Arbroath* (Edinburgh, 1970); A. A. M. Duncan, *The Nation of Scots and the Declaration of Arbroath* (Historical Association Pamphlet, 1970); G. W. S. Barrow, 'The Idea of Freedom in Late Medieval Scotland', *Innes Review*, 30 (1970), pp. 16–34.

10 John Major, *History of Greater Britain* (Scottish History Society, 1892). My debt in this section to the work of Professor J. H. Burns is very clear: see Burns, 'The Conciliarist Tradition in Scotland', *Scottish Historical Review*, 42 (1963), pp. 89–104, and '*Politia Regalis et Optima*: The Political Thought of John Mair', *History of Political Thought*, II (1981–2), 31–61; I also learned a great deal from his Carlyle Lectures on 'Lordship, Kingship and Empire, 1400–1525', given in the University of Oxford, 1988.

11 Hector Boece, *The History and Chronicles of Scotland . . . translated by John Bellenden*, ed. T. Maitland (Edinburgh, 1821). George Buchanan, *De Iure Regni apud Scotos* (Edinburgh, 1579: facsimile reprint, Da Capo Press, Amsterdam and New York, 1969). Among the wealth of writing on these authors, see in particular A. A. M. Duncan, 'Hector Boece and the Medieval Tradition', *Scots Antiquaries and Historians* (Abertay Historical Society, Dundee, 1972), pp. 1–11; J. H. Burns, 'The Political Ideas of George Buchanan', *Scottish Historical Review*, 30 (1951), 60–8; H. R. Trevor-Roper, 'George Buchanan and the Ancient Scottish Constitution', *English Historical Review*, Supplement 3,

1966; R. A. Mason, '*Rex Stoicus*: George Buchanan, James VI and the Scottish Polity', in *New Perspectives on the Politics and Culture of Early Modern Scotland*, ed. J. Dwyer, R. A. Mason and A. Murdoch (Edinburgh, 1982), pp. 9–33; and, most recently, the excellent new approach by D. Norbrook, '*Macbeth* and the Politics of Historiography' in *Politics of Discourse: The Literature and History of Seventeenth-Century England*, ed. Kevin Sharpe and Steven N. Zwicker (Berkeley, 1987), pp. 78–116. For the development of theories of resistance, Q. Skinner, *The Foundations of Modern Political Thought* (Cambridge, 1978), II, part 3.

12 John Knox, *Appellation to the nobility and estates of Scotland* and *Letter addressed to the Commonalty of Scotland* (both 1558) in *The Works of John Knox*, ed. D. Laing (Edinburgh, 1864), IV, pp. 469–520 and 521–38; the quotation is on p. 495. The reference to 'the rascal multitude' is in John Knox, *History of the Reformation in Scotland*, ed. W. C. Dickinson (Edinburgh, 1949), I, p. 162.

13 *Ibid.*, II, pp. 82–3; David Calderwood, *The History of the Kirk of Scotland* (Wodrow Society, Edinburgh, 1842–9), II, pp. 277–9. John Ponet, *A Short Treatise of Politic Power* (Scolar Press facsimile, London, 1970).

14 Jenny Wormald, *Lords and Men in Scotland: Bonds of Manrent, 1442–1603* (Edinburgh, 1985). As king, James recognized and made use of the idea of contract for political purposes; he entered into bonds himself, and in 1587 he revived the idea of the General Band, which formally bound highland and border lords to take responsibility for their followers and tenants: *Lords and Men*, pp. 130, 153, 165. But unlike Mair and Buchanan, he did not subsume practice into his political theory; he was no 'contractualist'. Not surprisingly, he shared his predecessors' belief in hereditary succession as the basis for his position as King of Scotland – and potential King of England: *Trew Law*, ed. Craigie, pp. 73, 80–1.

15 Maurice Lee Jr, *James I and Henry IV: An Essay in English Foreign Policy, 1603–1610* (Illinois, 1970), p. 10. *Trew Law*, ed. Craigie, p. 71.

16 Allen, *Political Thought*, pp. 252–3.

17 'The Library of James VI, 1573–1583' is listed in *Scottish History Society, Miscellany 1* (Edinburgh, 1893), pp. xi–lxxv; references to Budé and Bodin are on pp. xli–ii and lvi – there were two copies of Budé. An appealing aspect of this list is that it includes bows, arrows, a shooting glove and golf clubs (p. lxx): 'mens sana in corpore sano'! Jean Bodin, *The Six Bookes of a Commonweale*, ed. K. D. McRae (Harvard, 1962), p. 84.

18 M. Lee Jr, *John Maitland of Thirlestane and the Foundation of the Stewart Despotism in Scotland* (Princeton, 1959); *Government by Pen: Scotland under James VI and I* (Illinois, 1980); 'James VI and the Revival of Episcopacy in Scotland, 1596–1600', *Church History*, 43 (1974), pp. 55–7.

19 I. H. Stewart, *The Scottish Coinage* (London, 1967), pp. 92–6.

20 *Calendar of State Papers Scottish*, VI, p. 523.

21 'Mr Henry Yelverton, his Narrative of what passed on his being restored to the King's favour in 1609 ... ', *Archaeologia*, 15 (1806), p. 51.

22 *Acts of the Parliaments of Scotland*, ed. T. Thompson and C. Innes (12 vols., Edinburgh, 1814–75), III, pp. 292–3, 296, cc. 2, 8; p. 293, c. 3.

23 *Ibid.*, III, p. 443, c. 16; pp. 509–10, c. 120, an act which revived legislation first passed in 1428 but never put into effect.

24 For greater control before 1603, see, for example, *ibid.*, III, p. 443, c. 16, and p. 530; IV, pp. 8, 56, 69, c. 28. In the second parliament held after his departure to England, the king tried to nominate the Lords of the Articles, probably unsuccessfully: *ibid.*, IV, p. 280 (the record is mutilated here, and the king's list does not survive). James's visit to Scotland in 1617, when he spent twelve days sitting with the Lords of the Articles, produced something of a show-down. He was forced to concede that no more than eight from each estate, and from among the officers of state – the real point of the demand – would be elected to the Articles: *ibid.*, IV, p. 527. Despite this, royal control of the Articles seems to have reached a new level in the parliament of 1621, when James was straining every nerve to push through his ecclesiastical policy and a new form of taxation; for the extent of royal manipulation in this parliament, Calderwood, *History*, VII, pp. 488–507.

25 *Trew Law*, ed. Craigie, pp. 70–1. This description of the effect of the Norman Conquest on English law and government – reinforced by the point that the laws in England were written in a foreign language – was certainly touching on a somewhat raw English nerve: see Christopher Hill, 'The Norman Yoke' in *Puritanism and Revolution* (Penguin Books reprint, 1986), pp. 58–125; J. P. Sommerville, 'History and Theory: The Norman Conquest in Early Stuart Political Thought', *Political Studies*, 34 (1986), pp. 249–61. That being so, the passage may support the argument suggested on p. 50, that the *Trew Law*, when written, was not primarily directed towards an English readership.

26 *Trew Law*, ed. Craigie, pp. 70, 71, 64–6, 81.

27 According to Castelvetro, in his dedication to James, the king had asked to see this work. Whether it was genuine or not remains uncertain. There are, as Craigie has pointed out, certain similarities between *Basilikon Doron* and Charles V's 'Instrucciones' to Philip in 1543 and 1548; and James may well have known about these. But the Castelvetro manuscript was his holograph of the dubious 'political testament' of 1555. An English translation of this work by Lord Henry Howard was presented to Queen Elizabeth in the 1590s; and Castelvetro had ties with the English court. The literary link between two royal fathers, Charles V and James VI, writing for their sons, is therefore tenuous; more probably the manuscript given to James had only the spurious authority of Charles's name rather than the genuine one of his authorship. This does not, however, affect the idea that James saw himself as following Charles's example. *Basilikon Doron*, ed. Craigie, II, pp. 63–7; *The Works of William Fowler*, ed. H. W. Meikle, J. Craigie and J. Purves (Scottish History Society, Edinburgh, 1940), III, pp. cxxvi–xxxi; R. B. Merriman, *The Rise of the Spanish Empire* (New York, 1962), III, pp. 407–9; Karl Brandi, *The Emperor Charles V* (London, 1949), pp. 484–95, 582–6.

28 *Basilikon Doron*, ed. Craigie, I, pp. 24–5.

29 *Ibid.*, I, pp. 39, 140–3, 82–93, 120–35.
30 *Ibid.*, I, pp. 174–5, 180–1, 188–91.
31 This became immediately apparent at the beginning of the reign, even before James had left Scotland, in an exchange of letters between the king and the English councillors, in which James talked of the blessings of God, while the councillors, instructed to keep things going until his arrival, had to send messengers post-haste to Scotland to tell him the right form of words to authorise them to do so. Apparently English government ceased to function for a few days! Bodleian MS Ashmole 1729, ff. 41r–42r, 56r–v.
32 S. R. Gardiner, *History of England, 1603–1642* (London, 1884–9), II, pp. 38–9.
33 *Parliamentary Debates in 1610*, ed. S. R. Gardiner, Camden Society o.s. 81 (London, 1861), p. 10. M. Lee Jr, 'James VI and the Aristocracy', *Scotia*, 1 (1977), p. 19.
34 British Library, Royal MS 18 B xv (Basilikon Doron); 18 B xiv, f. 1 (Revelations).
35 Godfrey Goodman, *The Court of King James the First*, ed. J. S. Brewer (London, 1839), I, p. 173.
36 *Basilikon Doron*, ed. Craigie, II, pp. 8–15.
37 *Register of the Privy Council of Scotland*, ed. J. H. Burton and others (Edinburgh, 1877–), VI, p. 63.
38 *Basilikon Doron*, ed. Craigie, II, pp. 117, 6.
39 *Ibid.*, I, p. 13; II, pp. 7–8.
40 I am deeply indebted to Dr Blayney for the information contained here, and for his permission to use it; and I should like to record the pleasure and fascination which his discussion of his discovery gave me.
41 *Basilikon Doron*, ed. Craigie, I, pp. 21, 13, 14, 18.
42 One manifestation of this is, however, a good deal more remarkable than the average mug. As a pleasing compliment to the king and his son Henry, the classical scholar and artist Henry Peacham produced two delightful books containing emblems illustrating quotes from *Basilikon Doron*, accompanied by appropriate classical tags; one, with pen-and-ink drawings, was dedicated to the king, the other, using water-colour, to Henry Prince of Wales: British Library, Royal MS 12 A lxvi and Harleian MS 6855, art. 13.
43 Calderwood, *History*, V, p. 680.
44 *Political Works of James I*, ed. McIlwain, pp. 306–25; Sommerville, *Politics and Ideology*, p. 134.
45 *Commons Debates, 1621*, ed. W. Notestein, F. H. Relf and H. Simpson (New Haven, 1935), II, pp. 3–4. A similar note had been struck in the first speech James ever made to the English parliament, on 29 March 1604. In the opening sentences, he stated his view of parliament: 'you who are here presently assembled to represent the Body of this whole Kingdome'. Later in the speech he was even more specific, when he talked of the 'making of Lawes at certain times, which is onely at such times as this in Parliament'. There is no doubt that this is how he saw it. But he immediately followed it up by promising 'that I will ever preferre the weale of the body and of the whole Common-wealth, in making of good Lawes and constitutions, to any particular or private ends of mine, thinking ever the wealth and weale of the Common-wealth to bee my greatest weale and

worldly felicitie: A point wherein a lawful King doeth directly differ from a Tyrant.' It might have been more tactful to resist the temptation to talk about his 'special subject' on this occasion; it was an intrusion of his personal role in the making of law which could too easily give rise to confusion and misinterpretation. *Political Works of James I*, ed. McIlwain, pp. 269 and 277.

46 Edward Seymour, Protector Somerset, 'Epistle or exhortacion to uniti & peace to the inhabitauntes of Scotland', appendix to *The Complaynt of Scotlande*, ed. J. A. H. Murray (Early English Text Society, Extra Series 17, 18, London, 1872).

47 Thomas Craig of Riccarton, *Scotland's Sovereignty Asserted* (London, 1695), p. 3. He wrote his rebuttal of Holinshed because 'none of our Country-men had answered that Calumny, as if they seem'd to own the Truth of it by their Silence': he himself would not have bothered, 'except that learned men, such as Bodin, fell into this error' (pp. 3–4). Bodin's opinion clearly mattered. In *The Right of Succession to the Kingdom of England, in Two Books: against the Sophisms of Parsons the Jesuite, who assumed the counterfeit Name of Doleman* (London, 1703), Craig took up the theme of royal power and the law, and cited with approval Bodin's distinction between mutable and immutable laws, which 'pleases me much better than other distinctions' (p. 129), while making clear the grounds for his disagreement. So far, indeed, did he emphasize the supremacy of law that, in the passage referred to here, he invoked the testimony of Jeremiah, 'that God himself is bound, as it were, by Laws to observe his Covenant with Mankind' (pp. 128–9). These works set out the position held by a man very much in James's confidence; the king undoubtedly knew about Craig's ideas. They were not published in his day, however, because the ease with which James succeeded to the throne of England made them unnecessary. But the battle went on. A century after Craig wrote *Scotland's Sovereignty*, an edition and translation by George Ridpath was produced in 1695 because, as Ridpath complained, English historians were still attacking the honour of Scotland, including 'now by Mr Rymer Historiographer to his Majesty king William, who hath publish'd a Form of Homage said to be performed by Malcolm the Third King of Scots to Edward the Confessor for the Kingdom of Scotland' (pp. x–xi); and this in turn provoked William Atwood's *The Superiority and direct dominion of the Imperial Crown of England over the Crown and Kingdom of Scotland asserted. In answer to Scotland's Sovereignty asserted, tr. by G. Ridpath, 1695* (London, 1704). But this was, of course, all very topical because of a very different union.

4 James I and the divine right of kings: English politics and continental theory

In the notes below, the dates are Old Style but the year is taken to begin on 1 January; however, in bibliographical references dates of books are those given on the title-pages. Unless otherwise stated the place of publication is London. Quotations have been modernized, and obvious errors have been silently corrected.

1 Sir Roger Twysden, *Certaine considerations upon the government of England,*

ed. John Mitchell Kemble (Camden Society, 1849), pp. 142, 144. W. J. Jones, *Politics and the Bench: The Judges and the Origins of the English Civil War* (1971), pp. 80–3 briefly discusses the question of whether the meetings of 1614 and 1621 counted as parliaments in law. On annual parliaments see the excellent article by Pauline Croft, 'Annual Parliaments and the Long Parliament' in *Bulletin of the Institute of Historical Research*, 59 (1986), 155–71, and J. P. Sommerville, *Politics and Ideology in England 1603–1640* (1986), pp. 104, 111n41, 139, 179.

2 A brief introduction to the methodological literature may be found in David Wootton (ed.), *Divine Right and Democracy: an Anthology of Political Writing in Stuart England* (Harmondsworth, 1986), pp. 10–14.

3 C. H. McIlwain (ed.), *The Political Works of James I* (Cambridge, Mass., 1918), pp. xiii–cxi. Discussing one of James I's most famous political speeches in his *The High Court of Parliament and its Supremacy* (New Haven, 1910), p. 348, McIlwain pronounced that 'the theory here layed down is plain absolutism'. One aim of this chapter is to reassert McIlwain's central conclusions on James's thinking. Both McIlwain's arguments and his evidence are now regularly ignored by revisionists; it is therefore timely once more to draw attention to them. The account given in this chapter of James's political views departs from McIlwain's on a number of points of detail, and draws on much material which McIlwain did not use, but its broad conclusions are close to his.

4 Easily the most accomplished of revisionist works is Conrad Russell, *Parliaments and English Politics 1621–1629* (Oxford, 1979). Brief guides to the debate between revisionists and their opponents include R. Zaller, 'The Concept of Opposition in Early Stuart England' in *Albion*, 12 (1980), 211–34, and Stephen White, 'Observations on early Stuart Parliamentary history' in *Journal of British Studies*, 18 (1979), 160–70.

5 J. G. A. Pocock, *The Ancient Constitution and the Feudal Law* (Cambridge, 1957), pp. 54 (quotations), 30–69 (insularity). The question of the insularity of English thinking is also discussed in D. R. Kelley, 'History, English Law and the Renaissance', *Past and Present*, 65 (1974), 24–51 and in J. P. Sommerville, *Politics and Ideology in England 1603–1640*, pp. 77–9. See also J. P. Kenyon, *The Stuart Constitution* (Cambridge, 1969), pp. 8–9.

6 Austin Woolrych, 'Political Theory and Political Practice' in *The Age of Milton: Backgrounds to Seventeenth-Century Literature*, eds. C. A. Patrides and B. Waddington (Manchester, 1980), pp. 34–71, at p. 39; Conrad Russell, *Parliaments and English Politics 1621–1629*, pp. 53–4.

7 J. P. Sommerville, *Politics and Ideology, passim.*

8 On the king's fears of assassination see David Harris Willson, *King James VI and I* (1956), pp. 227, 274, 277, 279, 348, 364, 367, 425, and Sarmiento to Lerma, 16 May 1615 in *Spain and the Jacobean Catholics, II. 1613–1624*, ed. A. J. Loomie (Catholic Record Society, 1978), pp. 47–8.

9 The two works written in Scotland were *Basilikon Doron* and *The Trew Law of Free Monarchies*. They are discussed by Jenny Wormald in chapter 3 above. Later, James produced *Triplici nodo, triplex cuneus, or an apologie for the oath*

of allegiance (1608), referred to below as *Triplici nodo; An apologie for the oath of allegiance . . . together with a Premonition of his Maiesties, to all most Mightie Monarches, Kings, free Princes and States of Christendom* (1609), referred to below as *Premonition*; and *Déclaration du serenissime roy Jacques I . . .Pour le droit des rois & independance de leurs couronnes, contre la harangue de l'illustrissime Cardinal du Perron prononcée en la chambre du tiers estat le xv de Ianvier 1615* (1615), which was later translated into English as *A remonstrance of the most gratious King Iames I. King of Great Brittaine . . . For the Right of Kings* (Cambridge, 1616), and which is referred to below as *Remonstrance*. The composition of James's works is discussed in D. H. Willson, 'James I and his Literary Assistants' in *Huntington Library Quarterly*, 8 (1944–5), 35–57. All of James's books went through a variety of editions though the alterations made in their texts were often only minor.

10 James I, *Basilikon Doron* in C. H. McIlwain (ed.), *The Political Works of James I*, p. 40; *Remonstrance* in *ibid.*, p. 260. Jacques Davy, Cardinal Du Perron, *Harangue faicte de la part de la chambre ecclésiastique* (Paris, 1615), translated into English as *An Oration made on the Part of the Lordes Spirituall* (St Omer, 1616); the English translator may have been the Jesuit Joseph Creswell; A. F. Allison, 'The Later Life and Writings of Joseph Creswell', *Recusant History*, 15 (1979), 79–144 at pp. 92–5. The background to Du Perron's oration is discussed in P. Blét, 'L'article du tiers aux Etats Generaux de 1614' in *Revue d'histoire moderne et contemporaine*, 2 (1955), 81–106, and in J. M. Hayden, *France and the Estates General of 1614* (Cambridge, 1974), pp. 131–48. The bibliographical details of the debate between James I and Du Perron have sometimes caused confusion because there were in fact two distinct disputes between them – one over religious matters and the other (which featured Du Perron's *Oration* and James's *Remonstrance*) over royal rights: McIlwain's account (in *The Political Works of James I*, p. lxx) is defective; an accurate list of the works involved in the two disputes is in Peter Milward, *Religious Controversies of the Jacobean Age: A Survey of Printed Sources* (1978), pp. 128–31.

11 James I, *Premonition* in *Political Works of James I*, ed. McIlwain, p. 153. In *ibid.*, p. 151, James advocates the summoning of a General Council, 'All the incendiaries and Novelist fire-brands on either side being debarred from the same, as well Iesuites as Puritanes.'

12 James's *Premonition* was placed on the Index on 13 July 1609: *Librorum post indicem Clementis VIII prohibitorum decreta* (Rome, 1624), p. 37. The pope also sent condemnations of the book to Catholic princes: Sir Henry Wotton to James I, 4 August 1609, in *The Life and Letters of Sir Henry Wotton*, ed. Logan Pearsall Smith, (2 vols.; Oxford, 1907), I, p. 465. France and Venice accepted the king's book but several other Catholic states refused it; these included Spain, Savoy, Milan and Florence. The subject is discussed in R. S. Peters, 'Some Catholic Opinions of King James VI and I' in *Recusant History*, 10 (1969–70), 292–303, at 300–3, and in Ludwig van Pastor, *History of the Popes*, vol. XXVI, translated by Dom Ernest Graf (1937), pp. 174–5; there is detailed material on

the king's attempts to get his book accepted by Catholic rulers in Raffaele Belvederi (ed.), *Guido Bentivoglio diplomatico*, (2 vols.; Rovigo, Genoa, 1947–8), II, pp. 138–43 and in *C.S.P. Venetian, 1607–1610*, pp. 283, 287–91, 297–9, 302, 307, 315–17, 321. In Venice, the king's book was accepted, but a decree was rapidly issued prohibiting its circulation; Wotton, the English ambassador, complained in the strongest terms about this, and the Venetians had to despatch a courier – who reached England in nine days – in order to smooth over the incident; *ibid.*, pp. 302, 328–9, 331–5, 337–41, 343–5, 347–51; Smith (ed.), *The Life and Letters of Sir Henry Wotton*, II, pp. 468–74.

13 Material on James's conduct towards Vorstius, and on his sensitivity about his reputation may be found in Frederick H. Shriver, 'Orthodoxy and Diplomacy: James I and the Vorstius Affair' in *English Historical Review*, 85 (1970), 449–74, especially at 453–6. Another instance of James's sensitivity is his reaction to two polite French works criticizing him: on each occasion James took it 'in no better part' than if the author 'shold bid a T[urd] in his teeth and then crie sir reverence': N. E. McClure (ed.), *The Letters of John Chamberlain*, 2 vols. (Philadelphia, 1939), I, pp. 292, 294. The main source for the king's attitude and actions towards Vorstius is James I, *His Maiesties declaration concerning his proceedings with the states generall of the United Provinces of the Low Countreys, In the cause of D. Conradus Vorstius* (1612). *C.S.P. Domestic, 1611–18*, pp. 142–3; *C.S.P. Venetian, 1610–13*, p. 400 (James, Du Moulin and Tilenus). *Corona regia* (1615), pp. 100–1 (legs); pp. 67–8, 89–92, 105 (homosexuality). There is material on the affair of *Corona regia* in *C.S.P. Domestic, 1611–18*, pp. 424–6, 514, 603 and in Smith (ed.), *The Life and Letters of Sir Henry Wotton*, II, pp. 88, 92–3, 280–1.

14 *H.M.C. Downshire*, IV, p. 380; *C.S.P. Venetian, 1613–15*, pp. 108–9, 547.

15 Belvederi (ed.), *Guido Bentivoglio diplomatico*, II, p. 361 (the Franciscan Filippo Bosquiero, and his book *Vegetio Christiano*). D.N.B. s.v. Drebbel; R. J. W. Evans, *Rudolf II and His World: A Study in Intellectual History 1576–1612* (Oxford, 1973), pp. 81, 189–90, 238, 284 (Drebbel). Marjorie Nicholson, 'Kepler, the Somnium and John Donne' in *Journal of the History of Ideas*, 1 (1940), 259–80, and Smith (ed.), *The Life and Letters of Sir Henry Wotton*, I, pp. 171–2, II, pp. 205–6 (Kepler).

16 James I, *Basilikon Doron* in *The Political Works of James I*, ed. McIlwain, p. 47. Information on the Barclays may be found in D. B. Smith, 'William Barclay' in *Scottish Historical Reivew*, 11 (1914), 136–63; John Barclay, *Euphormionis Lusinini Satyricon*, ed. D. A. Fleming (Nieuwkoop, 1973), introduction, pp. x–xiv; D. H. Willson, 'James I and his Literary Assistants', in *Huntington Library Quarterly*, 8 (1944–5), 45 and n. On John Barclay's rewards see *H.M.C. Salisbury*, XIX, pp. 27, 309; *C.S.P. Domestic, 1603–1610*, p. 579; *C.S.P. Domestic, 1611–1618*, pp. 60, 102. In 1615 Barclay went to Rome, became reconciled with his erstwhile opponent Bellarmine, and published the anti-Protestant *Paraenesis ad sectarios* (Rome, 1617): Gondomar to Bellarmine, 24 June 1618, in *Spain and the Jacobean Catholics*, ed. Loomie, II, pp. 108–9, and 110n6; John Barclay, *Paraenesis ad sectarios*, sig. *4a–2*2a. Du Moulin's

role in the composition of James's *Remonstrance* is discussed in Willson, 'James I and his Literary Assistants', 51. In 1610, Du Moulin published a defence of James's *Premonition*, entitled *Défense de la foy Catholique* (Paris, 1610), which was rapidly translated into English (cf. *H.M.C. Downshire*, II, pp. 389–90); another work, defending James's views on the pope as Antichrist, was translated into English in 1613 as *The Accomplishment of the Prophecies* (Oxford, 1613). On Du Moulin's rewards see: D.N.B., sub. verb. Du Moulin. Evidence on attitudes towards Du Moulin is in Sarmiento to Philip III, 20 June 1615 in *Spain and the Jacobean Catholics*, ed. Loomie, II, p. 55 (Sarmiento); and in Lancelot Andrewes to Casaubon, 24 August 1612, Andrewes, *Two Answers to Cardinal Peron and other Miscellaneous Works*, ed. James Bliss (Oxford, 1854), pp. xliii–iv.

17 Mark Pattison, *Isaac Casaubon 1559–1614*, second edn (Oxford, 1892), pp. 262–411, especially pp. 271–2, 307–10. Isaac Casaubon, *De libertate ecclesiastica liber singularis* (Paris, 1607), pp. 89–90.

18 *Controversiae memorabilis inter Paulum V Pontificem Max. et Venetos* (1607), *passim*, e.g. II, p. 88 (Venetian ideas). Noel Malcolm, *De Dominis (1560–1624): Venetian, Anglican, Ecumenist and Relapsed Heretic* (1984), pp. 37–8 (invitation to Sarpi), pp. 41–74 (De Dominis in England). *C.S.P. Venetian, 1610–1613*, p. 305 (James and Marsilius). Paolo Sarpi, *Lettere ai Protestanti*, ed. M. D. Busnelli, 2 vols. (Bari, 1931), e.g. I, pp. 10, 52, 53, 207, 230, 245, II, pp. 50, 58, 61 (Sarpi's interest in controversy over James's books); II, p. 219 (Sarpi to Casaubon). A stimulating discussion of Sarpi may be found in David Wootton, *Paolo Sarpi: Between Renaissance and Enlightenment* (Cambridge, 1983).

19 Saravia is discussed in Willem Nijenhuis, *Adrianus Saravia (c. 1532–1613)* (Leiden, 1980) and in J. P. Sommerville, 'Richard Hooker, Hadrian Saravia, and the Advent of the Divine Right of Kings', *History of Political Thought*, 4 (1983), 229–45. Diego Panizza, *Alberico Gentili, giurista ideologo nell'Inghilterra Elisabettiana* (Padua, 1981), pp. 158–9 (Gentili and Bodin). Another of Casaubon's correspondents was Jean Hotman, who translated James's *Basilikon Doron* into French; Hotman later complained that the king had not rewarded him: David Baird Smith, 'Jean Hotman' in *Scottish Historical Review*, 14 (1947), 147–66, especially 147, 155.

20 James I refers to himself in *Serenissimi et potentissimi Principis Iacobi . . . Opera* (1619; references in brackets are to McIlwain (ed.), *Political Works*): pp. 286 (111), 304 (126), 343 (162), 344 (163), 345 (164), 417 (174), 451 (221), 594; to Reginald Scot in *Opera*, p. 87; to Northampton in *ibid.*, p. 344 (163); to Andrewes in *ibid.*, p. 399; and to Gordon at p. 406. On Northampton's ideas, see especially Linda Levy Peck's excellent *Northampton: Patronage and Politics at the Court of James I* (1982), particularly at 181–4. Andrewes is discussed by Peter Lake in this volume, at pp. 113–33 below. The 1619 Latin *Opera* was the last edition of James's works to appear in his lifetime. There exists no really thorough study of the differences between the various editions of the king's books.

21 James's relationship with Coke is discussed in S. R. Gardiner, *History of England from the Accession of James I to the Outbreak of the Civil War, 1603–1642*, 10 vols. (1883–4), III, pp. 1–36. John Selden, *Ioannis Seldeni Vindiciae secundum integritatem existimationis suae* (1653), p. 16.

22 The relationship between historical and political thought in the years before the Civil War is discussed in J. P. Sommerville, 'History and Theory: The Norman Conquest in Early Stuart Political Thought' in *Political Studies*, 34 (1986), 249–61. James I, in *Political Works*, ed. McIlwain, pp. 473–4 (civil law); *Remonstrance* in *ibid.*, p. 170, and quoted in W. J. Jones, *Politics and the Bench* (1971), p. 155 (tennis balls). The passage from the *Remonstrance* is briefly discussed in J. M. Hayden, *France and the Estates General of 1614*, p. 144, which reads 'from his throne' instead of 'his throne'; this reading makes good sense, but is not supported by either James's *Workes*, p. 382, or his *Remonstrance for the Right of Kings*, sig. A2a.

23 James I, speech of 21 March 1610, in *Political Works*, ed. McIlwain, p. 309. On James's earlier attitude towards parliament see e.g. Gardiner, *History of England*, I, pp. 190–2; James I, *Political Works*, ed. McIlwain, pp. 288–9.

24 E. R. Foster (ed.), *Proceedings in Parliament 1610*, 2 vols. (New Haven, 1966), pp. 102, 104 (impositions and Bellarmine). James had in mind a passage in Bellarmine's letter to George Blackwell (printed in James's *Triplici nodo* in *Political Works*, ed. McIlwain, p. 83) and perhaps also Bellarmine's *Responsio Matthaei Torti presbyteri, et theologi papiensis, ad librum inscriptum, Triplici nodo triplex cuneus* (Cologne, 1608), p. 99. The views of James's ideological supporters are discussed in J. P. Sommerville, *Politics and Ideology in England 1603–1640* (1986), chapter 1.

25 J. P. Kenyon, *The Stuart Constitution: Documents and Commentary* (Cambridge, 1969), p. 8.

26 Paul Christianson in this volume, pp. 76–8. James I, *Trew Law of Free Monarchies* in *Political Works*, ed. McIlwain, p. 63.

27 Pauline Croft, 'Fresh Light on Bate's Case' in *Historical Journal*, 30 (1987), 523–39, especially 538. E. R. Foster (ed.), *Proceedings in Parliament 1610*, II, p. 102. J. P. Sommerville, *Politics and Ideology in England 1603–1640*, pp. 160–3. Aspects of the career of Sir John Davies are discussed in Hans Pawlisch, *Sir John Davies and the Conquest of Ireland: A Study in Legal Imperialism* (Cambridge, 1985).

28 James I, *Political Works*, ed. McIlwain, p. 310. Jenny Wormald, 'James VI and I: Two Kings or One?' in *History*, 68 (1983), 187–209, at 205. Examples of the king's willingness to compromise in R. C. Munden, 'James I and "the growth of mutual distrust": King, Commons, and Reform, 1603–1604' in Kevin Sharpe (ed.), *Faction and Parliament: Essays on Early Stuart History* (Oxford, 1978), pp. 43–72; J. P. Sommerville, *Politics and Ideology in England 1603–1640*, pp. 121–7 (Cowell).

29 E. R. Foster (ed.), *Proceedings in Parliament 1610*, II, p. 103 (1610); Hadrian Saravia, *De imperandi authoritate* in *Diversi tractatus theologici* (1611), IV, p. 175, and Roger Maynwaring, *Religion and Allegiance: In Two Sermons*,

II, p. 46 (clipping wings). James I, *Political Works*, ed. McIlwain, p. 333 (1616).

30 On the Apology see especially J. H. Hexter, 'The Apology' in Richard Ollard and Pamela Tudor-Craig (eds.), *For Veronica Wedgwood These Studies in Seventeenth-Century History* (1986), pp. 13–44. A somewhat different approach is taken in G. R. Elton, 'A High Road to Civil War' in his *Studies in Tudor and Stuart Politics and Government*, II (Cambridge, 1974), pp. 164–82. Anthony G. Petti (ed.), *Recusant Documents from the Ellesmere Manuscripts*, Catholic Record Society, vol. LX (1968), pp. 148–50 (Catholic report of 1604). Zuñiga to Philip III, 23 February 1609 in *Spain and the Jacobean Catholics*, ed. Loomie, I, p. 128 (Spanish ambassador). J. R. Tanner, *Constitutional Documents of the Reign of James I* (Cambridge, 1930), p. 247 (House of Commons).

31 James quoted in D. H. Willson, 'Summoning and Dissolving Parliament' in *American Historical Review*, 45 (1939–40), 279–300, especially 281–2. The king's disagreements with the Commons in 1614 and 1621 are discussed in Gardiner, *History of England*, II, pp. 216–58, IV, pp. 232–71. The standard works on these parliaments are T. L. Moir, *The Addled Parliament* (New York, 1958) and R. Zaller, *The Parliament of 1621: A Study in Constitutional Conflict* (Berkeley, 1971).

32 Conrad Russell, 'The Foreign Policy Debate in the House of Commons in 1621' in *Historical Journal*, 20 (1977), 289–309; *Parliaments and English Politics 1621–1629*, pp. 133, 140; J. P. Sommerville, *Politics and Ideology in England 1603–1640*, p. 182.

33 James I, *His Maiesties declaration, touching his proceedings in the late assemblie and convention of Parliament* (1621), pp. 14–15, 61; *Political Works*, ed. McIlwain, p. 340 (1616); p. 126 (Puritan–papists).

34 James I, *His Maiesties declaration, touching his proceedings in the late assemblie and convention of Parliament* (1621), pp. 23–4.

35 *Ibid.*, pp. 24–5, 32, 28.

36 James I, *A proclamation declaring his Maiesties pleasure concerning the dissolution of the present convention of Parliament* (1621), 18; *His Maiesties declaration, touching his proceedings in the late assemblie and convention of Parliament* (1621), p. 47. Twysden, *Certaine considerations upon the government of England*, p. 144. Attempts to revive the central points of the Protestation are discussed in J. P. Sommerville, 'The Powers and Privileges of Parliament and the Liberty of the Subject' in a forthcoming volume by J. H. Hexter, Derek Hirst and others, in a series on the making of modern freedom.

37 J. P. Sommerville, *Politics and Ideology in England 1603–1640*, pp. 57–85.

5 **Royal and parliamentary voices on the ancient constitution, *c.* 1604–1621**

1 See the recent attempts to unlock the meaning of this imagery in D. J. Gordon, 'Rubens and the Whitehall Ceiling' in *The Renaissance Imagination*, ed. Stephen Orgel (Berkeley, 1975); Oliver Millar, *Rubens: The Whitehall Ceiling* (London, 1958); Per Palme, *Triumph of Peace: A Study of the Whitehall Banqueting*

House (London, 1957); and Roy Strong, *Britannia Triumphans: Inigo Jones, Rubens and Whitehall Palace* (London, 1980).

2 Strong, *Britannia Triumphans*, pp. 44–5; for almost the same words, see Roy Strong, *Van Dyck: Charles I on Horseback* (London, 1972), p. 89; and Stephen Orgel and Roy Strong, *Inigo Jones: The Theatre of the Stuart Court* (2 vols., London, 1973), I, p. 50.

3 In addition to the works cited above, see Jonathan Goldberg, *James I and the Politics of Literature: Jonson, Shakespeare, Donne and Their Contemporaries* (Baltimore, 1983); Stephen Orgel, *The Illusion of Power* (Berkeley, 1975) and Graham Parry, *The Golden Age Restor'd: The Culture of the Stuart Court, 1603–42* (London, 1981).

4 J. P. Sommerville, *Politics and Ideology in England 1603–1640* (London, 1986). Sommerville displays an acute awareness of the European context of English political thought.

5 Goldberg, *James I and the Politics of Literature*, and Sommerville, *Politics and Ideology*, provide fuller and more nuanced readings.

6 For these arguments, see the essay by Sommerville in this collection.

7 For 'mixed monarchy', see Paul Christianson, 'Young John Selden and the Ancient Constitution, *ca.* 1610–18', *Proceedings of the American Philosophical Society*, 128 (1984), 271–315 and 'John Selden, the Five Knight's Case, and Discretionary Imprisonment in Early Stuart England', *Criminal Justice History*, 6 (1985), 65–87.

8 James Daly, 'The Idea of Absolute Monarchy in Seventeenth-Century England', *Historical Journal*, 21 (1978), 227–50.

9 Charles Howard McIlwain (ed.), *The Political Works of James I: Reprinted from the Edition of 1616* (Cambridge, Mass., 1918), p. 54.

10 *Ibid.*, pp. 54–5.

11 *Ibid.*, p. 55.

12 The absolutist writings of James VI and I read more like theological than civil law treatises. I would like to thank Professor Donald Kelley for raising this point.

13 McIlwain (ed.), *Political Works of James I*, p. 62. Contrast the image of Fergus, who founded the kingdom of Scotland 'by his owne friendship, and force' with that of William, 'the Bastard of *Normandie*', who took England by 'a mighty army', 'changed the Lawes, inverted the order of governement, set downe the strangers his followers in many of the old possessours roomes, as at this day well appeareth a great part of the Gentlemen in *England*, beeing come of the *Norman* blood, and their old Lawes, which to this day they are ruled by, are written in his language, and not in theirs', *ibid.*, pp. 62–3.

14 *Ibid.*, p. 328. This argued that he had inherited the throne.

15 *Ibid.*, pp. 269, 272. This speech appeared in two English and one Scottish editions and a Latin translation in 1604; see A. W. Pollard and G. R. Redgrave, W. A. Jackson and F. S. Ferguson, and Katharine F. Pantzer (eds.), *A Short-Title Catalogue of Books Printed in England, Scotland, and Ireland and of English Books Printed Abroad 1475–1640*, 2nd edn (2 vols.; London, 1976), II, *14390–1. The images of James drew upon profound depths of religious

association: God and Christ as the shepherd, Christ as the bridegroom and his people as the bride. The speech which engendered the 'Apology' of the Commons of 1604 has not survived; only the incautious would speculate on its contents; for a different interpretation, see J. H. Hexter, 'The Apology' in *For Veronica Wedgwood These Studies in Seventeenth-Century History*, eds. Richard Ollard and Pamela Tudor-Craig (London, 1986), pp. 13–44.

16 *Ibid.*, p. 287. Published in three editions in 1605 and a Latin translation in 1606; see Pantzer (ed.), *S.T.C.*, II, *14392–5. The king's experience of parliaments in Scotland probably still continued to influence his perception of English parliaments; see the *Trew Law*, where James mentioned the parliament of Scotland: 'we daily see that in the Parliament (which is nothing else but the head Court of the king and his vassals) the lawes are but craved by his subjects, and onely made by him at their rogation, and with their advice'; *ibid.*, p. 62.

17 *Ibid.*, pp. 288–9.

18 For an account that stresses dispute, see Wallace Notestein, *The House of Commons, 1604–1610* (New Haven, 1971); for more recent accounts of particular aspects, see R. C. Munden, 'James I and "the growth of mutual distrust": King, Commons and Reform' in *Faction and Parliament: Essays on Early Stuart History*, ed. Kevin Sharpe (Oxford, 1978), ch. 2; Bruce Galloway, *The Union of England and Scotland, 1603–1608* (Edinburgh, 1986); Pauline Croft, 'Fresh Light on Bate's Case', *H.J.*, 30 (1987), 523–39; and Eric N. Lindquist, 'The Failure of the Great Contract', *Journal of Modern History*, 57 (1985), 617–51. Also see Glen Burgess, 'Common Law and Political Theory in Early Stuart England', *Political Science*, 40 (1988), 4–17.

19 McIlwain (ed.), *Political Works of James I*, p. 292. Printed in 1607; see Pantzer (ed.), *S.T.C.*, II, *14395. For the law of conquest, see Hans S. Pawlisch, *Sir John Davies and the Conquest of Ireland: A Study in Legal Imperialism* (Cambridge, 1985), ch. 1.

20 For more extensive discussions of the relationship of civil to common law, see Paul Christianson, 'Political Thought in Early Stuart England', *H.J.*, 30 (1987), 955–71; Brian P. Levack, *The Civil Lawyers in England 1603–1641: A Political Study* (Oxford, 1973); Luigi Moccia, 'English Law Attitudes to the "Civil Law"', *Journal of Legal History*, 2 (1981), 157–68; and C. P. Rogers, 'Humanism, History, and the Common Law', *J.L.H.*, 6 (1985), 129–56.

21 McIlwain (ed.), *Political Works of James I*, pp. 292–3.

22 Including the Attorney General of Ireland; see Sir John Davies, *Le Primer Report des Cases et Matters en Ley Resolves et Adjudges en les Courts del Roy en Ireland* (Dublin, 1615), sig. *2ᵛ-3ʳ.

23 Sir Edward Coke, *Le Quart Part des Reportes* (London, 1604), sig. B3; for the question of law reform in early seventeenth-century England, see Louis A. Knafla, *Law and Politics in Jacobean England: The Tracts of Lord Chancellor Ellesmere* (Cambridge, 1977), ch. 5.

24 McIlwain (ed.), *Political Works of James I*, p. 299. So did his advisors; see the discussion which preceded Calvin's Case in *A Complete Collection of State Trials*, ed. T. B. Howell (London, 1809), II, pp. 561–76.

25 John Cowell, *The Interpreter* (Cambridge, 1607), sig. 2Q1ʳ, 3A3ᵛ.
26 McIlwain (ed.), *The Political Works of James I*, p. 307. Printed in three editions in 1609/10; see Pantzer (ed.), *S.T.C.*, II, *14396–96.7.
27 *Ibid.*, p. 309; the covenants God made with Noah, Abraham, Moses, and through Christ provided the starting points of the 'covenant theology' so favoured by the early seventeenth-century Reformed; for the classic discussion, see Perry Miller, 'The Marrow of Puritan Divinity' in his *Errand into the Wilderness* (Cambridge, Mass, 1954) and for a fuller account, see John von Rohr, *The Covenant of Grace in Puritan Thought* (Atlanta, 1986).
28 In the *Trew Law*, James had stressed the duty of kings to obey their coronation oaths, but had attacked any attempt to see the oath as a contract between king and people which both parties could judge; McIlwain (ed.), *The Political Works of James I*, pp. 68–9. Here he made the duty of the king to obey the laws more binding by likening it to the binding covenant of God. In the *Basilikon Doron*, James had discussed at length the difference between the good king who established and executed good laws and the tyrant who ruled according to his passions, pp. 18–20. Here he redefined a tyrant not as a ruler who ruled for his own pleasures, but as one who did not rule 'according to his Lawes', a more than subtle shift.
29 Cf. James Daly, *Cosmic Harmony and Political Thinking in Early Stuart England,* Transactions of the American Philosophical Society, LXIX, part 7; (Philadelphia, 1979), p. 25. For a different reading of this speech and the meaning of covenant, see Francis Oakley, *Omnipotence, Covenant, and Order: An Excursion in the History of Ideas from Abelard to Leibniz* (Ithaca, 1984), ch. 4, especially pp. 96–7, 103–5; in earlier chapters, Oakley unravels the differences between the 'absolute' and 'ordinary' powers of God as developed by medieval theologians.
30 McIlwain (ed.), *Political Works of James I*, p. 310.
31 *Ibid.*, pp. 310–11. In the previous sentences the king had defended the continued practice and study of the civil law in England. See the similar interpretation in Burgess, *P.S.*, 40 (1988), 13–14.
32 *Ibid.*, pp. 309, 310. Ironically, the *Reports* and *Institutes* of Sir Edward Coke came to remedy most of the problems in the common law noted by the king in these speeches; I would like to thank Professor Richard Helgerson for stressing this point. Of course, Coke was dismissed from his position of Chief Justice of the King's Bench by James in 1616; for details about Coke's constitutional position, see note 74 below.
33 *Ibid.*
34 *Ibid.*, pp. 311–12.
35 Elizabeth Read Foster (ed.), *Proceedings in Parliament 1610* (2 vols., New Haven, 1966), II, p. 102. Although James delivered this speech to both houses in Whitehall on 21 May 1610, he pointedly singled out members of the Commons for criticism.
36 *Ibid.*
37 *Ibid.*, p. 103.

38 *Ibid.*, pp. 104–5.
39 *Ibid.*, p. 109; for the debate of 22 May, see pp. 108–10.
40 *Ibid.*, pp. 114–17.
41 *Ibid.*, pp. 152–252, and Samuel Rawson Gardiner (ed.), *Parliamentary Debates in 1610* (Camden Society, LXXXI; London, 1862), pp. 58–120; these took place on 23, 28 and 29 June and 2 July 1610. Many of the speakers on both sides later became royal judges in the Chancery, Common Pleas, or King's Bench. For another reading of these speeches, see Notestein, *Commons 1604–1610*, pp. 361–92.
42 For Hobart's speeches, see Gardiner, *Parliamentary Debates in 1610*, pp. 89–93, 118–20, and Foster, *Proceedings in Parliament 1610*, II, pp. 198–201; for Bacon's able speech which drew forth a good number of answers, including that made by Hedley, see Gardiner, *Debates*, pp. 66–72; and for the solid defence made by Doderidge, see *ibid.*, pp. 98–103, and Foster, *Proceedings*, II, pp. 201–21, 223.
43 Although neither seems to grasp the implications of the chronology of Hedley's speech in relation to the prefaces of Coke and Davies, which appeared later, both Professor Pocock and Dr Sommerville pay considerable attention to Hedley; see J. G. A. Pocock, *The Ancient Constitution and the Feudal Law: English Historical Thought in the Seventeenth Century: A Reissue with a Retrospect* (Cambridge, 1987), pp. 270–3 and the numerous shorter references noted in the index of Sommerville, *Politics and Ideology*.
44 Foster, *Proceedings in Parliament 1610*, II, p. 175. Hedley sat for the borough of Huntingdon and, according to Notestein, became a 'well-known judge'; see Notestein, *Commons 1604–1610*, p. 365. For a fuller discussion of Hedley's speech and its place in early seventeenth-century English constitutional discourse, see Paul Christianson, 'Ancient Constitutions in the Age of Sir Edward Coke and John Selden', a paper delivered at the Liberty Fund Symposium on 'Magna Carta and Ancient Constitution: Medieval and Renaissance Roots of American Liberty', held at Windsor Castle, on 17 June 1988, pp. 7–18.
45 *Ibid.*, pp. 178–9.
46 *Ibid.*, pp. 179–80.
47 *Ibid.*, p. 180. Lord Chancellor Ellesmere interpreted the civil law as unwritten law, as well; see Knafla, *Law and Politics*, pp. 217–18.
48 *Ibid.* Obviously, Hedley did not invent the concept of 'immemorial custom'; other members of parliament had traced individual liberties or privileges back beyond memory; however, Hedley combined custom and immemoriality together as organizing principles, applied them to the whole of the common law, and used them to support a particular version of the ancient constitution in which the common law distributed power to the Crown and parliament.
49 See Pocock, *Ancient Constitution and Feudal Law*, chs. 2, 3.
50 C. W. Brooks, 'The Place of Magna Carta and the Ancient Constitution in Sixteenth Century English Legal Thought', a paper delivered at the Liberty Fund Symposium on 'Magna Carta and Ancient Constitution: Medieval and

Renaissance Roots of American Liberty', held at Windsor Castle, on 17 June 1988, p. 34. This greatly reinforces the interpretations put forward in my articles on John Selden cited in note 8 above.

51 See note 74 below.

52 Howell, ed., *State Trials*, II, p. 469.

53 *Ibid.*, p. 470.

54 *Ibid.* This portion of Hakewill's argument would have benefited from the interpretation of the English constitution as a mixed monarchy published by John Selden several months later; see Christianson, *P.A.P.S.*, 128 (1984), 276, 280, and 282–3.

55 *Ibid.*, p. 483.

56 *Ibid.*

57 *Ibid.*, pp. 483–4.

58 Foster, *Proceedings in Parliament 1610*, II, p. 258.

59 *Ibid.*

60 *Ibid.*, pp. 258–9.

61 *Ibid.*, pp. 266–7.

62 In comparison, the 'Apology' of the Commons of 1604, with its attempt to identify 'the fundamentall priviledges of our House' with 'the rights and liberties of the whole Commons of your realme of England, which they and their auncestors from tyme immemoriall have undoubtedly enjoyed under your Majesties most noble progenitors' looked quite crude and fumbling; by attempting to derive the liberties of the people from the privileges of the House of Commons, the 'Apology' presented a weak case for both; Historical Manuscripts Commission, *Calendar of the Manuscripts of the Most Honourable the Marquess of Salisbury . . . preserved at Hatfield House Hertfordshire* (Part XXII Addenda 1562–1605, London, 1973), IX, p. 141; for the complete text, see pp. 140–52.

63 Dedicated to the Earl of Salisbury, and entered at the Stationers' Register on 26 November 1610, the *Jani Anglorum Facies Altera* (London, 1610) probably appeared in print early in 1610/11. For a full account of this work, see Christianson, *P.A.P.S.*, 128 (1984), 274–83.

64 John Selden, 'The Reverse or Back Face of the English Janus' in his *Tracts*, translated by Redman Westcot [Dr Adam Littleton] (London, 1683), pp. 13–19. English quotations will come from this translation. In his discussion of the major marks of sovereignty near the end of the *Jani Anglorum*, Selden systematically dismissed any attempt to read a single lawmaking sovereign into the British portion of the ancient constitution; *Jani Anglorum*, pp. 123–33 and 'English Janus', pp. 93–9.

65 *Ibid.*, p. 94.

66 *Ibid.*, pp. 94, 32 and Selden, *Jani Anglorum*, pp. 43, 124–5.

67 *Ibid.*, pp. 58–91.

68 See Maija Jansson, *Proceedings in Parliament 1614 (House of Commons)* (Memoirs of the American Philosophical Society, CLXXII, Philadelphia, 1988), pp. 7–9, 13–20, 43–6, 138–44, 379, 383, and 427; H.M.C., *Report on the*

Manuscripts of the Late Reginald Rawdon Hastings . . . (London, 1947), IV, 230–4, and 239–41. For accounts of this parliament, see Thomas L. Moir, *The Addled Parliament of 1614* (Oxford, 1958) and the introduction to Jansson, *Proceedings*.

69 See Jansson, *Proceedings in Parliament 1614*, pp. 130–1, 146–54, 156–60, 211–14, 219–20, 221–2, 223–7, 285–8, 311–12, 390 and 397–400; also see Moir, *Addled Parliament*, pp. 94–5, 100–1, 110–12, and 114–16.

70 H.M.C., *Hastings MS*, IV, pp. 249–64 and 267–8; also see Moir, *Addled Parliament*, pp. 116–23.

71 Jansson, *Proceedings in Parliament 1614*, pp. 320–1, 325–6, 340–7, 348, 354, 355–64, 365, 370, 373, 377, 381, 386, 387, 390, 391, 396, 398, 402–3, 404, 407 and 410.

72 H.M.C., *Hastings MS*, IV, pp. 249, 253, 259, 267–72, 273–7 and 278; also see Moir, *Addled Parliament*, pp. 123–33.

73 Jansson, *Proceedings in Parliament 1614*, pp. 379, 374, 364–75, and 383.

74 See Sir Edward Coke, *Le Tierce Part Des Reportes* (London, 1602), sig. C3^v, C4^r–D2^r, E1^v; Sir Edward Coke, *Quinta Pars Relationum* (London, 1605); Sir Edward Coke, *La Sept Part des Reports* (London, 1608), ff. 2–3; Sir Edward Coke, *La Huict^{me} Part des Reports* (London, 1611); Sir Edward Coke, *La Neuf^{me} Part des Reports* (London, 1613), sig. c1–3; Sir Edward Coke, *La Dix^{me} Part des Reports* (London, 1614), sig. d3 and d3^v–[e2^r]; and Davies, *Primer Report*, sig. *1^v–2^r, *3^r.

75 J. G. A. Pocock, *The Ancient Constitution and the Feudal Law: English Historical Thought in the Seventeenth Century* (Cambridge, 1957), chs. 2, 3. For the civil law side of Davies which emerged in the cases, as opposed to the preface, of the *Primer Report*, see Pawlisch, *Sir John Davies, passim*.

76 See Christianson, *P.A.P.S.*, 128 (1984), 286–307.

77 McIlwain (ed.), *Political Works of James I*, p. 326. This speech was printed in three editions in 1616; see Pantzer (ed.), *S.T.C.*, II, *14397–7.7. For the context in which it appeared, see Anthony Fletcher, *Reform in the Provinces: The Government of Stuart England* (New Haven, 1986), pp. 52–5.

78 McIlwain (ed.), *Political Works*.

79 *Ibid.*, p. 327.

80 *Ibid.*, p. 329.

81 *Ibid.*, pp. 332, 331. By 'longer custome' in the above quotation James could have meant that the civil and canon laws had exercised jurisdiction for a longer time in England than had the common law, but he probably meant, more simply, that the common law had received portions of the civil and canon laws as custom long ago.

82 *Ibid.*, p. 333, see 332–5.

83 *Ibid.*, p. 335.

84 *Ibid.*, p. 339.

85 *Ibid.*, p. 337.

86 For example, even Ellesmere's fairly particular observations on the parliament of

1604–10 and criticisms of Coke's *Reports* remained in manuscript; see Knafla, *Law and Politics*, ch. 8.

87 Wallace Notestein, Frances Helen Relf, and Hartley Simpson (eds.), *Commons Debates 1621*, (7 vols.; New Haven, 1935), II, p. 3; for the reading of 'estates', see *ibid.*, IV, p. 2; for the whole speech, see II, pp. 1–13, IV, pp. 1–6, V, pp. 425–9 and VI, pp. 365–73. For the parliament of 1621, see Robert Zaller, *The Parliament of 1621: A Study in Constitutional Conflict* (Berkeley, 1971) and Conrad Russell, *Parliaments and English Politics 1621–1629* (Oxford, 1979), ch. 2.

88 For the disagreement on this point between James and Coke, see Russell, *Parliaments and Politics*, p. 141; curiously, this discussion comes in Russell's account of the second session.

89 Notestein, ed., *Commons Debates 1621*, II, p. 3; cf. IV, p. 2.

90 *Ibid.*, II, p. 4.

91 *Ibid.*, cf. IV, pp. 2–3.

92 *Ibid.*, II, p. 5.

93 *Ibid.*, II, p. 12.

94 *Ibid.*, II, p. 13.

95 *Ibid.*, II, p. 148; see IV, p. 116. Hakewill also carried out research for the Lords; see Lady de Villiers (ed.), 'The Hastings Journal of the Parliament of 1621' in *Camden Miscellany*, 20 (C.S., series 3, LXXXIII; London, 1953), p. 48. For the revival of parliamentary judicature, see especially Elizabeth Read Foster, *The House of Lords 1603–1649: Structure, Procedure, and the Nature of its Business* (Chapel Hill, 1983), ch. 9, and Colin G. C. Tite, *Impeachment and Parliamentary Judicature in Early Stuart England* (London, 1974).

96 *Ibid.*, IV, pp. 115–16.

97 *Ibid.*, II, pp. 197–8. For another comparison of these speeches, see White, *Sir Edward Coke*, pp. 149–51.

98 De Villiers (ed.), 'Hastings Journal', p. 25; this speech from 10 March 1621 represented an aggressive act on the part of the king.

99 *Ibid.*, pp. 26–7.

100 *Ibid.*, p. 28.

101 See the passage cited in note 96 above.

102 De Villiers (ed.), 'Hastings Journal', p. 27; see also p. 31. Of course, Coke had drawn many of his most telling precedents from the reigns of Richard II and Henry VI!

103 *Ibid.*, p. 28.

104 *Journals of the House of Lords* (London, 1767+), III, pp. 10, 17, 21, 65, and 74, de Villiers (ed.), 'Hastings Journal', pp. 7, 15, and 21, and Helen Relf (ed.), *Notes of the Debates in the House of Lords* (C.S., series 3, XLII; London, 1929), pp. 1–2 and 48. The committee for privileges was first appointed on 5 February, a working subcommittee appointed on 14 February, and permission to hire scholars to carry out the research granted on 17 February. For the importance of this task, see Foster, *House of Lords*, chs. 8, 9.

105 Maurice F. Bond (ed.), *Manuscripts of the House of Lords* (Historical Manuscripts Commission, London, 1953), X, 1712–1714, pp. 1–6, prints this

draft; pp. 1–11 contain all of the standing orders for the period before 1660. Lady de Villiers thought that the standing orders in the 'Remembrances for Order and Decency', were part of the report made on 7 February; de Villiers, 'Hastings Journal', pp. vi–vii, 8, and 8n3. Since the committee had just started to meet, however, this seems very unlikely. For the later date, see Tite, *Impeachment and Parliamentary Judicature*, p. 32, n. 24. Judging from the collection of precedents made by Sir Charles Howard, the Commons probably could have put together such standing orders; see Notestein (ed.), *Commons Debates 1621*, VI, pp. 343–62. For the procedural innovations developed in this parliament by the Commons, see G. A. Harrison, 'Innovation and Precedent: A Procedural Reappraisal of the Parliament of 1625', *English Historical Review*, 102 (1987), 31–62.

106 De Villiers (ed.), 'Hastings Journal', p. 33.
107 *L.J.*, III, pp. 196–7, and David S. Berkowitz, 'Young Mr. Selden, Essays in Seventeenth-Century Learning and Politics, being a Prolegomena to Parliament' (PhD thesis, Harvard, 1946), ch. 5, pp. 39–47. The original resides in the record office of the House of Lords, a number of contemporary manuscript copies exist in various libraries, and a modified and expanded version appeared in print as *The Priviledges of the Baronage in England* (London, 1642); my quotations will come from the original. Berkowitz, 'Young Mr. Selden', ch. 5, p. 48n85, lists some fifteen manuscript copies; for his detailed account of Selden's work for the Lords, see pp. 28–48.
108 John Selden, 'The Priviledges of the Baronage in England', ff. 2ᵛ and 98ʳ.
109 Selden, 'Priviledges', ff. 9ᵛ–10ʳ.
110 For the revival of judicature in the Lords, see Foster, *House of Lords*, ch. 9 and Jess Stoddart Flemion, 'Slow Process, Due Process, and the High Court of Parliament: A Reinterpretation of the Revival of Judicature in the House of Lords in 1621', *H.J.*, 17 (1974), 3–16; cf. Tite, *Impeachment and Judicature*, ch. 4; Stephen D. White, *Sir Edward Coke and 'The Grievances of the Commonwealth', 1621–1628* (Chapel Hill, 1979), pp. 142–64, and Zaller, *Parliament of 1621*, pp. 59–61, 69–70, and ch. 2.
111 For the passage of the petition, see Notestein (ed.), *Commons Debates 1621*, II, pp. 487–99; for the warnings of Sackville and Weston, see *ibid.*, II, pp. 487–8, 489, V, p. 229, and VI, p. 220; for Coke's answer to their objections, see *ibid.*, II, pp. 457–9, VI, pp. 222–3. For the text of most of the petition, see J. R. Tanner (ed.), *Constitutional Documents of the Reign of James I, 1603–1625* (Cambridge, 1930; reprinted 1961), pp. 276–9.
112 Tanner (ed.), *Constitutional Documents*, p. 279.
113 Notestein (ed.), *Commons Debates 1621*, II, p. 500, V, p. 232 and VI, p. 224.
114 Tanner (ed.), *Constitutional Documents*, pp. 281–2.
115 *Ibid.*, p. 283.
116 Tanner (ed.), *Constitutional Documents*, p. 284; for the king's use of the same argument in 1614, see the passage cited in note 73 above. My account draws upon those portions of the letter not printed by Tanner, but available in John Rushworth, *Historical Collections . . .* (London, 1659), I, pp. 46–52.

117 *Ibid.*, pp. 286–7.
118 *Ibid.*
119 Notestein (ed.), *Commons Debates 1621*, VI, p. 332.
120 *Ibid.*, VI, pp. 334–5.
121 *Ibid.*, II, p. 533 and VI, p. 336.
122 *Ibid.*, VI, pp. 340, 341 and II, p. 542; see II, pp. 535–42 and VI, pp. 336–43.
123 *Ibid.*, II, p. 542.
124 Tanner (ed.), *Constitutional Documents*, pp. 288–9.
125 For an extension of the argument presented in this essay into the parliament of 1628–9, see Christianson, *C.J.H.*, 6 (1985), 65–87 and 'Ancient Constitutions in the Age of Sir Edward Coke and John Selden', pp. 20–36. Earlier versions of portions of this paper were read at the Tudor and Stuart Seminar at the Henry E. Huntington Library, the University of Santa Barbara, and the Renaissance and Reformation Colloquium at the University of Toronto; I would like to thank Professors David Cressy, Sears McGee, and Jacqueline Murray for the invitations and those in attendance for their helpful comments.

6 Cultural diversity and cultural change at the court of James I

1 See, in particular, Douglas Brooks-Davies, *The Mercurian Monarch* (Manchester, 1984); Norman Council, 'Ben Jonson, Inigo Jones and the Transformation of Chivalry', *E.L.H.*, 47 (1980); Jonathan Goldberg, *James I and the Politics of Literature* (Baltimore, 1983); John Harris, 'Inigo Jones and the Cavalier Style', *Architectural Review*, 154 (1973); D. J. Howarth, *Lord Arundel and his Circle* (New Haven and London, 1985); Stephen Orgel, *The Jonsonian Masque* (Cambridge, Mass., 1965) and *The Illusion of Power* (Berkeley and Los Angeles, 1975); Per Palme, *The Triumph of Peace: A Study of the Whitehall Banqueting House* (Stockholm, 1956); John Peacock, 'Inigo Jones's Stage Architecture and its Sources', *Art Bulletin*, 64 (1982); Richard W. Peterson, *Imitation and Praise in the Poems of Ben Jonson* (New Haven, 1981); Roy Strong, *The English Icon* (London, 1969), *Britannia Triumphans: Inigo Jones, Rubens and Whitehall Palace* (London, 1980); 'Inigo Jones and the Revival of Chivalry' in *Apollo*, 86 (1967) and 'Some Early Portraits at Arundel Castle' in *Connoisseur*, 197 (1978); Sir John Summerson, *Inigo Jones* (Harmondsworth, 1966); Frances Yates, *The Rosicrucian Enlightenment* (London, 1972). Two works of synthesis are Graham Parry, *The Golden Age Restor'd* (Manchester, 1981) and R. Malcolm Smuts, *Court Culture and the Origins of a Royalist Tradition in Early Stuart England* (Philadelphia, 1987).

2 M. W. Thompson, *The Decline of the Castle* (Cambridge, 1987), ch. 4.

3 For the European and Elizabethan background see, esp. Frances Yates, *The French Academies of the Sixteenth Century* (London, 1947); *Giordano Bruno and the Hermetic Tradition* (London, 1964); *Astrea: The Imperial Theme in the Sixteenth Century* (London, 1975); Roy Strong, *Splendour at Court* (London and Boston, 1973). Studies of English court culture deriving from the same tradition include Yates, *The Rosicrucian Enlightenment* (London, 1972), ch. 1; D. J. Gordon, *The Renaissance Imagination*, ed. Stephen Orgel (Berkeley and

Los Angeles, 1980) and, most recently, Roy Strong, *Henry Prince of Wales and England's Lost Renaissance* (London, 1985). An earlier study that also stresses European and Neoplatonic influences in English court culture is Per Palme, *The Triumph of Peace*.

4 As Strong puts it, 'artists and poets were essential to a court, not only as overt political propagandists through image, masque and portrait, but also as interpreters of messianic hopes' (*Henry Prince of Wales*, p. 86).

5 The most systematic attempt to trace Hermeticism in both Jacobean and Caroline masques is Brooks-Davies, *The Mercurian Monarch*. Palme, *Triumph of Peace*, contains a good discussion of Neoplatonic imagery in the Banqueting House. Gordon Toplis, 'The Sources of Jones's Mind and Imagination' in *The King's Arcadia: Inigo Jones and the Stuart Court*, eds. John Harris, Stephen Orgel and Roy Strong (London, 1973), pp. 60–2, attempts to trace Neoplatonic influences upon Jones's thought. For a more sceptical view of this last topic see Smuts, *Court Culture*, pp. 162–71 and 253–5.

6 For a listing see Harris *et al.*, *King's Arcadia*, pp. 217–18.

7 The administration of cultural patronage under James I badly needs more systematic study. Smuts, *Court Culture*, pp. 120–30, is concerned with the administration of Caroline patronage, though its general conclusions also apply to the Jacobean period.

8 In particular Ben Jonson in the seventeenth century and Stephen Orgel in the twentieth. See, especially, *The Illusion of Power* and 'Platonic Politics' in Orgel and Strong, *Inigo Jones*. Orgel's brilliant reconstruction of the theoretical underpinnings of Renaissance court spectacles has immeasurably increased our understanding of the topic. But he is sometimes too ready to assume, without corroborating evidence, that the pronouncements of theorists provide a reliable guide to the mentality of court patrons. Kevin Sharpe, *Criticism and Compliment: the Politics of Literature in the England of Charles I* (Cambridge, 1987), is an impressive example of a historian's effort to use masques and other pieces of literature as the basis for a reinterpretation of the court's outlook.

9 For Bacon's views see 'Of Masques and Triumphs', *Francis Bacon: Essays and New Atlantis* (New York, 1942), pp. 159–62. Most accounts of masques in newsletters concentrate on evidence of lavish expenditure, especially in costume. See, e.g., N. E. McLure (ed.), *The Letters of John Chamberlain* (Philadelphia, 1939), I, pp. 252–3. Some comment on stage machinery or poetic devices, but never, to my knowledge, in a way that suggests that masque imagery was anything more than an interesting curiosity.

10 Jonson satirized hermetic ideas in *Mercury Vindicated from the Alchemists at Court*, for example. As Kevin Sharpe has recently shown, one must always be alert to ironic overtones and deliberate ambiguities when interpreting masque texts. See Sharpe, *Criticism and Compliment*, ch. 5.

11 The importance of gauging audience reactions is briefly noted by David Sacks in a far-reaching but in some ways problematical discussion of the relationship between politics and cultural forms in the early Stuart period, 'Searching for "Culture" in the English Renaissance' in *Shakespeare Quarterly*, 39, p. 470. I am

not convinced that the holistic approach Sacks advocates, which allegedly 'overcomes the rigid dichotomy between the aesthetic and anthropological concepts of culture' by focusing on 'the ritual aspects' of the masques, solves as many problems as he appears to think. Replacing a literary and art historical analysis of masque iconography with an anthropological analysis of masque ritual does not solve the underlying problem. The historian still needs to show that his reading of the masque's original meaning was one that contemporaries recognized and found significant.

12 These accusations are rooted in contemporary complaints, but there is sometimes a curiously puritanical and Victorian air about the way in which modern scholars paraphrase them. See, for example, P. W. Thomas's polemical account, 'Two Cultures? Court and Country under Charles I' in *The Origins of the English Civil War*, ed. Conrad Russell (London, 1973).

13 See, in particular, P. W. Thomas, 'Two Cultures?'; Perez Zagorin, *The Court and the Country* (New York, 1969), esp. pp. 71–3; and Lawrence Stone, *The Causes of the English Revolution, 1529–1642* (London, 1972), e.g. p. 106.

14 For Cotton see Kevin Sharpe, *Sir Robert Cotton* (Oxford, 1979).

15 I have provided a more extended discussion of this point in Smuts, *Court Culture*, ch. 3.

16 David Starkey, *et al.*, *The English Court* (London, 1987). Neil Cuddy's essay in this volume, 'The Revival of the Entourage: the Bedchamber of James I, 1603–1625', is a valuable starting point for detailed study of the Jacobean court.

17 He does address this side of court life in 'Representations through Intimacy' in *Symbols and Sentiments*, ed. I. Lewis (London, 1977).

18 See G. R. Elton, 'Tudor Government: The Points of Contact, III: The Court', *Transactions of the Royal Historical Society*, 26 (1976), pp. 211–28.

19 Cuddy, 'Revival of the Entourage' in *English Court*. eds. Starkey *et al.*, p. 197; P.R.O. S.P. 14/95/12.

20 See Kevin Sharpe, 'The Earl of Arundel, his Circle, and the Opposition to the Duke of Buckingham, 1618–1628' in *Faction and Parliament: Essays on Early Stuart History* (Oxford, 1978), pp. 209–44 for Arundel, and Strong, *Prince Henry*, pp. 71–85 for the Prince.

21 In this context D. J. Howarth, *The Earl of Arundel and his Circle* (New Haven and London, 1985) provides some illumination with respect to one major aristocratic patron. The cultural patronage and influence of the Earl of Salisbury and other members of the Cecil family is a subject that particularly needs fuller investigation. Strong, *Prince Henry*, indicates that there were important connections between the Prince and both Salisbury and several younger members of the Cecil family, including Salisbury's heir, Lord Cranborne, and Edward Cecil, son of Thomas Lord Burghley (pp. 41–50). It may be more than a coincidence that Inigo Jones enjoyed Salisbury's patronage before becoming Surveyor, first to Prince Henry and eventually to the king.

22 Sir Dudley Carleton and Sir Francis Cottington are two prominent examples of figures who began as Jacobean diplomats and ended up as powerful members of

the king's government; Sir Henry Wotton and Sir Thomas Roe were diplomats who wished to rise in a similar fashion but never succeeded. The importance of Jacobean diplomatic careers in shaping the cosmopolitan outlook of many courtiers who became prominent late in James's reign or under Charles I is another topic deserving more systematic study. Smuts, *Court Culture*, p. 185, touches on this issue briefly.

23 For Carleton's art-collecting see Ruth Magurn (ed.), *The Letters of Peter Paul Rubens* (Cambridge, Mass., 1955), pp. 5, 50, and 59–68. Mayerne also had contacts with Rubens, among other luminaries. A single fashionable street near the court, like St Martin's Lane, might at any time contain the houses of artists (Daniel Mytens and Paul van Somer), diplomats (Sir Thomas Roe), major officers of state (Sir Thomas Lake, the Secretary of State), and courtiers of foreign extraction, like Mayerne. The court's neighbourhood was an extraordinarily sophisticated and cosmopolitan place. Information about residential patterns is most easily obtainable from the overseers' accounts for parishes adjacent to the court found in the Westminster Public Library Archives Division. For St Martin's Lane and nearby areas see F 330–67.

24 Donne failed, although he was eventually given ecclesiastical preferment as a sort of consolation prize after his failure to win political office. Jonson succeeded for a time, though only up to a point, and then fell from favour in Charles's reign. Jones was a success in the end. Donne sought a very different kind of patronage from Jones and Jonson, since he was never a professional poet. But it is Jonson rather than Donne who seems anomalous as a court poet, since court poetry had traditionally been written by amateurs.

25 As Howarth, *Arundel*, shows. See, for example, p. 13.

26 One obvious exception was theology, in which James took a very strong interest. The king's tastes and cultural interests need to be studied more carefully but it seems unlikely that he will emerge as a major trendsetter even in many fields in which he took some interest. James wrote poetry, for example, but his verse was derivative and there appears to be no evidence that he significantly influenced literary styles at court. See Jonathan Goldberg, *James I and the Politics of Literature* (Baltimore, 1983) for an extended discussion.

27 See, however, the analysis of Sharpe, *Criticism and Compliment*, ch. 5. I have used the plural form, households, since those of Henry and Queen Anne were also involved in producing masques.

28 I have discussed this topic at somewhat greater length in Smuts, *Court Culture*, pp. 73–82.

29 See, e.g., Salisbury's complaint to Sir John Harington: 'good knight . . . give heed to one that hath sorrowed in the bright lustre of a Court . . . Tis a great task [there] to prove one's honesty and yet not spoil one's fortune . . . I am pushed from the shore of comfort and know not where the winds and waves of a Court will bear me. I know it bringeth little comfort on earth, and he is, I reckon, no wise man that looketh this way to heaven'. Quoted in Wallace Notestein, *The House of Commons, 1604–1610* (New Haven, 1971), p. 38.

30 It is possible that the instability of court politics after Somerset's fall contributed

to the desire for reliable news. For those seeking office and patronage from the Crown it was crucial to know who was in and who out of favour at any given moment, and also what offices and crumbs of patronage might be available. Cuddy, 'Revival of the Entourage', provides a good discussion of how shifts in the influence of those in the inner circle around James affected the larger course of politics.

31 See Richard Cust, 'News and Politics in Seventeenth Century England', *Past and Present*, 112 (1986), 60–90.

32 *Volpone*, the Yale Ben Jonson (New Haven, 1962), p. 30: 'I know nothing can be so innocently writ or carried, but may be made obnoxious to construction ... Application is now grown a trade with many, and there are [those] that profess to have a key for deciphering of everything; but let wise and noble persons take heed how they be too credulous, or give leave to these invading interpreters to be overfamiliar with their fames, who cunningly, and often, utter their own virulent malice under other men's simplest meanings.' Cf. Samuel Calvert's comment, in 1605, 'the players do not forbear to represent upon their Stage the whole course of this present time, not sparing either King, State or Religion, in so great absurdity and with such liberty, that any would be afraid to hear them'. Quoted in John Nichols, *Progresses of James I* (London, 1828), I, p. 500.

33 For a fuller discussion see Smuts, *Court Culture*, ch. 4.

34 Especially J. G. A. Pocock, who has done more than any other scholar to enlarge our appreciation for the role of classical influences in reshaping the political languages of seventeenth-century Britain. His *The Machiavellian Moment* (Princeton, 1975), in particular, pays virtually no attention to political thought within early Stuart milieux associated with the court. It is also striking that most accounts of this subject pay little attention to poetry, despite the very prominent role of verse in this period as a vehicle for political and social ideas and polemics. Educated English gentlemen often read Horace and Jonson (and later Dryden and Pope) as avidly as they read Tacitus, Camden and, later, James Harrington. Poets and antiquarians also frequently had close links: Jonson was Camden's pupil and the close friend of Selden and Cotton. Poetry, analytic history and political discourse were all part of an undifferentiated literary and intellectual culture shared by courtiers, London men of letters and the more sophisticated country gentry.

35 PRO E/405/265. B.L. Add. MS 58833 provides additional information on the enormous cost of great public rituals in James's reign, which dwarf expenditures on masques and art collections.

36 C. H. Herford and Percy Simpson, *Ben Jonson: The Man and his Work*, IV (Oxford, 1932), p. 33.

37 We may have an example here of the process Lawrence Stone attempted to trace, through which the early Stuart nobility gradually reduced traditional forms of conspicuous consumption that had become ruinously expensive. See Lawrence Stone, *The Crisis of the Aristocracy* (Oxford, 1965), esp. p. 584.

38 On this point see Smuts, *Court Culture*, p. 104.

39 Smuts, *Court Culture*, pp. 106–8.

40 J. M. Shuttleworth (ed.), *The Autobiography of Lord Herbert of Cherbury* (London, 1976).

41 For the decline of the epic see Richard Helgerson, *Self-Crowned Laureates: Spenser, Jonson, Milton and the Literary System* (Berkeley and Los Angeles, 1983). Helgerson does not take into account the point raised here: that there may have been political reasons for the declining prestige of epic poetry among leading poets and patrons.

7   Lancelot Andrewes, John Buckeridge and avant-garde conformity at the court of James I

1 Peter Lake, *Anglicans and Puritans? Presbyterianism and English Conformist Thought from Whitgift to Hooker* (London, 1988), pp. 145–238. The problems of continuity linking Hooker to developments in the early seventeenth century are sketched in the conclusion, pp. 239–52.

2 *Correspondence of John Cosin*, ed. J. Ormsby, Surtees Society (1869), I, p. 70; see also R. Montague, *Appello Caesarem* (London, 1625), pp. 215, 265; *The Folger Edition of the Works of Richard Hooker*, ed. W. Speed Hill, III, p. xxviii. For the Durham House faction, see N. R. N. Tyacke, *Anti-Calvinists: The Rise of English Arminianism, c. 1590–1640* (Oxford, 1987), ch. 5.

3 K. Fincham and Peter Lake, 'The Ecclesiastical Policy of James I', *Journal of British Studies*, 24 (1985), 169–207.

4 For Presbyterianism see *The Works of Lancelot Andrewes* (Library of Anglo-Catholic Theology, Oxford, 1854) (cited hereafter as Andrewes, *Sermons*), II, pp. 33–5, from a sermon preached before Elizabeth at Greenwich, 24 February 1590; *ibid.*, pp. 280–3, from a sermon preached before James at Whitehall, 24 March 1611; *ibid.*, IV, pp. 11–12, from a sermon before James, 5 August 1607, being the anniversary of the Gowrie conspiracy; *ibid.*, p. 306, from a sermon preached before James at Whitehall, 5 November 1614.

5 *Ibid.*, II, pp. 407–9, from a sermon before the king at Whitehall, 5 April 1618.

6 *Ibid.*, I, p. 288, from a sermon before the king, 25 December 1624; *ibid.*, p. 311, from a sermon preached before Elizabeth, 4 March 1598; *ibid.*, V, p. 38, from a sermon preached during the Wednesday of Easter Week 1588; *ibid.*, p. 58, from a sermon preached at St Giles, Cripplegate, 9 January 1592. J. Buckeridge, 'A sermon preached at the funeral of . . . Lancelot Andrewes . . . 11th November, 1626' in Andrewes, *Sermons*, V, p. 269. Hereafter cited as Buckeridge, *Sermon*.

7 *Ibid.*, pp. 197–8, from a sermon preached before James at Greenwich in 1607; *ibid.*, II, pp. 387–8, from a sermon preached before James at Durham Cathedral, 20 April 1617; *ibid.*, V, p. 55, from a sermon preached at St Giles, Cripplegate, 9 January 1593.

8 *Ibid.*, I, pp. 407–8, from a sermon preached before James at Whitehall, 6 March 1622; *ibid.*, III, p. 141, from a sermon preached before James at Greenwich, Whitsunday, 1608; *ibid.*, III, pp. 267–8, 274–5, from a sermon preached before

James at Greenwich, 19 May 1616; *ibid.*, I, pp. 420–1, from a sermon preached before James at Whitehall, 26 February 1623; *ibid.*, III, p. 97, from a sermon prepared to be given at court on Easter day, 1624; *ibid.*, IV, p. 379, from a sermon preached before James, at Whitehall, 5 November 1617. J. Buckeridge, *A Sermon preached before his majesty . . . touching prostration and kneeling in the worship of God, to which is added a discourse concerning kneeling at the communion* (London, 1618), pp. 10–11. Hereafter cited as Buckeridge, *Kneeling*.

9 Andrewes, *Sermons*, III, p. 328, from a sermon preached before James at Greenwich, 16 May 1619; *ibid.*, p. 32, from a sermon preached before James at Whitehall, 1 April 1621; *ibid.*, V, p. 398, from an undated sermon on the Lord's Prayer, first published in 1611.

10 Buckeridge, *Kneeling*, p. 172. Andrewes, *Sermons*, III, p. 363, from a sermon before James at Greenwich, 20 May 1621; *ibid.*, I, p. 230, from a sermon preached before James at Whitehall, 25 December 1619; *ibid.*, V, p. 531, from the fifth sermon of a series of seven on the combat of Christ and the devil first published in 1592; *ibid.*, p. 521, from the fourth sermon of the same series; *ibid.*, V, p. 530, from the fifth sermon on the combat of Christ and the devil; *ibid.*, I, p. 428, from a sermon preached before James at Whitehall, 26 February 1623; also see *ibid.*, p. 184, from a sermon before James at Whitehall, 25 December 1616.

11 *Ibid.*, I, pp. 288–9, from a sermon preached before James at Whitehall, 25 December 1624; *ibid.*, V, pp. 59–60, from a sermon preached at St Giles, Cripplegate, 9 January 1593; *ibid.*, I, pp. 395–6, from a sermon preached before the king at Whitehall, 14 February 1621; *ibid.*, p. 451, from a sermon to be preached at court on Ash Wednesday, 1624; *ibid.*, III, pp. 193–4, from a sermon preached before the king at Whitehall, 31 May 1612.

12 Buckeridge, *Kneeling*, pp. 16, 32, 69–70, 224–5; also see *ibid.*, pp. 92, 148–50, 185–6, 223. Andrewes, *Sermons*, I, pp. 261–2, from a sermon preached before James at Whitehall, 25 December 1622; *ibid.*, III, p. 33, from a sermon preached before James at Whitehall, 1 April 1621.

13 *Ibid.*, II, p. 408, from a sermon preached before the king at Whitehall, 5 April 1618; *ibid.*, p. 338, from a sermon preached before James at Whitehall, 24 April 1614. Buckeridge, *Kneeling*, pp. 241–2.

14 Andrewes, *Sermons*, I, p. 411, from a sermon preached before James at Whitehall, 6 March 1622; *ibid.*, II, p. 408, from a sermon preached before the king at Whitehall, 5 April 1618.

15 Buckeridge, *Kneeling*, pp. 7, 13, 25, 112–13; Andrewes, *Sermons*, IV, p. 375, from a sermon preached before James at Whitehall, 5 November 1617.

16 *Ibid.*, III, pp. 32–3, from a sermon preached before James at Whitehall, 1 April 1621; *ibid.*, IV, p. 60, from a sermon preached before James at Holdenby, 5 August 1610, being the anniversary of the Gowrie conspiracy; *ibid.*, pp. 305–6, 310, from a sermon preached before James at Whitehall, 5 November 1614; *ibid.*, III, p. 133, from a sermon preached before the king at Greenwich, 24 May 1608; *ibid.*, IV, p. 65, from a sermon preached before James at Holdenby,

5 August 1610, being the anniversary of the Gowrie conspiracy; *ibid.*, V, p. 128, from a sermon preached at Whitehall, 15 November 1601.

17 *Ibid.*, IV, pp. 136–7, from a sermon preached before James at Burleigh, near Oakham, 5 August 1616, being the anniversary of the Gowrie conspiracy; *ibid.*, III, pp. 277–8, from a sermon preached before James at Greenwich, 19 May 1616.

18 *Ibid.*, II, p. 122, from a sermon preached at court on Good Friday, 1597; *ibid.*, I, p. 141, from a sermon preached before the king at Westminster, 25 December 1614; *ibid.*, I, pp. 215–17, from a sermon preached before James at Whitehall, 25 December 1619; *ibid.*, II, pp. 122, 128, from a sermon preached at court, Good Friday 1597, also see *ibid.*, p. 159, from a sermon preached before James at Greenwich, on Good Friday 1605; *ibid.*, pp. 125–6, from a sermon preached at court, Good Friday, 1597; *ibid.*, pp. 178–80, from a sermon preached before James at Greenwich, Good Friday 1605.

19 *Ibid.*, III, pp. 66–73, on harrowing of hell, from a sermon preached before James at Whitehall, 13 April 1623; *ibid.*, pp. 82–3, from a sermon prepared to be delivered at court at Easter 1624; *ibid.*, II, pp. 188–9, from a sermon preached before James at Whitehall, 6 April 1606; *ibid.*, III, p. 380, from a sermon prepared to be preached at court on Whitsunday 1622; *ibid.*, II, p. 199, from a sermon preached before James, 6 April 1606.

20 On the particular stages of Christ's earthly journey as models for the stages of the spiritual journey of the Christian see *ibid.*, III, p. 83, from a sermon prepared to be preached at court at Easter 1624; *ibid.*, I, p. 439, from a sermon prepared to be preached at court on Ash Wednesday 1624; *ibid.*, p. 417, from a sermon preached before James at Whitehall, 26 February 1623 being Ash Wednesday; *ibid.*, p. 443, from a sermon prepared to be preached before the king 10 February 1624, being Ash Wednseday; *ibid.*, p. 426, from a sermon preached before James at Whitehall, 26 February 1623, being Ash Wednesday. Buckeridge, *Kneeling*, pp. 10, 86 and *Sermon*, pp. 267, 269, 273.

21 Andrewes, *Sermons*, III, p. 243, from a sermon preached before James at Greenwich, Whitsunday 1615; *ibid.*, p. 309, from a sermon preached before James at Greenwich, 24 May 1618, being Whitsunday; *ibid.*, p. 365, from a sermon preached before James at Greenwich, 20 May, being Whitsunday; *ibid.*, pp. 151–2, a sermon preached before James at Whitehall, 27 May 1610, being Whitsunday 1621; *ibid.*, V, ppl. 116–17, from a sermon preached at Whitehall, 23 November 1600. For the distinction between imputed and inherent righteousness see Buckeridge, *Sermon*, p. 272.

22 Andrewes, *Sermons*, III, p. 341, from a sermon preached before the king at Greenwich, 16 May 1619, being Whitsunday; *ibid.*, I, p. 289, from a sermon preached before James 25 December 1624; *ibid.*, III, p. 336, a sermon preached before James at Greenwich, 16 May 1619, being Whitsunday. Also see Buckeridge, *Kneeling*, pp. 20–1 and *Sermon*, pp. 262, 282.

23 Andrewes, *Sermons*, V, pp. 373–4, from sermon 8 of a series expounding the Lord's Prayer; *ibid.*, p. 464, from sermon 18 of the series on the Lord's Prayer; *ibid.*, V, pp. 527, 531, from sermon 5, of a series of seven on the combat

between Christ and Satan, first published in 1592; *ibid.*, pp. 49–50, from a sermon preached at St Mary's Hospital, 10 April 1588. Buckeridge, *Kneeling*, pp. 20–1.

24 R. T. Kendall, *Calvin and English Calvinism* (Oxford, 1979), *passim.*

25 Andrewes, *Sermons*, I, p. 450, from a sermon prepared to be preached at court on Ash Wednesday, 1624; also see *ibid.*, V, pp. 82–103, a sermon preached at Whitehall, 30 March 1600, on the power of absolution.

26 *Ibid.*, III, p. 69, from a sermon preached before James at Whitehall, 13 April, being Easter day 1623; *ibid.*, V, pp. 190, 191, from a sermon preached before James at Greenwich in 1607; *ibid.*, I, p. 35, from a sermon preached before James at Whitehall, 25 December 1607; *ibid.*, II, p. 64, from a sermon preached at Hampton Court before Elizabeth, 6 March 1594.

27 *Ibid.*, I, p. 116, from a sermon preached at Whitehall before James, 25 December 1612. Buckeridge, *Kneeling*, pp, 99, 106–10.

28 Andrewes, *Sermons*, III, p. 319, from a sermon preached before James at Greenwich, 24 May 1618, being Whitsunday; *ibid.*, IV, pp. 377–8, from a sermon preached before James at Whitehall, 5 November 1617; *ibid.*, I, p. 116, from a sermon preached before James at Whitehall, 25 December 1612; *ibid.*, II, p. 205, from a sermon preached before James at Whitehall, 6 April 1606, being Easter day; *ibid.*, III, p. 219, from a sermon preached before James at Whitehall, 23 May 1613, being Whitsunday. Buckeridge, *Kneeling*, p. 29.

29 Andrewes, *Sermons*, III, p. 128, from a sermon preached before James at Greenwich, 8 June 1606, being Whitsunday; *ibid.*, V, p. 311, from sermon 2 of a series – 'a preparation to prayer'; *ibid.*, III, p. 198, from a sermon preached before James at Whitehall, 31 May 1612, being Whitsunday.

30 *Ibid.*, III, p. 311, from a sermon preached before James at Greenwich, 24 May 1618, being Whitsunday; *ibid.*, V, pp. 355–6, from sermon 6 of the series 'a preparation for prayer'; *ibid.*, p. 231, from a sermon preached at Chiswick, 25 August 1603.

31 *Ibid.*, V, p. 231, 'The prayer of a prophet in that he is a prophet is more effectual'; 'the priest shall make an atonement for them before the lord, and their sins shall be forgiven them', he shall 'lift up his prayer for the remnant that were left', from a sermon preached at Chiswick, 21 August 1603, at a time of pestilence.

32 *Ibid.*, III, p. 318, from a sermon preached before James at Greenwich, 24 May 1618, being Whitsunday; Buckeridge, *Kneeling*, pp. 38–40.

33 Andrewes, *Sermons*, V, p. 323, from sermon 3 of the series 'a preparation to prayer'; *ibid.*, V, p. 352, sermon 6 of the same series; *ibid.*, IV, p. 376, from a sermon preached before James at Whitehall, 5 November 1617. Buckeridge, *Kneeling*, pp. 40, 77.

34 Buckeridge, *Kneeling*, pp. 40, 43–4.

35 Andrewes, *Sermons*, I, p. 381, from a sermon preached before James at Whitehall, 14 February 1621, being Ash Wednesday; Buckeridge, *Kneeling*, pp. 86, 229.

36 The phrase was Buckeridge's, *Kneeling*, p. 103.

37 Andrewes, *Sermons*, I, p. 213, from a sermon preached before James at White-hall, 25 December 1618; *ibid.*, p. 152, from a sermon preached before James at Whitehall, 25 December 1614; Buckeridge, *Kneeling*, p. 117. Also see *ibid.*, pp. 60–71 for the four ways in which the sacrament could be termed a sacrifice. Also see Buckeridge, *Sermon*, p. 263.

38 Andrewes, *Sermons*, II, p. 333, from a sermon preached before James at White-hall, 24 April 1614, being Easter day; *ibid.*, V, p. 349, from sermon 5 of the series 'a preparation to prayer'; Buckeridge, *Kneeling*, pp. 19, 46–7.

39 Buckeridge, *Kneeling*, pp. 11, 114–15. Also see Andrewes, *Sermons*, IV, p. 372, from a sermon preached before James at Whitehall, 5 November 1617, in which Andrewes ranked holiness in the service of God before moral righteousness as a Christian duty.

40 Andrewes, *Sermons*, III, pp. 113–14, from a sermon preached before James at Greenwich, 8 June 1606, being Whitsunday.

41 Buckeridge, *Kneeling*, pp. 8, 18, 166–7, 243; Andrewes, *Sermons*, II, pp. 323–43, from a sermon on the text 'at the name of Jesus every knee shall bow' preached before James at Whitehall, 24 April 1614, being Easter day.

42 On the argument from divine right see P. Lake, 'Presbyterianism, the Idea of a National Church and the Argument from Divine Right' in *Protestantism and the National Church in Sixteenth Century England*, eds. P. Lake and M. Dowling (London, 1987).

43 L. Andrewes, *Responsio ad apologiam cardinallis Bellarmini* in *The Works of Lancelot Andrewes*, ed. J. Bliss (Oxford, 1854), VIII, pp. 38–9, 161, 162, 290–1, 473–4, 486. I owe this point and these references to the kindness of Anthony Milton. Pressure of this sort did not only come from the king. According to Peter Heylin, writing in the 1630s, 'when bishop Andrewes had learnedly asserted the episcopal order to be of Christ's institution . . . some who were then in place did secretly intercede with King James to have it altered, for fear forsooth of offend-ing our neighbour churches', P. Heylin, *Antidotum Lincolniense* (London, 1637), section III, p. 8. The quote comes from a passage in which Heylin was trying to label Bishop John Williams as a secret enemy to episcopacy for defending what had been the orthodox *iure divino* claim under Elizabeth and James, that episcopacy was an institution of apostolic rather than of directly divine foundation. Evidently the constraints which had been placed on Andrewes at the Jacobean court were no longer operative at the court of his son.

44 On this point see Kenneth Fincham's study of the Jacobean episcopate forth-coming from Oxford University Press. I should like to thank Dr Fincham for allowing me to see this work in advance of publication and for many discussions on the subject of Lancelot Andrewes.

45 Abbot notes Andrewes's discomfort and silence during the Essex divorce trial; 'my lord of Ely sat little less than dumb', 'my Lord of Ely, who from the first beginning of the process had always been very silent'. This was in marked con-trast to Abbot's account of the conduct of Bishops Neile, Buckeridge and Bilson all of whom were active in the affair and exploited and enjoyed Abbot's

intransigence over the divorce. See T. B. Howell (ed.), *A Complete Collection of State Trials* (1816), II, pp. 806–50 especially, 815, 817, 823–4, 827, 829, 833–45. From the other side Montague's comparison between Andrewes and Gamaliel may have been a little double-edged, for while Gamaliel may have been a great scholar he was also something of an equivocator. Indeed, Montague's view, expressed to Cosin, that 'if our Gamaliel will now open his mouth and speak out, haply he will do that good for which God will reward him, and all posterity thank him' may betoken a certain concern about Andrewes's reliability as a political ally during a crisis. *Cosin Correspondence*, p. 70. I owe this point to the kindness of Ken Fincham.

46 On this see Fincham and Lake, 'Ecclesiastical Policy of James I' and N. R. N Tyacke, *Anti-Calvinists*, pp. 45, 91.

47 Buckeridge, *Kneeling*, pp. 246–8; compare the peroration to one of Andrewes's sermons (IV, pp. 116–19) preached before James at Salisbury, 5 August 1615. There, having established that it was 'the highest perfection God can bestow on David' to allow him to restore the temple and having, conventionally enough, compared James to David, Andrewes went on to exhort the king to 'do somewhat for which God may rejoice in him, somewhat for the sanctuary'. *Ibid.*, I, pp. 284–302, from a sermon preached before the king at Whitehall, 25 December 1624.

48 See P. Collinson, *The Religion of Protestants* (Oxford, 1982) and Dr Fincham's forthcoming book on the Jacobean episcopate.

49 Buckeridge, *Kneeling*, p. 8.

50 Fincham and Lake, 'Ecclesiastical Policy of James I'.

8   Robert Cecil and the early Jacobean court

1 *Letters of King James VI and I*, ed. G. P. V. Akrigg (California/London, 1984), pp. 173–5. Sir Robert Cecil became Baron Essendon in May 1603, Viscount Cranborne in August 1604 and Earl of Salisbury in May 1605. For the sake of simplicity he has been referred to as 'Cecil' throughout this essay.

2 Akrigg, pp. 178, 198–9, 209, 264. Sir William Evers was sent to the Tower for contacts with James: *The Letters of John Chamberlain*, ed. N. E. McClure (Philadelphia, 1939), I, p. 113; P. M. Handover, *The Second Cecil* (London, 1959), pp. 297–8; John Stow and Edmund Howes, *Annales or a General Chronicle of England* (London, 1631), p. 816.

3 'A collection of several speeches and treatises of the late lord treasurer Cecil', ed. P. Croft, *Camden Miscellany*, 29 (Royal Historical Society, London, 1987), p. 305; Handover, p. 299. *Calendar of the Carew MSS 1601–3 Preserved in the Archiepiscopal Library at Lambeth*, ed. J. S. Brewer and W. Bullens (London, 1870), pp. 157, 221, 260, 358–9. Writing later to James, Cecil remembered his service to the unreliable Elizabeth as a time when 'the age and sex were full of passion', *Historical Manuscripts. Commission, Salisbury (Cecil) Mss.*, XIX, p. 21.

4 Linda Levy Peck, *Northampton: Patronage and Policy at the Court of James I*

(London, 1982), pp. 16–22. J. Nichols, *The Progresses, Processions and Magnificent Festivities of James I . . .* (1828), I, p. 110. Bodleian Library Oxford MS Ashmole 1729.30.

5 Pam Wright, 'A Change in Direction: The Ramifications of a Female Household 1558–1603' in *The English Court from the Wars of the Roses to the Civil War*, eds. David Starkey *et al.* (London, 1987), pp. 147–72. Neil Cuddy, 'The Revival of the Entourage: The Bedchamber of James I, 1603–1625', *ibid.*, pp. 176–7.

6 J. Nichols, *Progresses and Public Processions*, III, pp. 369–490; *Calendar of State Papers Domestic 1598–1601*, p. 251.

7 E. Lodge, *Illustrations of British History . . . from the MSS of the Noble Families of Howard, Talbot and Cecil* (2nd edn, 1838), III, pp. 20–4, 33–4, 38, 52; P. Croft, 'Parliament, Purveyance and the City of London 1589–1608', *Parliamentary History*, 4 (1985), 13.

8 Sir Ralph Winwood, *Memorials of Affairs of State . . .* , ed. E. Sawyer (London, 1725), II, p. 155; *Calendar of State Papers Venetian 1603–1607*, pp. 267, 285; Croft, 'Parliament, Purveyance and the City of London', p. 19; Lodge, *Illustrations*, III, pp. 108–9, 217; *Calendar of Talbot Papers in the College of Arms*, ed. G. R. Batho (Derbyshire Archaeol. Society, 1968), p. 227. Cecil echoed Munck's complaints, looking back to the time when it had been possible to wait on a monarch and still enjoy 'ease at my board and rest in my bed', H. Harington, *Nugae Antiquae* (1804), I, p. 345.

9 Akrigg, p. 233, *HMC Salisbury*, XIX, p. 210.

10 For the need to define terms for the early seventeenth century see Sir Geoffrey Elton, 'Tudor Government: The Points of Contact. (3) The Court', *Trans. Royal Historical Society*, 5th ser., 26 (1976), 211. There is no discussion of this in either Cuddy, 'The Revival of the Entourage' or Graham Parry, *The Golden Age Restor'd: The Culture of the Stuart Court 1603–42* (Manchester, 1981). For the diffusion of court culture, R. Malcolm Smuts, pp. 99–112 of this volume. The court of Philip III of Spain, another passionate huntsman, poses exactly the same problem of definition and had the same effect of cultural diffusion: J. H. Elliott, 'The Court of the Habsburgs: A Peculiar Institution?' in *Politics and Culture in Early Modern Europe: Essays in Honour of H. G. Koenigsberger*, eds. P. Mack and M. C. Jacob (Cambridge, 1987), p. 18. P.R.O. State Papers Domestic James I, SP 14/9, f.137. *Winwood's Memorials*, II, p. 57.

11 Akrigg, pp. 239, 246–7, 255: *Cal. S.P. Ven. 1603–7*, pp. 331, 395, 397.

12 *Cal. S.P. Ven.*, pp. 39, 332; *HMC Salisbury*, XIX, p. viii. British Library Cotton Caligula MS E X. f.217. There were reports later of accidents to Prince Henry when James took him hunting: *HMC Salisbury*, XX, p. 120.

13 *HMC Salisbury*, XVI, p. 383. *Calendar of Carew MSS*, p. 318. *Winwood's Memorials*, II, p. 171; 'A Collection', ed. Croft, p. 295. Lodge, *Illustrations*, II, p. 550; Thomas Birch, *The Life of Henry Prince of Wales* (London, 1760), p. 240.

14 Akrigg, p. 227; Lodge, *Illustrations*, III, pp. 262, 265; *HMC Salisbury*, XIX, p. 185; XX, pp. 76–7, 79, 81, 98, 102, 120, 130; XXI, p. 92.

15 Lodge, *Illustrations*, III, pp. 265, 267; Akrigg, pp. 221, 257; *HMC Salisbury*, XXI, pp. 83, 173.

16 Akrigg, pp. 232, 259, 265. *HMC Salisbury*, XIX, pp. 136, 143, 209, 247, 285, 335; XX, pp. 89, 120; XVII, p. 3; XXI, pp. 33, 35, 157, 215; XXII, pp. x–xi. *Letters of John Chamberlain*, ed. McClure, I, p. 180, BL Lansdowne 92/114: BL Egerton 1525 f. 33.

17 *Cal. S.P. Ven. 1603–7*, pp. 25, 27, 240, 349, 354. *HMC Salisbury*, XVI, p. 389. S.P. 14/2/33. S.P. 14/1/73. *HMC Salisbury*, XX, p. 118; XXI, p. 45. Lodge, *Illustrations*, III, p. 12. In considering the membership of his Privy Council in May 1603 James wished to add representatives of 'the ancient nobility (whose birth and merit makes them more capable than others'. Bodleian Library MS Ashmole 1729 f. 97.

18 Lawrence Stone, *Family and Fortune: Studies in Aristocratic Finance in the Sixteenth and Seventeenth Centuries* (Oxford, 1973), pp. 62–105. BL Add. MS 36767 f. 319.

19 *Cal. S.P. Ven. 1603–7*, pp. 26, 308. 'A Collection', ed. Croft, pp. 257–9. Roy Strong, *Henry Prince of Wales and England's Lost Renaissance* (London, 1986), pp. 25–6, 46–7, 65, 74, 154, 188–9. *HMC Salisbury*, XIX, pp. 158, 447; XX, pp. 273–4; XXI, pp. 285–6. Birch, *Life of Henry Prince of Wales*, pp. 95, 127, 133.

20 'A Collection', ed. Croft, pp. 259, 282. Cecil also tried to use the prince's tutor Adam Newton to restrain his generosity to suitors: Birch, *Life of Henry Prince of Wales*, pp. 134, 138. *HMC Downshire*, II, p. 211. Elizabeth Read Foster, *Proceedings in Parliament 1610* (New Haven and London, 1966), I, pp. 12–13, 95–6; II, pp. 161–3. The embroidery alone for the suit and cloak worn by Cecil cost £79.10s: Stone, *Family and Fortune*, p. 29.

21 Strong, *Henry Prince of Wales*, pp. 151–74. 'A Collection', ed. Croft, p. 259.

22 Lodge, *Illustrations*, III, pp. 64–8, 148–9, 247, Appendix p. 207; *HMC Salisbury*, XVI, p. 415; XXII, p. xv; XIX, p. 151; XX, p. 41, 108; XXI, pp. 30, 149, 151; Akrigg, pp. 233, 259, 279, 285; Stone, *Family and Fortune*, p. 30. *Letters of John Chamberlain*, ed. McClure, I, p. 338; 'A Collection', ed. Croft, pp. 257–9. S.P. 14/1/47.

23 'A Collection', ed. Croft, pp. 257, 278.

24 The best account of the negotiations for the Union is contained in Bruce Galloway, *The Union of England and Scotland 1603–1608* (Edinburgh, 1986). Evidence for the covert dislike of members of the House of Lords for the Union proposals is summarized by Angela Britton, 'The House of Lords in English Politics 1604–1614' (DPhil. thesis, Oxford, 1982), pp. 143–84. Akrigg, p. 311, *HMC Salisbury*, XX, p. 5. Lodge, *Illustrations*, III, pp. 99, 101–3. *The Memoirs of Robert Carey*, ed. F. H. Mares (Oxford, 1972), pp. 66–7.

25 The treatises are printed in full in 'A Collection', ed. Croft; cf. especially pp. 267, 304–5, 309–10.

26 Cuddy, 'The Revival of the Entourage', p. 193 in *The English Court*, ed. Starkey, summarizing N. Cuddy, 'The King's Chambers: The Bedchamber of James I in Administration and Politics 1603–1625' (DPhil. thesis, Oxford, 1987).

27 Cuddy, 'The King's Chambers', pp. 1, 91–107. For the return to Cecil of documents bearing the king's signature see *HMC Salisbury*, XXI, pp. 18, 27, 85, 93, 138, 192–3, 197, 205, 207, 277, 293, 297, 334, 342, 347, 358, 359, 364, 368, 372. The examples could be multiplied. For the eager expectation of Cecil's visits and the welcome accorded him, *HMC Salisbury*, XXI, pp. 47, 92, 115–16, 130, 137, 171, 210, 235. Again the examples could be multiplied. Peck, *Northampton*, pp. 26–8; *HMC Salisbury*, XX, p. 89; XXI, pp. 30–1.

28 Roy Strong, 'England and Italy: The Marriage of Henry Prince of Wales' in *For Veronica Wedgwood These Studies in Seventeenth Century History*, eds. Richard Ollard and Pamela Tudor-Craig (London, 1986), pp. 59–87. For some important criticisms of Strong's conclusions see T. V. Wilkes, *The Court Culture of Prince Henry and his Circle 1603–1613* (DPhil thesis, Oxford, 1987), pp. 50–3. There is a sketchy discussion of Cecil's career after 1610 in E. Lindquist, 'The Last Years of the First Earl of Salisbury 1610–1612', *Albion*, 1 (1986).

29 Stone, *Family and Fortune*, pp. 13–15, 20–32.

30 *Opera Medica . . . Consilii, Epistolae, Observationes Pharmacopeia . . . Theo. Turquet Mayernii* (London, 1703), pp. 78–90. *Letters of John Chamberlain*, ed. McClure, I, pp. 338, 347. 'The character of Robert earle of Salesburye lord treasuror of Englande &c: written by Mr. William Turneur', printed in *The Works of Cyril Tourneur*, ed. Allardyce Nicoll (London, 1929), pp. 259–63. William Turneur cannot be safely identified with the playwright Cyril Tourneur: S. Tannenbaum, 'A Tourneur Mystification', *Modern Language Notes*, 47 (1932), 141–3.

9   The mentality of a Jacobean grandee

I am most grateful to A. R. Braunmuller, John Guy, John Salmon and Jenny Wormald for commenting on earlier drafts of this essay.

1 N. E. McClure (ed.), *The Letters of John Chamberlain* (2 vols., Philadelphia, 1939), I, p. 542. It was rumoured that Northampton received extreme unction and his body was covered by a velvet pall with a white cross. As his funeral procession slowly wound through Kent to Dover Castle, at each inn where the procession stopped, the coffin was surmounted by burning tapers while six of his men stood guard all night surrounded by flaming torches.

2 Quoted in A. J. Loomie, *Spain and the Jacobean Catholics, 1613–1624*, Catholic Record Society, vol. 68 (1978), pp. 38–40. Don Diego Sarmiento de Acuna, afterwards Conde de Gondomar, stressed Northampton's longtime support for Spain and his recent return to Catholicism.

3 Charles V had recognized twenty-five; by 1650 there were over 100 grandees in Spain. James Stuart, son of Esmé, Duke of Lennox, was created a grandee by Phillip IV while on the Grand Tour in the 1620s.

4 *OED*: 'grandee'.

5 Increasingly pejorative connotations attached to the great man in early seventeenth-century England as it became increasingly the label of the royal favourite, the Duke of Buckingham. See Robert Shepherd, 'Royal Favorites in the

Political Discourse of Tudor and Stuart England' (PhD thesis, Claremont Graduate School, 1985).

6 Linda Levy Peck, *Northampton: Patronage and Politics at the Court of James I* (London, 1982), pp. 18–22. Howard served as intermediary and sometime secretary for Essex. His commonplace book contains summaries of letters to Don Antonio Perez, the Spanish Secretary of State and exile in France whom Essex used as an emissary to the King of France, Henry IV. British Library, Titus C VI, f. 323ff. See Logan Pearsall Smith (ed.), *The Life and Letters of Sir Henry Wotton* (2 vols.; Oxford, 1907), I, p. 30 and n.; Thomas Birch, *Memoirs of the Reign of Queen Elizabeth* (2 vols.; London, 1754). Northampton also established ties to Cecil and was the principal English participant in the secret correspondence which secured James's successful and peaceful succession to the throne. John Bruce (ed.), *Correspondence of King James VI of Scotland with Sir Robert Cecil and Others in England*, Camden Society, o.s., vol. 68 (London, 1861); David Dalrymple, Lord Hailes (ed.), *The Secret Correspondence of Sir Robert Cecil with James VI of Scotland* (Edinburgh, 1766).

7 James McConica, *English Humanists and Reformation Politics* (Oxford, 1965), pp. 210–11.

8 Peck, *Northampton*, p. 8. B.L. Lansdowne MS 109, no. 49, Lord Henry Howard to Michael Hickes (undated). The titles of the Norfolk branch had been restored by Mary Tudor and in the 1560s while teaching at Cambridge Howard, as grandson and brother to Earls had the courtesy title of Lord Henry Howard.

9 Oxford, Bodl. Lib. MS 616, f. 3. This work on natural philosophy showed the influence of Renaissance Aristotelianism; see Charles Schmitt, *John Case and Aristotelianism in Renaissance England* (Kingston, Ontario, 1983), p. 59n. Bent Juel-Jensen in 'The Poet Earl of Surrey's Library', *Book Collector*, 5 (1956), 172, described a 1541 Italian edition of *The Courtier* with Henry Howard's name and numerous manuscript annotations both in Italian and Latin with citations to an edition of Cicero which he suggests is Surrey's.

10 Quentin Skinner, *The Foundations of Modern Political Thought* (2 vols.; Cambridge, 1978), I, pp. 30-1.

11 Anthony Grafton and Lisa Jardine, *From Humanism to the Humanities* (Cambridge, Mass., 1986), pp. 210–20. Discussing the writings and marginalia of Gabriel Harvey, Cambridge lecturer in rhetoric, they argue that Harvey adopted views from Peter Ramus that led to the separation of virtue and learning. Harvey never achieved his ambition for public service. Northampton, one of the two University readers who, in 1569–70 ranked Harvey ninth on his senior examinations, attacked the work of Gabriel's brother Richard in *A Defensative against the Poyson of Supposed Prophecies* (London, 1583). Virginia F. Stern, *Gabriel Harvey, His Life, Marginalia and Library* (Oxford, 1979), pp. 72–3. Making explicit his role as public orator before the commission negotiating union with Scotland, Northampton referred to 'my last hallowe and applause', B.L. Cotton MS Titus C VI, f. 433. James referred to 'Your orations in parliament in advancement of the union', Titus C VI, f. 178.

12 *Letters of Francis Bacon* (London, 1702), pp. 18–19.

13 Grafton and Jardine, *From Humanism to the Humanities*, pp. 210–20.

14 B.L. Cotton MS Titus C I, f. 140.

15 J. G. A. Pocock, *The Ancient Constitution and the Feudal Law* (Cambridge, 1957); Johann Sommerville, *Politics and Ideology in Early Stuart England* (London, 1986).

16 B.L. Titus C VI, f. 213v–214. Howard's unfinished tract on the power of the king begins at f. 212. Internal evidence suggests that it was composed in the 1580s. In addition to classical authors, Howard makes heavy use of Bodin's *Six Livres de la République* but only occasionally provides citations. His target is George Buchanan but he does not identify the works to which he refers.

17 B.L. Titus C VI, ff. 263–4; 'A Dutiful Defense of the Lawful Regiment of Women', f. 14v. James I, 'A Speech to the Lords and Commons of the Parliament at Whitehall', 21 March 1610 in C. H. McIlwain, *The Political Works of James I* (Cambridge, Mass., 1916), p. 309.

18 Newberry Library, 'The Dutiful Defense of the Lawful Regiment of Women', f. 82v.

19 I am grateful to John Salmon for advice on Bodin and his English reception. See his *The French Religious Wars in English Political Thought* (Oxford, 1959); David Parker, 'Law, Society and the State in the Thought of Jean Bodin', *History of Political Thought*, II (1981), pp. 253–85; Quentin Skinner, *The Foundations of Modern Political Thought*, II, pp. 284–301; Julian Franklin, *Jean Bodin and the Rise of Absolutist Theory* (Cambridge, 1973). Howard's admiration and imitation of Bodin was shared by other civil lawyers such as Alberico Gentili; see Brian Levack, *The Civil Lawyers in England, 1603–41* (Oxford, 1973), p. 97. E. J. L. Scott, *Letterbook of Gabriel Harvey A.D. 1573–1580*, Camden Society, n.s., vol. 33 (London, 1884), p. 79.

20 B.L. Cotton MS Titus C VI contains Northampton's correspondence, drafts of religious works and tracts on monarchy. His other works include *A Defense of the Ecclesiasticall Regiment in Englande defaced by T.C. in his Replie against Whitgifte* (London, 1574); B.L. Egerton MS 944, 'Regina Fortunata' (1576); 'An Answer to Stubbs' Gaping Gulf' in *John Stubb's Gaping Gulf*, ed. Lloyd E. Berry (Charlottesville, Virginia, 1968); *A Defensative against the Poyson of Supposed Prophesies*; Oxford, Bodl. Lib. MS 903, 'Dutiful Defense of the Lawful Regiment of Women' (*c.* 1590).

21 This appears in the midst of praise for Queen Elizabeth for her honesty in 'A Dutiful Defense of the Lawful Regiment of Women', p. 14.

22 Bodleian MS 616, f. 2v. 'I am not ignorant how ready this carping age of ours doth show itself with poisons . . . and out of sweet and savory herbs rather with the spider suck poison than with the busy bee collect the pleasant honey and as the verdure of wits is now most delectable so is the gaul of taunts and cavills most bitter.'

23 He appealed to 'the touch and trial of antiquity . . . [and] learned writers and preachers of the church, to whom the keys of knowledge and authority are given' *A Defensative against the Poyson of Supposed Prophecies*, pp. 10 ff.

24 I am grateful to David McKitterick, Librarian of Trinity College, Cambridge, for

invaluable discussions on Northampton's library. Arundel's collections are reflected in early lists of his library such as B.L. Sloane 862 and *Bibliotheca Norfolciana* (London, 1681), the catalogue of books and manuscripts presented by Arundel's grandson, the sixth Duke of Norfolk, to the Royal Society at the urging of John Evelyn. Arundel's library was made up of the Pirckheimer collection of Aldine Press editions of classical authors and Reformation tracts by Luther and his contemporaries which the Earl bought in the 1630s in Vienna, other Howard family books and Northampton's library. The Royal Society gave many of the manuscripts to the British Library and to the College of Heralds, and a few deeds to the Duke of Norfolk in 1831, and sold some books to Bernard Quaritch in 1873. In 1925 the Royal Society sold the remaining 226 items. Of these, several of Northampton's books can be positively identified from the Sotheby's sale catalogue, some bound with Northampton's crest and circled by the order of the garter. Others had dedicatory inscriptions. Further investigation of research library holdings for volumes with the Royal Society stamp will yield information about his library. See Bent Juel-Jenson, 'The Poet Earl of Surrey's Library', p. 172.

25 The Folger Shakespeare Library holds the de Morales and Campi volumes. Cotton obtained Northampton's manuscripts and amongst his loan lists is a record of 'Prayers of my Lord of Northampton in velom', loaned to Mr Fowler (Sarmiento's Secretary). B.L. Harl. MS 6018, f. 173v. I am grateful to Colin Tite for this reference.

26 James I collected Gretser's works. T. A. Birrell, *English Monarchs and their Books: From Henry VII to Charles II* (London, 1987), p. 27. In 1610 Gretser published a book entitled *Basilikon Doron*, dedicated to Mary Queen of Scots, 'now in heaven' challenging the king's writings on behalf of the oath of allegiance.

27 *Bibliotheca Norfolciana, passim.* Arundel's library also contained one copy of *The Prince*, a copy of a work by Northampton's tutor Hadrian Junius, Adam Blackwood's *Contra Buchanani* of 1581 and the treaty between James I and Philip III of Spain of which Northampton was a principal negotiator.

28 See Loomie, *Spain and the Jacobean Catholics*, pp. 38–40; Northampton was asked to acknowledge publicly his return to Catholicism: B.L. Arundel Mss. 300. 'A formulary of psalms and prayers made by Henry Earl of Northampton and writ with his own hand' and B.L. Titus C VI, ff. 516–83 were two of his religious writings.

29 *A Defence of the Ecclesiasticall Regiment in Englande defaced by T.C. in his Replie against Whitgifte* (London, 1574).

30 *The Poyson of Supposed Prophesies* was republished in 1620 under the auspices of his nephew, the Earl of Arundel.

31 As chief of state the Queen was superior yet her husband might try to 'extort the very sceptre of government . . . The lamentable example of the most unfortunate and poor afflicted Queen of Scotland doth yield hereof an evident testimony.' Howard blamed Mary's misfortunes on her unhappy match with Darnley. Elizabeth faced a great threat by marrying at home, especially 'the more bloody

the families be whereof the champions are descended'. Such a match would produce 'an implacable dislike and discontentment of all the nobility', 'Answer to Stubbs' Gaping Gulf', in *John Stubb's Gaping Gulf*, ed. Berry, pp. 173–5.

32 See Peck, *Northampton*, p. 11. While John Aylmer had written against John Knox's *The First Blast of the Trumpet Against the Monstrous Regiment of Women* on behalf of Elizabeth in the 1550s, John Leslie, Bishop of Ross, had published tracts from 1567 on attacking Knox for questioning Mary's right to rule, one of which was republished in 1584. Constance Jordan, 'Woman's Rule in Sixteenth-Century British Political Thought', *Renaissance Quarterly*, 40 (1987), 421–51; Dennis Moore is preparing an edition of Northampton's treatise.

33 Howard's translation exists in different versions: 'The summe of diverse directions of government which Charles 5th lefte unto his sonne Philip ye III k of Spaine', Yale University, Beinecke Library, Osborn Shelves, b. 31; B.L. Kings MS 166; and 'The Emperor Charles V's political instructions to his son from Philip II', B.L. Lansdowne MS 792. James Craigie, *The Basilikon Doron of James I* (Edinburgh, 1950), II, pp. 63–9.

34 See, for instance, his support for the French match in 'An Answer to Stubbs' Gaping Gulf', pp. 156, 177.

35 See Nannerl L. Keohane, *Philosophy and the State in France* (Princeton, 1980), p. 43; Donald L. Kelley, *Foundations of Modern Historical Scholarship* (New York, 1970).

36 John Bossy, *The English Catholic Community, 1570–1850* (London, 1975); Peck, *Northampton*, pp. 9, 70–1; Northampton represents, what has been called Catholic 'survivalism'. See Christopher Haigh, *The English Reformation Revised* (Cambridge, 1987), pp. 176–208.

37 *A Defense of the Ecclesiasticall Regiment in Englande*, pp. 192–3.

38 *Ibid.*, pp. 27, 28.

39 *Ibid.*, pp. 3, 4, 8, 111–15.

40 Howard does present two definitions of tyrants, one of which could be resisted under Roman law, 'that by murder of the rightful heires . . . aspireth to the state without title, right, etc.' B.L. Titus C VI, f. 224v.

41 Peck, *Northampton*, pp. 179–80. B.L. Titus C VI, ff. 409v.

42 Constance Jordan, 'Woman's Rule in Sixteenth-Century British Political Thought'.

43 'Dutiful Defense of the Lawful Regiment of Women', ff. 248–248v. Howard dedicated his first treatise on natural philosophy to his sister, Katherine Berkeley, and in it endorsed the education of women.

44 'Dutiful Defense of the Lawful Regiment of Women', f. 33v. 'Lipsius a learned wryter of our tyme speaketh of this matter in my conceite neither soe clearely as he ought nor soe plainely as weare requisite. First he alleageth out of Seneca that nature gave not force to weomen but onely filled their breasts with deciets: Concealing the cheefe point which is that Seneca durst not avowe those words out of his owne conceyt but in the person of that Tyrant Nero at such tyme as he was working how to bee dyvorsed from his chast and lawfull wyfe Octavia' f. 103.

45 'Dutiful Defense of the Lawful Regiment of Women', f. 34v; see Constance Jordan who discusses the importance of the notion of effeminacy to arguments against women's rule, 'Women's Rule in Sixteenth-Century British Political Thought', pp. 421–51.

46 Howard, 'A Dutiful Defense', f. 14–14v. See Bodin, *Six Bookes of a Commonweale*, trans. Richard Knolles (London, 1606), Book II, ch. 3, p. 204 for some similar limitations on the monarch. Howard seemed to suggest in a work of 1580 that parliament had historically played a role in electing the monarchy. 'Edward the Second was for his insufficiency and intolerable imperfections deposed from the crown, we see, notwithstanding that Edward the Third, his son, was elected in his place by the general consent of the Parliament, which was not willing to discontinue so lineal a descent in succession although desirous to report those abuses in government.' 'An Answer to Stubbs' Gaping Gulf', pp. 162–3.

47 B.L. Cotton MS Titus C VI, ff. 213, 218.

48 *Ibid.*, ff. 213v–214. Bodin, *The Six Bookes of a Commonweale*, Book II, pp. 200–1.

49 B.L. Cotton MS Titus C VI, f. 214.

50 *Ibid.*, ff. 215, 219. See *The Trew Law of Free Monarchies* in C. H. McIlwain (ed.), *The Political Works of James VI and I* (Cambridge, Mass., 1918), pp. 61–2.

51 B.L. Titus C VI, ff. 213v–214. Book VIII was not published until 1648: 'Touching the supremacy of power which our kings have in this case of making laws, it resteth principally in the strength of a negative voice', ch. 6, 112v–113, R. A. Houk, *Hooker's Ecclesiastical Polity, Book VIII* (New York, 1931), p. 244.

52 B.L. Titus C VI, f. 263. Because Northampton's English translation or paraphrase of passages from Bodin's *Six Livres de la République* differs from that of Richard Knolles first published in 1606, it would appear that the Earl worked from an earlier French edition, probably the original edition of 1576. In other contexts Northampton turned to origins to understand the powers of political institutions as in his speech to parliament in 1606–7 when he argued that members of the House of Commons were 'not fit to examine or determine secrets of state' because their original foundation was to provide 'a private and local wisdom', Peck, *Northampton*, p. 194.

53 B.L. Titus C VI, ff. 262v–264. Bodin, *Six Bookes*, Book II, chs. 3 and 4.

54 *A Defense of the Ecclesiastical Regiment in England*, p. 193.

55 Berosus wrote a history of Babylonia in the third century BC.

56 Peck, *Northampton*, pp. 101–21 and *passim*; Kevin Sharpe, *The Political Career of Sir Robert Cotton* (Oxford, 1979), pp. 114–28.

57 Grafton and Jardine, *From Humanism to the Humanities*, pp. 210–20.

58 Castiglione, *The Courtier*, pp. 346–7.

59 The Venetian ambassador said that the fact that Northampton was considered a Catholic gave his writing greater stature. *Cal. S.P. Venetian 1603–1607*, pp. 438–9, 7 December 1606.

60 See Northampton's speech in the parliament of 1604 in *Northampton*, p. 182.

61 Philip Watson's *A History of the Reign of Philip III*, 2nd edn (2 vols.; London,

1786), II, p. 245. A report of the negotiations by Sir Thomas Edmondes, now catalogued as B.L. Add. MS 14033, was published as an appendix to Watson's work. Another account exists in HMC *Appendix to the 8th Report*, the Earl of Jersey's Manuscripts. After Northampton's speech, the senator of Milan presented an oration in Latin at greater length, and more religious, learned and elaborate than that of Northampton. J. H. Burns and Quentin Skinner argue that Calvinist resistance theory was based on the arguments developed during the conciliar movement by writers such as John Major. Lutherans and Calvinists used such arguments precisely because they would be recognizable to their opponents. Similarly, Northampton used natural law theory and Catholic theorists to make his points. J. H. Burns, *John Major*; Quentin Skinner, 'Calvinist Resistance Theory' in *After the Reformation*, ed. B. Malament (Philadelphia, 1980), pp. 309–30; see also Richard Tuck, *Natural Rights Theories* (Cambridge, 1979).

62 Here I go beyond my discussion in *Northampton*, pp. 104–10.

63 P.R.O. S.P.94/10, f. 215, Northampton to Sir Thomas Edmondes (1605). Northampton worked with Sir Thomas Edmondes, who prepared a report, perhaps for publication. Peck, *Northampton*, pp. 109–10.

64 Watson, *A History of the Reign of Philip III*, II, p. 265. Even if the pope as pastor had to settle disputes within his fold, 'yet as St. Paul refused plainly to judge of those that are without the Church, so likewise it might be thought hard by some princes which were not within the fold, to hearken to the voice of a strange shepherd'. In 1635 John Selden used natural right theory and the work of Grotius, which he challenged at some points, to make precisely the opposite claim on behalf of Charles I and English fishing against Dutch claims. Tuck, *Natural Rights Theories*, pp. 86–8.

65 In making his argument he provided examples of papal conflict with the Emperors, cited Giucciardini, contemporary Catholic writers, such as de Soto and Bellarmine, even 'a discreete Cardinall', at the recent conclave that chose the new pope, Pius V. *A True and Perfect Relation*, Dd, Gg2, Qq–Qq4v, Ddd 4. See also *Northampton*, pp. 111–13.

66 The Venetian ambassador reported that 'The Earl of Northampton, one of the great Lords of this kingdom, a man of letters, member of the Privy Council has . . . complete[d] a book on the late plot . . . hostile to the pretended superiority of popes over princes in matters temporal. The work is highly commended by all, by the king in particular', *Cal. S.P. Ven. 1603–1607*, 438–9, 7 December 1606.

67 *Ibid.*; 'A Premonition to All Most Mightie Monarches, Kings, Free Princes, and States of Christendome' in *The Political Works of James I*, ed. McIlwain, pp. 161–4.

68 William Bouwsma, *Venice and the Defense of Republican Liberty* (Berkeley, 1968), p. 309. The work to which Northampton referred was *Avviso delle ragioni della serenissima repubblica di Venezia intorno alle difficoltà, che le sono promosse dalla Santità di Papa Paolo V* (Venice, 1606). There is a suggestion that this may have been written by Marcantonio De Dominis not Querini, see John Lievsay, *Venetian Phoenix: Paolo Sarpi* (Kansas, 1973), pp. 28 and 212n.

69 Bouwsma, *Venice and the Defense of Republican Liberty*, p. 365n113.
70 Bouwsma, 'Venice and the Political Education of Europe' in *Renaissance Venice*, ed. J. R. Hale (London, 1973), p. 445.
71 'The Republic, as free and independent prince, has by the nature of its principate, authority over all its subjects indifferently.' Quoted in Bouwsma, *Venice and the Defense of Republican Liberty*, p. 440. In his own manuscript on government, Northampton, like other contemporary theorists, denied that the Duke of Venice was a sovereign prince. 'The Duke of Venice's prerogative is only to give his voice first without any prerogative in matters of state above any ordinary senator', B.L. Titus C VI, f. 234.
72 See Bouwsma, *Venice and the Defense of Republican Liberty*, p. 440. Paolo Sarpi defended Venetian interests in similar terms:

> no injury penetrates more deeply into a principate than when its majesty, that is to say sovereignty, is limited and subjected to the laws of another . . .He who takes away a part of his state from a prince makes him a lesser prince but leaves him a prince; he who imposes laws and obligations on him deprives him of the essence of a prince, even if he possessed the whole of Asia.

Quoted in Bouwsma, *Venice and the Defense of Republican Liberty*, pp. 437–8, 445.
73 Bouwsma, 'Venice and the Political Education of Europe', p. 457. 'Venetian freedom . . . was the most widely celebrated element in the myth of Venice; its attractiveness signified resistance to the idea of a universal empire.' If Northampton was an odd republican ally, Venice was an odd republic, but one which continued to be emblematic in English politics into the 1620s and beyond. In 1621 Richard Crakanthorp, drew on Querini for similar propositions: that Christ had 'refused to meddle with temoral causes' and that 'the Venetian Commonwealth is as a free prince . . . which by the nature of principality depends on none' and that the Venetian commonwealth claimed dominion from God only, and this is the very fundamental law of their state'. Quoted in Lievesay, *Venetian Phoenix*, pp. 117 and 224n. The history of *The True and Perfect Relation*, which the king called 'The Earl of Northampton's Book', did not end with these Jacobean controversies. It was republished in 1679 under the editorship of the Calvinist bishop, Thomas Barlow, who used it to attack the future James II during the Exclusion crisis. Northampton who had embraced the legitimist theories of the Stuarts would, no doubt, have been uncomfortable with this use of his speeches to challenge the right of James Stuart to succeed to the throne. Barlow omitted Northampton's lengthy treatise: 'After this, the Earl of Northampton, made a learned speech which in itself was very copious, and the intention being to contract this volume as much as might be, and to keep only to matter of fact, it was thought convenient to omit the same', p. 223. Barlow used the rest of the book in which Northampton and Salisbury strongly questioned papal authority and stressed responsibility of Catholics to their prince. Barlow made the Venetian connection in the introduction by citing 'Father Paul's History of Trent'.
74 *A True and Perfect Relation of the Whole proceedings against the late most*

barbarous Traitors, Garnet, a Jesuite, and his Confederats, STC 11619 (London, 1606), sig. Ee3v.

75 *A Publication of His Majesty's Edict, and Severe Censure Against Private Combats and Combatants*, STC 8498, pp. 24–5, 36–9, 34, 95, 41–2. This tract accompanied 'A Proclamation against private Challenges and Combats: With Articles annexed for the better directions to be used therein, and for the more judicial proceeding against offenders', 4 February 1614; Larkin and Hughes, *Stuart Royal Proclamations*, no. 136, p. 305.

76 Peck, *Northampton*, pp. 181–4, 194.

77 B.L. Egerton MS 2877, f. 167v.

78 Peck, *Northampton, passim*; E. R. Foster, *Proceedings in Parliament, 1610* (2 vols.; New Haven, 1966), I, pp. 270, 274–5.

79 B.L. Cotton MS Titus B IV, f. 178. Northampton attacked the practices of 'pensions paid private' that is 'not recorded in the receipt but taken from the . . . receivers or farmers' so that income was not only not certain but consistently fell short.

80 B.L. Cotton MS Cleo F VI, ff. 102, 100–100v.

81 See Peck, *Northampton*, pp. 200–4. Northampton's speech of 14 November 1610 in Elizabeth Read Foster, *Proceedings in Parliament, 1610* (2 vols.; New Haven, 1966), I, pp. 259–75.

82 Norbert Elias, *The Court Society*, trans. Edmund Jephcott (Oxford, 1983), p. 50.

83 Peck, *Northampton*, pp. 26–7.

84 He also reburied a Howard infant who had died in the previous century at the urging of the antiquary Sir Henry Spelman. The lack of any religious statement may be due to Northampton's Catholicism or to the fact that the tomb was completed by his secretary, John Griffith.

85 Peck, *Northampton*, p. 182; *A True and Perfect Relation*, Ddd4v–Eee.

86 D. C. Peck (ed.), *Leicester's Commonwealth* (Columbus, Ohio, 1985), pp. 172–3.

87 Peck, *Northampton*, p. 20.

88 *Ibid.*, p. 21.

89 See Ellery Schalk, *From Valor to Pedigree* (Princeton, 1986), for sixteenth-century France.

90 Peck, *Northampton*, pp. 156–60; W. H. Dunham, Jr, 'William Camden's Common Place Book', *Yale Library Gazette*, 43 (January 1969), 152. He shared the view put forward by Essex as Earl Marshal in 1599 that 'all nobility is from the prince . . . the upholding of nobility is a most necessary and religious care, for in holy histories the succession of nobility is recorded.'

91 Folger Shakespeare Library, Vb7, pp. 88–9.

92 *Northampton*, p. 182. The king's order shows competing demands of the ancient nobility and the Scots. It boded ill for the remaining Elizabethan councillors. While the king did not want greatly to increase numbers of councillors, he wanted to allow 'entry for such of the ancient nobility whose birth and merit makes them more capable than others, nor to forbear to prefer such of our

subjects of Scotland at this time as we shall have occasion to use, and desire to grace about us', P.R.O. S.O. 3/2, 10 May 1603.

93 P.R.O. S.P. 14/19/12.

94 Preface, *A Defensative against the Poyson of Supposed Prophecies.*

95 Peck, *Northampton*, pp. 81–3, 166–7.

96 Quoted in J. F. Bradley and J. Q. Adams, *The Jonson Allusion Book* (New Haven, 1922), pp. 71–2.

97 In his tract on monarchy Northampton had described a problem uncomfortably familiar to Jacobeans:

> When a prince is to pitifull and almost refuseth no pardone flatterers and bribers doo what theie liste and even as rewmes fall to the weaker partes in a sickelie bodie so doo all dangeres and disgraces during this distemper upon the common people. The example is Henry 2 of Fraunce who by his immoderate gifts uppon to great facility brought himself into that want as he was glad to recover himself againe by setting offices and [honor?] etc to sale and by spoylinge one to content another.
>
> B.L. Titus C VI, f. 264.

98 *Ibid.*, f. 483.

99 Loomie, *Spain and the Jacobean Catholics, 1613–1624*, pp. 38–40. Edward Hasted, *History of Kent* (4 vols.; Canterbury, 1778) I, p. 21.

100 E. P. Shirley, 'An inventory of the effects of Henry Howard, K.G., Earl of Northampton . . . with a transcript of his will', *Archaeologia*, 42 (1869), 364; in the Lowe Wardrobe was 'a carpet and cupboord clothe of purple velvett with silver and silke frindge belonginge to the bed where my Lord died'.

101 I am grateful to Philippa Glanville, Curator of Metalwork at the Victoria and Albert Museum, for drawing these objects to my attention and for advice on Jacobean silver generally. See her *Silver in Tudor and Early Stuart England* (London, 1990).

102 Shirley, 'An inventory', *Archaeologia*, 42 (1869), 364. Amongst his silver can be found New Year's gifts from ambassadors and clients such as the Earl of Rutland.

103 This picture is probably the Robert Peake portrait now at Parham Park showing Prince Henry armed, mounted on horseback, and leading Opportunity by the forelock. I am grateful to A. R. Braunmuller for this information.

104 Andrew Lang, *Portraits and Jewels of Mary Stuart* (Glasgow, 1906).

105 See B. L. Titus C VI, f. 204 where in a fragment of an undated entertainment he referred to the 'coming of a Fairy Queen' and to himself as 'this old doting hermit'. The motif of the old hermit was a common one in the Elizabethan period: Sir Robert Cecil presented an entertainment at Theobalds in which he made 'An Old Hermit' speech and Sir Francis Bacon wrote several speeches for an entertainment a year later for a soldier, squire, secretary of state and an old hermit. See Nichols, *Progresses*, pp. 241–50. Such a figure, important in Shakespeare's *Timon of Athens*, appears to be a figure of folklore and perhaps of religious or alchemical significance. I am grateful to Werner Gundersheimer, David Bevington, Lena Orlin and Barbara Mowat and A. R. Braunmuller for discussion of this point.

106 Eugene Rice, *St. Jerome in the Renaissance* (Baltimore, 1985).
107 Northampton's will and inventory is in *Archaeologia*, 42 (1869), 347–78.
108 In the trial of the Earl of Somerset and Frances Howard for the murder of Sir Thomas Overbury, the evidence included the encoded writings between Somerset and Overbury in which 'the King was called Julius in respect of Empire; the Queen, Agrippina, Nero's mother, agreeable to that Northampton said that Prince Henry if he reigned would prove a Tyrant; The Archbishop, Unctious, The Chancellor, The Lawyer, Suffolk, first Laerma and after Woolsey, Pembroke, Niger, Northampton, Dominican, The Countess of Essex, Catopard, Salisbury Ignatius founder of all mischiefe, Nevill, simimilis, as being king: H: etc', HEH, Ellesmere MS 5979, f. 7.
109 B.L. Titus C VI ff. 203–4. Northampton apotheosized James as 'Rex pacificus . . . which according to Merline's prediction was to hold in one paw the Battlements of new Troy, in an other Sylvan Caledoniam', *A True and Perfect Relation*, Dd, Gg2, Qq1v, Ddd 4.
110 Folger Shakespeare Library, Loseley Manuscripts, L.B. 638, Inventory of the Effects of Robert Carr, Earl of Somerset, 29 November 1615. Somerset too lavished his apartments with tapestries on classical and scriptural themes such as Moses and Aaron, but more celebrated the Trojan War, Venus and Adonis and other classical love themes, and see A. R. Braunmuller in this volume.
111 David Howarth, *Lord Arundel and his Circle* (New Haven, 1985); Kevin Sharpe, *Sir Robert Cotton, 1586–1631* (Oxford, 1979).
112 See Howarth, *Lord Arundel and his Circle*, pp. 2, 37.
113 *Ibid.*, pp. 53–4.
114 Edward Hasted, *History of Kent* (London, 1886), I, p. 31.
115 HMC *Downshire*, IV, pp. 433–4.
116 HMC *Downshire*, V (London, 1988), p. 143.

10 Seneca and Tacitus in Jacobean England

In a longer and differently arranged version, this paper has been published as 'Stoicism and Roman Example: Seneca and Tacitus in Jacobean England' in Journal of the History of Ideas, 50 (1989), 199–225.

1 Tacitus's references to Seneca are at *Annals*, xiii.2, 6, 20; xiv.52–6; xv.60–5.
2 Peter Burke, 'Tacitism' in *Tacitus*, ed. T. A. Dorey (London, 1969), pp. 149–71; Theodore G. Corbett, 'The Cult of Lipsius: A Leading Source of Early Modern Spanish Statecraft', *Journal of the History of Ideas*, 36 (1975), 139–52; Morris W. Croll, *Style, Rhetoric and Rhythm* (Princeton, 1966); Else-Lilly Etter, *Tacitus in der Geistes Geschichte des 16. und 17. Jahrhunderts* (Basel, 1966); J. H. M. Salmon, 'Cicero and Tacitus in Sixteenth-Century France', *American Historical Review*, 85 (1980), 307–31; Jurgen von Stackelberg, *Tacitus in der Romania* (Tübingen, 1960); André Stegmann, 'Le Tacitisme' in his *Machiavellismo e Antimachiavellici nel Cinquecento* (Florence, 1969), pp. 117–30; F. E. Sutcliffe, *Politique et Culture, 1560–1660* (Paris, 1973); Giuseppe Toffanin, *Machiavelli e*

il 'Tacitismo' (Paris, 1921); L. Zanta, *La Renaissance du Stoicisme au XVIe siècle* (Paris, 1914).

3 Many particular studies on the influence of Stoicism on Elizabethan and Jacobean literature have been consolidated and extended by Gilles D. Monsarrat, *Light from the Porch: Stoicism and English Renaissance Literature* (Paris, 1984). On the significance of Tacitus in English historiography see F. J. Levy, *Tudor Historical Thought* (San Marino, 1967), and 'Hayward, Daniel and the Beginnings of Politic History', *Huntington Library Quarterly*, 50 (1987), 1–34. Introductory sketches of Tacitean influence on English political thought are provided by Mary F. Tenney, 'Tacitus in the Politics of Early Stuart England', *Classical Journal*, 37 (1941), 151–63; Alan T. Bradford, 'Stuart Absolutism and the "Utility" of Tacitus', *Huntington Library Quarterly*,m 45 (1983), 127–55; and Kenneth C. Schellhase, *Tacitus in Renaissance Political Thought* (Chicago, 1976), pp. 157–68.

4 Gerhard Oestreich, *Neostoicism and the Early Modern State* (Cambridge, 1982), p. 14.

5 *Two Bookes of Constancie Written in Latin by Iustus Lipsius, Englished by Sir John Stradling*, ed. with intr. Rudolf Kirk, notes by Clayton Morris Hall (New Brunswick, 1939), p. 116.

6 Jason Lewis Saunders, *Justus Lipsius: The Philosophy of Renaissance Stoicism* (New York, 1955), p. 111.

7 *Constancie* (ed. Kirk), p. 197.

8 *Ibid.*, p. 207.

9 Oestreich, *Neostoicism*, p. 58.

10 Montaigne, *The Essays or Moral, Politic Discourses*, trans. John Florio (London, 1603); Du Vair, *The Moral Philosophy of the Stoics*, trans. Thomas Page (London, 1598); *A Buckler against Adversity*, trans. Anthony Court (London, 1622); *The True Way to Virtue and Happiness*, trans. Anthony Court (London, 1623); Charron, *Of Wisdom*, trans. Samson Lennard (London, n.d. [1606?]). Spelling of titles and quotations has been modernized throughout, except for titles of modern reprints and quotations in verse.

11 Levy, 'Hayward, Daniel . . . ', p. 9.

12 Du Plessis-Mornay, *A Work concerning the Trueness of the Christian Religion* (London, 1587), pp. 36–7.

13 Monsarrat, *Light from the Porch*, p. 23.

14 Lennard translated Mornay's *The Mystery of Iniquity* (London, 1611), an anti-papal diatribe. His version of Charron's *Of Wisdom* had several reprintings in 1612 at the height of the Jacobean Neostoic movement.

15 Levy, 'Hayward, Daniel . . . ', p. 10.

16 Mary Herbert's rendering of Mornay's *Life and Death* was accompanied by her translation of a tragedy in the Senecan mode by the French poet, Robert Garnier: *A Discourse of Life and Death: Antonius a Tragedy. Both done into English by the Countess of Pembroke* (London, 1592). On the fashion for Senecan tragedy see F. L. Lucas, *Seneca and Elizabethan Tragedy* (Cambridge, 1922).

17 *The End of Nero and Beginning of Galba. Four Books of the Histories of*

Cornelius Tacitus. The Life of Agricola, trans. Savile (Oxford, 1591); *The Annals of Cornelius Tacitus. The Description of Germany*, trans. Greneway (London, 1598). Joint editions appeared in 1598, 1604/1605, 1612, 1622.

18 *The Life and Letters of Francis Bacon*, ed. James Spedding *et al.* (London, 1890), II, p. 320.

19 *The Essayes of Michael Lord of Montaigne translated by John Florio* (London, n.d. – Everyman edn), III.8, 'The Art of Conferring', V, p. 265.

20 *Histories*, trans. Savile, unpaginated prefatory material.

21 Thomas Lodge, *The Wounds of Civil War lively set forth in the true tragedies of Marius and Scilla* (London, 1594); William Fulbecke, *The Historical Collection of the Continued Factions, Tumults and Massacres of the Romans and Italians* (London, 1601); Samuel Daniel, *The First Four Books in the Civil Wars between the Two Houses of Lancaster and York* (London, 1595); Michael Drayton, *The Barons' Wars in the Reign of Edward the Second* (London, 1603); John Hayward, *The First Part of the Life and Reign of King Henry IV* (London, 1599). To these, of course, many of Shakespeare's history plays could be added.

22 *Annals*, trans. Greneway, unpaginated prefatory material.

23 Cited by F. J. Levy in his introduction to *Francis Bacon, the History of the Reign of Henry VII* (Indianapolis, 1972), p. 41.

24 Levy, 'Hayward, Daniel . . . ', pp. 17–19.

25 Logan Pearsall Smith, *The Life and Letters of Sir Henry Wotton* (Oxford, 1907), I, p. 236. Cf. Wotton's despatch to Salisbury, 18 September 1609, in *ibid.*, p. 471.

26 *Ibid.*, I, p. 30. See in general Gustav Ungerer, *A Spaniard in Elizabethan England: The Correspondence of Antonio Perez's Exile* (2 vols., London, 1974–8).

27 Logan Pearsall Smith, *Wotton*, II, pp. 109, 210.

28 Spedding, *Bacon*, II, p. 8.

29 *Ibid.*, p. 22. The recipient is shown as Fulke Greville, but it cannot possibly be Sidney's friend and contemporary.

30 Bacon, *Essays* (London, n.d. [1597, 1625]), pp. 55, 95–7, 105, 41 (against the Stoics).

31 Schellhase, *Tacitus*, pp. 161–2. In general see Edwin B. Benjamin, 'Bacon and Tacitus', *Classical Philology*, 60 (1965), 102–10.

32 Vincent Luciani, 'Bacon and Guicciardini', *Publications of the Modern Language Association of America*, 62 (1947), 96–113.

33 R. Johnson, *Essays or rather Imperfect Offers* (London, 1601), unpaginated. Cited by Benjamin, 'Bacon and Tacitus', p. 103.

34 On Henry Howard see Linda Levy Peck, *Northampton: Patronage and Policy at the Court of James I* (London, 1982).

35 *Essayes by Sir William Cornwallis the Younger*, ed. Don Cameron Allen (Baltimore, 1946), p. 51.

36 *Ibid.*, p. 234.

37 *Ibid.*, p. 63.

38 Sir William Cornwallis, *Discourses upon Seneca the Tragedian*, introd. Robert Hood Bowers (Gainesville, 1952), unpaginated.

39 Roy Strong, *Henry Prince of Wales and England's Lost Renaissance* (New York, 1986), p. 223.
40 Sir Charles Cornwallis, 'A Discourse of the Most Illustrious Prince Henry, late Prince of Wales' in *The Somers Collection of Tracts* (London, 1809), II, p. 218.
41 Cited from D'Ewes's *Autobiography* by R. Malcolm Smuts, *Court Culture and the Origins of a Royalist Tradition in Early Stuart England* (Philadelphia, 1987), p. 26.
42 Barbara K. Lewalski, 'Lucy, Countess of Bedford: Images of a Jacobean Courtier and Patroness' in *Politics and Discourse: The Literature and History of Seventeenth-Century England*, eds. Kevin Sharpe and Steven N. Zwicker (Berkeley, 1987), pp. 52–77.
43 Peck, *Northampton*, p. 1.
44 Thomas Greene, 'Ben Jonson and the Centered Self', *Studies in English Literature*, 10 (1970), 325–48; Katharine Eisaman Maus, *Ben Jonson and the Roman Frame of Mind* (Princeton, 1984), pp. 15–20.
45 *Ben Jonson's Sejanus His Fall*, ed. Henry de Vocht (Louvain, 1935), p. 15.
46 Anne Barton, *Ben Jonson, Dramatist* (Cambridge, 1984), p. 92.
47 *Ibid.*, p. 100.
48 *Ibid.*, p. 96.
49 *Sejanus* (ed. Vocht), p. 41, lines 1331–40.
50 Barbara N. De Luna, *Jonson's Romish Plot: A Study of Catiline in its Historical Context* (Oxford, 1967).
51 *Sejanus* (ed. Vocht), p. 17, lines 441–56.
52 Karl Joseph Höltgen, 'Sir Robert Dallington (1561–1637): Author, Traveler and Pioneer of Taste', *Huntington Library Quarterly*, 47 (1984), 153–4. Dallington, *The View of France* (London, 1604); *A Survey of the Great Duke's State of Tuscany* (London, 1605).
53 Montaigne, *Essayes*, III.8, V, p. 265.
54 Francesco Sansovino, *The Quintessence of Wit*, trans. Richard Hitchcock (London, 1590); Remigio Nannini, *Civil Considerations upon many and sundry Histories as well ancient as modern, done into French by G. Chappuys and into English by W.I.* (London, 1602). Cf. Levy, 'Hayward, Daniel . . . ', p. 9.
55 *Aphorisms Civil and Military, amplified with authorities and exemplified out of the first quarterne of Guicciardini* (London, 1613), pp. 314–15.
56 *Ibid.*, p. 176.
57 Huntington Library MS EL 6857.
58 Gainsford, *Observations*, pp. 17–47.
59 *Ibid.*, p. 57.
60 *Ibid.*, p. 23.
61 *Ibid.*, pp. 9, 16, 36.
62 *Ibid.*, p. 10.
63 *Ibid.*, p. 34.
64 *The History of the Most Renowned and Victorious Princess Elizabeth*, ed. Wallace T. MacCaffrey (Chicago, 1970), p. 7.

65 Kevin Sharpe, *Sir Robert Cotton, 1586–1631: History and Politics in Early Modern England* (Oxford, 1979), p. 106.

66 Audrey Chew, 'Joseph Hall and Neo-Stoicism', *Publications of the Modern Language Association of America*, 65 (1950), 1130; Monsarrat, *Light from the Porch*, p. 98. A recent biography is by F. L. Huntley, *Bishop Joseph Hall, 1574–1656: A Biographical and Critical Study* (Cambridge, 1979).

67 *Heaven upon Earth and Characters of Vertues and Vices*, ed. Rudolf Kirk (New Brunswick, 1948), p. 84. Hall's autobiographical fragment is printed in his *Works*, ed. Peter Hall (12 vols., Oxford, 1837), I, pp. xi–xxxiv.

68 *Heaven upon Earth* (ed. Kirk), pp. 88–94.

69 Theophrastus antedated Zeno. Du Plessis-Mornay (*Trueness*, p. 34) was among those who took him for a Stoic.

70 *Heaven upon Earth* (ed. Kirk), pp. 200–1.

71 *Ibid.*, p. 181.

72 Hall, *Works*, I, pp. xix–xxi; Edward Andrews Tenney, *Thomas Lodge* (Ithaca, New York, 1935), p. 173.

73 Saunders, *Lipsius*, pp. 51–3.

74 *The Famous and Memorable Works of Josephus, a Man of Much Honor and Learning among the Jews, faithfully translated out of the Latin and French by Thomas Lodge, Doctor of Physic* (London, 1632 [1602]), 'To the Courteous Reader Touching the Use and Abuse of History', unpaginated.

75 N. Burton Paradise, *Thomas Lodge: The History of an Elizabethan* (New Haven, 1931), p. 171.

76 Montaigne, *Essayes*, II.35, 'Of Three Good Women', II, pp. 323–4.

77 *The Works both Moral and Natural of Lucius Annaeus Seneca translated by Thomas Lodge, Doctor in Physic* (London, 1614). An additional title page bears the date 1613.

78 *Epictetus his Manual and Cebes his Table* (London, 1610). Healey added to Epictetus the *Pinax*, attributed to the Pythagorean philosopher Cebes, but in fact a late Stoic work. Another English translation of the *Manual*, by J. Sanford, had been published in 1567.

79 Monsarrat, *Light from the Porch*, pp. 118–25.

80 *A Learned Summary upon the Famous Poem of William of Saluste* (London, 1621); *Philip Mornay, Lord of Plessis, his Tears for the Death of his Son* (London, 1609); Hall, *The Discovery of a New World* (London, 1609).

81 Montaigne, *Essayes*, II.32, IV, p. 275.

82 Monsarrat, *Light from the Porch*, p. 106.

83 *Ibid.*, p. 107.

84 Mark Pattison, *Isaac Casaubon, 1559–1614* (Oxford, 1892, 2nd edn), pp. 280–1.

85 Bradford, 'Stuart Absolutism', pp. 135–7; Schellhase, *Tacitus*, pp. 145–9. John Florio and others translated the *Ragguagli* as *The New-Found Politic* (London, 1626).

86 Bradford, 'Stuart Absolutism', pp. 139–45.

87 Wheare, *De Ratione et Methodo Legendi Historias Dissertatio* (Oxford, 1623).

The quotation comes from Edmund Bohun's translation, *The Method and Order of Reading both Civil and Ecclesiastical History* (London, 1698), pp. 106–7. Lipsius's original text is in *C. Cornelii Taciti Opera Omnia quae extant* (Antwerp, 1581), p. 4^r.

88 Wheare, *Method and Order*, p. 7.

89 Mark H. Curtis, 'The Alienated Intellectuals of Early Stuart England', *Past and Present*, 23 (1962), 26–7.

90 Mary F. Tenney, 'Tacitus', p. 60.

91 Sharpe, *Cotton*, p. 106.

11 The court of the first Stuart queen

1 See Pam Wright, 'A Change in Direction: The Ramification of a Female Household, 1558–1603' in *The English Court*, eds. David Starkey *et al.* (London, 1987), pp. 147–72. See also Neil Cuddy, 'The Revival of the Entourage: the Bedchamber of James I, 1603–1625' in Starkey (ed.), *The English Court*, pp. 173–225, esp. 177–8, 195–6.

2 See Roy Strong, *Henry Prince of Wales, and England's Lost Renaissance* (London, 1986), pp. 16 ff. See also Agnes Strickland, *Lives of the Queens of England* (London, 1842–88), IV, pp. 62–5; Frances Yates, *John Florio* (Cambridge, 1934), pp. 248–9; Maurice Lee, Jr, *John Maitland of Thirlestane* (Princeton, 1959), pp. 204, 286–8; G. P. V. Akrigg, *Jacobean Pageant* (Cambridge, Mass., 1962), *passim*. In a book-length biography, Anna has been given quite a silly character, perhaps unconsciously, by E. C. Williams, *Anne of Denmark* (London, 1971). This biography is full of errors of fact and assumption: the most reliable life is still the essay in *DNB* by Adolphus William Ward, but even he summarizes Anna with the term 'frivolous'.

3 John Florio became a groom of the Queen's Privy Chamber in 1604 and Samuel Daniel in 1614; see Yates, *Florio*, p. 246. For a list of Anna's household before 18 March 1606, see *Salisbury MSS* (London: 1883–1976), XXIV, pp. 65–7.

4 Uraniborg held sixteen stone furnaces for distilling, while on the floors above were a library and a museum, and on the second floor, a large sitting-room adjoining four apartments. The towers contained observatories and the whole was supplied with running water powered by a pressure pump from a well eighty feet deep. See Joakim A. Skovgaard, *A King's Architecture* (London, 1973), pp. 15–16.

5 Anna's mother also helped Tycho gain power of appointment over the succession to the control of Uraniborg. See J. L. E. Dreyer, *Tycho Brahe* (Edinburgh, 1890), p. 200n1.

6 For the comment to Burghley, see Sir Henry Ellis, *Original Letters*, 2nd ser. (London, 1827), III, p. 149: the letter of Daniel Rogers to Lord Burghley in 1588. It is also noted by Adolphus William Ward in *DNB*, I, p. 431.

7 Ellis, *Original Letters*, III, p. 149. The formal wedding was planned for November, 1589, but Anna's crossing was so delayed by autumn storms that James sailed to Norway, where he married her again on 23 November. See David Moysie, *Memoires of the Affairs of Scotland* (Edinburgh, 1830), pp. 81–3.

8 For the texts see James I, *New Poems*, ed. Allan F. Westcott (New York, 1911), pp. 26–7, and James VI, *Poems*, ed. James Craigie (Edinburgh, 1958), II, pp. 100–1.

9 This is so far as can be determined from the regular reports of the English agent in Scotland to Lord Burghley, reports that were minutely attentive to the states of James and Anna. But in the nine years which would extend from the birth of her first son to Anna's accession as Queen of England, she would bear five children, two of whom would not survive beyond the age of two, and become pregnant with another.

10 See Jennifer M. Brown, 'Scottish Politics 1567–1625' in *The Reign of James VI and I*, ed. Alan G. R. Smith (London, 1973), 22–40 and Keith M. Brown, *Bloodfeud in Scotland 1573–1625* (Edinburgh, 1986), pp. 107–44.

11 Brown, 'Scottish Politics', p. 172; see *Calendar of State Papers Relating to Scotland*, ed. W. K. Boyd and H. W. Meikle (Edinburgh, 1936), X, p. 437; hereafter cited as *SPS*. See also Moysie, *Memoires*, p. 102, and *Complete Peerage*, ed. H. A. Doubleday *et al.* (London, 1910–59), VI, p. 680.

12 See Maurice Lee, Jr., *John Maitland of Thirlestane* (Princeton, 1959), pp. 38–41.

13 See Lee, *Maitland*, p. 177, and David Mathew, *James I* (London, 1967), p. 55.

14 See *The Warrender Papers*, ed. Annie I. Cameron (Edinburgh, 1932), third ser., XIX, p. 10 and n. 2. For the more general question of the French influence in Scotland, see Denys Hay, 'Scotland and the Italian Renaissance' in *The Renaissance and Reformation in Scotland*, eds. I. B. Cowan and Duncan Shaw (Edinburgh, 1983), pp. 114–24.

15 See *SPS*, XIII, part 1, pp. 398–9 where she is described as 'a very subtle, wise lady'. In 1600 the Countess of Huntley was one of Prince Charles's godparents at his baptism: XIII, part 2, p. 758. For the Countess's Catholicism, see *Warrender Papers*, XIX, p. 328. For other instances of Anna's friendship with the Countess of Huntley, see *SPS*, XI, pp. 296, 359, 385, 390.

16 *SPS*, X, p. 591; XII, part 2, pp. 730, 758. Gordon Donaldson suggested that Anna's influence on the culture of the court and of Scotland may have been considerable: see *Scotland: James V to James VI* (Edinburgh, 1965), p. 186.

17 *SPS*, X, pp. 507, 450, 543–4. Anna also twice sided in those early days with Maitland in persuading King James to readmit nobles forbidden the court such as Sir Walter Scott, Laird of Buccleuch, in December 1591 – see *SPS*, X, pp. 602–10.

18 *SPS*, XI, p. 150; *Salisbury MSS*, IV, p. 178. The emotions generated in 1592 may be gathered from another report to Burghley. The queen many times 'falleth into tears, wishing herself either with her mother in Denmark, or else that she might see or speak with her majesty [Queen Elizabeth]', *SPS*, X, p. 722. For Anna's later pressure on the Chancellor, see *SPS*, X, pp. 788, 803, 824.

19 *SPS*, XI, pp. 78, 180, 88–100, 234, 237, 280, 554. For Aston, see Cuddy in Starkey (ed.), *The English Court*, pp. 188–9.

20 *SPS*, XI, p. 602. For Maitland's role here, see Lee, *Maitland*, pp. 286–8.

21 For the report of an extremely emotional confrontation between the king and queen at this time, see *SPS*, XI, pp. 662–3.

22 She intervened, for instance, to try to resolve Mar's feud with Livingston. See Keith M. Brown, *Bloodfeud*, pp. 130–2.

23 See *SPS*, XI, pp. 681–3; XII, pp. 313, 317; XIII, pp. 133, 264. A month before the birth of her third child on Christmas Eve 1598, for example, Anna informed King James of a plot being hatched against him by the Lords Erroll, Home, Cessford and others (*SPS*, XIII, p. 333).

24 *SPS*, XIII, pp. 679, 691. Sir Roger Aston, for one, and Sir George Home suggested to King James Anna's complicity in the plot, as did the Earl of Mar. But in this famously tangled ambiguity, we also note the Duke of Lennox, Anna's usual ally, observing that if there was a plot, he himself did not know 'whether the practice proceeded from Gowrie or the King'. See *SPS*, XIII, part 2, pp. 721–37.

25 See *SPS*, XIII, pp. 719, 727, 737. Two months later, in January 1601, the queen was again angry with the Earl of Mar and his faction and, by March, offended at the kirk's support, through Patrick Galloway, of James's procedure with the Gowries, she refused to hear Galloway's sermons and was busy trying to circumvent the kirk and to 'insinuate herself in the people's hearts' (*SPS*, XIII, p. 789).

26 *SPS*, XIII, p. 795. The ruling group referred to included the Earl of Mar, Sir Thomas Erskine and Sir George Home (see *SPS*, XIII, p. 762), all of whom would accompany James to England where Erskine would replace Sir Walter Raleigh as Captain of the Yeomen of the Guard (James's personal protectors) and Home would become Baron Home of Berwick (and Earl of Dunbar in Scotland).

27 *SPS*, XIII, pp. 1095–6. See also Strickland, IV, p. 55.

28 All of them would be sworn to the English Privy Council by 4 May 1603. See *Acts of the Privy Council of England*, ed. J. R. Dasent (London, 1890–1907), XXXII, pp. 496–7.

29 I have not been able to determine the political purpose of this group that may merely have been disaffected because they had not gone south with James. For the participants see *Register of the Privy Council of Scotland* (Edinburgh, 1884), ed. David Masson, pp. 571–2.

30 This reporter, writing on 18 May, was a little late in his news for according to another account, Anna 'parted with child' on 10 May. See David Calderwood, *History of the Kirk of Scotland* (Edinburgh, 1845), VI, pp. 230–1. For the Venetian ambassador's account, see *Calendar of State Papers . . . Venice*, ed. Horatio F. Brown (London, 1900), X, pp. 40, and 42 for a parallel account by the Venetian ambassador in France.

31 Before relinquishing Prince Henry into the care of the queen and of the Duke of Lennox while still in Scotland, Mar demanded formal action so the Privy Council of Scotland signed a 'warrand for delyverie of the Prince to the Duke of Lenox', officially discharging Mar from his guardian position. King James, however, delayed. He would register his own discharge in the 'Books of Secret Council' absolving Mar and his descendants forever from any further responsibility for heirs apparent, only after Mar should have undertaken in June 1603 'to

continue his careful and vigilant attendance upon the person of the Prince, his preservation and safe convoy in company of the Queen, his dearest mother, till he present him in safety to his Majesty. At the which time his Highness promises in his princely word to see him [Mar] gratified with a condigne remembrance to him and his in a perpetual record of his said service.' See *MSS of the Earl of Mar and Kellie at Alloa House* (London, 1904), 50–2, and *PCS*, VI, p. 571.

32 For example, Cuddy has argued that Anna was important in the appointments to James's Bedchamber (see Starkey (ed.), *The English Court*, pp. 194–5) while Roger Lockyer has noted Coventry's account of Anna's role in the advancement of George Villiers into James's favour – see *Buckingham* (London, 1981), pp. 19–20. John Chamberlain wrote in 1617 that the queen dreamt of 'a regencie' during the time James would return to Scotland for his visit (in N. E. C. McClure, *The Letters of John Chamberlain* (2 vols., Philadelphia, 1939), II, p. 47). But she was indeed appointed a member of a six-person committee to rule the kingdom in James's absence (*SPV*, XIV, p. 412). She also supported Sir Edward Coke for a baronage (*SPD*, IX, p. 413) and defended him when he was falling out of favour (*Chamberlain Letters*, II, p. 29).

33 *Salisbury MSS*, XII, p. 43. Elizabeth Lady Russell was the widow (first) of Sir Thomas Hoby and (second) of John Lord Russell who had been heir apparent to the 2nd Earl of Bedford but died before his father: she was the aunt of the 3rd Earl of Bedford, husband to the well-known Countess of Bedford. Elizabeth, daughter of Anthony Cook, had a sister, Mildred, who married the 1st Lord Burghley.

34 For these matters see also *Peerage*, XI, p. 550; *MSS of the Lord de L'Isle and Dudley*, ed. C. L. Kingsford and William A. Shaw (London: HMSO, 1936), II, pp. 204, 400; Robert Carey, *Memoirs*, ed. F. H. Mares (Oxford, 1972), p. 25n.

35 See John Stow, *Annals [as continued by Edmond Howes]* (London, 1615), sig. 3Z3ᵛ.

36 The mother of Dorothy and Penelope, Lettice, Countess of Leicester was married to Sir Christopher Blount, one of the five or six persons connected with the special performance of Shakespeare's *Richard II* before the Essex rebellion. See 'A New History for Shakespeare and His Time', *SQ*, 39 (1988), 441–64.

37 For these matters see Webb's 'Memoirs' prefixed to Inigo Jones, *Stonehenge . . . Restored*, ed. John Webb (London, 1725) – these remarks do not appear in the first, 1665, edition (Wing STC 654); Sir Sidney Lee in *DNB*, IX, pp. 677 ff.; E. K. Chambers, *Elizabethan Stage* (Oxford, 1923), II, p. 308.

38 See Sir Robert Naunton, *Fragmenta Regalia*, ed. J. S. Cerovski (Washington, DC: Folger Books: Associated University Presses, 1985).

39 See M. S. Rawson, *Penelope Rich and Her Circle* (London, 1911); Ben Jonson, *Conversations with Drummond*; *Epigram 79*.

40 For Lucy Bedford's age, see B. H. Newdigate, *Michael Drayton and his Circle*. Corrected edn (Oxford, 1961), ch. 5. This chapter, *DNB*, scattered remarks in R. C. Bald, *John Donne: A Life* (New York, 1970), and Barbara Kiefer Lewalski, 'Lucy Countess of Bedford: Images of a Jacobean Courtier and Patroness' in Kevin Sharpe and Steven N. Zwicker, *Politics of Discourse*

(Berkeley, 1987), pp. 52–77, are the best accounts I have been able to find of the countess's life.

41 George Chapman wrote a sonnet to Lady Bedford in the preface to his (1598) *Iliad*, and Ben Jonson in 1601 presented Bedford a printed copy of *Cynthia's Revels* in which was inserted a leaf containing a set of verses to her. Jonson also mentioned the countess in an ode which was his contribution to 'The Phoenix and the Turtle'. See Newdigate, *Drayton*, p. 64n1. Lady Bedford was also patroness to Samuel Daniel and John Donne: indeed, she stood as godmother to Donne's second daughter.

42 For these two passages, see *De L'Isle MSS*, II, p. 322; *Chamberlain Letters*, I, p. 179.

43 See Edmund Lodge, *Illustrations of British History* (London, 1838), III, p. 12; *The Diary of Anne Clifford*, ed. V. Sackville-West (London, 1923), p. 9n; *Dudley Carleton to John Chamberlain*, ed. Maurice Lee Jr (New Brunswick, NJ, 1972), p. 35.

44 *Clifford*, p. 8. John Nichols, *The Progresses of James I* (London, 1828), I, p. 190.

45 Lady Anne Clifford's diary significantly mentions an earlier date for Lady Harington's connection with Princess Elizabeth. Before July 1603 she notes *both* 'my Lady Kildare and the Lady Harrington' as being the princess's 'governesses'. See *Clifford*, p. 9.

46 The following were the officers of the queen's household, appointed, for the most part, in July 1603: Sir Robert Cecil, *Lord High Steward*; Sir Robert Sidney, *Lord High Chamberlain and Surveyor General*; Sir George Carew, *Vice Chamberlain and Receiver*; Sir Thomas Monson, *Chancellor*; The Earl of Southampton, *Master of the Game*; Thomas Somerset, *Master of the Horse*; Mr William Fowler, *Secretary and Master of Requests*: see Lodge, *History*, III, p. 65. For Anna's English jointure, worth £6,376 annually in rents, see *Salisbury MSS*, XV, pp. 347–8 and *SPV*, X, p. 87. For later revenue and details regarding the Queen Consort's legal position in England, see Leonore Marie Glanz, *The Legal Position of English Women* (PhD Dissertation, Loyola University of Chicago, 1973), ch. 4.

47 See *Malone Society Collections 6*, ed. David Cook and F. P. Wilson (Oxford, 1961), Appendix B.

48 See Lodge, *History*, III, pp. 11–12. The queen's Lord Chamberlain in Scotland was Henry Wardlaw. See *Register of the Privy Council of Scotland*, ed. David Masson (Edinburgh, 1889), first ser. VI, p. 302 and VI *passim*. For the group that would manage the queen's affairs in Scotland after 1603 see Masson, VI, pp. 556–7.

49 For Carew's correspondence with Cecil, see *The Letters of Sir Robert Cecil to Sir George Carew*, ed. John Maclean, Camden Society, 88 (London, 1864). Sir George Carew is sometimes confused by literary scholars with other Carews and Careys. This was the second son of George Carew, D.D., Dean of Windsor and of Exeter. See *Peerage*, XII, part 2, p. 798. A Robert Carey, Lord Hunsdon's younger brother, and the future Earl of Monmouth had a *wife* in the queen's Privy Chamber.

50 M. V. Hay, *The Life of Sir Robert Sidney* (Washington, DC, 1984) has quite a different view of Sidney's career, assuming that King James himself appointed Sidney as the queen's Chamberlain: see ch. 10, *passim.*

51 *De L'Isle MSS*, II, pp. 194, 238. *Clifford*, p. 8. Although Worcester (probably with more authority than most) described Bedford as being of the 'Bed Chamber', Dudley Carleton described her as having been sworn to the 'Privy Chamber'. See Nichols, *James I*, p. 190. For a general discussion of the Privy Chamber, see Chambers, *Elizabethan Stage*, I, p. 54; Wright and Cuddy in Starkey (ed.), *The English Court*, pp. 147–72, 173–225.

52 Frances, Countess of Hertford, daughter of Thomas (Howard) Viscount Bindon, was twenty-five in 1603 and attracted Anna early on. The queen, before July 1603, 'wore her picture' (see Anne Clifford as quoted by Nichols, I, p. 196n2). Hertford was at court long enough to dance in *The Vision of the Twelve Goddesses* of Christmas 1603–4 but then her sixty-four-year-old husband 'called her home' (Lodge, *History*, III, p. 88), and she was not a courtier during Anna's reign. But she returned to court after her husband's death and married the Duke of Lennox. For her patronage of the poet Samuel Daniel, see John Pitcher, 'Samuel Daniel, the Hertfords, and a Question of Love', *RES*, 25 (1984), 449–62.

53 See *Calendar of State Papers Domestic*, ed. Mary Anne Everett Green (London, 1857), VIII, p. 32. He also created Essex's young son one of the Companions of the young Prince Henry: see Thomas Birch, *Henry Prince of Wales* (London, 1760), and also below.

54 For these matters, see *Peerage*, IX, p. 185, and Robert Kenny, *Elizabeth's Admiral* (Baltimore, 1970), p. 93 and n. 11. Lady Walsingham was probably Audrey Shelton Walsingham, a member of the group sent to Scotland by the Privy Council and, with her husband (Sir Thomas), Keeper of the Queen's Wardrobe (see *SPD*, XII, p. 427).

55 Some literary scholars have therefore confused the two Countesses of Derby: Alice, Dowager Countess of the 5th Earl coexisting with Elizabeth, her daughter-in-law, Countess of Derby to the 6th Earl.

56 See *Dudley Carleton*, pp. 66–7.

57 For Derby's patronage, see Virgil B. Heltzel, 'English Literary Patronage 1550–1630' (unpublished typescript): Folger Shakespeare Library, 'Stanley', and Thomas Heywood, 'The Earls of Derby and the Verse Writers and Poets of the Sixteenth and Seventeenth Centuries' in *Remains . . . of Lancaster and Chester* (London, 1853), p. 29. See also *Salisbury MSS*, XIII, p. 609 and Chambers, *Elizabethan Stage*, II, p. 194. The Countess of Derby's mother-in-law was married now to Sir Thomas Egerton (later Baron Ellesmere), himself well-known as a patron to whom John Donne had been secretary.

58 John Donne, *Letters to Several Persons of Honor* (London, 1651), sigs. D4v–Ev, wrote the Countess in 1619. For Susan de Vere, see also Graham Parry, *The Golden Age Restor'd* (Manchester, 1981), pp. 108–11. For Oxford, see Chambers, *Elizabethan Stage*, II, pp. 99–102 and for Rich see Heltzel, 'Rich'.

59 See *SPV*, X, p. 26.

60 See J. W. Williamson, *The Myth of the Conqueror* (New York, 1978), pp. 27–30.

61 See Strong, however, for a contrary view arguing that the queen was indifferent and opportunistic regarding her son (pp. 16, 25).

62 See E. C. Wilson, *Prince Henry and English Literature* (Ithaca, NY, 1946), pp. 11 ff.

63 Lodge, *History*, III, p. 96.

64 During the interview, the English ambassador apparently remained standing, the more to honour Harington. Salisbury seems to have grasped Harington's position as early as the previous year when he enjoined Thomas Edmondes to be sure to show deference to the youth (*SPV*, XI, pp. 215–16 and *Salisbury MSS*, XX, pp. 232–3). Cecil had no interest, however, in marrying his daughter to John Harington despite his sister's vigorous pursuit of the match (*Salisbury MSS*, XVII, pp. 629–30). Instead, Frances Cecil married Henry Clifford, son and heir of the 4th Earl of Cumberland: see Lawrence Stone, *The Crisis of the Aristocracy* (Oxford, 1965), pp. 633, 651.

65 John Harington himself died two years after the prince and many noted his death. James Whitelocke, a judge of the Court of the King's Bench observed that young Harington was 'the most complete young gentleman of his age', while even the Doge of Venice had commented 'We do not wonder the Prince loves him; he deserves it.' See Sir James Whitelocke, *Liber Famelicus*, ed. John Bruce, Camden Society 70 (London, 1858), p. 39; *SPV*, XI, p. 389.

66 See Roy E. Schreiber, 'The First Carlisle' in *Transactions of the American Philosophical Society*, 74 (1984), p. 7.

67 For these matters see *SPD*, IX, pp. 214, 413; *Chamberlain Letters*, I, pp. 214, 358, 542, II, pp. 29, 32, and Linda Levy Peck, *Northampton* (London, 1982), pp. 40, 74.

68 See, for these matters, *SPV*, X, p. 393, XV, p. 513.

69 See Michael Brennan, *Literary Patronage in the English Renaissance: The Pembroke Family* (London, 1988), p. 109.

70 See also Yates, *Florio*, p. 246. In Scotland Anna's Secretary had been a literary figure: the poet and scholar William Fowler who, significantly, became her Secretary and Master of Requests in England (see n. 46). For his other activities, see *DNB* and William Fowler, *Works* (Edinburgh: STS, 1949–40), ed. H. W. Meikle, James Craigie and John Purves, III; see also James K. Cameron, 'Some Continental Visitors to Scotland in the Late Sixteenth and Early Seventeenth Centuries' in *Scotland and Europe*, ed. T. C. Smout (Edinburgh, 1986), pp. 45–61. He regularly entertained intellectuals visiting Scotland, including the nephew of Tycho Brahe in 1602. See also Edward J. Cowan, 'The Darker Vision of the Scottish Renaissance' in I. B. Cowan and Duncan Shaw (eds.), *The Renaissance and Reformation in Scotland* (Edinburgh, 1983), p. 138.

71 Graham Parry, *The Golden Age Restor'd* (London, 1981), p. 149; *Chamberlain Letters*, II, p. 56. Lady Carey who, by 23 February 1605, had been chosen to bring up Prince Charles, was one of the ladies of Queen Anna's Privy Chamber (see *SPD*, XII, p. 458). Arundel, who married a sister of the Earl of Pembroke's wife, both daughters of the Earl Shrewsbury and co-heiresses of Shrewsbury's

fortune, travelled with Princess Elizabeth, along with Inigo Jones, when the princess, accompanied by the Countess of Bedford's mother and father, left for the Continent.

12 The masque of Stuart culture

1 David Lindley, *The Court Masque* (Manchester, 1984), p. 1. In addition to such essential works as Stephen Orgel, *The Jonsonian Masque* (Cambridge, Mass, 1965); Orgel (ed.), *Ben Jonson, The Complete Masques* (New Haven, 1969); Orgel, *The Illusion of Power* (Berkeley, 1975); Orgel and Roy Strong, *The Theatre of the Stuart Court* (2 vols.; Berkeley, 1973), see Lindley's extensive bibliography for secondary literature on the masque.

2 See discussion of this concept in George R. Kernodle, *From Art to Theatre* (Chicago, 1944), p. 47; E. Panofsky, *Meaning in the Visual Arts* (New York, 1955).

3 See Samuel Y. Edgerton, Jr, *The Renaissance Rediscovery of Linear Perspective* (New York, 1975), pp. 74–5.

4 See Majorie Hope Nicolson, *The Breaking of the Circle* (New York, 1960), *passim*.

5 Joseph A. Mazzeo, 'Universal Analogy and the Culture of the Renaissance', *Journal of the History of Ideas*, XV, no. 2 (1954), 304.

6 H. James Jensa, *The Muses' Concord* (London, 1976), pp. 3, 19.

7 See Jensa, *The Muses' Concord*, pp. 50–5.

8 This was often the case with masques 'invented' by Inigo Jones.

9 *Art and Power* (Berkeley, 1984), pp. 40–1.

10 See an interesting discussion of this problem in Dobrochna Ratajczak, 'Teatralność i sceniczność' in: *Miejsce Wspólne. Szkice o komunikacji literackiej i artystycznej*, eds. E. Balcerzan and S. Wyslouch (Warsaw, 1985), p. 66.

11 This was first printed 'from the manuscript', now apparently lost, in Peter Cunningham, *Inigo Jones and Ben Jonson*, The Shakespeare Society (London, 1853), pp. 131–42.

12 See, for instance, *The Masque of Augurs*: 'Then he advanced with them to the King' (F2, II, p. 87); 'After which *Appolo* went up to the King and sung' (*ibid*, p. 90); *The Fortunate Isles*: 'Proteus, Portunus, and Saron come forth, and goe up singing to the *State* . . . ' (*ibid.*, p. 139); *Love's Triumph Through Callipolis*: 'Here hee goes up to the State' (Q1, 1631, sig. A3v); *The Lord's Masque*: 'Sixteen pages, like fiery spirits . . . come forth below dancing a lively measure'.

13 The distinction between the stage and the proscenium is, of course, of later date than the period under discussion.

14 Allardyce Nicoll, *Stuart Masques and the Renaissance Stage* (New York, 1963), p. 35. (The book was first published in 1938).

15 Hence the masque's similarity to liturgical drama; for some interesting comments on the latter see Rainer Warning, 'On the Alterity of Medieval Religious Drama', *NLH*, 10, no. 2 (1970), 267.

16 David Woodman, *White Magic and English Renaissance Drama* (Rutherford, NJ, 1973), p. 88.

17 David Norbrook, 'The Reformation of the Masque' in *The Court Masque*, ed. David Lindley (Manchester, 1984).

18 Keir Elam, *The Semiotics of Theatre and Drama* (London and New York, 1980), pp. 102–9.

19 Elam, *Semiotics of Theatre and Drama*, p. 109.

20 Orgel, *The Jonsonian Masque*, p. 14.

21 This is also the case of those masques in which elements of 'drama' are introduced.

22 This masque was first published by Rudolf Brotanek in *Die Englische Maskenspiel* (Wien and Leipzig, 1902), pp. 328–37. Similarly in the *Masque of Augurs* (1622) the antimasque characters are 'frighted away' by the appearance of Apollo, which is a sign for the main masque to begin. I am using the second folio edition of Jonson's *Works* (London, 1640), II, p. 86.

23 Jonson, *The Masque of Queenes* (London, 1609).

24 Jonson, *Pleasure Reconciled to Virtue*. An emblem showing sleeping Hercules surrounded by Pigmys was very well known in England at that time.

25 This is Jonson's *The Vision of Delight* (London, 1617).

26 See the discussion of this problem in Nicoll, *Stuart Masques and the Renaissance Stage*, pp. 36–8.

27 Jonson's *Time Vindicated* was first published in a quarto edition in 1623, a unique copy of which is in a private collection; I have used the second folio edition: II, p. 98.

28 Characteristically, Cupid addresses also the Masquers and the Ladies urging them to love and dance; second folio, II, pp. 100 ff.

29 F2, II, p. 87.

30 In many masques, the source of light was concealed – hence the initial effect of a magical self-illuminated reality. However, in many texts we are told that the king himself is the source of light: after all he is the Sun. Light played an important role in most cosmologies of natural philosophers of the Renaissance. The three-dimensional space, made visible by self-emanating light, the entity that is neither corporeal nor immaterial, serves as the intermediary between the corporeal concrete world of nature and the incorporeal world of spirits. It is therefore significant that the major source of light in the masque world is the king himself. It is through this light that the way to the divine sphere is visualized in ritualistic spectacle. See Max Jammer, *Concepts of Space. The History of Theories of Space in Physics* (2nd edn, Cambridge, Mass., 1969), p. 40.

31 Thomas Middleton, *The Masque of Heroes* (London, 1619), sig. C3.

32 Jonson, *Loves Triumph* (London, 1631), sig. A2. See also Orgel and Strong, *Inigo Jones, The Theatre of the Stuart Court* (2 vols.; London, 1973), I, p. 2.

33 Quoted in Elam, *The Semiotics of Theatre and Drama*, p. 68.

34 Elam, *The Semiotics of Theatre and Drama*, pp. 29–30.

35 Many of the emblematic designs for the masques were commonplace in seventeenth-century England.

36 Orgel and Strong, *Inigo Jones. The Theatre of the Stuart Court*, I, p. 21.

37 Elam discusses this phenomenon in a similar context; see *The Semiotics of Theatre and Drama*, p. 68.
38 *On Translation*, ed. by Reuben A. Brower (Cambridge, Mass., 1959), p. 233.
39 Q1, sig. B3v–B4v.
40 Strong, *Art and Power*, p. 155.
41 Nicoll, *Stuart Masques and the Renaissance Stage*, p. 155.
42 Richard Southern, *Changeable Scenery* (London, 1952), p. 34.
43 Rosemary Freeman, *English Emblem Books* (London, 1948), pp. 96–7.
44 Margery Corbett and Ronald Lightbown, *The Comely Frontispiece. The Emblematic Title-Page in England 1550–1650* (London, 1979), pp. 4–5.
45 *Masque of Flowers* (London, 1614), sig. A1.
46 Corbett and Lightbown, *The Comely Frontispiece*, p. 6. Orgel and Strong, *Inigo Jones: The Theatre of the Stuart Court*, vols. I and II.
47 Corbett and Lightbown, *The Comely Frontispiece*, p. 6; Orgel and Strong, *Inigo Jones: The Theatre of the Stuart Court*.
48 Corbett and Lightbown, *The Comely Frontispiece*, p. 35.
49 Roy Strong noted in his *Britannia Triumphans, Inigo Jones, Rubens and Whitehall Palace* (London, 1980) the general similarity of the masque allegory to the Whitehall ceiling as painted by Rubens; he also gives several examples of direct iconographic relationship between particular masque designs and the murals (see, for instance, p. 15).
50 This masque was presented by Lord Hay in 1617 and published in the second folio of Jonson's *Workes* (London, 1640).
51 Corbett and Lightbown, *The Comely Frontispiece*, p. 47.
52 See also Nicoll, *Stuart Masques and the Renaissance Stage*, p. 47.
53 See Plate 4.
54 It may be noted that in emblem books the icons were sometimes accompanied by dialogue, as in F. Quarles, *Emblems* (London, 1635), sig. G2v–G4.
55 D. J. Gordon, *The Renaissance Imagination*, ed. S. Orgel (Berkeley, 1975), p. 311n6.
56 *English Emblem Books*, p. 73.
57 *Sermons*, ed. L. P. Smith (Oxford, 1920), p. 67.
58 *Emblems*, sig. A3.
59 See Strong, *Britannia Triumphans, Inigo Jones, Rubens and Whitehall Palace, passim*.
60 See Robert J. Clements, *Picta Poesis. Literature and Humanist Theory in Renaissance Emblem Books* (Rome, 1960), pp. 68 ff.
61 For Neoplatonic views of human and divine movements, see Paul Oskar Kristeller, *The Philosophy of Marsilio Ficino* (New York, 1943), p. 387.
62 Orgel and Strong, *Inigo Jones, The Theatre of the Stuart Court*, I, p. 7.
63 Yuri Lotman and Boris Uspensky observed in their essay 'On the Semiotic Mechanisms of Culture': 'it is clear that the very fact of emphasis on expression, of strictly ritualized forms of behaviour, is usually a consequence of seeing a one-to-one correlation (rather than an arbitrary one) between the level of expression and the level of content', *NLH*, 9, no. 2 (1978), p. 217.

64 *Ibid.*

65 With the exception of those texts that in their printed form try to free themselves from the spectacle and become autonomous literary texts.

66 Lotman and Uspensky, 'On the Semiotic Mechanisms of Culture', p. 218.

67 This is [Richard Mocket's?] *God and the King: Or, A Dialogue shewing that our Souereigne Lord King Iames, being immediate under God . . . Doth rightfully claime . . . the Oath of Allegeance* (London, 1615).

13   Robert Carr, Earl of Somerset, as collector and patron

1 Royal Commission on Historical Manuscripts, *Report on the Manuscripts of the Marquis of Downshire* (5 vols. in 6, London, 1924–88), II, p. 278 (Samuel Calvert to William Trumbull, 29 March 1611), hereafter cited as *HMC Downshire*. Menna Prestwich, *Cranfield: Politics and Profits under the Early Stuarts* (Oxford, 1966), p. 109; Martin J. Havran, *Caroline Courtier: The Life of Lord Cottington* (London, 1973), p. 73; P. R. Seddon, 'Robert Carr, Earl of Somerset', *Renaissance and Modern Studies*, 14 (1970), p. 68. Compare the more general statement in Roger Lockyer, *Buckingham* (London and New York, 1981), p. 464. For some qualification to the traditional views see Neal Cuddy, 'Anglo-Scottish Union and the Court of James I, 1603–1625', *TRHS*, 5th ser., 39 (1989), 107–24.

2 Henry, Lord Danvers, compliments the taste of his artistic agent, Sir Dudley Carleton, when asking for pictures 'of the best hands wherein I have noted your eye excellent' (Public Record Office (London) SP 14/86, f. 237, 9 April 1616), although he also criticized Rubens's paintings as unsuitable for English domestic architecture (SP 14/110/11*, f. 14 [formerly SP 14/88/47], Danvers to Carleton, 7 August [reassigned to 1619]). European taste could be an embarrassment; Sir Henry Savile wrote Carleton, thanking him for a medal he had sent, but remarking that he will not wear it until its setting is completed because 'as it is, it would be taken for some whistle or instrument of a wood drawer among these ignorant people of ours, who know not . . . what belongs to good manners' (SP 14/77/77, 14 August 1614). Sir Walter Cope had complained that Italian artists' 'intentions are a little too light, not fitting for any place of gravity' (SP 14/61/33; Cope to Carleton, 26 January 1611, quoted by Erna Auerbach, 'Part One – up to 1632', in Auerbach and C. Kingsley Adams, *Paintings and Sculpture at Hatfield House* (London, 1971), p. 79).

3 Traditional views of Tudor taste have been modified but not substantially revised for elite collectors. Susan Foister, 'Paintings and other works of art in sixteenth-century English inventories', *Burlington Magazine*, 123 (1981), 273–82, presents evidence from sixty-three probate inventories, 1468–1582, but none of the collectors Foister studied was an aristocrat, though there is a sprinkling of knights; most of the collections contained fewer than a half-dozen items, and the largest contained thirty. For a more general survey, see Denys Sutton, 'Early Patrons and Collectors', *Apollo*, 114 (1981), 282–97.

4 See Roy Strong, *Henry, Prince of Wales, and England's Lost Renaissance*

(London, 1986); T. V. Wilks, 'The Court Culture of Prince Henry and his Circle 1603–1613', (DPhil. thesis, Oxford, 1987); David Howarth, *Lord Arundel and his Circle* (New Haven, 1985); Oliver Millar (ed.), *Abraham Van der Doort's Catalogue of the Collections of Charles I*, Walpole Society, 37 (1960); Per Palme, *The Triumph of Peace: A Study of the Whitehall Banqueting House* (Stockholm, 1956), pp. 29–32; Lionel Cust, 'The Lumley Inventories', Walpole Society 6 (1917–18), 16–35; Evelyn P. Shirley, 'An Inventory of the Effects of Henry Howard, K.G., Earl of Northampton . . .', *Archaeologia*, 42 (1869), 347–78 ('14 Venetian pictures of one bigness' are listed on p. 372 as purchased by 'Mr H. Howarde'; Linda Levy Peck, *Patronage and Policy at the Court of James I* (London, 1982), pp. 74–5.

5 Auerbach, *Paintings and Sculpture at Hatfield House*, pp. 26, 73–4, and 102.

6 The letter, 23 July 1609, is now in the Forster collection, Victoria and Albert Museum; see the facsimile in J. Irene Whalley, 'Italian Art and English Taste: An Early-Seventeenth-Century Letter', *Apollo*, 94 (1971), 184–91. As Whalley says (p. 186), such an early recommendation of a Roman artist is quite remarkable: English taste was typically Venetian. For the longevity of English preferences among foreign artistic traditions, preferences formed in the early Stuart period, see Iain Pears, *The Discovery of Painting: The Growth of Interest in the Arts in England, 1680–1768* (New Haven, 1988), pp. 166–8 and appendix to chapter 6.

7 Paul Shakeshaft, ' "To much bewiched with thoes intysing things": The Letters of James, Third Marquis of Hamilton and Basil, Viscount Feilding, Concerning Collecting in Venice 1635–39', *Burlington Magazine*, 128 (1986), 114–32, quotation from p. 116; Shakeshaft refers initially to Buckingham and Hamilton, but then extends his comment retrospectively to Carr and, oddly, to Robert Dudley, Earl of Leicester, sometime favourite of Elizabeth I. Only three of Leicester's pictures have titles associating them with Venice.

8 There are, for example, no books dedicated to Philip Howard, Earl of Arundel, after his committal to the Tower; no books dedicated to Raleigh after 1603; one book (Aemilia Lanier's *Salve deus rex Judaeorum*, entered for printing 2 October 1610) is jointly dedicated to Arabella Stuart after her imprisonment, but that may be an accident of timing; the second edition (1614) of *The Golden Mean*, an anonymous book attributed to John Ford, is the only title dedicated to Henry Percy, Earl of Northumberland, during his long imprisonment. See Appendix for a chronological list of dedications to Carr.

9 See Arthur Wilson, *History of Great Britain* (London, 1653), p. 54 and Anthony Weldon, *The Court and Character of King James* (London, 1650), p. 63.

10 *HMC Downshire*, III, p. 369 (Overbury to Trumbull); SP 77/10, ff. 231v–232r (Trumbull to Overbury, 8 October 1612) and SP 77/10, ff. 352r–v (Trumbull to Carr, 5 November 1613). I owe transcripts of the second and third letters to the kindness of Louis A. Knafla.

11 Folger MS. G.b. 10, f. 87v, a contemporary collection of copies of diplomatic correspondence; I owe this reference to Linda Levy Peck. Date, sender and addressee are inferential and based on abbreviations and initials, but the

copyist's habits elsewhere, an internal reference to 'Mr. Dowricke' (i.e. John Dowrishe, mentioned as a messenger in another Wotton letter of 7 June 1615 (see L. P. Smith, *The Life and Letters of Sir Henry Wotton*, 2 vols. (Oxford, 1907), II, p. 80 and II, pp. 469–70) and the dates of Wotton's tenure as special envoy to the States strongly suggest that f. 87v is a copy of a Wotton letter to Carr, probably from June 1615. The painting might be the 'perspective Church' mentioned in the 1619 list of Carr's pictures discussed below.

12 BL Add. MS 6115, f. 87 (Thomas Roe to Carr, from 'the Mogulls Court', 14 February 1616).

13 For incomplete and slightly inaccurate accounts, see W. Noel Sainsbury, *Original Unpublished Papers Illustrative of the Life of Sir Peter Paul Rubens* (London, 1859), pp. 269–79 and Howarth, *Arundel*, pp. 59–61. Since this essay was accepted for publication, Timothy Wilks has published a detailed study of the events of 1615, placing Carr's collecting (of 1612–15) in context; see 'The Picture Collection of Robert Carr, Earl of Somerset (*c.* 1587–1645), Reconsidered', *Journal of the History of Collections*, 1 (1989), 167–77. I am pleased that Dr Wilks and I agree on ascribing the Copenhagen Bassano to Carr's collection and on identifying 'Mr Palmer' (for both, see below).

14 Nys's list of paintings is SP 14/80/88A where he names John Packer as Carr's secretary; to the invoice of 25 April reciting Nys's list (SP 14/80/88), Carleton adds 'two several tables of Paulo Veronese' and 'The creation of old Bassan' which Nys had acquired 26 March 1614 – 'duo quadri grandi di Paulo Veronese' and 'la Creatione di animali del Bassan vecchio' – according to a still earlier invoice of Nys to Carleton covering purchases for the period 24 October 1613–12 May 1614 (SP 14/77/22*), and they are repeated in Carleton's holograph 'Account of such things as I have bought for the Earle of Somerset' (SP 14/80/87). The statues are listed in SP 14/80/88B. There is no summary invoice listing valuations for the pictures: Nys lists pictures to the value of 800 ducats, to which Carleton adds others he values at 100 and 500 pounds, respectively.

15 Using Sainsbury's excerpts, Howarth traces the statues' movements beginning in March 1616 (*Arundel*, pp. 60–1 and p. 239n9), but inaccurately states (p. 60) that Somerset never took possession of the paintings (see below). At least some of the statues were shipped to Carleton in the Netherlands: see SP 14/89, f. 1 (Sherburn to Carleton, 1 November 1616; invoice in Sainsbury, *Original Unpublished Papers*, pp. 302–3). Carleton then negotiated an exchange of the statuary with Rubens for pictures (March–May 1618; see Sainsbury, pp. 22–45), and Buckingham eventually acquired the statues when he bought Rubens's collection (see Lockyer, *Buckingham*, p. 410). By this circuitous route, one favourite gained what his predecessor lost.

16 BL MS Stowe 175, f. 310 (Winwood to Sir Thomas Edmondes, 26 April 1615).

17 Sir John Holles to George Holles, his brother, 10 May 1615: *The Letters of Sir John Holles*, ed. P. R. Seddon, 3 vols. (Nottingham, 1975–86), I, p. 66, modernized. Cited hereafter as *Holles Letters*. John Chamberlain to Dudley Carleton, 20 May 1615, in N. E. McClure (ed.), *The Letters of John Chamberlain*, 2 vols. (Philadelphia, 1939), I, p. 597. It is not clear whether Carleton's date of 25 April

is old (English) or new (Venetian) style; Holles's letter is thus written either fifteen or twenty-five days after the invoice's date.

18 The standard modern account is Beatrice White, *Cast of Ravens* (London, 1965), but the gallimaufry of human interests still appears best in *Cobbett's Complete Collection of State Trials*, ed. and comp. T. B. Howell, 33 vols. (London, 1809–26), II, pp. 951–1022.

19 The most circumstantial account of Carr's incriminating behaviour is by the Spanish ambassador; see the translation in S. R. Gardiner, 'On Certain Letters of Diego Sarmiento de Acuña, Count of Gondomar . . .', *Archaeologia*, 41 (1867), 151–86, citation to p. 172, and Howell, *State Trials*, II, p. 922.

20 The inventory, begun 29 November 1615, is now Folger MS L.b. 638.

21 See Gondomar to the Duke of Lerma, 20 October 1615, trans. Gardiner, *Archaeologia*, 41 (1867), 173. The inventory-makers mention the Earl's tent among other things stored in the Cockpit (Folger MS L.b. 638, f. 8v), and there are no records of the space being prepared for its better-known functions as a gaming arena and theatre between January–March 1613 and March–April 1615; see David Cook, 'Dramatic Records in the Declared Accounts of the Treasurer of the Chamber 1558–1642', *Malone Society Collections* 6 (1962 for 1961).

22 Although James built separate accommodation for his favourite at the principal royal hunting lodge, Royston (see H. M. Colvin (gen. ed.), *History of the King's Works*, 5 vols. [London, 1963–82], IV, p. 237), he often insisted on Carr's attendance. In an angry, accusatory letter usually dated 'early 1615', James complained of Carr's 'long creeping back and withdrawing yourself from lying in my chamber, notwithstanding my many hundred times earnest soliciting you to the contrary' (G. P. V. Akrigg, ed., *Letters of King James VI & I* [Berkeley and Los Angeles, 1984], p. 337). On the Bedchamber more generally, see Neil Cuddy, 'The Revival of the Entourage: the Bedchamber of James I, 1603–1625' in David Starkey (ed.), *The English Court: from the Wars of the Roses to the Civil War* (London and New York, 1987), pp. 173–225.

23 The first entry is apparently incomplete, while the second seems to combine two counts (a 'dozen' and '99').

24 Folger MS L.b. 638, ff. 6, 6v, 7, 9v, respectively. The last named pictures were found 'In Mr Palmers howse'; on f. 6, Palmer is cited as the authority for the ownership of certain picture frames. It seems likely that Palmer had charge of Carr's pictures and perhaps guided his collecting; he is probably the James Palmer (knighted 1629) who 'had lodgings in the tennis-court at Whitehall [adjacent to Carr's apartments], and is often mentioned as a domestic servant' (Horace Walpole, *Anecdotes of Painting in England*, 3rd edn, 4 vols. [London, 1782], II, p. 223). Palmer (1584–1657) was himself a painter, Gentleman of the Bedchamber to James (1622), Gentleman Usher of the Privy Chamber to Charles I, Chancellor of the Order of the Garter, governor of the Mortlake tapestry works, and involved in Charles's collecting. A miniature dated 1619 and long said to be of Robert Carr but now thought to be of Sir Peter Young (Fitzwilliam Museum, Cambridge) has been ascribed to Palmer. See: Millar (ed.), *Catalogue of the Collections of Charles I*; Graham Reynolds, 'A newly identified

Miniaturist of the early seventeenth century, probably Sir James Palmer', *Burlington Magazine*, 91 (1949), 196–7 and fig. 14; Daphne Foskett, *A Dictionary of British Miniature Painters*, 2 vols. (New York, 1972), I, pp. 434–5 and figs. 648–9; Robert Bayne-Powell, *Catalogue of Portrait Miniatures in the Fitzwilliam Museum* (Cambridge, 1985), p. 174.

25 Folger MS L.b. 638, f. 14. For Frances Carr's house arrest and transfer to the Tower, see the warrant (27 March 1616) printed in William Bray, 'Original Letters of King James I. to Sir George More . . . ', *Archaeologia*, 18 (1817), 358, and confirmed by Chamberlain, *Letters*, I, p. 619.

26 Folger MS L.b. 638, f. 9v. I have here reproduced the inventory as exactly as possible so my inferences may be checked.

27 See SP 14/86, f. 134.

28 See SP 14/88, f. 12v and SP 14/89, f. 1, original emphasis.

29 See, respectively, the following letters of Sherburn to Carleton: SP 14/86, f. 167 (23 March 1616); SP 14/86, f. 233 (9 April 1616); SP 14/88, f. 12v (11 July 1616); SP 14/86, f. 154 (14 March 1616). Danvers mentions 'that special picture of the creation' in a letter to Carleton (SP 14/86, f. 237, 9 April 1616), and calling it 'exquisite work', Danvers again (SP 14/88/29, 23 July 1616) asked Carleton to exchange it; on the painting's 'gravity' see SP 14/88/118 and 133 (Danvers to Carleton, 7 and 23 October 1616). Howarth, *Arundel*, pp. 60–1, names the paintings Arundel bought, but I know of no evidence for the claim.

30 See John Shearman, *The Early Italian Pictures in the Collection of Her Majesty the Queen* (Cambridge, 1983), catalogue number 263.

31 For the post-1684 provenance, see Harald Olsen, *Italian Paintings and Sculpture in Denmark* (Copenhagen, 1961), p. 38; for this reference and generous assistance, I thank Olaf Koester, Curator of Old Foreign Paintings and Sculpture, Statens Museum for Kunst, Copenhagen.

32 See M. F. S. Hervey, *The Life, Correspondence, and Collections of Thomas Howard, Earl of Arundel* (Cambridge, 1921), Appendix V, numbers 345, 402, 405, 353, 373, 502. Howarth, *Arundel*, p. 61, says that of the paintings Arundel bought from Carleton 'all except the *Benediction* were destroyed along with the house in the Greenwich fire six months later', but provides no reference. For the fire, see SP 14/90/16 (Sherburn to Carleton, 11 January 1617).

33 'Susanna bathing her selfe. By old Tintaret' appears in Van der Doort's inventory of Charles I's collection (ed. Millar, p. 227); this may be the Louvre painting on the same (but very popular) subject (*ibid.*, p. 235) and might be the 'Susanna di Tintoretto' of Nys's 25 April 1615 list. Some of the pictures listed in 1615 remained in Carr's possession until 1637; see below.

34 See, for example, SP 14/88/52 (Sherburn to Carleton, 25 July 1616); on their behaviour in prison generally, see Chamberlain, *Letters*, II, pp. 13, 19, 77, 85, 156 (6 July 1616–10 April 1618). James worried about how his leniency might be perceived; see Folger MS L.b. 663 (George Villiers to Sir George More, 25 August 1616). On what Carr and his wife brought into the Tower, see the inventory in Loseley MS 1124, Kent Archive Office (cited from Folger [micro]Film Acc 571, reel 9); the Whitehall inventory mentions 'Six of these

books were delivered out for my Lord's use [in the Tower] . . . 15 February 1615 [i.e. 1616]' (Foger MS L.b. 638, f. 6v).

35 Despite the murder conviction, Carr retained, controversially but by King James's direct order, his Garter and wore it publicly (as Garter statutes dictated) in the Tower and in the streets of London after his release; see SP 14/88, f. 26 (Sherburn to Carleton, 13 July 1616); Chamberlain, *Letters*, II, pp. 13, 17; *Holles Letters*, III, p. 391 (20 June 1629).

36 Folger MS L.b. 638, f. 20v. The first George listed may be the 'large agate George circled with gold and set with 57 small diamonds' bequeathed to Carr by the Earl of Northampton; see Shirley, 'An Inventory . . . ', *Archaeologia*, 42 (1869), 350.

37 SP 16/238/71; the second passage continues, 'Besides, your present condition is not fit for a servant & his Majesty will be no longer delayed but is resolved to take another way in case of a second refusal . . . ' On 21 January 1631, Inigo Jones and others had been instructed to collect and organize the King's Greek and Roman coins and medals, including those in others' hands; see SP 16/183/1 and Sainsbury, *Original Unpublished Papers*, p. 173n228.

38 See SP 16/239/24 (Sir Thomas Lake to Sir John Coke, 22 May 1633) and *HMC Cowper*, II, p. 15 (Sir Francis Windebank to Coke, 27 May 1633).

39 Millar, *Catalogue of the Collections of Charles I*, p. 128, modernized; the text in angle brackets appears in another manuscript of Van der Doort's inventory. The claim that Frances Carr broke the jewel while her husband was Lord Chamberlain is probably not inconsistent with the statement that Charles had the jewel when he was prince, but if the latter statement is accurate this agate (or cameo) is not the one Charles recovered from Carr in 1633.

40 For an illustration of this gem and the claim that it is a contemporary representation of Claudius, see C. Drury E. Fortnum, 'Notes on some of the Antique and Renaissance Jewels in Her Majesty's Collection at Windsor Castle', *Archaeologia*, 45 (1880), 1–28 and plate 1.

41 Folger MS L.b. 638, ff. 13 and 21.

42 *Ibid.*, f. 24.

43 Surprisingly, Charles I approved and forwarded the match, despite the Earl of Bedford's having given his son 'leave and liberty to choose in any family but in that'; see George Garrard to Earl of Strafford, 5 April 1636, in William Knowler, ed., *The Earl of Strafforde's Letters and Dispatches*, 2 vols. (London, 1739), II, p. 2. The Russells and the Carrs were neighbours in Chiswick. In a later letter to Strafford, Garrard says, '*Somerset* told the Lord Chamberlain [i.e. Philip Herbert, Earl of Pembroke], who hath been a great Mediator in this Business, before his Daughter, that one of them was to be undone, if that Marriage went on; he chose rather to undo himself than to make her unhappy' (23 March 1637; *ibid.*, II, p. 58). The dowry was the same at that the much wealthier William Cecil, second Earl of Salisbury, had trouble raising for 'his favourite daughter . . . the equivalent [for Cecil] of one and a half years gross landed income' (Lawrence Stone, *Family and Finance: Studies in Aristocratic Finance in the Sixteenth and Seventeenth Centuries* (Oxford, 1973), p. 122).

44 Both documents are in the file of Carr materials among the first Duke of

Bedford's papers in the Bedford Estate Office, London; they are here cited with the kind permission of the Trustees of the Bedford Estates and the Marquess of Tavistock. Pembroke also took a mortgage on Carr's Chiswick house (Knowler (ed.), *Strafforde's Letters*, II, p. 58; Garrard to Strafford, 23 March 1637) and eventually foreclosed (Daniel Lysons, *The Environs of London*, 4 vols. (London, 1794–6), II, p. 194). Mrs M. P. G. Draper, Archivist, Bedford Estate Office, generously assisted my research and showed me Thomas Ingram's partial transcript of the 1637 inventory.

45 See Allan Braham, *El Greco to Goya: The Taste for Spanish Paintings in Britain and Ireland* (London, 1981), pp. 5–9. The attribution could also be a translated nickname ('Lo Spagna', 'Lo Spagnuolo', 'Lo Spagnoletto').

46 The Florentine government gave Prince Henry portraits of Machiavelli, Pico, and Castruccio (Wilks, 'The Court Culture of Prince Henry', p. 169); and Carr's Machiavelli and Castruccio might have come from the same source. Similarly, the portraits of 'The Prince of Peimont' and 'The 2 daughters of Savoy' on the 1619 list may have come to England as part of the marriage negotiations for Princess Elizabeth and Prince Henry, respectively.

47 Except for the portrait of Catherine of Aragon, which appears on the 1619 list only, the subjects and quoted phrases in this sentence are from the 1637 inventory, although several of the same subjects appear on the 1619 list.

48 Randall Davies, 'An Inventory of the Duke of Buckingham's Pictures, etc., at York House in 1635', *Burlington Magazine*, 10 (1907), 376.

49 For an analysis of Buckingham's collection – 'not initiating, but rather following, a trend' – see Lita-Rose Betcherman, 'The York House Collection and its Keeper', *Apollo*, 92 (1970), 250–9; quotation from p. 250.

50 For this argument applied to Restoration examples, see Eugene Waith, 'The Voice of Mr. Bayes', *Studies in English Literature*, 3 (1963), 335–43.

51 See F. B. Williams, Jr., 'Special Presentation Epistles before 1641: A Preliminary Check-List', *The Library*, ser. 5, 7 (1952), 15–16 and for Abraham Darcie's devious dedicatory practices, pp. 20 and 22. Without Williams's valuable *Index of Dedications and Commendatory Verses* (London, 1962), this essay would have been impossible.

52 Another issue, probably the second, of Darcie's translation elaborately appeals to an entirely different set of patrons, a 'godly', Calvinist group associated with the Earl of Bridgewater, none of whom had suffered public falls from power. Peter W. M. Blayney helped me understand the relation between the two issues of Darcie's translation.

53 In most copies, the dedication is signed 'H.T.' [*sic*], but the British Library copy is signed 'T. Heywood'. Barckley's work had previously been published in 1598 and 1603, dedicated both times to Queen Elizabeth.

54 For Chapman's relation with Essex, see below; for his references to Prince Henry's request that he complete the English translation of Homer, his many years of unpaid work on the project, the Prince's promise of £300 for the translation, and his deathbed promise of a life-pension, see P. B. Bartlett (ed.), *The Poems of George Chapman* (New York, 1941), pp. 199–200, 385–9, hereafter

cited as *Poems*, and *A Seventeenth-Century Letter-Book: A Facsimile Edition of Folger Library MS. V.a. 321*, with transcription, annotation, and commentary by A. R. Braunmuller (Newark, Delaware and London, 1983), pp. 293–4 (item 88), 396 (item 139), 443, and 457.

55 'To the most Honord . . . Earle', prefixed to *Seaven Bookes of the Iliades*; see *Chapman's Homer*, ed. Allardyce Nicoll, 2 vols., Bollingen Series, 41 (New York, 1956), I, p. 504, with some corrections; hereafter cited as *Homer*. For a persuasive argument that Chapman's first Homeric work is 'topical translation' 'doctored' to appeal to, advise and encourage Essex in his military ambitions, see John C. Briggs, 'Chapman's *Seaven Bookes of the Iliades*: Mirror for Essex', *Studies in English Literature*, 21 (1981), 59–73. Briggs also shows that Chapman removed many of the topical distortions when he republished his translation in the new century, almost a decade after Essex's rebellion.

56 *Calendar of State Papers Venetian, 1610–13*, p. 135 (Correr to the Doge and Senate, 21 April 1611); Gondomar to the Duke of Lerma, trans. Gardiner, in *Archaeologia*, 41 (1867), 174.

57 For Carr's original modesty and his later arrogance, see: Wilson, *History*, p. 83 and *HMC Portland*, IX, p. 41 (Thomas Erskine, Viscount Fenton to John, Earl of Mar; mid-1612). For Carr's own self-interested claims of disinterested service to the state and throne, see SP 14/71/6, ff. 9–9v (Carr to Northampton, 8 October 1612); SP 16/524/65 (Carr to Charles I, 19 July 1636); SP 16/310/89 (Carr to Charles I, ?1635). For James's sense that Carr's 'unquietness, passion, fury and insolent pride' had increased 'especially of late', see *Letters of James VI and I*, ed. Akrigg, pp. 336–7 ('Early 1615').

58 This copy, now British Library shelfmark C 28.m.11–12, was purchased at Sotheby's sale of the Archibald Fraser of Lovat collection 18 February 1852 (see *Notes and Queries*, 5 (28 February 1852), 193); it has the Earl of Lothian's arms (*pace ibid.*) on the covers and a plausible ownership inscription of the Duke of Newcastle ('1676'). It may have originally been Carr's since he had no male heirs and might not have been able to acquire the first folio published (1616) during his imprisonment; Lothian was the son of Sir Robert Kerr, Earl of Ancram, a long-time friend and distant relative of Carr. The only book I know certainly to have been in Carr's possession is a copy of the expensive Braun-Hogenberg *Civitates Orbis Terrarum*, 6 vols. (1572–1618), once at Newbattle (Abbey) Library and inscribed, 'This booke the Earle of Somerset sent to the E. of Lothiane, Marche 1636' (or 1637?); see David Laing, ed., *Correspondence of Sir Robert Kerr, first Earl of Ancram and . . . William, third Earl of Lothian*, 2 vols. (Edinburgh, 1875), II, p. 539. For Jonson's poem and the masques, see C. H. Herford and P. and E. Simpson (eds.), *Ben Jonson*, 11 vols. (Oxford, 1925–54), II, p. 298, VIII, p. 384, XI, p. 138, and David Lindley, 'Embarrassing Ben: The Masques for Frances Howard' in Arthur F. Kinney and Dan S. Collins (eds.), *Renaissance Historicism* (Amherst, Mass., 1987), pp. 248–64.

59 See R. C. Bald, *John Donne: A Life* (Oxford, 1970), pp. 271–4, 289–95, 313–15.

60 John Pitcher, *Samuel Daniel: The Brotherton Manuscript*, Leeds Texts and Monographs, n.s. 7 (Leeds, 1981), pp. 66 ff. and Appendix C.

61 *Holles Letters*, III, p. 511, undated letter to Carr.

62 Lisle also published the masque Thomas Campion wrote for the wedding as well as eleven editions or impressions of Thomas Overbury's 'A Wife' and other literary characters from the first in 1614 through 1622. Overbury is generally believed to have opposed the Carr–Howard marriage and to have been poisoned for his opposition; some scholars have argued that 'A Wife' and/or 'A very very Woman' represent Overbury's attack on Frances Howard Carr. See James E. Savage (ed.), *The 'Conceited Newes' of Sir Thomas Overbury and his Friends* (Gainesville, Florida, 1968), pp. xiii–xviii.

63 W. W. Greg, *Licensers for the Press, &c. to 1640* (Oxford, 1962), p. 87.

64 For a selection of the scurrilous poems evoked by the marriage and trial, see White, *Cast of Ravens*, Appendix IV and James L. Sanderson, 'Poems on an Affair of State – The Marriage of Somerset and Lady Essex', *Review of English Studies*, n.s. 17 (1966), 57–61. According to Chamberlain, the 'common people' were so angered by Frances Carr's pardon that they threatened a riot when the queen and her companions were mistaken for Frances and her mother; see Chamberlain, *Letters*, II, pp. 17–18 (20 July 1616).

65 BL Cotton MS. Titus B 7, f. 447v (28 November 1615); SP 14/87/29 (Edward Sherburn to Dudley Carleton, 25 May 1616).

66 See Norma Dobie Solve, *Stuart Politics in Chapman's 'Tragedy of Chabot'*, University of Michigan Publications in Language and Literature, 4 (Ann Arbor, 1928). Albert Tricomi strongly attacks Solve's thesis in 'The Dates of The Plays of George Chapman', *English Literary Renaissance*, 12 (1982), 261–3.

67 Ties of family and friendship may partly explain the dedication to Carr: Horace Vere was Frances Carr's first cousin twice removed (her great-grandmother was Vere's grandmother), and the elder son of Carr's friend John Holles married Vere's daughter in 1626.

68 The absence is speculative: see C. J. Sisson and Robert Butman, 'George Chapman, 1612–1622: Some New Facts', *Modern Language Review*, 46 (1951), 185–90.

69 Jonathan Goldberg thinks Chapman is referring to himself here (poet becoming patron's patron), and Chapman seems at times to have confused himself with Homer; line 77 does, however, refer to 'your *Homer*'. See *James I and the Politics of Literature* (Baltimore, 1983), p. 134.

70 'Those that came to the Princes service seem'd (compared with the places they liv'd in before) to rise from death to the fields of life' ('An Epicede or Funerall Song: On the most disastrous Death, of . . . Henry Prince of Wales'; *Poems*, p. 257).

71 James Maidment and W. H. Logan (eds.), *The Dramatic Works of Sir William D'Avenant*, 5 vols. (Edinburgh, 1872–4), I, p. 17; this quotation and others have been corrected from the first quarto. Subsequent quotations from the play are cited parenthetically by Act and page number(s) from volume I.

72 *Ibid.*, I, p. 14.

73 Arthur Nethercot, *Sir William Davenant: Poet Laureate and Playwright-Manager* (Chicago, 1938), p. 82. Contrary to common scholarly belief, Carr was

far from destitute after his release from the Tower, and Davenant could plausibly hope for financial reward.

74 See, e.g., Act I, pp. 23–4; Act II, p. 36; Act III, p. 48.

75 Compare Albovine's remark to Paradine: 'I am in love too violent. / My embraces crush thee, thou art but yet / Of tender growth' (Act I, p. 23); Rhodolinda calls Albovine's behaviour 'sincere dotage' (Act V, p. 90).

76 Thomas Howard (second son to Thomas Howard, Earl of Suffolk, and later [1626] Earl of Berkshire) to Sir John Harington, about 1607, in Henry Harington (ed.), *Nugae Antiquae*, rev. edn, Thomas Park, (2 vols., London, 1804), I, p. 392. The date (probably correct) is conjectured in *Letters and Epigrams of Sir John Harington*, ed. N. E. McClure (Philadelphia, 1930), p. 31.

77 Francis Osborne, *Traditionall Memoyres of the Raigne of King James*, the second, separately paginated part of *Historical Memoires on the Reigns of Queen Elizabeth and King James* (1658), pp. 127–9. The 1615 inventory of Carr's possessions includes many soberly black garments, but even more brightly coloured and richly decorated outfits (see Folger MS L.b. 638, ff. 6v–8r). For other accounts of James's embracing and kissing Carr, see Weldon, *Court and Character of King James*, pp. 102–3 and Wilson, *History*, p. 68.

78 See, for example, Nethercot, *Sir William Davenant: Poet Laureate and Playwright-Manager*, pp. 82–3, and Mary Edmonds, *Rare Sir William Davenant* (Manchester, 1987), p. 40.

79 In his fatal struggle with Paradine, Albovine cries, 'Tis time that I were dead, for I shall else / Outlive my chief prerogative. I have / Forgot how to command' (Act V, p. 98).

80 In early August 1628, Buckingham 'was present at the acting of of [*sic*] K. Hen. 8 at the Globe, a play bespoken of purpose by himself; whereat he stayd till the Duke of Buckingham was beheaded, & then departed. Some say he should rather have seen the fall of Cardinall Woolsey, who was a more lively type of himself having governd this kingdom 18 yeares, as he hath done 14' (BL Harl. MS 383, f. 65; Robert Gell to Sir Martin Stuteville, 9 August 1628). A slightly inaccurate excerpt appears in J. O. Halliwell, 'Early notice of Shakespeare's play of Henry the Eighth', *Shakespeare Society Papers*, 2 (1845), 151. Buckingham's beheading is the first and Wolsey's dismissal the last of three falls from eminence represented in Shakespeare's *Henry VIII*.

81 Kevin Sharpe also makes this suggestion in *Criticism and Compliment: The Politics of Literature in the England of Charles I* (Cambridge, 1987), p. 55.

82 SP 16/524/65 (Carr to Buckingham, 19 July 1626); for accounts of James's promise to replace the lands he had confiscated upon Carr's conviction, see SP 16/310/89, 16/341/94, and *Holles Letters*, III, p. 487.

83 James to Carr, 'early 1615' in Akrigg (ed.), *Letters of King James VI & I*, p. 336.

84 *HMC Downshire* V, p. 58 (John Throckmorton to William Trumbull, 14 November 1614); *Holles Letters* III, p. 387 (Holles to Sir Horace Vere, 4 August 1628). Buckingham left London on 12 August and was murdered 23 August (Lockyer, *Buckingham*, pp. 452–3).

85 This suggestion is hypothetical because the history of English collecting before the activities of Prince Henry, Arundel, Buckingham and Charles I has not been thoroughly studied; see above, n. 4, Hervey, *Arundel*, pp. 140 and 297, John Buxton, *Elizabethan Taste* (London, 1963), pp. 96–104.

86 Chamberlain, *Letters*, II, p. 582 (9 October 1624). This essay was largely written while I was the grateful holder of a National Endowment for the Humanities–Folger Shakespeare Library Fellowship, and I received valuable criticism and assistance from F. J. Levy, Linda Levy Peck and Joanna Udall.

Appendix

Books dedicated ('ded.') to Robert Carr individually or jointly are arranged chronologically with brief annotations where appropriate; initial numbers refer to *A Short-Title Catalogue . . . 1475–1640*, 2nd edn rev. by W. A. Jackson, F. S. Ferguson and Katharine F. Pantzer, 2 vols. (London, 1976–86); when known, dates of entry ('ent.') in the Stationers' Register are listed.

1611

13634 Homer, trans. Chapman, *Iliads* (1 of 3 sonnets added to those in 13633, *Iliads* 1–12 [1609?])

1612

6246 Samuel Daniel, *The First Part of the Historie of England* (2nd edn, 1618, ded. to Queen Anne)

1613

18697 Angelo Notari, *Prime musiche nuove*
25174 John Webster, *A Monumental Columne . . . to . . . Henry, Prince of Wales*

1614

18611 John Norden, *The Labyrinth of Mans Life* (ent. 17 January)
338 William Alexander, *Doomsday*
3609 (= 21462) Henry Brereton, *News of Rushia*
4964 George Chapman, *Andromeda Liberata*
13636 Homer, trans. Chapman, *Odysseys*, Books 1–12 [1614?]
15710 William Lithgow, *A Peregrination* 1614 (1st issue ded. to Carr; 2nd ded. to 'Gentlemen')

1615

73 John Abernethy, *A Christian and Heavenly Treatise* (ent. 17 August 1614)
6580.4 T. Dempster, *Votum Divae Virgini Sanlucianae*
13637 Homer, trans. Chapman, *Odysseys* 1–24

1616

13624   Homer, trans. Chapman, *Whole Works* [1616?] (*Odysseys* ded. retained)

1622

4988   George Chapman, *Pro Vere, Autumni Lachrymae*

1624/1624?

7326.5   Pierre Du Moulin, *Teares of Heraclitus, or, meditations . . . misery . . . mankind*, trans. Abraham Darcie (one issue ded. to Carr among others)
13628   Homer, trans. Chapman, *Crown of all Homers Workes* [1624?]

1625

6270   Abraham Darcie, *Honors true arbor . . . Nobilitie of the Howards* (family tree includes Frances Carr; multiple dedications)
17331   Francis Markham, *Book of Honor* (volume of 50 'epistles' each ded. to an individual; entire volume ded. to King Charles)

1629

6307   William Davenant, *The Tragedie of Albovine*

1631

1383   Richard Barckley, *Discourse of Felicity* 3rd edn (assigned to new publisher, 6 December 1630)

1637

10667   Mary Fage, *Fames roule, or Names . . . anagrammatiz'd* (includes Carr's name; ent. 22 April)

1638

10693   Robert Farley, *Kalendarium humanae vitae* (ent. 20 February)

14   John Donne, kingsman?

1 See George R. Potter and Evelyn M. Simpson, *The Sermons of John Donne*, (10 vols.; Berkeley and Los Angeles, 1953–62), I, p. 83.
2 See Thomas Docherty, *John Donne, Undone* (London and New York, 1986), p. 1. Docherty updates his topic primarily by his allegiance to deconstructive criticism. He avoids all but the most passing reference to Donne's biography, and understands history as the history of philosophy, or at best the history of science.
3 Compare the argument of Ernest Gilman, in ' "To adore, or scorn an image": Donne and the Iconoclastic Controversy', *John Donne Journal*, 5 (1986), that 'the surviving portraits offer a series of shifting, carefully contrived poses that

vividly reflect the several different selves Donne would fashion for himself – the resolute "gentleman volunteer" at eighteen, the fastidious melancholiac at twenty-three, the sober courtier at thirty-four, the august divine at forty-nine' (p. 68).

4 Ben Jonson, *Works*, eds. C. H. Herford, P. Simpson and E. Simpson, (11 vols.; Oxford, 1925–52), I, p. 135.

5 Donne, *Poetical Works*, ed. H. J. C. Grierson (Oxford, 1929), p. 14. I refer to this paperback version of the first volume of Grierson's edition on the grounds of its accessibility. The pagination differs from the original two-volume edition (Oxford, 1912), which contains annotation.

6 *Poetical Works*, pp. 14, 84.

7 If there remains any doubt that the king's passion for hunting was a frontal issue early in the reign, James settled that doubt by issuing, on 9 September 1609, a proclamation against poaching that began: 'We had hoped, seeing it is notorious to all our subjects how greatly we delight in the exercise of hunting'.

8 Donne, *Poetical Works*, p. 98.

9 Donne, *Biathanatos* (London, 1610), p. 187.

10 *The Courtier's Library, or Catalogus Librorum Aulicorum*, ed. E. M. Simpson (London, 1930), pp. 40–1.

11 John Donne, *Essays in Divinity*, ed. E. M. Simpson (Oxford, 1952), pp. ix–x, 3.

12 *Poetical Works*, p. 189.

13 In a letter to Sir Henry Goodyer printed in the 1633 edition of Donne's *Poems* (p. 352), Donne asked for the return of several of his manuscripts, including the *Catalogus librorum satyricus*, so that he could revise them.

14 Donne, *Essays in Divinity*, p. 3.

15 See *The Life and Letters of John Donne*, ed. Edmund Gosse (2 vols.; London, 1899), I, p. 108 facing.

16 For Donne's difficulties under Charles, see Bald, *A Life*, pp. 491–4; and my *Censorship and Interpretation* (Madison, 1984), pp. 100–5. Since many of the sermons are only hypothetically dated, we cannot be certain how many were Jacobean; but in November 1625, perhaps partly motivated by the king's death, Donne wrote to Sir Thomas Roe that he had copied out eighty of his sermons for the use of his son, and intended to continue this project. See Edmund Gosse, *Life and Letters of John Donne* (2 vols.; London, 1889), II, pp. 222–5.

17 Donne, *A Sermon Upon the VIII Verse of the 1 Chapter of the Acts of the Apostles. Preach'd To the Honourable Company of the Virginia Plantation. 13 Novemb. 1622* (London, 1622), p. 33. For an instance of Donne's resistance to the role of king's man in the pulpit, see my account, in *Censorship and Interpretation*, pp. 97–101, of the sermon Donne was commanded to preach in September 1622 supporting James's *Directions to Preachers*, restraining the pulpit from discussing the affairs of the Palatinate.

18 R. C. Bald, *John Donne: A Life* (Oxford, 1970).

19 John Carey, *John Donne: Life, Mind and Art* (New York, 1981).

20 Jonathan Goldberg, *James I and the Politics of Literature* (Baltimore, 1983). Goldberg makes Donne one of the chief exhibits of his thesis that James totally

dominated early seventeenth-century culture by the constitutive force of his Word, hypostasized as *Works* in 1616.

21 John Carey, *John Donne*, pp. 19, 11.

22 *Ibid.*, pp. 109, 115.

23 Goldberg, *James I*, p. 219.

24 Carey, *John Donne*, p. 21.

25 See especially T. K. Rabb and D. M. Hirst, 'Revisionism Revised', *Past and Present*, 92 (1981), 55–99.

26 Donne, *Letters to Severall Persons of Honour* (1651), p. 224.

27 Donne, *Biathanatos. A Declaration of that Paradoxe, or Thesis, that Selfe-homicide is not so Naturally Sinne, that it may never be otherwise* (London, 1646), pp. 48–9.

28 Compare *The Courtier's Library*, p. 24: 'Edward Hoby's Afternoon Belchings; or, A Treatise of Univocals, as of the King's Prerogative'. This shows that Donne was certainly capable of irony on the subject.

29 A dinner meeting of the Mermaid Club took place at the end of Michaelmas Term, in either 1609 or 1610, and included, as well as Hoskyns and Brooke, Richard Martin, Sir Henry Neville, Sir Robert Phelips, Lionel Cranfield and Arthur Ingram. See I. A. Shapiro, 'The "Mermaid Club"', *Modern Language Review*, 45 (1950), 6–17; and my own 'All Donne', in *Soliciting Interpretation*, ed. Elizabeth Harvey and Katharine Maus (Chicago, 1990), pp. 37–67.

30 See *Proceedings in Parliament 1610*, ed. Elizabeth Read Foster, 2 vols. (New Haven, 1966), II, p. 94.

31 Among the items in *The Courtier's Library* were 'A few small Treatises supplementary to the Books of Pancirolli; to the Book of Things Lost is added *A Treatise on Virtue and on Popular Liberty*, begun by a chaplain of John Cade and finished by Buchanan'. And in another, more economical joke Donne added, 'Tarlton, *On the Privileges of Parliament*' (pp. 48, 53). The first item associates popular liberty both with outright and unsuccessful rebellion, in the form of Jack Cade's 1450 insurrection, and with James's formidable Scottish tutor George Buchanan, a name that stood for the theory of contractual monarchy, classical republicanism and, if necessary, tyrannicide. The second item associates the privileges of parliament, which from 1604 onwards were consistently identified with freedom of speech, with a famous theatrical clown. It is impossible to determine, however, from which direction Donne's irony is coming.

32 John Donne, *Pseudo-Martyr*, ed. F. J. Sypher (Delmar, NY, Scholars' Facsimiles, 1974), A2.

33 Donne, *Pseudo-Martyr*, A2r.

34 *Ibid.*, B2v.

35 Donne's grandfather, John Heywood, married Sir Thomas More's niece Joan Rastell. Heywood himself fled to Europe in 1564 to escape the effects of the Elizabethan settlement of the church, and his brother Thomas was executed a decade later for saying mass. Donne's uncle, Jasper Heywood, became head of the Jesuit mission in England, and was captured and imprisoned in the Tower in 1583.

36 James I, *Triplici Nodo, Triplex Cuneus. Or an Apologie for the Oath of Allegiance* in *The Political Works of James I*, ed. C. H. McIlwain (2 vols.; Cambridge, Mass., 1918), I, p. 106.

37 James I, 'A Speach to the Lords and Commons of the Parliament at White-Hall, on Wednesday the XXI of March. Anno 1609', in McIlwain, pp. 306–7.

38 See *A Booke of Proclamations, published since the beginning of his Majesty's most happy reign over England, etc. until this present moneth of February 3. Anno Domini 1609* (London, 1610).

39 See *Proceedings*, II, p. 22.

40 See *ibid.*, II, pp. 321, 338n. A list of grievances 'delivered at a committee in writing by some of the lower House whose names were concealed' contained the item 'parliaments to be from 7 year to 7 year with provision that there be no proclamation law', II, p. 71. And see also James Larkin and Paul Hughes (eds.), *Stuart Royal Proclamations* (2 vols.; Oxford, 1973), I, pp. v–vi: 'The Jacobean proclamations are pointed expressions of attitudes and axioms of the Crown and of its wearer . . . Constitutionally, these documents are perhaps most significant as a prime source of friction between Crown and Parliament, especially the Commons, which repeatedly advanced them as grievances against the common law.'

41 *Proceedings*, II, p. 103.

42 *Ibid.*, II, p. 101.

43 Chamberlain, *Letters*, I, p. 301. For an immediate response in the House, see James Whitelocke's statement that 'he heard the speech yesterday and came ther with great desire and hope but went away exceeding sad and heavy and . . . saw nothing in that speech any way to restrain the power of imposing, even upon our lands and goods' (*Proceedings*, II, p. 108).

44 See also the warning of Sir Thomas Hedley in the 1610 debates that those who maintain 'an unlimited and transcendent prerogative may peradventure be holden like the lovers of Alexander with Ephestion but never true lovers of the king with Craterus' (*Proceedings*, II, p. 197).

45 Donne, *Pseudo-Martyr*, pp. 167–8. And in a letter to Sir Henry Goodyer written just before he began work on *Pseudo-Martyr*, Donne commented: 'the Supremacy which the Ro. church pretend, were diminished, if it were limited, will as ill abide that, or disputation, as the Prerogative of temporall Kings, who being the onely judges of their prerogative, why may not Roman Bishops . . . be good witnesses of their own supremacie, which is now so much impugned?' See *Letters to severall persons of Honour* (London, 1651), p. 161.

46 Donne, *Pseudo-Martyr*, pp. 171–2; italics added.

47 J. P. Sommerville, *Politics and Ideology in England, 1603–1640* (London and New York, 1986), p. 30.

48 Donne, *Pseudo-Martyr*, p. 83.

49 *Ibid.*, p. 169.

50 Donne, *Essays in Divinity*, p. 4.

51 Donne, *Poetical Works*, p. 146.

52 Donne, *Courtier's Library*, pp. 51–2.
53 The Latin is still more potent: 'Autorem quaeris? Frustra.' It is worth noting that when Kepler read the *Conclave* and noted its dependence on his own *Somnium*, he was unable to attach a name to it. See Marjorie Nicolson, *Science and Imagination* (Ithaca, 1956), pp. 63, 67.
54 Donne, *Ignatius his Conclave* (London, 1611), A3r–5v; italics added.
55 Bald, *A Life*, p. 228.
56 Donne, *Ignatius his Conclave*, 5v.
57 *Ibid.*, pp. 55, 33.
58 *Ibid.*, p. 13.
59 *Ibid.*, p. 27.
60 *Ibid.*, p. 17. T. S. Healey (ed.), *Ignatius his Conclave* (Oxford, 1969), p. xxx, suggests that Donne did not wish to satirize Galileo and was uneasy with the attack on Copernicus.
61 *Ibid.*, pp. 78–9.
62 Donne, *Poetical Works*, p. 144.
63 *Ibid.*, p. 118.
64 *Ibid.*, p. 135. For the 1633 omission, see W. Milgate (ed.), *The Satires and Verse Letters* (Oxford, 1967), p. 135.
65 See *Censorship and Interpretation*, pp. 100–1; and for the same meaning in Ben Jonson, pp. 53, 56, 134–5.
66 Donne, *Poetical Works*, p. 129.
67 John Chamberlain, *Letters*, ed. Norman McClure, 2 vols. (Philadelphia, 1939), I, p. 539.
68 See Maija Jansson (ed.), *Proceedings in Parliament 1614 (House of Commons)* (Philadelphia, 1988), pp. xxiii–xxx.
69 See Clayton Roberts and Owen Duncan, 'The Parliamentary Undertaking of 1614', *English Historical Review*, 93 (1978), 481–98. Roberts subsequently published a second version of his argument (without his collaborator) in *Schemes and Undertakings: A Study of English Politics in the Seventeenth Century* (Columbus, Ohio, 1985). It is worth noting that this book, which makes Henry Neville the heroic pioneer of undertaking, seen as a valuable innovation in political practice, concludes with praise of Margaret Thatcher as the heroic inheritor who brings the practice to perfection: 'She, and only she, can undertake to manage the Queen's affairs in Parliament successfully' (p. 251).
70 It was presented to James in July 1612. The full text is printed in S. R. Gardiner's *History of England from the accession of James I to the outbreak of civil war*, 10 vols. (London, 1883–4), II, pp. 389–94.
71 Sir John Holles to Lord Norris, 28 April 1614; H.M.C. Portland Mss. IX, p. 27.
72 Gosse, *Life and Letters of John Donne*, II, p. 34. In the second version of his argument, Clayton Roberts mentioned Donne's letter (mistakenly referring to him as the Dean of St Paul's at this time) and claimed that it was the first recorded use of the term 'undertaker' in this sense. See *Schemes and Undertakings*, p. x. 'Within three months', Roberts continued, 'the word *undertaker* was on every man's lips.'

73 After the session collapsed, the immediate provocation having been John Hoskyns's imprudent attack on the Scottish favourites and the reference to a Sicilian Vespers, John Chamberlain suggested that the Phelips, father and son, might have been responsible: 'for there be many presumptions that his hand was in it, his son being so busy and factious in the House, and Hoskyns one of his chief consorts and minions so far engaged, besides divers untoward speeches of his own.' See John Chamberlain, *Letters*, I, p. 540; and Linda Levy Peck, *Northampton: Patronage and Policy at the Court of James I* (London, 1982), p. 210, who cites Chamberlain's suggestion as part of her argument that the conspiracy theory involving Northampton – that Hoskyns's speech was planted in *order* to abort the session – was merely one of multiple rumours.

74 *Journal of the House of Commons*, I, pp. 494, 496.

75 R. C. Bald, *John Donne: A Life*, p. 289; italics added.

76 John Carey, *John Donne*, p. 88. When added to the misleading statement that Donne acquired his seat through 'court influence' (p. 87), when in fact he owed it to the father of one of the leading oppositionists, Carey's language quite unjustly suggests betrayal of friendship, another form of apostasy.

77 Donne, *Poetical Works*, pp. 90, 22, 78.

78 Donne, *Essays in Divinity*, p. 87.

79 Donne, *Poetical Works*, pp. 118–19.

80 *Ibid.*, p. 145.

81 See also the ironic metaphor, in *Loves growth*, that the relationship expands 'as princes doe in times of action get/New taxes, and remit them not in peace', *ibid.*, p. 31.

82 *Ibid.*, pp. 28–9.

83 *Ibid.*, p. 49.

84 *Ibid.*, p. 32.

85 See *Proceedings*, II, p. 241–4. This speech took place on 2 July 1610.

86 Donne, *Essays in Divinity*, p. 81. J. P. Sommerville, *Politics and Ideology*, p. 37, cited this passage as demonstrating that Donne supported the concept of free or unlimited monarchy. See also Donne's funeral elegy for Lord Harington, brother of Lucy, Countess of Bedford, where, in reference to his early death in 1614, Donne commented: 'Yet I am farre from daring to dispute/With that great soveraigntie, whose absolute/Prerogative hath thus dispens'd with thee,/'Gainst natures lawes' (p. 254). The context here, of course, made the belief in divine absolutism appropriate.

87 Donne, *Essays in Divinity*, p. 94.

88 Donne, *Poetical Works*, p. 237.

89 See *Proceedings*, II, pp. 164, 190.

90 Donne, *Poetical Works*, p. 103.

91 Donne, *Sermons*, 1:161.

INDEX

Abbot, George, archbishop of Canterbury
(1611–33), 90, 133, 307n45
Admonition Controversy, 154
Aggas, Edward:
The Defence of Death, 171
Alfred, king of the West Saxons (871–99), 88–9
Allde, Edward, 51
Allen, J. W., 36
Allen, Cardinal William, 154
ancient constitution, 8, 13, 40, 56, 63, 64, 65, 70,
78–95 *passim*, 150
Andrewes, Lancelot, bishop of Chichester
(1605–9), Ely (1609–19), Winchester
(1619–26), 6, 14, 60, 61, 62, 113–31 *passim*,
plate 30
and the beauty of holiness, 6, 128–30
his character, 132
and Christian liberty, 117–18
and Christocentricity, 120–3
and prayer, 125–6
and preaching, 124–5
and predestination, 116–17
and reverence, 118–19
and the sacrament, 127–8
and sermons, 116
Angus, earl of, *see* Douglas, William
Anne of Denmark, queen of England, also known
as queen Anna, 6–7, plate 9
arrival in England, 200, 202
character, 192, 207
coronation, 6
court, 138, 191–208 *passim*
family, 192–3
House, 10, 12, plate 10
household, 3, 7, 14, 330n46
patronage 15, 192, 202–3, 205, 207–8
and Prince Henry, 196–7, 198–9, 205–6, 207
relationship with Robert Cecil, 142–3
and Scottish politics, 193–200

Arianism, 118
Aristotle, 15, 73, 151, 155, 157, 158
Ethics, 101
Arminianism, 14, 113, 114, 131, 132
Arschot, duke of, *see* Croy family
art, 7, 12, 18, 25, 27, 34, 192, 201, 208, 210,
211, 221, 222, 231
see also subheadings under Carr, Robert; court
culture; Howard, Henry earl of
Northampton
Arundel, Charles, 153
Arundel, countess of, *see* Howard, Alatheia
Arundel, earl of, *see* Howard, Philip; Howard,
Thomas
Arundel House, 10, 104
Ascham, Roger, 149
Aston, Roger, 197
Audley End, Essex, 10, 99, 110, plate 17
Aylmer, John bishop of London (1577–94),
315n32

Bacon, Sir Edmund, 184
Bacon, Sir Francis, 9, 79, 86, 89, 101, 107, 108,
109, 110, 172, 173, 174–5, 177, 186,
320n105
Advancement of Learning, 149, 150, 175
Apophthegms, 174
Essays, 175
*History of the Reign of King Henry the
Seventh*, 175
Baggris, Antoine Rascas de, 4
Bald, R. C., 254, 263, 268
Bancroft, Richard, bishop of London
(1597–1604), archbishop of Canterbury
(1604–10), 5, 61
Banqueting House, Whitehall, 6, 7, 10, 12, 71,
99–100, 103, 110, 224, plate 18
Barckley, Sir Richard:
Discourse of Felicite, 240

353

Barclay, John, 60
Barclay, William:
  De Regno, 60
Barkham, Sir Edward 276n37
Barlow, Thomas, bishop of Lincoln (1675–91), 318n73
Bartas, Salluste du, 185
Bate's case, 64–5, 78, 79
Bedford, countess of, *see* Harington, Lucy
Bellarmine, Robert, cardinal, 37, 59, 60, 64, 65, 68, 152, 159, 164, 167, 258
Berkeley, Katherine, 315n43
Beza, Theodore, 41
Bilson, Thomas, bishop of Winchester (1597–1616), 307n45
Blayney, Peter W. M., 4, 51
Blount, Charles, Lord Mountjoy, later earl of Devonshire, 172, 175, 177, 200, 201, 203
Boccalini, Traiano:
  Ragguagli di Parrasso, 186
Bodin, Jean, 54, 61, 62, 150–1, 155, 156–7, 172
  Methodus ad facilem historiarum cognitionem, 152
  Six livres de la Republique, 43, 152, 153, 155
Boece, Hector, 40–1, 45
Bolton, Edmund, 9, 164, 186
  Nero Caesar, 186–7
Bossuet, Jacques, 40
Bothwell, earl of, *see* Stewart, Francis
Bouwsma, William, 160
Bowes, Robert, 196
Brahe, Tycho, 193
Brandon, Charles, 1st duke of Suffolk, 29
Bridges, John, 113
Bridgewater, earl of, *see* Egerton, John
Brooke, Christopher, 257, 268
Brooke, Henry, 11th Lord Cobham, 202
Brooks, Christopher, 80
Bruce, Edward, Lord of Kinloss, 198
Bruce, Robert, 39
Buchanan, George, 38, 40–6, 50, 54, 58, 73, 149, 151, 155, 156, 313n16, 349n31
  De Iure Regno apud Scotos, 44
  History of Scotland, 44
Buckeridge, John, bishop of Rochester (1611–28), 6, 14, 113–33 *passim*, plate 30
  and the beauty of holiness, 128–31
  and faith, 121, 123
  and irreverence, 118, 119
  and prayer, 126
  and the sacrament, 124–5, 126–8
Buckingham, duke of, *see* Villiers, George
Budé, Guillaume:
  Institut du Prince, 43
Burbage, Richard, 143, 201
Burgess, John, 7
Burghley, Lord, *see* Cecil, Sir William (d. 1598)
Burns, J. H., 40
Butler, Martin, 2
Byrd, William, 201

Caesar, Sir Julius, 136, 242–3
Calvert, Samuel, 302n32
Calvin, John, 40
Calvinism, 123, 131, 132, 133, 316n61
Camden, William, 103, 167, 183, 187
  Annals of Queen Elizabeth, 183
  Brittania, 8
Campi, Antonio, 152
Carew, Sir George, later earl of Totnes, 203
Carey, John, 254, 268
Carey, Philadelphia, Lady Scrope, 200
Carey, Sir Robert, 144
Carleton, Sir Dudley, 11, 101, 105, 137, 202, 232, 234–5, 238, 260, 300n22, 336n2, 340n32
Carlisle, earl of, *see* Hay, Sir James
Carr, Anne, 236–7
Carr, Frances, *see* Howard, Frances
Carr, Robert, 1st earl of Somerset, 7, 12, 15, 16, 164, 167, 183, 207, 230–50 *passim*, 252, 264–6 *passim*, 267, 268, 269
  books dedicated to him, 345–7
  and jewellery, 235–6
  literary patronage, 231, 239–50
  and painting, 230–5, 237–8, plates 21, 22
  and tapestries, 233–4
Carr, Sir Robert, earl of Ancram, 255, 260, 343n58
Cartwright, Thomas, 153, 154
Casaubon, Isaac, 61, 174, 183, 186, 187
Cassirer, Ernst, 210
Castelvetro, Giacomo, 47
Castiglione, Baldassare, 150, 158
  The Courtier, 164
Castle, John, 244
Catesby, conspiracy of (1605), 177
Cavendish, Thomas, 237
Cecil, Sir Edward, 141
Cecil, Sir Robert, viscount Cranborne, 1st earl of Salisbury (d. 1612), 1, 10, 12, 13, 14, 15, 33–4, 44, 50, 51, 60, 105, 107, 134–47 *passim*, 149, 162, 164, 174, 197, 203, 205, 206, 231, 242, 259, 320n105, plate 14
  and building programme, 140
  death, 147
  and the Household, 143–4
  and the Jacobean Scots, 144–6
  and the Order of the Garter, 139–40
  physique, 138
  and relations with James I, 134–7, 138, 140, 144–6
  and relations with Prince Henry, 140–2
  and relations with Queen Anne, 142–3
  and Theobalds, 135, 139
  wealth, 140, 146
Cecil, Thomas, Lord Burghley, 1st earl of Exeter (d. 1623), 146
Cecil, William, later 2nd earl of Exeter (d. 1640), 231

Cecil, Sir William, later Lord Burghley (d. 1598), 29–31 *passim*, 33, 135, 143, 146, 155, 183, 193, 195, 196
Cecil, William, viscount Cranborne, later 2nd earl of Salisbury (d. 1668), 139, 140–1, 341n43
Chaloner, Sir Thomas, 177, 206
Chamberlain, John, 101, 147, 233, 235, 260, 266, 352n73
Chapman, George, 16, 178, 205, 240–6 *passim*, 250
  Andromeda Liberata, 242–4
  The Crowne of all Homers Workes, 244, 245
  Pro Vere, Autumni Lacrymae, 244–5
Charles I, king of England (1625–49):
  as prince, 3, 11, 58, 60, 67, 91–2, 180, 198, 231, 235, 236
  as king, 1, 7, 11, 55, 67, 93, 95, 99, 112, 133, 249, 262, 341n39
Charles V, Holy Roman Emperor:
  Political Testament, 47, 50
Charron, Pierre, 171
  De la Sagesse, 172
Christianson, Paul, 36
Chrysippus, 185
Chrysostom, St John, 127–8
Cicero, 15, 151, 154, 169, 173, 312n9
  De Officiis, 181
Clifford, Lady Anne, 202
Cobham, Lady, *see* Howard, Elizabeth
Cobham, William Lord, 162
Coke, Sir Edward, 48, 52, 56, 62, 63, 65, 69–70, 75, 80, 84–90 *passim*, 93, 95, 174, 207, 239, 244, 292n32
Collinson, Patrick, 133
Commines, Philippe de, 176
Conciliar Movement, 40; *see also* Mair, John
conquest of England, 43, 50, 63
Cooper, Thomas, 113
Cope, Sir Walter, 143, 326n2
Copernicus, Nicolaus, 264
Cornwallis, Sir Charles, 176, 177
Cornwallis, Sir William, 175–81 *passim*
  Discourses upon Seneca the Tragedian, 175, 176
  Essays, 175, 180
Corona Regiae, 59
Correr, Marc Antonio, Venetian ambassador, 241
Cortes, Ferdinand, 237
Cottington, Sir Francis, 300n22
Cotton, Sir Robert, 8, 103, 110, 150, 152, 157, 158, 160, 183, 188
  Short View of the Long Life and Reign of Henry III, 183
court, 23–4, 25, 28, 30, 31, 32
  definitions of, 3–4, 102–5, 137–8
court culture, 1–16 *passim*, 100–112 *passim*, 137
  and architecture, 10–11, 99–100
  and art, 7, 11–12
  and the chivalric, 8
  cultural images of court society, 107–8

and foreign policy, 110–11
and iconography, 5, 6
and maps, 6, 9–10, plates 23–5
and medals and coins, 4–5, 43, 44, plates 1, 2
patterns of conspicuous consumption, 108–10
and the study of history, 8–9
and woodcuts, 5
and the written word, 4, 5–6
see also Anne of Denmark; James I; masques
Cowell, John:
  The Interpreter, 76, 77
Craig, John, 41
Craig, Sir Thomas, 53–4
Craigie, Dr James, 50
Crakanthorp, Richard, 318n73
Cranborne, viscount, *see* Cecil, William, later 2nd earl of Salisbury (d. 1668)
Cranfield, Sir Lionel, later earl of Middlesex, 143, 160, 163, 349n29
Cranmer, Thomas, archbishop of Canterbury (1533–53), 154
Crew, Sir Randolph, 93
Critz, John de, 140
Croft, Pauline, 65
Cromwell, Thomas, 1st earl of Essex, 24–7 *passim*
Croy family:
  Charles, duc de Croy de d'Arschot, 231
Cuddy, Neal, 3, 14
Cuffe, Henry, 172–3, 174
Cunningham, James, 7th earl of Glencairne, 198
Cusanus, Nicolaus, 210

Dallington, Sir Robert, 178, 180–1
  Aphorisms Civil and Military, 180
Daly, James, 72
Daniel, Samuel, 171, 178, 192, 201
  First Part of the Historie of England, 242
  Vision of the Twelve Goddesses, 226
Danvers, Henry Lord, 235, 336n2
Darcie, Abraham, 239–40, 250
Darcy, Elizabeth, Lady Lumley, 206
Davenant, William:
  The Tragedy of Albovine, King of the Lombards, 246–8, 250
Davidson, John, 52
Davies, Sir John, 65, 80, 84–7 *passim*
Declaration of Arbroath (1320), 39
Derby, countess of, *see* Stanley, Elizabeth
Devereux, Robert, 2nd earl of Essex (d. 1601), 8, 13, 33–5, 110, 134, 165, 172–5 *passim*, 240, 246, 253, 319n90; *see also* Essex circle
Devereux, Robert, 3rd earl of Essex (d. 1646), 15, 140, 205, 242, 244, 264, 307n45
D'Ewes, Sir Simonds, 177
Dio Cassius, 172, 179, 185–6
Diodati, Theodore, 201
divine right, *see* kingship
Docherty, Thomas, 251
Doderidge, Sir John, 79

Dominis, Marc'Antonio de, 4, 61
Donne, John, 6, 15, 16, 103, 105–6, 108, 226, 242, 251–72 *passim*, plate 33
  Anniversaries, 252, 268, 270
  Biathanatos, 251, 253, 256, 257, 260
  Conclave Ignati, 262–3
  The Courtier's Library, 252, 253, 262
  Elegies, 252, 268–9, 271
  Essays in Divinity, 253, 262, 269, 270
  Holy Sonnets, 210
  Loves Exchange, 252, 270
  Pseudo-Martyr, 252, 253, 258–63 *passim*
  Satire 2, 268, 269
  A Valediction: of the booke, 269–70
Dorislaus, Isaac, 187
Dorset, earl of, *see* Sackville, Thomas
Dort, synod of (1618), 120, 133, 184
Douglas, James, 4th earl of Morton, 44
Douglas, William, earl of Angus, 51
Dowland, John, 201
Drake, Francis, 237
Drayton, Michael, 100, 110, 201
Drebbel, Cornelis, 60
Drummond, Jane, later countess of Roxborough, 7
Drummond of Hawthornden:
  A Cypress Grove, 210
Drury, Elizabeth, 270
Du Moulin, Pierre, 59, 60, 62
  Teares of Heraclitus, 239
Du Perron, Jacques, 58–9, 60, 63
Du Plessis-Mornay, Philippe, 41, 171, 185
  De La Vérité, 171
  Excellent Discours, 171
Dudley, John, 1st earl of Warwick, 1st duke of Northumberland, 26, 27
Dudley, Robert, earl of Leicester, 29–31 *passim*, 33, 34, 153, 162, 337n7
Dunbar, earl of, *see* Home, Sir George
Durham House Group, 114
Dyer, Edward, 237

Edmondes, Sir Thomas, 202, 203
Edward IV, king of England (1461–9; 1471–83), 23
Edward VI, king of England (1547–53), 26, 27, 136
Egerton, John, earl of Bridgewater, 342n52
Egerton, Sir Thomas, 1st Lord Ellesmere, lord chancellor, 84, 86, 103, 181–2, 267, 293n47
Elam, Keir, 216, 221
Elias, Norbert, 161
Eliot, Sir John, 188
Elizabeth I, queen of England (1558–1603), 5, 8, 13, 21, 26–35 *passim*, 39, 41, 44, 48, 51, 58, 65, 88, 89, 93, 134, 136, 152–3, 165, 167, 173, 174, 191, 195–6, 313n21
  court of, 3–4, 137, 162
  court culture of, 112

Elizabeth, princess, daughter of James I, sister to Charles I, 109, 142, 146, 202, 206, 207, 233, 252, 342n46
Ellesmere, Lord, *see* Egerton, Sir Thomas
Elphinstone, Alexander, 4th Lord, 198
Elphinstone, Sir James, 197, 198
Elsyng, Sir Henry, 90, 91
Elton, G. R., 3, 104
emblems, 10, 16, 210, 214, 221, 222–7 *passim*, 229; *see also* Ripa, Cesare
Epictetus, 169, 170, 171
  Manual, 185
Erroll, earl of, *see* Hay, Francis
Erskine, John, 3rd earl of Mar, 140, 195–9 *passim*, 242–3
Erskine, Thomas, 197
Essex circle, 149, 172, 174–8 *passim*, 182, 200–1, 203, 204, 268; *see also* Devereux, Robert, 2nd earl of Essex
Essex, earl of, *see* Devereux, Robert (d. 1601); Devereux, Robert (d. 1646)
Estates General of France, 58, 59
Exeter, earl of, *see* Cecil, Thomas; Cecil, William

faction, 26, 27, 29, 30, 31, 115
Fanshawe, Sir Henry, 233, 234
favourites, 26, 29, 30, 33; *see also* Carr, Robert; Villiers, George
Fergus, king of Scots, 8, 46, 73, 156
Filmer, Sir Robert, 151
Finch, Heneage, 79, 270
Fincham, Ken, 114–15, 132, 133
Fitzgerald, Frances countess of Kildare, 200, 202
Florio, John, 178, 192, 201, 208
Fortescue, Sir John, 23, 37, 38, 56, 57, 63, 84
  De Laudibus Legum Angliae, 63, 84
Foxe, John, 149, 262
Frederic, Elector Palatine, 165, 245, 252
Frederick II, king of Denmark and Norway, 192–3
Freeman, Rosemary, 223
Fuller, Nicholas, 37, 48, 78, 79, 271

Gainsford, Thomas, 181–2
Gardiner, Stephen bishop of Winchester (1531–51; 1553–55), 26, 149, 167
Garnet, Father Henry, 158, 159, 167, 264
garter, order of the, 8, 139–40, plates 26, 27
General Assembly of Scotland (1564), 41
Gentili, Alberico, 313n19
  De Potestate Regis Absoluta, 62
Gerson, Jean, 39
Gheeraerts, Marcus, 140
Gibb, Sir Henry, 237
Glanville, Philippa, 11
Goldberg, Jonathan, 2, 8, 254, 255, 275n18
Golding, Arthur, 171
Gondomar, *see* Sarmiento, Count Gondomar
Gonzaga, dukes of, 11

Goodman, Godfrey, bishop of Gloucester (1625–40), 49
Gordon, D. J., 226
Gordon, George, 6th earl and marquis of Huntly, 51, 195, 197
Gordon, Henrietta, countess of Huntly, 194–5
Gordon, John, dean of Salisbury, 62
Goring, Sir George, 67
Gowrie Conspiracy (1600), 42, 45, 114, 197–8
Gowrie, earl of, *see* Ruthven, William
grandees, definition of, 148–9
Great Contract (1610), 141, 146, 161
Greenblatt, Stephen, 2
Greg, Walter, 243
Greneway, Richard, 172, 173, 185
Gretser, Jacob, 152
Greville, Fulke, 172, 174, 175, 177, 187
Grotius, Hugo, 159
Gucciardini, Francesco, 9, 101, 175, 176, 181
Gunpowder Plot (1605), 58, 62, 114, 152, 158, 159, 177, 179
Gwynne, Matthew, 201

Hakewill, William, 79, 80, 83, 88, 93
Hall, Arthur, 88
Hall, Joseph, bishop of Norwich (1641–56), 178, 183–4, 185
    Characters of Virtues and Vices, 183
    Heaven upon Earth, 183
Hamilton, John, 1st marquis of Hamilton, 50, 198
Hampton Court Conference (1604), 5
Harington family, 175, 352n86
Harington, John, 206, 207
Harington, Lucy, countess of Bedford, also known as Lucy Russell, 15, 178, 200–8 *passim*, 242, plate 11
Harington, Sir John, 178, 200, 201, 202, plate 12
Harp, 39
Harrison, Stephen:
    Arches of Triumph, 7
Harte, Percival, 152
Harvey, Gabriel, 151, 312n11
Hatfield House, Herts, 10, 110, 140
Hatton, Sir Christopher, 29, 30, 33
Hay, Francis, earl of Erroll, 51
Hay, Gilbert, 39
Hay, Sir James, later 1st earl of Carlisle, 167, 207, 231
Hayward, Sir John, 172, 174, 175, 177
    First Part of the Life and Reign of King Henry IV, 174
Healey, John, 185
Hedley, Thomas, 72, 79–80, 81, 82, 84, 86, 94, 95, 271, 350n44
Henrietta Maria, queen of England, 11
Henry III, king of France (1574–89), 58
Henry IV, king of France (1589–1610), king of Navarre, 4, 8, 42, 58, 139

Henry VI, king of England (1422–61; 1470–1), 63, 88, 89, 93
Henry VII, king of England (1485–1509), 21, 23, 34, 89, 134
Henry VIII, king of England (1509–47), 21, 23–4, 25, 62, 88, 89, 136, 137, 145, 164, 167
Henry of Navarre, *see* Henry IV
Henry, prince (d. 1612), 8, 15, 48, 49, 71, 109, 110, 111, 172, 192, 199, 205–6, 208, 231, 240, 282n42, 342n46, plates 6, 12
    birth, 158
    court and household, 3, 14, 105, 177–8, 183
    patronage, 177, 207
    and Robert Cecil, 140–2, 146
    St James' House, 104
Herbert, Lady Anne, 200
Herbert, Lord of Cherbury, 110
Herbert, Mary countess of Pembroke, 171, 172, 200
Herbert, Philip, earl of Montgomery, later 4th earl of Pembroke (d. 1650), 104, 205, 237, 341nn43, 44
Herbert, William, 3rd earl of Pembroke (d. 1630), 12, 105, 140, 149, 167, 200–1, 202, 207–8
Hermetic tradition, 100, 102
Herodotus, 101
Hertford, countess of, *see* Seymour, Frances
Heylin, Peter, 307n43
Heywood family, 349n35
Heywood, Thomas, 179, 239–40, 250
Hilliard, Nicholas, 5, 201
historiography, 1, 8–9, 15, 38, 56–7, 108; *see also* individual historians
Hobart, Sir Henry, attorney general, 79
Hoby, Sir Edward, 262, 267
Holinshed, Raphael, 53–4
    Chronicles of England, Scotland and Ireland, 53–4
Holles, Francis, 276n37
Holles, Sir George, 276n37
Holles, Sir John, 9, 16, 233, 243, 267
Home, Sir George, Lord Home, later 1st earl of Dunbar, 137, 142, 144, 195, 198
Homer:
    Iliad, 241, 243, 246
Hooker, Richard, 14, 113–14, 131
    Of the Laws of Ecclesiastical Polity, 156
Hoskyns, John, 257, 352n73
Howard, Alatheia, countess of Arundel, 10, 12
Howard, Catherine, countess of Suffolk, 204
Howard, Charles, 1st earl of Nottingham, 136, 161, 204
Howard, Elizabeth, Lady Cobham, 191
Howard family, 23, 26, 29, 161–2, 166, 177, 184, 230, 237, 247, 248, 266
Howard, Frances, countess of Somerset, also known as Frances Carr, 7, 162, 167, 230, 233, 234, 235, 236, 242, 243, 244, 252, 264–5

Howard, Henry, Lord Howard, after 1604 earl of
  Northampton (d. 1614), 8, 11, 15, 62, 134,
  135, 140, 148–68 *passim*, 176, 177, 178,
  183, 186, 207, 231, 237, 257, plates 28, 29
  his collections, 165–6
  and court politics, 162, 164
  *A Defensative against the Poyson of Supposed
    Prophesies*, 153, 167
  *A Defense of the Ecclesiasticall Regiment in
    Englande*, 154
  and Howard family, 161–2
  and James I, 149, 153, 159, 160, 166
  his library, 151–2
  Northampton House, 165, 166
  as orator, 158
  and Roman Catholicism, 152, 154, 158,
    319n84
  views on kingship, 154–8
  view of nobility, 163
  work as privy councillor, 160–1
Howard, Henry, *styled* earl of Surrey (d. 1547),
  149, 312n9, plate 19
Howard, Lord Henry, *see* Howard, Henry, Lord
  Howard (d. 1614)
Howard, Philip, earl of Arundel, 337n8
Howard, Thomas, 3rd duke of Norfolk (d. 1554),
  149, 164, 167
Howard, Thomas, 4th duke of Norfolk (d. 1572),
  29, 152, 162
Howard, Thomas, earl of Arundel (d. 1646), 1, 8,
  10, 11–12, 104, 105, 106, 109, 110, 111,
  151, 152, 167, 183, 231, 235, 238, plate 20
Howard, Thomas, lord treasurer, 1st earl of
  Suffolk (d. 1626), 10, 141, 142, 163, 164,
  167, 233, 234, 242
Huntly, countess of, *see* Gordon, Henrietta
Huntly, earl of, *see* Gordon, George
Hutton, Matthew, archbishop of York
  (1595–1606), 160
Hyde, Edward, earl of Clarendon, 247, 248

iconography, 1, 4, 5, 162, 215, 224, 225; *see also*
  court culture
Inns of Court, 3, 14, 105, 106
Ireland, 9–10, 30, 32, 34
Ireland, John:
  Merroure of Wisdome, 39

Jacobean Scots, 3, 107, 135–6, 144–5
Jakobson, Roman, 222
James I, king of England (1603–25); king of
  Scotland as James VI (1567–1625), 178,
  plates 1–8
  his accession, 33–5, 134, 177
  his bedchamber, 136, 143, 144–5, 146, 147
  and ceremony, 7
  character, 49, 132
  and constitutional monarchy, 13, 85–6, 93, 94
  and coronation, 6, 43, 77, 156
  and the court of queen Anne, 203

as emperor, 5, 7–8, 9
  and the English church, 114–15, 133
  and ideology of family, 6–7
  and impositions, 64–5, 66, 67, 72, 78–9, 80,
    83
  interference in European affairs, 59–60
  and masques, 214, 217, 226, 227
  opinion of Tacitus, 186–7
  his political ideas, 56, 57–9, 63, 65–7, 70
  and privy councillors, 319n92
  and progresses, 136–9
  and relations with parliaments, 37–8, 53,
    55–6, 63–70 *passim*, 74–6, 78–9, 80–1,
    83–4, 86–94, 259–60
  royal patronage, 12–13, 60–2, 106
  and the Scottish kirk, 43, 58, 154, 194
  and Scottish reign, 42–4, 193–4
  and Robert Carr, 235, 236, 238, 242, 247–9,
    339n22
  and Robert Cecil, 134–7, 138–9, 140, 144–6
  and John Donne, 254, 258–9, 260
  and Henry Howard, 149, 153, 159, 160, 161
  his writings, 4, 6–7, 37, 38, 48–9, 58–9, 60,
    62–3, 72, 73; *see also* individual books
  Basilikon Doron, 4, 13, 16, 42, 43,
    47–52 *passim*, 71, 72, 153, 166, 186, 225,
    226, 292n28, plate 3; printing history, 50–2;
    intended readers, 48–50
  Daemonologie, 49
  Paraphrase on Revelations, 49
  Premonition to all Christian Monarchies, 49
  Reulis and Cautellis of Poesie, 49
  Trew Law of Free Monarchies, 6, 7, 13, 36,
    42, 43, 45–7, 49–54 *passim*, 64, 71, 73, 76,
    94, 153, 260, 292n28; intended readers,
    48–9
  *Triplici Nodo Triplex Cuneus. Or an Apologie
    for The Oath of Allegiance*, 49, 152, 258
  Workes, 62
  see also court culture; King James Bible
James II, king of England (1685–88), 318n73
James IV, king of Scotland (1488–1513), 39
James VI, king of Scotland, *see* James I
Jesuits, 65, 66, 68, 69, 70, 259, 262–4
John, master of Orkney, 198
John XXII, pope, 39
Johnson, Robert, 175
Jones, Inigo, 8, 10, 12, 99, 100, 106, 110, 111,
  201, 208, 222, 223, 227, 235, 300n21,
  341n37, plates 9, 11, 16, 18
  his books, 101
  Tempe Restord, 211
Jones, William, 172
Jonson, Ben, 15, 99, 100, 101, 103, 104, 106,
  107, 108–11 *passim*, 164, 178–80, 201, 205,
  208, 216, 220, 221, 242, 251, 252
  Cataline, 179
  Haddington Masque, 226
  Hymenai, 222, 225
  Lovers Made Men, 224

Newes from the New World, 226
Pleasure Reconciled to Virtue, 216–17, 223, 226
Poetaster, 178
Sejanus, 178, 179–80, 188
Volpone, 107
Jordan, Constance, 155
Julius II, pope, 237
Junius, Hadrian, 149
Juvenal, 179, 181

Kelley, Edward, 237
Kendall, Dr, 123
Kenyon, J. P., 57
Kepler, Joannes, 60
Kerr, Robert, earl of Roxborough, 7
Kerr, Sir Robert, earl of Ancram, *see* Carr, Sir Robert
Key, William, 238
Kildare, countess of, *see* Fitzgerald, Frances
King James Bible, 5–6, plate 31
kingship, 22–3, 28, 36–40 *passim*, 44, 45, 47, 48, 52, 54, 154–8
    absolute monarchy, 13, 36, 42, 43, 56–7, 61, 62, 71–4, 76, 93, 94, 150, 157, 160, 255, 256, 259, 261, 268
    contractual theories of kingship, 41, 42, 43, 45, 61, 70, 80, 349n31
    divine right, 6, 13, 46, 48, 50, 53, 55–70 *passim*, 71–2, 160, 186, 228, 229, 256, 262
    mixed monarchy, 62, 69, 72, 73, 81, 83, 84, 86, 94, 96, 294n54
    resistance theory, 39, 41, 58, 60, 66, 70, 154, 156, 159
    see also political theory, Scottish
Kingston, Felix, 51
Kishlansky, Mark, 2
Knollys, William, Lord Wallingford, 143
Knox, John, 41, 46, 58
    First Blast of the Trumpet, 155
    History of the Reformation, 50

Lake, Sir Thomas, 145, 301n23
Laud, William, archbishop of Canterbury (1633–45), 14, 113, 114, 131, 133
law:
    civil law, 75, 77–8, 79, 85–6, 153, 157
    common law discourse, 56, 58, 62–5 *passim*, 72, 75–95 *passim*
    see also Inns of Court
Le Roy, Louis, 151
Lee, Maurice, 48
Leicester, earl of, *see* Dudley, Robert; Sidney, Robert
Lennard, Samson, 172
Lennox, duke of, *see* Stuart, Esmé; Stuart, Ludovic
Leslie, John, bishop of Ross (1567–8; 1575–89), 315n32

Lipsius, Justus, 15, 151, 155, 169–72, 174–5, 176, 178, 181, 183, 184, 185, 186, 187
    Constancy, 170, 172, 188
    Manuductio ad Stoicam Philosophiam, 171
    Monita et Exempla, 171, 181
    Six Books of Politics, 170, 171, 172, 175, 181
Lisle, Lawrence, 243
Livingstone, Alexander, earl of Linlithgow, 198
Livy, 155, 169
    Historia, 152
Lodge, Thomas, 184–5
    Wit's Misery, 184
    Workes of Seneca, plate 32
    The Wounds of Civil War, 184
London, bishop of, *see* Ridley, Nicholas; Aylmer, John; Bancroft, Richard; Abbot, George
Lords of the Articles, 45, 281n24
lordship, 23
Lotman, Yuri, 220, 228
Love's Triumph Through Callipolis, 218
Loyola, Ignatius, 237, 262, 264
Lumley, John Lord, 231
Luther, Martin, 262, 313–14
Lyly, John, 205

Machiavelli, Niccolò, 9, 151, 155, 157, 162, 186, 264
    Discorsi, 152
    Historia Fiorentina, 152
McIlwain, C. H., 56
Magna Carta, 38, 271
Main and Bye Plots (1603), 177, 202
Mair, John, 40–1, 42, 46
    History of Greater Britain, 40
Maitland, William of Lethington, chancellor of Scotland, 41, 195–6, 197
Manners, Elizabeth, countess of Rutland, 201, 202
Manners, Roger, earl of Rutland, 11, 172, 174, 175, 177, 180, 200, 201, plates 28, 29
Mantegna, Andrea, 11
Mar, earl of, *see* Erskine, John
Marsilius, Joannes, 61
Marston, John, 179
    The Fawn, 164
Mary, queen of England (1553–8), 26, 27, 65
Mary, queen of Scotland (1542–67), also known as Mary Stuart and Mary, queen of Scots, 29, 39, 41, 42–3, 44, 152, 153, 162, 163, 166, 183
Mary Stuart, *see* Mary, queen of Scotland
Masque of Augurs, 218
Masque of Beauty, 217
Masque of Flowers, 224
Masque of Queenes, 216
Masque of Twelve Months, 214
masques, 7, 16, 60, 101–2, 103, 107, 109, 110, 111, 139, 142, 208, 209–29 *passim*, plate 11
    and antimasque, 212, 214, 215, 216–17, 219, 229

masques (*cont.*)
    and the court, 218–20
    and emblems, 16, 210, 214, 221,
        222–7 *passim*, 229
    theatres for masques, 212–15, 217–18
Matthieu, Pierre 188
Mayerne, Sir Theodore, 105, 147
Maynwaring, Roger, 66
Melville, Andrew, 43, 46, 52
Melvillians, 43, 47, 49, 50, 52
Meres, Francis, 205
Meutys, Jane, 178
Middleton, Thomas:
    The Masque of Heroes, 219–20
Miller, James, 244
Mirror for Magistrates, 151
Mirror of Justices, 88
Molino, Nicolo, 207
Mompesson, Sir Giles, 88
monarchy, *see* kingship
Montague, James, bishop of Bath and Wells
    (1608–16), Winchester (1616–18), 133
Montague, Richard, bishop of Lichfield
    (1628–38), Norwich (1638–41), 114, 131,
    133
Montaigne, Michel de, 171, 173, 180, 185, 186,
    201
    Essays, 178
Montgomery, earl of, *see* Herbert, Philip
Mor, Antonis, 238
Morales, Ambrosio de:
    La Corònica General de España, 152
Moray, earl of, *see* Stewart, James
More, Sir George, 235, 267
More, Sir Thomas, 258–9
Moreau, Philippe, 152
Mornay, Philippe, *see* Du Plessis-Mornay,
    Philippe
Morrill, John, 2
Morton, earl of, *see* Douglas, James
Morton, Thomas, 258
Mountjoy, Lord, *see* Blount, Charles
Munck, Levinus, 137
Mytens, Daniel, 10, 100, 110, 301n23, plates 8,
    20

Nabbes, Thomas:
    Microcosm. A Moral Maske, 210
Nannini, Remigio, 181
National Covenant (1638), 42
Naunton, Sir Robert, 139, 201
Neile, Richard, bishop of Rochester (1608–10),
    Lichfield (1610–14), Lincoln (1614–17),
    Durham (1617–28), 83–4, 114, 267, 307n45
Nero, 169, 173
Neville, Charles, 6th earl of Westmorland, 29
Neville, Sir Henry, 266, 267, 349n29
New Exchange, London, 10, 140, plate 16
Nicoll, Allardyce, 214, 222
Nicolson, George, 50

Norbrook, David, 215
Norfolk, duke of, *see* Howard, Thomas (d. 1554);
    Howard, Thomas (d. 1572)
Norris, Sir John, 246
Northampton, earl of, *see* Howard, Henry
    (d. 1614)
Northampton House, London, 10, 165
Northumberland, countess of, *see* Percy, Dorothy
Northumberland, duke of, *see* Dudley, John
Northumberland, earl of, *see* Percy, Thomas;
    Percy, Henry
Norton, John, 51
Nottingham, countess of, *see* Stuart, Margaret
Nottingham, earl of, *see* Howard, Charles
Noy, William, 88, 93
Nys, Daniel, 232, 235

Oestreich, Gerhard, 15, 169
office holding, 23, 24, 27, 28, 31–2
Olivares, Count, 164
Oliver, Isaac, 208, plates 6, 33
Orgel, Stephen, 213, 216, 217, 224, 227
Orkney, earl of, *see* Sinclair, William
Osborne, John, 233, 234
Overbury, Sir Thomas, 16, 107, 167, 230, 231,
    233, 235, 244, 264–5, 344n62
    Characters, 253, 265
Owen, Sir Roger, 79

Packer, John, 232
Palmer, James, 339n24
Panofsky, Erwin, 210
papal authority over rulers, 58–9, 61, 63–4, 65,
    68–9, 159, 160
parliament, of England, 13, 24, 25, 45, 55–6, 57,
    74, 77–8, 83, 95, 150, 316n46
    of 1604, 66, 67, 74–5, 78–81, 92, 93, 94, 154,
        282n45, 294n62, 316n52
    of 1610, 37, 52–3, 64, 66, 67, 72, 76, 81–2,
        92, 93, 141–2, 144, 146, 259, 271
    of 1614, 67, 83, 230, 266, 272
    of 1621, 53, 67–9, 84, 87–94
    of 1628, 94
parliament, of Scotland, 45
    of 1584, 44
    of 1587, 45
Parsons, Father Robert, 73, 148, 154
patronage, 21–35 *passim*, 40, 101, 104–5, 171,
    172, 176, 178, 180, 200, 201, 203, 205,
    207–8; *see also subheadings under* Anne,
    queen of England; Carr, Robert; Henry,
    prince; James I
Paul V, pope, 259
Peacham, Henry, 16, 225, 282n42, plate 4
Peake, Robert the Elder, 100, 205, plate 12
Pembroke, countess of, *see* Herbert, Mary
Pembroke, earl of, *see* Herbert, William; Herbert,
    Philip
Percy, Dorothy, countess of Northumberland,
    200

Percy, Henry, 3rd earl of Northumberland
    (d. 1632), 135
Percy, Sir Thomas, 202
Percy, Thomas, 1st earl of Northumberland
    (d. 1572), 29
Perez, Don Antonio, 174, 312n6
Perth, articles of, 133
Petition of Right (1628), 63
Petrarch, 108
Phelips, Sir Edward, 267
Phelips, Sir Robert, 70, 93, 267, 349n29
Philip IV, king of Spain, 12
Pigott, Sir Christopher, 144
Plato, 102, 151, 155, 158, 211, 215
    Republic, 101
Plutarch, 15, 101, 151, 156, 181
Pocock, J. G. A., 56, 80, 84, 159
Pole, Reginald, cardinal, archbishop of
    Canterbury (1556–8), 28
political theory, Scottish, 13, 38–45, 54
Polybius, 101
Ponet, John, 41
Ponte, Jacopo da, *see* Vecchio, Bassano
Powel, Gabriel, 186
predestination, 113–14, 116–17, 119, 120, 121,
    123, 131, 132
Presbyterianism, 65, 69, 113–14, 115, 116, 119,
    130, 131, 132, 151
    Scottish, 43, 58, 68, 133
Prince Henry's Barriers, 111
Privy Council, 25, 104
    of Edward VI, 26
    of Mary, 26, 136
    of Elizabeth, 28, 29, 32, 33, 34, 35, 134, 135,
        136, 175
    of James I, 3, 135, 136–7, 138, 139, 140, 143,
        163, 164, 178, 200, 243, 267, 282n31,
        310n17, 319n92
Provisions of Oxford (1258), 38
puritanism, 66, 68, 113–20 *passim*, 123, 130,
    131, 132, 133
Pym, John, 70

Quarles, Francis, 226
Querini, Antonio, 159, 160

Raleigh, Sir Walter, 110, 162–3, 177, 337n8
Ramus, Peter, 312n11
Riccio, David, 42
Rich, Henry, earl of Holland, 247
Rich, Penelope, 172, 200–5 *passim*
Richard II, king of England (1377–99), 63, 88,
    89, 174
Richelieu, cardinal, 67
Ridley, Nicholas, bishop of Rochester (1547–50),
    London (1550–3), 154
Ripe, Cesare:
    Iconologia, 209
Roe, Sir Thomas, 232, 300n22, 301n23
Romano, Giulio, 11

Roos, Lord, 180
Roxborough, earl of, *see* Kerr, Robert
Rubens, Peter Paul, 6, 7, 12, 71, 94, 301n23,
    336n2, 338n15
Russell, Conrad, 2, 57, 67
Russell, Lucy, *see* Harington, Lucy
Russell, William, 5th earl and 1st duke of
    Bedford, 237
Ruthven, Barbara, 197, 198
Ruthven, Beatrix, 197, 198
Ruthven, William, earl of Gowrie, 194
Rutland, countess of, *see* Manners, Elizabeth
Rutland, earl of, *see* Manners, Roger

Sackville, Sir Edward, 91
Sackville, Thomas, earl of Dorset, 145, 165
St Jerome, 166
St Martin's Lane, London, 301n23
Salisbury, earl of, *see* Cecil, Robert (d. 1612);
    Cecil, William (d. 1668)
Salisbury House, London, 104, 140
Sallust, 15, 181
Sandys, Sir Edwin, 70, 78
Sansovino, Francesco, 181
Saravia, Hadrian, 61–2, 66
Sarmiento, Don Diego de, Count Gondomar,
    Spanish ambassador, 61, 148, 241, 311n2
Sarpi, Paolo, 61, 159
Savile, Sir Henry, 172, 173, 174, 175, 177, 178,
    336n2
Schoppe, Kaspar, 60
Scot, Reginald, 62
Scott, Sir Walter, 36
Scrope, Lady, *see* Carey, Philadelphia
Secreta Secretorum, 39
Segal, Sam, 11
Selden, John, 63, 84–7 *passim*, 90, 94, 95,
    317n64
    Historie of Tithes, 63, 84
    Jani Anglorum Facies Altera, 72, 83
    Titles of Honor, 84
Seneca, 15, 151, 168–88, 315n44
    De Providentia, 171
    De Tranquillitate Animi, 176
Seymour, Frances, countess of Hertford, 204
Seymour, Sir Edward, 1st earl of Hertford, 1st
    duke of Somerset, also known as Protector
    Somerset, 26, 53
Shakespeare, William, 201
    A Midsummer Night's Dream, 205
Sharpe, Kevin, 2
Sharpe, Lionel, 177
Sherburn, Edward, 235, 238
Shirley, James:
    The Triumph of Peace, 220
Shrewsbury, countess of, *see* Talbot, Mary
Shrewsbury, earl of, *see* Talbot, Gilbert
Sidney, Barbara, 200
Sidney circle, 175–6, 178
Sidney, Sir Philip, 110, 171–2, 200, 237

361

Sidney, Sir Robert, viscount L'Isle, later earl of Leicester, 167–8, 172, 175, 177, 200–2, 203, 205, 207

Sinclair, William, 3rd earl of Orkney, 39

Skinner, Quentin, 36

Smith, Thomas, 38

Smith, Sir William, 234

Society of Antiquaries, 8–9, 105, 183

Solve, Norma Dobie, 244

Somerset, earl of, *see* Carr, Robert

Somerset, Edward, earl of Worcester, 142, 200, 204

Somerset, Elizabeth, countess of Worcester, 200

Somerset House Conference (1604), 158, plate 13

Somerset, Protector, *see* Seymour, Sir Edward

Somerset's Masque, 224

Sommerville, J. P., 36, 53, 72, 261

Sophia, queen of Denmark and Norway, 193, 197

Southampton, earl of, *see* Wriothesley, Henry

Southern, Richard, 223

Southwell, Lady Elizabeth, 204

Speed, John, 6, 9–10, 165, plate 23
  The Theatre of the Empire of Great Britaine, 9, plates 24, 25

Spelman, Sir Henry, 9, 319n84

Stafford, Anthony, 185

Stanley, Elizabeth, countess of Derby, 204

Stanley family, 23

Starkey, David, 2, 3, 103–4

Stately Tragedy of Claudius Tiberius Nero, 179

Stewart, Francis, Lord Darnley, earl of Bothwell, 195, 196, 197

Stewart, Ian, 43

Stewart, James, earl of Moray, 195, 197

Stoicism, 169–88

Stone, Lawrence, 10, 102

Stone, Nicholas, 8, 167

Stradling, Sir John, 172

Strode, Sir William, 267

Strong, Roy, 3, 8, 71, 100, 192, 205, 211, 213, 215, 222, 224, 227

Stuart, Arabella, 337n8

Stuart, Esmé, earl and 1st duke of Lennox (d. 1583), 194

Stuart, James, 311n3

Stuart, Ludovic, earl and 2nd duke of Lennox (d. 1624), 140, 167, 195, 198, 199, 242–3

Stuart, Margaret, countess of Nottingham, 191, 204

Stubbs, John:
  Gaping Gulf, 153

Suetonius, 179

Suffolk, countess of, *see* Howard, Catherine

Suffolk, duke of, *see* Brandon, Charles

Suffolk, earl of, *see* Howard, Thomas (d. 1626)

Surrey, earl of, *see* Howard, Henry (d. 1547)

Sutcliffe, Matthew, 113, 262

Tacitus, 9, 15, 83, 108, 151, 155, 162, 169–88
  Annals, 169, 170, 172, 173
  Histories, 169, 170, 172, 173, 174

Talbot, Gilbert, earl of Shrewsbury, 106, 136, 138, 144, 203, 231

Talbot, Mary, countess of Shrewsbury, 206

Tethys' Festival, 214

Theophrastus, 184

Thomas, P. W., 102

Thomson, George, 186

Thornton, Peter, 11

Time Vindicated, 218

Tintoretto, 232, 235, 238, plate 22

Titian, 232, 235, 238

Topcliffe, Richard, 262

Tornielli, Agostino:
  Annales Sacri et Profani, 152

Trumbull, William, 168, 231

Twysden, Sir Rober, 55, 69

Union of England and Scotland, 2, 9, 50, 53–4, 75, 143–4, 145

Uspensky, Boris, 228

Vair, Guillaume du, 171

Valkenborch brothers, 238

Van der Doort, Abraham, 236

Van Dyck, Sir Anthony, 7, 12, 99

Van Somer, Paul, 100, 110, 208, 301n23, plate 9

Vane, Sir Henry, 253

Vasquez, Ferdinando, 158–9

Vecchio, Bassano, also known as Jacopo da Ponte, 232, 235, 238

Vedel, Anders Sorensen, 193

Venetian Interdict, 4, 8, 15, 61, 159

Vere, Elizabeth de, 204

Vere, Sir Horace, 245

Vere, Susan de, 204, 205, 208

Veronese, 232, 235, 238

Villiers, George, earl, marquis and duke of Buckingham, 6, 11–12, 16, 25, 29, 67–8, 104–5, 109, 149, 164, 167, 187, 188, 207, 233, 248–50, plate 15

Virginia Company, 254

Waldegrave, Robert, 50–1

Walsingham, Lady Audrey, 142, 202, 204

Walsingham, Sir Francis, 28, 30, 33, 153

Walton, Isaac, 253, 254

Weldon, Sir Anthony, 36, 54

Wentworth, Thomas, 37

Westmorland, earl of, *see* Neville, Charles

Weston, Sir Richard, 91

Wheare, Degory, 187

White, John, bishop of Winchester (1556–9), 149–50

Whitelocke, Sir James, 78, 79, 80–3, 95, 164, 350n43

Whitgift, John, archbishop of Canterbury (1583–1604), 113, 154

Wilkes, William:
  Obedience or Ecclesiastical Union, 152
William I, king of England (1066–87), also
    known as William the Conqueror, 62, 80,
    84, 290n13
Williams, John, bishop of Lincoln (1621–41),
    archbishop of York (1641–50), 307n43
Williams, Mr (goldsmith), 236–7
Windebank, Sir Francis, 236, 239, 249
Windood, Sir Ralph, 168, 233
Wolsey, Thomas, cardinal, archbishop of York
    (1514–30), lord chancellor, 24, 25, 26, 27
Woodman, David, 215
Woolrych, Austin, 57
Worcester, countess of, *see* Somerset, Elizabeth

Worcester, earl of, *see* Somerset, Edward
Wormald, Jenny, 65
Wotton, Sir Edward, 143
Wotton, Sir Henry, 11, 59, 143, 172, 174, 177,
    183, 207, 232, 238, 253, 300n22
Wriothesley, Henry, 4th earl of Southampton,
    135, 140, 200, 201, 202, 203

Xenophon, 101, 155

Yates, Frances, 100
Yelverton, Sir Henry, 44, 90

Zagorin, Perez, 3, 102
Zeno, 169, 171, 175, 185

Printed in Great Britain
by Amazon

17034767R00231